by
Siegfried Haenisch

AGS Publishing
Circle Pines, Minnesota 55014-1796
800-328-2560

About the Author

Siegfried Haenisch, Ed.D., holds a master's degree in mathematics and has taught mathematics at every level, from elementary to graduate school, most recently as Professor in the Department of Mathematics and Statistics at the College of New Jersey. The Mathematical Association of America granted him the 1995 Award for Distinguished Teaching of Mathematics. Dr. Haenisch was the site director for the training of teachers in the New Jersey Algebra Project. He was a member of the National Science Foundation Institutes in Mathematics at Rutgers University, Oberlin College, and Princeton University. At Yale University, he was a member of the Seminar in the History of Mathematics, sponsored by the National Endowment in the Humanities. Dr. Haenisch currently serves as a mathematics curriculum consultant to school districts.

Content Reviewer, Robert F. Cunningham, Ed. D., Department of Mathematics and Statistics, The College of New Jersey.

Photo credits for this textbook can be found on page 539.

The publisher wishes to thank the following educators for their helpful comments during the review process for *Geometry.* Their assistance has been invaluable.

Candise Campbell, Special Education Teacher, Montclair High School, Montclair, CA; **Sharon Chapman**, Assistant Director of Special Education, Flour Bluff High School, Corpus Christi, TX; **Betty Davis**, Academic Dean of Mathematics and Science, Jefferson High School, Shenandoah Junction, WV; **Reva Halloran**, Learning Disabilities Teacher, Cabell Midland High School, Ona, WV; **Carolyn Hansen**, Instructional Specialist for Mathematics and Technology, Williamsville Schools, Williamsville, NY; **Deborah Horn**, Special Education Teacher, Wayne City High School, Wayne City, IL; **Sandy Hough**, Program Manager, Adult Learning Center, University of Alaska, Anchorage, AK; **Lee E. Kucera, Ph.D.**, Mathematics Department Chair, Capistrano Valley High School, Mission Viejo, CA; **Kim Newhouse**, Algebra Teacher, Port Charlotte High School, Port Charlotte, FL; **Niki J. Pennington**, Department Head, Exceptional Student Education, Durant High School, Plant City, FL; **Peter Saarimaki**, Educational Consultant—Mathematics, Psycan Corporation, Scarborough, Ontario, Canada; **Carolyn Scott**, Secondary Educational Coordinator, Terrebonne Parish School Board, Houma, LA; **Chet Singer**, Supervisor of Mathematics, Business and Computer Education, Hicksville UFSD, Hicksville, NY; **Elin Snyder Smith**, Special Education Teacher, Muhlenberg South High School, Greenville, KY; **Marlinda Stull**, Special Vocational Teacher and Special Education Instructor, Meade County High School, Brandenburg, KY; **Aimee Swann**, Mathematics and Special Education Teacher, Flour Bluff High School, Corpus Christi, TX; **Suzanne R. Swartz**, Special Educator, Jefferson High School, Shenandoah Junction, WV; **Nancy J. Williamson**, Mathematics Teacher, Dana Hills High School, Dana Point, CA; **David Wright**, Special Education Teacher, King High School, Corpus Christi, TX

Publisher's Project Staff

Vice President, Product Development: Kathleen T. Williams, Ph.D., NCSP; Director, Curriculum Development: Teri Mathews; Assistant Editor: Sarah Brandel; Development Assistant: Bev Johnson; Graphic Designer: Katie Sonmor; Director, Creative Services: Nancy Condon; Production Artists: Jack Ross, Peggy Vlahos; Purchasing Agent: Mary Kaye Kuzma; Product Manager, Curriculum: Brian Holl

4201 Woodland Road
Circle Pines, MN 55014-1796
800-328-2560 • www.agsnet.com

Printed in the United States of America

ISBN 0-7854-3829-7

Product Number 93980

A 0 9 8 7 6 5 4 3 2 1

Contents

Chapter 3

Chapter 4

Chapter 5

Chapter 6

Chapter 7

Chapter 8

Chapter 9

Chapter 10

How to Use This Book: A Study Guide

Welcome to *Geometry.* Geometry is the study of how points, lines, and planes can be used to picture the space around us. In this book, the main attention will be placed on *plane* geometry. Plane geometry studies geometric figures in a plane, like squares, triangles, and circles. Later, we will consider *solid* geometry. In solid geometry, you will learn about solid figures like cubes, prisms, and spheres.

You may be asking yourself, "Why do I need to learn about geometry?"

Knowing about geometry will help you in many ways. Any time you read a map, look at a floor plan for a house, or set up a baseball diamond, you are using the basic ideas of geometry. When you describe a shape as rectangular, round, or at right angles, you are using terms from geometry. Every day, carpenters, graphic designers, architects, engineers, and many others use geometry in their jobs. Knowing about geometric shapes and measurements for length, area, and volume will give you skills you can use throughout your life. Geometry will also teach you about thinking and problem solving.

How to Study

These tips can help you study more effectively:

- Plan a regular time to study.
- Choose a desk or table in a quiet place where you will not be distracted. Find a spot that has good lighting.
- Gather all the books, pencils, paper, and other equipment you will need to complete your assignments.
- Decide on a goal. For example: "I will finish reading and taking notes on Chapter 1, Lesson 1, by 8:00."
- Take a five- to ten-minute break every hour to keep alert.
- If you start to feel sleepy, take a short break and get some fresh air.

Chapter

4 Using Algebra: Lines in the Coordinate Plane

This weather map shows Hurricane Irene moving over Florida in October 1999. While satellites can photograph an area around the storm, we can find its exact location using latitude and longitude. On the map, latitude lines run east and west (left and right). Longitude lines run north and south (up and down). Any place on the earth can be named by its latitude and longitude. For example, Orlando, Florida, is located at 28°N, 81°W.

A Global Positioning System, or GPS, uses a process called triangulation to find the latitude and longitude of a place. Once, GPSs were only used by the military. Now drivers, sailors, and hikers use them to keep from getting lost. A system that defines locations with pairs of numbers is called a coordinate system.

In Chapter 4, you will learn about points, lines, and angles in the coordinate plane.

Goals for Learning

- To identify the algebraic equation for a line
- To use ordered pairs to graph lines on a coordinate plane
- To define and find the slope of a line
- To write and calculate the equations for lines
- To graph lines given slope and ordered pairs
- To find the midpoint of a line segment

103

Before Beginning Each Chapter

- Read the chapter title and study the photograph. What does the photo tell you about the chapter title?
- Read the opening paragraphs.
- Study the Goals for Learning. The Chapter Review and tests will ask questions related to these goals.
- Look at the Chapter Review. The questions cover the most important information in the chapter.

Note the Chapter Features

Application

A look at how a topic in the chapter relates to real life

Algebra Connection

Relates geometry to algebra in each chapter

Technology Connection

Use technology to apply math skills . . . . .

Writing About Mathematics

Opportunities to write about problems and alternate solutions . . . . . .

Try This

New ways to think about problems and solve them . . . . TRY THIS

Estimation Activity

Use estimation as a way to check reasonableness of an answer . . . . .

Notes

Hints or reminders that point out important information . . . .

Look for this box for helpful tips!

Calculator Practice

How to solve problems using a calculator . . . .

Geometry in Your Life

Relates geometry to the "real world" . . . . .

Geometry in Your Life

Algebra Review

Reviews concepts from earlier algebra courses . . . .

Before Beginning Each Lesson

Read the lesson title and restate it in the form of a question.

For example, write: *What are points and lines?*

Look over the entire lesson, noting the following:

- bold words
- text organization
- exercises
- notes in the margins
- photos

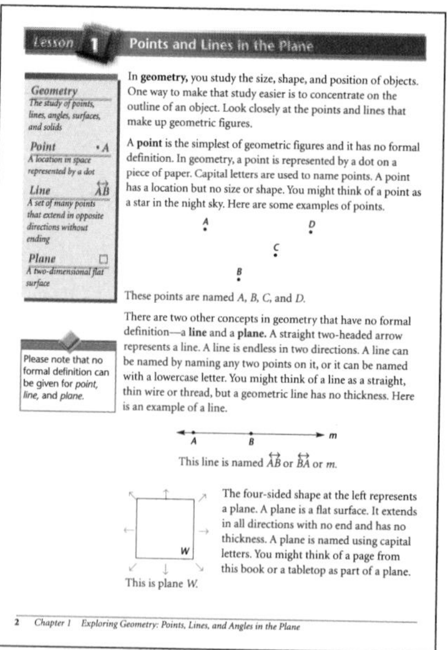

Lesson 1 Points and Lines in the Plane

Geometry — *The study of points, lines, angles, surfaces, and solids*

Point • A — *A location in space represented by a dot*

Line $\overleftrightarrow{AB}$ — *A set of many points that extend in opposite directions without ending*

Plane — *A two-dimensional flat surface*

In **geometry,** you study the size, shape, and position of objects. One way to make that study easier is to concentrate on the outline of an object. Look closely at the points and lines that make up geometric figures.

A **point** is the simplest of geometric figures and it has no formal definition. In geometry, a point is represented by a dot on a piece of paper. Capital letters are used to name points. A point has a location but no size or shape. You might think of a point as a star in the night sky. Here are some examples of points.

These points are named *A*, *B*, *C*, and *D*.

There are two other concepts in geometry that have no formal definition—a **line** and a **plane.** A straight two-headed arrow represents a line. A line is endless in two directions. A line can be named by naming any two points on it, or it can be named with a lowercase letter. You might think of a line as a straight, thin wire or thread, but a geometric line has no thickness. Here is an example of a line.

Please note that no formal definition can be given for *point, line,* and *plane.*

This line is named $\overleftrightarrow{AB}$ or $\overleftrightarrow{BA}$ or m.

The four-sided shape at the left represents a plane. A plane is a flat surface. It extends in all directions with no end and has no thickness. A plane is named using capital letters. You might think of a page from this book or a tabletop as part of a plane.

This is plane *W*.

2 Chapter 1 Exploring Geometry: Points, Lines, and Angles in the Plane

As You Read the Lesson

- Read the major headings.
- Read the subheads and paragraphs that follow.
- Read the content in the example boxes.
- Before moving on to the next lesson, see if you understand the concepts you read. If you do not, reread the lesson. If you are still unsure, ask for help.
- Practice what you have learned by doing the exercises in each lesson.

Bold type

Words seen for the first time will appear in bold type

Glossary

Words listed in this column are also found in the glossary

Using the Bold Words

Knowing the meaning of all the boxed words in the left column will help you understand what you read.

These words appear in **bold type** the first time they appear in the text and are often defined in the paragraph.

Parallel lines are lines that have equal slopes.

All of the words in the left column are also defined in the **glossary**.

Parallel lines (par´ ə lel līnz) Lines with equal slopes (p. 66)

What to Do with a Word You Do Not Know

When you come to a word you do not know, ask yourself:

- **Is the word a compound word?**
  Can you find two words within the word? This could help you understand the meaning. For example: *rainfall.*
- **Does the word have a prefix at the beginning?**
  For example: *improper.* The prefix *im-* means "not," so this word refers to something that is not proper.
- **Does the word have a suffix at the end?**
  For example: *variable, -able.* This means "able to vary."
- **Can you identify the root word? Can you sound it out in parts?** For example: *un known.*
- **Are there any clues in the sentence that will help you understand the word?**

Look for the word in the margin box, glossary, or dictionary. If you are still having trouble with a word, ask for help.

Using the Chapter Reviews

- For each Chapter Review, answer the multiple choice questions first.
- Answer the questions under the other parts of the Chapter Review.
- To help you take tests, read the Test-Taking Tips at the end of each Chapter Review.

When learning math vocabulary, make flash cards with words and abbreviations on one side and definitions on the other side. Draw pictures next to the words, if possible. Then use the flash cards in a game to test your vocabulary skills.

Preparing for Tests

- Complete the exercises in each lesson. Make up similar problems to practice what you have learned. You may want to do this with a classmate and share your questions.
- Review your answers to lesson exercises and Chapter Reviews.
- Test yourself on vocabulary words and key ideas.
- Practice problem-solving strategies.

Using the Answer Key

Pages 462–501 of this book show answers and solutions to selected problems. The problems with black numbers show answers. The problems with red numbers also show step-by-step solutions. Use the answers and solutions to check your work.

Getting Ready to Study Geometry

What will you need to study geometry? Make sure you have enough paper, sharp pencils, and an eraser. You'll also need some basic tools.

- **Straightedge** A straightedge is a ruler without numbers. You'll use your straightedge to draw lines.
- **Compass** A compass is used to draw circles and arcs and to measure lengths.
- **Protractor** A transparent plastic protractor is used to measure angles.
- **Calculator** A calculator will help with calculations.

Using a Graphing Calculator

There are many different kinds of calculators available. Below are some tips for using the keys on most graphing calculators. You will use a graphing calculator in many of the Calculator Practice activities in this textbook. To learn more about your own calculator, read the instructions that come with it.

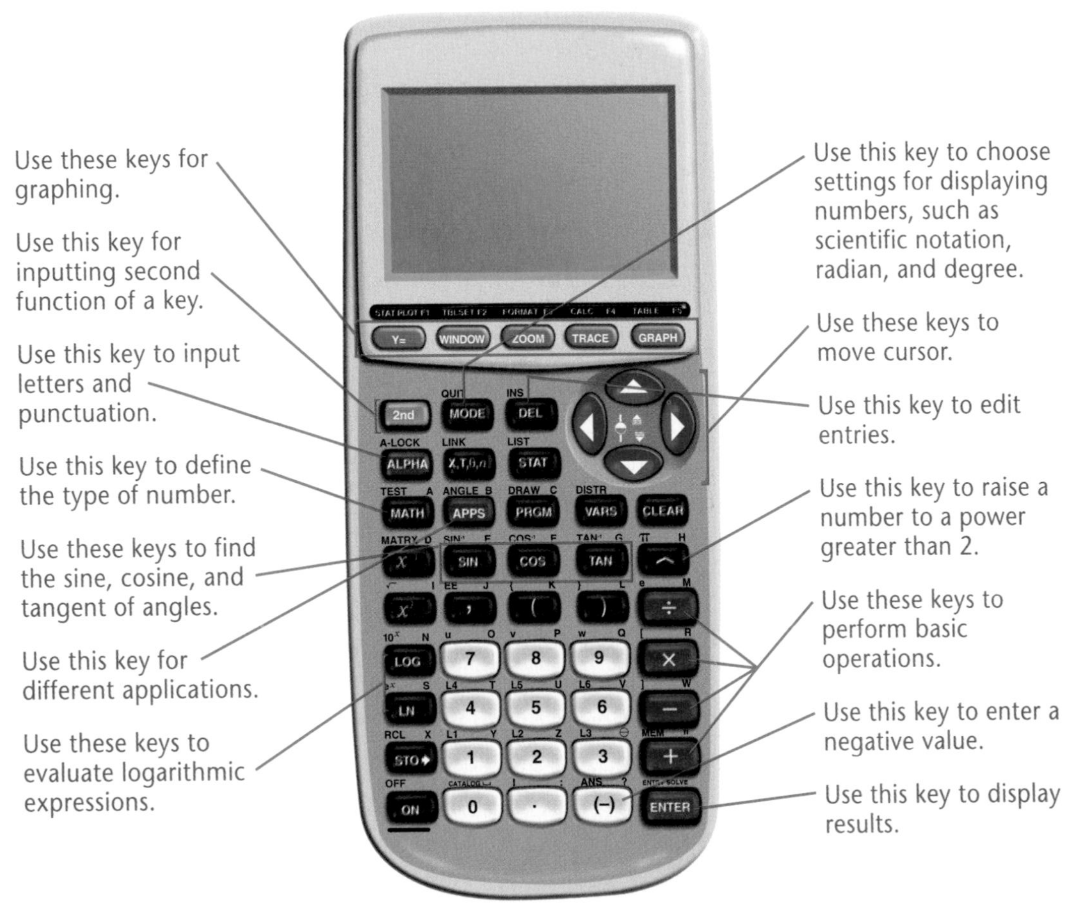

Problem-Solving Strategies

The main reason for learning geometry skills is to help us use mathematics to solve everyday problems. You will notice sets of problem-solving exercises throughout your text. When you learn a new math skill, you will have a chance to apply this skill to a real-life problem or the solution of a more complex mathematical problem. Following these steps will help you to solve the problems.

1 Read

Read the problem to discover what information you are to gather. Study the problem to decide if you have all the information you need or if you need more data. Also study the problem to decide if it includes information you do not need to solve the problem. Begin thinking about the steps needed to solve the problem.

Ask yourself:

- Am I looking for the measure of an angle?
- Am I looking for a geometric shape?
- Am I looking for a line or line segment?
- Am I looking for a length, area, or volume?
- Am I looking for more than one answer?
- Will solving the problem require multiple steps?

For example, read this problem

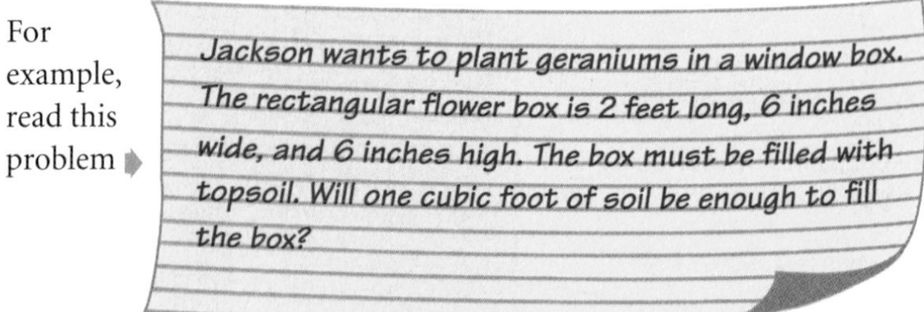

This problem asks you to decide if one cubic foot of soil is enough to fill the window box. First, you'll need to find the volume of the flower box. Then you will need to compare the volume of the box to one cubic foot. You'll decide if the volume is less than, equal to, or more than one cubic foot. The fact that geraniums are to be planted is unnecessary information.

2 Plan

Think about the steps you will need to do to solve the problem. Decide if you are going to calculate this mentally, on paper, or with a calculator. Will you need to add, subtract, multiply, or divide? Will you need to do more than one step? Will you need to write an equation or use a formula? Can you estimate the answer?

These strategies may help you to find a solution:

✔ Simplify or reword the problem
✔ Draw a picture
✔ Make a chart or graph to illustrate the problem
✔ Divide the problem into smaller parts
✔ Look for a pattern
✔ Use a formula or write an equation

For the example problem, you can use more than one strategy.

✔ Divide the problem into smaller parts.
✔ Draw a picture and label the parts.
✔ Change the dimensions of the box to feet, because the volume of the topsoil is in cubic feet. You know that 6 inches = $\frac{1}{2}$ foot so the dimensions of the box are 2 ft long by $\frac{1}{2}$ ft wide by $\frac{1}{2}$ ft high.
✔ Use a formula.

$$V = l \cdot w \cdot h = \text{(length)(width)(height)}$$

3 Solve

Follow your plan and do the calculations. Check your work. Make sure to label your answer correctly.

4 Reflect

Reread the problem. Does your answer make sense? Did you answer the question? You can also check your work to see if your answer is correct.

Flowers
$\frac{1}{2}$ ft
$\frac{1}{2}$ ft
2 ft

$V = l \cdot w \cdot h$

$V = 2(\frac{1}{2})(\frac{1}{2}) = \frac{2}{4} = \frac{1}{2}$ cubic foot

$\frac{1}{2}$ cu ft < 1 cu ft

$\frac{1}{2}$ cubic foot is less than one cubic foot, so one cubic foot of topsoil is more than enough to fill the flower box.

The volume of the flower box is $\frac{1}{2}$ cubic foot. You will need $\frac{1}{2}$ cubic foot of topsoil to fill the flower box. You have one cubic foot of topsoil. One cubic foot is more than $\frac{1}{2}$ cubic foot, so you have plenty of topsoil to fill the flower box. The answer is correct.

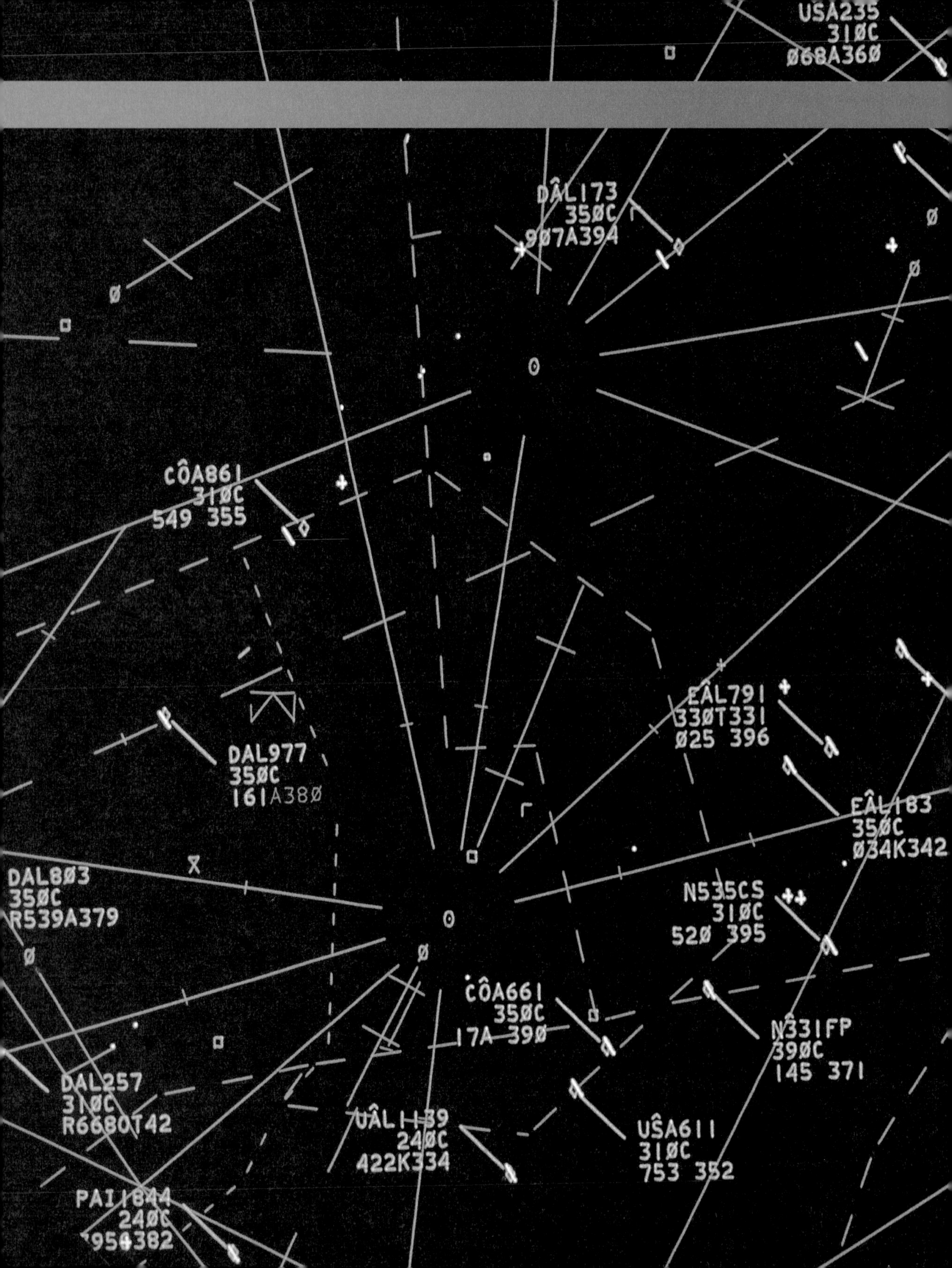
USA235
31ØC
Ø68A36Ø
DAL173
35ØC
9Ø7A394
CÔA861
31ØC
549 355
DAL977
35ØC
161A38Ø
EÂL791
33ØT331
Ø25 396
EÂL183
35ØC
Ø34K342
DAL8Ø3
35ØC
R539A379
N535CS
31ØC
52Ø 395
CÔA661
35ØC
17A 39Ø
N331FP
39ØC
145 371
DAL257
31ØC
R668ØT42
UÂL1139
24ØC
422K334
USA611
31ØC
753 352
PAI1844
24ØC

Chapter

Exploring Geometry: Points, Lines, and Angles in the Plane

Air traffic controllers keep airplanes moving in a safe and orderly way. Each air traffic controller watches one or more "sectors" or sections of airspace. They direct airplanes in their sector when to take off, land, or change flight paths. Therefore, they must keep track of the speed, altitude, and direction the airplanes are traveling.

An air traffic controller's computer screen uses points and lines to show airplanes and their routes. Even though the airplanes are all flying at different altitudes, their routes are shown on a flat screen, or plane. Points and lines are two building blocks in your study of plane geometry.

In Chapter 1, you'll learn about points, lines, and angles in the plane.

Goals for Learning

- To recognize a point, a line, and a plane
- To identify line segments and rays
- To use postulates to determine how to use a ruler with geometric figures
- To construct angles—copying and bisecting
- To measure and classify angles
- To identify complementary and supplementary angles
- To use algebra to solve problems in geometry

Lesson 1 Points and Lines in the Plane

Geometry
The study of points, lines, angles, surfaces, and solids

Point • *A*
A location in space represented by a dot

Line $\overleftrightarrow{AB}$
A set of many points that extend in opposite directions without ending

Plane □
A two-dimensional flat surface

In **geometry,** you study the size, shape, and position of objects. One way to make that study easier is to concentrate on the outline of an object. Look closely at the points and lines that make up geometric figures.

A **point** is the simplest of geometric figures and it has no formal definition. In geometry, a point is represented by a dot on a piece of paper. Capital letters are used to name points. A point has a location but no size or shape. You might think of a point as a star in the night sky. Here are some examples of points.

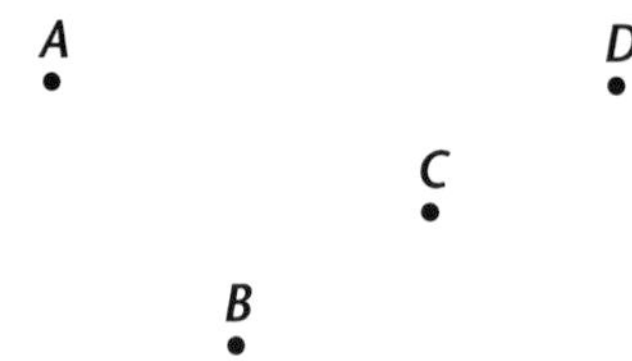

These points are named *A*, *B*, *C*, and *D*.

Please note that no formal definition can be given for *point, line,* and *plane.*

There are two other concepts in geometry that have no formal definition—a **line** and a **plane.** A straight two-headed arrow represents a line. A line is endless in two directions. A line can be named by naming any two points on it, or it can be named with a lowercase letter. You might think of a line as a straight, thin wire or thread, but a geometric line has no thickness. Here is an example of a line.

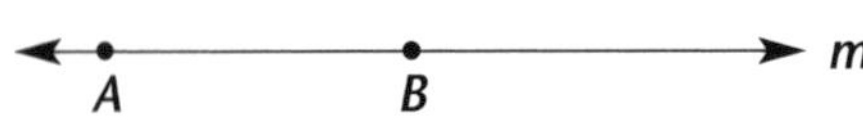

This line is named $\overleftrightarrow{AB}$ or $\overleftrightarrow{BA}$ or *m*.

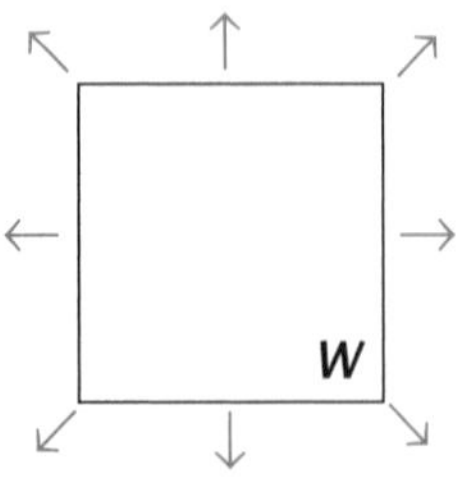

This is plane *W*.

The four-sided shape at the left represents a plane. A plane is a flat surface. It extends in all directions with no end and has no thickness. A plane is named using capital letters. You might think of a page from this book or a tabletop as part of a plane.

Collinear

Points on the same line

Line segment $\overline{AB}$

$\overline{AB}$ is the set of points A, B, and all the points between A and B

Endpoints $\overset{\bullet\!-\!\bullet}{A\;B}$

A and B are the endpoints of $\overline{AB}$ where $\overline{AB}$ is the set of points A, B, and all the points between A and B

EXAMPLE 1 Name this line in nine different ways.

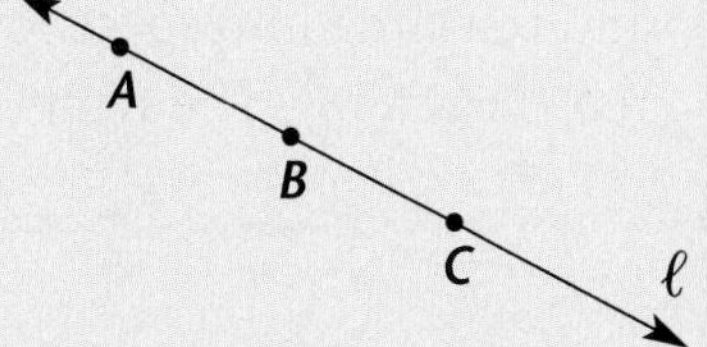

This line can be named $\overleftrightarrow{AB}$, $\overleftrightarrow{BA}$, $\overleftrightarrow{AC}$, $\overleftrightarrow{CA}$, $\overleftrightarrow{BC}$, $\overleftrightarrow{CB}$, $\overleftrightarrow{AC}$, $\overleftrightarrow{CA}$, or ℓ.

Points on the same line are called **collinear points.** In the example above, *A, B,* and *C* are collinear points on line ℓ.

EXAMPLE 2 Which three of these points are collinear?

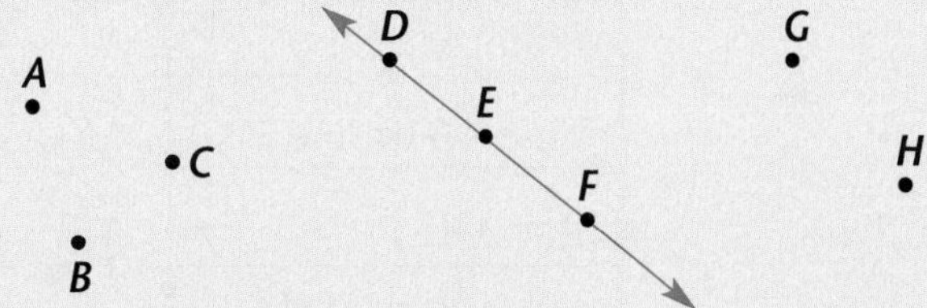

Points *D, E,* and *F* appear to be on the same line.

Recall that a *set* is a collection of particular things, like the set of points on a line segment.

If you draw a line between any two points, such as *A* and *B*, you have drawn a **line segment.** A line segment is part of a line.

A •———• B

This segment is named $\overline{AB}$ or $\overline{BA}$.

$\overline{AB}$ is a line segment, the set of points *A, B,* and all points between *A* and *B. A* and *B* are called the **endpoints** of the segment. The symbol $\overline{AB}$ is read "line segment *AB*."

EXAMPLE 3 Draw and name all the line segments between points *P, Q,* and *R.*

P •   • R

Q •

Remember that you need two endpoints for each segment. You can draw $\overline{PQ}$, $\overline{QR}$, and $\overline{RP}$.

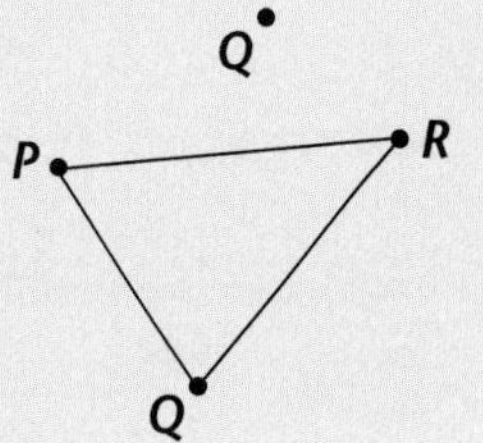

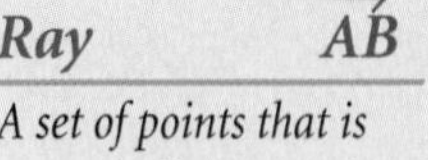

Ray $\overrightarrow{AB}$

A set of points that is part of a line; a ray has one endpoint and extends in one direction with no end

Another part of a line is called a **ray.** A ray is a line with one endpoint. You might think of it as a ray of light leaving the sun and traveling into space forever. A straight arrow is used to represent a ray. The symbol $\overrightarrow{AB}$ is read "ray *AB*."

This ray is named $\overrightarrow{AB}$. *A* is its endpoint.

A ray extends from its endpoint in one direction with no end.

This chart brings together all of the geometric figures and their definitions. Come back to this chart if you have any questions about what a diagram or symbol means.

Name	Symbol	Diagram
Point *A*	*A*	•*A*
Line *AB* or line *BA*	$\overleftrightarrow{AB}$ or $\overleftrightarrow{BA}$	A B
Ray *AB*	$\overrightarrow{AB}$	A B
Line segment *AB* or line segment *BA*	$\overline{AB}$ or $\overline{BA}$	A B
Length of $\overline{AB}$ or distance from *A* to *B*	*AB*	AB, A B
Plane *W*	□*W*	W

Exercise A Which three points are collinear? There may be more than one correct answer.

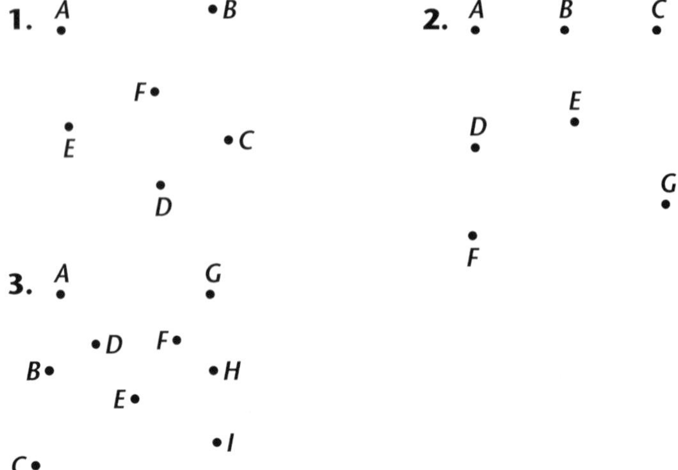

Exercise B Tell whether each figure is a line, a line segment, or a ray.

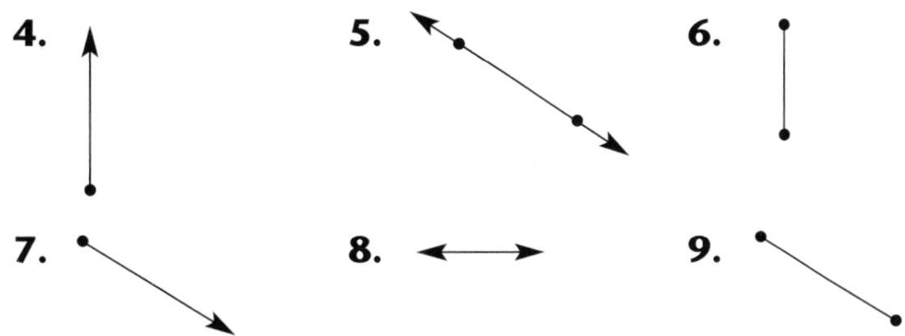

Exercise C Name the line as many ways as you can.

10.

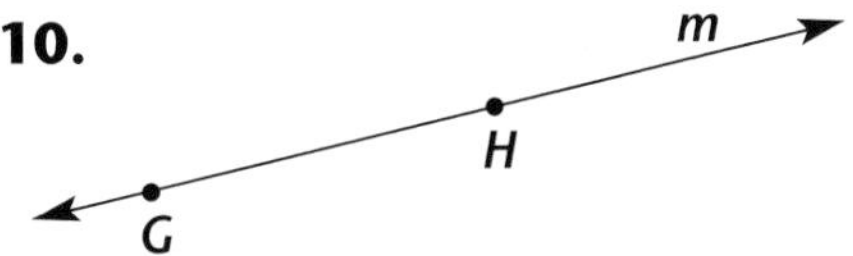

Exercise D Answer each question.

11. How many endpoints does a line segment have?

12. How many endpoints does a line have?

13. How many endpoints does a ray have?

14. Are two points always collinear? Explain why or why not.

15. What geometric term(s) can you use to describe the lights in this picture?

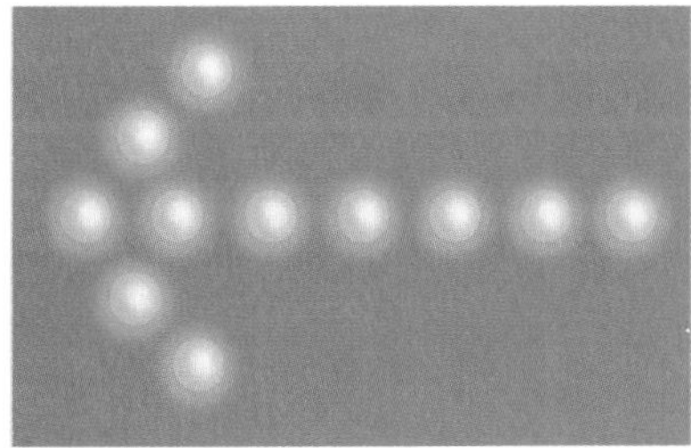

16. What geometric term(s) can you use to describe the lights on a straight string of holiday lights?

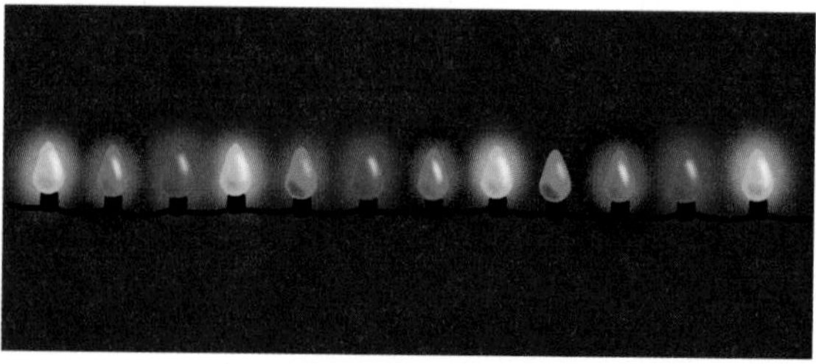

17. What geometric term can you use to describe the light from a flashlight?

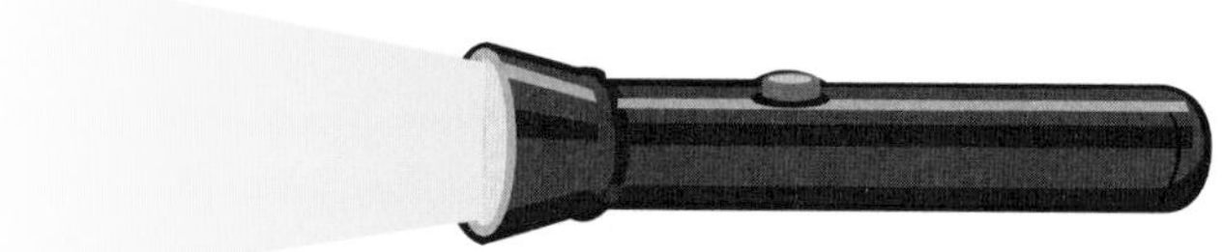

PROBLEM SOLVING

Exercise E Answer the following questions.

18. How many line segments can you draw using 2 points as endpoints?

19. How many line segments can you draw using 3 points as endpoints?

20. Complete the following table to show how many segments can be drawn using the given number of points as endpoints. Hint: Draw a triangle (3 sides), square (4 sides), 5-sided figure, 6-sided figure, and 8-sided figure. Connect the corners (endpoints). Count the segments.

Number of points	2	3	4	5	6	8
Number of segments						

TRY THIS You experimented by counting segments. Can you discover a pattern or formula to give you the answer? Hint: Let n = the number of sides or points.

Lesson 2 Ruler Postulates

Postulate

A statement about geometric figures accepted as true without proof

Measurement is an important part of geometry. You use measurement every day. The measuring tool you use most often is a ruler. You can think of a ruler as a line with numbers on it. Modern geometry has set some rules on how to use a ruler for geometric figures. The rules are called **postulates.** A postulate is a statement about geometric figures accepted as true without proof. Here are three postulates involving rulers.

Ruler Postulate:
The points on a line can be placed in a one-to-one correspondence with real numbers so that

1. for every point on the line, there is exactly one real number.
2. for every real number, there is exactly one point on the line.
3. the distance between any two points is the absolute value of the difference of the corresponding real numbers.

Line

Line as Ruler

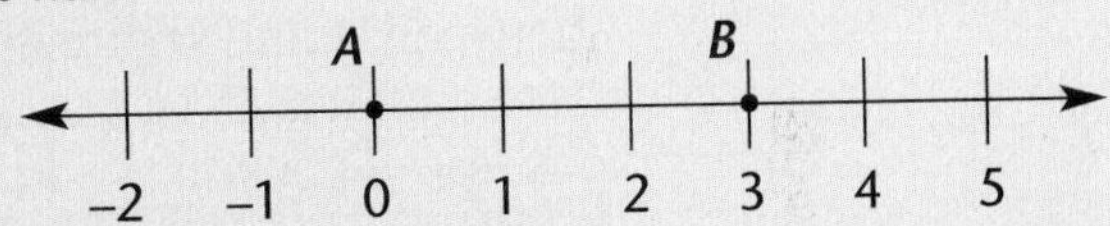

A corresponds to 0. *B* corresponds to 3.

The distance between *A* and *B* is 3.

Caution: When writing a distance, use *AB* without a bar to represent a number. $\overline{AB}$ with a bar names a line segment, not its length.

Ruler Postulate $AB = |3 - 0|$ or $|0 - 3| = 3$

Remember that the *absolute value* of a number is equivalent to its distance from zero on the number line. $|n|$ is the symbol for the absolute value of *n*. For example, $|-3| = 3$.

Notice that *A* was placed at 0 and *B* at 3. This makes it easy to find the distance between *A* and *B*—you can read it directly from the number line. The following postulate allows you to do this for any two points.

The set of real numbers contains rational and irrational numbers. A *rational number* can be written as a fraction whose numerator and denominator are whole numbers. Any number that is not rational is called *irrational*. For example, π and $\sqrt{2}$ are irrational numbers.

Ruler Placement Postulate:
Given two points, *A* and *B* on a line, the number line can be chosen so that *A* is at zero and *B* is at a positive number.

EXAMPLE 2 Given $\overline{AB}$. Find *AB*, the length of $\overline{AB}$.

Ruler Postulate

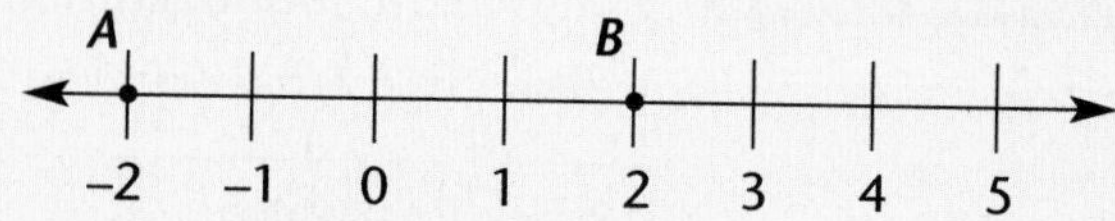

$AB = |-2 - 2| = 4$ or $|2 - (-2)| = 4$

Ruler Placement Postulate

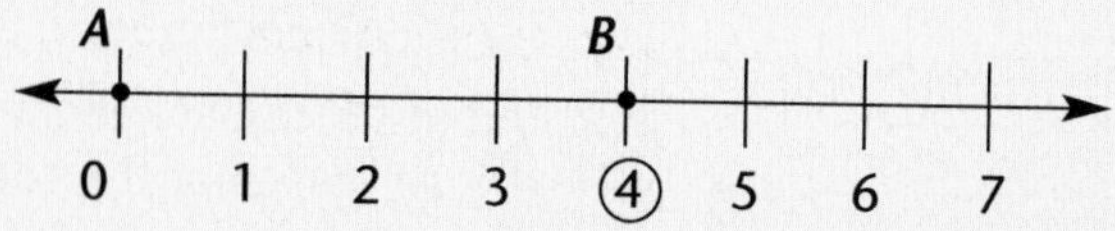

The distance between *A* and $B = |4 - 0|$ or $|0 - 4|$.
$AB = 4$

Using the Ruler Placement Postulate, you can read the distance between *A* and *B* directly from the number line "ruler."

Segment Addition Postulate:
If *B* is between *A* and *C* on a line, then $AB + BC = AC$.

EXAMPLE 3 Prove that *B* is between *A* and *C*.

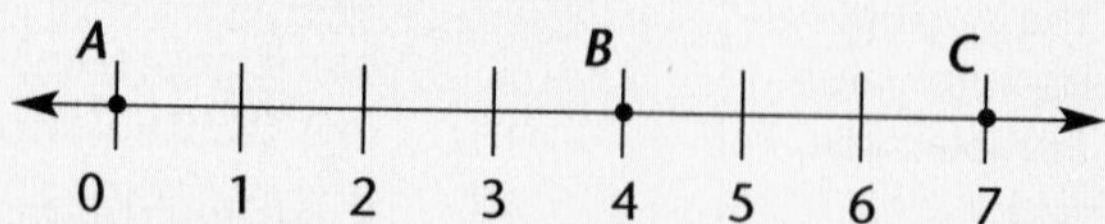

Segment Addition Postulate

$AB = 4,\ BC = 3,\ AC = 7$
$AB + BC = 4 + 3 = 7$
B is between *A* and *C* because $4 + 3 = 7$.
Also, 4 is between 0 and 7 on the number line.

EXAMPLE 4 Prove that D is between C and E.

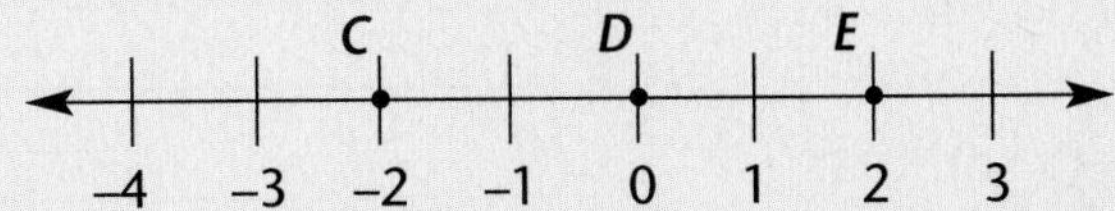

Segment Addition Postulate

$CD = 2$, $DE = 2$, $CE = 4$

$CD + DE = 2 + 2 = 4$

D is between C and E because $2 + 2 = 4$.

Also, 0 is between -2 and 2 on the number line.

Exercise A Use the Ruler Postulate to name the real number corresponding to each letter.

1.

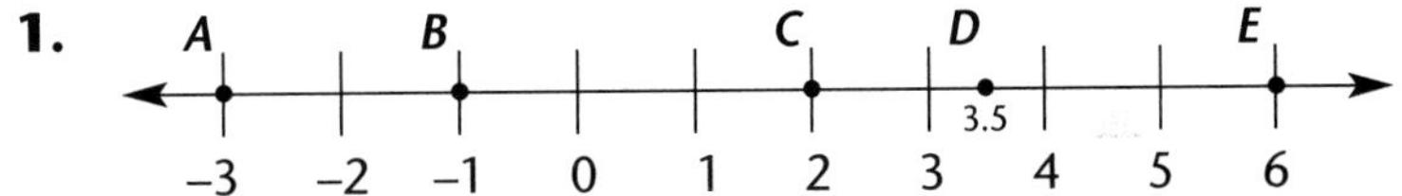

Exercise B Use the Ruler Postulate to name the letter corresponding to each real number.

2.

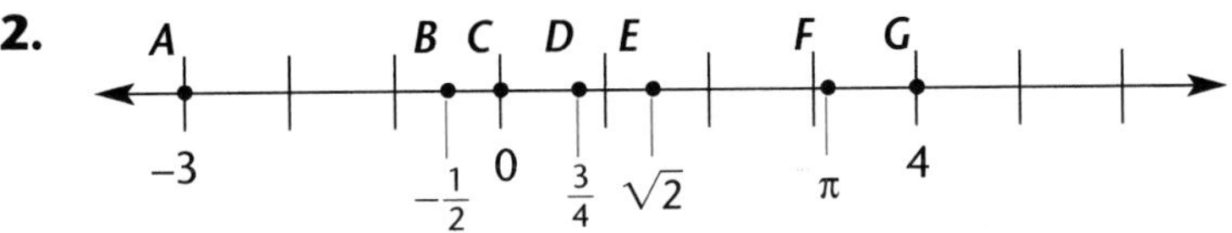

Exercise C Use the Ruler Placement Postulate to find the distance between the points. (Hint: Think 0 at the point at the left.)

3.

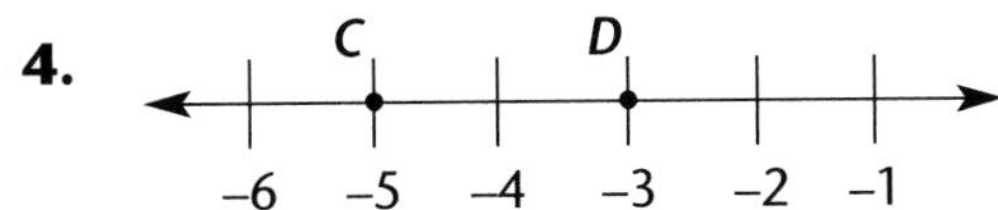

4.

Exercise D Use a ruler to measure these segments in inches. Round to the nearest inch.

5. ______________________

6. ________________________________

Exercise E Use a ruler to measure these segments in centimeters. Round to the nearest centimeter.

7. ____ **8.** ________ **9.** ____________

Exercise F Use the Segment Addition Postulate to prove that *B* is between *A* and *C*.

10.

A (0), B (2), C (6)

11.

A (0), B (4), C (12)

Exercise G Answer the questions.

12. Which postulate places numbers on a line?

13. Which postulate can you use to measure distances between points?

14. How did you use the Ruler Postulate in problems 5–9?

15. Do you think you can use the Ruler Postulate if the points *A*, *B*, and *C* are not collinear? Why or why not?

A • C • B •

Technology Connection

Accurate measurements of distances and angles, such as flight paths and re-entry angles, are important to space exploration. The Mars Climate Orbiter, which traveled 416,000,000 miles to Mars, may have failed because it came about $12\frac{1}{2}$ miles too close to the planet's surface. That's an error of about 0.000003%!

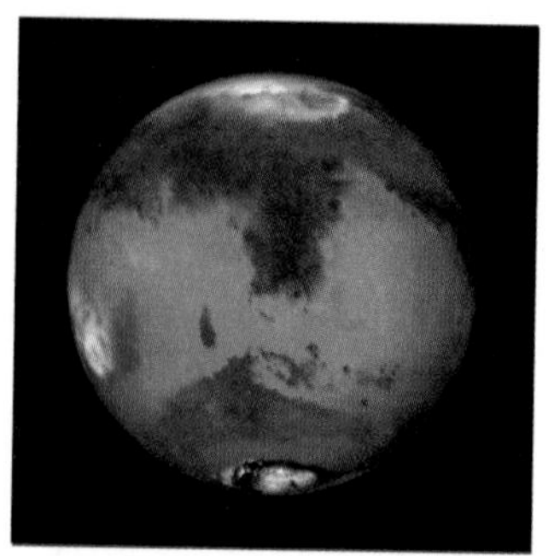

Lesson 3 Copying and Bisecting Angles

Angle ∠

A figure made up of two sides, or rays, with a common endpoint

Vertex

The point common to both sides of an angle

Geometric figures exist in a variety of shapes and sizes. As you look around, you will see one of the most important geometric figures, angles.

An **angle** is a geometric figure made up of two rays with a common endpoint called the **vertex.**

Examples of angles

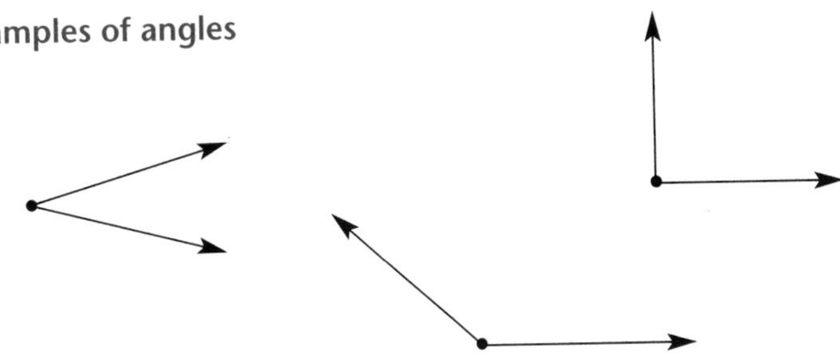

The symbol for an angle is ∠. Angles can be named in several ways.

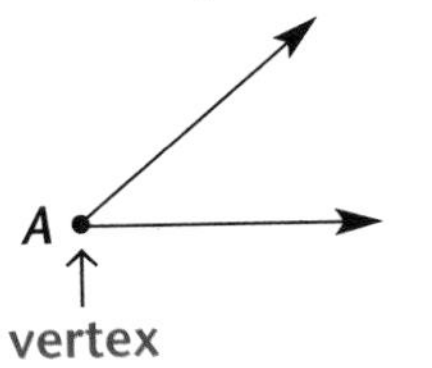

An angle can be named by its vertex.
Angle A or $\angle A$

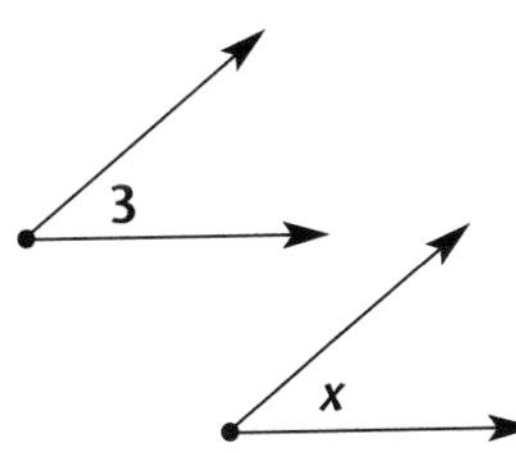

An angle can be named by a letter or number "inside" the angle.
Angle 3 or $\angle 3$
Angle x or $\angle x$

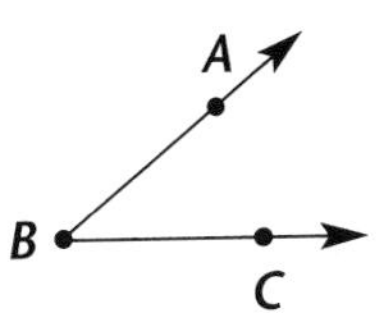

An angle can be named by the rays that form it. The vertex is always in the middle of the name.
$\angle ABC$ or $\angle CBA$

Copy $\angle A$ using a compass and straightedge.

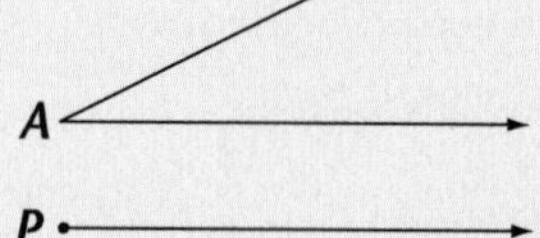

Step 1 Draw a ray. Label the endpoint *P*.

Step 2 Place the needle of the **compass** at *A*, the vertex of $\angle A$. Draw any size **arc** that crosses each ray of $\angle A$. Once you draw the arc, do not change the opening of the compass. Label the points where the arc crosses the rays *B* and *C*.

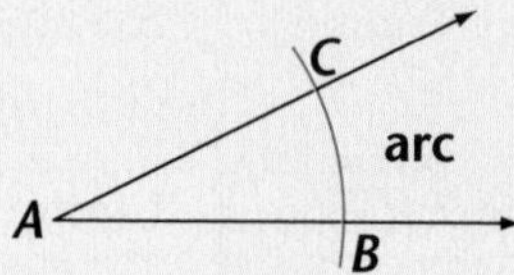

Step 3 Place the compass needle at point *P*. Keeping the compass opening the same, draw an arc that crosses the ray. Label that point *Q*.

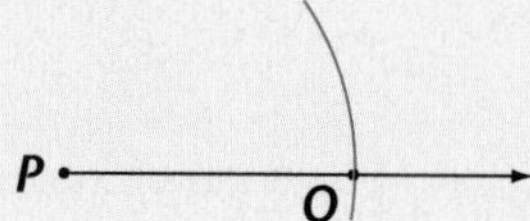

Step 4 Place the compass needle at point *B*. Fix the compass opening so that the pencil touches point *C*. Keeping the same opening, place the needle at point *Q*. Draw an arc that crosses the arc that passes through *Q*. Label the point where the arc crosses *R*.

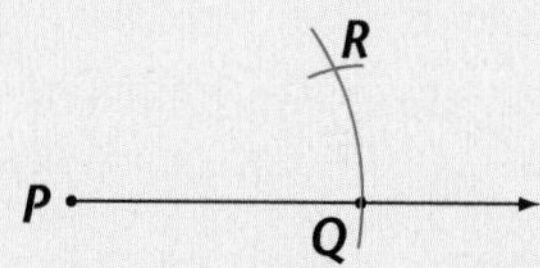

Step 5 Draw $\overrightarrow{PR}$. $\angle RPQ$ is a copy of $\angle A$.

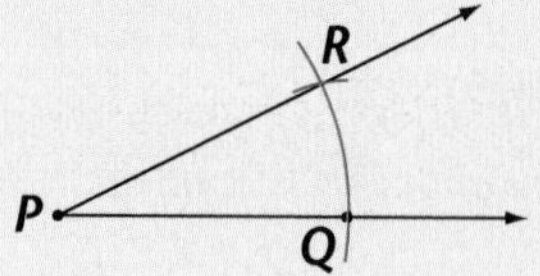

Compass

A tool used to draw circles and parts of circles called arcs

Arc

Part of a circle

Construction

Process of making a line, angle, or figure according to specific requirements

If you are asked to copy an angle, you will be expected to do all five steps on the given angle and its copy. The **construction** will look like this.

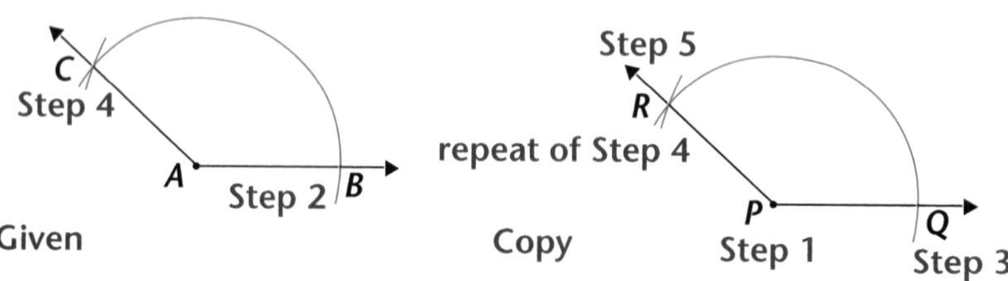

To **bisect** an angle means to divide an angle into two equal parts.

CONSTRUCTION Bisect $\angle A$ using a compass and straightedge.

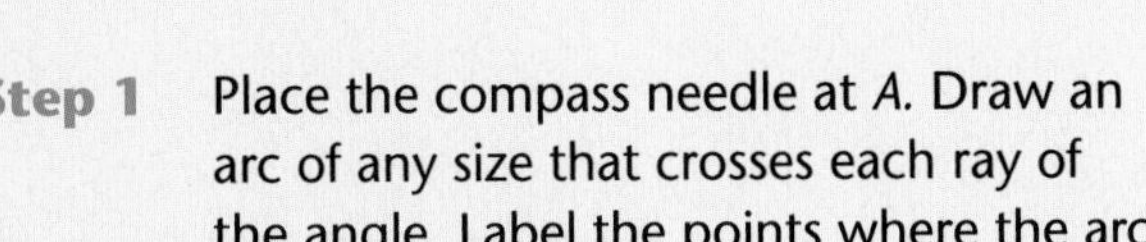

Step 1 Place the compass needle at *A*. Draw an arc of any size that crosses each ray of the angle. Label the points where the arc crosses the rays *B* and *C*.

Step 2 Place the compass needle at *B*. Draw an arc. Once you draw the arc, do not change the opening of the compass. Place the needle at C and draw an arc that crosses the arc you just drew. Label the point where the arcs cross *D*.

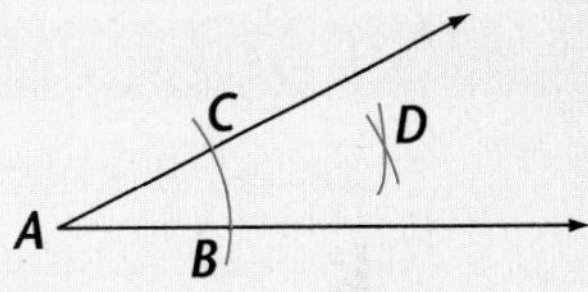

Step 3 Draw $\overrightarrow{AD}$. $\overrightarrow{AD}$ bisects $\angle A$.

Angle *A* has been bisected. $\overrightarrow{AD}$ is the **angle bisector.** Two angles are formed. $\angle CAD$ and $\angle DAB$ are equal.

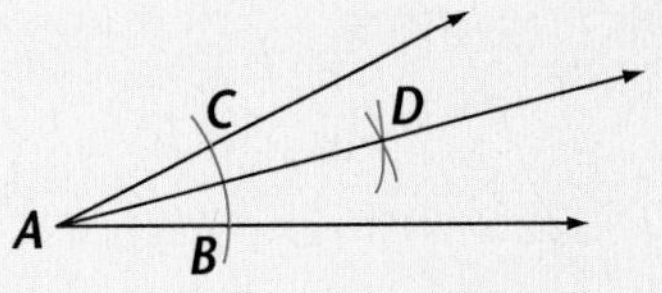

Bisect

To divide into two equal parts

Angle bisector

Ray that divides an angle into two equal parts

If you are asked to bisect an angle, you will be expected to do all three of the steps on the given angle. The construction will look like this.

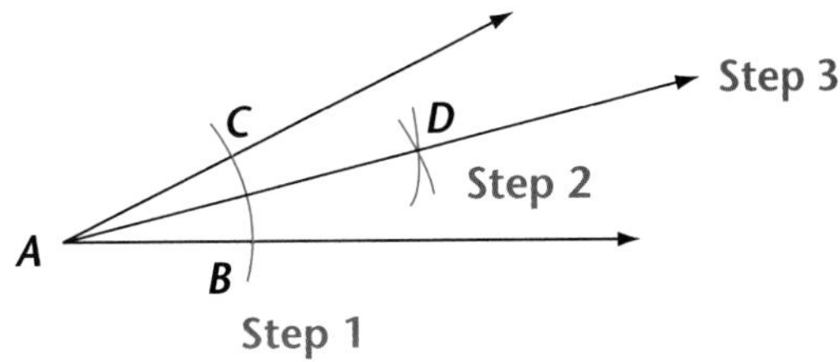

Exercise A Name each angle in two other ways.

1. $\angle PQR$

2. $\angle y$

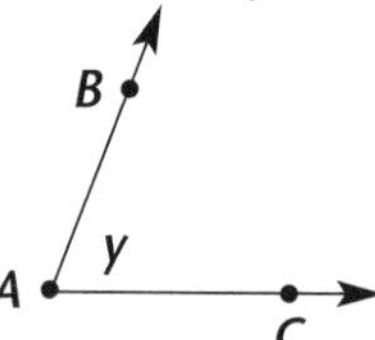

3. $\angle R$

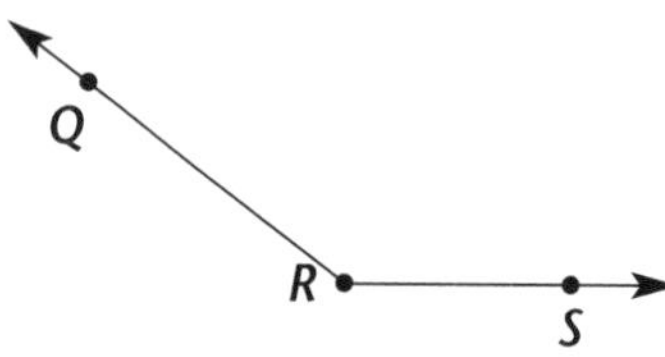

CONSTRUCTION

Exercise B On a separate sheet of paper, draw an angle similar to each of the angles shown. Be sure to use a ruler or straightedge and be neat and accurate. Then copy each angle you have drawn.

4.

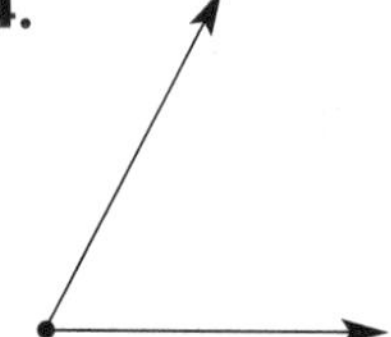

5.

6.

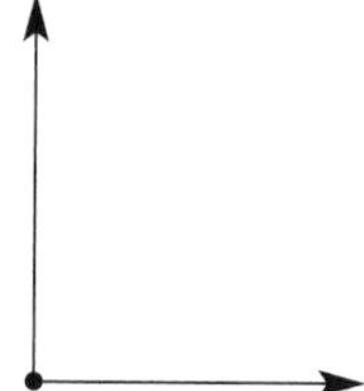

Exercise C On a sheet of paper, draw an angle similar to each of the angles shown. Remember to be accurate. Then bisect each angle you have drawn. You will need to use a compass and straightedge.

7.

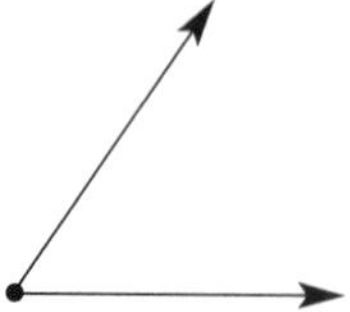

8.

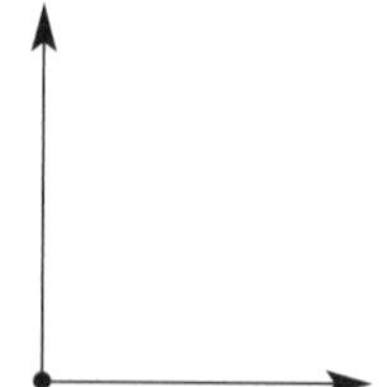

9.

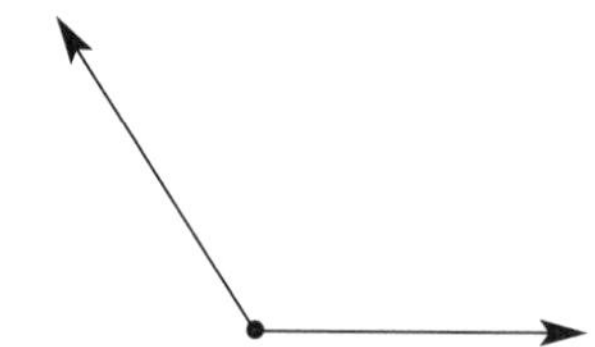

PROBLEM SOLVING

Exercise D Answer the following question.

10. Can $\overrightarrow{BA}$ and $\overrightarrow{BC}$ form an angle? Why or why not?

Lesson 4 Angle Measurement

Degree
A unit of angle measure

Protractor
A tool used to draw or measure angles

The ancient Babylonians created several systems of measurement. Historians believe that they were the first to divide a circle into 360 equal parts, called **degrees.** No matter who invented them, we all use degrees to measure angles.

Note that the numbers increase in a counterclockwise direction —the direction opposite to the direction the hands of a clock move.

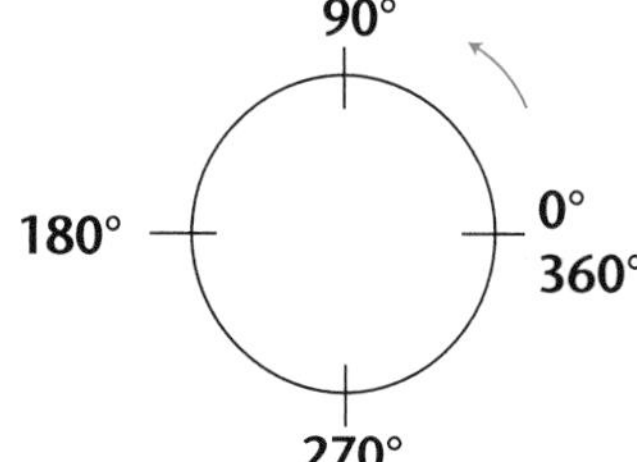

The symbol for a degree is °. An angle measurement of 10 degrees is written 10°. To measure an angle, you can use a **protractor.** A protractor is a tool shaped like half a circle with degree markings from 0° to 180°.

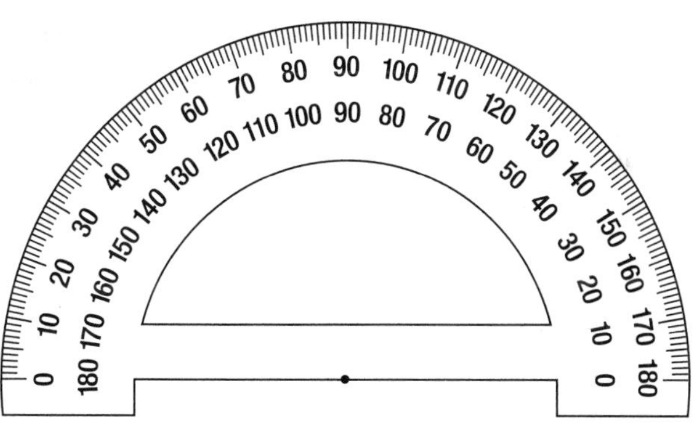

EXAMPLE 1 Find the measure of $\angle a$.

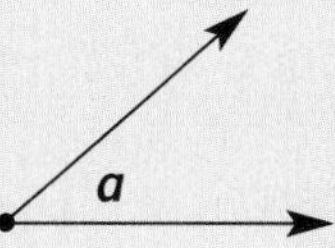

EXAMPLE 1 *(continued)*

Step 1 Place the center point (labeled *O* below) on the base of the protractor at the vertex of the angle. Turn the protractor so that one ray of the angle passes through the 0° mark on the protractor.

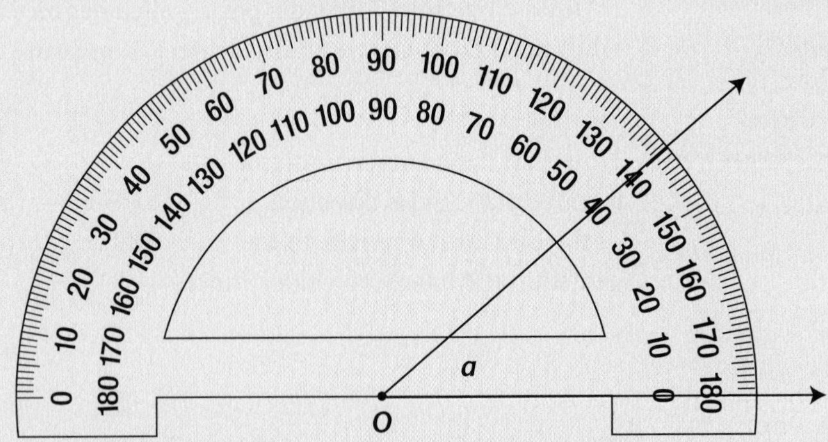

Step 2 Follow the second ray outward from point *O* on the protractor. Read the degree mark where the ray crosses the protractor.

The measure of angle a is 40°. You can write this as $m\angle a = 40°$.

Acute angle

An angle whose measure is greater than 0° and less than 90°

Right angle

An angle whose measure is 90°

You can classify an angle using its measure.

An **acute angle** is an angle whose measure is greater than 0° and less than 90°.

Examples of acute angles

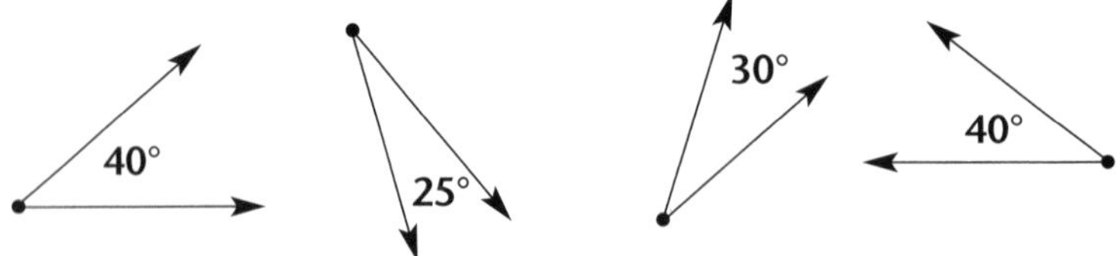

The symbol □ is sometimes used to show a right angle.

A **right angle** is an angle whose measure = 90°.

Examples of right angles

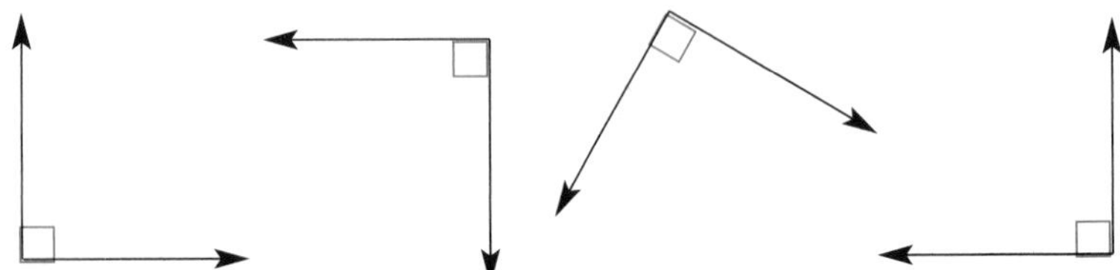

Obtuse angle

An angle whose measure is greater than 90° but less than 180°

Straight angle

An angle whose measure is 180°

Perpendicular lines ⊥

Lines that form right angles

An **obtuse angle** is an angle whose measure is greater than 90° and less than 180°.

Examples of obtuse angles

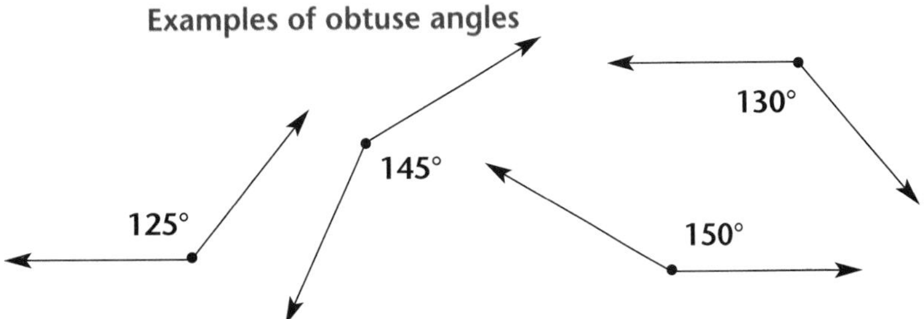

A **straight angle** is an angle whose measure = 180°.

Examples of straight angles

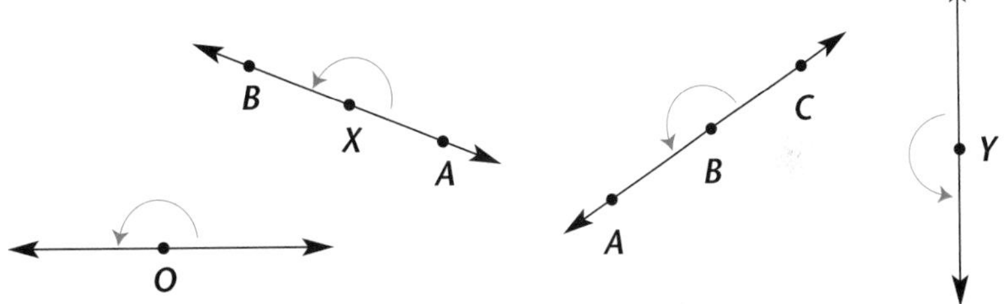

Writing About Mathematics

Write a description of three objects. Tell whether the objects have acute, right, or obtuse angles. Point out any perpendiculars.

Look again at the right angles. Notice the rays that make up the angles.

Lines that form right angles are said to be **perpendicular lines.**

Examples of perpendicular lines, rays, and segments

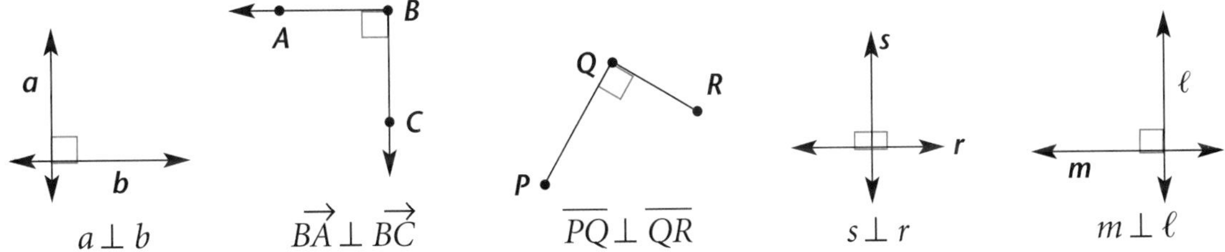

$a \perp b$ $\quad \overrightarrow{BA} \perp \overrightarrow{BC}$ $\quad \overline{PQ} \perp \overline{QR}$ $\quad s \perp r$ $\quad m \perp \ell$

The symbol for "is perpendicular to" is ⊥. Here, a is perpendicular to b, $\overrightarrow{BA}$ is perpendicular to $\overrightarrow{BC}$, $\overline{PQ}$ is perpendicular to $\overline{QR}$, s is perpendicular to r, and m is perpendicular to ℓ. As part of your geometry study, you will need to know how to construct perpendicular lines.

Construct a line perpendicular to a given line ℓ and passing through a given point *P*.

Step 1 Place the needle of the compass at *P*. Draw any size arc that crosses ℓ on both sides of point *P*. Label one place where the arc crosses *A*. Label the other place *B*.

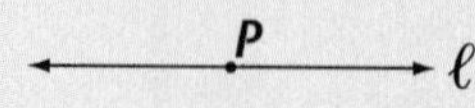

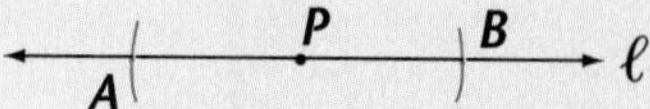

Step 2 Place the compass needle at *A*. Open the compass so that it reaches past point *P*. Keep the needle on *A* and draw an arc above *P*.

Step 3 Then, keeping the same compass opening, place the compass needle at point *B*. Draw a second arc above *P*. Be sure the arcs cross one another. Label the point where the arcs cross *C*.

Step 4 Draw $\overline{PC}$. $\overline{PC} \perp \ell$.

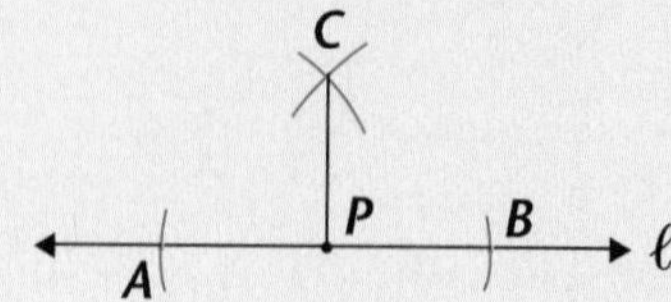

Exercise A Classify each angle. Write *acute, right, obtuse,* or *straight.*

1. $m\angle a = 15°$

2. $m\angle ABC = 100°$

3. $m\angle z = 180°$

4. $m\angle d = 90°$

5.

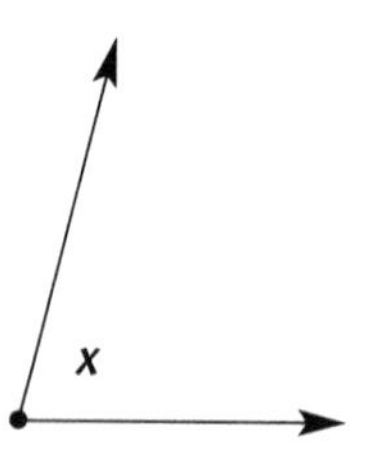

6.

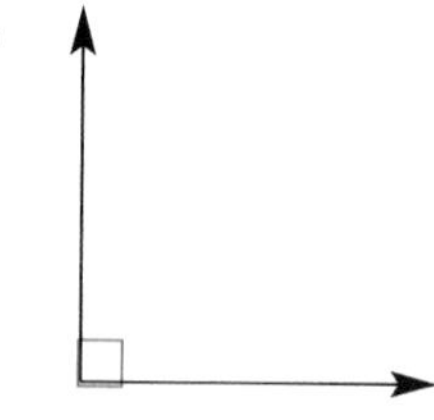

7.

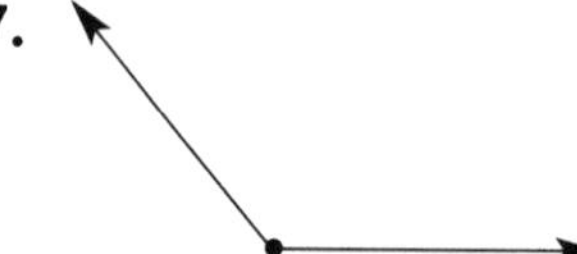

8. ←•→ O

CONSTRUCTION

Exercise B Draw an example of each type of angle. Then use a protractor to measure your angle.

9. acute **10.** right **11.** obtuse

Exercise C For each exercise, name a pair of perpendicular lines, rays, or segments.

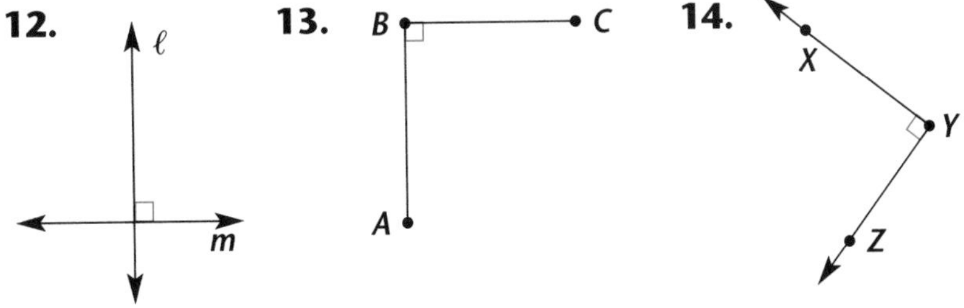

PROBLEM SOLVING

Exercise D Answer the following question.

15. Explain with a sentence or a construction how you can make four right angles using only two lines.

Talking over geometry problems and definitions with friends can help you to learn the fundamental ideas of geometry. This is also a terrific way to study.

Lesson 5 Complementary and Supplementary Angles

Adjacent angles

Angles with a common vertex and one common side

Complementary angles

Two angles whose measures add to 90°

You have seen that angles can be classified by their measures. Now you will see that pairs of angles can be classified by their positions and their measures.

In the drawing on the right, $\angle a$ and $\angle b$ are classified as **adjacent angles.** They have a common vertex, C. They also have a common side, ℓ.

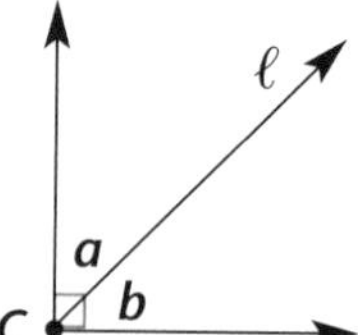

Adjacent angles have a common vertex and one common side.

The □ symbol in the drawing tells you that $m\angle C = 90°$. So, $m\angle a + m\angle b = 90°$.

Two angles whose measures add to 90° are called **complementary angles.** In this case, angles a and b are also called complementary angles. Note: Two angles do not have to be adjacent in order to be complementary. For example, the following pairs of angles are complementary angles.

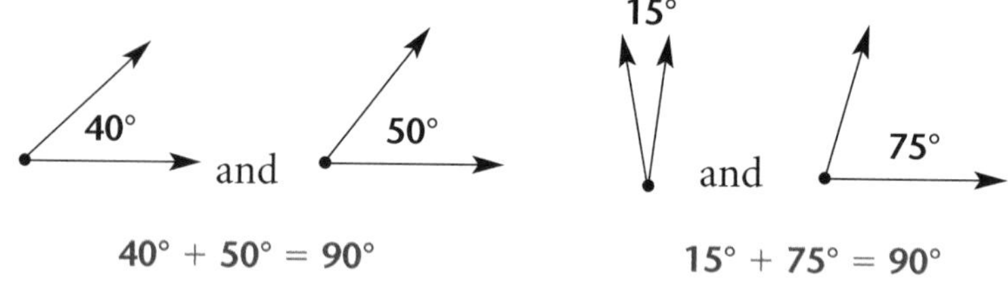

Suppose you have a straight angle such as the angle below.

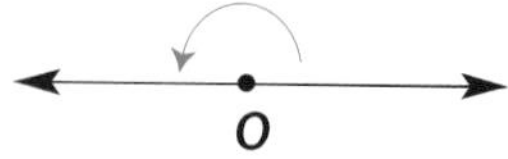

If you draw any ray from O, you will form two adjacent angles, c and d.

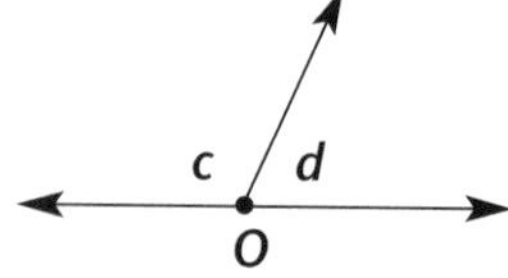

The drawing tells you that $m\angle O = 180°$.

Supplementary angles

Two angles whose measures add to 180°

Intersect

To meet at a point; to cross or overlap each other

Vertical angles

Angles that have a common vertex and whose sides are formed by the same lines

Two angles whose measures add to 180° are **supplementary angles.** So, $m\angle c + m\angle d = 180°$. In this case, angles c and d are also called supplementary angles. Note: Two angles do not have to be adjacent in order to be supplementary. For example, the following pairs of angles are supplementary angles.

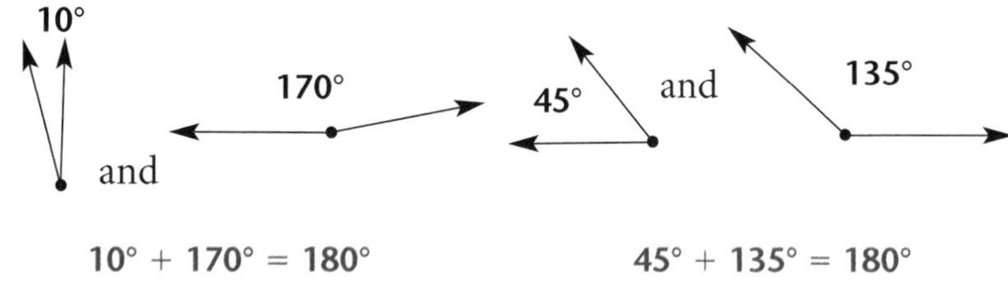

When two lines **intersect,** four angles are formed.

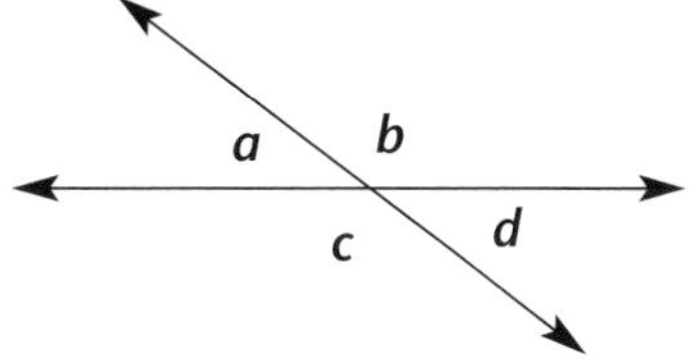

Writing About Mathematics

Find three other words that mean the same thing as *intersect*. Use these words to write three sentences about angles.

Vertical angles are angles that have a common vertex and whose sides are formed by the same lines. In the drawing above, $\angle a$ and $\angle d$ are vertical angles and $\angle b$ and $\angle c$ are vertical angles. Whenever two lines intersect, two pairs of equal vertical angles are formed. If $m\angle a = 45°$, then $m\angle d = 45°$. If $m\angle b = 135°$, then $m\angle c = 135°$. That is, $m\angle a = m\angle d$, and $m\angle b = m\angle c$.

Note that if the two lines are perpendicular, then four right angles are formed.

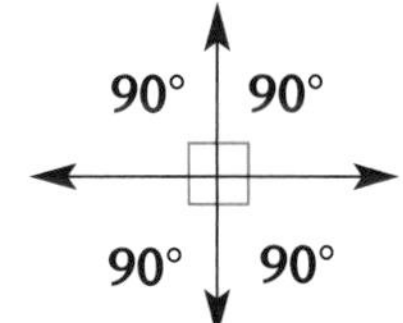

In this drawing, more than two lines intersect to create three pairs of vertical angles: $\angle n$ and $\angle q$, $\angle o$ and $\angle r$, and $\angle s$ and $\angle p$.

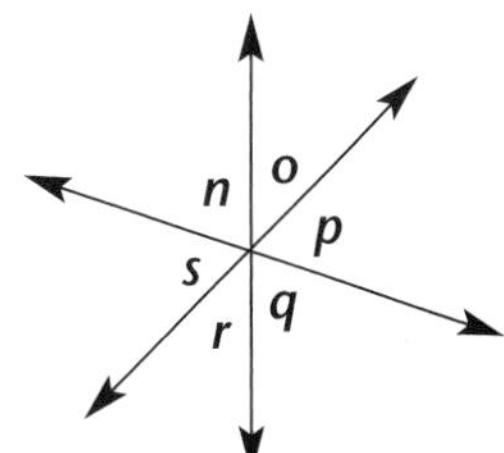

Exercise A Classify each pair of angles. Write *supplementary* or *complementary.* Identify any pairs that are *adjacent.*

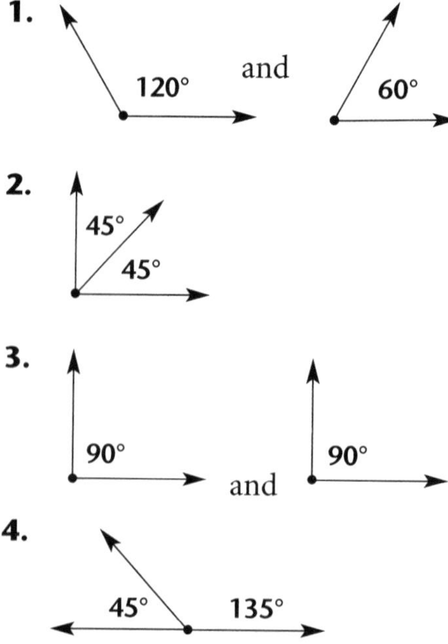

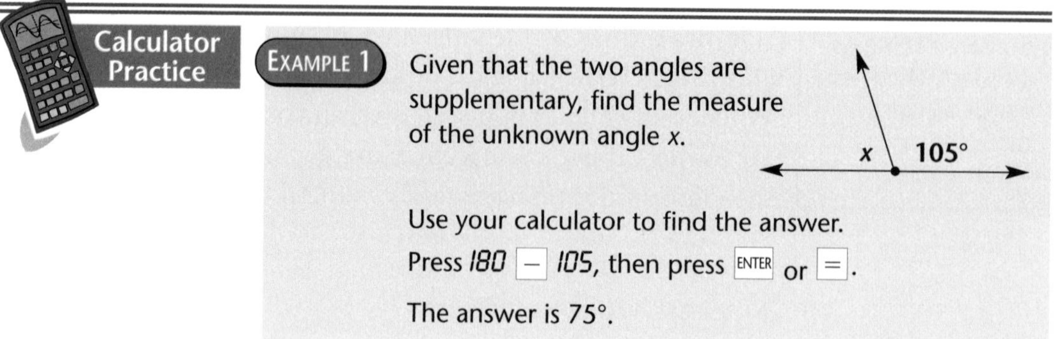

Calculator Practice

EXAMPLE 1 Given that the two angles are supplementary, find the measure of the unknown angle x.

Use your calculator to find the answer.

Press *180* [–] *105*, then press [ENTER] or [=].

The answer is 75°.

Exercise B Use your calculator to find the measure of an angle that is supplementary to the given angle measure.

5. 100°

6. 70°

7. 62°

8. 78°

9. 53°

10. 125°

11. 81°

12. 67°

Exercise C Name the pairs of vertical angles in each figure.

13.

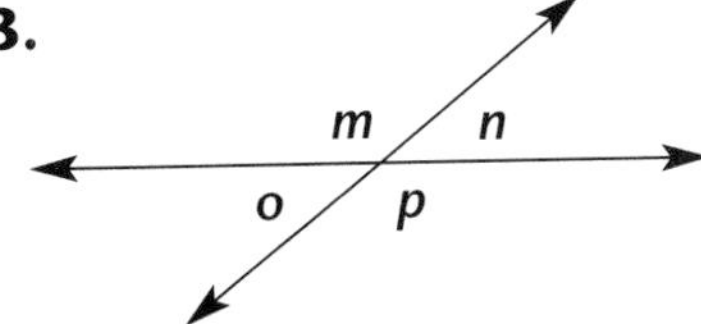

14.

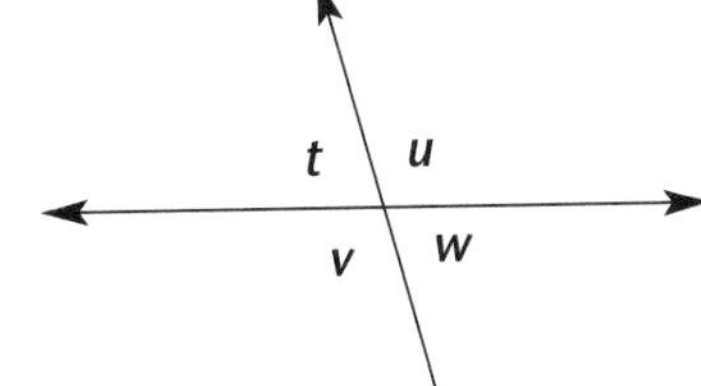

15.

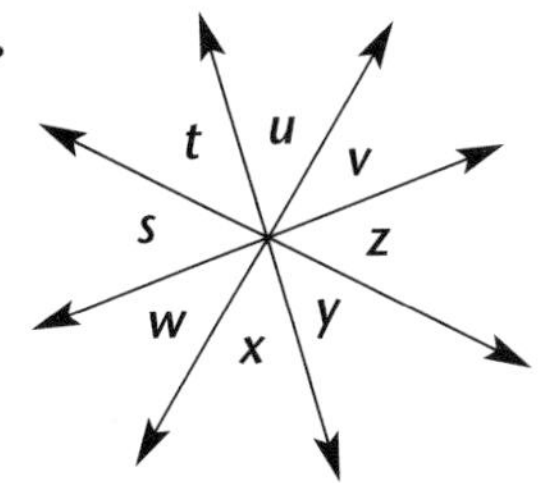

16.

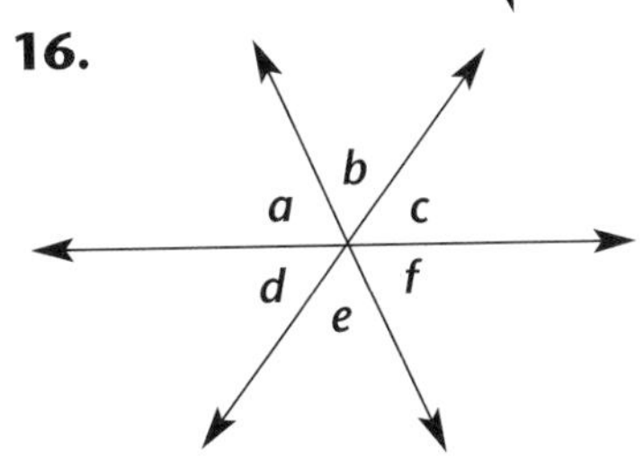

Writing About Mathematics

Think of a real-world example of vertical angles. Describe the example, telling about the angles.

Exercise D Find the measure of each angle.

17. $\angle f$

18. $\angle b$

19. $\angle d$

20. $\angle e$

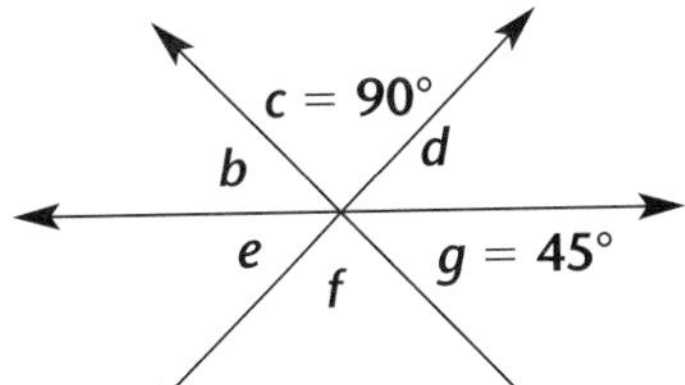

Geometry in Your Life

Urban planners try to lay out cities so that the streets are parallel and perpendicular, making a grid. This is not always possible. Study a map of your city. Find streets that are not perpendicular and measure the angles they form. Are there any streets that form complementary, supplementary, or vertical angles? Are there any adjacent angles? Which type of angle did you find most often? Explain why you think this is so.

Lesson 6 Algebra and Angles

You can use the definitions of complementary, supplementary, and vertical angles along with algebra to solve problems in geometry.

Algebra Review

To solve for x in an algebraic equation, you must get x by itself. To do this, you might use addition, subtraction, multiplication, or division. For example, to solve $x + 18 = 40$, you subtract 18 from both sides of the equation. To solve $5x = 95$, you divide both sides of the equation by 5.

EXAMPLE 1 The measure of one of two complementary angles is 20°. What is the measure of the second angle?

Step 1 Call the unknown angle measure x.

Step 2 $20° + x = 90°$ by definition of complementary angles

Step 3 $x = 90° - 20°$

$x = 70°$

The measure of the second angle is 70°.

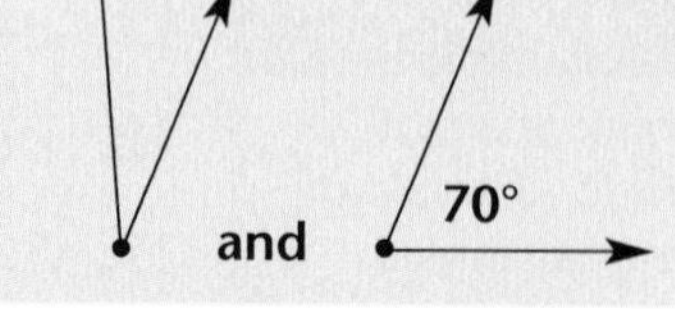

Use algebra and the definitions of angles to solve this problem.

EXAMPLE 2 The measure of one of two supplementary angles is 35°. What is the measure of the second angle?

Step 1 Call the unknown angle measure y.

Step 2 $35° + y = 180°$ by definition of supplementary angles

Step 3 $y = 180° - 35°$

$y = 145°$

The measure of the second angle is 145°.

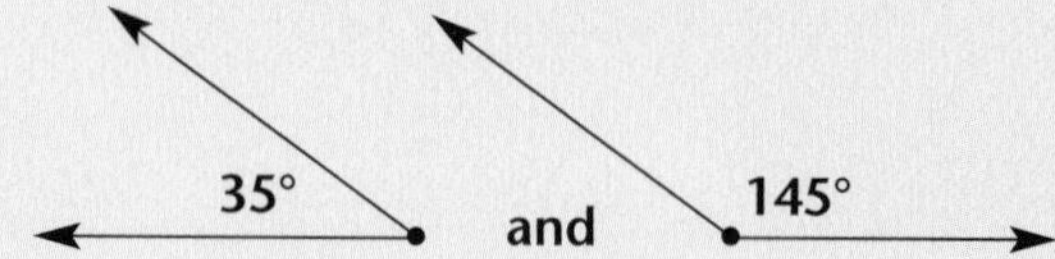

Writing About Mathematics

Two perpendicular lines always form four right angles. Write an explanation of why this is so.

Example 3 Two lines cross each other, creating two pairs of supplementary angles. The measure of one supplementary angle is twice the measure of the second supplementary angle. What are the measures of each of the four angles?

Step 1 Let w be the measure of the smaller angle.
Let $2w$ be the measure of the larger angle.

Step 2 $2w + w = 180°$ by definition of supplementary angles

Step 3
$$3w = 180°$$
$$w = 60°$$

The measure of one of the four angles is 60°.

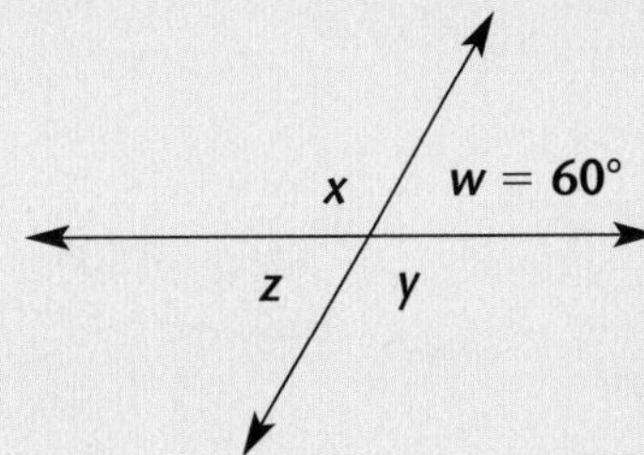

Now, find the measures of the other three angles.

Step 4 $x + 60° = 180°$ by definition of supplementary angles
$$x = 180° - 60°$$
$$x = 120° \text{ so } m\angle x = 120°$$

Step 5 $y + 60° = 180°$ by definition of supplementary angles
$$y = 180° - 60°$$
$$y = 120° \text{ so } m\angle y = 120°$$
OR $m\angle y = 120°$ because vertical angles are equal

Step 6 $z + 120° = 180°$ by definition of supplementary angles
$$z = 180° - 120°$$
$$z = 60° \text{ so } m\angle z = 60°$$
OR $m\angle z = 60°$ because vertical angles are equal

Exercise A Solve for the missing angles.

1.

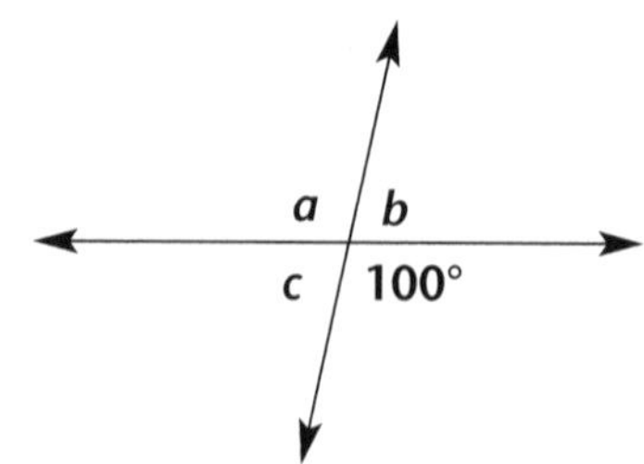

2.

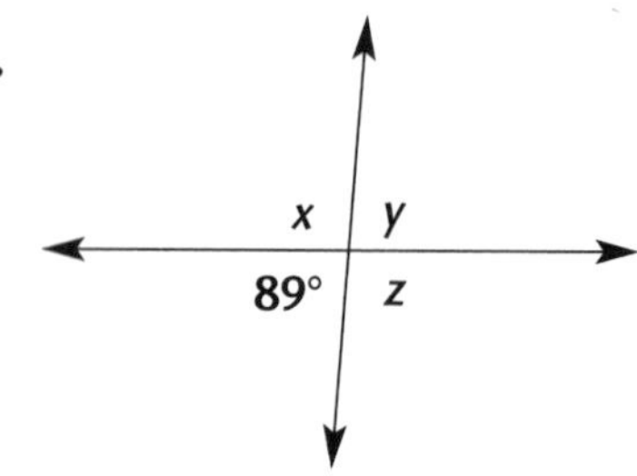

3.

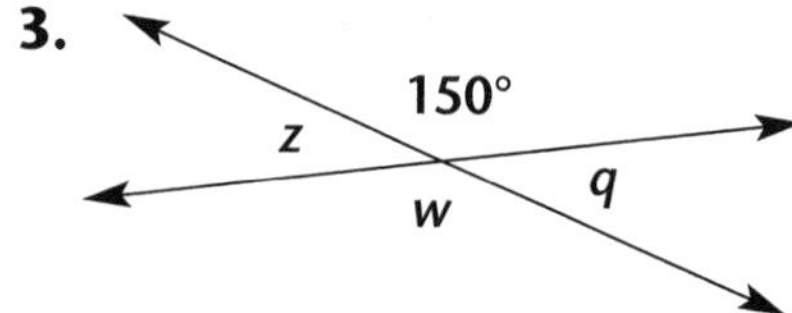

Estimation Activity

Estimate: Estimate m∠2, if m∠1 = 58° and ∠1 and ∠2 are complementary angles.

Solution: m∠1 = 58° ≈ 60° Round the measure of ∠1.
90° – 60° = 30° Subtract.

The solution, m∠2, should be close to 30°.

Exercise B Find the measure of each numbered angle, given m∠2 = 42°.

4. m∠1

5. m∠3

6. m∠4

7. m∠5

8. m∠6

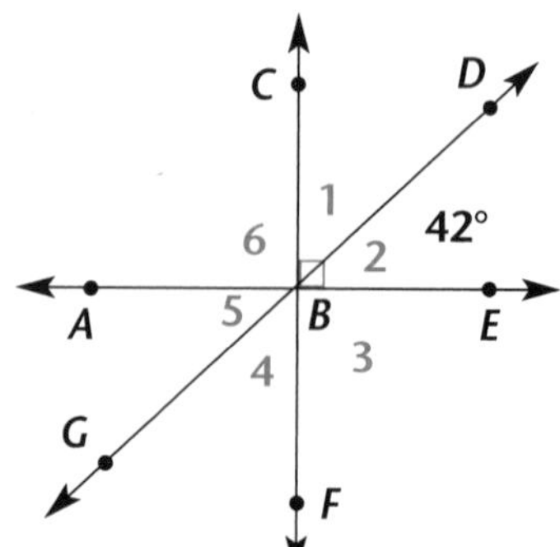

Exercise C Use the figure from Exercise B to do the following.

9. Add m∠6 and m∠3.

10. Give another name for ∠6.

11. Name a pair of vertical angles.

12. Name a pair of complementary angles.

PROBLEM SOLVING

Exercise D Answer the following questions.

13. Draw a set of vertical angles. Compare the measures of the vertical angles. Write a statement that describes your observation about the measures of vertical angles.

14. The measure of one complementary angle is five times as large as the measure of the second angle. What is the measure of each angle?

15. The measure of one supplementary angle is four times as large as the measure of the second angle. What is the measure of each angle?

16. One complementary angle is half as large as the second angle. What is the measure of each angle?

17. One supplementary angle is two-thirds as large as the second angle. What is the measure of each angle?

18. The measure of one complementary angle is four times as large as the measure of the second angle. What is the measure of each angle?

19. The measure of one supplementary angle is five times as large as the measure of the second angle. What is the measure of each angle?

20. One complementary angle is two-thirds as large as the second angle. What is the measure of each angle?

Geometry in Your Life

Many companies have logos that are based upon the letters of their name. Use straws to create a logo design based on the first letters of your first, middle, and last name. Use at least one of each of the following angles: acute, obtuse, right, straight, vertical, supplementary, adjacent, and complementary. Glue your design to construction paper. Label one of each type of angle formed in your design.

Lesson 7 Algebra Connection: Positive Exponents

Exponent

The number of times a base is multiplied by itself

Base

The number being multiplied by itself

The expression 10^3 is shorthand for $10 \cdot 10 \cdot 10$.

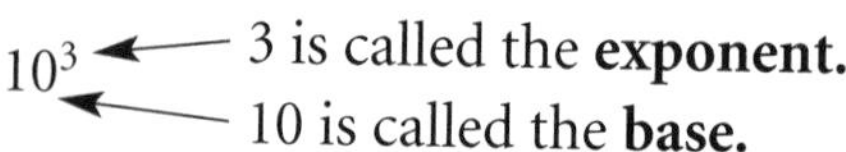

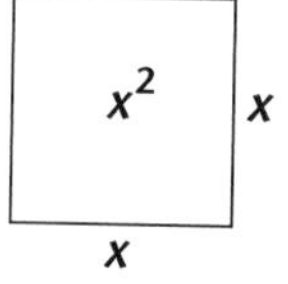

In $x \cdot x = x^2$, x is the base and 2 is the exponent. Read "x to the second power" or "x squared."

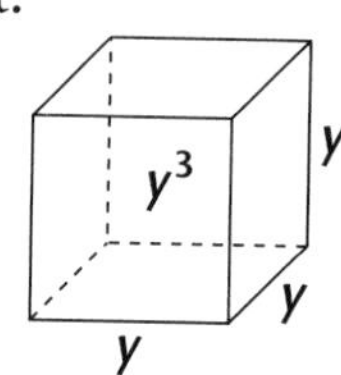

In $y \cdot y \cdot y = y^3$, y is the base and 3 is the exponent. Read "y to the third power" or "y cubed."

In $a \cdot a \cdot a \cdot a = a^4$, a is the base and 4 is the exponent. Read "a to the fourth power."

Understanding exponents is important when working with area or volume. These topics will be covered later in this textbook.

We can multiply or divide expressions with the same base by adding or subtracting the exponents.

EXAMPLE 1 $x^4 \bullet x^2 = \underbrace{x \bullet x \bullet x \bullet x}_{x^4} \bullet \underbrace{x \bullet x}_{x^2} = x^6$

$x^4 \bullet x^2 = x^{4+2} = x^6$

To multiply expressions with the same base, add the exponents.

EXAMPLE 2 $y^5 \div y^2 = \frac{y^5}{y^2} = \frac{y \bullet y \bullet y \bullet y \bullet y}{y \bullet y} = y^3$

So, $y^5 \div y^2 = y^{5-2} = y^3$

To divide expressions with the same base, subtract the exponents.

Special Cases: Any number (except 0) divided by itself equals 1.

$1 = \frac{x^2}{x^2} = x^{2-2} = x^0$

$1 = \frac{a^3}{a^3} = a^{3-3} = a^0$

$1 = \frac{y^n}{y^n} = y^{n-n} = y^0$

For any m and any $x \neq 0$, $1 = \frac{x^m}{x^m} = x^{m-m} = x^0$, so $1 = x^0$.

Also, for any y, $y^1 = y$.

EXAMPLE 3 For what value of n is the statement true?

$$a^3 \bullet x^5 \bullet a^4 = a^n \bullet x^5$$
$$\downarrow$$

Solution: $a^3 \bullet x^5 \bullet a^4 = a^{3+4} \bullet x^5 = a^7 \bullet x^5$

The statement is true for $n = 7$.

Rule: $x^m \bullet x^n = x^{m+n}$

For $x \neq 0$, $x^m \div x^n = x^{m-n}$

Special Case: For $x \neq 0$, $x^m \div x^m = x^{m-m} = x^0 = 1$

Exercise A Simplify multiplication.

1. $a^7 \cdot a^3$

2. $x^5 \cdot x^2$

3. $y^5 \cdot y^5$

4. $w^4 \cdot w$

5. $b^4 \cdot b^9$

6. $x^2 \cdot x^4 \cdot x^5$

7. $y^3 \cdot y^{10} \cdot y^2$

8. $a^7 \cdot a^4 \cdot a \cdot a^3$

Exercise B Simplify division.

9. $y^3 \div y^2$

10. $a^{10} \div a^5$

11. $x^7 \div x$

12. $w^4 \div w^4$

13. $z^{15} \div z^5$

14. $x^{13} \div x^{10}$

15. $y^{10} \div y^2$

16. $b^8 \div b$

17. $n^{21} \div n^{16}$

18. $c^9 \div c^9$

19. $m^{19} \div m^{19}$

20. $a^4 \div a^3$

Exercise C Find the value of n that makes each statement true.

21. $y^3 \cdot b^2 \cdot y^2 = b^2 \cdot y^n$

22. $a^5 \cdot b^3 \cdot a^8 = a^n \cdot b^3$

23. $\frac{e^{10}}{e^4} = e^n$

24. $\frac{x^{15}}{x^n} = x^8$

25. $w^n \div w^2 = w^{10}$

26. $\frac{y^n}{y^4} = y^7$

27. $a^3 \cdot x^2 \cdot a^4 \cdot x^5 = a^n \cdot x^7$

28. $b^4 \cdot c^3 \cdot b^4 \cdot c^6 = b^8 \cdot c^n$

29. $p^5 \cdot r^6 \cdot p^2 \cdot r = p^n \cdot r^7$

30. $x^3 \cdot y^3 \cdot x \cdot y^4 = x^n \cdot y^7$

Application

Drawing Networks Do you go to school the same way every day? If you walk you can take any route you want. However, if you ride a bus you travel on the same streets and make the same turns every day. School and city buses travel along the routes that cover the most distance in the shortest amount of time. They save time and money by not traveling over the same roads more than once.

This diagram shows what a bus route may look like. The route is made of points connected by lines. This is called a *network*. You could easily start at a point and trace each part of the route only once without lifting your finger off the page. Any network that can be traced this way is called *traversable*.

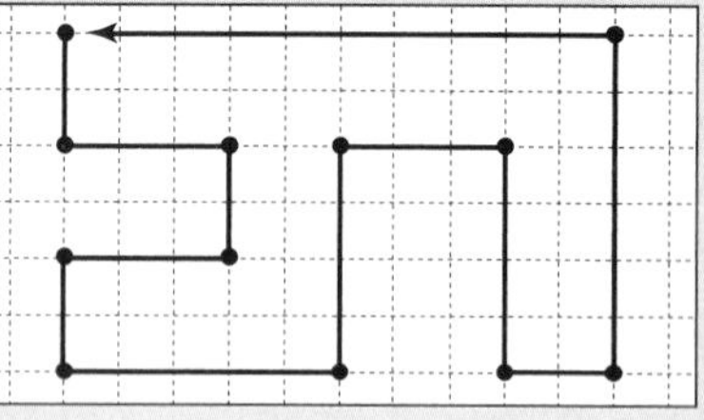

EXAMPLE 1 Decide if the network is traversable.

You may have to keep tracing different routes until you are convinced a network is traversable. If it is traversable you should be able to describe the path.

The network is traversable. Follow this path: *B-G-F-E-D-C-B-A-H-G-D*.

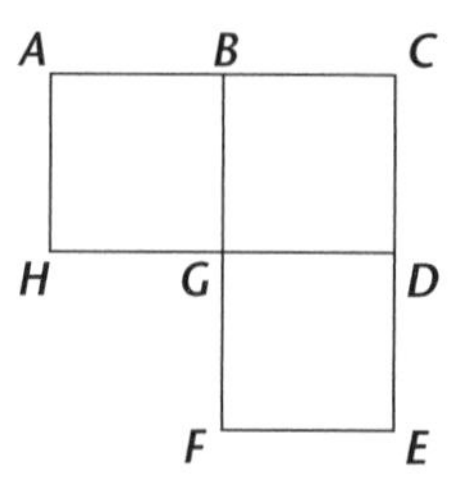

Exercise Trace the following networks. Decide if they are traversable or not. Explain why they do not all work.

1. 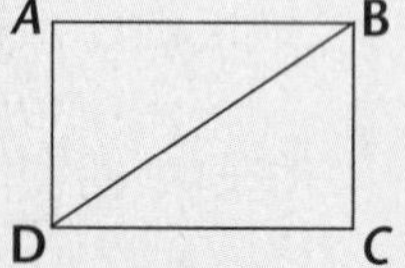

2. 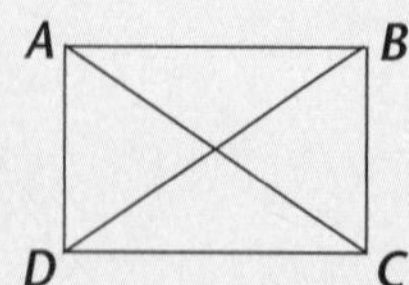

3. 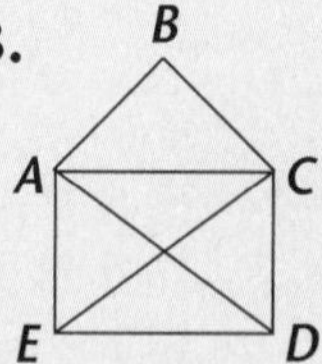

4. 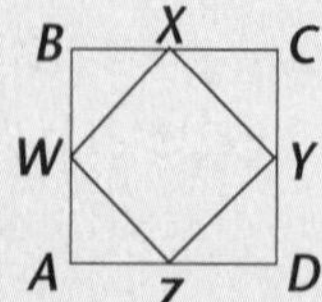

5. 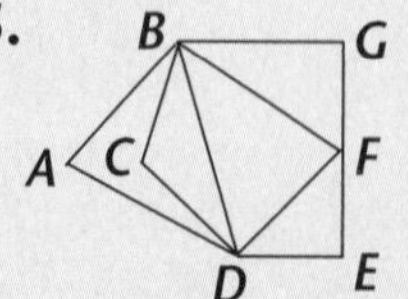

Chapter 1 REVIEW

Write the letter of the correct answer.

1. How many endpoints does a line segment have?

A 0 **C** 2
B 1 **D** more than 2

2. How many endpoints does a ray have?

A 0 **C** 2
B 1 **D** more than 2

3. Which of the following *cannot* be used to name the angle shown to the right?

A $\angle ABC$ **C** $\angle C$
B $\angle B$ **D** $\angle CBA$

4. What is the measure of $\angle x$? Use a protractor to measure the angle.

A 102° **C** 78°
B 82° **D** 72°

5. Two lines intersect to form the four angles shown. Which statement is true?

A $\angle 1$ and $\angle 2$ are complementary.
B $\angle 1$ and $\angle 2$ are right angles.
C $\angle 1$ and $\angle 2$ are supplementary.
D $\angle 1$ and $\angle 2$ are vertical angles.

6. The measure of one of two complementary angles is 48°. What is the measure of the second angle?

A 42° **B** 48° **C** 52° **D** 132°

7. Two angles are supplementary. The larger angle has measure 4 times as great as the measure of the smaller angle. What is the measure of the smaller angle?

A 18° **B** 30° **C** 36° **D** 144°

Tell whether each figure is a point, a line, a line segment, or a ray. Then use symbols to name each figure.

Example: Q W Solution: line segment, $\overline{QW}$

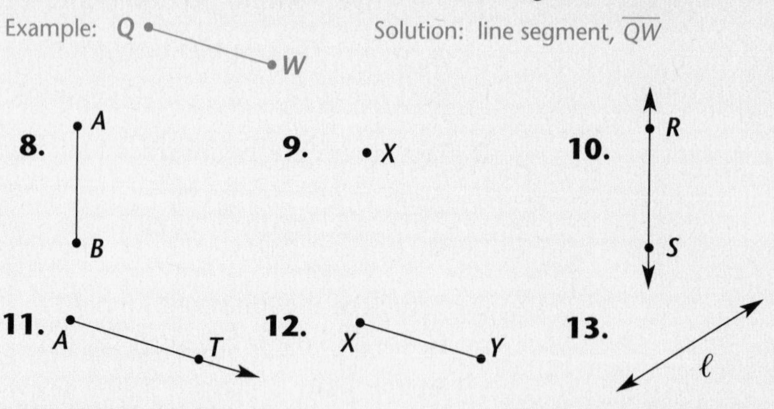

Use a ruler to measure these segments in inches. Round to the nearest inch.

Example: Solution: 2 in.

14.

15.

Use a ruler to measure these segments in centimeters. Round to the nearest centimeter.

Example: Solution: 2 cm

16.

17.

18.

Use a straightedge and compass to copy and bisect each angle.

Example: Solution:

19.

20.

Classify each angle. Write *acute, right, obtuse,* or *straight.*

Example: m∠C = 90° Solution: right

21. m∠x = 105°

22. m∠XYZ = 90°

23.

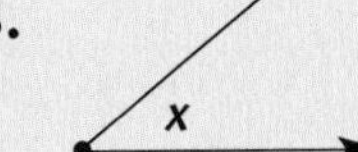

Find the measure of an angle complementary to the given angle.

Example: m∠C = 35° Solution: 90° − 35° = 55°

24. m∠y = 15° **25.** m∠x = 30° **26.** m∠w = 45°

Find the measure of an angle supplementary to the given angle.

Example: m∠C = 135° Solution: 180° − 135° = 45°

27. m∠m = 115° **28.** m∠n = 60° **29.** m∠o = 40°

Draw an example of each type of angle, then use a protractor to measure your angle.

Example: right Solution:

30. obtuse **31.** straight

Solve to find the measure of the unknown angles.

Example: The measure of an angle is two times the measure of its complement. What is the measure of the smaller angle?

Solution: $x + 2x = 90$
$3x = 90$
$x = 30$
So, the smaller angle measures 30°.

32. Supplementary angles, one angle = 65°.

33. Complementary angles, one angle = 12°.

34. One supplementary angle is half as large as the second supplementary angle. What is the measure of the larger angle?

35. One complementary angle is nine times as large as the second complementary angle. What is the measure of the smaller angle?

Test-Taking Tip

To prepare for a geometry test, study in short sessions for several days rather than one long session the night before the test.

Chapter

Thinking Geometrically: Using Proofs

In a trial, the prosecutor's job is to prove that the defendant is guilty. The prosecutor uses evidence, reasoning, and knowledge of laws and earlier court cases to do this. From the other side of the courtroom, a defense attorney uses the same tools to defend his or her client.

In geometry, you will use evidence to help form ideas about what is true and what is false. It will be your job to prove, step by step, that statements called theorems are true using logical reasoning.

In Chapter 2, you will learn about proofs as you apply some of the axioms and postulates of geometry.

Goals for Learning

- ◆ To evaluate and write conditionals
- ◆ To identify and apply the postulates that define lines and angles
- ◆ To identify postulates that apply to constructions
- ◆ To construct geometric lines and shapes based on postulates
- ◆ To use axioms in explanations
- ◆ To prove the Vertical Angle Theorem and to use it to find measures of angles

Lesson 1 If . . . Then Statements

Condition

Something on which something else depends; a requirement

Conditional

A statement in the form "If . . . then . . ."

Hypothesis

The given or "If . . ." part of a conditional

Conclusion

The "then . . ." part of a conditional

Every day you hear statements in the form "If . . . then . . . ." "**If** you use Clean & Bright toothpaste, **then** your teeth will be sparkling." You know this may or may not be true depending on Clean & Bright toothpaste. "If . . . then . . ." statements are also used in geometry and mathematics. These statements describe the necessary **conditions** for a conclusion to be true. In geometry and mathematics there are strict rules for "If . . . then . . ." statements to be true.

EXAMPLE 1 Study this example.

If two angles are complementary,	→	**then** the sum of their measures equals 90°.
Given or Hypothesis		**Conclusion**
"Two angles are complementary" is the given statement, also called the *hypothesis*.		"The sum of their measures equals 90°" is the *conclusion.*

The entire "If . . . then . . ." statement is called a **conditional.** A statement of the form "If . . . then . . ." is a *conditional.*

The statement that follows the "If" in a conditional is the **hypothesis.**

The statement that follows the "then" in a conditional is the **conclusion.**

Writing About Mathematics

Copy an "If . . . then . . ." statement from an advertisement. Tell which part is the hypothesis and which is the conclusion. Tell whether you think the conditional is true or false. Explain why.

The rules of logic tell you if a conditional statement is true or false.

Rule for Conditionals:

A conditional is always **true** except when a *true hypothesis* is followed by a *false conclusion.* A conditional in which a true hypothesis is followed by a false conclusion is **false.**

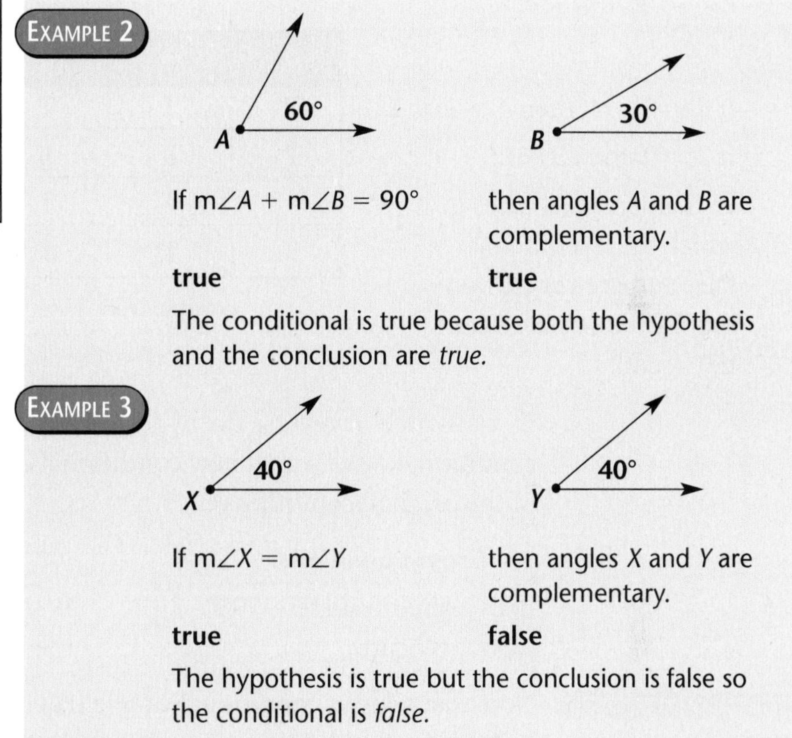

Example 2

If $m\angle A + m\angle B = 90°$	then angles A and B are complementary.
true	**true**

The conditional is true because both the hypothesis and the conclusion are *true.*

Example 3

If $m\angle X = m\angle Y$	then angles X and Y are complementary.
true	**false**

The hypothesis is true but the conclusion is false so the conditional is *false.*

Technology Connection

"If . . . then . . ." statements are at the heart of many computer programs. Here is an excerpt from a program designed to classify angles.

```
110    INPUT "ENTER MEASURE OF ∠A": A
120    IF (A > 0) AND (A < 90) THEN 170
130    IF (A = 90) THEN 180
```

What information do you think is given on line 170?

Converse

A new conditional formed from a given conditional in which the hypothesis and conclusion are switched

The Rule for Conditionals can also be written with symbols. The symbols are arranged in a table called a *truth table.* *T* stands for true, *F* stands for false.

In words—A conditional is always true except when a true hypothesis is followed by a false conclusion.

In a truth table—Let p stand for the hypothesis, let q stand for the conclusion, use $\rightarrow$ to mean "If . . . then . . ."

	p	$\rightarrow$	q
If $2 + 2 = 4$, then $4 - 2 = 2$.	T	T	T
If $3 > 0$, then $3 < 0$.	T	F	F
	F	T	T
	F	T	F

conditional

In mathematics, cases in which the hypothesis is false and the conclusion may be true or false are not useful.

Conclusion may be true or false.

If you switch or reverse the hypothesis and conclusion in a conditional, you form a new conditional called the **converse** of the original conditional.

Given Conditional	Converse
If an angle measures $< 90°$, then it is acute.	If an angle is acute, then it measures $< 90°$.

Let p = The figure is a square.

Let q = The figure has four sides.

Note that a given conditional can be true, and its converse can be false. Here is such an example.

If a figure is a square, then it has four sides.

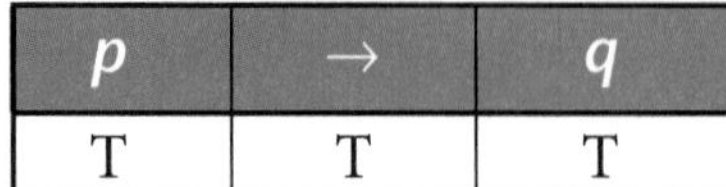

p	$\rightarrow$	q
T	T	T

If a figure has four sides, then it is a square.

p	$\rightarrow$	q
T	F	F

Exercise A Copy each statement. Draw one line under the hypothesis. Circle the conclusion.

1. If a figure is a triangle, then it has three sides.

2. If an angle is obtuse, then it measures $> 90°$.

3. If the sum of the measures of two angles is 90°, then the angles are complementary.

4. If two angles are supplementary, then the sum of their measures is 180°.

5. If you use SuperBright detergent, then your clothes will be clean.

Exercise B Write *True* or *False* for each of the conditionals.

6. If an angle is a right angle, then it measures 90°.

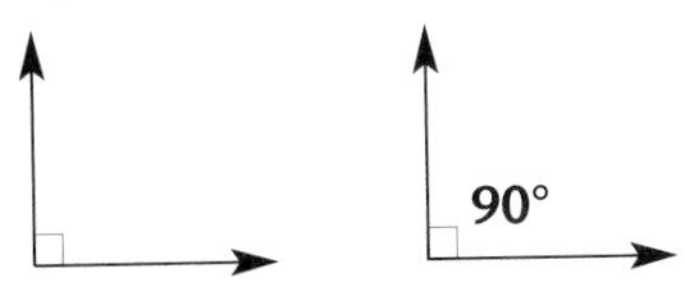

7. If $\angle A$ and $\angle B$ are supplementary, then their angle sum is 180°.

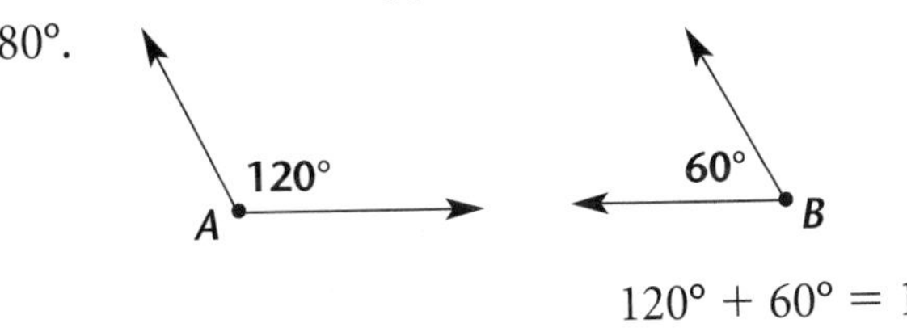

8. If an angle is a straight angle, then it measures 180°.

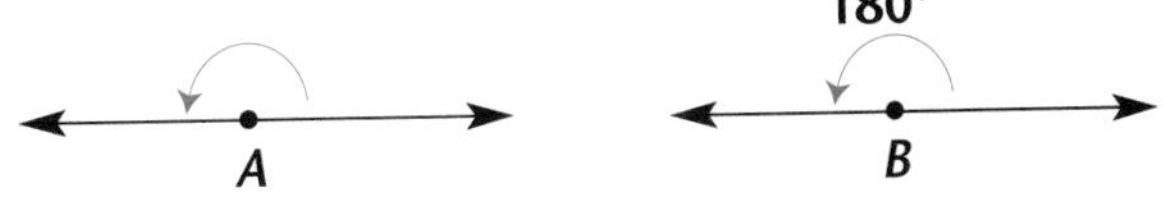

9. If $\angle Y$ and $\angle Z$ are equal, then they are supplementary.

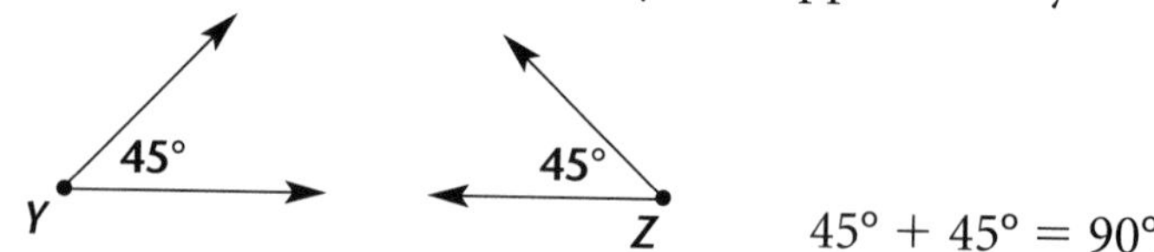

$45° + 45° = 90°$

10. If *ABCD* is a square, then it is a rectangle.

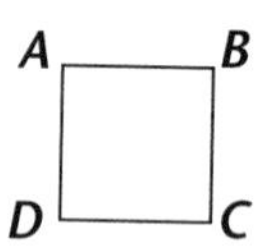

Exercise C Write the converse of each conditional.

11. If an angle is obtuse, then its angle measure is $90° < m < 180°$.

12. If a figure has four sides, then it is a rectangle.

13. If the sum of the measures of two angles is 90°, then the angles are complementary.

14. If a figure is a triangle, then it has three sides.

15. If an animal is a dog, then it has four legs.

Exercise D Write *True* or *False* for each conditional and each converse in Exercise C.

TRY THIS Collect six newspaper or magazine advertisements. See how many claims for the product you can write in the form of an "If . . . then . . ." statement.

Lesson 2 Euclid's Five Postulates

Euclid wrote the first complete geometry book. He lived in ancient Greece about 300 B.C. Euclid began his book with five "facts" or assumptions about geometry in a plane. He assumed these statements were true without proving them. These statements, called *Euclid's postulates,* form the building blocks for plane Euclidean geometry. They explain why certain constructions can be made. You will need to know these postulates as part of your study of geometry.

Euclid's Postulate 1

A straight line can be drawn from any point to any point.

Remember that a statement assumed to be true without proof is a postulate.

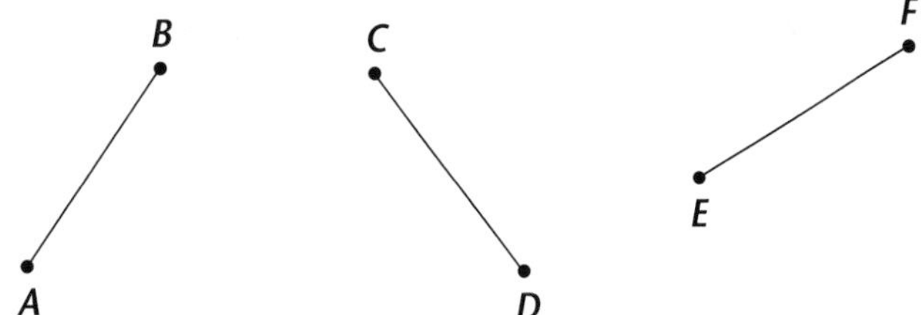

Algebra Review

Do you remember using equations to graph lines in an algebra class? To graph a line, you only need to plot two points. Then you can draw the line through these two points. This procedure from algebra is related to Euclid's Postulate 1.

You could connect point A not only with B, but with C, D, E, and so on.

The lines on this map represent airline routes showing where planes travel from one point to another.

Euclid's Postulate 2

A finite straight line can be extended continuously in a straight line. (A finite straight line is a line segment.)

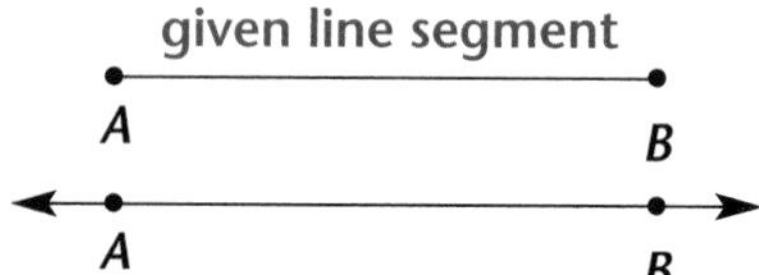

Postulate 2 allows you to extend the line segment in each direction.

Euclid's Postulate 3

A circle may be described with any center and distance. (The given distance is the radius of the circle.)

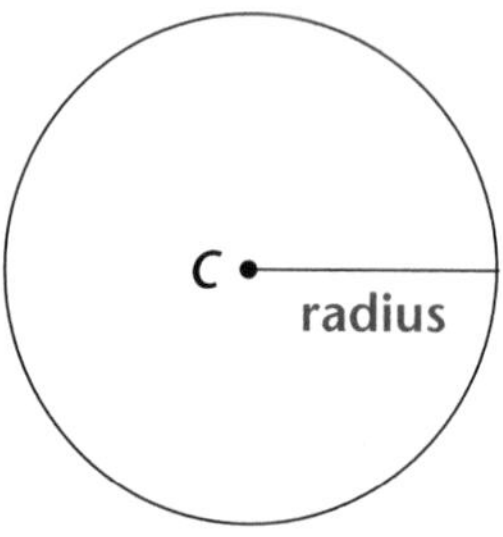

Postulate 3 means that if you are given a point *C* and a distance, you can draw a circle with the center at *C* and a radius equal to the given distance.

Euclid's Postulate 4

All right angles are equal to one another.

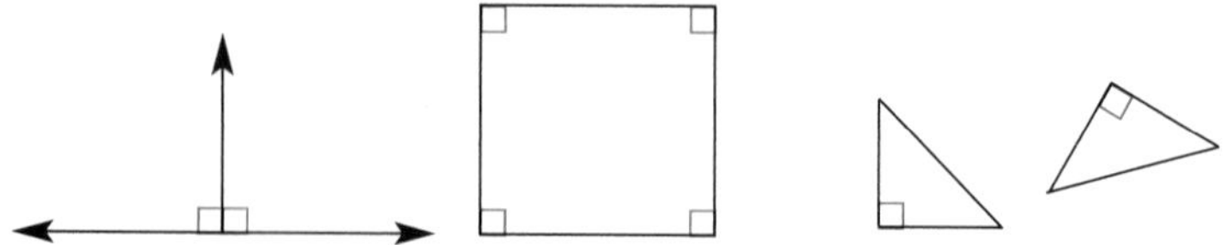

This postulate assumes that the measures of all right angles are equal to each other and to 90°.

Euclid's Postulate 5

If two lines ℓ and m are cut by a third line t, and the two inside angles, a and b, together measure less than two right angles, then the two lines ℓ and m, if extended, will meet on the same side of t as the two angles a and b.

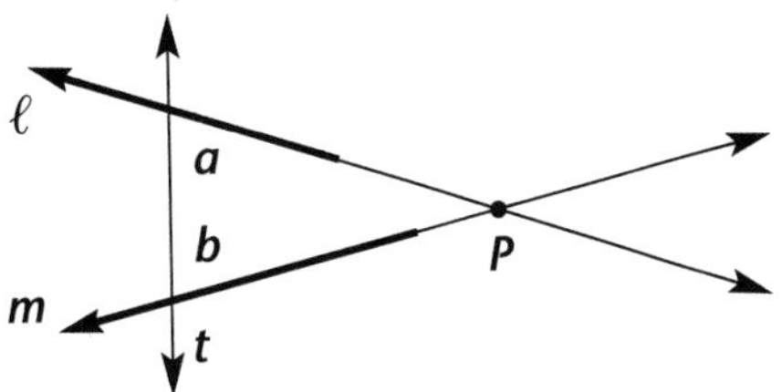

When two lines intersect, they cross each other.

This postulate actually defines the conditions necessary for two lines to meet or *intersect*. The illustration of the postulate shows that if $m\angle a + m\angle b < 2 \cdot 90°$, then ℓ intersects m at P.

There is a modern equivalent to Euclid's Postulate 5.

Parallel Postulate 5

If there is a line ℓ and a point P not on ℓ, then there is only one line that passes through P and is parallel to ℓ.

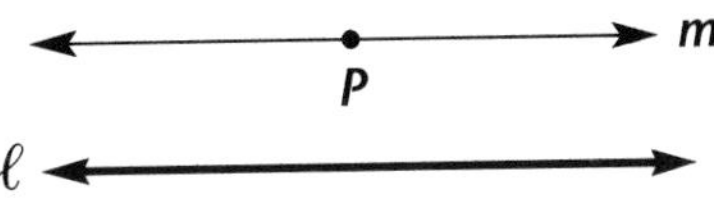

Line m is the only line through P that is parallel to the given line ℓ.

This statement has the same meaning as Euclid's Postulate 5. Therefore, Euclid's Postulate 5 is often called the "Parallel Postulate."

This chair is an example of Euclid's Postulate 5. Going from bottom to top, the legs are crossed by a third piece. The interior angles measure less than two right angles, so the legs intersect above the third piece.

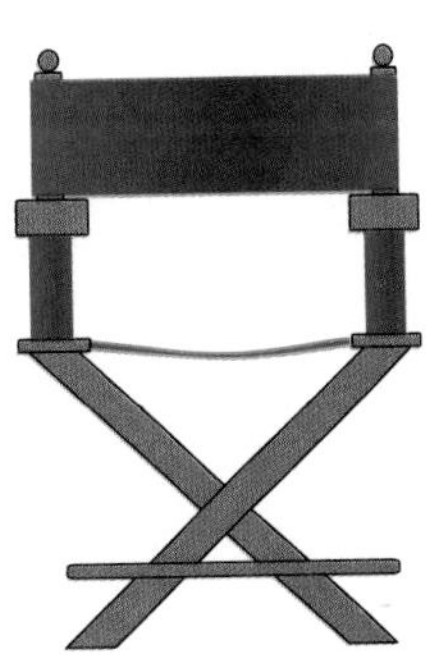

Exercise A Identify the postulate that allows each construction to be made.

1. Draw a circle with center *A* and distance *d.*

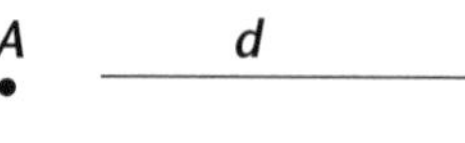

2. Use line segments to connect point *P* to points *A, B,* and *C.*

3. Draw a line that is parallel to line ℓ and passes through point *X.*

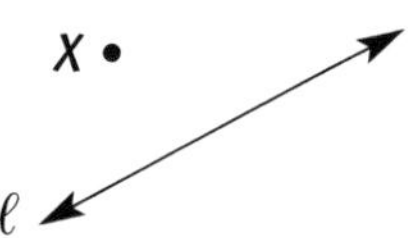

4. Draw a straight line segment between points *P* and *Q.* Then extend the line beyond each endpoint.

Exercise B Tell which of Euclid's postulates makes each of the following statements true.

5. Angles *A, B,* and *C* are all right angles; therefore, their measures are equal.

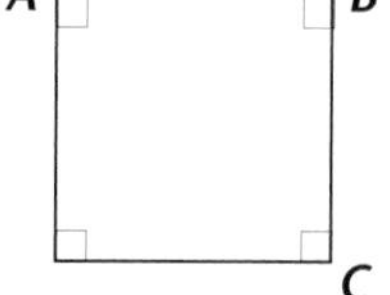

6. There is no line other than line *s* that can be parallel to ℓ and pass through *Q.*

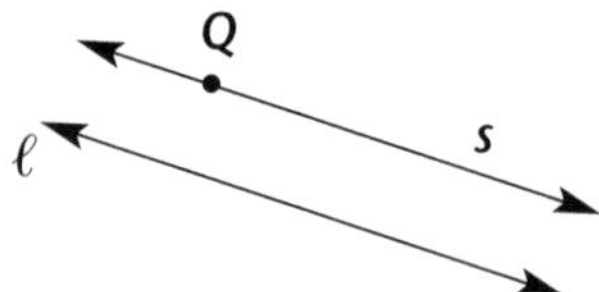

7. You can connect the points *W, X, Y,* and *Z* to form a geometric figure.

8. Lines s and t will intersect at some point to the right of line p.

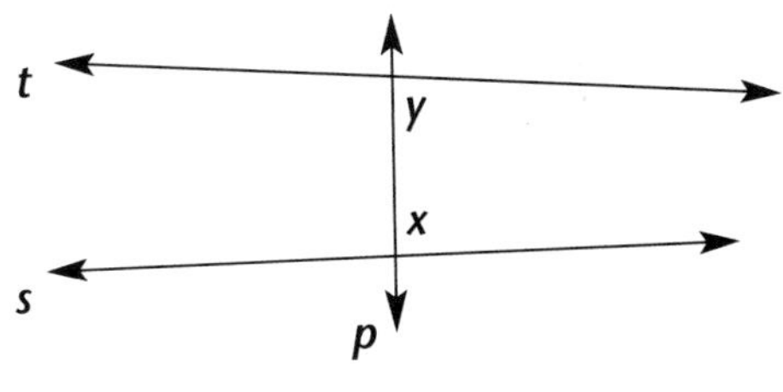

$$m\angle x + m\angle y < 2 \cdot 90°$$

9. You can use a point Q and a line segment AB to draw a circle.

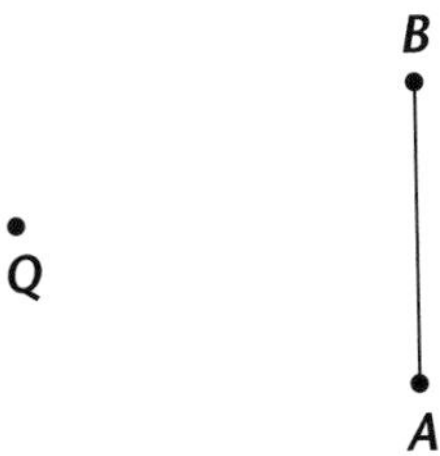

PROBLEM SOLVING

Exercise C Solve the following problem.

10. Line ℓ forms two right angles when it crosses lines m and n. Are lines m and n parallel? Why do you think so?

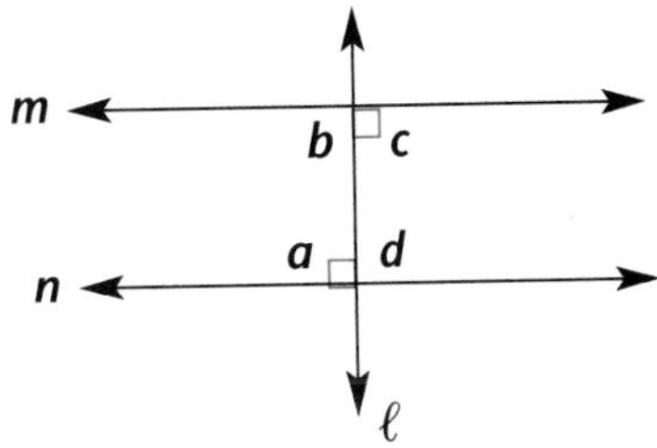

Geometry in Your Life

A builder uses a carpenter's square to mark a line across a board at a right angle to the edge before cutting. The line also makes a right angle with the opposite side of the board. You can see this by folding a sheet of lined paper so that the horizontal lines make right angles with the fold. Use your protractor to make sure that all the angles made by the fold are equal.

Lesson 3 Using Euclid's Postulates

In geometry, you must be able to explain why you can take certain steps. Euclid's five postulates form the basis of constructions in geometry. They provide the reasons for some of geometry's basic constructions.

Remember, $\overline{AB}$ is the symbol for line segment AB. $\overleftrightarrow{XY}$ is the symbol for line XY.

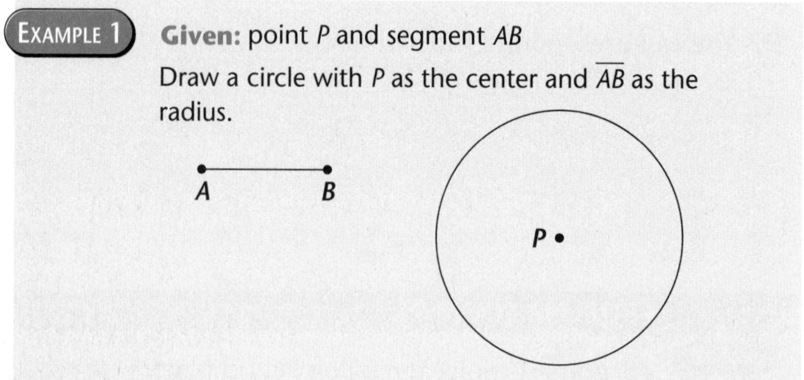

Euclid's Postulate 3 allows you to make this construction.

Euclid's Postulate 3 allows the greens keeper at a golf course to make a putting green with a radius of any size.

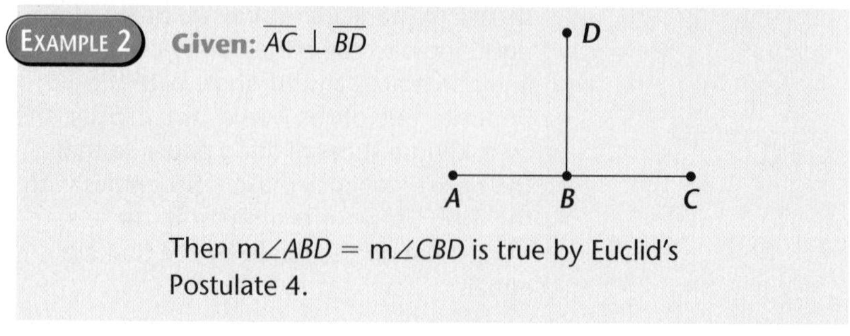

EXAMPLE 3 **Given:** three points A, B, and C that are not collinear
Draw all the lines that pass through these three points.

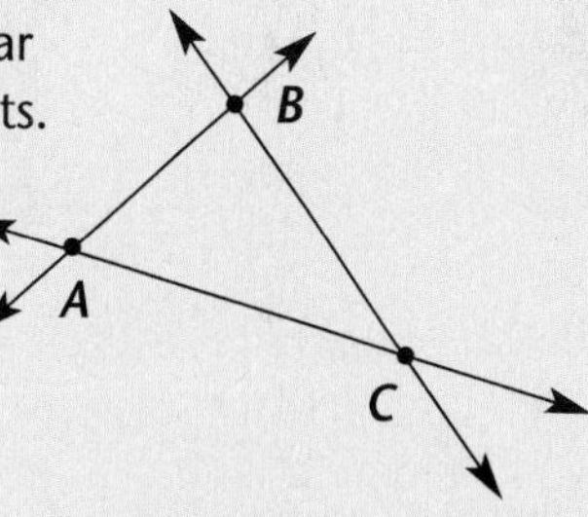

$\overleftrightarrow{AB}$, $\overleftrightarrow{AC}$, and $\overleftrightarrow{BC}$ can be drawn using Euclid's Postulate 1 and Postulate 2.

This draftsperson uses Euclid's postulates to draw geometric figures. A compass, a straightedge, and Euclid's Postulate 4 can be used to construct several right angles equal to each other.

Exercise A Name the postulate that makes each construction possible.

1. Draw lines passing through point A and points B and C.

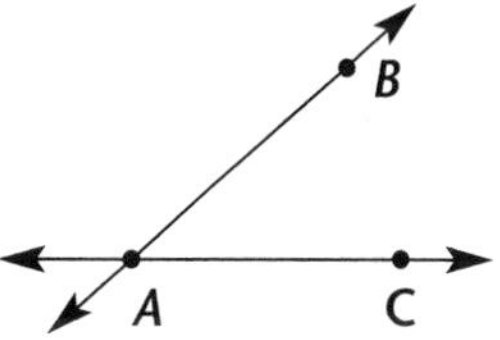

2. Draw two circles, one with center A, one with center B, and each with a radius $\overline{AB}$.

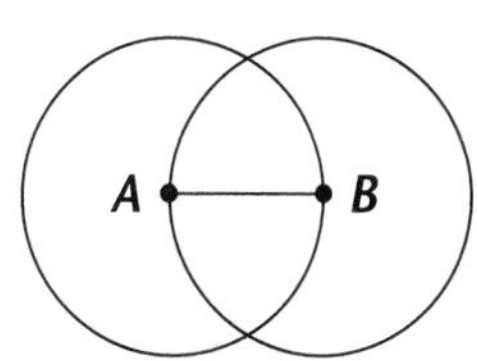

3. Extend all the sides of triangle ABC.

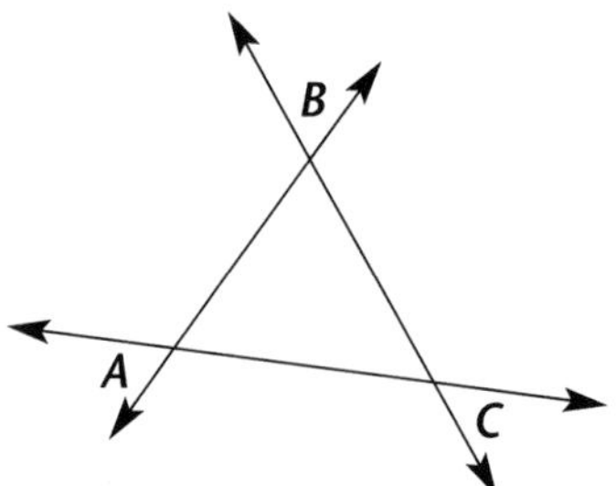

4. Draw four right angles equal to one another.

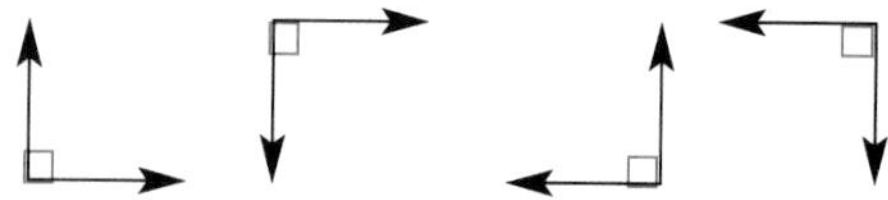

5. Extend all the sides of pentagon $ABCDE$.

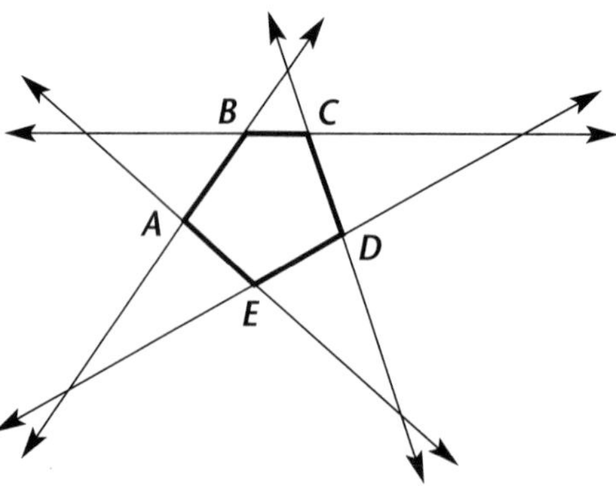

6. Draw line segments from point P to points A, B, C, D, E, and F.

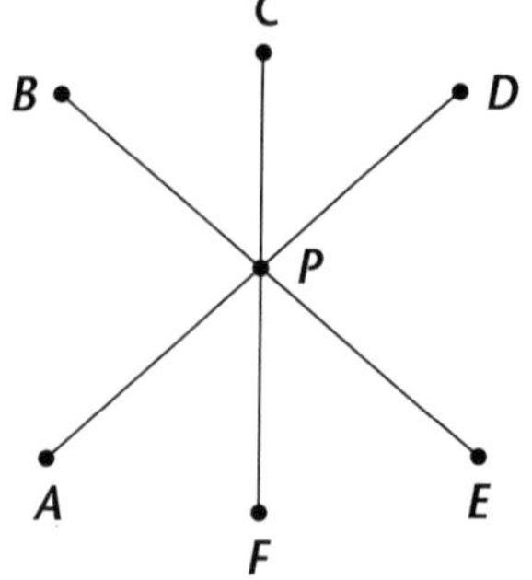

7. Draw three circles, each with radius $\overline{AB}$ and centers A, B, and C.

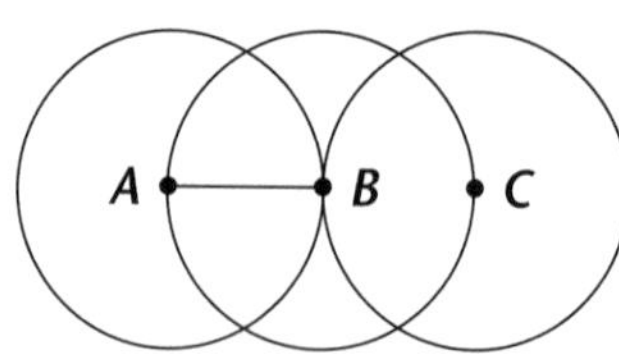

8. Draw two lines parallel to line ℓ, one through point P and one through point Q.

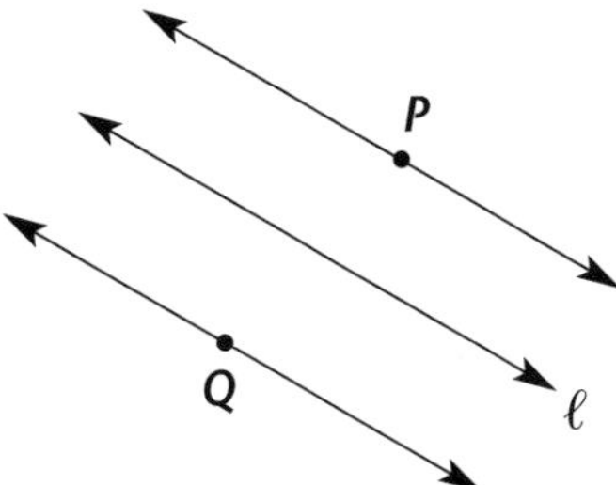

9. Draw a circle with center P and with a radius equal to PQ.

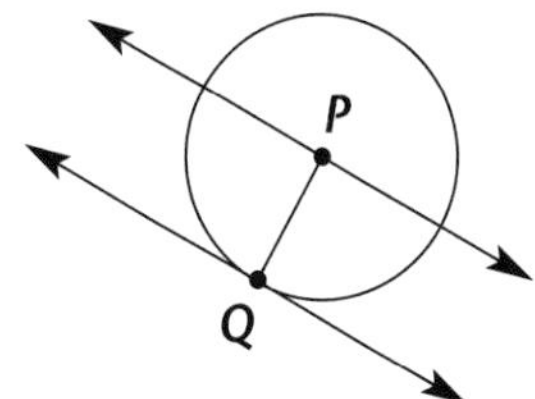

10. Draw a line and two perpendicular rays to form four equal angles.

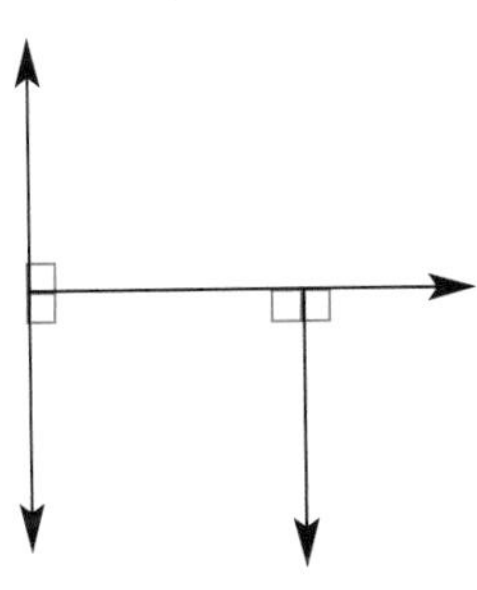

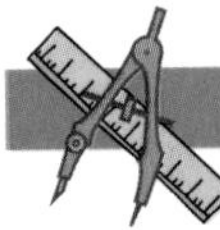

CONSTRUCTION

Exercise B Do these constructions on a separate sheet of paper. Tell which postulate(s) you used to make each construction.

11. Draw a line between points K and L.

12. Draw a line segment MN; then extend each end.

13. Draw a rectangle; state which angles are equal.

14. Given point P and a distance of 2 inches, draw a circle.

15. Given line ℓ and point Q not on the line, draw a line through Q and parallel to ℓ.

16. Given $\overline{FG}$, extend the line to include points H and J.

17. Connect points A, B, and C to form a triangle.

18. Draw a circle with center at point P, and a radius twice the length of $\overline{CD}$. Let $CD = 3$ cm.

19. Given line ℓ and points A and B not on line ℓ, draw two lines parallel to ℓ, one passing through A, one passing through B.

20. Given $\overline{QR}$ and point P, draw a circle with radius equal to three times QR and center at point P. Let $QR = 4$ cm.

Writing About Mathematics

Which version of the parallel postulate do you use to draw parallel lines? Why? Which version do you use to draw intersecting lines? Why?

Geometry in Your Life

Suppose there are four friends you want to visit. Copy the points at the right on a sheet of paper. Use these points to represent their houses and your house. Connect the points to show how you can visit each person's house only once and return home. You cannot cross any path you have already walked on. Think about which postulate allows you to complete this puzzle.

Lesson 4 Axioms or Common Notions

Axiom

A statement assumed to be true without proof

An **axiom,** like a postulate, is a statement taken to be true without proof. Axioms are statements about properties of equality. Axioms give us a formal way to refer to facts that seem obviously true. You may remember some axioms from your study of algebra. You used them to solve equations.

In addition to his postulates, Euclid included five axioms or common notions (ideas) in his geometry text. The fact that Euclid included statements about algebra in a book about geometry shows that he saw a clear connection between the two subjects.

Euclid		Algebra
Axiom 1	Things that are equal to the same thing are equal to each other.	If $a = b$ $b = c$ then $a = c$ You might think of this as substituting c for b.
Axiom 2	If equals are added to equals, the sums are equal.	If $a = b$ $c = d$ then $a + c = b + d$
Axiom 3	If equals are subtracted from equals, the differences are equal.	If $a = b$ $c = d$ then $a - c = b - d$
Axiom 4	Things that are alike or coincide with each other are equal to one another.	Two figures that can be made to match each other, point for point, are equal.
Axiom 5	The whole, or sum, is greater than the parts.	If $a + b = c$ a and $b > 0$ then $c > a$ and $c > b$

EXAMPLE 1

Given:

$$\begin{array}{r} x - 3 = 10 \\ +3 = +3 \\ \hline x = 13 \end{array}$$

Reason

Axiom 2
If equals are added to equals, the sums are equal.

EXAMPLE 2

Given:

$$\begin{array}{r} x + 3 = 10 \\ -3 = -3 \\ \hline x = 7 \end{array}$$

Reason

Axiom 3
If equals are subtracted from equals, the differences are equal.

EXAMPLE 3

Given:

1 yard = 3 feet
1 foot = 12 inches
1 yard = 3(12 inches)
= 36 inches

Reason

Axiom 1
Equals can be substituted for equals.

EXAMPLE 4

Given: The upper half circle, called a *semicircle,* completely matches the lower half. (Think of folding them together along the center line or diameter.)

Therefore, the semicircles are equal.

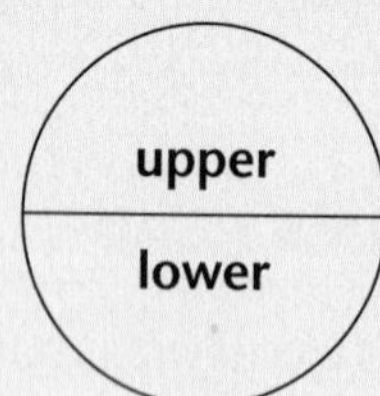

Reason

Axiom 4
Things that coincide, point for point, are equal.

EXAMPLE 5

Given: $m\angle ABD + m\angle DBC = 180°$

Therefore, $180° > m\angle ABD$ and $180° > m\angle DBC$.

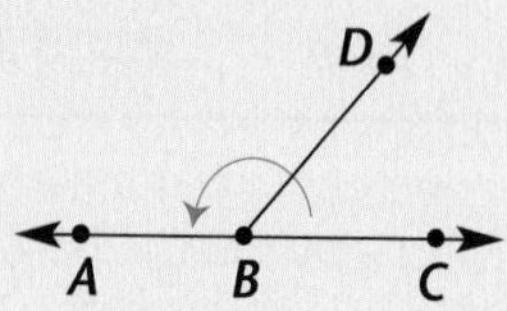

Reason

Axiom 5
The whole is greater than the parts.

Exercise A Name the axiom that gives the reason for each step.

1. $$\begin{aligned} y - 5 &= 10 \\ +5 &= +5 \\ \hline y &= 15 \end{aligned}$$

2. $$\begin{aligned} w + 5 &= 10 \\ -5 &= -5 \\ \hline w &= 5 \end{aligned}$$

3. $$\begin{aligned} z + 7 &= 30 \\ -7 &= -7 \\ \hline z &= 23 \end{aligned}$$

4. $$\begin{aligned} q + 6 &= 12 \\ -6 &= -6 \\ \hline q &= 6 \end{aligned}$$

5. $$\begin{aligned} m - 4 &= 10 \\ +4 &= +4 \\ \hline m &= 14 \end{aligned}$$

Exercise B Answer each question. Tell which axiom you used.

6. Which angles are less than 90°? Why?

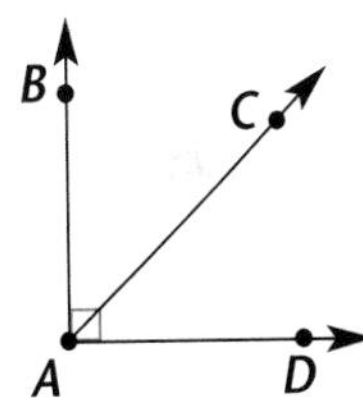

7. The m∠a = m∠b, and m∠b = m∠c. Does m∠a = m∠c? Why?

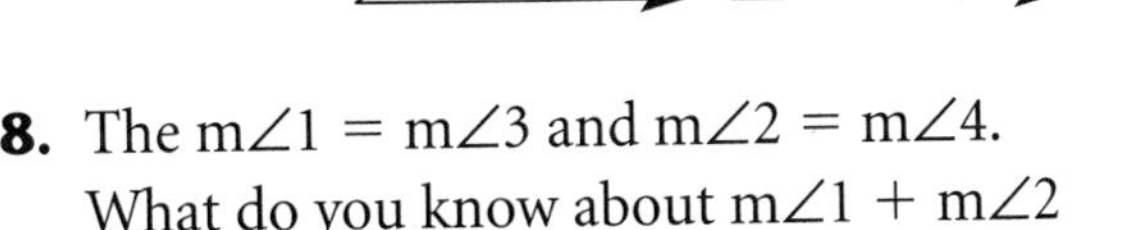

8. The m∠1 = m∠3 and m∠2 = m∠4. What do you know about m∠1 + m∠2 and m∠3 + m∠4? Why?

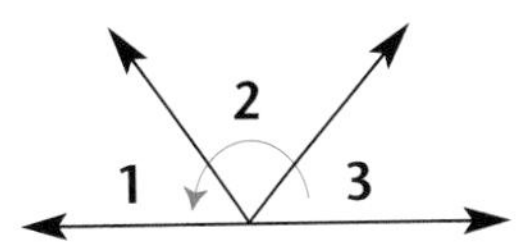

9. Which angles are less than 180°? Why?

10. Every point on square *ABCD* can be matched to a point on *EFGH*. What can you say about the two squares? Why?

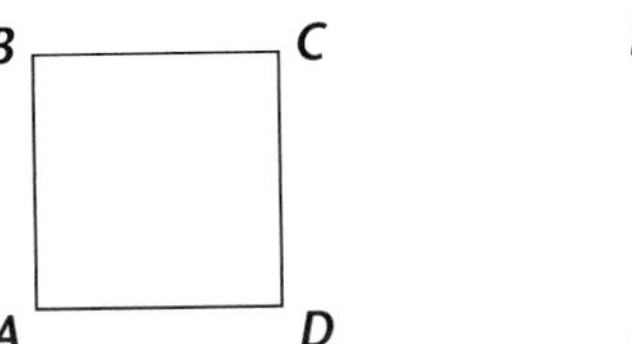

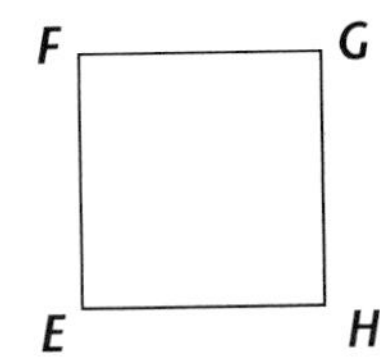

EXAMPLE 6 1 week = 7 days
1 day = 24 hours
1 week = ____ hours

Press 7 × 24 ENTER.

The answer is 168 hours.

Exercise C Complete each of the following. Tell which axiom you used. Use your calculator to check your computation.

11. 1 gal = 4 qt
1 qt = 2 pt
1 gal = ____ pt

12. 1 qt = 2 pt
1 pt = 16 oz
1 qt = _____ oz

13. 1 pt = 2 c
1 c = 8 oz
1 pt = ___ oz

14. 1 day = 24 hr
1 hr = 60 min
1 day = ___ min

15. 1 decade = 10 years
1 year = 365 days
1 decade = ____ days

Estimation Activity

Estimate: Before using a calculator, estimate the answer first. Check your estimate with the answer in the display.

Solution:

1 week	= 7 days ≈ 10 days	Round the number of days.
1 day	= 24 hours ≈ 20 hours	Round the number of hours.
1 week	= __ hours ≈ 200 hours	Multiply 10 × 20.

One number was rounded up and one number was rounded down. Therefore you can't tell whether the answer will be less than or greater than the estimate.

Lesson 5 A Simple Proof

Proof
A series of true statements leading to a desired conclusion

Theorem
A statement that can be proven true

Given
Specified

Prove
To show that a conclusion is true

In your study of geometry in this book, you have learned about points, lines, and planes. You have also learned that axioms and postulates are assumed to be true without proof. Definitions, too, are true statements. **Theorems,** however, are statements that need to be proven true. A **proof** is a series of true statements. The last statement in a proof is the desired conclusion.

Vertical Angle Theorem (2.5.1):
If angles are vertical angles, then their measures are equal.

Theorems in this book are numbered to help you locate them. For example, the first theorem in Chapter 2, Lesson 5, is numbered 2.5.1.

Adjacent angles have a common vertex and one common side.

EXAMPLE 1 To start a proof, clearly state what is **given** and what is to **prove.** In this case the *given,* or *hypothesis,* is "angles are vertical." The *conclusion* to be proved true is "their measures are equal."

Next, use a construction to draw a picture of the given. You may also write out the given information.

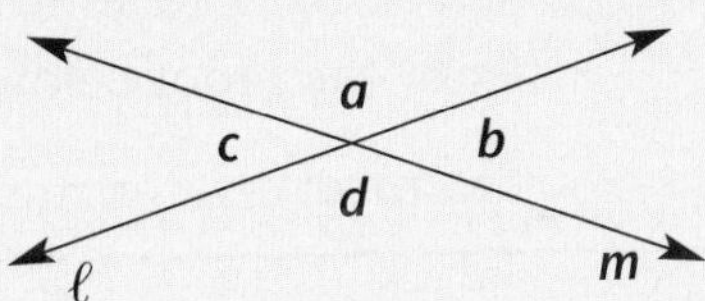

Recall that vertical angles have a common vertex and the same sides.

$\angle a$ and $\angle d$ are vertical angles.

$\angle c$ and $\angle b$ are vertical angles.

You may use symbols to write what you need to prove.

To Prove: $m\angle a = m\angle d$ and
$m\angle c = m\angle b$

Now you are ready to start your proof. You will need to work in two columns. On the left, list the true statements you need to reach the conclusion. On the right, list the definition, axiom, or postulate that makes the statement true.

Refer to the figure in the example on page 55. Prove m$\angle a$ = m$\angle d$.

PROOF

Statement	Reason
1. Lines ℓ and m intersect to form vertical angles a and d.	1. Given.
2. m$\angle a$ + m$\angle b$ = 180°	2. $\angle a$ and $\angle b$ are adjacent on m and are supplementary.
3. m$\angle b$ + m$\angle d$ = 180°	3. $\angle b$ and $\angle d$ are adjacent on ℓ and are supplementary.
4. m$\angle a$ + m$\angle b$ = m$\angle b$ + m$\angle d$	4. Axiom 1, substitution, and steps 2 and 3.
5. ∴ m$\angle a$ = m$\angle d$	5. Axiom 3. If equals are subtracted from equals, the differences are equal.

∴ means "therefore" and is used to signal the last step of the proof.

The vertical angles a and d have been proved equal. Notice that angles c and b also form vertical angles, so they too must be equal. For practice, you can work out the proof that shows angles c and b are equal in the following exercises.

Exercise A Refer to the figure in the example on page 55. Copy the proof below. Write the reason(s) for each step.

To Prove: m$\angle c$ = m$\angle b$

PROOF

Statement	Reason
1. Lines ℓ and m intersect to form vertical angles b and c.	**1.** ________
2. m$\angle a$ + m$\angle c$ = 180°	**2.** ________
3. m$\angle a$ + m$\angle b$ = 180°	**3.** ________
4. m$\angle a$ + m$\angle c$ = m$\angle a$ + m$\angle b$	**4.** ________
5. ∴ m$\angle c$ = m$\angle b$	**5.** ________

Exercise B Use the Vertical Angle Theorem to find the measures of angles x, y, and z.

6.

x 120°

y z

7.

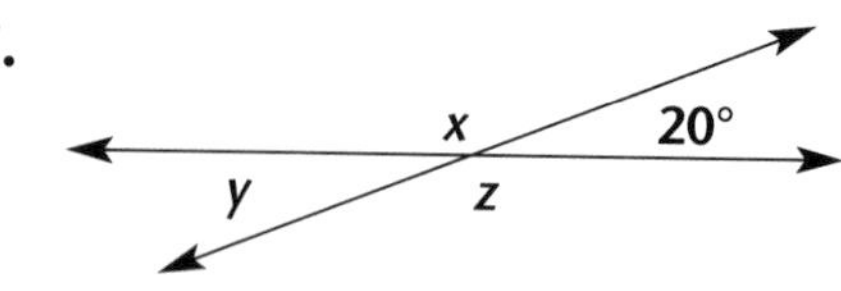

8.

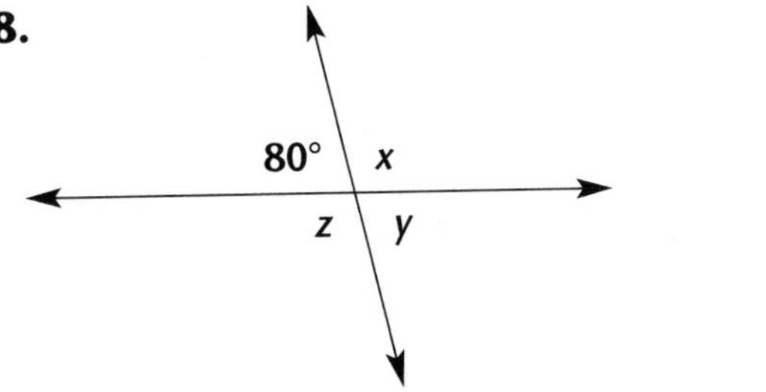

9.

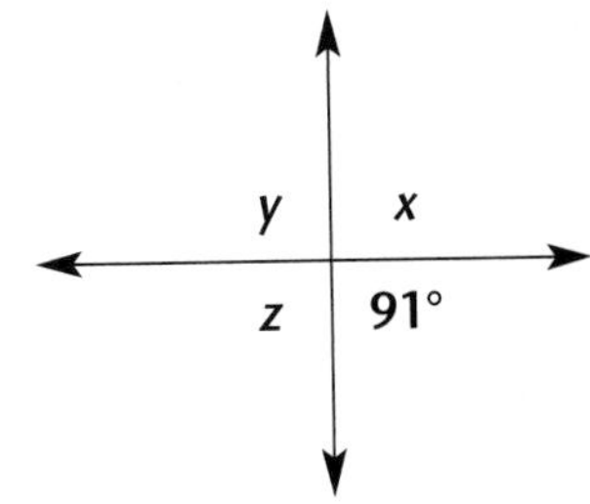

10.

Exercise C Give a reason for each of the following statements. Use the diagram at the right.

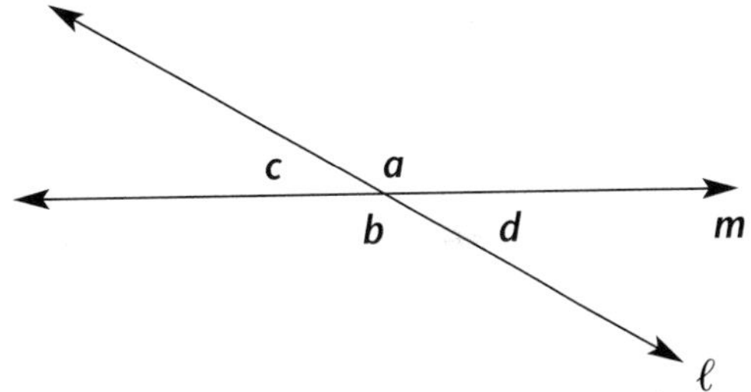

Given: ℓ intersects m

11. $m\angle a = m\angle b$

12. $m\angle a < 180°$

13. $m\angle b < 180°$

14. $180° - m\angle a = 180° - m\angle b$

PROBLEM SOLVING

Exercise D Follow the directions.

15. Give two different reasons for each of the following statements. Use the diagram at the right.

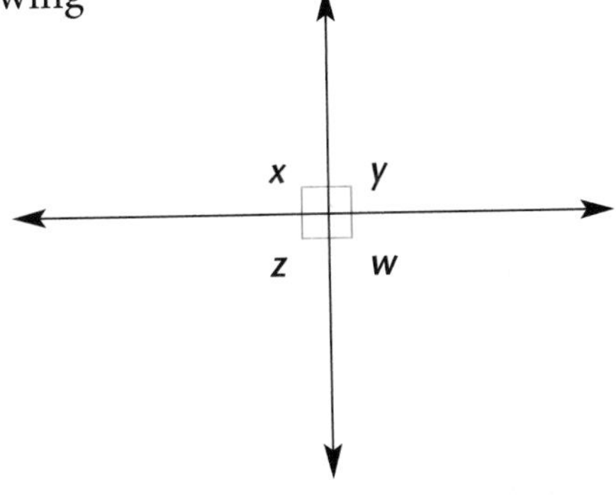

a. $m\angle x = m\angle w$

b. $m\angle y = m\angle z$

c. $m\angle x = m\angle y = m\angle w = m\angle z$

Lesson 6 Algebra Connection: The Distributive Property

Distributive property

a(b + c) = ab + ac

Factor

To write an expression as the product of its multipliers

Common factor

A multiplier shared by the terms in an expression

Remember that multiplication can be written several ways. For example, $3 \bullet a$ can also be written $3a$. Subtracting a number can be written as adding a negative number. For example, $5x - 15$ can be written as $5x + (-15)$.

Suppose you want to multiply $3 \cdot 14$ in your head. One way is to break apart 14 to make two easier products. Multiply 10 by 3 *and* multiply 4 by 3. Then add the products.

$$3 \cdot (10 + 4) = (3 \cdot 10) + (3 \cdot 4)$$

$$= 30 + 12 = 42$$

You have spread out or *distributed* multiplication by 3 over addition. You can use the **distributive property** to multiply and simplify at the same time. You can also use the distributive property to **factor** an expression.

EXAMPLE 1 Multiply: $3(a + b)$

You can multiply and then simplify.

$3(a + b) = a + b + a + b + a + b = 3a + 3b$

It is faster and easier to use the distributive property. Multiply a by 3 and multiply b by 3. Then add.

$3(a + b) = 3 \bullet a + 3 \bullet b = 3a + 3b$

Factor: $3a + 3b$

3 is a factor of $3a$ and 3 is a factor of $3b$. So, 3 is a **common factor** of $3a + 3b$.

When there is a common factor, you can use the distributive property.

product of 3 and $(a + b)$

$3a + 3b = 3(a + b)$

3 and $(a + b)$ are factors.

EXAMPLE 2 Multiply: $5(x - 3)$

$5(x - 3) = 5(x) + 5(-3) = 5x - 15$

Factor: $5x - 15$

5 is a factor of $5x$ and 5 is a factor of -15.

So, 5 is a common factor of $5x - 15$.

$5x - 15 = 5(x) + 5(-3) = 5(x - 3)$

EXAMPLE 3 Multiply: $a(x + y)$

$$a(x + y) = ax + ay$$

In this case, we are using the distributive property to multiply.

Factor: $ax + ay$

Think: a is a factor of ax and a is a factor of ay.

So, we can rewrite $ax + ay$ as the product of two factors.

$$a(x) + a(y) = a(x + y)$$

EXAMPLE 4 Multiply: $3(x - y + z)$

$$3(x - y + z) = 3x - 3y + 3z$$

Factor: $3x - 3y + 3z$

3 is a common factor, so you can rewrite $3x - 3y + 3z$ as a product of two factors.

$$3(x) - 3(y) + 3(z) = 3(x - y + z)$$

In general, for any real numbers a, b, and c, $a(b + c) = ab + ac$.

Exercise A Copy and complete.

1. $3(10 + 8) = 3 \cdot ■ + 3 \cdot ■$
2. $7(m + 3) = 7 \cdot ■ + 7 \cdot ■$
3. $a(b + x) = a \cdot ■ + a \cdot ■$
4. $5(x - y) = 5 \cdot ■ + 5 \cdot ■$
5. $y(5 - y) = y \cdot ■ + y \cdot ■$
6. $c(x + w) = c \cdot ■ + c \cdot ■$

Exercise B Use the distributive property to multiply.

7. $4(x + y)$
8. $9(4 + a)$
9. $a(x - y)$
10. $6(2x + 1)$
11. $c(y - w)$
12. $5(x + y + z)$
13. $a(x + y - z)$
14. $5(3 - x + z)$
15. $b(x - 3 + y)$

Exercise C Factor.

16. $am + ax$
17. $3x - 3y$
18. $5x + 15$
19. $ax + 3ay - aw$
20. $6x - 15y + 21z$

Application

Logical Deductions Detectives solve crimes by collecting as many clues as possible, then making conclusions based on facts. This process is called *logical deduction.* Mathematicians studying geometry use this process. They start with what they know and use the facts to discover new facts.

You can use logical deduction to solve problems.

EXAMPLE 1 Bob has two brothers. The oldest boy is 21. Henry is one year older than Bob. When Bob was born, John had just turned three. List the brothers' names from oldest to youngest. Give their current ages.

B = Bob's age
H = Henry's age = $B + 1$
J = John's age = $B + 3$
John is the oldest, so $J = 21$, $B = 21 - 3 = 18$, and $H = 18 + 1 = 19$

John is 21, Henry is 19, and Bob is 18.

Exercises Solve each using logical deductions.

1. Emmanuel, Javier, and Isaac are 8, 13, and 16 years old. Javier is older than Isaac. Emmanuel is twice as old as Isaac. Find each person's age.

2. Ben stacks five different colored blocks in a tower. The green block is between the orange and the blue blocks. The yellow block is below the orange block and above the green block. The red block is below the yellow block and is not touching the green block. List the colors of the blocks from bottom to top.

3. Selva, Patricia, Cindy, and Alicia played a game of basketball. They scored 12, 16, 17, and 20 points. Cindy scored 4 points less than Patricia. Patricia scored three points more than Selva. Selva scored more points than Alicia. How many points did each person score?

4. A jar contains \$5.61 worth of coins. There are more quarters than any other coin. There are two times as many dimes as nickels. There are five more pennies than nickels. The value of the nickels is the same as the value of 1 quarter plus 1 nickel. How many of each coin are there?

Chapter 2 REVIEW

Choose the letter of the correct answer.

1. Which conditional is false?

   A If an angle is acute, then it has a measure of less than 45°.

   B If two angles are complementary, then the sum of their measures is 90°.

   C If the sum of the measures of two angles is 90°, then the angles are complementary.

   D If an angle has a measure of less than 45°, then it is acute.

2. Which statement has a converse that is true?

   A If *ABCD* is a square, then it is a rectangle.

   B If *ABCD* is a square, then it has four sides.

   C If *ABCD* has four sides, then it is a rectangle.

   D If *ABCD* is a rectangle, then it contains a 90° angle.

3. *P* is a point that does not lie on line *m*. How many lines are there that pass through *P* and are parallel to *m*?

   A 0 **C** 2
   B 1 **D** more than 2

4. Points *X*, *Y*, and *Z* are not on a straight line. How many lines can be constructed that contain two of these points?

   A 0 **C** 2
   B 1 **D** more than 2

Use the diagram to the right for problems 5–6.

5. What is the measure of $\angle b$?

   A 42° **C** 138°
   B 132° **D** 180°

6. What is the measure of $\angle c$?

   A 42° **C** 132°
   B 48° **D** 180°

Euclid's Postulates
1 A straight line can be drawn from any point to any point.
2 A finite straight line can be extended continuously in a straight line.
3 A circle may be described with any center and distance.
4 All right angles are equal to one another.
5 If two lines ℓ and m are cut by a third line t, and the two inside angles, a and b, together measure less than two right angles, then the two lines will meet on the same side as the two angles a and b.
Parallel Postulate 5
If there is a line ℓ and a point P not on ℓ, then there is only one line that passes through P and is parallel to ℓ.
Axioms
1 Things that are equal to the same thing are equal to each other.
2 If equals are added to equals, the sums are equal.
3 If equals are subtracted from equals, the differences are equal.
4 Things that are alike or coincide with each other are equal to each other.
5 The whole, or sum, is greater than the parts.

Use statements 1 and 2 for problems 7–12.

Example: Statement: If an angle is a straight angle, then it measures 180°.
Hypothesis: An angle is a straight angle.
Conclusion: It measures 180°.
Converse: If an angle measures 180°, then it is a straight angle.

Statement 1: If an angle is acute, then it measures less than 90°.

Statement 2: If the sum of the measures of two angles is 90°, then the angles are complementary.

7. Write the hypothesis for Statement 1.

8. Write the hypothesis for Statement 2.

9. Write the conclusion for Statement 1.

10. Write the conclusion for Statement 2.

11. Write the converse of Statement 1.

12. Write the converse of Statement 2.

Write which postulate allows each construction to be made.

Example: A B / A B

Solution: Postulate 2, A finite straight line can be extended continuously in a straight line.

13. Connect point P to points A, B, C, and D.

A B P C D

14. Draw a line that is parallel to line m and passes through point X.

m X

15. Draw a circle with center A and distance, r.

A r

Write which axiom allows each operation.

Example: $m + 13 = 17$
$-13 = -13$
$m = 4$

Solution: Axiom 3, If equals are subtracted from equals, the differences are equal.

16. $m - 9 = 20$
$+9 = +9$
$m = 29$

17. Angle $x + y$ is less than 180°.

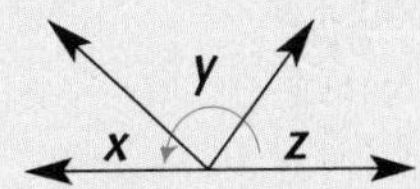

Copy the proof. Write the missing steps to prove m∠c = m∠b.

Statement: Lines ℓ and m intersect.
Reason: Given.

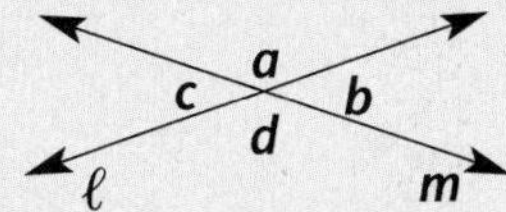

Proof Statement	Reason
1. Lines ℓ and m intersect. ∠b and ∠c are vertical angles.	1. **18.** ____
2. **19.** ____	2. ∠a and ∠b are adjacent on line m and are supplementary.
3. m∠a + m∠c = 180°	3. **20.** ____
4. **21.** ____	4. Axiom 1, substitution, and steps 2 and 3.
5. **22.** ____	5. Axiom 3. If equals are subtracted from equals, the differences are equal.

Find the measure of each angle.

Example: ∠z

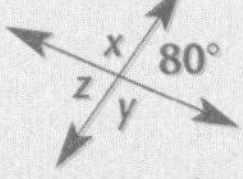

Solution: Angle z and the angle marked 80° are vertical angles. Since vertical angles are equal, m∠z = 80°.

Use the illustration below for problems 23–25.

23. ∠x

24. ∠y

25. ∠z

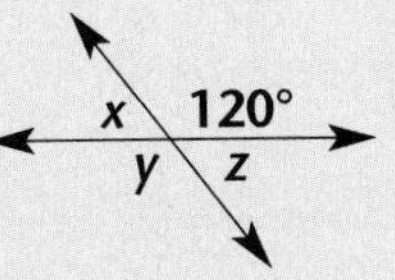

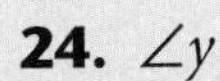

Test-Taking Tip

When you read test directions, restate them in your own words. Tell yourself exactly what you are expected to do.

Chapter

Parallel Lines and Transversals

These train tracks appear to get closer together as they head off into the distance. But this is just an illusion. The trails of a train track are set a constant distance apart to match the wheels of the trains. Because these rails stay the same distance apart, they will never cross. Parallel lines in the same plane have these qualities.

Beneath the rails are wooden boards called ties that are used to keep the rails in place. From above, the ties intersect the rails in the same way that transversals intersect parallel lines. They meet both rails at the same angle.

In Chapter 3, you will learn how to identify and measure angles in parallels and quadrilaterals.

Goals for Learning

- To distinguish parallel, intersecting, and skew lines
- To identify and name angles formed by transversals crossing parallel lines
- To use theorems to compare and find the measures of angles and identify parallel lines
- To construct squares, rectangles, and trapezoids
- To use postulates and theorems to construct parallel lines
- To define quadrilaterals and parallels and apply theorems to them

Lesson 1 Parallel Lines

Parallel lines ||
Lines in the same plane that never meet

Coplanar
Lines or points in the same plane

Skew lines
Lines in space that are not coplanar and never meet

Parallel lines are all around us. Look at a race track and you will see that the lanes are parallel to one another. The lines that divide the lanes are parallel to one another as well.

Look for parallel lines. You'll see them everywhere. Parallel lines are in the same plane and never meet.

Remember, a *plane* is one of geometry's undefined terms. You can think of a page from this book or a desktop as part of a plane.

Parallel lines are lines that do not meet or intersect. Another condition for parallel lines is that the lines must be in the same plane. Lines in the same plane are called **coplanar.** Look at the picture of the shoe box below. Notice that the bottom and side edges indicated do not meet. These lines are not in the same plane. Lines in space that never meet and are not in the same plane are **skew lines.**

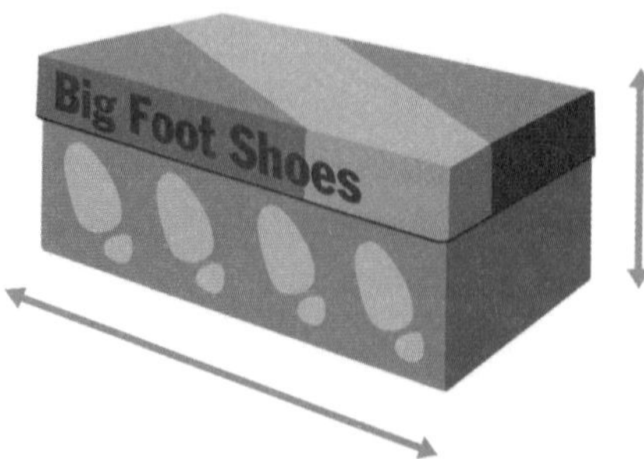

These bottom and side edges do not meet. The lines are not in the same plane. The lines are skew. What other lines or edges on the shoe box are skew?

Writing About Mathematics

Describe a pair of skew lines you find in the classroom.

Parallel lines are coplanar lines that never meet. The symbol for parallel lines is ||.

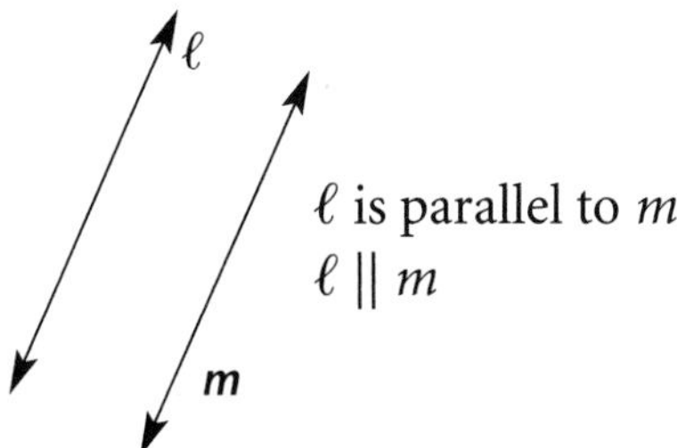

ℓ is parallel to m

$\ell \parallel m$

p

q

p is not parallel to q

$p \nparallel q$

Parallel

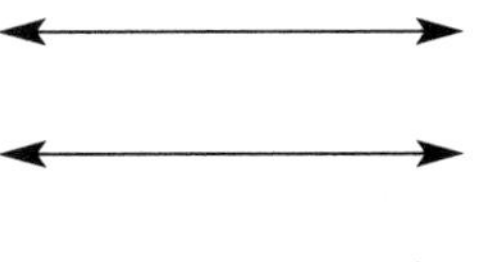

in the same plane

Not Parallel

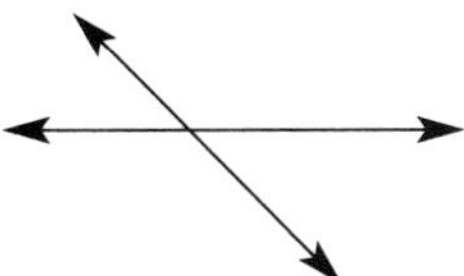

intersect in the same plane

Skew

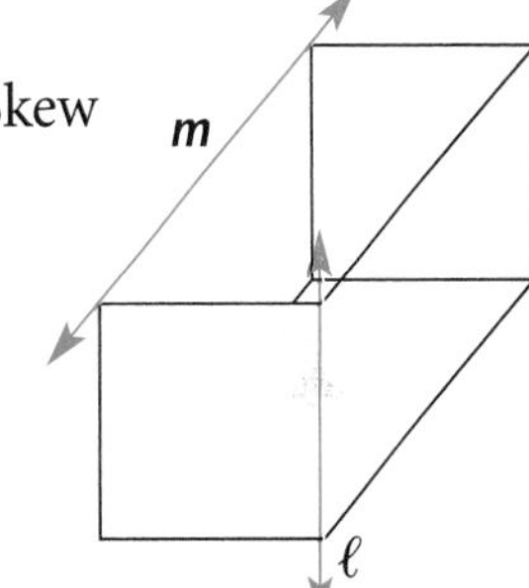

ℓ and m are skew lines not in the same plane

Technology Connection

Circuit boards are used to run everything from calculators to airplanes. There are many parallel lines on this circuit board. The people who make this board must be careful that the lines stay straight and parallel so that the circuits are accurate. One way to do this is to make a grid that covers the entire circuit board. By keeping the angles at which the circuits cross the grid equal, the manufacturer can be sure the lines are parallel.

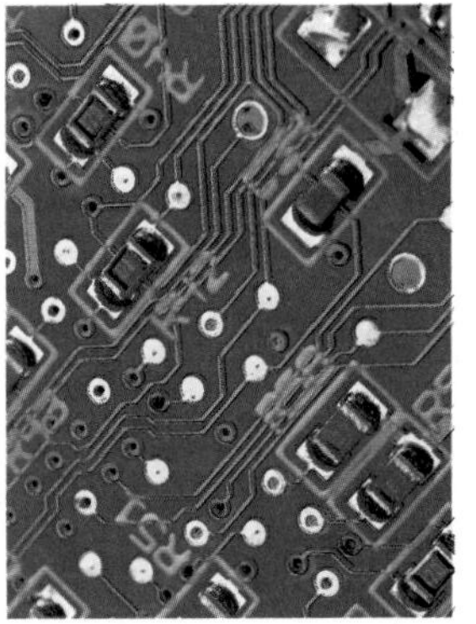

Exercise A Use the figure below. Write *T* if you think the statement is *true*. Write *F* if you think the statement is *false*.

1. $\overline{AE} \parallel \overline{BD}$
2. $\overline{BE} \parallel \overline{ED}$
3. $\overline{FC} \nparallel \overline{BE}$
4. $\overline{AB} \parallel \overline{ED}$
5. $\overline{FC} \nparallel \overline{ED}$
6. $\overline{AB} \parallel \overline{FC}$
7. $\overline{AB} \nparallel \overline{BE}$
8. $\overline{AF} \parallel \overline{FE}$
9. $\overline{AF} \parallel \overline{CD}$
10. $\overline{AB} \parallel \overline{FC} \parallel \overline{ED}$

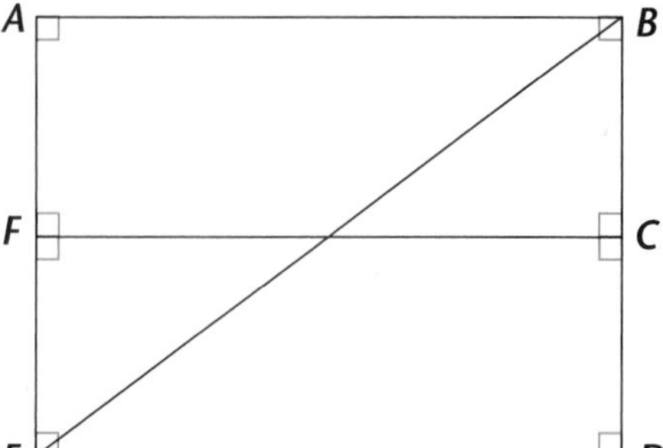

Exercise B Use symbols $\parallel$ or $\nparallel$ to describe each pair of lines.

11. 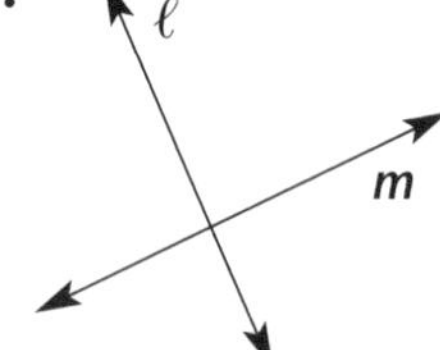

12. 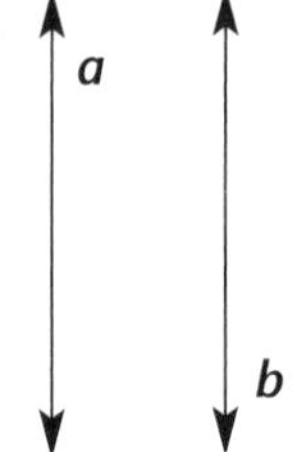

13. 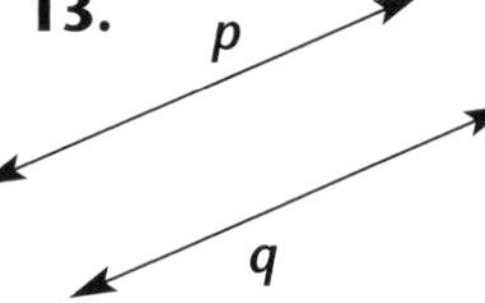

14. 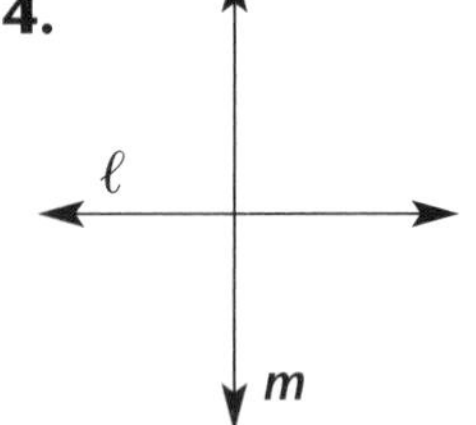

15. 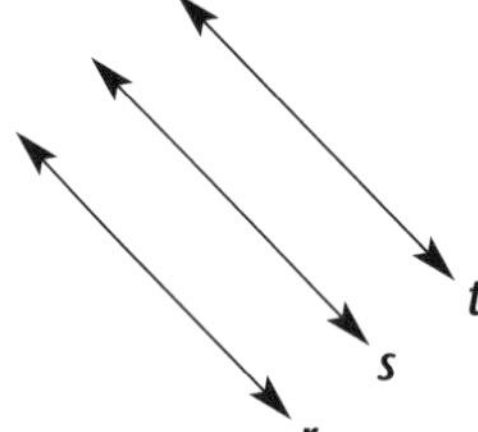

TRY THIS Are these lines parallel or skew? Why?

Lesson 2 Transversals

Transversal
A line that crosses parallel lines

Exterior angle
Angle outside the parallel lines

Interior angle
Angle inside the parallel lines

When one line is crossed by a second line, four angles are formed.

If two parallel lines are crossed by a third line, eight angles are formed. The line that crosses the parallel lines is a **transversal.** The eight angles formed have names that identify their location.

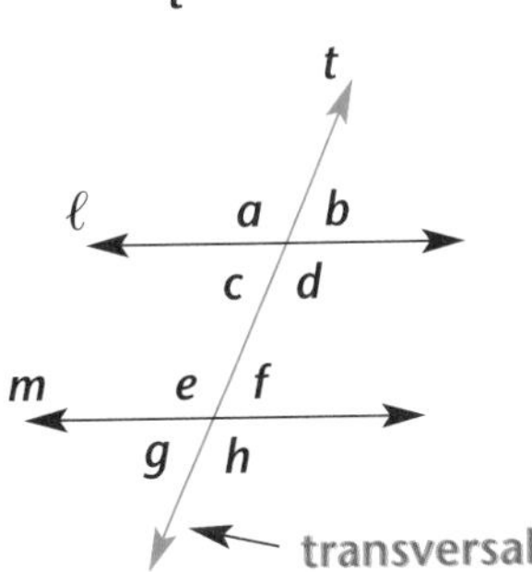

In the diagram, *a–h* are labels for the angles. When a measure is assigned to these letters, however, they can be used as algebraic variables.

▶ **Exterior Angles**—angles outside the parallel lines ℓ and m

There are four exterior angles—*a*, *b*, *g*, and *h*.

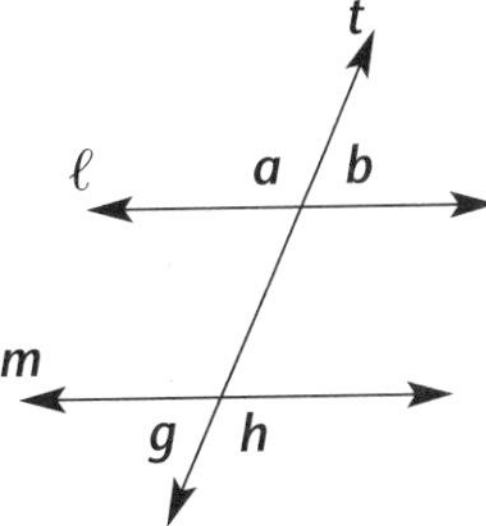

▶ **Interior Angles**—angles inside the parallel lines ℓ and m

There are four interior angles—*c*, *d*, *e*, and *f*.

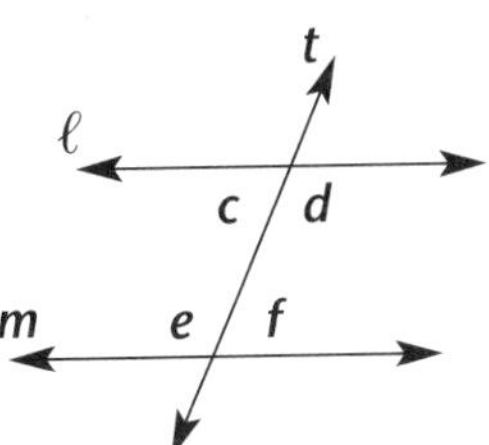

▶ **Corresponding Angles**—pairs of angles that are in similar positions

There are four pairs of corresponding angles:

a and *e*	*c* and *g*
b and *f*	*d* and *h*

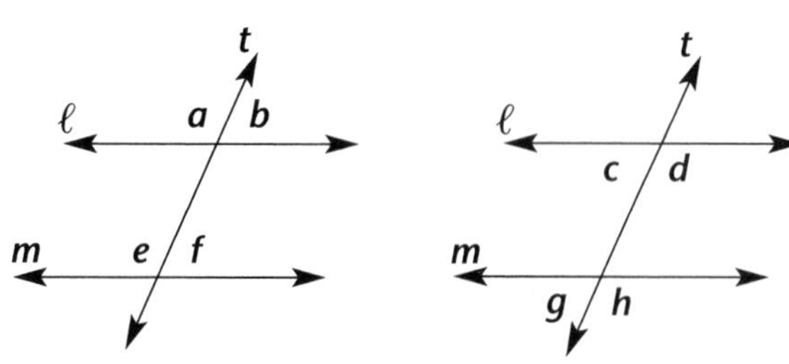

▶ **Alternate Interior Angles**—pairs of interior angles on opposite sides of the transversal

Angles *c* and *f* are alternate interior angles; so are angles *d* and *e*.

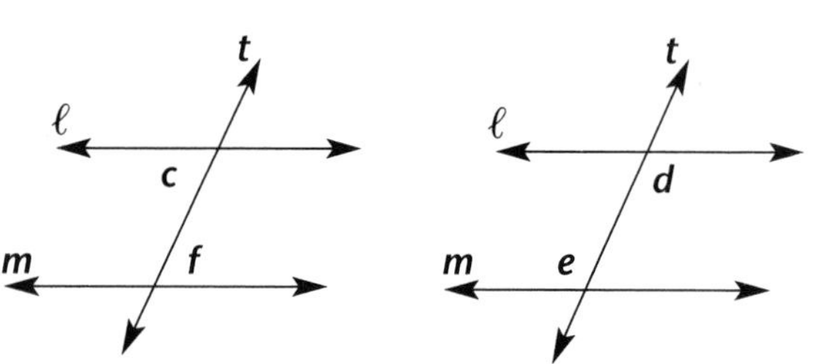

▶ **Alternate Exterior Angles**—pairs of exterior angles on opposite sides of the transversal

Angles *a* and *h* are alternate exterior angles; so are angles *b* and *g*.

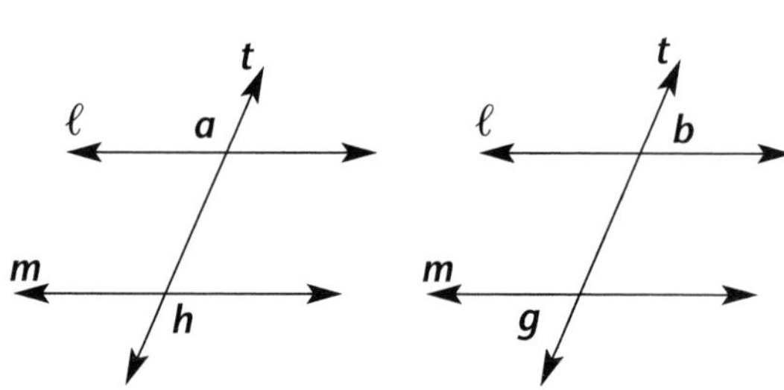

Corresponding angles

Pairs of angles in similar positions

Alternate interior angles

Pairs of interior angles on opposite sides of the transversal

Alternate exterior angles

Pairs of exterior angles on opposite sides of the transversal

EXAMPLE 1 Look closely at the diagram and you can see that adjacent angles whose exterior sides are in a straight line are supplementary angles.

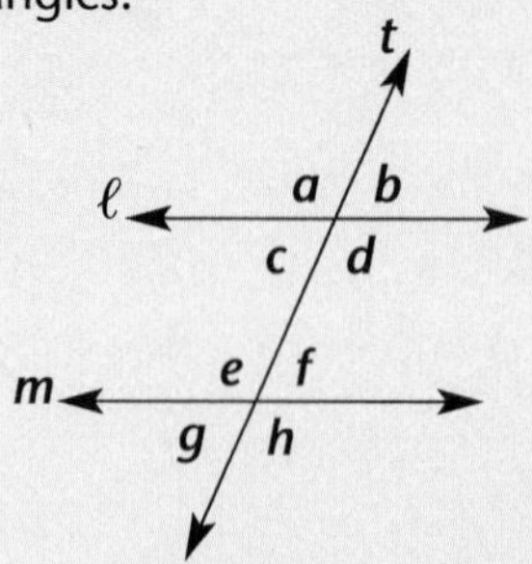

There are eight pairs of supplementary angles: *a* and *b*, *b* and *d*, *a* and *c*, *c* and *d*, *e* and *f*, *f* and *h*, *e* and *g*, *g* and *h*.

Writing About Mathematics

Discuss what you think will happen to the eight angles if the transversal is perpendicular to the two lines.

Exercise A Use the figure shown for problems 1–5.

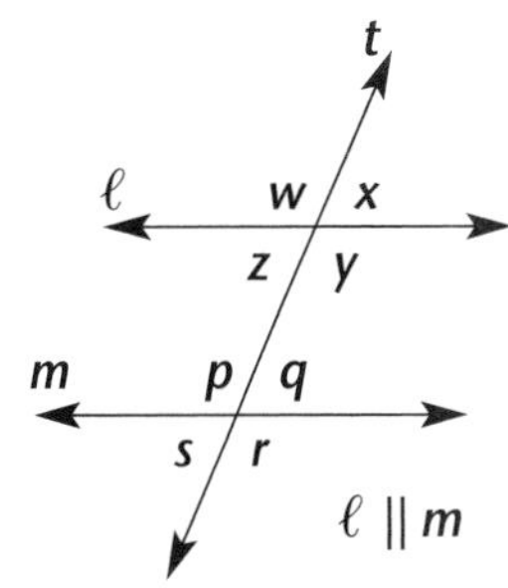

1. Name the exterior angles.
2. Name the interior angles.
3. Name all pairs of corresponding angles.
4. Name all pairs of alternate interior angles.
5. Name eight pairs of supplementary angles.

Exercise B Use the figure shown for problems 6–15. Name the angles as *exterior, interior, alternate exterior, alternate interior, corresponding,* or *supplementary.*

6. *f* and *k*
7. *k* and *l*, *e* and *f*
8. *g* and *j*
9. *g* and *k*
10. *h* and *i*, *j* and *g*
11. *e* and *f*
12. *j* and *l*
13. *h* and *l*
14. *i* and *h*
15. *i* and *j*

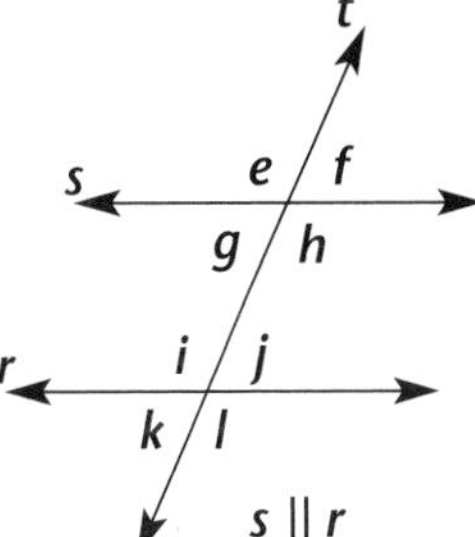

CONSTRUCTION

Exercise C Construct two parallel lines using the two edges of your straightedge. Draw a transversal that is not perpendicular to the parallels. Use a protractor to measure the angles. Which of the following angles appear to be equal? Write *yes* or *no.*

16. Corresponding angles
17. Supplementary angles
18. Alternate interior angles
19. Alternate exterior angles
20. Interior angles on the same side of the transversal

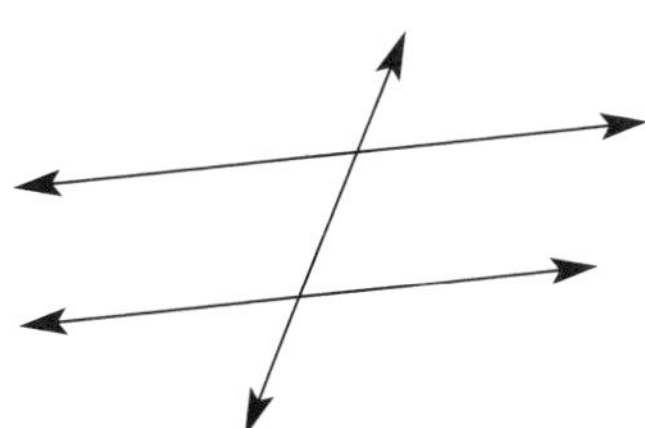

Lesson 3 Theorems About Parallel Lines

Indirect proof

A proof that shows that the conclusion cannot be false because accepted facts would be contradicted

At the end of the last lesson you measured certain angles. In your drawing, you may have found that the corresponding angles were equal. In geometry, measurement is not enough. We need a formal proof about corresponding angles before we can say that all corresponding angles are equal. There are several theorems about which angles are equal. The first, and most important, depends on Euclid's original Parallel Postulate. (Now would be a good time to turn back to page 43 and review Euclid's Postulate 5, the Parallel Postulate.)

A statement can be either *true* or *false*. An argument, or proof, can be either *valid* or *invalid*. A proof is valid if the conclusion is true whenever the given (the hypothesis) is true.

Theorem 3.3.1: If two lines are parallel, then the interior angles on the same side of the transversal are supplementary.

For this theorem, we will use a method of proof called *proof by contradiction,* also known as an **indirect proof.** In an indirect proof, you begin with the *opposite* of the desired conclusion. Then you work, in logical steps, to find a contradiction. When the same statement is shown to be true as well as false, it is a contradiction. If you reach a contradiction, then you know it was incorrect, or *false,* to assume the opposite of the conclusion. Therefore the conclusion must be true.

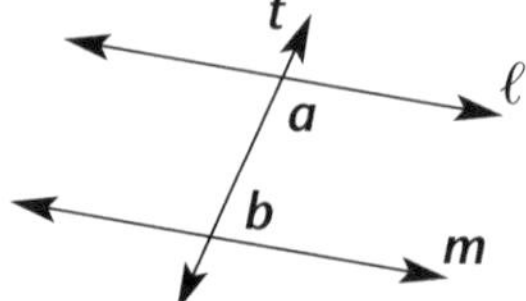

Proof by Contradiction (Indirect Proof)

To Prove: $\angle a$ and $\angle b$ are supplementary

PROOF

Statement	Reason
1. $\ell \parallel m$, transversal t	1. Given.
2. $\angle a$ and $\angle b$ are not supplementary	2. Indirect proof assumption (something taken to be true without proof); the opposite of "To prove."
3. $m\angle a + m\angle b \neq 180°$	3. Definition of angles that are not supplementary.
4. $m\angle a + m\angle b < 180°$ or $m\angle a + m\angle b > 180°$	4. Definition of not equal, greater than or less than.
5. ℓ must intersect m This contradicts the given: $\ell \parallel m$ $\therefore$ Theorem is valid and proof is complete.	5. Euclid's Postulate 5.

Remember, ∴ is the symbol for "therefore," and notes the last statement of a proof.

What does this theorem mean? It means every time you have two parallel lines, ℓ and m, then you know that

$m\angle a + m\angle c = 180°$

and

$m\angle b + m\angle d = 180°$.

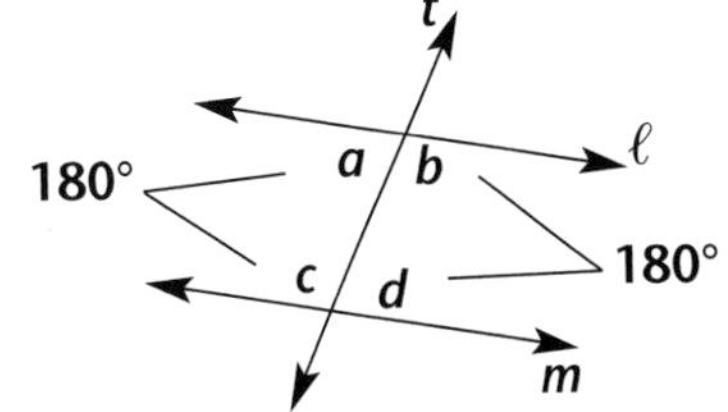

This theorem about supplementary angles forms the foundation for the proofs of other theorems about parallel lines.

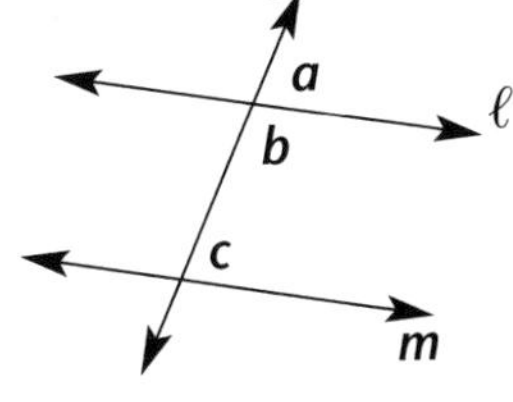

Theorem 3.3.2: If two lines cut by a transversal are parallel, then the corresponding angles are equal.

To Prove: $m\angle a = m\angle c$. Use the figure to the left.

Proof

Statement	Reason
1. ℓ ∥ *m*, transversal *t*	1. Given.
2. $m\angle b + m\angle c = 180°$	2. Theorem, interior angles on the same side of the transversal are supplementary.
3. $m\angle a + m\angle b = 180°$	3. Adjacent angles whose exterior sides are a straight line are supplementary. Definition of adjacent and supplementary.
4. $m\angle b + m\angle c = m\angle a + m\angle b$	4. Axiom 1, things equal to the same thing are equal to each other, and steps 2 and 3.
5. ∴ $m\angle c = m\angle a$.	5. Axiom 3, equals subtracted from equals give equal differences.

What does this theorem mean? It means every time you have two parallel lines, ℓ and *m*, and a transversal *t*, you know that the angles in each pair of corresponding angles are equal.

$m\angle x = m\angle y$

So, if you know the $m\angle x$, you also know the $m\angle y$.

$m\angle x = 80° = m\angle y$

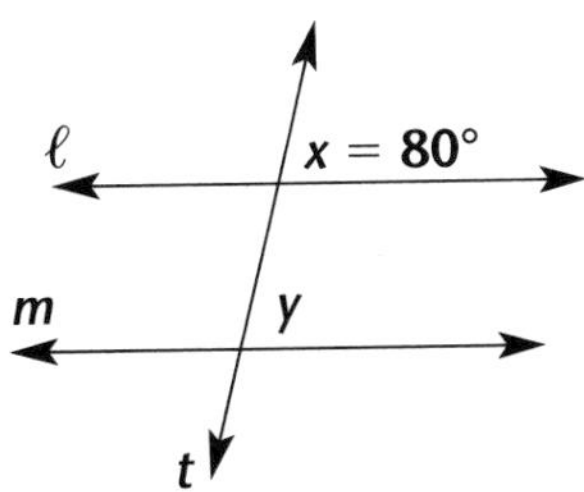

There is one more parallel line theorem left to prove.

> **Theorem 3.3.3:** If two lines cut by a transversal are parallel, then the alternate interior angles are equal.

To Prove: m$\angle a$ = m$\angle b$

PROOF

Statement	Reason
1. $\ell \parallel m$, transversal t	**1.** Given.
2. $\angle c$ is supplementary to $\angle a$. m$\angle a$ + m$\angle c$ = 180°	**2.** Definition of adjacent and supplementary.
3. m$\angle b$ + m$\angle c$ = 180°	**3.** Theorem, interior angles on the same side of the transversal are supplementary.
4. m$\angle a$ + m$\angle c$ = m$\angle b$ + m$\angle c$	**4.** Axiom 1, things equal to the same things are equal to each other, and steps 2 and 3.
5. $\therefore$ m$\angle a$ = m$\angle b$	**5.** Axiom 3, equals subtracted from equals give equal differences.

Let's look at the meaning of this theorem. It means that if ℓ and m are parallel, then any pair of alternate interior angles created by transversal t are equal. You can prove this to yourself by writing a proof of the theorem for angles c and d.

Exercise A Complete the following statements. For problems 1 and 2, use the figure shown and the theorem, if $\ell \parallel m$, then interior angles on the same side of the transversal are supplementary.

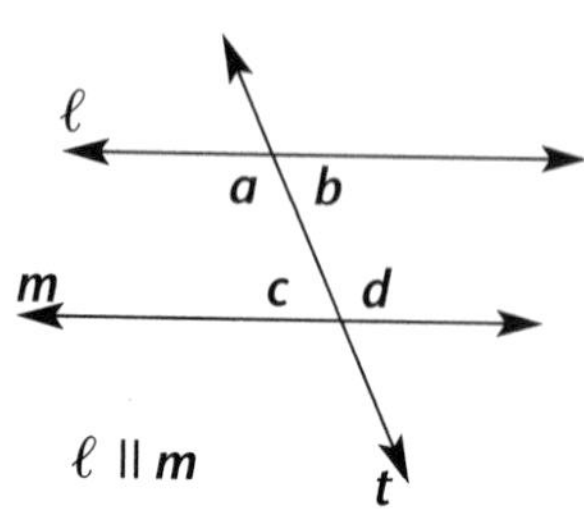

1. m$\angle a$ + m$\angle c$ = ____

2. m$\angle b$ + m$\angle d$ = ____

For problems 3 and 4, use the figure shown and the theorem, if $\ell \parallel m$, then alternate interior angles are equal.

3. m$\angle a$ = ____

4. m$\angle b$ = ____

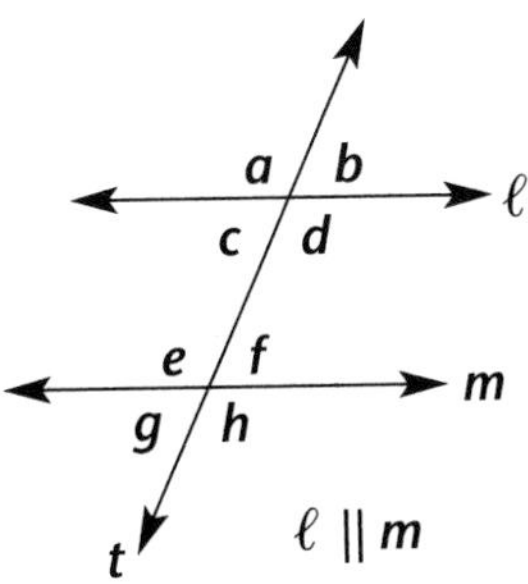

For problems 5–12, use the figure shown and the theorem, if $\ell \parallel m$, then corresponding angles are equal.

5. $m\angle a =$ ____

6. $m\angle b =$ ____

7. $m\angle c =$ ____

8. $m\angle d =$ ____

9. $m\angle e =$ ____

10. $m\angle f =$ ____

11. $m\angle g =$ ____

12. $m\angle h =$ ____

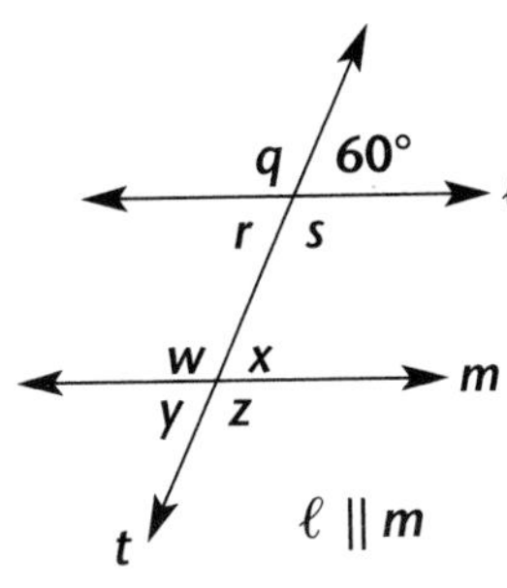

Exercise B Find the measures of the angles in the figure shown. Write your reason for each measure. Use the three theorems about parallel lines and what you know about supplementary and vertical angles.

13. $\angle q$

14. $\angle r$

15. $\angle s$

16. $\angle w$

17. $\angle x$

18. $\angle y$

19. $\angle z$

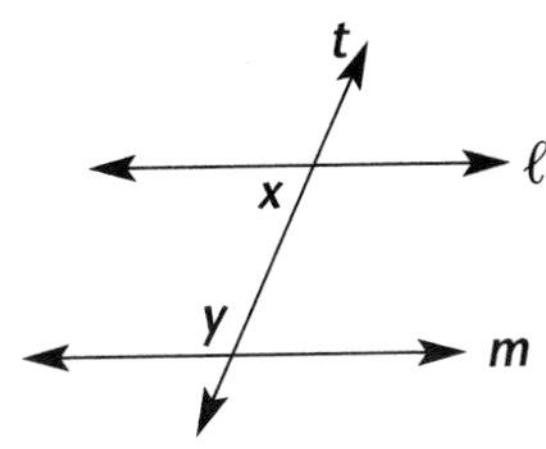

Exercise C Copy and then complete the following indirect proof (proof by contradiction). Use the proof of the theorem on page 72 as a guide.

If $\ell \parallel m$ with transversal t, then $m\angle x + m\angle y = 180°$.

To Prove: $\angle x$ and $\angle y$ are supplementary

Proof

Statement	Reason
1. $\ell \parallel m$, transversal t	1. Given.
2. **20.** ____	2. Indirect proof assumption; the opposite of "To prove."
3. $m\angle x + m\angle y \neq 180°$	3. **21.** ____
4. **22.** ____	4. Definition of not equal means greater than or less than.
5. ℓ must intersect m This contradicts the given: $\ell \parallel m$ $\therefore m\angle x + m\angle y = 180°$	5. **23.** ____

PROBLEM SOLVING

Exercise D Solve the following problems.

24. Each sailboat will cross under the bridge during a race. Boat 2 will cross at a right angle to the bridge. If the boats are following parallel courses, what will be the measure of angle *x*? Why?

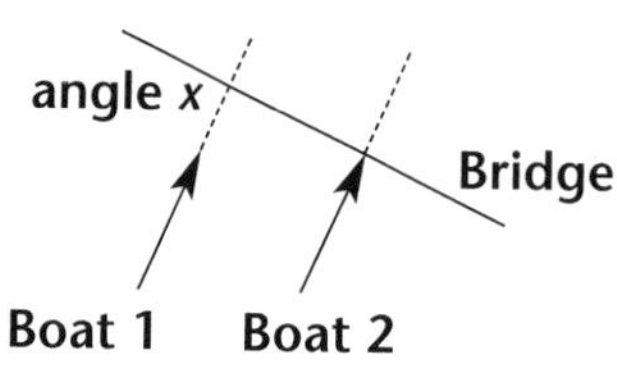

25. Find the measures of angles *w*, *x*, *y*, *z*, *h*, *i*, *j*, and *k*. Use the figure shown and any theorems or information about supplementary angles.

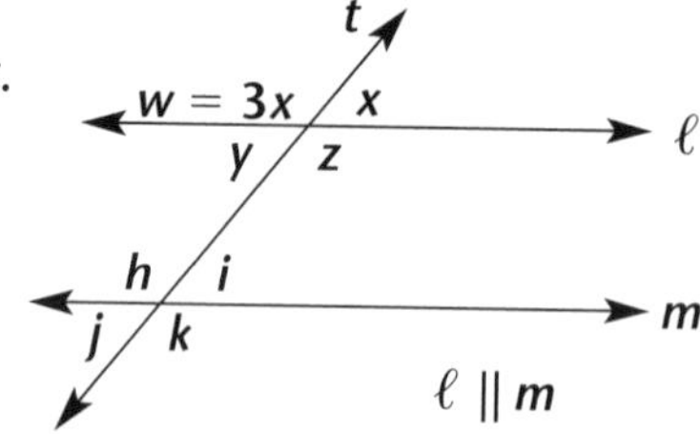

Exercise E Use a calculator to find the measure of the second angle.

26. supplementary angles, one angle = 52°

27. supplementary angles, one angle = 28°

28. supplementary angles, one angle = 36°

29. supplementary angles, one angle = 63°

30. supplementary angles, one angle = 74°

Estimation Activity

Estimate: Supplementary angles, one angle = 123°
Before using your calculator, estimate the answer.

Solution: 123° ≈ 120° Round to the nearest ten.
180° − 120° = 60° Subtract.

The number was rounded down, so the calculator display should be less than 60.

Lesson 4 Constructions and Problem Solving

You now know three useful theorems about parallel lines and their angles. You can use the information from these theorems to develop other information about parallel lines. You can also use the information to construct parallel lines.

Remember, if $p \rightarrow q$ is any conditional, then $q \rightarrow p$ is its *converse.*

Recall the theorem, if two lines are parallel, then alternate interior angles are equal. You will need the *converse* of this theorem: if alternate interior angles are equal, then the lines that are not common to the angles are parallel. This statement will be taken to be true as a postulate. It is called the Alternate Interior Angles Postulate. You can use this postulate to construct parallel lines.

Alternate Interior Angles Postulate:
If a transversal intersects two lines so that the alternate interior angles are equal, then the lines are parallel.

Remember, to copy an angle:

Draw arc through rays of angle *x*.

Draw same size arc at vertex *P*.

Then complete the construction for copying the angle.

See page 12 for more review.

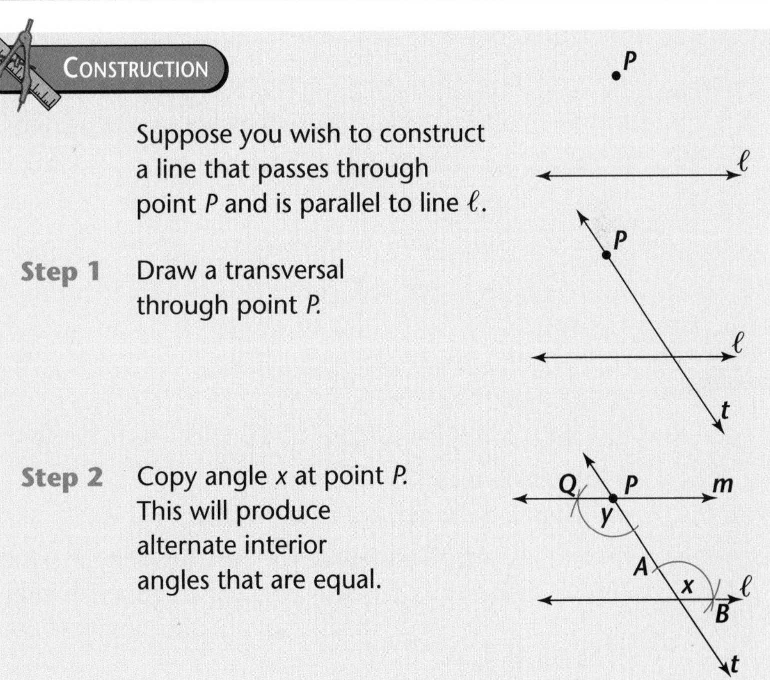

You have now constructed line m parallel to line ℓ using only a straightedge and a compass.

Using the theorems, you can solve for the measure of any angle formed by a transversal and a set of parallel lines. Then you can use algebra to determine the angle measure. Here are some examples.

EXAMPLE 1 The measure of $\angle b$ is twice the measure of $\angle a$. What is the measure of each angle?

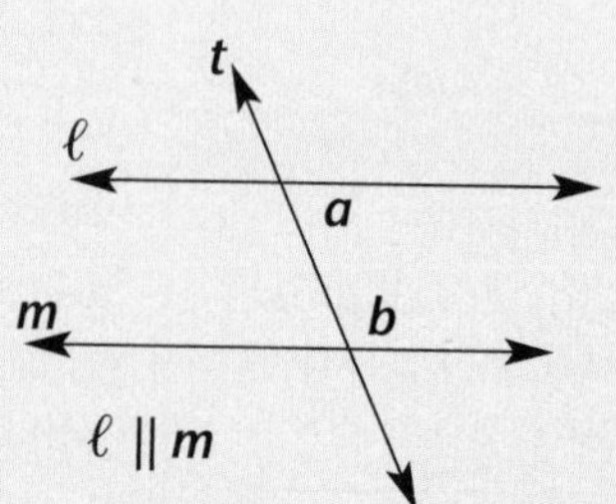

Let $x = m\angle a$ and $2x = m\angle b$

$m\angle a + m\angle b = 180°$ by theorem, interior angles are supplementary

so $x + 2x = 180°$ by substitution

$3x = 180°$

$x = 60°$

$m\angle a = 60°$ and $m\angle b = 120°$

EXAMPLE 2 The measure of $\angle a$ is five times the measure of $\angle b$. What is the measure of $\angle y$?

By theorem, you know that corresponding angles are equal and $m\angle b = m\angle y$. So you need only to solve for $m\angle b$.

Let $x = m\angle b$ and $5x = m\angle a$

$m\angle a + m\angle b = 180°$, because they are supplementary angles

so $5x + x = 180°$ by substitution

$6x = 180°$

$x = 30°$

$m\angle b = 30° = m\angle y$

EXAMPLE 3 Using the figure shown, give two ways to find $m\angle y$.

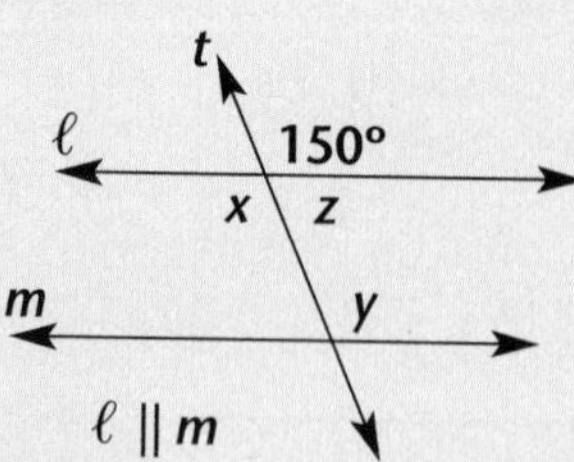

First, the angle of 150° and $\angle y$ are corresponding angles. By theorem, corresponding angles are equal, so $m\angle y = 150°$.

Second, $\angle z$ and the angle of 150° are supplementary angles, so $m\angle z = 180° - 150° = 30°$. Since $\angle x$ and $\angle z$ are supplementary, $m\angle x + 30° = 180°$, so $m\angle x = 150°$. Note that $\angle x$ and $\angle y$ are alternate interior angles, so by theorem, they are equal.

$m\angle x = m\angle y = 150°$

Exercise A Use the three theorems to find the measure of each angle. State the theorem or tell how you found the measure of each angle. (Note: Use reasoning to find the answer and do not measure with a protractor.)

1. The measure of $\angle z$ is three times that of $\angle y$.

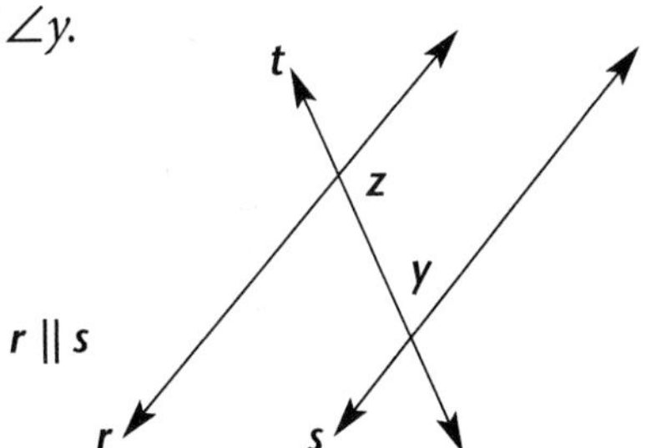

2. Eight times the $m\angle p = m\angle q$.

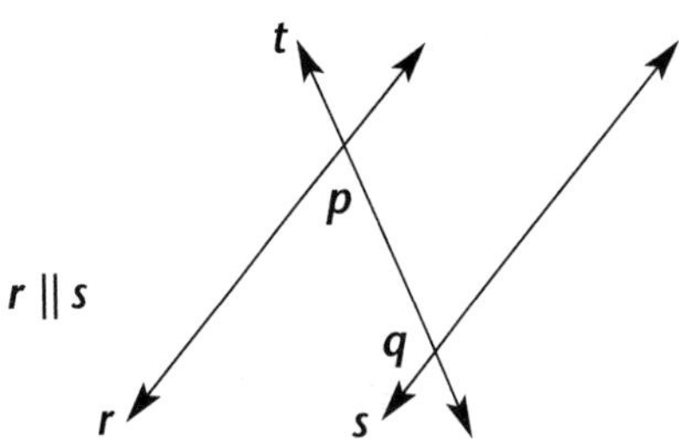

3. Nine times the $m\angle w = m\angle z$.

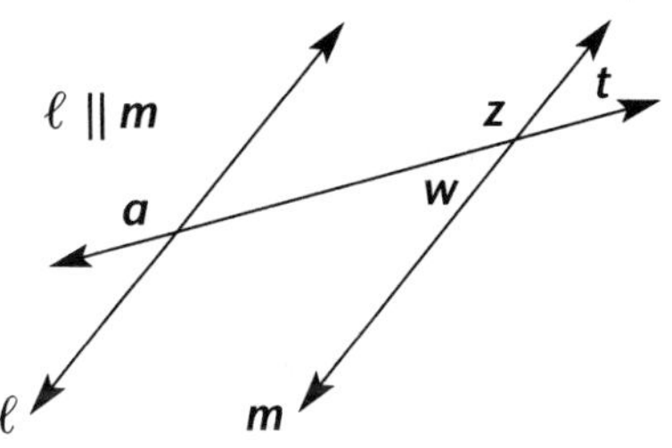

4. Three times the $m\angle a$ equals two times the $m\angle b$.

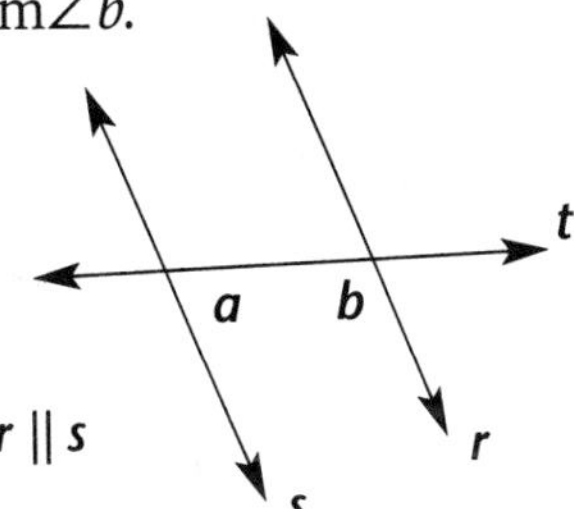

5. $m\angle b$ is $\frac{1}{3}$ $m\angle a$. What is $m\angle x$?

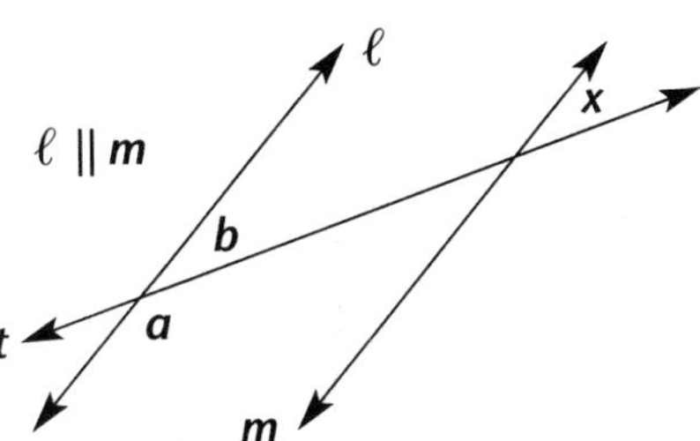

6.

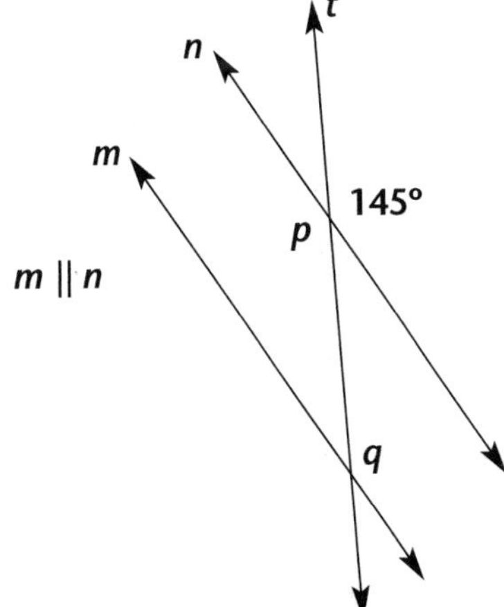

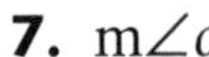

Exercise B Find the measures of all angles in the figure.
Hint: find the measures of the angles for $\ell \parallel m$ first, then $m \parallel n$.

7. m$\angle o$

8. m$\angle p$

9. m$\angle q$

10. m$\angle r$

11. m$\angle s$

12. m$\angle u$

13. m$\angle v$

14. m$\angle w$

15. m$\angle x$

16. m$\angle y$

17. m$\angle z$

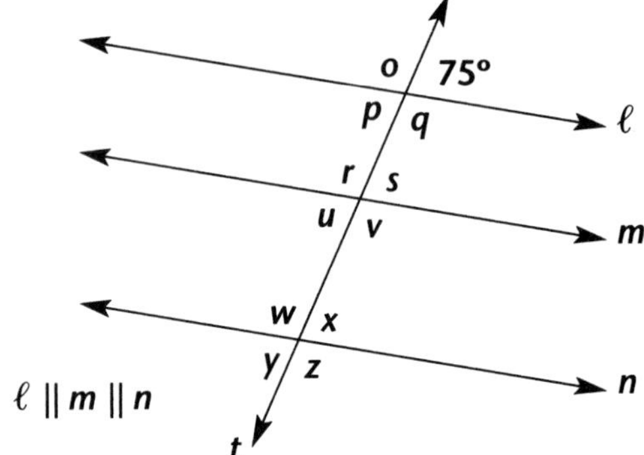

CONSTRUCTION

Exercise C Copy and complete the following constructions on a separate sheet of paper. Use the Alternate Interior Angles Postulate.

18. Construct line m parallel to line ℓ and through point P.

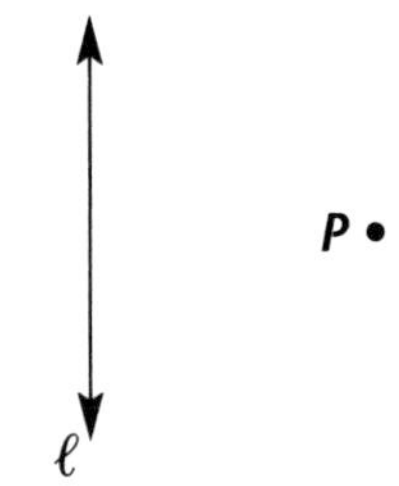

19. Construct line t, parallel to line m and through point X.

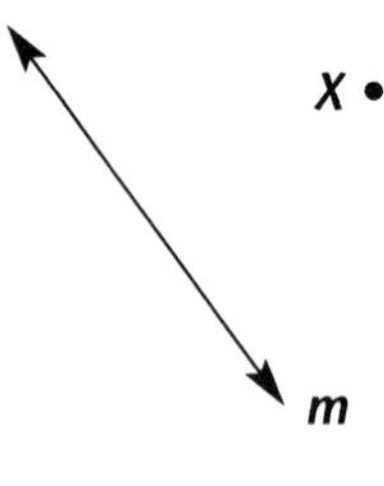

20. Construct m, parallel to ℓ and through X. Also construct n, parallel to m and through Y.

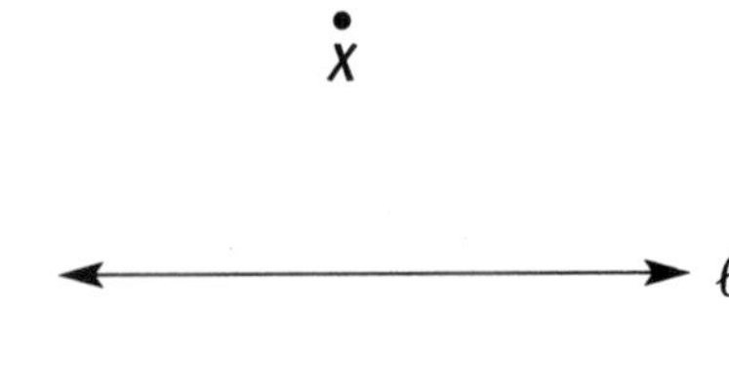

Lesson 5 Quadrilaterals and Parallels

Quadrilateral
A geometric figure with four sides

Rectangle
A parallelogram with four right angles

Square
A rectangle with sides of equal length

Parallelogram
A quadrilateral whose opposite sides are parallel

Rhombus
A parallelogram with four equal sides

Look around you. Concentrate on the shapes and outlines of buildings, parking lots, and houses. Notice that many of the things you see could be drawn using a four-sided geometric figure called a **quadrilateral.** In fact, many of the things you see can be drawn using specific kinds of quadrilaterals such as **rectangles** and **squares.**

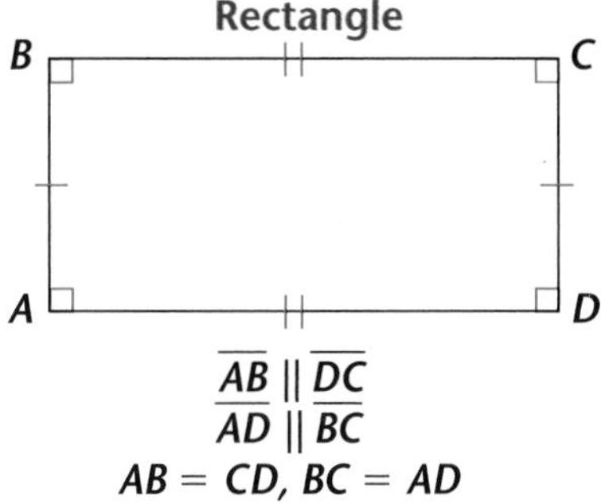

$\overline{AB} \parallel \overline{DC}$
$\overline{AD} \parallel \overline{BC}$
$AB = CD$, $BC = AD$

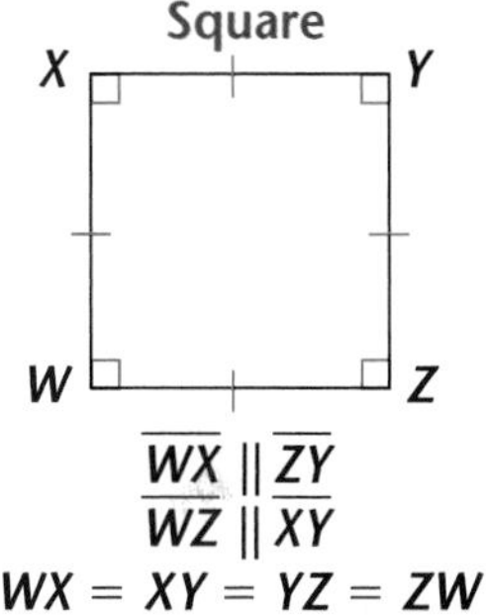

$\overline{WX} \parallel \overline{ZY}$
$\overline{WZ} \parallel \overline{XY}$
$WX = XY = YZ = ZW$

The **parallelogram** and **rhombus** are two other figures whose opposite sides are parallel and equal.

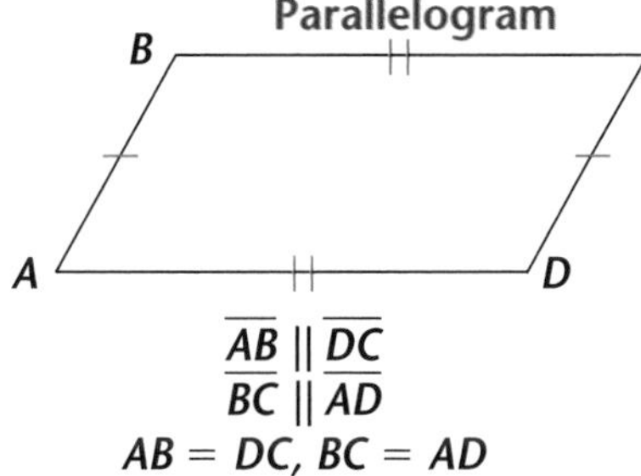

$\overline{AB} \parallel \overline{DC}$
$\overline{BC} \parallel \overline{AD}$
$AB = DC$, $BC = AD$

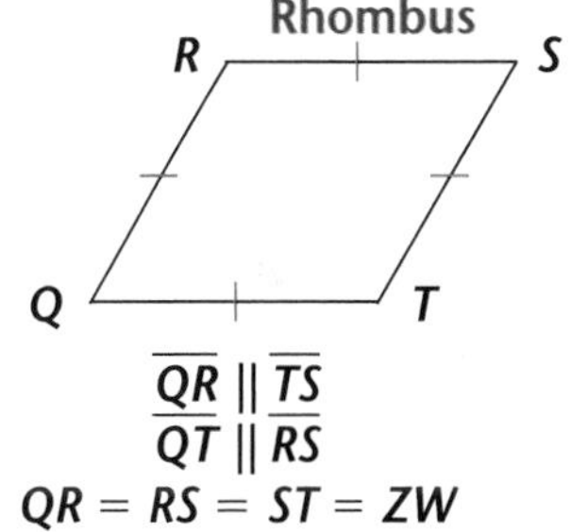

$\overline{QR} \parallel \overline{TS}$
$\overline{QT} \parallel \overline{RS}$
$QR = RS = ST = ZW$

These figures have some characteristics in common. They are made up of two pairs of parallel lines. Another way to describe these figures is to say that their opposite sides are parallel.

A parallelogram is a quadrilateral whose opposite sides are parallel. A rectangle is also a parallelogram, but its angles are all right angles. A rectangle is a parallelogram with four right angles.

If you wished, you could shorten this definition to read, "A rectangle is a parallelogram with one right angle." Let's see why this is possible.

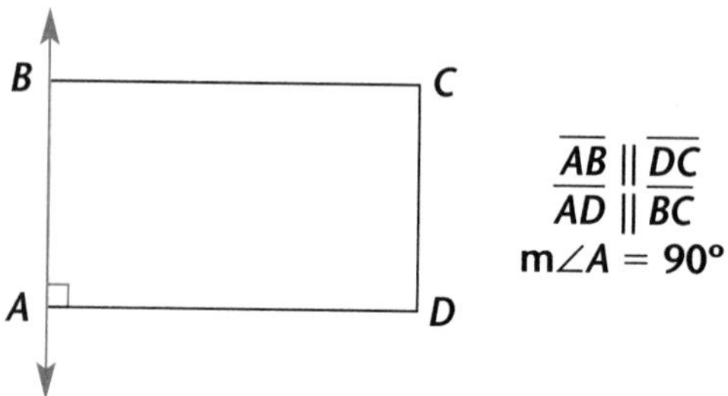

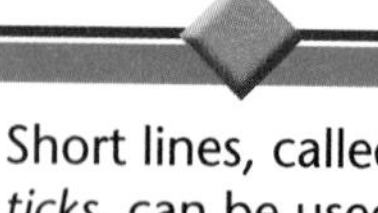

EXAMPLE 1 Suppose *ABCD* is a rectangle with right angle ∠*A*. What is true about ∠*B*? It must also be a right angle! You know this because one theorem states that interior angles on the same side of a transversal are supplementary.

If $\overline{AD} \parallel \overline{BC}$, with transversal $\overleftrightarrow{AB}$, then m∠*A* + m∠*B* = 180°.

m∠*A* = 90°, so

90° + m∠*B* = 180°

m∠*B* = 90°

You can make the same argument to show that m∠*C* and m∠*D* are also 90°. Therefore, all four angles are right angles.

Short lines, called *ticks,* can be used to mark equal sides of a figure. A single line represents one length. If the figure has all its sides marked with a single line, then all the sides are of equal length. More than one tick may be used in the same manner.

Now look at the next figure. This figure is a rhombus. It has four sides of equal length. A rhombus is a parallelogram with four equal sides.

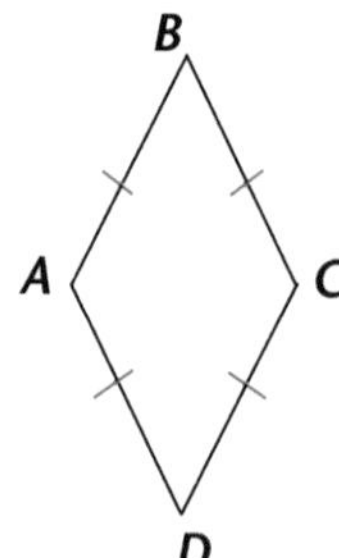

$\overline{AB} \parallel \overline{DC}$
$\overline{BC} \parallel \overline{AD}$
AB = *BC* = *CD* = *DA*

To construct a square, you need the length of one side.

Given: side $\overline{AB}$

Construct: a square with all sides equal to *AB*

Step 1 Draw line ℓ.
Use your compass to copy $\overline{AB}$ on ℓ.

Step 2 Construct a line perpendicular to line ℓ through point *A*. Copy $\overline{AB}$ on it. Name the segment $\overline{AC}$.

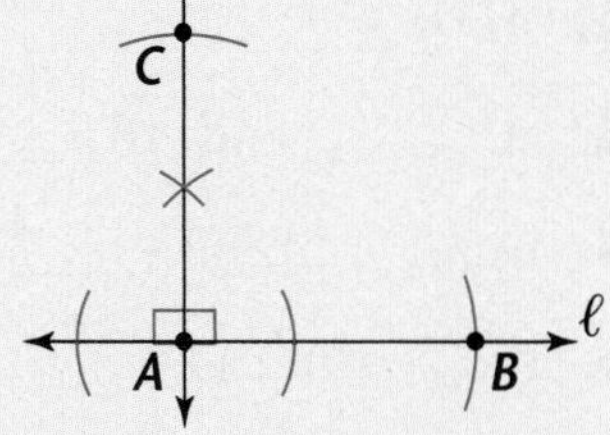

Step 3 Set the compass opening at $\overline{AB}$. Place the compass needle at *C*. Draw an arc. Place the compass needle at *B*. With the same opening, draw an arc. Name the intersection *D*. Draw $\overline{CD}$ and $\overline{BD}$.

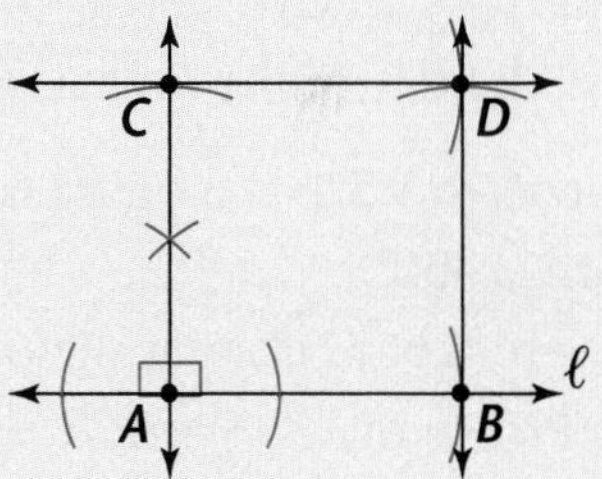

Given: $\overline{AB}$ and $\overline{AC}$

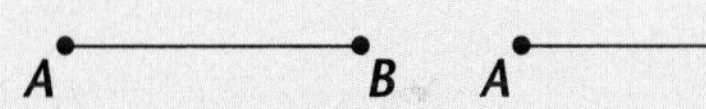

Construct: a rectangle with sides $\overline{AB}$ and $\overline{AC}$

Step 1 Draw line ℓ. Use your compass to copy $\overline{AB}$ on ℓ.

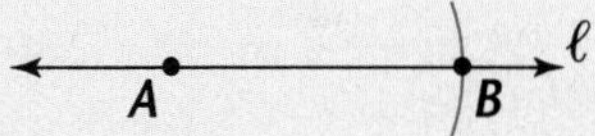

Step 2 Construct $\overline{AC} \perp \overline{AB}$.

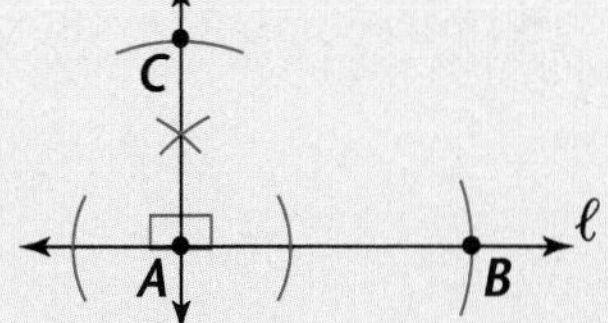

Step 3 Set the compass opening at $\overline{AB}$. Place the compass needle at *C*. Draw an arc. Set the compass opening at $\overline{AC}$. Place the compass needle at *B*. Draw an arc. Name the intersection *D*. Draw $\overline{CD}$ and $\overline{BD}$.

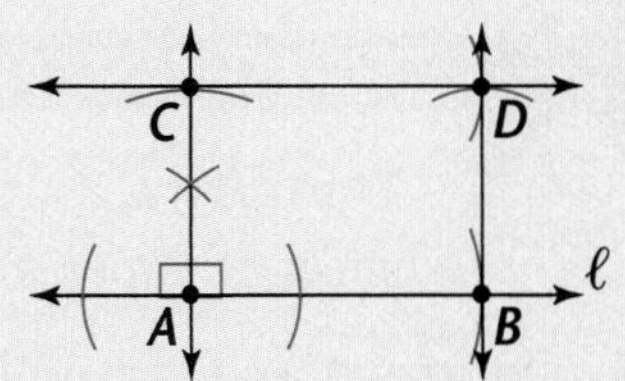

Exercise A Use definitions and theorems of parallels to complete the following statements. Think of $\overline{AD}$ and $\overline{BC}$ as transversals

Use the figure at right for problems 1–8.

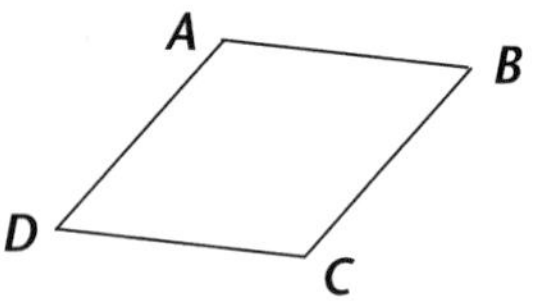

Given: *ABCD* is a parallelogram.

1. $\overline{AB} \parallel$ ___

2. $\overline{AD} \parallel$ ___

3. $\overline{AB} \nparallel$ ___ and $\overline{AB} \nparallel$ ___

4. $m\angle A + m\angle D =$ ___

5. $m\angle B + m\angle C =$ ___

6. $m\angle A + m\angle B =$ ___

7. $m\angle C + m\angle D =$ ___

8. $m\angle A + m\angle B + m\angle C + m\angle D =$ ___

9. A parallelogram has opposite sides that are equal and __________ .

Exercise B Give the missing reasons for this proof. Use the figure shown at right for problems 10–13.

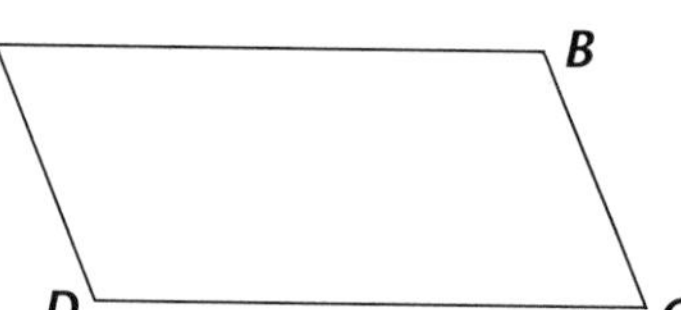

Theorem 3.5.1: If a figure is a parallelogram, then its angle sum is 360°.

Given: *ABCD* is a parallelogram.

To Prove: $m\angle A + m\angle B + m\angle C + m\angle D = 360°$

PROOF

Statement	Reason
1. $\overline{AB} \parallel \overline{CD}$ and $\overline{AD} \parallel \overline{BC}$	1. Given: **10.**
2. $m\angle A + m\angle D = 180°$	2. (Hint: Think of $\overline{AD}$ as a transversal) **11.**
3. $m\angle B + m\angle C = 180°$	3. **12.**
4. $\therefore m\angle A + m\angle B + m\angle C + m\angle D = 360°$	4. **13.**

CONSTRUCTION

Exercise C Complete the following constructions. Use a separate sheet of paper. You will need a straightedge and a compass.

14. Construct a square with a base of 2 inches.

15. Construct a rectangle with 5-in. sides and 2-in. sides.

Lesson 6 Trapezoids

Trapezoid
A quadrilateral with exactly one pair of parallel sides

Isosceles
A geometric figure with two sides of equal length

Scalene
A geometric figure with sides of unequal lengths

Angle sum
The sum of the measures of all the interior angles in a closed figure

It is possible to have a quadrilateral with *exactly one pair* of parallel sides. A **trapezoid** is a quadrilateral with exactly one pair of parallel sides. Here are some examples.

$\overline{AB} \parallel \overline{CD}$ for each figure

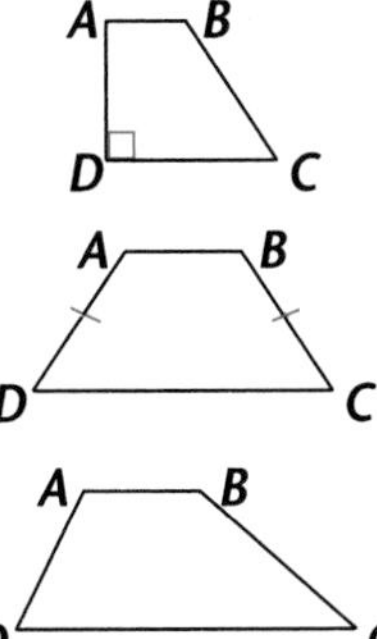

Right-Angled Trapezoid
m∠D = 90° makes *ABCD* a *right* trapezoid.

Isosceles Trapezoid
$\overline{AD} = \overline{BC}$ makes it **isosceles.** Figures with two sides of equal length are called isosceles.

Scalene Trapezoid
Figures with no sides of equal length are called **scalene.**

$\overline{AB} \parallel \overline{CD}$ and $\overline{AD} \nparallel \overline{BC}$ make *ABCD* a trapezoid in each case.

What do you know about the angles in each trapezoid?

$m\angle A + m\angle D =$ ■ (180°, supplementary, because they are on the same side between parallels)

$m\angle B + m\angle C =$ ■ (180°, supplementary)

From this we can conclude that, for any trapezoid *ABCD,* the **angle sum** $= m\angle A + m\angle B + m\angle C + m\angle D = 360°$.

With *inductive thinking,* you show how particular cases are similar to make a general statement. Look at the examples on this and previous pages. We can conclude that all parallelograms and trapezoids have similar properties. Here is an example of inductive thinking.

Parallelograms

Square

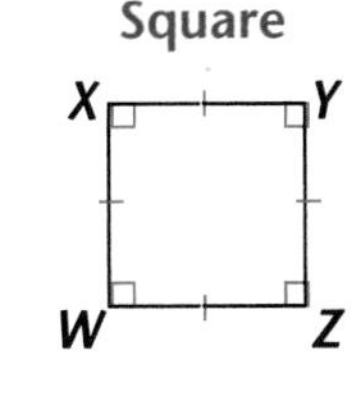

angle sum = 4 • 90°
= 360°

Rectangle

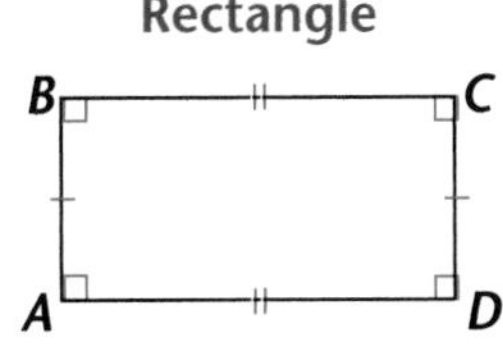

angle sum = 4 • 90°
= 360°

Rhombus

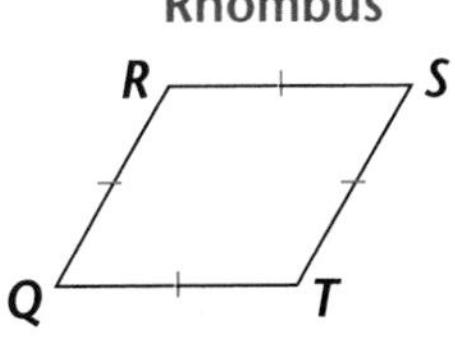

$m\angle Q + m\angle R = 180°$,
$m\angle S + m\angle T = 180°$
angle sum = 2 • 180° = 360°

Trapezoids

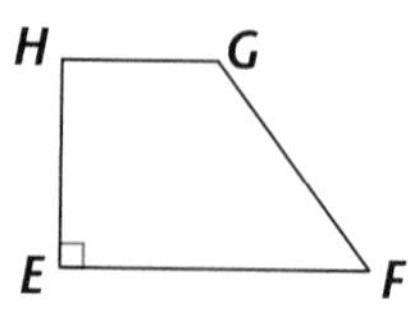

$m\angle E + m\angle H = 180°$, supplementary right angles
$m\angle F + m\angle G = 180°$, supplementary because they are on the same side between parallels
angle sum $= 2 \cdot 180° = 360°$

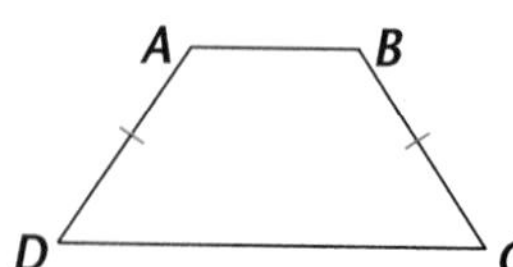

$m\angle A + m\angle D = 180°$, $m\angle B + m\angle C = 180°$
angle sum $= 2 \cdot 180° = 360°$
Think of $\overline{AD}$ and $\overline{BC}$ as transversals between parallels.

Conclusion: The sum of the angle measures inside a parallelogram or trapezoid is 360° for the examples shown. The formal proof follows in Exercise C.

Given: $\overline{AB}$, $\overline{DC}$, $\overline{AD}$; $\overline{AB} \parallel \overline{DC}$

Construct: a right-angled trapezoid with height $\overline{AD}$

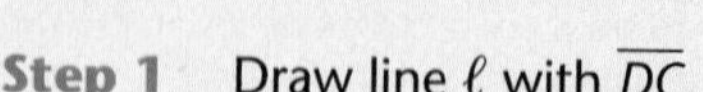

Step 1 Draw line ℓ with $\overline{DC}$.

Step 2 Construct $\overline{AD} \perp \overline{DC}$.

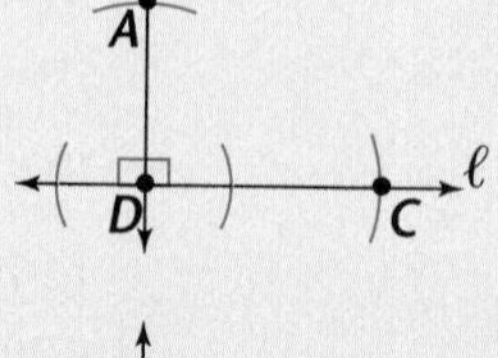

Step 3 Construct $\overline{AB} \perp \overline{AD}$. Draw $\overline{BC}$.

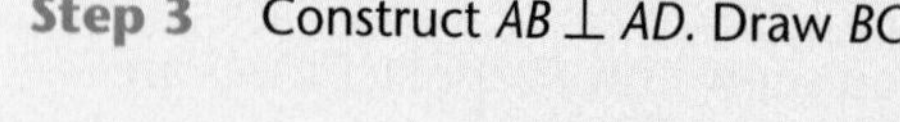

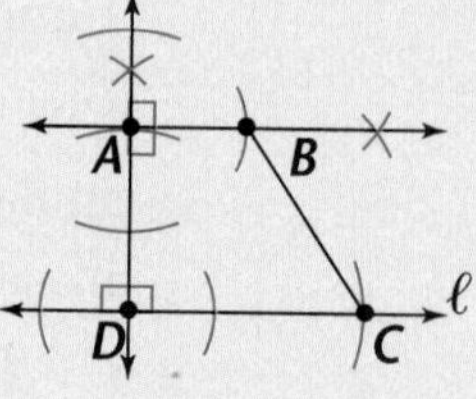

Given: height $\overline{AB}$

Construct: any trapezoid (not right-angled, not isosceles)

B

A

Step 1 Draw a line. Copy $\overline{AB}$ onto it.
Construct line $\ell \perp \overline{AB}$ at point B.
Construct line $m \perp \overline{AB}$ at point A.

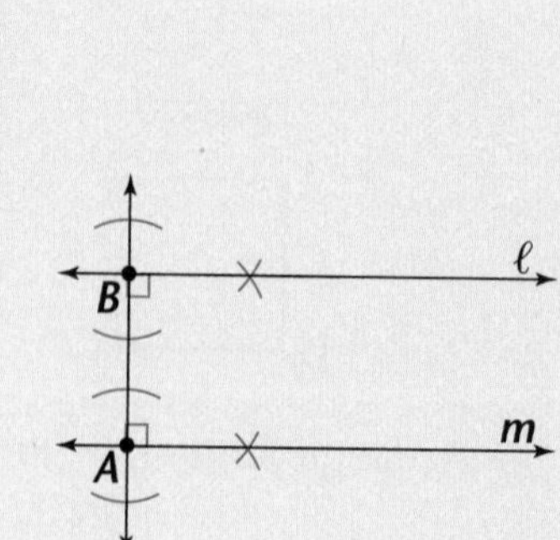

(continued)

Step 2 Choose a point C to the right of B on ℓ. Then draw $\overline{CA}$.

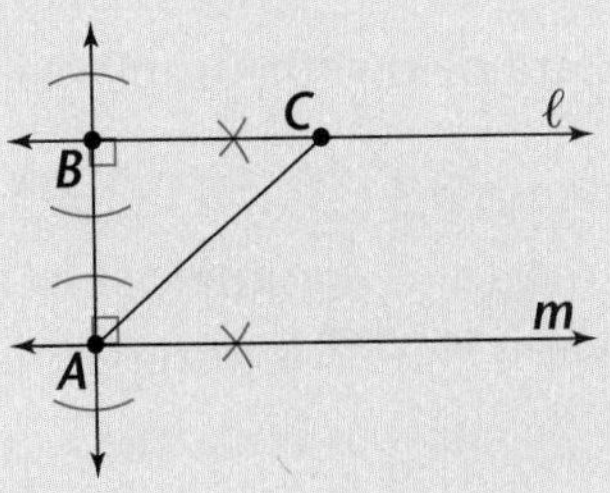

Step 3 Choose a point D to the right of C on ℓ. Open the compass to a width different than CA. Put the compass point on D. Make an arc that intersects m. Name the point of intersection E. Draw $\overline{DE}$.

$ACDE$ is a trapezoid that is neither right-angled nor isosceles.

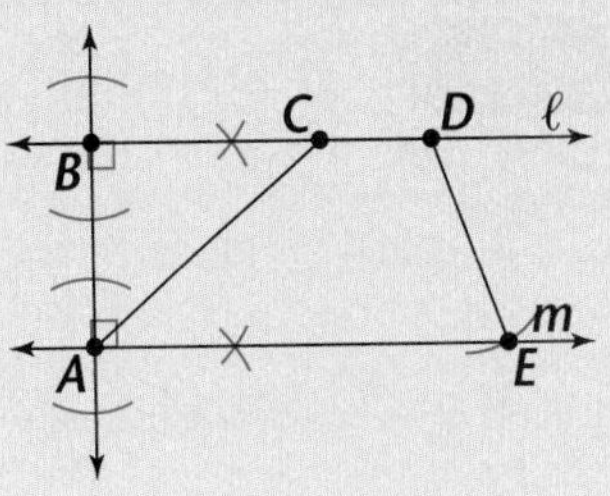

Exercise A Use the figure shown at right for problems 1–5.

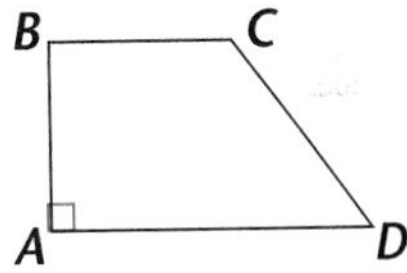

Given: *ABCD* is an right trapezoid.

1. $\overline{BC} \parallel$ ____
2. $\overline{AB} \perp$ ____ and ____
3. $m\angle A + m\angle B =$ ____
4. $m\angle C + m\angle D =$ ____
5. $\overline{AB} \nparallel$ ____

Exercise B Use the figure shown at right for problems 6–11.

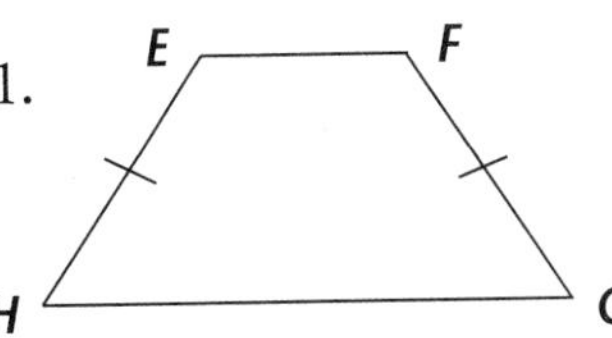

Given: *EFGH* is an isosceles trapezoid.

6. $\overline{EF} \parallel$ ___
7. $\overline{EH} \nparallel$ ___, $\overline{EH} \nparallel$ ___, $\overline{EH} \nparallel$ ___
8. $EH =$ ___
9. $m\angle E + m\angle H =$ ___
10. $m\angle F + m\angle G =$ ___
11. $m\angle E + m\angle F + m\angle G + m\angle H =$ ___

Exercise C Give the missing reasons in the proof. Use the figure below for problems 12–15.

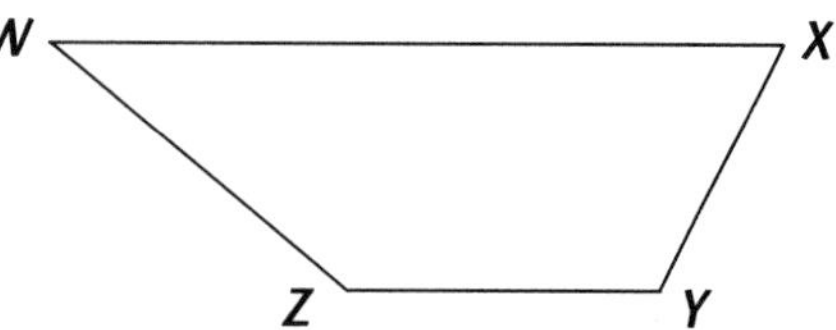

Theorem 3.6.1: If a figure is a trapezoid, then its angle sum is 360°.

Given: *WXYZ* is a trapezoid.

To Prove: $m\angle W + m\angle X + m\angle Y + m\angle Z = 360°$

PROOF

Statement	Reason
1. $\overline{WX} \parallel \overline{ZY}$	1. Given: **12.** ____
2. $m\angle W + m\angle Z = 180°$	2. **13.** ____
3. $m\angle X + m\angle Y = 180°$	3. **14.** ____
4. $\therefore m\angle W + m\angle X + m\angle Y + m\angle Z = 360°$	4. **15.** ____

Exercise D Tell whether each statement is *True* or *False.* Give reasons for your answer.

16. A square is a rhombus with one right angle.

17. A trapezoid with one right angle has at least two right angles.

18. Every square is also a rectangle.

CONSTRUCTION

Exercise E Complete the following constructions. Use a separate sheet of paper. You will need a straightedge and a compass.

19. Construct a right-angled trapezoid with height 1 in., bottom base 3 in., and top base 2 in.

20. Construct a trapezoid that is not right-angled or isosceles. Use your own dimensions.

Lesson  7 Proving Lines Parallel

Look closely at this picture of the Golden Gate Bridge in San Francisco, California. Try to find at least four sets of parallel lines. Then look for transversals to the parallel lines. How could you prove that some of the transversal lines are parallel too?

You have learned how to construct parallel lines using alternate interior angles. Here are the steps you use. Notice that in Step 2 you construct an angle equal to the existing angle and that the pair of angles are alternate and interior.

Construction **Given:** line ℓ and point P not on ℓ

Construct: a line || to ℓ, through point P.

Step 1 Draw a transversal t through P.

Step 2 Copy $\angle a$ at P. $\ell \parallel m$

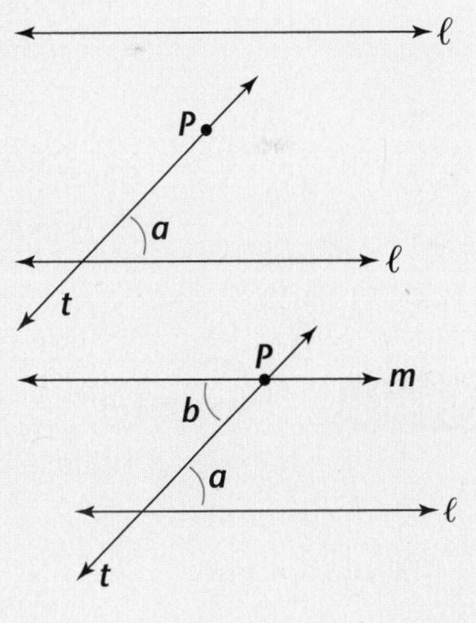

Legal

Allowed by mathematical laws

As with all constructions in geometry, there must be an axiom, postulate, or theorem that makes the construction **legal,** or allowed by mathematical laws. In this case, the construction is based on a postulate about alternate interior angles.

Arcs are used like ticks to show equal angles. If a pair of angles is marked with a single arc, those angles are of equal measure. Multiple arcs may be used in the same manner.

Look closely—this is the second time you've met a statement about alternate interior angles and parallel lines. This postulate is the converse of a theorem you've proved earlier: If two lines are parallel, then their alternate interior angles are equal. You used this postulate to construct parallel lines in Lesson 4.

Alternate Interior Angles Postulate:
If a transversal intersects two lines so that the alternate interior angles are equal, then the lines are parallel.

If $m\angle a = m\angle b$, then $m \parallel \ell$.

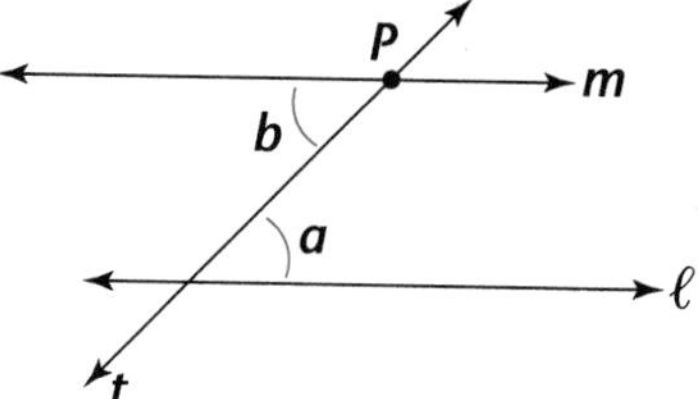

Suppose you wanted to construct parallel lines using equal corresponding angles. You would want to know that if corresponding angles are equal, then lines are parallel. Let's prove that theorem now.

Theorem 3.7.1: If corresponding angles are equal, then the lines are parallel.

Given: t is a transversal, $m\angle a = m\angle b$
To Prove: $\ell \parallel m$

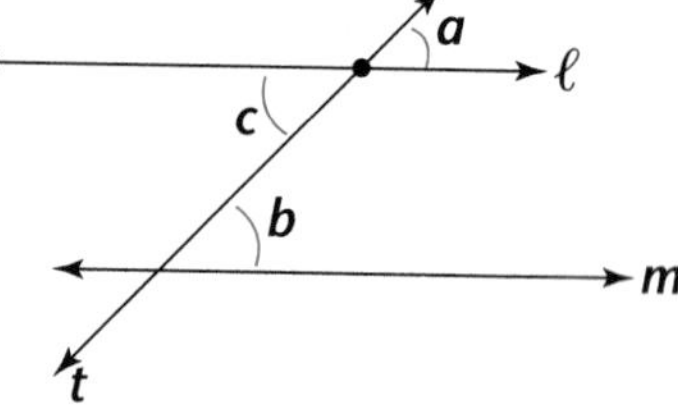

Proof

Statement	Reason
1. t is a transversal, $m\angle a = m\angle b$	**1.** Given.
2. $m\angle a = m\angle c$	**2.** Vertical angles are equal.
3. $m\angle b = m\angle c$	**3.** Substitution of equals and steps 1 and 2.
4. $\therefore \ell \parallel m$	**4.** Alternate Interior Angles Postulate.

This theorem allows you to construct parallel lines using equal corresponding angles. Study the following construction.

Given: line m and point R not on m

Construct: a line || to m, through point R, using equal corresponding angles.

Step 1 Draw a transversal t through R. Mark $\angle x$ at m.

Step 2 Copy $\angle x$ at R, corresponding to $\angle x$ at m. Label the new angle y and the new line n.

$m \parallel n$ based on the corresponding angles theorem.

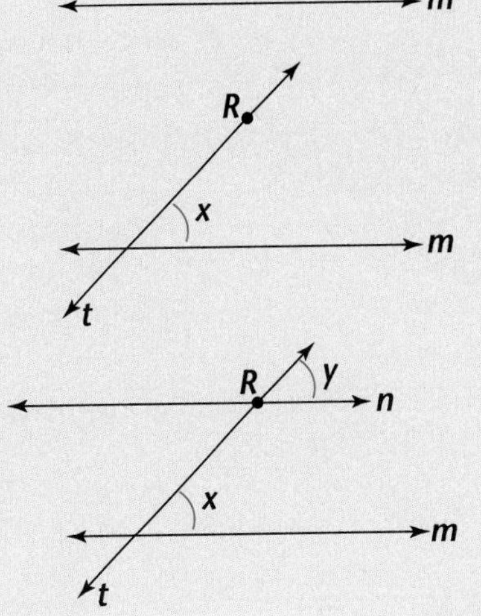

Exercise A What measure for x makes ℓ and m parallel?

1.

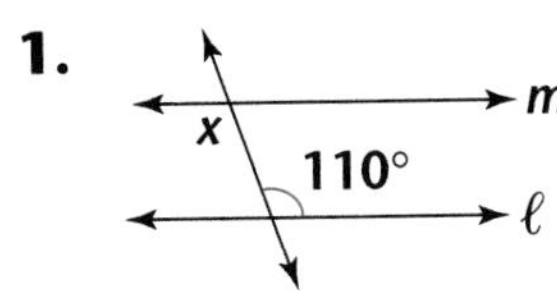

2.

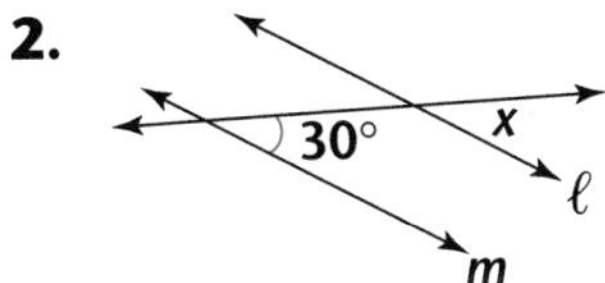

3.

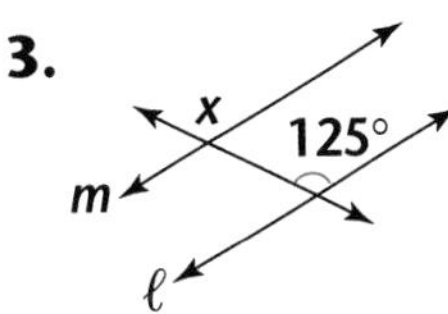

Exercise B Use the figure shown at the right. Write *T* if you think the answer is *true*. Write *F* if you think the answer is *false*.

4. $m\angle a = m\angle e$

5. $m\angle c = m\angle f$

6. $m\angle d = m\angle h$

7. $m\angle g = m\angle h$

8. $m\angle e = m\angle d$

$m \parallel \ell$

CONSTRUCTION

Exercise C Complete the following constructions on a separate sheet of paper. Use only a straightedge and a compass.

9. Draw line ℓ and point P not on ℓ. Construct m through point P, parallel to ℓ, using equal alternate interior angles.

10. Draw line ℓ and point Q not on ℓ. Construct k through point Q, parallel to ℓ, using equal corresponding angles.

Lesson 8 Parallel Lines: More Theorems and Converses

Recall the first theorem you learned about parallels. If parallel lines are cut by a transversal, then the interior angles on the same side of the transversal are supplementary. Here is the converse of that theorem.

> **Theorem 3.8.1:** If two lines are cut by a transversal so that the angles on the same side of the transversal are supplementary, then the lines are parallel.

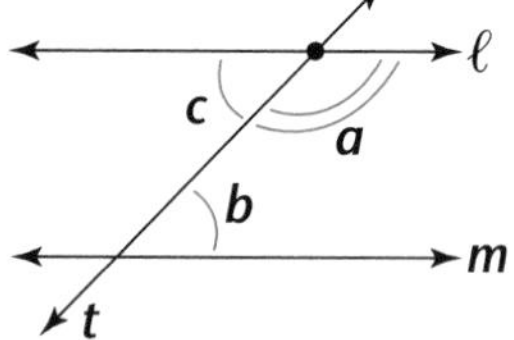

Let us prove this new theorem.

Given: t, a transversal for ℓ and m, and $m\angle a + m\angle b = 180°$

To Prove: $\ell \parallel m$

PROOF

Statement	Reason
1. t is a transversal for ℓ and m $m\angle a + m\angle b = 180°$	1. Given.
2. $m\angle a + m\angle c = 180°$	2. If exterior sides of adjacent angles form a straight angle, the angles are supplementary.
3. $m\angle a + m\angle b = m\angle a + m\angle c$	3. Axiom 1, things equal to the same things are equal to each other.
4. $m\angle b = m\angle c$	4. Axiom 3, equals subtracted from equals give equal remainders.
5. $\therefore \ell \parallel m$	5. Alternate Interior Angles Postulate.

Now you have a third method for constructing parallel lines.

CONSTRUCTION **Given:** line s and point X not on s

X•

Construct: a line $\parallel$ to s, through point X, using the theorem that if angles on the same side of the transversal are supplementary, then the lines are parallel.

Step 1 Draw a transversal t through X. Mark $\angle h$ and $\angle j$ at s.
$m\angle h + m\angle j = 180°$

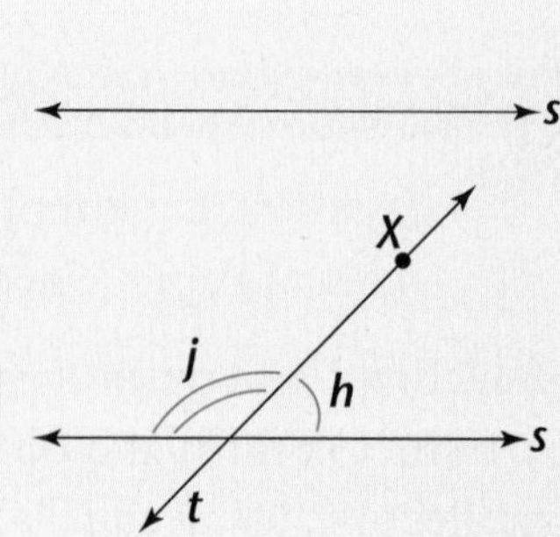

CONSTRUCTION (continued)

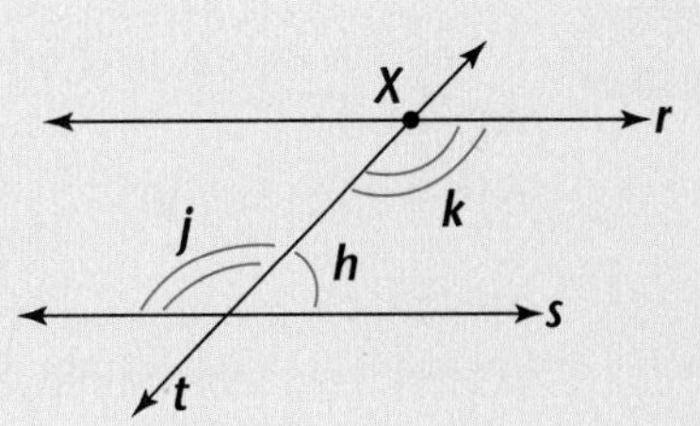

Step 2 Copy $\angle j$ at X and label it $\angle k$.
$m\angle h + m\angle k = 180°$

So $s \parallel r$ by the theorem just proved.

Writing About Mathematics

Which construction of parallel lines do you think is the easiest for you? Why?

The following table summarizes the three theorems and their converses from this and the previous lesson.

Theorems	Converses
Given Parallels: If parallel lines are cut by a transversal, then the alternate interior angles are equal. (Theorem 3.3.3)	**Given Angles:** **1.** If alternate interior angles are equal, then the lines are parallel. (Alternate Interior Angles Postulate)
If parallel lines are cut by a transversal, then the corresponding angles are equal. (Theorem 3.3.2)	**2.** If corresponding angles are equal, then the lines are parallel. (Theorem 3.7.1)
If parallel lines are cut by a transversal, then the sum of the interior angles on the same side of the transversal is 180°. (Theorem 3.3.1)	**3.** If the sum of the interior angles on the same side of the transversal is 180°, then the lines are parallel. (Theorem 3.8.1)

You will find the converses helpful when you need to prove lines are parallel. Notice the converses in the following examples.

EXAMPLE 1 Given the figure, prove that lines m and ℓ are parallel.

Alternate interior angles are equal.

$\therefore m \parallel \ell$

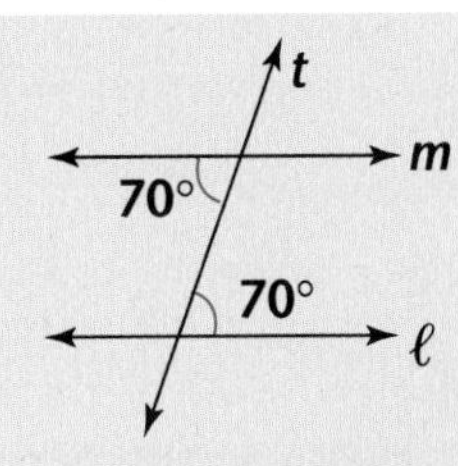

EXAMPLE 2 Given the figure, prove that lines s and ℓ are parallel.

Corresponding angles are equal.

$\therefore s \parallel \ell$

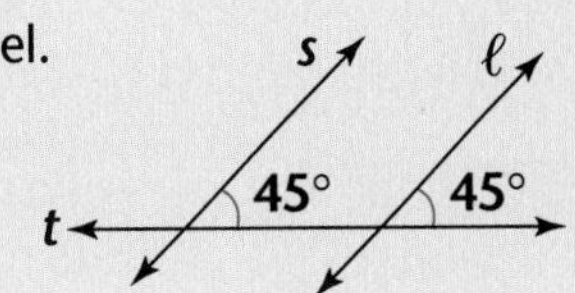

EXAMPLE 3 Given the figure, prove that lines m and n are parallel.

$60° + 120° = 180°$

The angles are supplementary and they are on the same side of the transversal.

$\therefore m \parallel n$

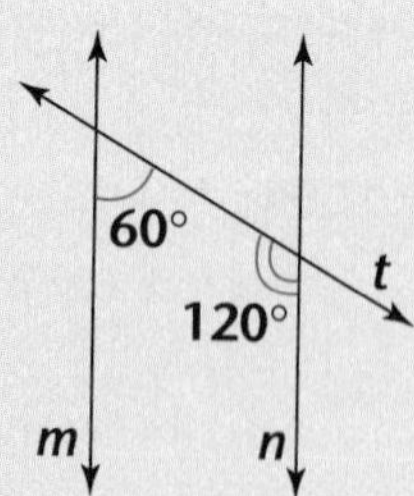

Conclusion: To prove lines parallel you need a pair of equal or supplementary angles.

Exercise A Use the diagram shown. Tell which converse you can use to prove $\ell \parallel m$ if the angles have the given values.

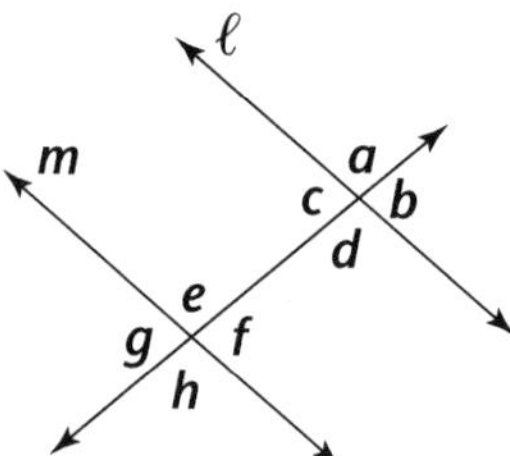

1. $m\angle d = m\angle e$
2. $m\angle b = m\angle f$
3. $m\angle c = m\angle f$
4. $m\angle a = m\angle e$
5. $m\angle g = m\angle c$
6. $m\angle d + m\angle f = 180°$
7. $m\angle c + m\angle e = 180°$
8. $m\angle d = m\angle h$
9. $m\angle g = 120°$, $m\angle c = 120°$
10. $m\angle d = 75°$, $m\angle e = 75°$
11. $m\angle c = 120°$, $m\angle e = 60°$
12. $m\angle h = 110°$, $m\angle d = 110°$

CONSTRUCTION

Exercise B Complete the following construction.

13. Draw line ℓ and point R not on ℓ on a separate sheet of paper. Construct line j through point R and parallel to ℓ using supplementary interior angles on the same side of the transversal.

PROBLEM SOLVING

Exercise C Solve the following problems.

14. A carpenter's bevel is used to draw parallel line segments. Jane, the carpenter, has set the tool to a 45° angle. Then she draws several lines using the bevel. How can she be sure the lines will be parallel?

15. Two bicyclists have crossed the 10 m mark. Each crossed at the angle marked in the diagram. If each cyclist stays on the same course, will they cross each other's path?

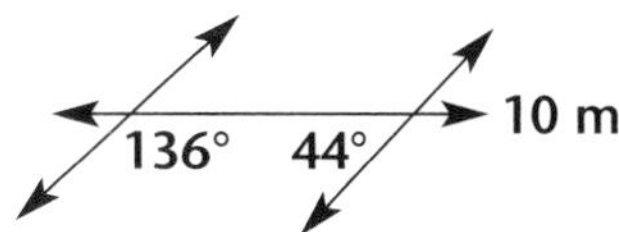

Geometry in Your Life

Gather a variety of different cardboard boxes. Remove the top and bottom of each box. Reshape the boxes by folding or pulling them so that the angles of the box change. Tell what shapes you can make with the edges of the boxes, such as a square, rectangle, rhombus, parallelogram, and so on. Look at these shapes and think about filling them with the same material that came out of the original box. Would it fit? Why do you think they don't use these other shapes to make containers?

Lesson 9 Algebra Connection: Solving Linear Equations

Equation
A mathematical sentence stating that two quantities are equal

Variable
An unknown quantity in an equation

Equations are mathematical statements saying that two things are equal. A **variable** is an unknown in an equation. To solve an equation, find the value of the variable that makes the equation true. These are ways to solve an equation:

- Add the same number or numbers to *both* sides.
- Subtract the same number or numbers from *both* sides.
- Multiply *both* sides by the same number.
- Divide *both* sides by the same number.

These operations can be used to isolate the variable, but only if they are applied to *both* sides of the equation.

These skills will be useful as you work with the equations of lines in Chapter 4.

EXAMPLE 1 Solve $\frac{1}{3}x = 15$ for x.

Step 1 Write the equation. $\frac{1}{3}x = 15$

Step 2 Multiply each side by 3 to get $1x$. $3 \bullet \frac{1}{3}x = 3 \bullet 15$

Step 3 Simplify. $\frac{3}{3}x = 45$

Solution: $x = 45$

Step 4 Check that $\frac{1}{3}(45) = 15$ is true. $15 = 15$

EXAMPLE 2 Solve $3y - 5 = 10$ for y.

Method 1

Step 1 Write the equation. $3y - 5 = 10$

Step 2 Multiply each side by $\frac{1}{3}$.

$$\frac{1}{3}(3y - 5) = \frac{1}{3} \bullet 10$$

$$y - \frac{5}{3} = \frac{10}{3}$$

Step 3 Add $\frac{5}{3}$ to each side.

$$y - \frac{5}{3} + \frac{5}{3} = \frac{10}{3} + \frac{5}{3}$$

$$y = \frac{15}{3} = 5$$

Step 4 Check that $3(5) - 5 = 10$ is true.

Method 2

$3y - 5 = 10$

Add 5 to each side.

$$3y - 5 + 5 = 10 + 5$$

$$3y = 15$$

Divide each side by 3.

$$3y \div 3 = 15 \div 3$$

$$y = 5$$

$3(5) - 5 = 15 - 5 = 10$

EXAMPLE 3 In one class, $\frac{2}{5}$ of the students are on a softball team. If 8 students are on the softball team, then how many students are in the class?

Solution: Write an equation. Let x = number of students in the class.

Then $\frac{2}{5}$ of the class is $\frac{2}{5}x$. The equation is $\frac{2}{5}x = 8$.

Solve.	$\frac{5}{2} \cdot \frac{2}{5}x = \frac{5}{2} \cdot 8$	Multiply both sides by $\frac{5}{2}$ to get $1x$.
	$\frac{10}{10}x = \frac{40}{2}$	Simplify.
	$x = 20$	There are 20 students in the class.
Check: Is $\frac{2}{5}(20) = 8$ true?		Yes, because $\frac{40}{5} = 8$.

Exercise A Solve for the variable. Check your answer.

1. $\frac{2}{3}x = 10$
2. $\frac{1}{2}y = 17$
3. $\frac{5}{3}x = 30$
4. $\frac{3}{2}x = -12$
5. $\frac{7}{8}y = 49$
6. $3x + 4 = 10$
7. $9y + 13 = 10$
8. $\frac{1}{2}w - 3 = 7$
9. $\frac{1}{2}z - 15 = -10$
10. $3x - 5 = 11 + x$

PROBLEM SOLVING

Exercise B Write an equation for each problem. Solve the equation. Check your answer.

11. 12 cubic yards of mulch is $\frac{3}{4}$ of a truckload. How much is a full load?

12. If you subtract 7 from three times some number, you get 23. What is the number?

13. Latisha is 3 years older than her brother William. Latisha is 15. How old is William?

14. Jorge served 36 pieces of pizza at a party. Each person ate 3 pieces. There were 6 pieces of pizza left over. How many people were at the party?

15. If you add 4 to $\frac{1}{5}$ of some number, you get 29. What is the number?

Application

Geometric Quilt Shapes Quilters sew one or more shapes together in a pattern that tells a story or creates a beautiful design. Some of the shapes in a quilt may be classified as *polygons.* A polygon is a closed figure that is made up of three or more line segments in the same plane. Each line segment intersects with one other line segment at each of its endpoints. Squares, rectangles, parallelograms, triangles, and trapezoids are only some of the polygons found in quilt patterns.

EXAMPLE 1 *ABCDE* is a polygon. Each segment intersects two others, one at each endpoint.

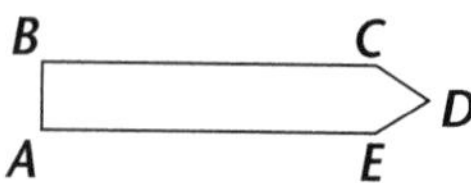

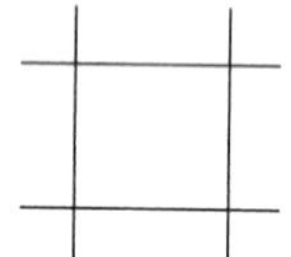

The figure at the left is not a polygon. Its segments do not intersect at the endpoints.

The figure at the right is not a polygon. More than two segments intersect at some of the endpoints.

Exercise Write *polygon* or *not a polygon* for each of the figures. Give reasons why you think any figure is not a polygon.

1. 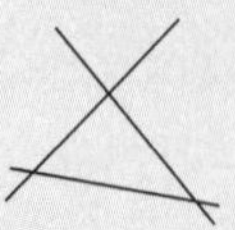

2. 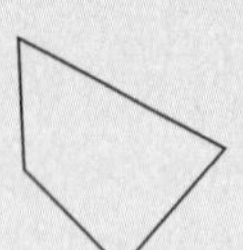

3. 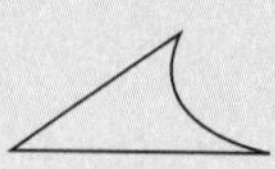

4. 

5. 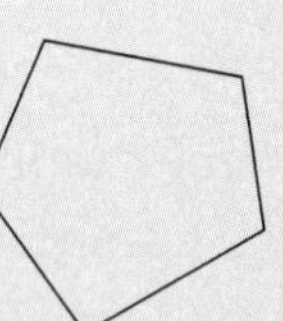

6. 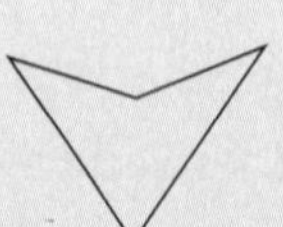

7. 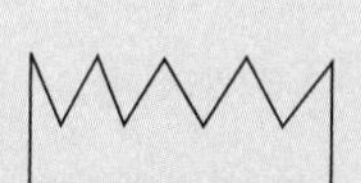

8. 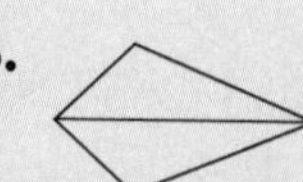

9. 

10. 

Chapter 3 REVIEW

Choose the letter of the correct answer.

1. Lines ℓ and m lie in the same plane but they never meet. What can you conclude?

A ℓ and m are parallel.
B ℓ and m are skew.
C ℓ and m intersect.
D ℓ and m bisect each other.

2. Lines ℓ and m never meet and do not lie in the same plane. What can you conclude?

A ℓ and m are parallel.
B ℓ and m are skew.
C ℓ and m intersect.
D ℓ and m bisect each other.

Use the figure to the right for problems 3–6.

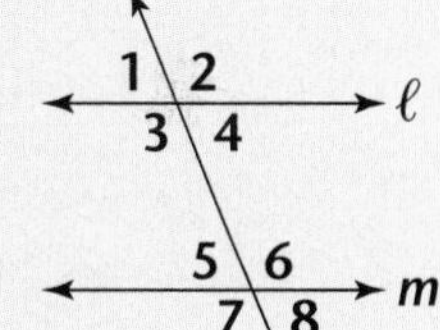

3. Which of the following forms a pair of corresponding angles with $\angle 2$?

A $\angle 1$
B $\angle 3$
C $\angle 5$
D $\angle 6$

4. Which of the following forms a pair of alternate exterior angles with $\angle 7$?

A $\angle 1$
B $\angle 2$
C $\angle 3$
D $\angle 8$

5. Which angle is *not* an interior angle?

A $\angle 3$
B $\angle 4$
C $\angle 5$
D $\angle 7$

6. If $m\angle 1 = 72°$, what is the measure of $\angle 5$?

A 108°
B 76°
C 72°
D 36°

7. What is a parallelogram with four sides of equal length called?

A rectangle
B rhombus
C quadrilateral
D trapezoid

Draw a picture to show the situation described.

Example: Lines a and b intersect. Solution:

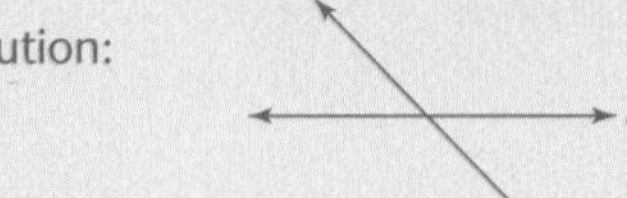

8. $\ell \parallel m \parallel n$

9. Lines x, y, and z intersect at point P.

In the figure below, ℓ and m are parallel lines crossed by transversal t. Identify the angles in the figure that match the description in each problem.

Example: alternate interior angles
Solution: $\angle c$ and $\angle f$, $\angle d$ and $\angle e$

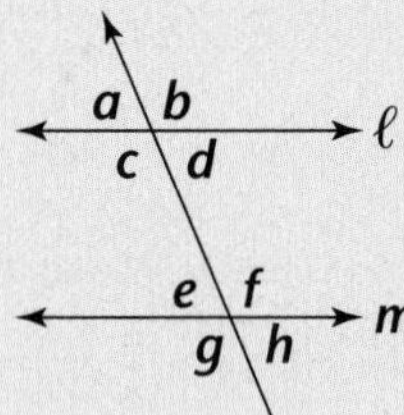

10. interior angles

11. exterior angles

12. alternate exterior angles

13. corresponding angles

14. angles equal in measure to $\angle a$

15. angles that are supplementary to $\angle a$

In this figure, $m \parallel \ell$, t is a transversal, and $m\angle q = 135°$. Find the measure (m) of each of the angles listed.

Example: $\angle p$ Solution: $\angle p$ and $\angle q$ are supplementary because they form a straight line. $m\angle q = 135°$, $m\angle p = 180° - 135° = 45°$

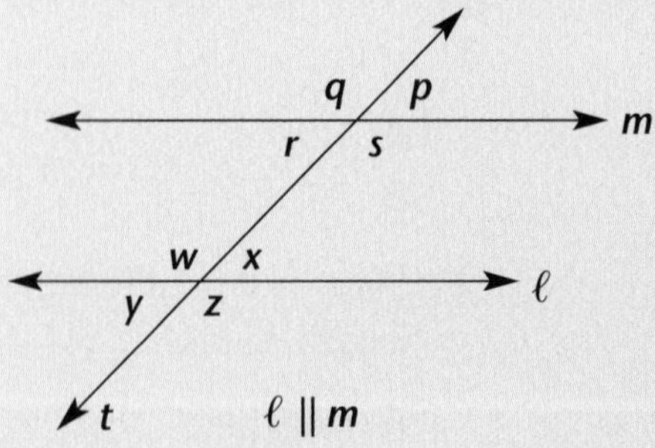

16. $\angle w$ **17.** $\angle r$ **18.** $\angle y$ **19.** $\angle x$ **20.** $\angle z$

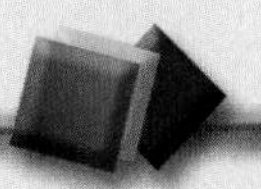

Find the measure of each angle. Use reasoning to determine the answer.

Example:
Given: m∠x = 2m∠y
Find m∠x.

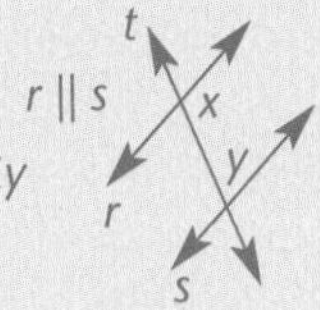

Solution: Since r || s, m∠x + m∠y = 180°. Let 2m∠y = m∠x; then m∠y + 2m∠y = 180°, 3m∠y = 180°, m∠y = 60°, m∠x = 120°

Given: Eight times m∠a = m∠b

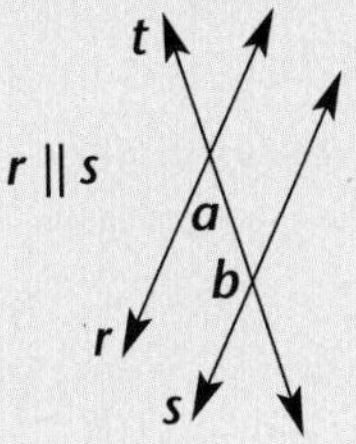

21. Find m∠a

22. Find m∠b

Name these geometric figures.

Example:

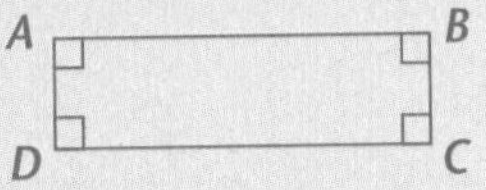

$\overline{AB} \parallel \overline{DC}$, $\overline{AD} \parallel \overline{BC}$ Solution: rectangle

23.

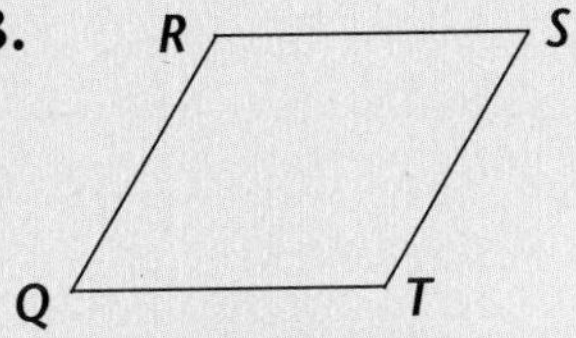

$\overline{RS} \parallel \overline{QT}$, $\overline{RQ} \parallel \overline{ST}$

24.

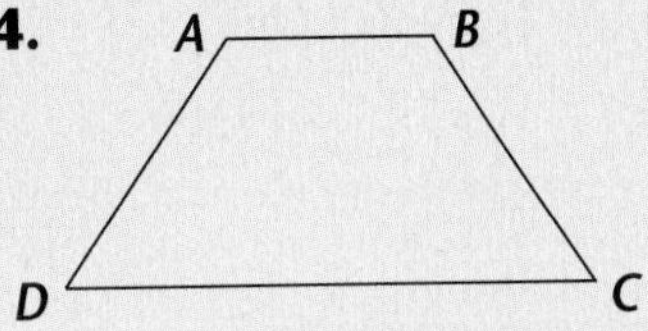

$\overline{AB} \parallel \overline{DC}$

Follow the directions.

25. Draw line ℓ and point X, not on ℓ. Construct line m parallel to ℓ using equal alternate interior angles.

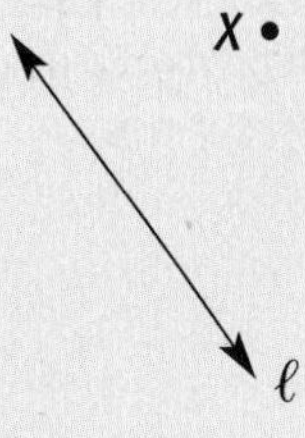

Test-Taking Tip

If a question shows a diagram, you probably need information from the diagram to answer the question. If the question doesn't have a diagram, it may help if you draw one to organize information.

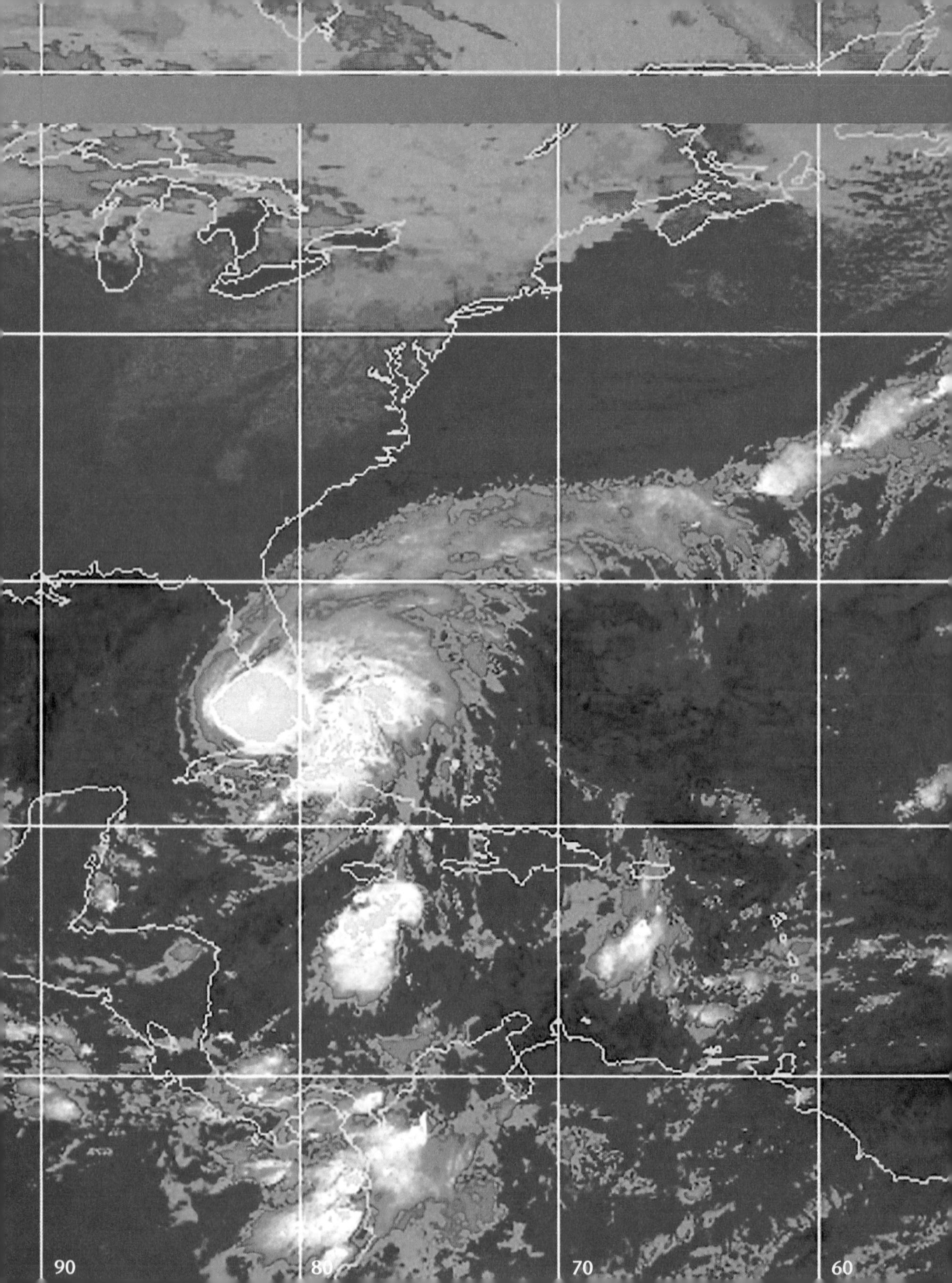
90
80
70
60

Chapter

Using Algebra: Lines in the Coordinate Plane

This weather map shows Hurricane Irene moving over Florida in October 1999. While satellites can photograph an area around the storm, we can find its exact location using latitude and longitude. On the map, latitude lines run east and west (left and right). Longitude lines run north and south (up and down). Any place on the earth can be named by its latitude and longitude. For example, Orlando, Florida, is located at 28°N, 81°W.

A Global Positioning System, or GPS, uses a process called triangulation to find the latitude and longitude of a place. Once, GPSs were only used by the military. Now drivers, sailors, and hikers use them to keep from getting lost. A system that defines locations with pairs of numbers is called a coordinate system.

In Chapter 4, you will learn about points, lines, and angles in the coordinate plane.

Goals for Learning

- To identify the algebraic equation for a line
- To use ordered pairs to graph lines on a coordinate plane
- To define and find the slope of a line
- To write and calculate the equations for lines
- To graph lines given slope and ordered pairs
- To find the midpoint of a line segment

Lesson 1 Naming Points

Horizontal
Parallel to the horizon

Vertical
Straight up and down

Coordinate plane
Plane formed by placing two real number lines at right angles

Graph
A diagram showing how one quantity depends on another

A plane, as Euclid saw it, has no named points except those that you place in it. Another way to think about a plane is to imagine that every point in the plane has a specific name. The Ruler Postulate allows you to do this. First assign real numbers on a **horizontal** line and on a **vertical** line.

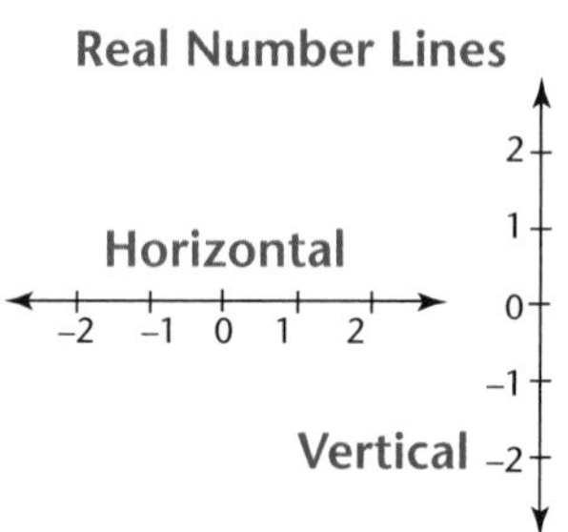

Then place the two number lines at right angles to each other, allowing the zero points of each to match. You have now formed a **coordinate plane.**

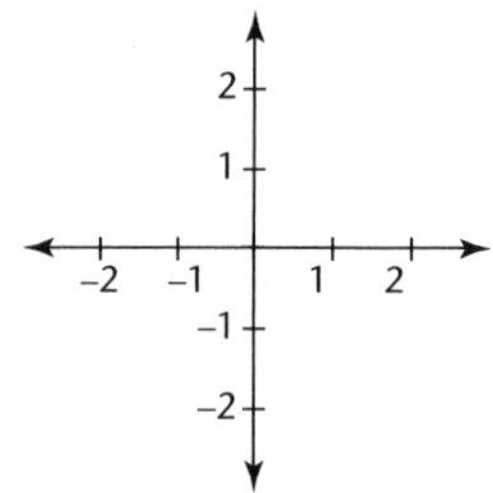

Points in the coordinate plane are named using their position relative to the *x*- and *y*-axes. The points are placed on a **graph.**

EXAMPLE 1 Name point *P*

Step 1 Draw a perpendicular from point *P* to the *x*-axis. Locate the point where the perpendicular meets the *x*-axis. This number is the *x*-value of point *P.*

Step 2 Draw a perpendicular from point *P* to the *y*-axis. Locate the point where the perpendicular meets the *y*-axis. This number is the *y*-value of point *P.*

Point *P* can be named by using both the *x*- and *y*-values together. In this case, $x = 2$ and $y = 3$. Therefore you can name the point $P = (2, 3)$.

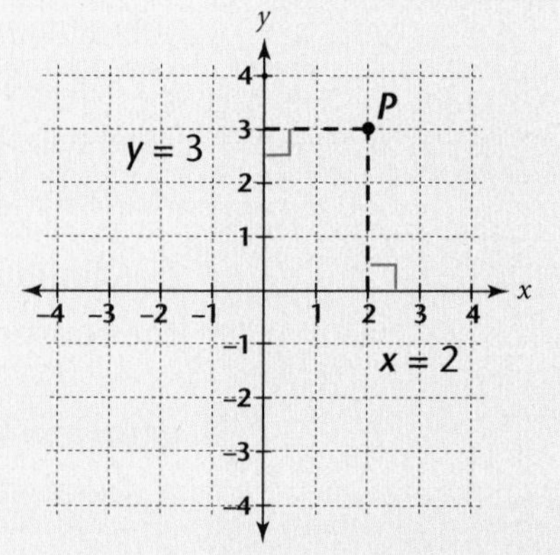

Ordered pair
A set of two real numbers that locate a point on a plane

Origin
The point at which the x-axis and y-axis intersect in the coordinate system

An **ordered pair** of real numbers (x, y) names each and every point on the coordinate plane. The pair is called an ordered pair because the x-value is always given first and the y-value is always given second.

First Second
(x, y) ordered pair of real numbers

EXAMPLE 2 Name the points A, B, and C as ordered pairs.

$A = (2, 3)$ x-value is 2, y-value is 3

$B = (2, 2)$ x-value is 2, y-value is 2

$C = (2, 1)$ x-value is 2, y-value is 1

Notice that the x-values for these three points are on the same vertical line, $x = 2$.

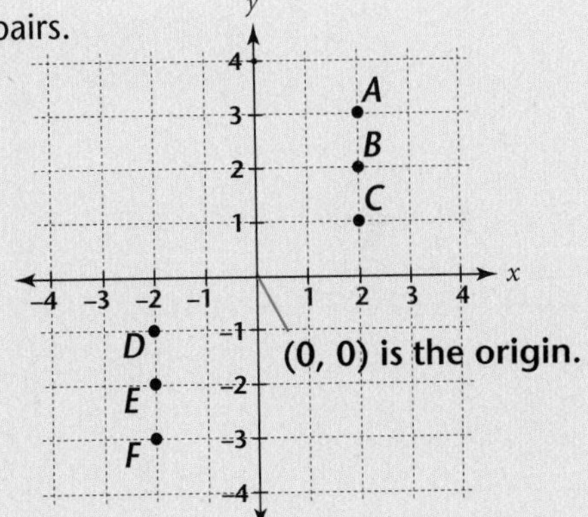

EXAMPLE 3 Name the points D, E, and F as ordered pairs.

$D = (-2, -1)$ x-value is -2, y-value is -1

$E = (-2, -2)$ x-value is -2, y-value is -2

$F = (-2, -3)$ x-value is -2, y-value is -3

The x-values for these three points are on the same vertical line, $x = -2$.

The ordered pair (0, 0) is called the **origin**.

EXAMPLE 4 Points on the axes can be named in two ways. Point A can be named (3, 0). The x-value is 3 and the y-value is 0.

B can be named $(0, -2)$. The x-value is 0, the y-value is -2.

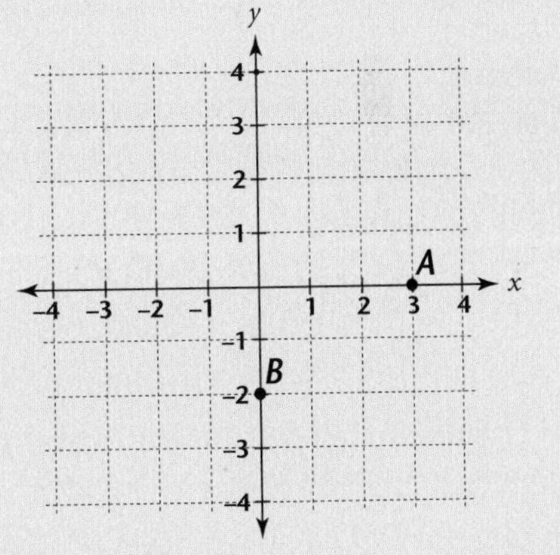

Even if a point is on the x- or y-axis, it should be identified by both coordinates. The ordered pair name specifies a single point and excludes all other points. This eliminates any confusion about the point's location.

Quadrant

One-fourth of the coordinate plane

EXAMPLE 5 Name each of the points as an ordered pair.

A = (−2, 0)
B = (−1, 0)
C = (0, 0)
D = (1, 0)
E = (2, 0)
F = (3, 0)

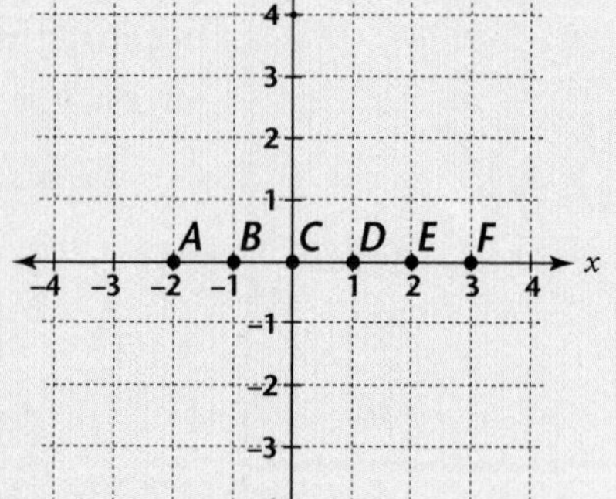

EXAMPLE 6 Name each of the points as an ordered pair.

U = (0, −2)
V = (0, −1)
W = (0, 0)
X = (0, 1)
Y = (0, 2)
Z = (0, 3)

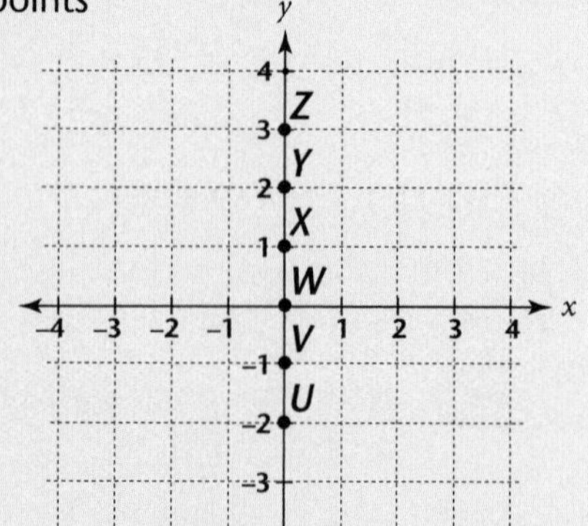

EXAMPLE 7 The x-axis and the y-axis divide the coordinate system into four regions called **quadrants.** Name the quadrant of each point's location.

Point $A = (2, 2)$ is in Quadrant I.

Point $B = (-3, 1)$ is in Quadrant II.

Point $C = (-1, -3)$ is in Quadrant III.

Point $D = (3, -3)$ is in Quadrant IV.

In Quadrant I, all points have x- and y-values greater than 0. That is, $x > 0$ and $y > 0$.

In Quadrant II, all points have $x < 0$ and $y > 0$.

In Quadrant III, all points have $x < 0$ and $y < 0$.

In Quadrant IV, all points have $x > 0$ and $y < 0$.

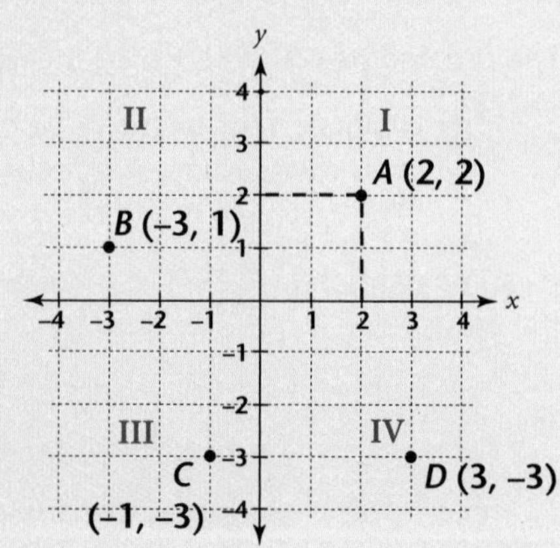

Exercise A Name the ordered pair that corresponds to each point.

1. A

2. B

3. C

4. D

5. E

6. F

7. G

8. H

9. I

10. J

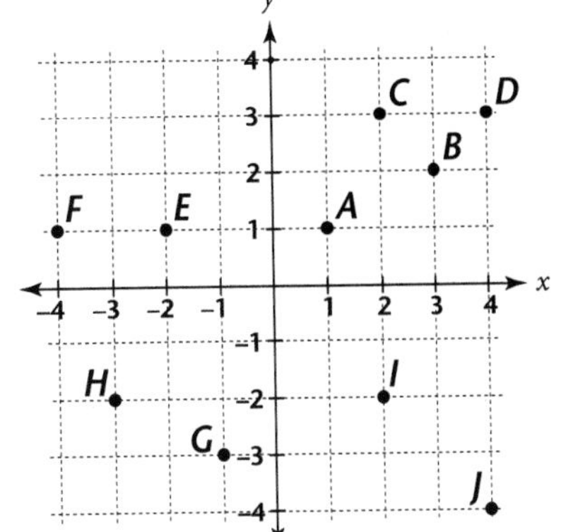

Exercise B Name the point located at each ordered pair.

11. $(-2, 2)$

12. $(3, -3)$

13. $(-3, -3)$

14. $(2, 2)$

15. $(1, -1)$

16. $(-2, -2)$

17. $(3, 5)$

18. $(-4, 3)$

19. $(-4, 0)$

20. $(0, 0)$

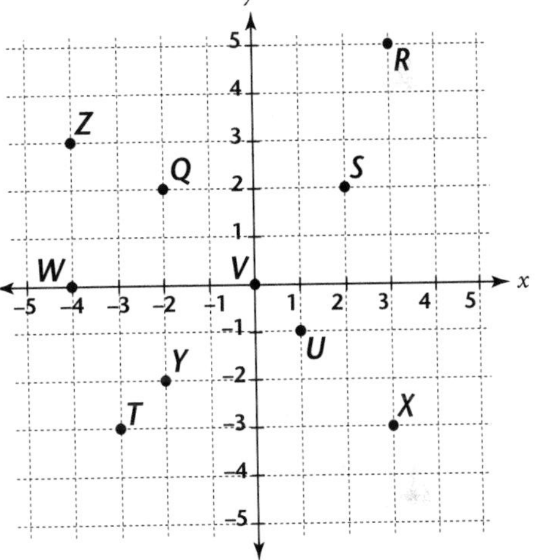

Exercise C Name the points on the x-axis using ordered pairs.

21. A

22. B

23. C

24. D

25. E

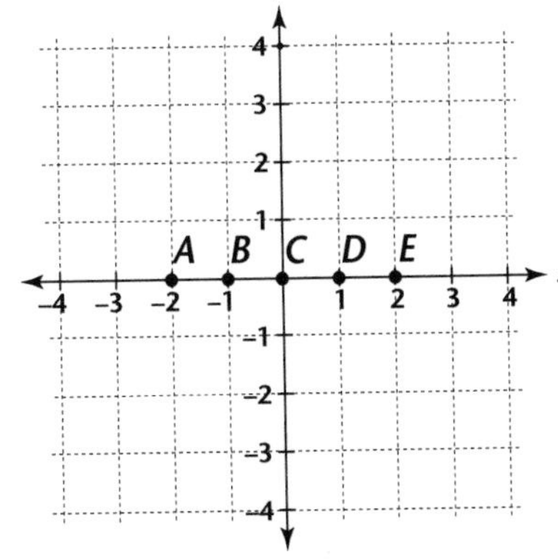

Exercise D Name the points on the y-axis using ordered pairs.

26. V

27. W

28. X

29. Y

30. Z

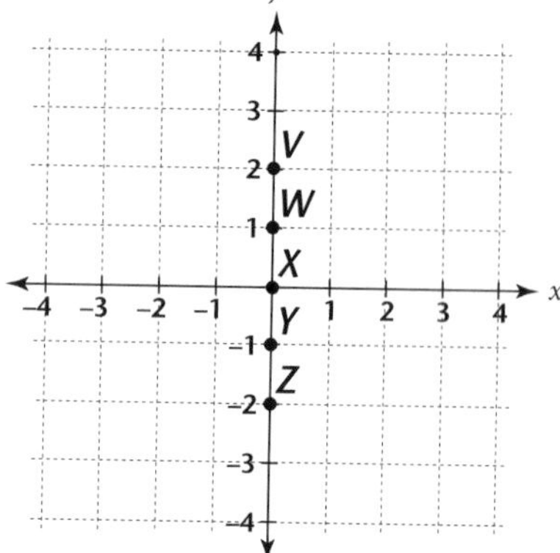

PROBLEM SOLVING

Exercise E Answer the following questions.

31. What can you say about the locations of these points in the coordinate plane: (3, 2), (3, 1), (3, 0), (3, -1), (3, -2) and (3, -3)?

32. What generalization can you make about the locations of these points in the coordinate plane: (-2, 2) (-1, 2), (0, 2), (1, 2), (2, 2), and (3, 2)?

33. Use algebraic terms to describe the points on the x-axis between Quadrant II and Quadrant III.

34. You can locate any city in the world using latitude and longitude. For example, Denver, Colorado, is located at 40°N, 105°W; Belo Horizonte, Brazil, is located at 20°S, 45°W. How are the lines of latitude and longitude on a map like a coordinate plane? How are they different?

35. In chess, each square has a name consisting of a letter and number, such as *b6* or *f8*. Why might this be useful to people playing chess by e-mail? How is the identification system for a chessboard like a coordinate plane? How is it different?

Lesson 2 Horizontal Lines

Horizontal lines are lines parallel to the x-axis. To help yourself remember this idea, think of the horizon. The horizon appears as a straight line as you look across a field, lake, or ocean.

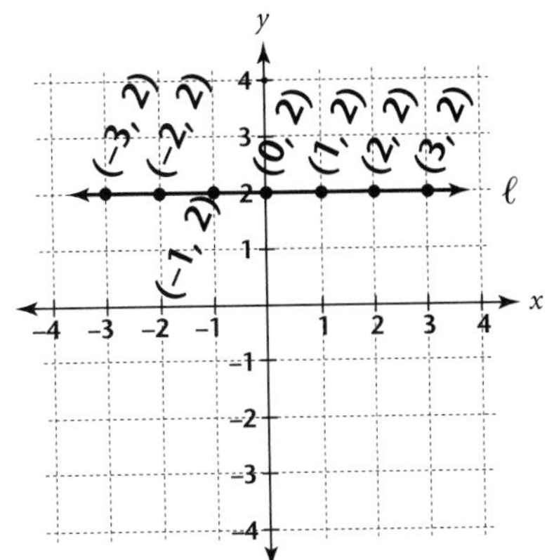

On the graph, line ℓ passes through the point (0, 2). Each point on ℓ has a different x-value, but all points have the same y-value, 2. If you wanted to describe the line using ordered pairs, it would be impossible to name all the points. For this reason, ℓ is often described as $y = 2$. A more useful way to describe ℓ is to say $y = 2$ and x is any real number. Or, you can describe the line using ordered pairs of the form $(x, 2)$.

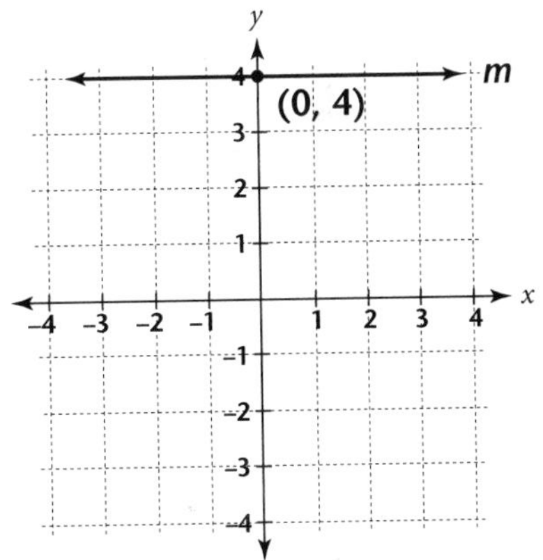

What is the algebraic expression, or equation, for line m? Since m passes through (0, 4) and is parallel to the x-axis, the algebraic expression is $y = 4$ and x is any real number. The ordered pairs are all of the form $(x, 4)$.

EXAMPLE 1 What are the algebraic expressions for these two lines, each parallel to the x-axis and exactly 5 units from the x-axis?

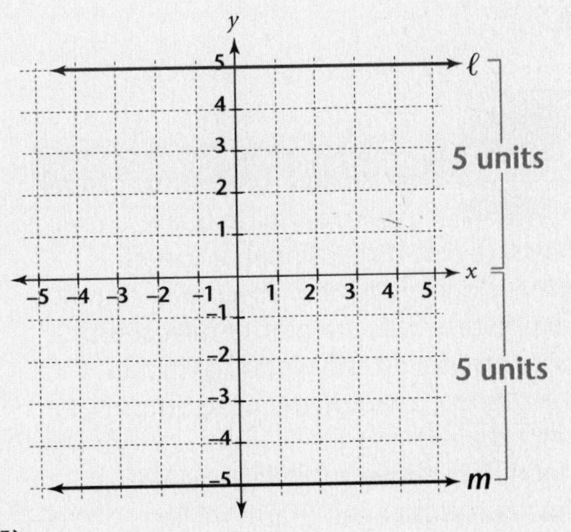

Solution:

Line ℓ passes through (0, 5) and the line m passes through (0, −5). Each of the lines is parallel to the x-axis so each has an x-value equal to any real number. Therefore the algebraic expression for ℓ is $y = 5$ and x is any real number. The algebraic expression for m is $y = -5$ and x is any real number.

The ordered pairs for ℓ are of the form $(x, 5)$. The ordered pairs for m are of the form $(x, -5)$.

EXAMPLE 2 What is the algebraic expression, or equation, for a line passing through (6, 4) and parallel to the line passing through (4, 2) and (6, 2)?

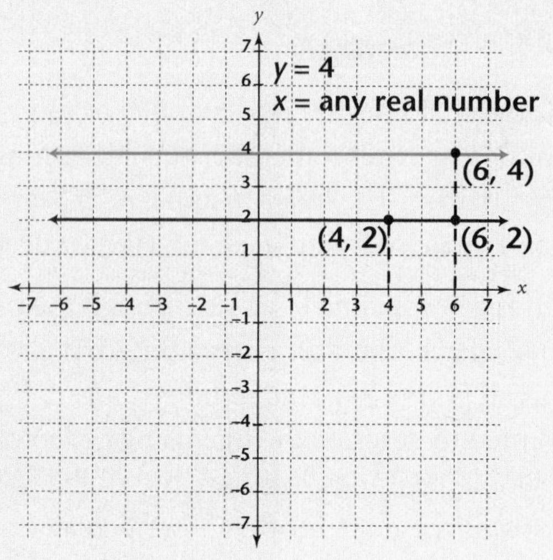

Solution:

The line passing through (4, 2) and (6, 2) is parallel to the *x*-axis. So the line passing through (6, 4) must also be parallel to the *x*-axis. The algebraic expression is $y = 4$ and x is any real number. The ordered pairs have the form $(x, 4)$.

Exercise A Write the algebraic expression for each line.

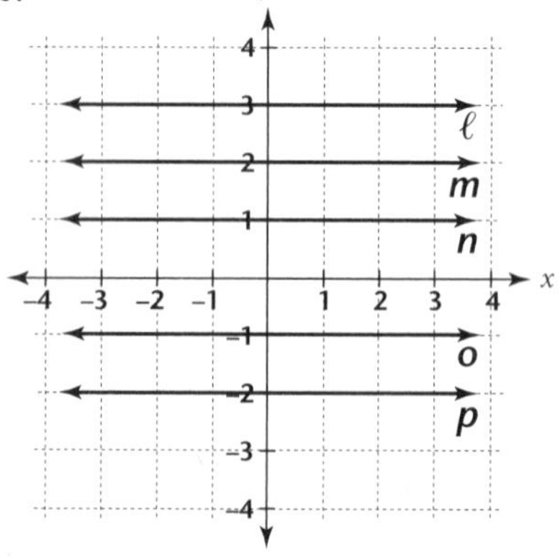

1. ℓ

2. m

3. n

4. o

5. p

Exercise B Write the ordered pairs for each line.

6. ℓ

7. m

8. n

9. o

10. p

Technology Connection

The coordinate plane is used to illustrate two-dimensional or three-dimensional images of equations. Benoit Mandelbrot was the mathematical artist who introduced the world to fractals. Fractals are created when the output of a function (the *y*-value) is put back into the function as the input (the *x*-value). Computers that can graph millions of these points from fractal functions are used to create and display these beautiful functions.

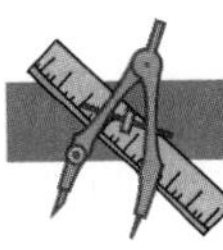

CONSTRUCTION

Exercise C Draw a graph of each line.

11. $y = 2$ and x is any real number

12. $y = -2$ and x is any real number

13. $y = 1\frac{1}{2}$ and x is any real number

14. $y = -3$ and x is any real number

Exercise D Graph all the ordered pairs.

15. $(x, 1)$ where x is any real number

16. $(x, -3)$ where x is any real number

17. $(x, -5)$ where x is any real number

18. $(x, 0)$ where x is any real number

PROBLEM SOLVING

Exercise E Answer the following questions.

19. What is the equation for the x-axis?

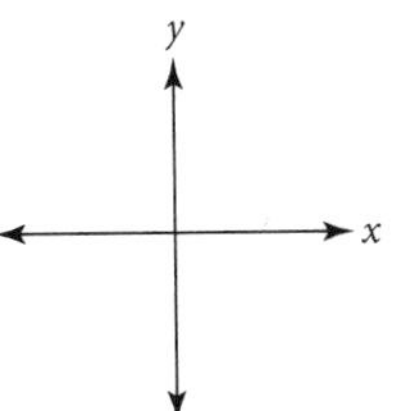

20. Downhill skiers and snowboarders often talk of "slopes." Beginning skiers look for gentle slopes, while more advanced skiers look for steeper slopes. Using your knowledge of slopes and the diagram below, what do you think is the slope of a level surface?

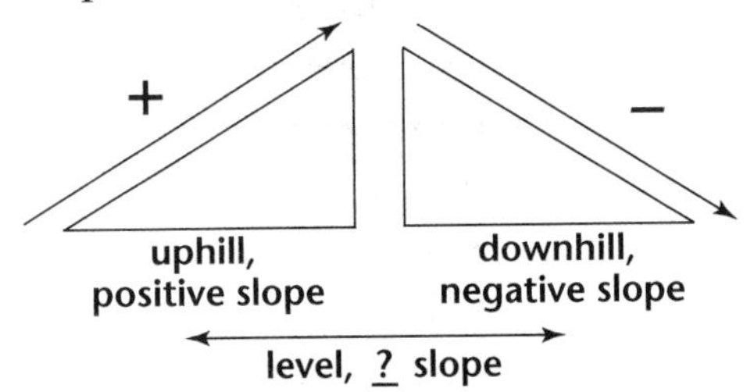

Geometry in Your Life

A grid system is used on local maps to make it easier to find roads and cities. These grid systems divide the map in to labeled rows and columns, like a chess board. Set up a coordinate grid on your classroom floor. Locate all of the objects in your classroom on the coordinate grid. Then give the coordinates of an object to another student and have him or her find it.

Lesson 3 Vertical Lines

Remember that the y-axis is the vertical axis. Therefore, lines parallel to the y-axis are vertical lines. These lines pass through a single point on the x-axis.

Line m is parallel to the y-axis and passes through the point (3, 0).

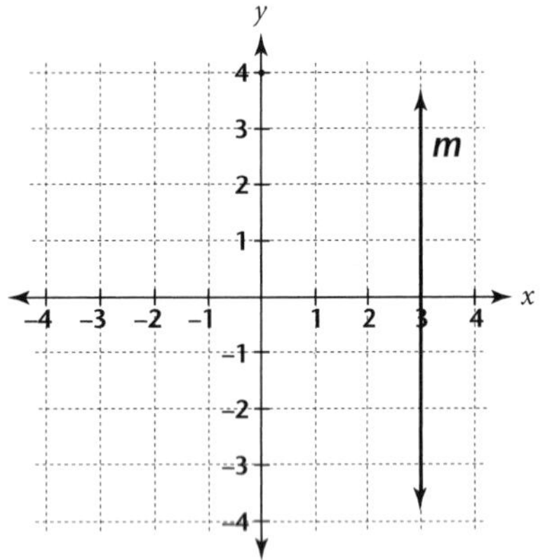

Each point on m has a different y-value, but all points have the same x-value, 3. If you tried to describe the line using ordered pairs, you would find it impossible to name all the points. However, you can say that line m consists of all ordered pairs where $x = 3$ and y is any real number. Notice that $m \perp$ the x-axis.

EXAMPLE 1 Here, line ℓ is parallel to the y-axis. What are the ordered pairs for points on ℓ?

$A = (5, 4)$

$B = (5, 3)$

$C = (5, 2)$

and so on to $G = (5, -2)$

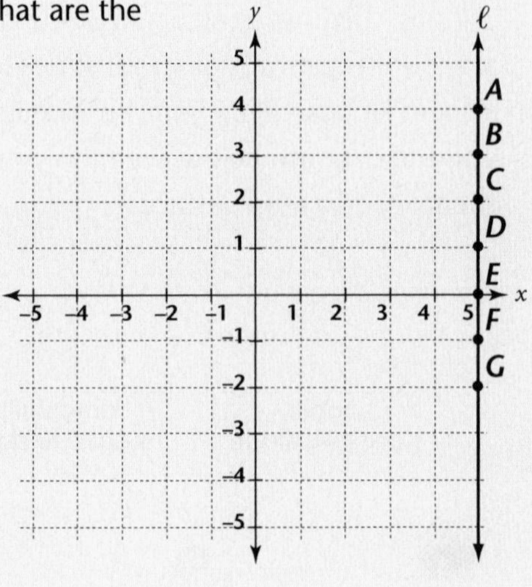

Notice that although all the x-values are 5, the y-values change. The algebraic expression for line ℓ is $x = 5$ and y is any real number. Since ℓ passes through (5, 0), the algebraic expression is $x = 5$ and y is any real number. The ordered pairs are all $(5, y)$.

EXAMPLE 2 What are the algebraic expressions for these two lines, each parallel to the y-axis at a distance of 3 units?

Solution:

Line ℓ passes through $(-3, 0)$ and line m passes through $(3, 0)$. Each of the lines is parallel to the y-axis so each has a y-value equal to any real number. Therefore the algebraic expression for ℓ is $x = -3$ and y is any real number. The algebraic expression for m is $x = 3$ and y is any real number.

The ordered pairs for ℓ are of the form $(-3, y)$. The ordered pairs for m are of the form $(3, y)$.

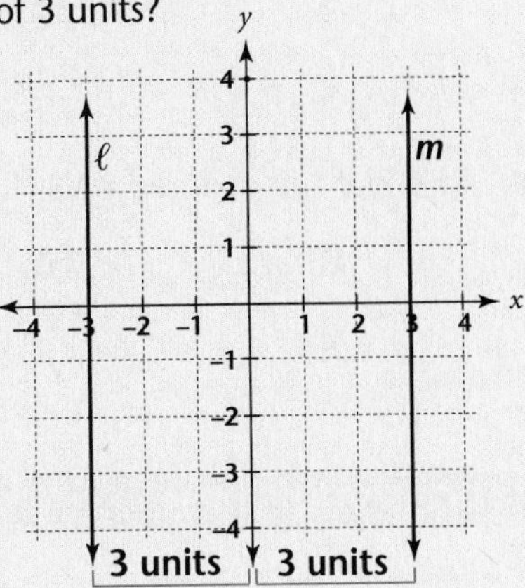

EXAMPLE 3 Is $\overline{BC}$ parallel to the y-axis? How do you know?

Solution:

$\overline{BC}$ passes through $x = 4$ because both B and C have the same x-value, 4. $\overline{BC}$ is a portion of the line that has the equation $x = 4$ and y is any real number. Therefore $\overline{BC}$ must be parallel to the y-axis.

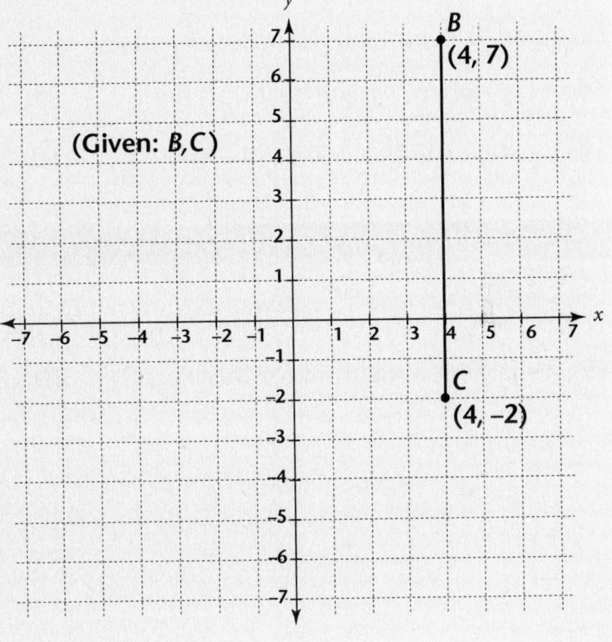

Exercise A Write the equation for each line.

1. ℓ

2. m

3. n

4. p

5. q

Exercise B Write the ordered pairs for each line.

6. ℓ

7. m

8. n

9. r

10. s

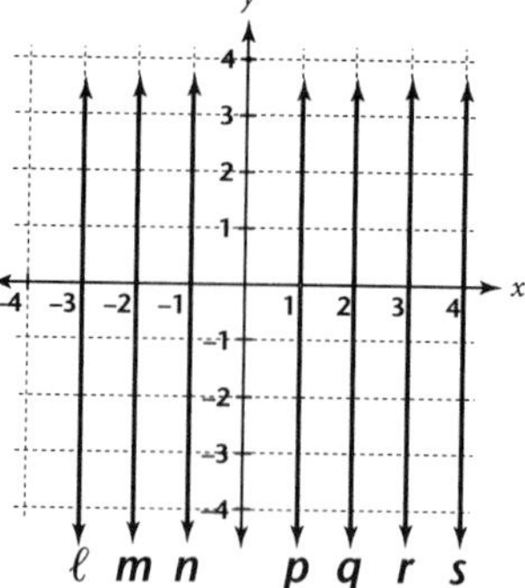

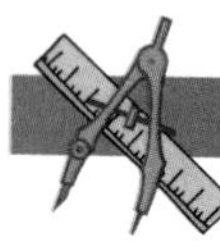

CONSTRUCTION

Exercise C Graph the line described by the equations.

11. $x = 2$ and y is any real number

12. $x = -2$ and y is any real number

13. $x = 1\frac{1}{2}$ and y is any real number

14. $x = -3$ and y is any real number

Exercise D Graph all the ordered pairs.

15. $(1, y)$ where y is any real number

16. $(-3, y)$ where y is any real number

17. $(-5, y)$ where y is any real number

18. $(0, y)$ where y is any real number

PROBLEM SOLVING

Exercise E Answer the following questions.

19. What is the equation for the y-axis?

20. Explain why any line parallel to the y-axis is perpendicular to the x-axis. (Hint: Review the definition of the coordinate plane and theorems from Chapter 3).

Lesson 4 Slope of a Line

Slope of a line

Ratio of the difference in y-values to the difference in x-values of any two points on the line

Carpenters and other craftspeople interested in the **slope of a line** define slope as rise divided by run.

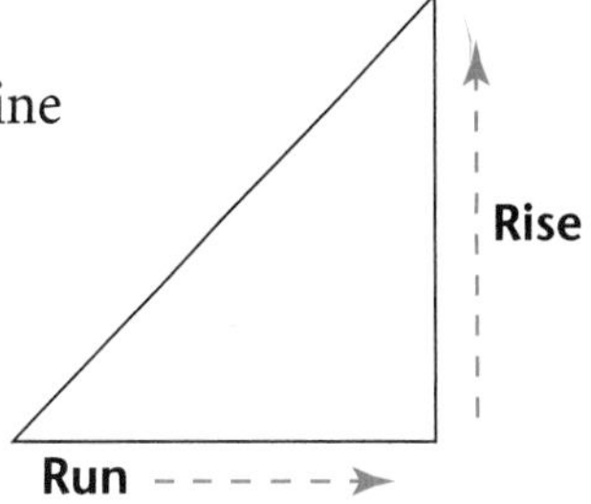

In the coordinate plane, slope has an algebraic definition.

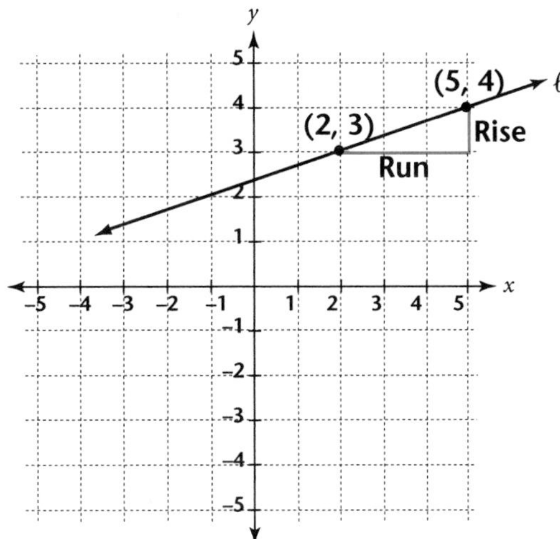

Here, line ℓ passes through points (2, 3) and (5, 4). Remember, Euclid's postulate states that any two points determine a line.

$$\text{slope of line } \ell = \frac{\text{rise}}{\text{run}} = \frac{\text{difference in } y\text{-values}}{\text{difference in } x\text{-values}}$$

$$\text{slope of } \ell = \frac{4-3}{5-2} = \frac{1}{3}$$

The slope is positive; the line is moving uphill from left to right.

Line m passes through points $(-1, 3)$ and $(4, -1)$.

$$\text{slope of line } m = \frac{\text{rise}}{\text{run}} = \frac{\text{difference in } y\text{-values}}{\text{difference in } x\text{-values}}$$

$$= \frac{3-(-1)}{-1-4} = \frac{4}{-5}$$

$$\text{slope} = -\frac{4}{5}$$

The slope is negative; the line is moving downhill from left to right.

When you use the formula for the slope of a line, it does not matter which point you label (x_1, y_1) and which you label (x_2, y_2); the results are the same.

The difference in y-values can be written as $y_1 - y_2$. The difference in x-values can be written as $x_1 - x_2$. We can use these expressions to write the slope of a line in symbol form.

The letter m is generally used to represent the value of the slope of a line. This leads to the following formula.

Formula for Slope of a Line:

$$m = \frac{y_1 - y_2}{x_1 - x_2}$$

where m is the slope of the line, and (x_1, y_1) and (x_2, y_2) are any two points on the line.

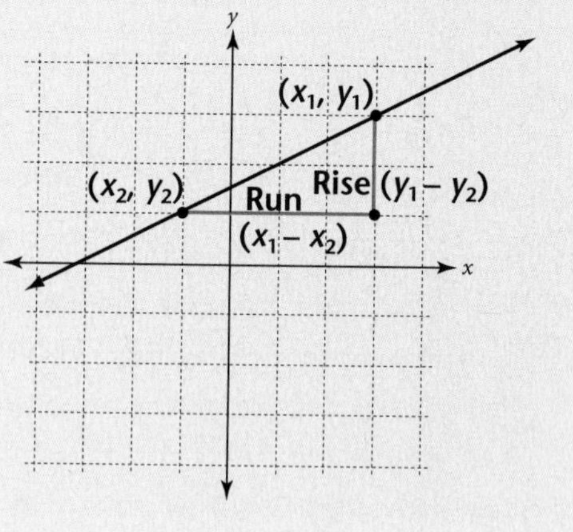

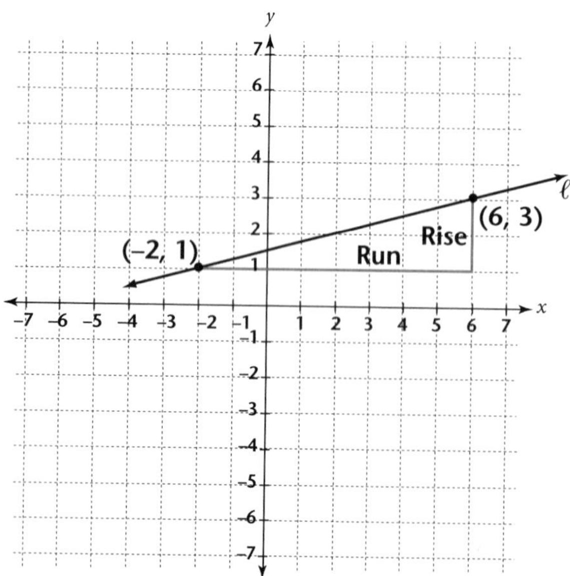

Let $(x_1, y_1) = (-2, 1)$

$(x_2, y_2) = (6, 3)$

$$\text{slope} = \frac{y_1 - y_2}{x_1 - x_2} = \frac{1 - 3}{-2 - 6} = \frac{-2}{-8} = \frac{1}{4}$$

OR

Let $(x_1, y_1) = (6, 3)$

$(x_2, y_2) = (-2, 1)$

$$\text{slope} = \frac{y_1 - y_2}{x_1 - x_2} = \frac{3 - 1}{6 - (-2)} = \frac{2}{8} = \frac{1}{4}$$

The slope is $\frac{1}{4}$ no matter which way you enter the points into the formula.

EXAMPLE 1 Calculate the slope of the line passing through (−4, 2) and (3, 1).

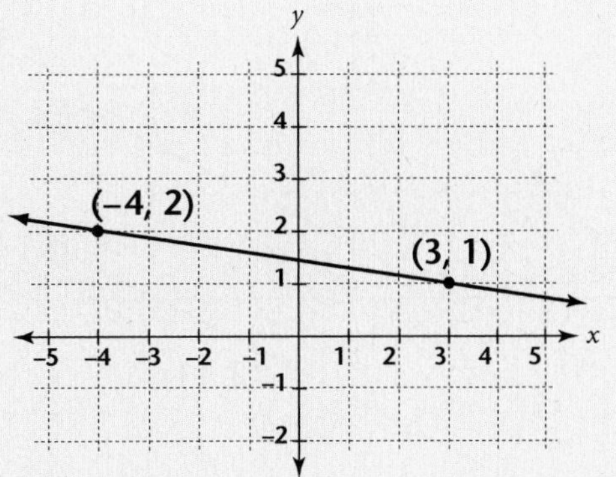

Solution: $m = \frac{y_1 - y_2}{x_1 - x_2}$

Let $(x_1, y_1) = (-4, 2)$

$(x_2, y_2) = (3, 1)$

then $m = \frac{2 - 1}{-4 - 3} = \frac{1}{-7} = -\frac{1}{7}$

$m = -\frac{1}{7}$

EXAMPLE 2 Calculate the slope of the horizontal line passing through (1, 4) and (3, 4).

Solution: $m = \frac{y_1 - y_2}{x_1 - x_2}$

Let $(x_1, y_1) = (1, 4)$

$(x_2, y_2) = (3, 4)$

then $m = \frac{4 - 4}{1 - 3} = \frac{0}{-2} = 0$

$m = 0$

Undefined

Cannot be expressed numerically

Notice that the y-values of all lines parallel to the x-axis are the same; their difference will always be zero. Therefore, the slope of any line parallel to the x-axis is zero. However, for vertical lines—lines parallel to the y-axis—the slope formula fails. Here is why.

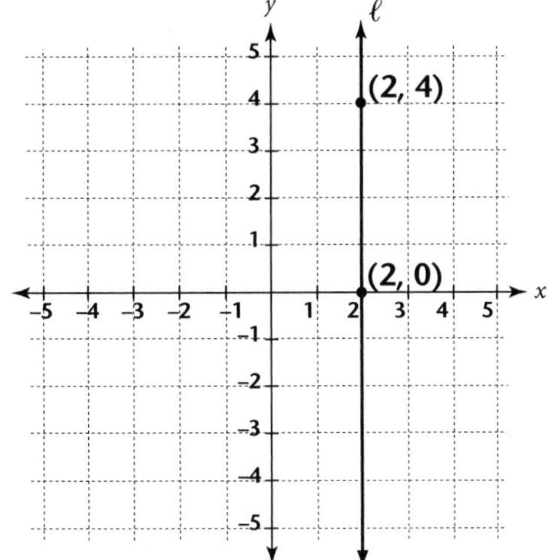

Suppose ℓ, parallel to the y-axis, passes through (2, 0) and (2, 4).

Let $(x_1, y_1) = (2, 0)$

$(x_2, y_2) = (2, 4)$

then $m = \frac{y_1 - y_2}{x_1 - x_2} = \frac{0 - 4}{2 - 2} = \frac{-4}{0}$

But division by zero is **undefined.** Therefore the slope of a line ℓ parallel to the y-axis is also undefined.

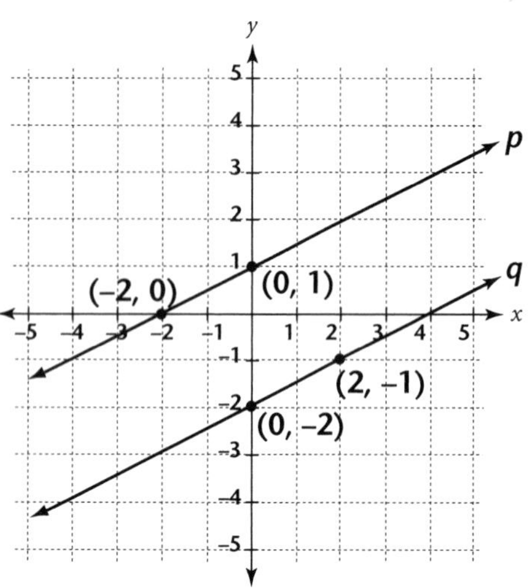

Any line parallel to the y-axis has equal x-values for all of its points. Therefore, the denominator of the slope formula, $(x_1 - x_2)$, will always equal zero and the fraction will be undefined.

Suppose you construct $p \parallel q$ on the coordinate plane as shown.

slope of $p = \frac{0 - 1}{-2 - 0} = \frac{-1}{-2} = \frac{1}{2}$

slope of $q = \frac{-2 - (-1)}{0 - 2} = \frac{-1}{-2} = \frac{1}{2}$

Parallel lines have equal slope.

Summary of Information about Slope

Negative Slope

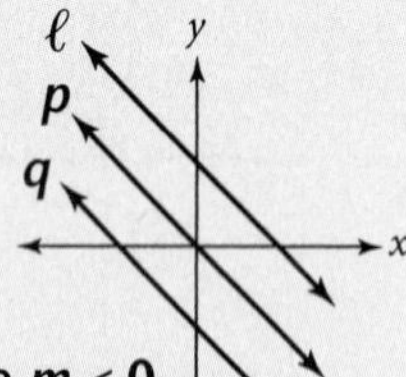

ℓ, p, q have $m < 0$

Positive Slope

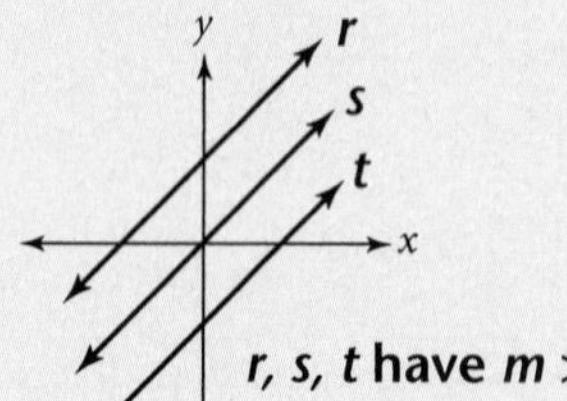

r, s, t have $m > 0$

Undefined Slope

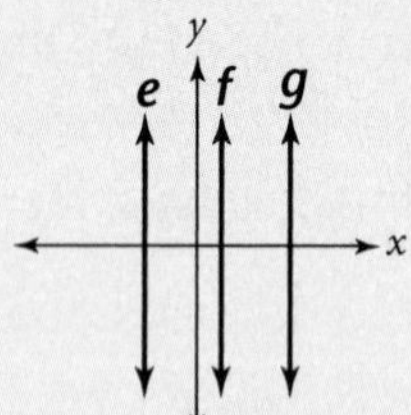

e, f, g have undefined slope

Zero Slope

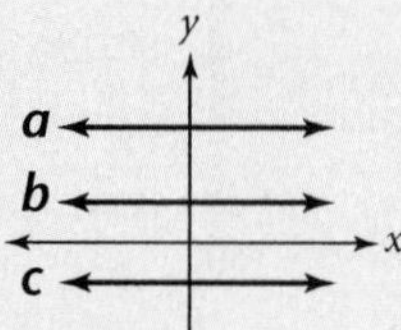

a, b, c have $m = 0$

Parallel lines have equal slopes

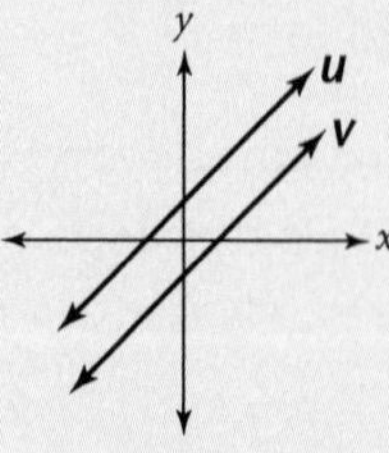

u, v have $m = 1$

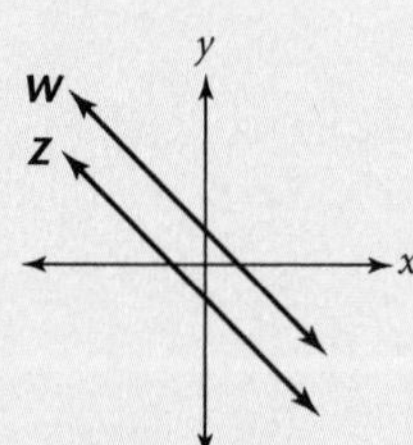

w, z have $m = -1$

Calculator Practice

Using the parentheses keys on your calculator can help you to find the slope of a line easily.

EXAMPLE 3 Let $(x_1, y_1) = (8, 6)$

$(x_2, y_2) = (4, 2)$

then $m = \frac{y_1 - y_2}{x_1 - x_2} = \frac{6 - 2}{8 - 4}$

Use your calculator to find the answer.

Press (6 − 2) ÷ (8 − 4) ENTER.

The answer is 1.

EXAMPLE 4 Let $(x_1, y_1) = (8, 6)$

$(x_2, y_2) = (4, -2)$

then $m = \frac{y_1 - y_2}{x_1 - x_2} = \frac{6 - (-2)}{8 - 4}$

Use your calculator to find the answer.

Press (6 − (−) 2) ÷ (8 − 4) ENTER.

The answer is 2.

Estimation Activity

Estimate: Estimate the slope of the solid line below.

45°

Solution: The broken line makes a 45° angle with the *x*-axis. The slope of the broken line is 1. The solid line is steeper than the broken line, so the slope of the solid line is greater than 1.

Exercise A Use a calculator to find the following quotients.

1. $\frac{6 - 3}{4 - (-2)}$
2. $\frac{20 - 15}{7 - (-3)}$
3. $\frac{4 - (-3)}{12 - (-2)}$
4. $\frac{9 - 3}{-15 - (-3)}$
5. $\frac{(-9) - (-3)}{15 - 3}$

Exercise B Find the slope, *m*, of each line.

6.

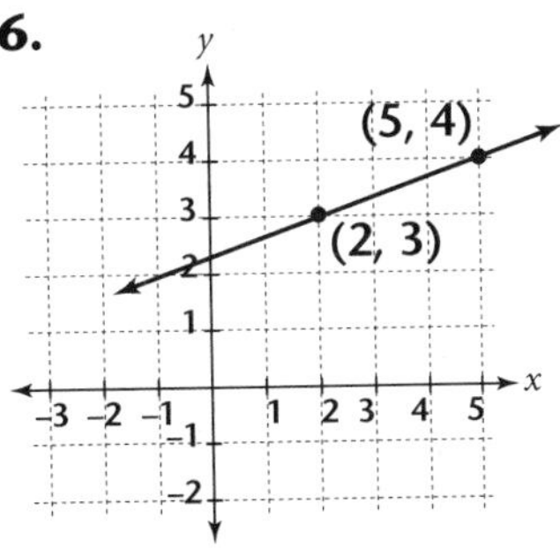

7.

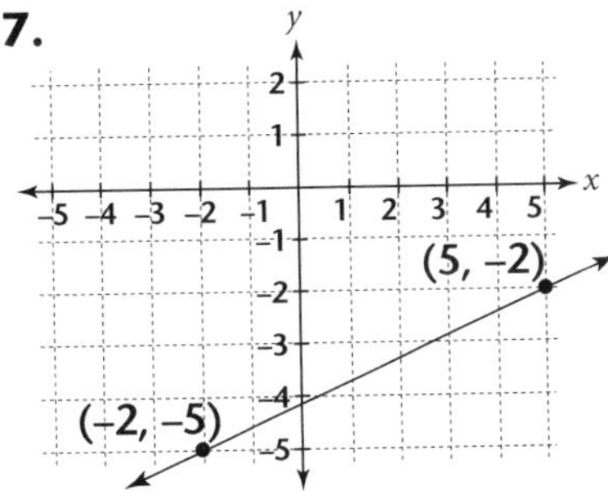

8.

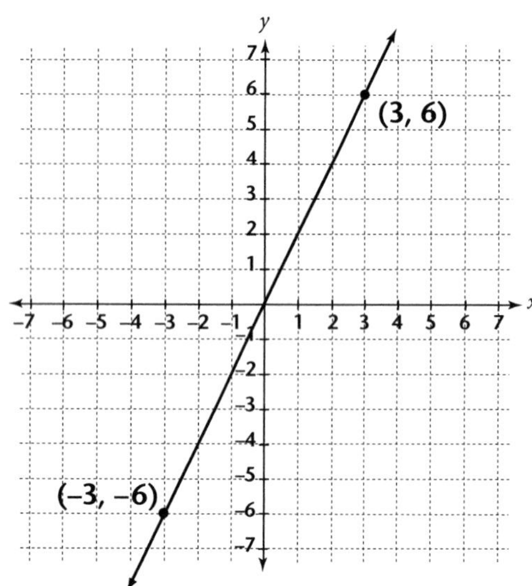

9.

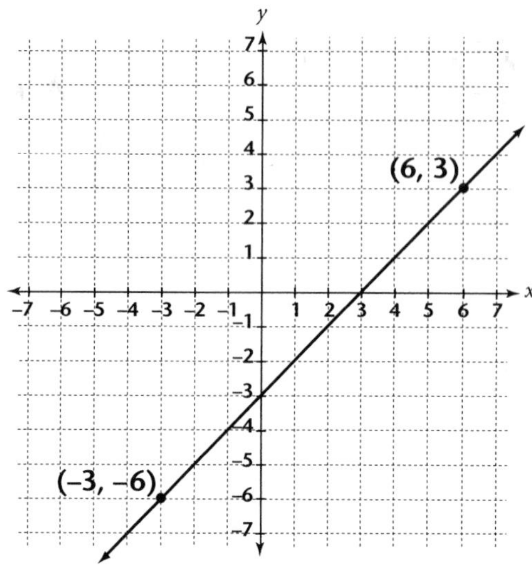

Exercise C Find the slope, m, of a line that passes through the given points.

10. (3, 4) and (7, 16)

11. (−3, 4) and (7, 16)

12. (4, 6) and (8, 12)

13. (−3, −7) and (−7, −3)

Exercise D Find the slope for each pair of lines.

14.

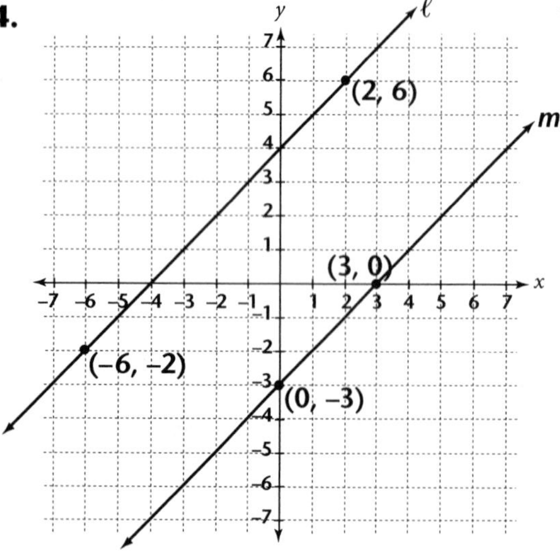

15.

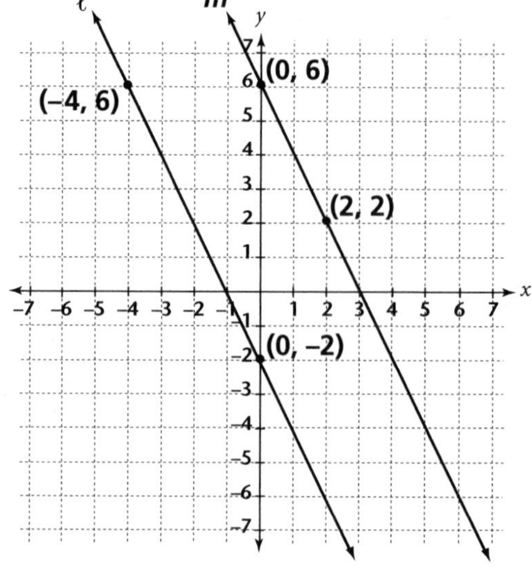

Lesson 5 Using Algebra: $y = mx + b$

In geometry, Euclid's first postulate states that for any two points there exists one, and only one, line passing through those points. If the points are A and B, then line AB or segment AB is determined.

Line *AB*

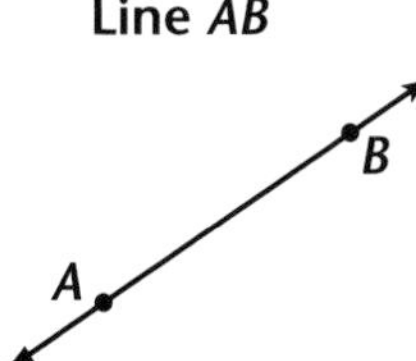

Segment *AB*

You can draw the line or line segment on the coordinate plane as well. All you need are the ordered pairs that locate points A and B.

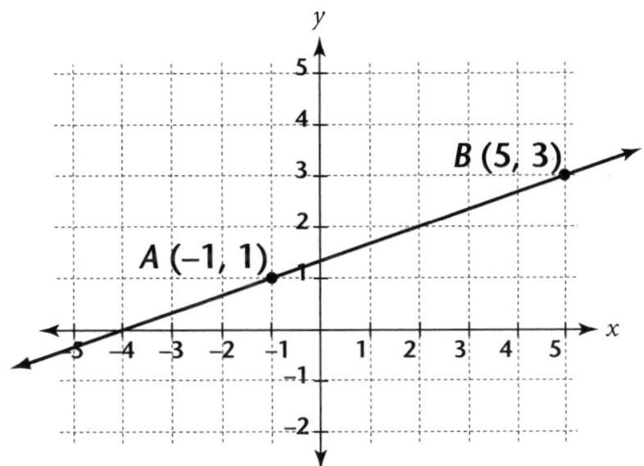

Graph line *AB*

Let $A = (-1, 1)$ and $B = (5, 3)$.

Place A and B in the plane.

Draw the line through A and B.

(Use a straightedge.)

You have now graphed $\overleftrightarrow{AB}$.

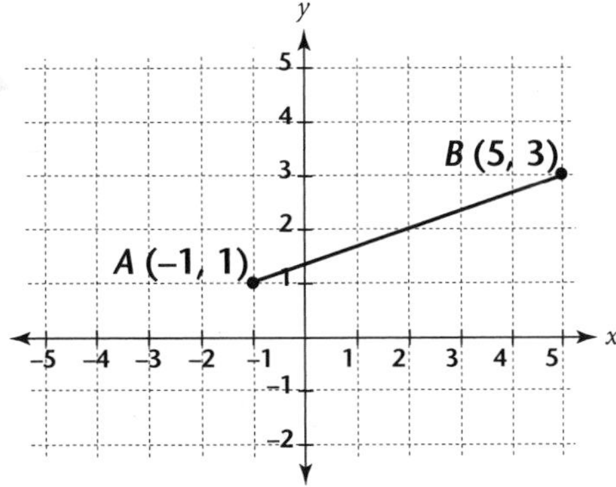

Graph segment *AB*

Let $A = (-1, 1)$ and $B = (5, 3)$.

Place A and B in the plane.

Draw a line between A and B.

(Use a straightedge.)

You have now graphed $\overline{AB}$.

Y-intercept

The y-value of the point where a line crosses the y-axis (when x = 0)

Function

A rule that pairs every x-value with one and only one y-value

Domain

The x-values of a function

Range

The y-values of a function

To represent $\overleftrightarrow{AB}$ and $\overline{AB}$ using only algebra, you need to use the equation for the line, $y = mx + b$. The equation $y = mx + b$ has three parts: an ordered pair, (x, y); the slope, m; and the y-intercept, b. The **y-intercept** is the y-value of a **function** when $x = 0$; it is the point at which the line crosses the y-axis.

$y = mx + b$ is a rule that pairs every x-value with one and only one y-value, therefore $y = mx + b$ is an example of a function. The graph of $y = mx + b$ is a straight line, so the equation is sometimes called the straight line function. Sometimes $y = mx + b$ is written as $f(x) = mx + b$ and read as "the function of x equals mx plus b."

The x-values of a function are called the **domain** of the function. The y-values of a function are called the **range** of the function. Let's see how we can represent $\overleftrightarrow{AB}$ using $y = mx + b$.

EXAMPLE 1 Write the equation for line AB when $A = (-1, 1)$ and $B = (5, 3)$.

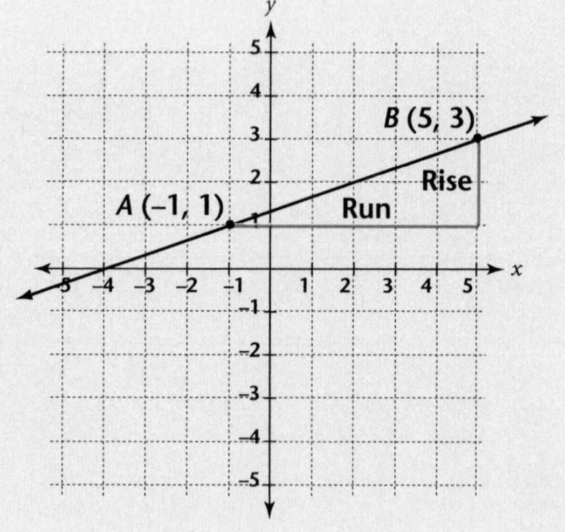

Step 1 Calculate $m = \frac{1 - 3}{-1 - 5} = \frac{-2}{-6} = \frac{1}{3}$

Step 2 The equation $y = \frac{1}{3}x + b$ is true for all ordered pairs on $\overleftrightarrow{AB}$. This means we can substitute the coordinates of any one point on the line for the x- and y-values in the equation. This will allow us to solve for b.

Take $A = (-1, 1)$

$x = -1, y = 1$

so $y = mx + b$ becomes

$1 = \frac{1}{3}(-1) + b$

$\therefore \frac{4}{3} = b$

Conclusion: $y = \frac{1}{3}x + \frac{4}{3}$

Take $B = (5, 3)$

$x = 5, y = 3$

so $y = mx + b$ becomes

$3 = \frac{5}{3} + b$

$\therefore \frac{4}{3} = b$

Conclusion: $y = \frac{1}{3}x + \frac{4}{3}$

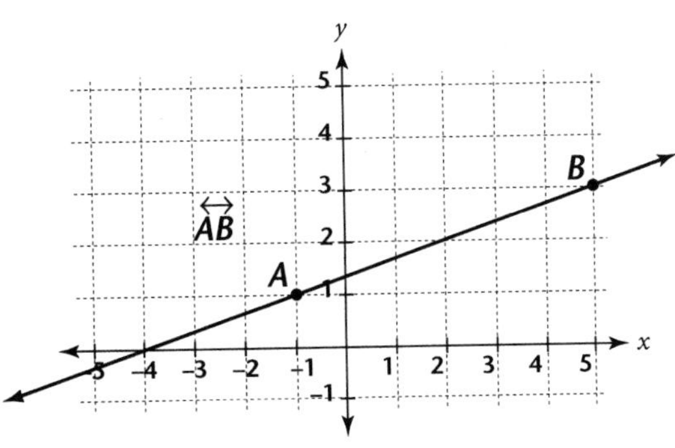

The substitution of either A or B in the equation leads to the same conclusion.

$y = \frac{1}{3}x + \frac{4}{3}$ represents $\overleftrightarrow{AB}$ for the domain of $x =$ all real numbers and the range of $y =$ all real numbers.

Here, the x- and y-values can be any real number for the ordered pairs on $\overleftrightarrow{AB}$ as long as $y = \frac{1}{3}x + \frac{4}{3}$ is true for each pair.

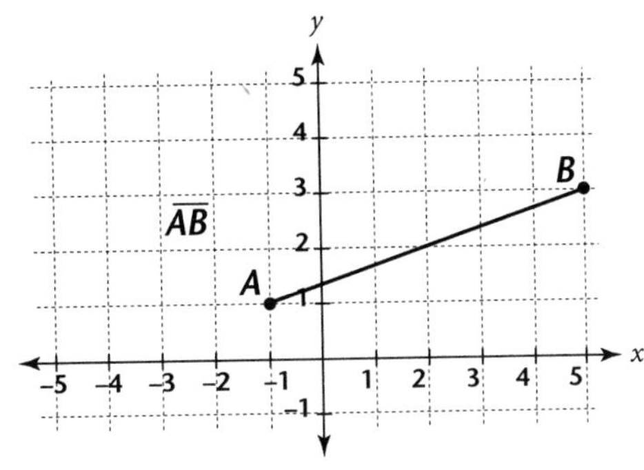

$y = \frac{1}{3}x + \frac{4}{3}$ represents $\overline{AB}$ for the domain of $-1 \leq x \leq 5$ and the range of $1 \leq y \leq 3$.

EXAMPLE 2 Write the equation for segment *CD* and line *CD* when $C = (2, 1)$ and $D = (6, 5)$.

Step 1 Calculate $m = \frac{1 - 5}{2 - 6} = \frac{-4}{-4} = 1$

If we substitute 1 for m in the equation, the equation for the line becomes $y = \ x + b$.

Step 2 Substitute the coordinates of any one point on the line for the x- and y-values in the equation. Then solve for b.

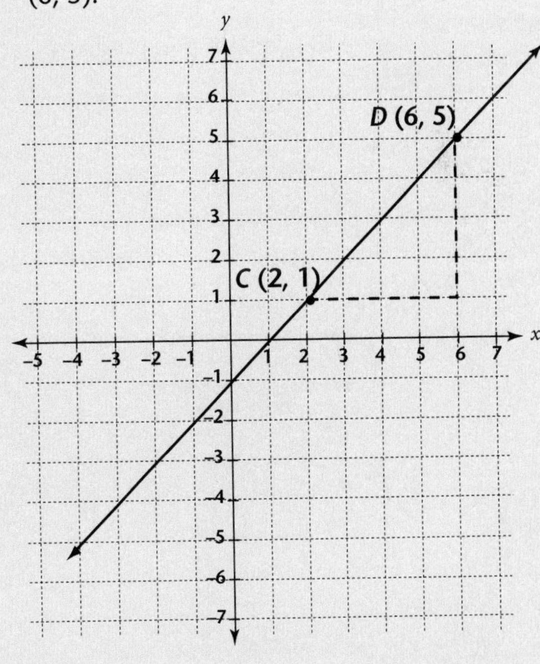

Example 2 continues on page 124

EXAMPLE 2 *(continued)*

Take $C = (2, 1)$	Take $D = (6, 5)$
$x = 2, y = 1$	$x = 6, y = 5$
so $y = mx + b$ becomes	so $y = mx + b$ becomes
$1 = 2 + b$	$5 = 6 + b$
$\therefore -1 = b$	$\therefore -1 = b$
Conclusion: $y = x - 1$	**Conclusion:** $y = x - 1$

For line *CD*, $y = mx + b$ becomes $y = x - 1$ or $f(x) = x - 1$; the domain equals all real numbers and the range equals all real numbers.

For segment *CD*, $y = mx + b$ becomes $y = x - 1$ or $f(x) = x - 1$; the domain is $2 \le x \le 6$ and the range is $1 \le y \le 5$.

You can generally read the domain and range of a function from the graph of that function.

The domain is all points on the *x*-axis needed to form the ordered pairs on $\overline{AB}$, and the range is all the *y*-values needed to form the ordered pairs on $\overline{AB}$.

EXAMPLE 3 Name the domain and range for each graph.

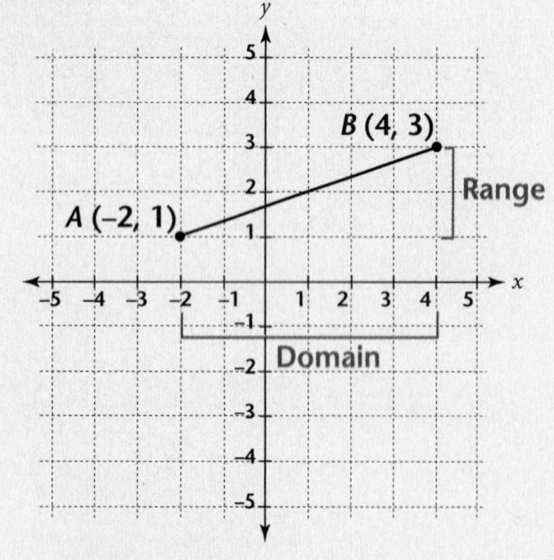

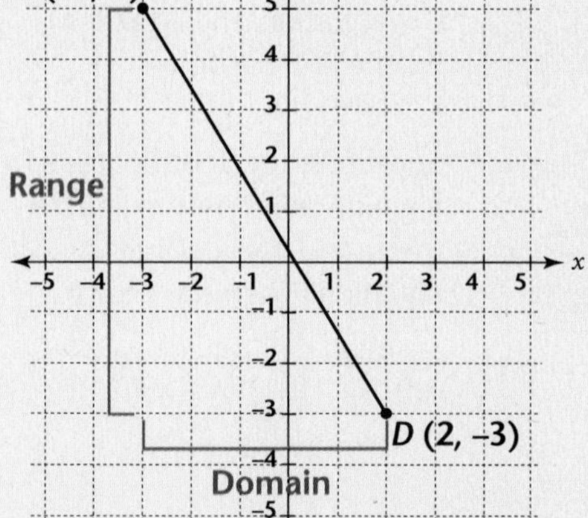

Solution:	**Solution:**
Domain is $-2 \le x \le 4$	Domain is $-3 \le x \le 2$
Range is $1 \le y \le 3$	Range is $-3 \le y \le 5$

EXAMPLE 3 *(continued)*

Special Case: Remember, $m = 0$ for lines parallel to the x-axis. In these cases $y = mx + b$ becomes $y = (0)x + b$ or $y = b$. In the example, the line passes through (1, 1) and (5, 1) and

$$m = \frac{1 - 1}{1 - 5} = \frac{0}{-4} = 0.$$

So, $y = mx + b$ becomes $y = b$, but $y = 1$ since the line intercepts the y-axis at 1. So $y = b = 1$.

Solution: The domain for this function is any real number and the range is 1.

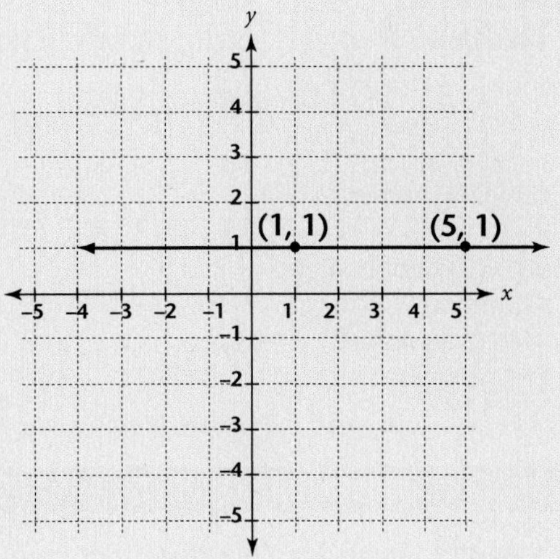

Writing About Mathematics

Why are lines at right angles to the x-axis not functions?

CONSTRUCTION

Exercise A Graph the line that passes through each pair of points. Use graph paper and a straightedge.

1. (2, 1) and (1, 2)

2. (3, 4) and (−3, −4)

3. (5, 1) and (10, 1)

4. (3, 2) and (2, 3)

5. (2, 2) and (5, 5)

6. (−3, −3) and (4, −3)

7. (−2, 3) and (4, −3)

Exercise B Graph the line segments for the following pairs of endpoints. Use graph paper and a straightedge. Give the domain and range of each.

8. (2, 1) and (1, 2)

9. (−2, 6) and (1, 1)

10. (3, 1) and (2, −5)

11. (4, 2) and (−1, 2)

12. (6, 3) and (−3, 4)

TRY THIS

Look in a magazine or newspaper for a line graph. Explain whether the graph is or is not an example of a function. If it is, what is its domain and range?

Exercise C Write the equation of the line that passes through each pair of points. Use the form $y = mx + b$.

13. (2, 1) and (1, 2)

14. (3, 4) and (−3, −4)

15. (5, 1) and (10, 1)

16. (3, 2) and (2, 3)

17. (2, 2) and (5, 5)

PROBLEM SOLVING

Exercise D Solve the following problems.

18. At the right is a design for a playground slide. What is the slope of the slide?

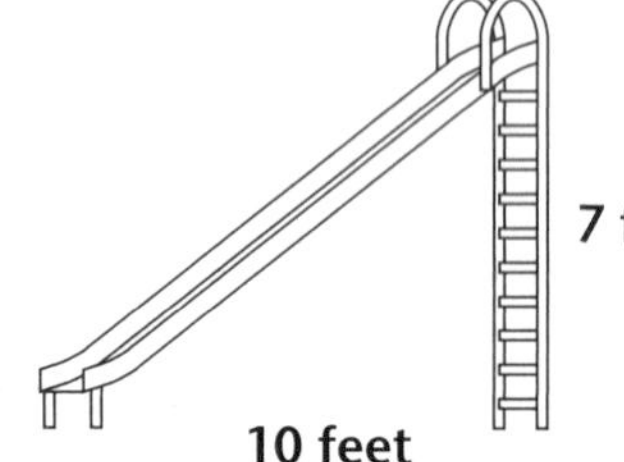

19. A ski lift carries skiers from an elevation of 5,200 ft to an elevation of 7,700 ft. The horizontal distance from the start to the end of the lift is 5,000 ft. Draw a diagram showing this information and find the slope of the lift line.

20. The distance between the first and second floor of a building is 10 ft. The horizontal distance between the bottom step and the top step is 72 in. What is the slope of the stairway?

Lesson 6 Writing the Equation of a Line

Suppose you are given a point A at $(1, 3)$ and a slope $m = \frac{1}{2}$. How would you graph the line and then write the equation for that line?

Given: Point A $(1, 3)$ and slope $m = \frac{1}{2}$

Graph: The line with slope $m = \frac{1}{2}$ that passes through A $(1, 3)$

Graph $\overleftrightarrow{AB}$.

Step 1 Locate (1, 3) on the plane, in Quadrant I.

Step 2 Use $m = \frac{1}{2}$ to locate a second point on the line. (Remember Euclid's Postulate 1 on page 41.)

$m = \frac{1}{2} = \frac{\text{change in } y}{\text{change in } x}$

from point A (1, 3)
count UP 1
count 2 to the RIGHT
to reach point B (3, 4)

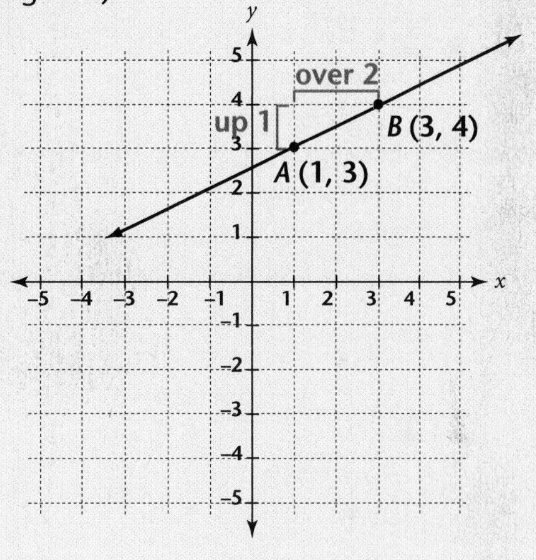

Draw $\overleftrightarrow{AB}$. This is your graph.

You can also calculate the coordinates for point B. The given slope, $m = \frac{1}{2}$, indicates that as the x-value increases by 2, the y-value increases by 1. If point A is (x, y), then the ordered pair for point B is $(x + 2, y + 1)$.

Point $A = (1, 3)$, so point $B = (1 + 2, 3 + 1) = (3, 4)$.

EXAMPLE 1 Write the equation for $\overleftrightarrow{AB}$.

Step 1 $y = mx + b$ and $m = \frac{1}{2}$, so $y = \frac{x}{2} + b$.

Step 2 The equation $y = \frac{x}{2} + b$ is true for all ordered pairs on $\overleftrightarrow{AB}$. Because (1, 3) is on the line, we can substitute $x = 1$ and $y = 3$ and solve for b.

$y = \frac{x}{2} + b$ becomes $3 = \frac{1}{2} + b$

$2\frac{1}{2} = b$

Step 3 Using this value for b, the equation becomes

$y = \frac{x}{2} + 2\frac{1}{2}$

$\therefore y = \frac{x}{2} + 2\frac{1}{2}$ is the equation for $\overleftrightarrow{AB}$.

CONSTRUCTION **Given:** Point $C(-1, -2)$ and slope $m = -2$

Graph: The line with slope $m = -2$ that passes through $C(-1, -2)$

Graph $\overleftrightarrow{CD}$.

Step 1 Locate $C(-1, -2)$ on the plane, in Quadrant III.

Step 2 Use $m = -2$ to locate a second point on the line. (Remember Euclid's Postulate 1.)

$m = -\frac{2}{1} = \frac{\text{change in } y}{\text{change in } x}$

From point $C(-1, -2)$ count DOWN 2 and count 1 to the RIGHT to reach point $D(0, -4)$.

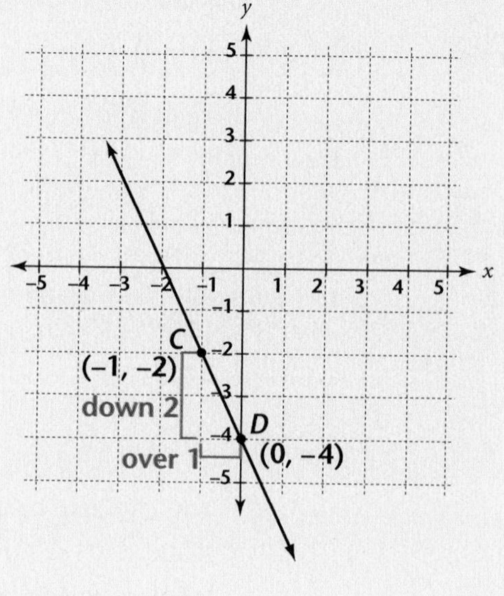

Draw $\overleftrightarrow{CD}$. This is your graph.

Check by calculating the coordinates for point D. The given slope, $m = -2 = -\frac{2}{1}$, indicates that as the x-value increases by 1, the y-value decreases by 2. If point C is (x, y), then the ordered pair for point D is $(x + 1, y - 2)$.

Point $C = (-1, -2)$, so point $D = (-1 + 1, -2 - 2) = (0, -4)$.

EXAMPLE 2 Write the equation for $\overleftrightarrow{CD}$.

Step 1 $y = mx + b$ and $m = -2$, so $y = -2x + b$.

Step 2 The equation $y = -2x + b$ is true for all ordered pairs on $\overleftrightarrow{CD}$. Because $(-1, -2)$ is on the line, we can substitute $x = -1$ and $y = -2$ and solve for b.

$y = -2x + b$ becomes $-2 = (-2)(-1) + b$

$-4 = b$

Step 3 Using this value for b, the equation becomes $y = -2x - 4$.

$\therefore y = -2x - 4$ is the equation for $\overleftrightarrow{CD}$.

Special Case: Suppose you are given any point and slope $m = 0$. You know that all lines with $m = 0$ are parallel to the x-axis. In these cases, you need only plot the point and draw a line through that point parallel to the x-axis.

CONSTRUCTION **Given:** Point P (3, 4) and slope $m = 0$

Graph: The line ℓ with slope $m = 0$ that passes through P (3, 4)

Graph line ℓ.

Step 1 Locate P (3, 4) on the plane.

Step 2 Draw a line parallel to the x-axis passing through (3, 4).

This is your graph.

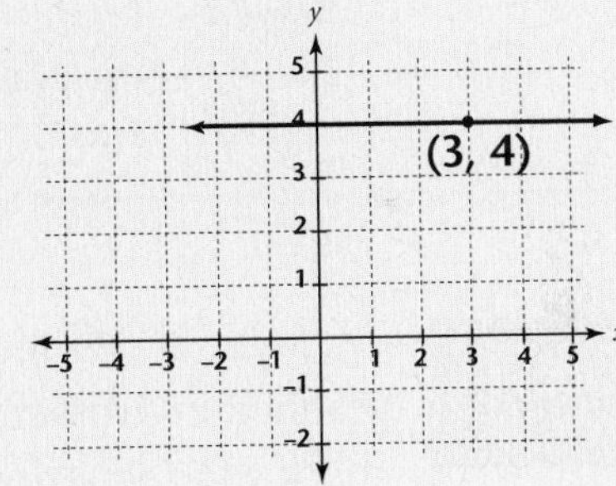

EXAMPLE 3 Write the equation for line ℓ.

Step 1 $y = mx + b$ and $m = 0$, so $y = 0x + b$, or $y = b$

Step 2 The equation $y = b$ is true for all ordered pairs on ℓ. Because (3, 4) is on the line, we can substitute $y = b = 4$ and solve for b.

$y = mx + b$ becomes $y = 4$.

$\therefore y = 4$ is the equation for ℓ. The domain is all real numbers.

CONSTRUCTION

Exercise A Graph each line using the slope and point given.

1. ℓ, $m = 1$, passes through (2, 3)

2. k, $m = -1$, passes through (−2, −3)

3. n, $m = -1$, passes through (3, 4)

4. o, $m = \frac{1}{3}$, passes through (4, 5)

5. p, $m = 0$, passes through (3, −2)

6. q, $m = 5$, passes through (1, −1)

7. r, $m = 3$, passes through (−6, 2)

8. s, $m = 2$, passes through (4, 3)

9. t, $m = -2$, passes through (4, 3)

10. u, $m = 0$, passes through (3, 6)

Calculator Practice

EXAMPLE 4 You can use a graphing calculator to produce the graph of a linear function such as $y = 3x + 2$.

Step 1 Press MODE ▼ ▼ ▼. Display is flashing "Func".

Step 2 Press Y= .

Step 3 Enter the equation of the line after the \Y₁ by pressing 3 X,T,θ,n + 2. You will see \Y₁ = 3x + 2. Press ENTER .

Step 4 Press GRAPH . The display will show x- and y-axes and the graph of $y = 3x + 2$.

To clear or "erase" a graph and its data, press Y= CLEAR .

Writing About Mathematics

Which method do you prefer for finding a second point on a line—counting on a graph or calculating using the slope and the ordered pair? Tell why.

Exercise B Write an equation for each of the lines you graphed in problems 1–10 above. Use your calculator to check your equations by comparing the graph to your answers for 1–10.

11. line ℓ

12. line k

13. line n

14. line o

15. line p

16. line q

17. line r

18. line s

19. line t

20. line u

Lesson 7 Finding the Midpoint of a Segment

Midpoint
Point that divides a line segment into two equal parts

When you do constructions in geometry, you must be careful to use only a straightedge and a compass. Remember that Euclid's Postulate 1—two points determine a line—allows you to use a straightedge. Euclid's Postulate 3—a circle may be described by any center and distance—allows you to use a compass.

You have used a straightedge and compass in your earlier constructions. In this lesson, you will learn how to use them to find the **midpoint** of any line segment.

Remember, a postulate is a statement accepted as true without proof. For a review of Euclid's postulates, turn back to Chapter 2.

CONSTRUCTION

Given: $\overline{AB}$

A B

Construct: Find midpoint of $\overline{AB}$

Step 1 Open your compass to a distance somewhat larger than $\frac{1}{2}$ of $\overline{AB}$.

Step 2 Using A as the center of a circle, draw an arc on each side of $\overline{AB}$. Do not change your compass opening.

Step 3 Using B as a center, draw an arc on each side of $\overline{AB}$. Make sure that these arcs intersect the arcs you have already drawn.

Step 4 Draw a line connecting the two points where the arcs intersect. This line is perpendicular to $\overline{AB}$ and bisects $\overline{AB}$. The point M, at which this line crosses $\overline{AB}$, is the midpoint of $\overline{AB}$. $AM = MB$.

A M B

Bisect
To divide into two equal parts

To **bisect** a line or an angle means to divide that line or angle into two equal parts.

You can also find the midpoint of a line using algebra, coordinate geometry, and arithmetic.

EXAMPLE 1 **Given:** $\overline{AB}$

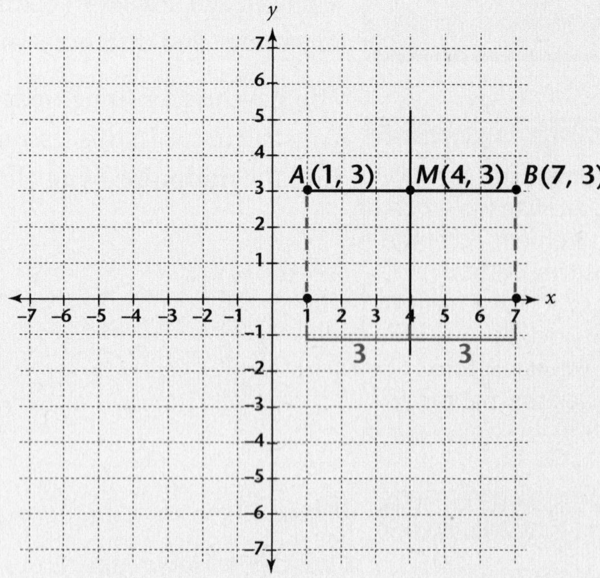

Construct: Find midpoint of $\overline{AB}$

The midpoint of $\overline{AB}$ is the point where the perpendicular bisector of the segment $1 \le x \le 7$ meets $\overline{AB}$.

The x-value of the midpoint can be found by dividing the sum of the x-values of the endpoints by 2.

$x\text{-value} = \frac{7 + 1}{2} = \frac{8}{2} = 4$

You already know the y-value of the midpoint of $\overline{AB}$; it is 3.

That means the midpoint M of $\overline{AB}$ is (4, 3).

EXAMPLE 2 **Given:** $\overline{CD}$

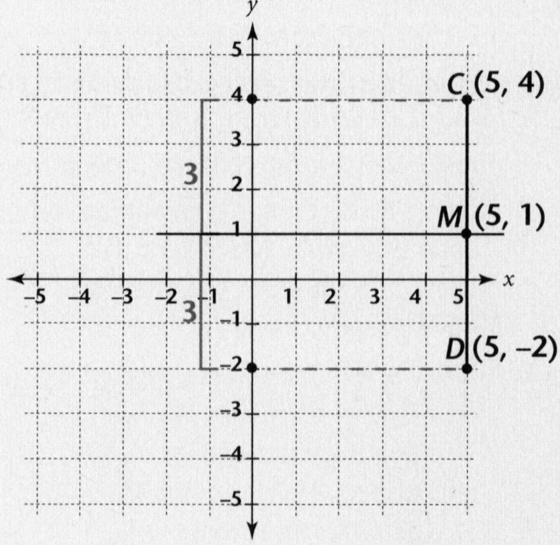

Construct: Find midpoint of $\overline{CD}$

The midpoint of $\overline{CD}$ is the point where the perpendicular bisector of the segment $-2 \le y \le 4$ meets $\overline{CD}$.

The y-value of the midpoint can be found by dividing the sum of the y-values of the endpoints by 2.

$y\text{-value} = \frac{4 + (-2)}{2} = \frac{2}{2} = 1$

You already know the x-value of the midpoint of $\overline{CD}$; it is 5.

That means the midpoint M of $\overline{CD}$ is (5, 1).

EXAMPLE 3 **Given:** $\overline{PQ}$

Construct: Find midpoint of $\overline{PQ}$

The midpoint of $\overline{PQ}$, which is not parallel to either the x-axis or the y-axis, can be calculated in three steps.

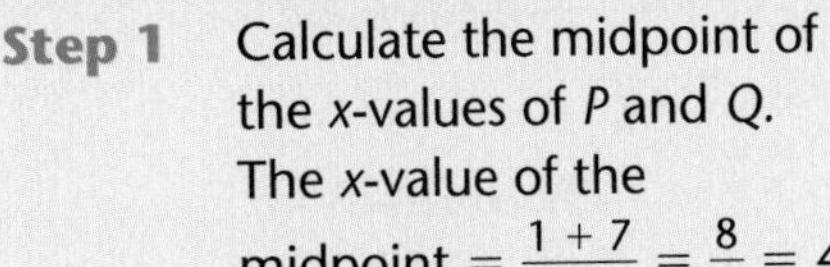

Step 1 Calculate the midpoint of the x-values of P and Q. The x-value of the midpoint $= \frac{1+7}{2} = \frac{8}{2} = 4$.

Step 2 Calculate the midpoint of the y-values of P and Q. The y-value of the midpoint $= \frac{1+3}{2} = \frac{4}{2} = 2$.

Step 3 Use the x- and y-values you calculated to form the ordered pair for the midpoint M.

$M = (4, 2)$

Note that when you calculated the midpoint, you calculated the midpoint of the domain ($1 \leq x \leq 7$) and the midpoint of the range ($1 \leq y \leq 3$) for segment $\overline{PQ}$.

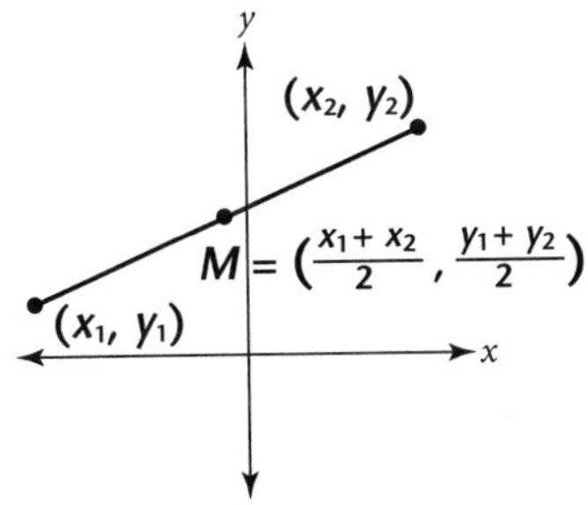

These examples lead to the following formula.

Midpoint Formula:

The midpoint of a segment between points (x_1, y_1) and (x_2, y_2) is

$$\left(\frac{x_1 + x_2}{2}, \frac{y_1 + y_2}{2}\right)$$

Use the midpoint formula to find the midpoint between $A = (3, 5)$ and $B = (4, -1)$.

$$\text{Let } x_1 = 3, x_2 = 4, y_1 = 5, y_2 = -1$$

$$\text{Midpoint} = \left(\frac{x_1 + x_2}{2}, \frac{y_1 + y_2}{2}\right)$$

$$= \left(\frac{3+4}{2}, \frac{5+(-1)}{2}\right) = \left(\frac{7}{2}, 2\right)$$

$\therefore$ Midpoint $M = \left(\frac{7}{2}, 2\right)$

You can graph the segment to check if your answer is reasonable.

Algebra Review

The midpoint formula can be used to find the endpoint of a line segment. If you know M and (x_1, y_1), you can insert them in the midpoint formula and solve for (x_2, y_2).

Calculator Practice

Using the parentheses keys on your calculator can help you find the midpoint of a line easily.

EXAMPLE 4 Let $(x_1, y_1) = (8, 6)$

$(x_2, y_2) = (4, 2)$

Then the x-value of $M = \frac{x_1 + x_2}{2}$ and the y-value of $M = \frac{y_1 + y_2}{2}$.

Use your calculator to find the answer.

Press (8 + 4) ÷ 2 ENTER 6 (the x-value)

Press (6 + 2) ÷ 2 ENTER 4 (the y-value)

$M = (6, 4)$

Exercise A Use the midpoint formula to find the midpoints of line segments having the following endpoints. Use a calculator to check your answers.

1. (6, 9) and (12, 18)

2. (2, 1) and (3, 7)

3. (−3, 1) and (−1, 4)

4. (4, −5) and (6, 3)

5. (−3, 5) and (−7, 10)

6. (2, −6) and (4, −12)

Writing About Mathematics

What happens to your construction of a bisector if your compass opening is less than $\frac{1}{2}$ AB?

CONSTRUCTION

Exercise B Draw lines having each of the given lengths on a separate sheet of paper. Using only a straightedge and compass, bisect each line.

7. 3 in.

8. 5 in.

9. 10 cm

10. 20 cm

11. a length of your choice

Exercise C Find the midpoints of the following line segments. Be sure to give both coordinates of each midpoint.

12.

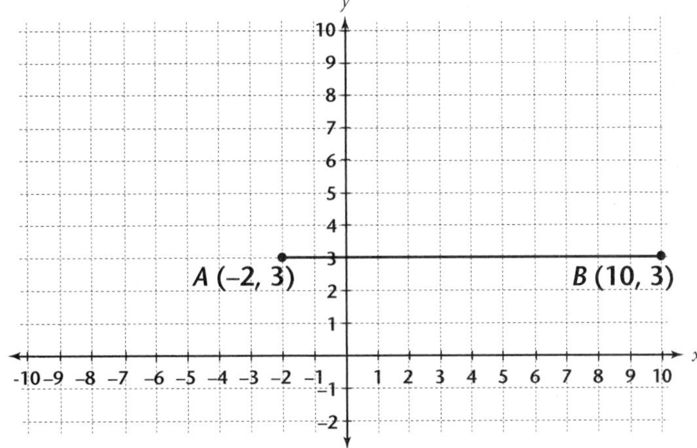

13.

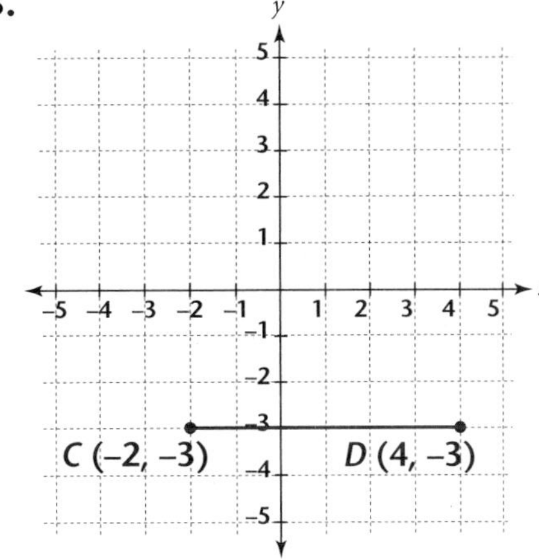

14.

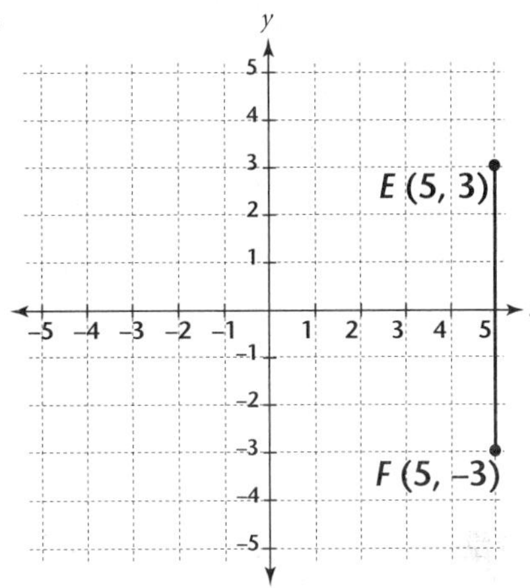

15.

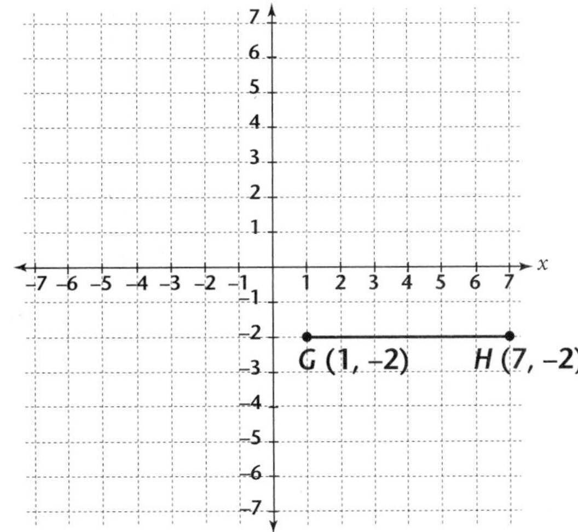

Lesson 8 Algebra Connection: Rate and Mixture Problems

> **Rate**
> *Quantity measured in proportion to something else*

The slope of a line tells you how much *y* changes as *x* changes. A **rate** is a quantity measured in proportion to something else. So, slope is one kind of rate. Other examples of rates are miles per gallon and dollars per hour. Each of these rates is calculated by a formula.

This formula relates distance, rate, and time:

Total distance = (Average rate of speed) • (Total time)

The same formula can be written three ways:

$d = rt \qquad r = \frac{d}{t} \qquad t = \frac{d}{r}$

The average rate of speed, *r*, is given in miles per *one* hour (mph) or in kilometers per *one* hour (kph).

EXAMPLE 1 Kalia traveled 315 miles in 5 h (hour). What was her average rate of speed?

Formula

$r = \frac{d}{t}$

$r = \frac{315 \text{ mi}}{5 \text{ h}}$

$r = 63$ mph

Diagram

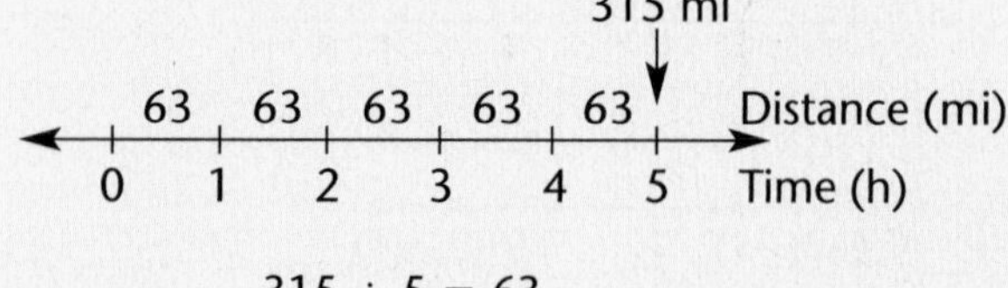

315 ÷ 5 = 63

Her average rate of speed was 63 mph.

EXAMPLE 2 Carlos traveled at 70 mph for $1\frac{1}{2}$ h then at 50 mph for $\frac{1}{2}$ h. What was his average rate of speed?

Use $d = rt$ two times. Add the two distances to get the total distance.

Formula

$r = \frac{\text{total distance}}{\text{total time}}$

$r = \frac{(70)(1\frac{1}{2}) + (50)(\frac{1}{2})}{1\frac{1}{2} + \frac{1}{2}}$

$r = \frac{105 + 25}{2}$

$r = \frac{130}{2} = 65$

Diagram

70 35 35 *d*

0 1 $1\frac{1}{2}$ 2 *t*

25 25 *d*

0 $\frac{1}{2}$ 1 *t*

105 mi in $1\frac{1}{2}$ h

+ 25 mi in $\frac{1}{2}$ h

130 mi in 2 h

or

65 mi in 1 h

His average rate of speed was 65 mph.

EXAMPLE 3 Denzel drove $2\frac{1}{2}$ h at an average rate of 100 kph. How far did he travel?

Formula

$d = rt$

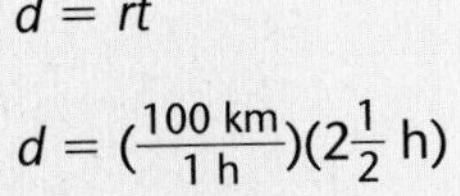

$d = (\frac{100 \text{ km}}{1 \text{ h}})(2\frac{1}{2} \text{ h})$

$d = 250$ km

Diagram

$100 + 100 + 50 = 250$

He traveled 250 km.

EXAMPLE 4 Peanuts cost \$2.00 per pound (lb). Pecans cost \$9.00 per pound (lb). You mix 3 lb of peanuts and $\frac{1}{2}$ lb of pecans. How much should 1 lb of the mixture cost?

Solution:

Peanuts: \$2.00 per lb × 3 lb =

Pecans: \$9.00 per lb × $\frac{1}{2}$ lb =

Mixture

3 lb peanuts for \$6.00

+ $\frac{1}{2}$ lb pecans for \$4.50

$3\frac{1}{2}$ lb mix for \$10.50

1 lb costs $\frac{\$10.50}{3\frac{1}{2}} = \$3.00$.

PROBLEM SOLVING

Exercise A Solve.

1. Mai traveled $2\frac{1}{2}$ h at an average rate of 60 mph. How many miles did she go?
2. Ron traveled at an average rate of 110 kph for 7 h. How many kilometers did he go?
3. Zoe biked at an average rate of 13 mph for 3 h. How many miles did she go?
4. Kwan biked at an average rate of 12 mph for $4\frac{1}{2}$ h. How many miles did he go?
5. LaToya traveled 480 mi in 8 h. What was her average rate of speed?
6. Fernando biked 42 mi in $3\frac{1}{2}$ h. What was his average rate of speed?
7. Maria traveled 225 mi in $4\frac{1}{2}$ h. What was her average rate of speed?
8. Yan traveled at 100 kph for $\frac{1}{2}$ h then at 120 kph for 2 h. What was his average rate of speed?
9. Gracia walked at 5 mph for $\frac{1}{2}$ h then at 4 mph for $1\frac{1}{2}$ h. What was her average rate of speed?
10. Peanuts cost \$2.00 per pound. Walnuts cost \$5.50 per pound. You mix 5 lb of peanuts and 2 lb of walnuts. How much does 1 lb of the mixture cost?

Application

Screaming Slopes Every amusement park wants to say it has the fastest, highest, or scariest rides in the world. Crowds flock to try out exciting new rides. Roller coaster designers work hard to design every part of the coaster for safety as well as thrills.

Roller coasters use gravity to reach their great speeds. They are pulled up a hill, released, and sent hurtling down the track. Designers must make the hill tall enough to give the coaster plenty of speed to drive it through the course. Or they can add more hills along the way. The steepness of the hill translates into slope. The bigger the slope, the bigger the thrill will be.

EXAMPLE 1 A coaster designer wants to build a new coaster with a 300-foot drop over a horizontal distance of 250 feet. What is the slope of the drop?

Slope $= \frac{\text{rise}}{\text{run}} = \frac{300 \text{ ft}}{250 \text{ ft}} = 1.2$ The slope of the drop is 1.2.

Exercise The table below gives the height of the first hill for several coasters. It also gives the distance, along the ground, covered during the first drop. Copy and complete the table, finding the slope for each drop. Then answer questions 8–10. Remember, slope $= \frac{\text{rise}}{\text{run}}$. Round to the nearest hundredth.

Coaster	Height of first hill (ft)	Horizontal distance covered (ft)	Slope
1. Cyclone	135	101	
2. Tornado	78	59	
3. Screamer	85	49	
4. Shaker	166	92	
5. Rattler	137	103	
6. Terror	155	121	
7. Beast	135	135	

8. Which coaster has the greatest slope?

9. Which coaster offers the gentlest slope?

10. What seems to be the "middle value" or median slope of these coasters?

Chapter 4 REVIEW

Write the letter of the correct answer.

Use the graph below for problems 1–4.

1. Which line has equation $x = -4$?

A Line ℓ **C** Line n
B Line m **D** Line p

2. Which line contains the point $(4, -3)$?

A Line ℓ **C** Line n
B Line m **D** Line p

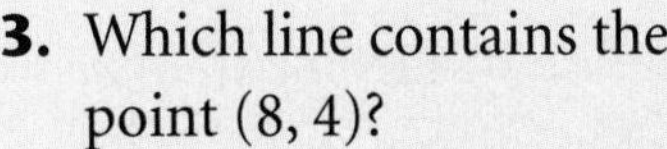

3. Which line contains the point $(8, 4)$?

A Line ℓ **B** Line m **C** Line n **D** Line p

4. What is the slope of line m?

A 0 **B** -1 **C** -4 **D** undefined

5. A line is parallel to the y-axis and contains the point $(2, 1)$. What is its equation?

A $x = 1$ **B** $x = 2$ **C** $y = 1$ **D** $y = 2$

6. What is the equation of the line with a slope of 3 that contains the point $(-2, -5)$?

A $x = 3y + 1$ **C** $y = 3x + 1$
B $x = 3y + 13$ **D** $y = 3x + 13$

7. What is the midpoint of $\overline{AB}$ on the graph to the right?

A $(2, 3)$ **C** $(-3, 1)$
B $(-1, -3)$ **D** $(-3, -1)$

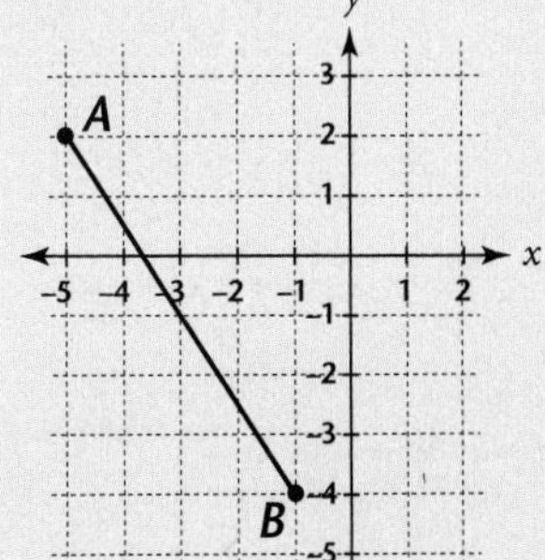

Find the slope m of a line that passes through the given points.

Example: (3, 4) and (−7, −16)

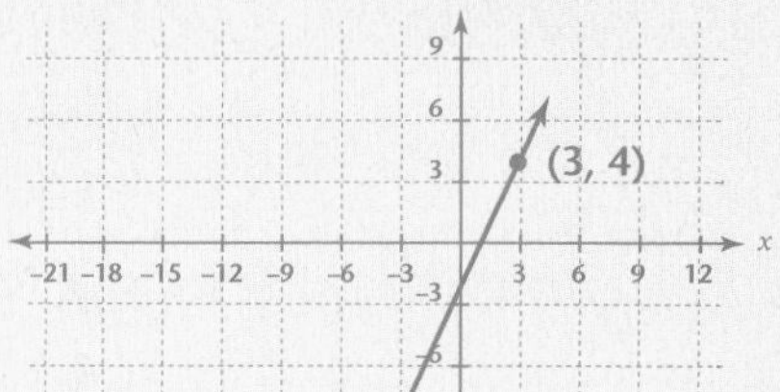

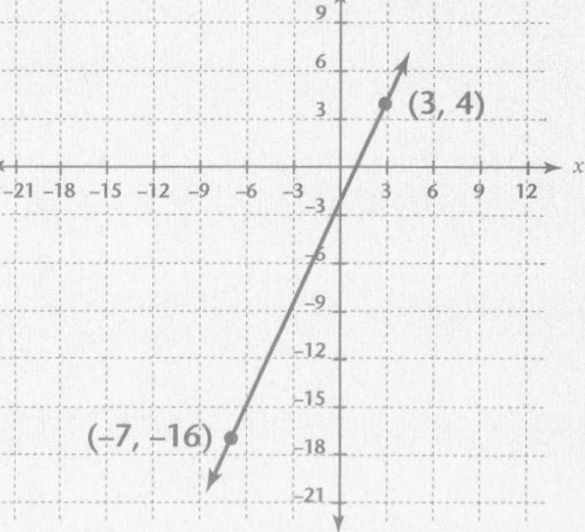

Solution: $m = \frac{y_1 - y_2}{x_1 - x_2}$

$m = \frac{4 - (-16)}{3 - (-7)} = \frac{4 + 16}{3 + 7} = \frac{20}{10} = 2$

8. (14, 2) and (2, 14)

9. (2, 2) and (8, 8)

10. (−2, −2) and (4, 12)

11. (0, −2) and (3, −12)

Write the equation of the line that passes through each pair of points. Use the form $y = mx + b$.

Example: (4, 3) and (8, 9)

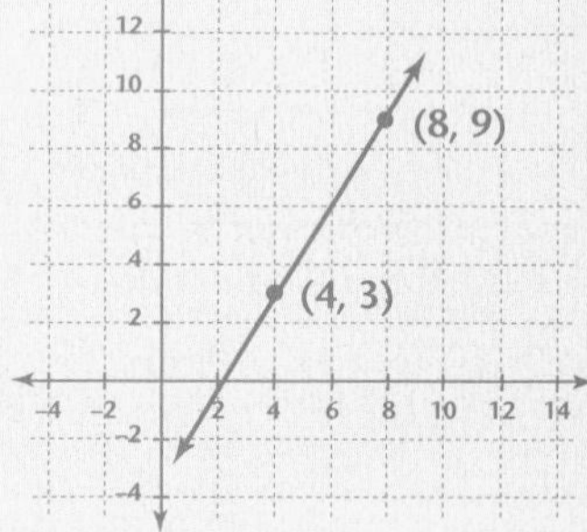

Solution: $m = \frac{y_1 - y_2}{x_1 - x_2} = \frac{3 - 9}{4 - 8} = \frac{-6}{-4} = \frac{3}{2}$

$\therefore y = \frac{3}{2}x + b$

Substitute x- and y-values from one of the ordered pairs.

Solve for b. $9 = (\frac{3}{2})(8) + b$ $9 = (\frac{24}{2}) + b$

$9 = 12 + b$ $-3 = b$ $\therefore y = \frac{3}{2}x - 3$

12. (3, 2) and (2, 3)

13. (8, 1) and (17, 1)

14. (3, 5) and (−6, 8)

15. (−6, −3) and (4, 2)

Use the midpoint formula to find the midpoints of line segments having the following endpoints.

Example: (2, 1) and (6, 4)

Solution: Midpoint $M = (\frac{x_1 + x_2}{2}, \frac{y_1 + y_2}{2})$

$M = (\frac{2 + 6}{2}, \frac{1 + 4}{2})$

$= (\frac{8}{2}, \frac{5}{2}) = (4, \frac{5}{2})$

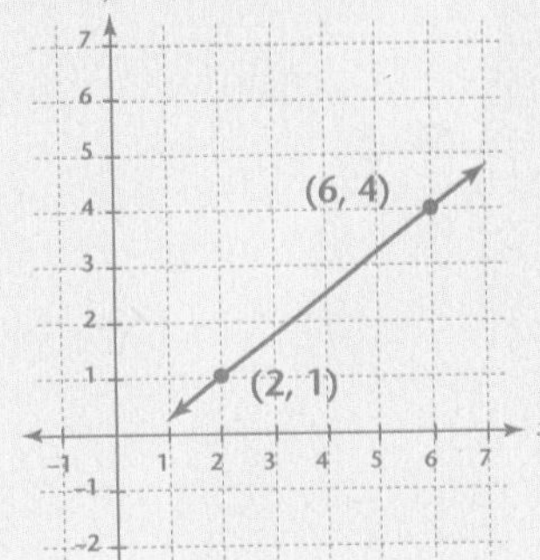

16. $(4, 3)$ and $(-2, 3)$

17. $(-6, 9)$ and $(-2, 7)$

18. $(-1, -1)$ and $(7, 7)$

19. $(-3, 4)$ and $(-3, 10)$

20. $(3, 6)$ and $(12, 4)$

Graph each line using the slope and point given. Use a separate sheet of graph paper and a straightedge.

Example: $m = -1$; (4, 2)

Solution: Mark (4, 2). Count down 1 and over 1 to (5, 1). Connect the points.

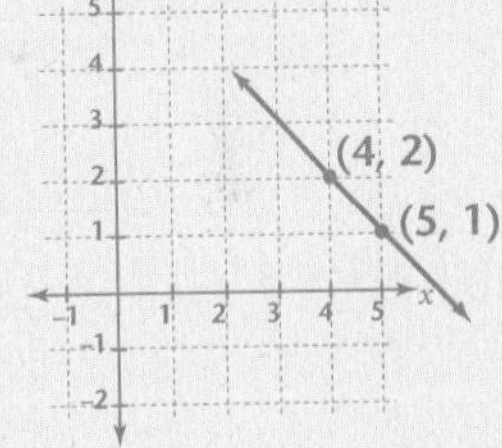

21. $m = -1; (-2, -3)$

22. $m = \frac{2}{3}; (0, 3)$

23. $m = \frac{1}{4}; (1, 1)$

24. $m = -2; (-2, -3)$

25. $m = 2; (1, 1)$

Always read the directions more than once to make sure you haven't missed anything. Remember to give the units if needed. Look out for the word *not* in directions.

Chapter

Triangles and Quadrilaterals

Bridges are marvelous examples of human skill and creativity. Bridges built during the Roman Empire, nearly 2,000 years ago, are still standing. Whether they are built of rope, stone, or steel, bridges can be works of art and architecture. The bridge to the left looks very modern and complicated. But look closer. It uses basic geometric figures: triangles and quadrilaterals.

Triangular design gives the best support, so triangles appear often in bridge structures. This is important to think about because hundreds of vehicles can cross a bridge at one time, each weighing thousands of pounds.

In Chapter 5, you will learn how to identify and measure sides and angles in triangles and quadrilaterals.

Goals for Learning

- To construct triangles using sides
- To name triangles using their angles
- To name and distinguish quadrilaterals
- To find the measures of angles in quadrilaterals and triangles
- To define quadrilaterals and parallels and apply theorems to them
- To construct perpendiculars
- To construct triangles based on angles and sides
- To use the Angle Sum Theorem to define triangles

Lesson 1 Naming Triangles Using Their Sides

Equilateral triangle

A triangle with three equal sides

Isosceles triangle

A triangle with two equal sides

Remember, a tick mark (|) is used to represent sides of the same length.

Look for triangles around you. You can find them in houses, bridges, and other structures. For example, this tower is built in the shape of a triangle with triangular supports.

As you look for triangles, you will see that they have different shapes. One way to name and identify triangles is to use their sides.

Examples of Triangles

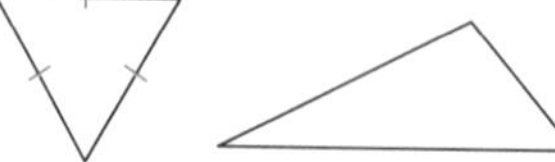

You may find it easy to recognize a triangle that has three equal sides. An **equilateral triangle** is a triangle with three sides of equal length. Below are some examples.

Equilateral Triangles

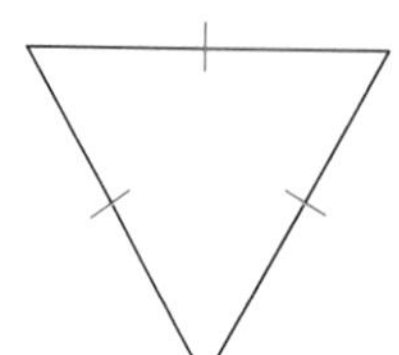

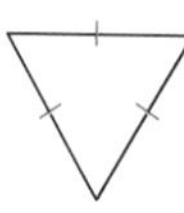

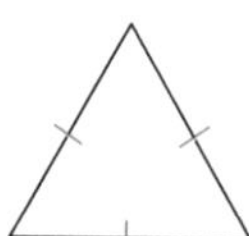

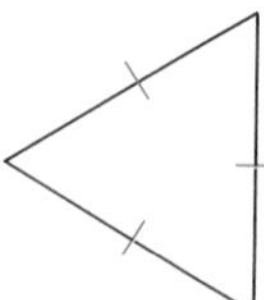

Another group of triangles has two equal sides. In an **isosceles triangle** the equal sides are called legs, and the remaining side is called the base. Below are some examples of isosceles triangles.

Isosceles Triangles

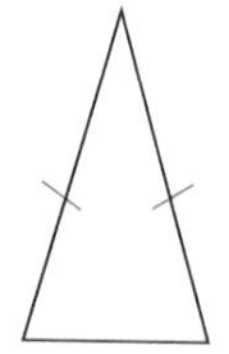

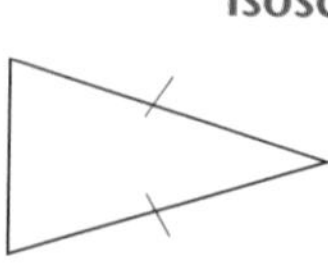

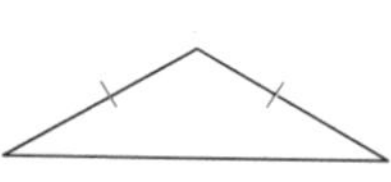

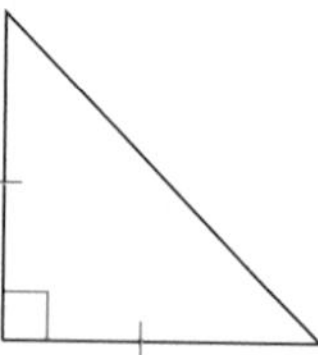

Scalene triangle

A triangle with no equal sides

Writing About Mathematics

When constructing a scalene triangle, what must be true about the lengths of sides b and c in relation to the length of side a?

Many triangles have no equal sides. A **scalene triangle** is a triangle with no sides of equal length. Below are some examples.

Scalene Triangles

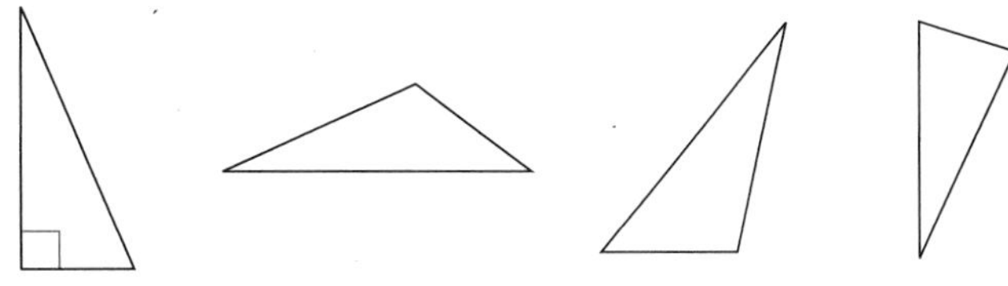

If you are given the length of a side, you can construct an equilateral triangle using only a straightedge and a compass.

Given: $\overline{AB}$

Construct: an equilateral triangle with each side equal to the given length AB

Step 1 Use your compass to copy $\overline{AB}$ on ℓ.

Step 2 Set your compass opening to match $\overline{AB}$. Draw an arc with its center at A. Draw a second arc with its center at B. Make sure the arcs intersect. (Note: The arcs may intersect both above and below ℓ. Choose one intersection to use.)

Step 3 Connect the point of intersection with point A and then point B. You have now constructed an equilateral triangle with each side equal to AB.

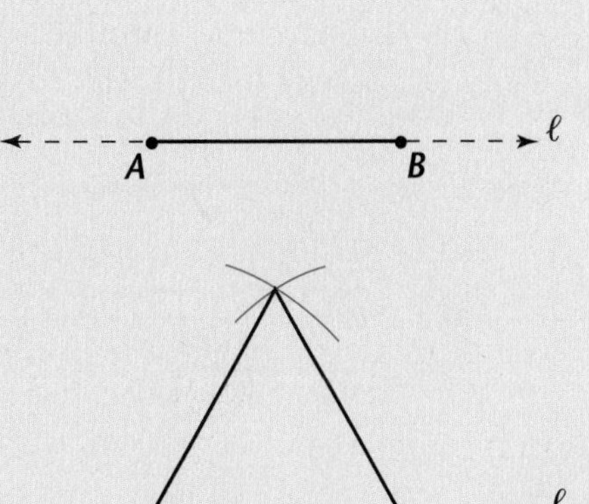

To construct an isosceles triangle, you need the length of one of the legs. You will also need the length of the base, which is not equal to the legs.

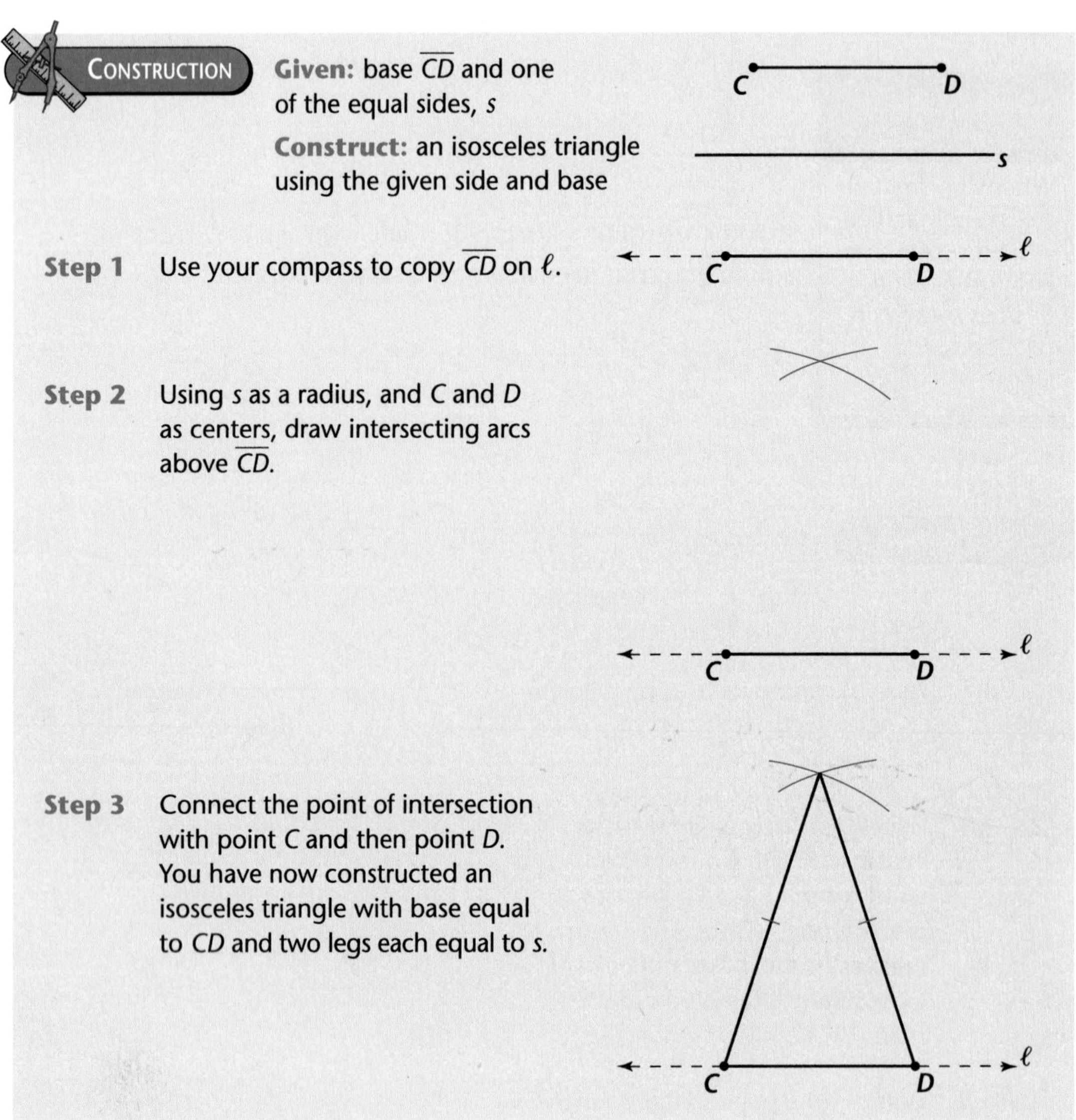

To construct a scalene triangle, you need to be given the lengths of all three sides.

Given: three line segments of unequal lengths: *a, b,* and *c*

Construct: a scalene triangle with the given line segments as side lengths

Step 1 Choose one side to be the base, $\overline{XY}$, of the triangle. For this example, we'll use line segment *a* as the base. Use your compass to copy *a* on ℓ. Label the segment $\overline{XY}$.

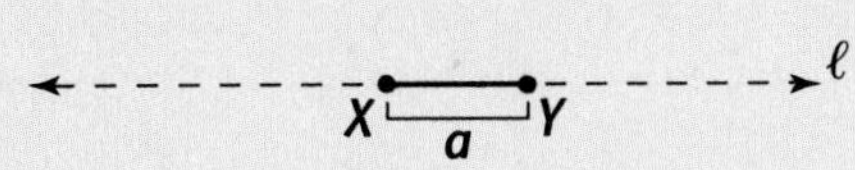

Step 2 Using *b* as a radius and *X* as the center, draw an arc above $\overline{XY}$.

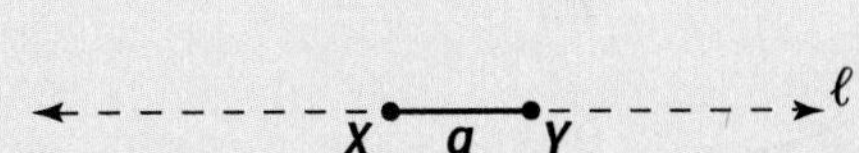

Step 3 Using *c* as a radius and *Y* as the center, draw a second arc above $\overline{XY}$. Make sure the arcs intersect.

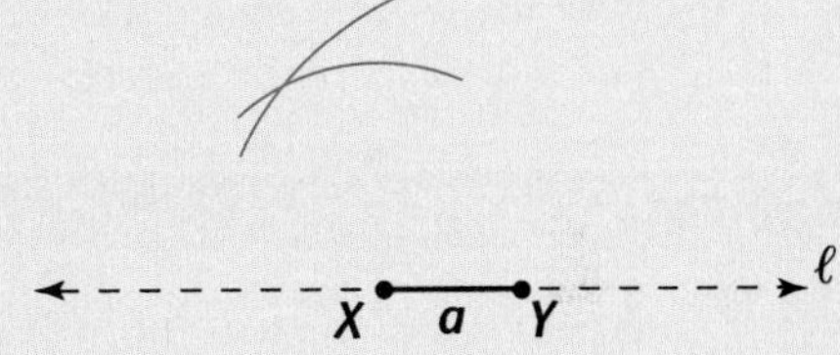

Step 4 Connect the point of intersection with point *X* and then point *Y*. You have now constructed a scalene triangle with sides equal to line segments *a, b,* and *c*. Because the line segments are different lengths, the triangle is scalene.

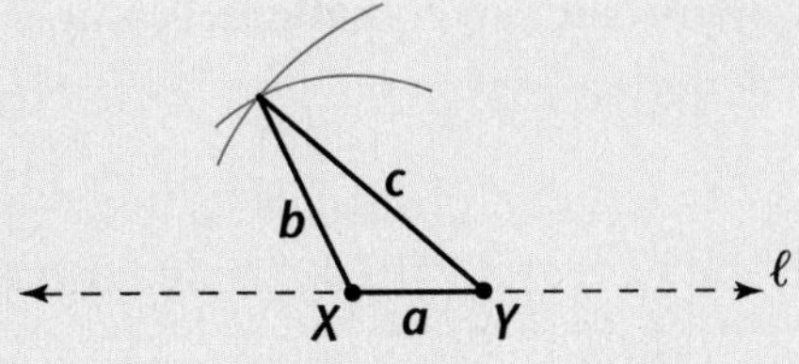

Exercise A Name the triangle shape. Write *equilateral, isosceles,* or *scalene.*

1. 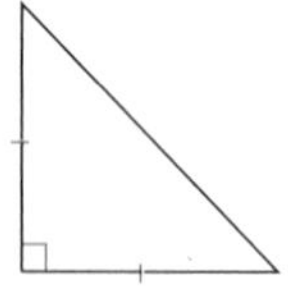

2. 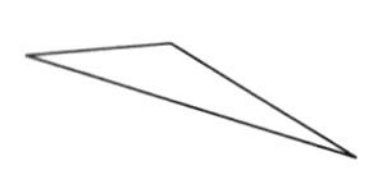

3. 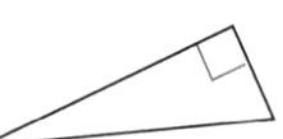

4. 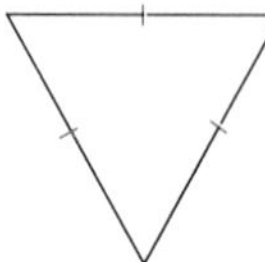

5. 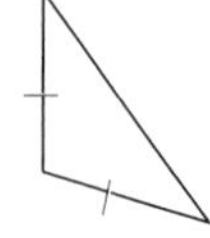

6. 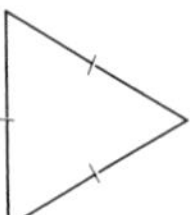

7. 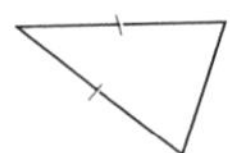

8. 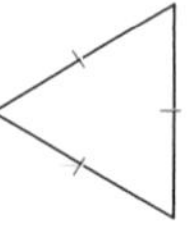

9. 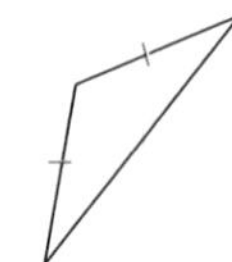

10. 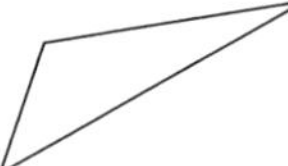

CONSTRUCTION

Exercise B Complete the following constructions. Use a separate sheet of paper. You will need a straightedge and a compass.

11. Construct an equilateral triangle whose sides are the same length as $\overline{AB}$.

12. Construct an isosceles triangle using the length of $\overline{CD}$ as the base and with two sides equal in length to $\overline{EF}$.

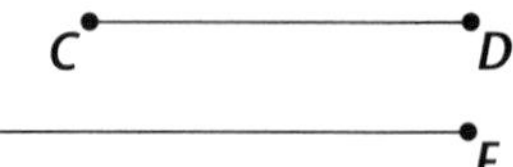

13. Construct a scalene triangle using the lengths of segments q, r, and s as the lengths of the sides.

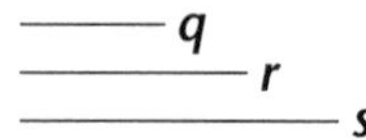

14. Construct triangle XYZ with $XY = RS$ and $XZ = YZ = 2(RS)$.

15. Construct triangle ABC with $AB = 5(MN)$, $BC = 4(MN)$, and $CA = 3(MN)$.

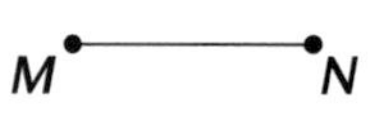

Lesson 2 Naming Triangles Using Their Angles

Acute triangle

A triangle whose angles are all less than 90°

Right triangle

A triangle having one right angle

Obtuse triangle

A triangle having one angle greater than 90°

A second way to name and identify triangles is to use their angles.

In some triangles, all the angles are less than 90°.

Acute Triangles

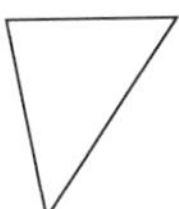

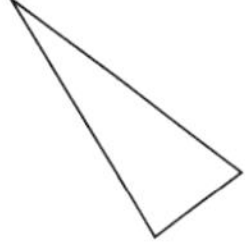
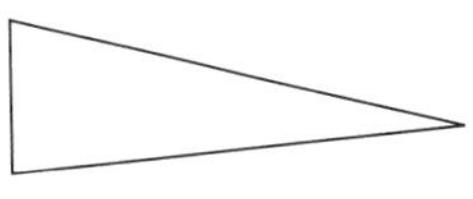

An **acute triangle** is a triangle with each angle less than 90°.

Some triangles have one 90° angle.

Right Triangles

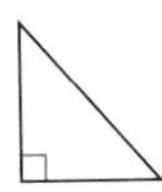

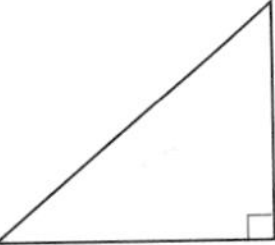
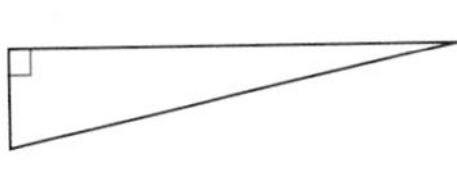

A **right triangle** is a triangle with a right angle. The sides adjacent to the right angle are often called the *legs* of a right triangle. The side opposite the right angle is called the *hypotenuse.*

The third group of triangles has one obtuse angle.

Obtuse Triangles

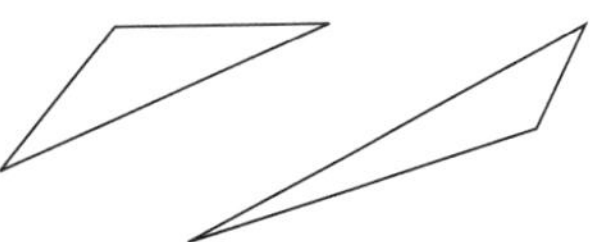
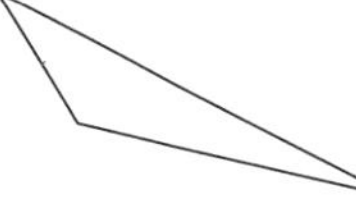

An **obtuse triangle** is a triangle with one angle greater than 90°.

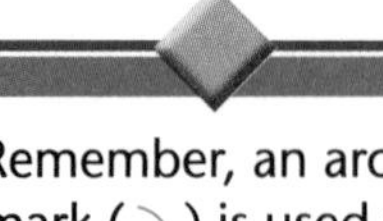

Remember, an arc mark (⌒) is used to represent angles of the same size.

Triangles can be named by the characteristics of their sides, the characteristics of their angles, or the characteristics of both. For example, an equilateral triangle is also acute.

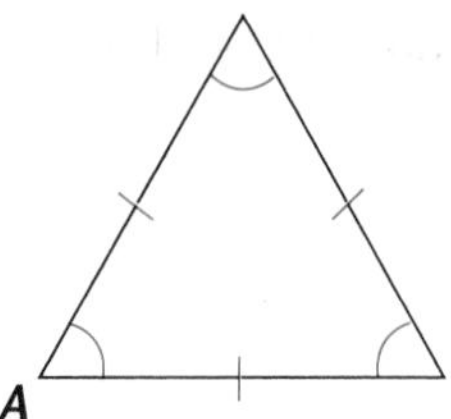

Later you will prove that an equilateral triangle has three equal angles that each measure 60°.

Remember, *AB* is a length, while $\overline{AB}$ is the symbol for a line segment.

A right triangle, ΔABC, can be isosceles.

$m\angle A = 90°$

$AB = AC$

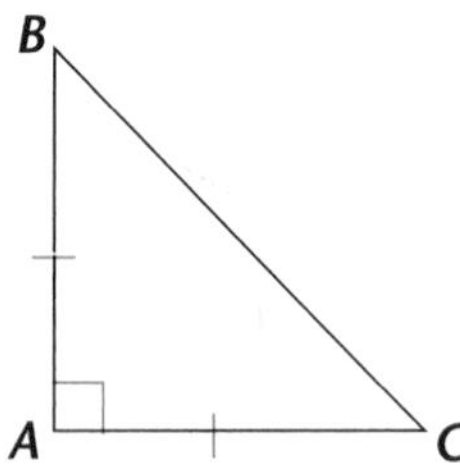

The symbol Δ is used to represent a triangle. ΔABC is read "triangle *ABC*."

An obtuse triangle, ΔABC, can be isosceles.

$m\angle B > 90°$

$AB = BC$

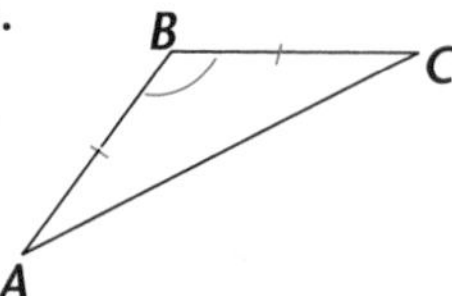

The base angles of any isosceles triangle (right, acute, or obtuse) are equal. You will learn why later.

An obtuse triangle, ΔABC, can be scalene.

$m\angle A > 90°$

$AB \neq BC$, $BC \neq AC$, and $AC \neq AB$

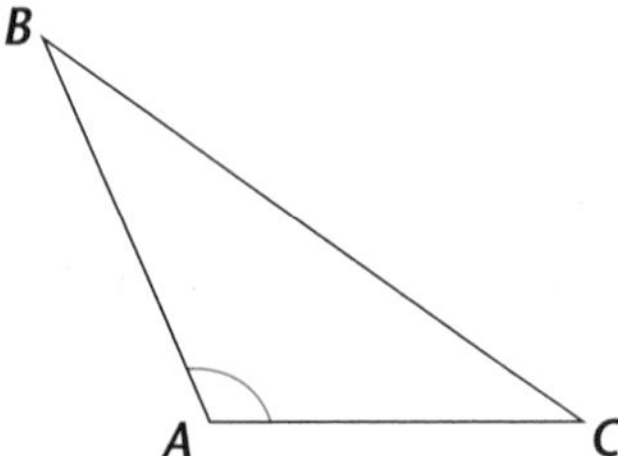

If you are given information about the sides and angles of a triangle, you can construct the triangle. Remember, you need to do the construction using only a straightedge and a compass.

Given: $AB = BC$ and $m\angle B = 90°$

Construct: an isosceles ΔABC with $AB = BC$ and $m\angle B = 90°$

Step 1 Draw a right angle. Label the angle *B*.

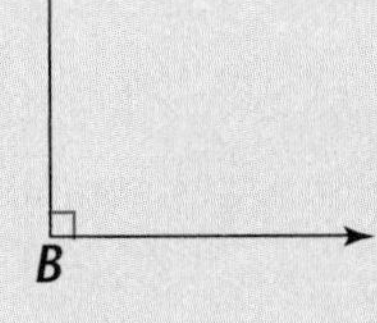

Step 2 Using your compass and *B* as the center, draw an arc that crosses each ray of angle *B*. Label the points where the arc crosses the rays *A* and *C*.

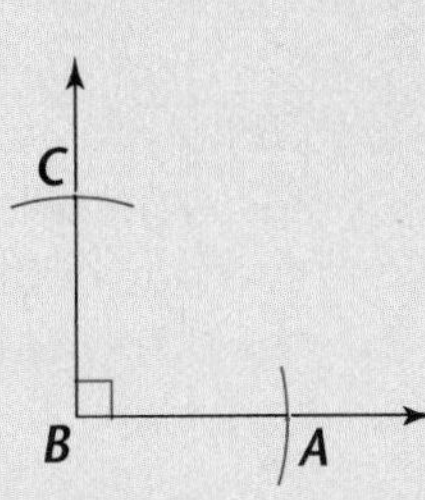

Step 3 Connect points *A* and *C*. You have now constructed a right triangle with two equal sides, or an right isosceles triangle.

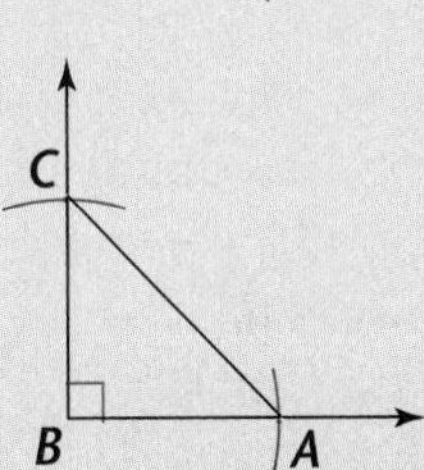

Given: two unequal segments, $\overline{AC}$ and $\overline{BC}$

Construct: a right scalene triangle with $m\angle C = 90°$ and sides of lengths *AC* and *BC*

Step 1 Draw a right angle. Label the angle *C*.

Step 2 Mark unequal segments $\overline{AC}$ and $\overline{BC}$.

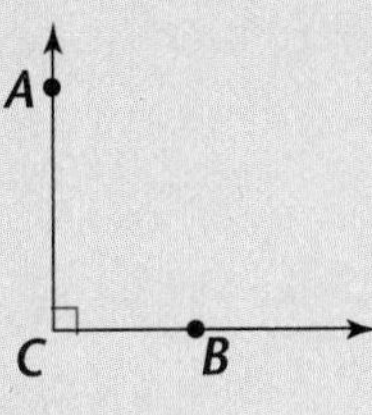

Step 3 Connect *A* and *B*.

You have now constructed a right scalene triangle.

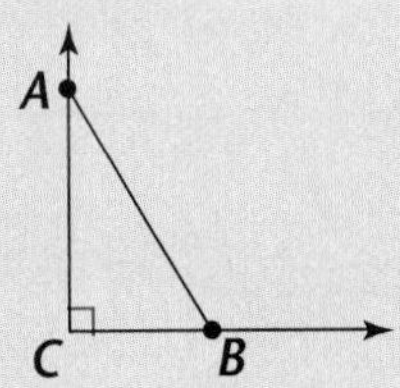

Given: $CD = DE$ and $m\angle D > 90°$

Construct: $\triangle CDE$ with $CD = DE$ and $m\angle D > 90°$, an obtuse isosceles triangle

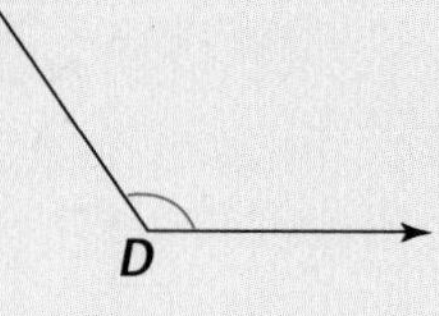

Step 1 Draw any obtuse angle. Label the angle *D*.

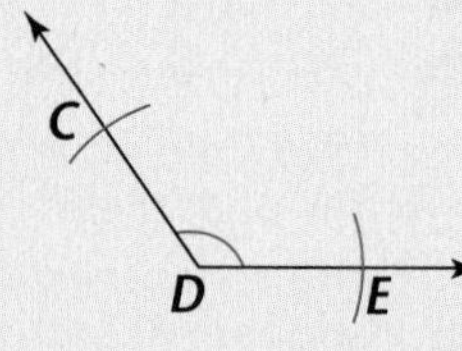

Step 2 Using your compass and point *D* as the center, draw an arc that crosses each ray of the obtuse angle. Label the points where the arc crosses the rays *C* and *E*.

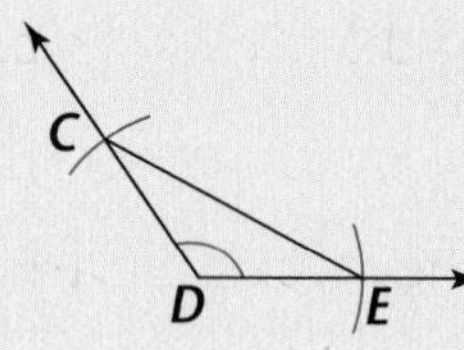

Step 3 Draw $\overline{CE}$. You have now constructed an obtuse isosceles triangle.

Theorem: In a 30°-60° right triangle, the side opposite the 30° angle is one-half the length of the hypotenuse. We can use this theorem to construct a right triangle. We will prove it in Chapter 8, Lesson 5.

Given: hypotenuse $\overline{AB}$

Construct: a 30°-60° right triangle

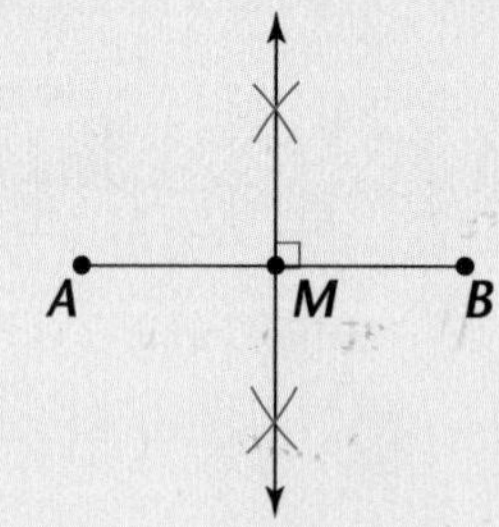

Step 1 Using your compass and *A* as the center, draw arcs above and below $\overline{AB}$. Using the same opening and *B* as the center, draw arcs above and below $\overline{AB}$. Connect the intersections. You have constructed a perpendicular bisector. Name the midpoint of $\overline{AB}$ point *M*.

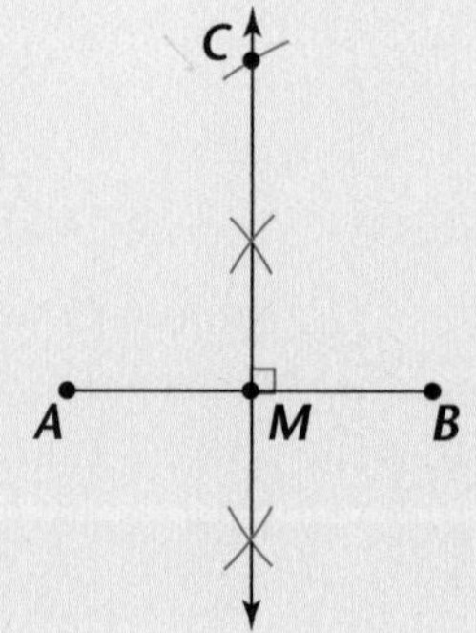

Step 2 Set the compass opening at the length of $\overline{AB}$ and the compass needle at *B*. Make an arc that intersects the perpendicular. Name the point of intersection *C*. Note that $AB = CB$ and $MB = \frac{1}{2}(AB) = \frac{1}{2}(CB)$.

(continued)

Step 3 Draw $\overline{BC}$. ΔMBC is a 30°-60° right triangle where $m\angle B = 60°$ and $m\angle C = 30°$.
You have now constructed a 30°-60° right triangle.

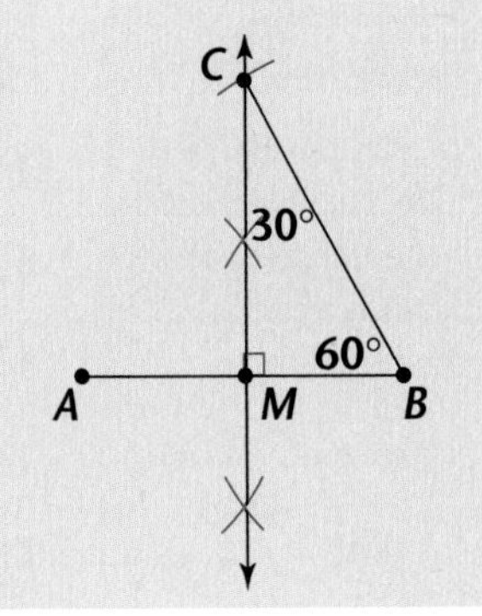

Exercise A Use the figure to the right and ΔBAD, ΔBFD, ΔBCD, and ΔBED for problems 1–6.

A F C E m
B D ℓ
$\ell \parallel m$ and $\overline{AB} \perp \ell$

1. Which of these triangles is a right triangle?
2. Which are obtuse triangles?
3. Which is an acute triangle but not a right triangle?
4. $\overline{BD}$ is what part of ΔBAD, ΔBFD, ΔBCD, and ΔBED?
5. Which angle has the same measure as $\angle DAF$? (Hint: Pretend $\overline{AD}$ is a transversal.)
6. If $BD = DE$, which angle has the same measure as $\angle EBD$?

Exercise B Use what you know about the construction in the figure to the right to answer problems 7–10.

7. What is true of line ℓ and line m?
8. What name is given to ray n?
9. Which angle has the same measure as $\angle x$?
10. $m\angle z = m\angle x +$ the measure of which angle?

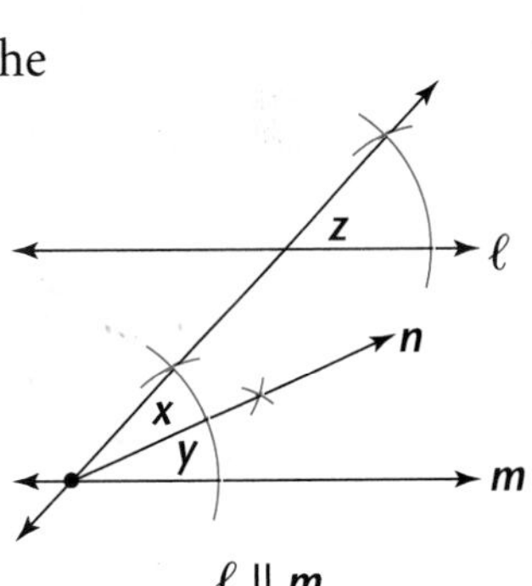

$\ell \parallel m$

Try to construct a right triangle with three equal sides. Explain your observations.

Exercise C Give the name of each triangle. Use the angles, sides, or both to name the triangles.

11. one right angle

12. one obtuse angle

13. three acute angles

14. one right angle and two equal sides

15. three equal angles

16. two equal sides and one obtuse angle

17. all acute angles and three equal sides

18. all acute angles and no equal sides

19. one right angle and no equal sides

20. two acute angles, one right angle, no equal sides

CONSTRUCTION

Exercise D Complete the following constructions. Use a separate sheet of paper. You will need a straightedge and a compass.

21. Construct ΔABC with $AC = BC$ and $m\angle C = 90°$.

22. Construct ΔDEF with $DE = DF$ and $m\angle D < 90°$.

23. Construct ΔGHI with $GH = HI$ and $m\angle H > 90°$.

24. Construct ΔJKL with $JK = 3s$, $JL = 4s$, and $m\angle J = 90°$.

s

25. Construct ΔMNO with $m\angle M = 90°$, $MO = r$, and $MN = 2r$.

r

Lesson 3 Special Quadrilaterals

Parallelogram

A quadrilateral whose opposite sides are parallel

Rectangle

A parallelogram with four right angles

Rhombus

A parallelogram with four equal sides

The word *quadrilateral* means "four sides."

In Chapter 3, you were introduced to geometric figures called quadrilaterals—figures with four sides. Here is some more information about quadrilaterals.

Examples of Quadrilaterals

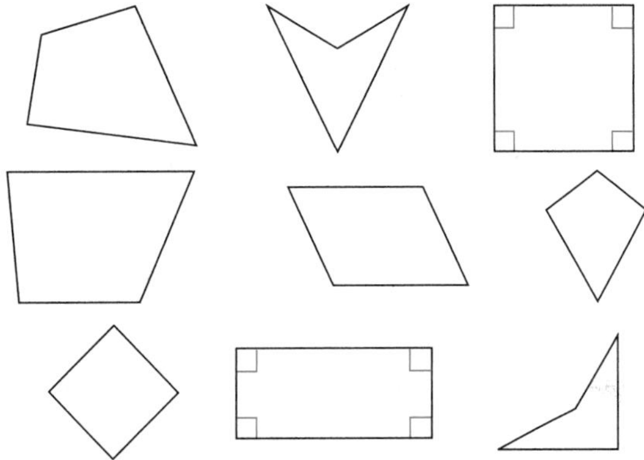

If we take a closer look at quadrilaterals, we will find that some of them have special characteristics. Some have parallel sides. Some have sides of equal length. During your study of parallel lines, you learned that **parallelograms** are quadrilaterals formed by two pairs of parallel sides.

Rectangles and squares are parallelograms with special properties. **Rectangles** have four equal angles; squares have four equal angles and equal sides.

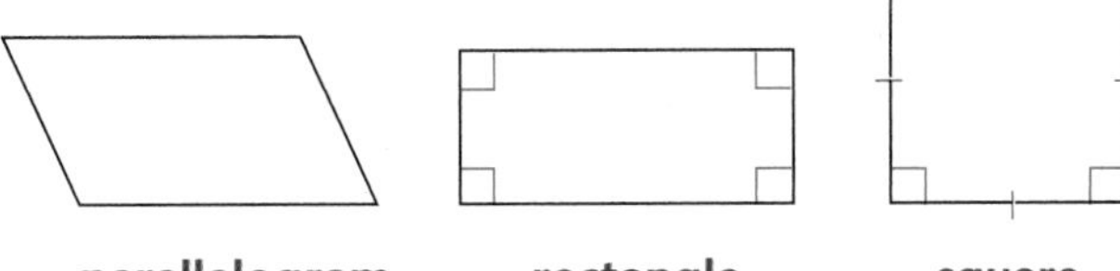

parallelogram rectangle square

A **rhombus** is a parallelogram with four equal sides. Note that this means you can call a square a rhombus with four equal angles.

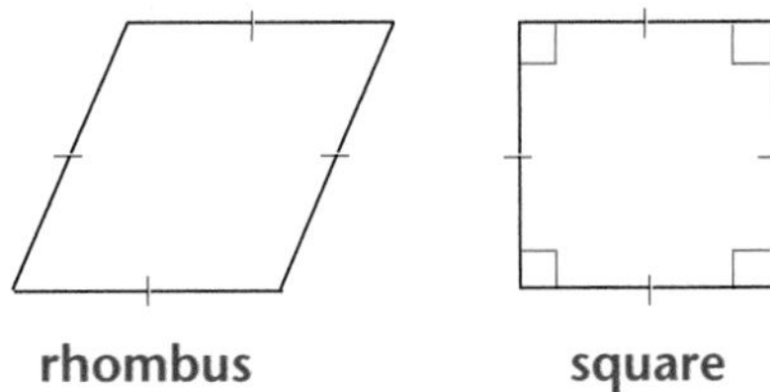

rhombus square

Trapezoid

A quadrilateral with exactly one pair of parallel sides

Counterexample

A single example that proves a statement false

Trapezoids are also quadrilaterals. All trapezoids share one characteristic—they have exactly one pair of parallel sides. However, some trapezoids have additional characteristics. You can use the same method you use to name triangles to name trapezoids.

Examples of Trapezoids

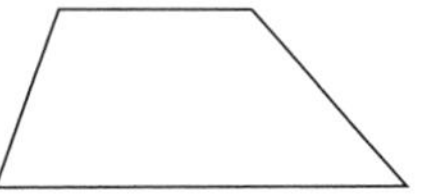

Scalene Trapezoid

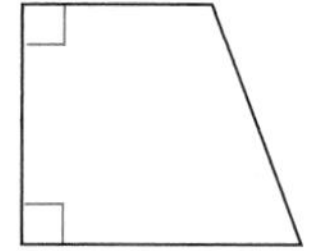

Right-Angled Trapezoid

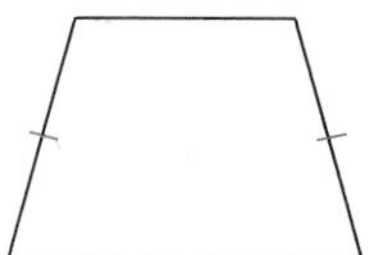

Isosceles Trapezoid

When you think about quadrilaterals and parallelograms, you will find there are some general statements that are always true—such as all squares are rectangles. But some statements are not always true. The following is an example.

EXAMPLE 1 **Statement:** All trapezoids are isosceles.

Question: Is this statement true?

Answer: No. It is possible to construct a trapezoid that does not have a pair of equal sides and so it is not isosceles.

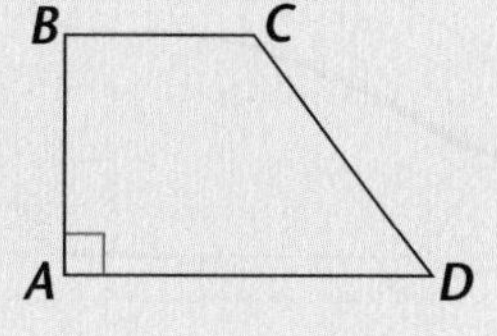

In this case, you were able to provide an example for which the statement was not true. Such an example is called a **counterexample.** One counterexample makes an *all*-statement false.

EXAMPLE 2 **Statement:** All parallelograms are rectangles.

Question: Is this statement true?

Answer: No. You can construct a parallelogram that is not a rectangle. Therefore, you can show a counterexample. The counterexample proves the statement false.

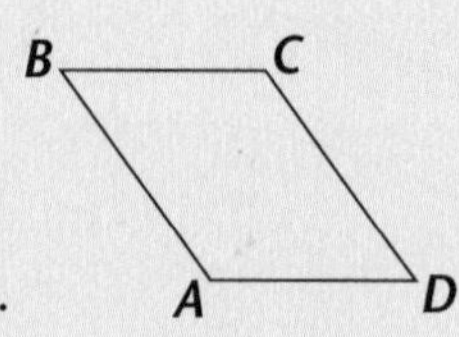

Writing About Mathematics

You know that "All rectangles are squares" is false because you can give a counter-example. Why is "Some rectangles are squares" a true statement?

Exercise A If the statement is true, write *True.* If the statement is false, write *False* and give a counterexample.

1. All parallelograms are squares.
2. All squares are parallelograms.
3. All trapezoids are scalene.
4. All squares are rhombuses.
5. All rhombuses are squares.
6. All rectangles are squares.
7. All squares are rectangles.

Exercise B Copy the chart. Fill in the missing information.

Quadrilateral	Parallelogram	Rectangle	Rhombus	Square
Figure with four sides	Figure with four sides	Figure with four sides	**8.** ____	Figure with four sides
No requirement for sides	Opposite sides are parallel and equal	Opposite sides are parallel and equal	Opposite sides are parallel and equal	Opposite sides are **9.** ____
No requirement for angles	Opposite angles are equal	Four **10.** ____	Opposite angles are equal	Four equal angles

Exercise C Name each figure as precisely as you can.

11.

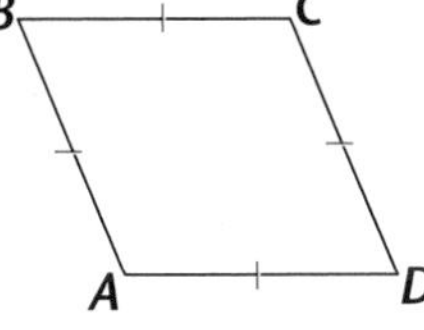

12.

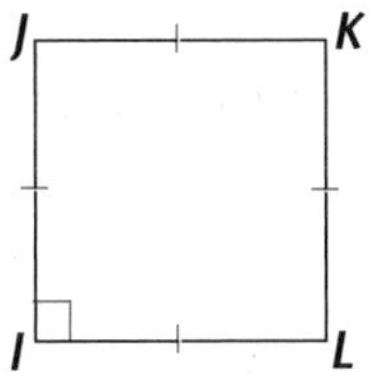

13.

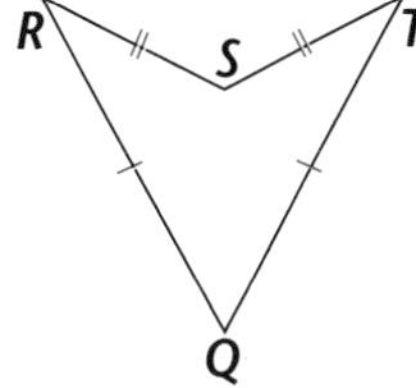

14.

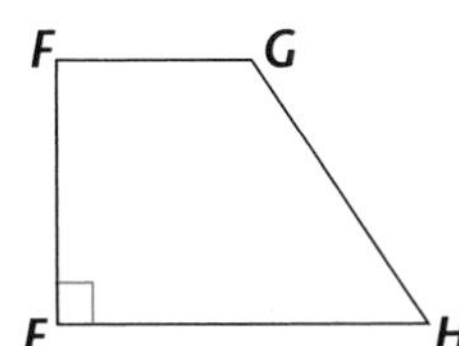

15.

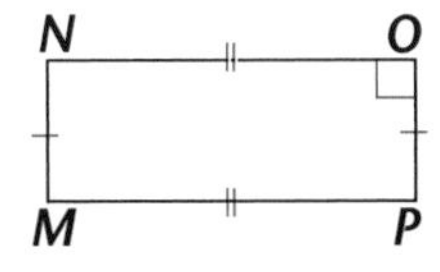

Lesson 4 Quadrilaterals and Their Diagonals

Diagonal

A line segment connecting any two nonadjacent vertices of a polygon

Quadrilaterals not only have four sides, they have four angles and four vertices. In quadrilateral *ABCD* below, *A*, *B*, *C*, and *D* are vertices.

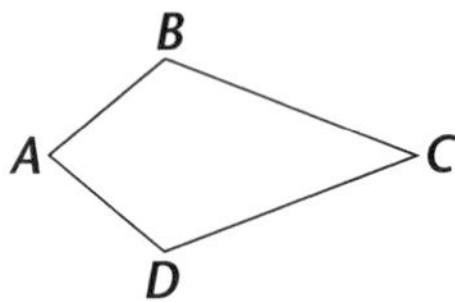

Remember, a *vertex* is the common endpoint of two rays that form an angle. The plural of vertex is *vertices. Adjacent* vertices share a common side. *Nonadjacent* vertices do not share a common side.

You can draw a line segment from each vertex to a vertex that does not share a common side. This is called a *nonadjacent* vertex. For example, you can draw a segment from *A* to *C*. $\overline{AC}$ is an example of a **diagonal.** The diagonal from *C* to *A* is also $\overline{AC}$ (or $\overline{CA}$).

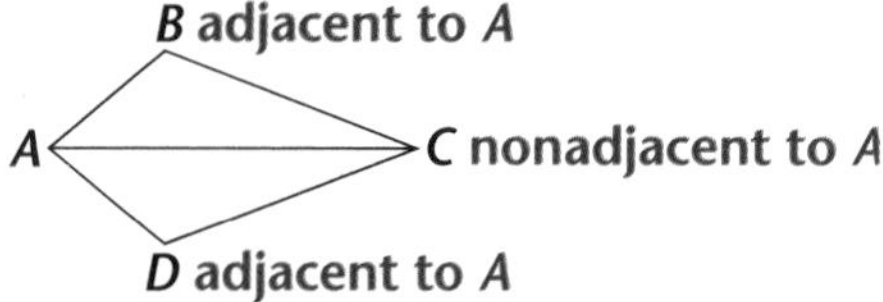

A diagonal is a line segment connecting any two nonadjacent vertices of a geometric figure. There is a second diagonal that can be drawn for *ABCD*. It is the segment from *B* to *D*, $\overline{DB}$. There are no other diagonals possible for quadrilateral *ABCD*.

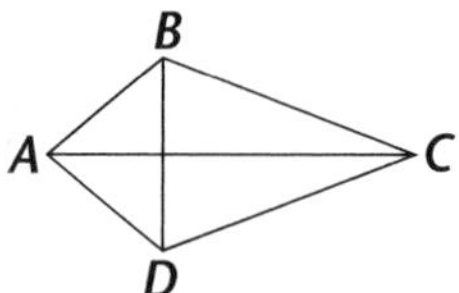

Suppose *ABCD* is a rectangle. Using Euclid's Postulate 1, you can draw diagonal $\overline{AC}$. This will form angles 1, 2, 3, and 4. Which, if any, of these angles are equal?

Theorem 5.4.1: In rectangle *ABCD* with diagonal $\overline{AC}$, $m\angle 1 = m\angle 4$ and $m\angle 2 = m\angle 3$.

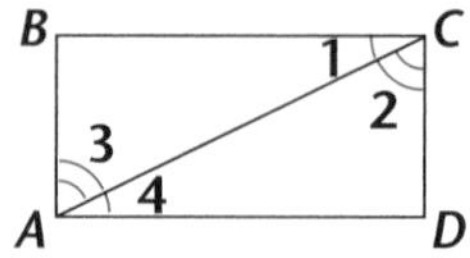

PROOF

Statement	Reason
1. $\overline{BC} \parallel \overline{AD}$ and $\overline{AC}$ is a transversal	1. Given; by definition of a rectangle and transversal.
2. $\therefore$ m$\angle 4$ = m$\angle 1$	2. By theorem, alternate interior angles are equal.
3. $\overline{AB} \parallel \overline{DC}$ and $\overline{AC}$ is a transversal	3. Given; by definition of a rectangle and transversal.
4. $\therefore$ m$\angle 2$ = m$\angle 3$	4. By theorem, alternate interior angles are equal.

You can use this information to solve problems like the following.

EXAMPLE 1 **Given:** *ABCD* is a rectangle, $\overline{AC}$ is a diagonal, and m$\angle 1$ = 40°

Find: measures of $\angle 2$, $\angle 3$, and $\angle 4$

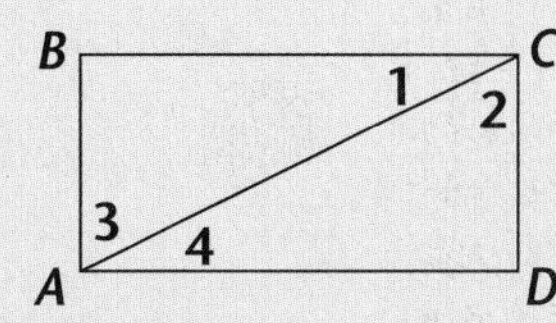

Solution:	**Reason:**
m$\angle 1$ = m$\angle 4$, so m$\angle 4$ = 40°	alternate interior angles
$\angle C$ is a right angle	definition of rectangle
so m$\angle 1$ + m$\angle 2$ = 90°, and 40° + m$\angle 2$ = 90°	substitution of equals
m$\angle 2$ = 50°	subtraction of equals
m$\angle 2$ = m$\angle 3$ = 50°	alternate interior angles
OR you can argue that $\angle A$ = 90°	definition of rectangle
so m$\angle 3$ + m$\angle 4$ = 90°, and m$\angle 3$ + 40° = 90°	substitution of equals
m$\angle 3$ = 50°	subtraction of equals

Geometry in Your Life

A square is one of the most basic shapes in geometry. It's found everywhere in daily life, from floor tiles to napkins. In fact, you can use a square napkin to find out something about the angles of a square. Label the corners of a square napkin *ABCD.* Draw diagonal $\overline{AC}$. Now fold the square in half along $\overline{AC}$, matching vertex *B* with vertex *D.* Label the interior angles 1, 2, 3, and 4. Notice that ΔABC matches ΔADC exactly. What can you say about the measures of angles 1, 2, 3, and 4? Give reasons for your answer.

Exercise A Copy the problem below. Fill in the missing reasons using the information in this lesson about rectangles.

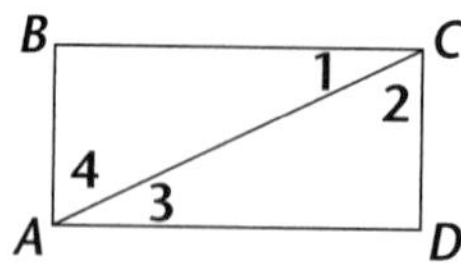

Given: $ABCD$ is a parallelogram, $\overline{AC}$ is a diagonal

Problem: show $m\angle 1 = m\angle 3$ and $m\angle 2 = m\angle 4$

Solution:	Reason:
1. $\overline{BC} \parallel \overline{AD}$	____________
2. $m\angle 1 = m\angle 3$	____________
3. $\overline{AB} \parallel \overline{DC}$	____________
4. $m\angle 2 = m\angle 4$	____________

Exercise B Use the information given to answer the questions.

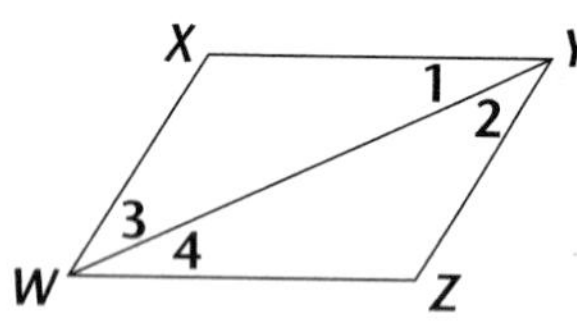

Given: $WXYZ$ is a parallelogram with diagonal $\overline{WY}$

5. If $m\angle 1 = 30°$, which remaining angle is also 30°?

6. If $m\angle 2 = 40°$, which remaining angle is also 40°?

Exercise C Use the information given to supply the angle measures.

Given: $EFGH$ is a rectangle with a diagonal $\overline{EG}$ and $m\angle 1 = 25°$

7. $m\angle 4$

8. $m\angle 1 + m\angle 2$

9. $m\angle 2$

10. $m\angle 3 + m\angle 4$

11. $m\angle 3$

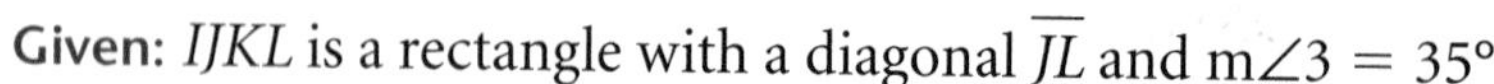

Given: $IJKL$ is a rectangle with a diagonal $\overline{JL}$ and $m\angle 3 = 35°$

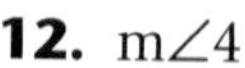

12. $m\angle 4$

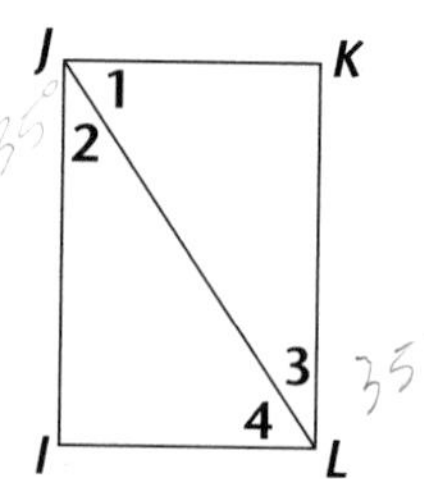

13. $m\angle 1$

14. $m\angle 2 + m\angle 1$

15. $m\angle 2$

Lesson 5 Angle Sum of Any Triangle

In Chapter 3, Lesson 6, you used inductive thinking to conclude that the sum of the angle measures inside a parallelogram or trapezoid is 360°.

Remember that the sum of the measures of the interior angles on the same side of a transversal is 180°.

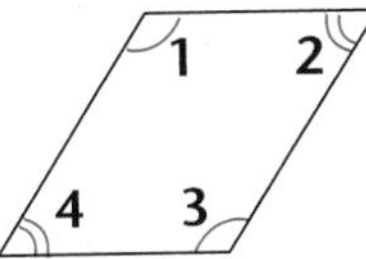

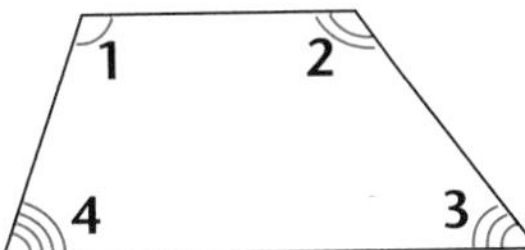

$m\angle 1 + m\angle 4 = 180°$
$m\angle 2 + m\angle 3 = 180°$ Angles on the same side of a transversal between parallels are supplementary.

With inductive thinking, you use the similarities of particular cases to make a general statement.

$m\angle 1 + m\angle 2 + m\angle 3 + m\angle 4 =$
$180° + 180° = 360°$ by addition of equals

If we draw a diagonal in each figure, we can conclude that the sum of the angles in two triangles is 360°.

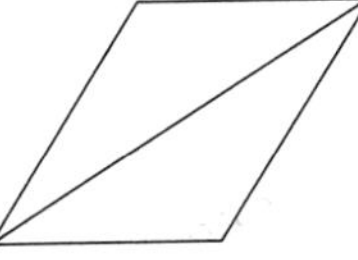

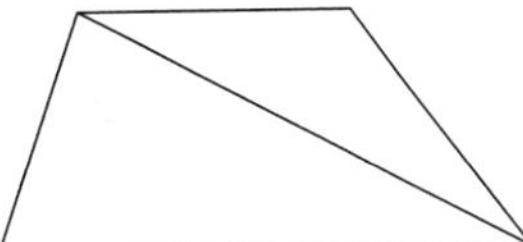

How can we find the sum of the angles in one triangle?

EXAMPLE 1 **Given:** *ABCD,* a square

Find: sum of the angles in a right triangle

$4 \bullet 90° = 360°$, $360° \div 2 = 180°$

Since the two right triangles in the square are identical, or coincide, we can see that the angle sum of right $\Delta ABC = 180°$.

Conclusion: The sum of the angles in a right isosceles triangle is 180°.

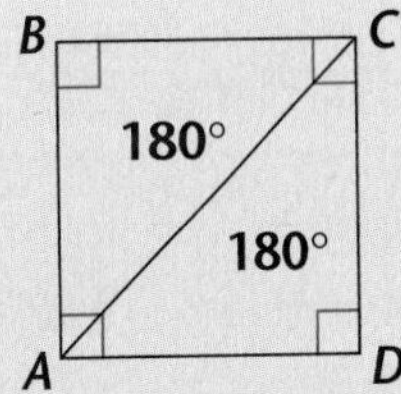

EXAMPLE 2 **Given:** *ABCD*, a rectangle, and diagonal $\overline{AC}$

Find: sum of the angles in a right triangle

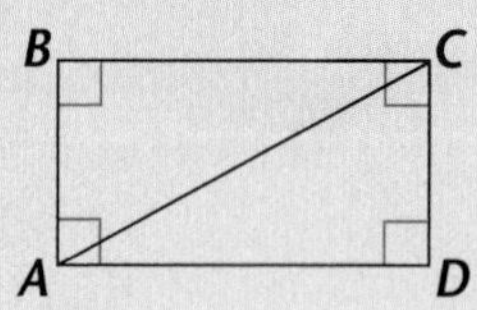

$4 \bullet 90° = 360°$

Separate the rectangle, along its diagonal, forming two right triangles. Turn ΔADC so that ΔABC can be placed on ΔADC, matching the angles and sides of the two triangles. From this we can see that the angles and sides of the triangles are equal.

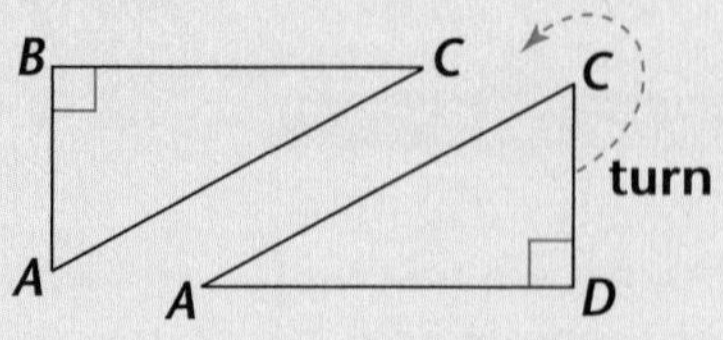

$360° \div 2 = 180°$ each

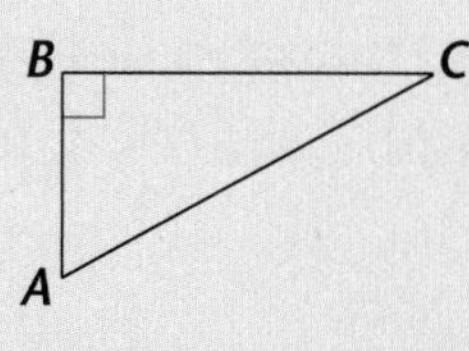

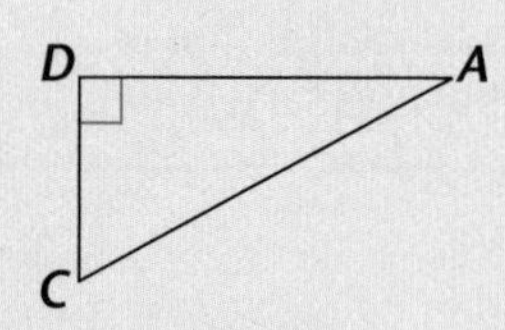

Conclusion: The sum of the angles in each right triangle is 180°.

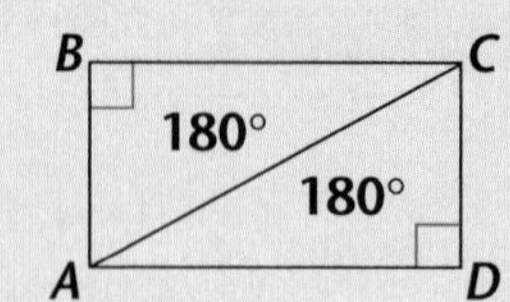

EXAMPLE 3 **Given:** ΔABC and $\overline{BD} \perp \overline{AC}$ at *D*

Find: sum of the angles in any triangle

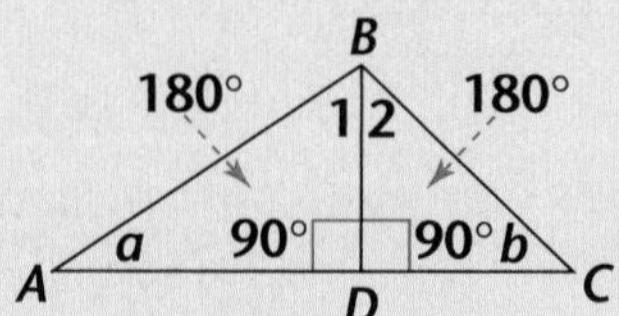

$m\angle a + (m\angle 1 + m\angle 2) + m\angle b =$ angle sum of ΔABC	Definition of sum of angles.
$m\angle a + m\angle 1 + 90° = 180°$, and $m\angle b + m\angle 2 + 90° = 180°$	The sum of the angles in every right triangle is 180°.
$m\angle a + m\angle 1 + m\angle 2 + m\angle b + 90° + 90° = 360°$	Addition of equals.
$m\angle a + (m\angle 1 + m\angle 2) + m\angle b = 180°$	Subtract 180° from each side.

Conclusion: The sum of the angles in any triangle is 180°.

Summary of Inductive/Informal Argument

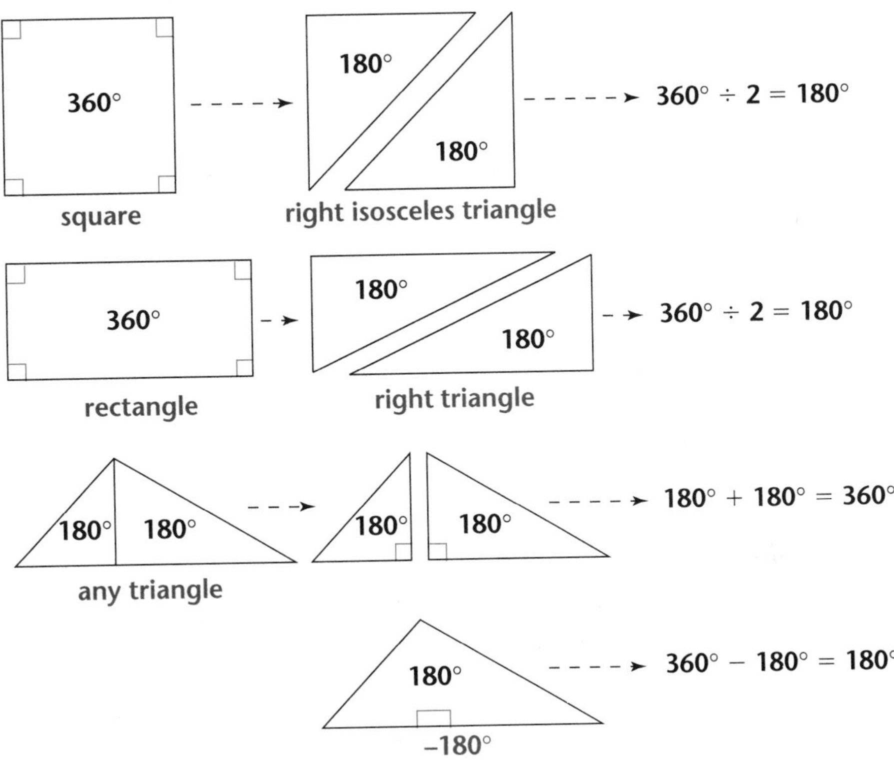

Conclusion: The sum of the angles in any triangle is 180°.

This conclusion is known as the Angle Sum Theorem. You will prove this theorem more formally later. Using this theorem, you can solve many kinds of angle measure problems involving triangles.

Technology Connection

Scientists and researchers rely on basic geometric terms to describe the physical world. Crystals are arrangements of solid chemical compounds that can be described using these terms. Models of crystals can be created using advanced computer software. This allows scientists to study the crystals on a computer as well as in a laboratory. Take a look at the crystals shown at the right. What geometric figures do you see?

EXAMPLE 4 **Given:** ΔABC is a right triangle with $m\angle A = 30°$

Find: measure of $\angle B$

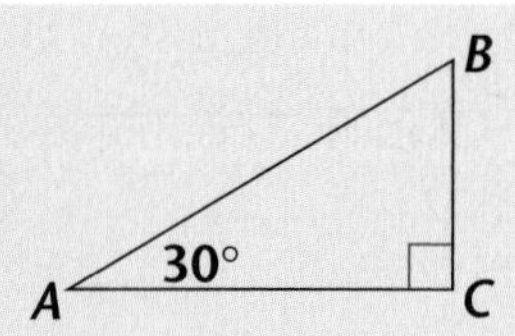

Solution:	**Reason:**
$m\angle A + m\angle B + m\angle C = 180°$	Angle Sum Theorem
$30° + m\angle B + 90° = 180°$	substitution
$120° + m\angle B = 180°$	simplification
$m\angle B = 60°$	subtraction of equals

EXAMPLE 5 **Given:** ΔABC is a right triangle with $m\angle BCD = 160°$

Find: measure of $\angle A$

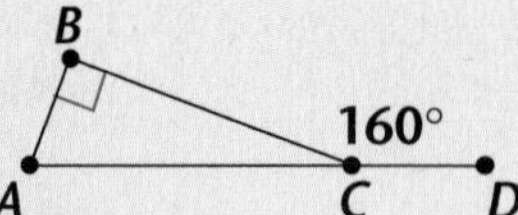

Solution:	**Reason:**
$m\angle ACB + 160° = 180°$	*ACD* forms a straight angle
$m\angle ACB = 20°$	subtraction of equals
$m\angle A + m\angle ACB + m\angle B = 180°$	Angle Sum Theorem
$m\angle A + 20° + 90° = 180°$	subtraction of equals
$m\angle A = 70°$	subtraction of equals

EXAMPLE 6 **Given:** ΔABC is an isosceles triangle with $m\angle ABC = 15°$

Find: measures of the base angles *A* and *C*

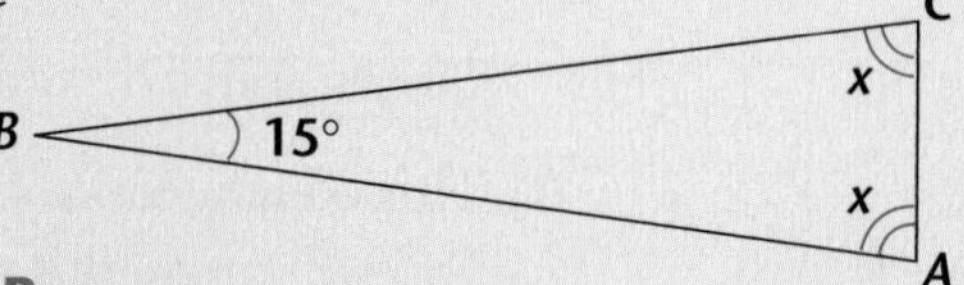

Solution:	**Reason:**
Let $x = m\angle A$ (or *C*)	$m\angle A = m\angle C$
$15° + x + x = 180°$	Angle Sum Theorem
$2x = 165°$	simplification
$x = 82.5°$	division of equals

Conclusion: The measure of each base angle, $\angle A$ and $\angle C$, $= 82.5°$.

Exercise A Find the measure of the angles.

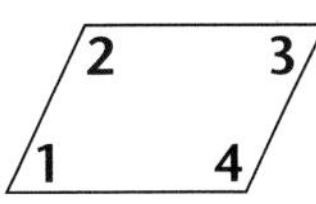

1. $m\angle 1 + m\angle 2$

2. $m\angle 3 + m\angle 4$

3. $m\angle 1 + m\angle 2 + m\angle 3 + m\angle 4$

4. $m\angle 1 + m\angle 2$

5. $m\angle 3 + m\angle 4$

6. $m\angle 1 + m\angle 2 + m\angle 3 + m\angle 4$

Exercise B Find the measure of $\angle x$.

7.

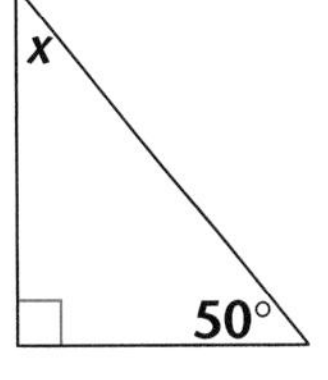

8.

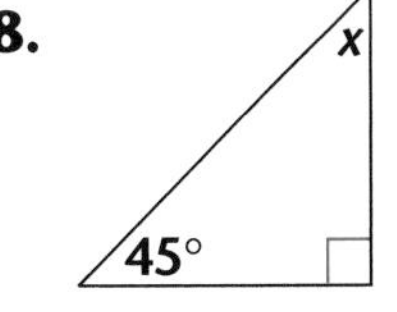

9.

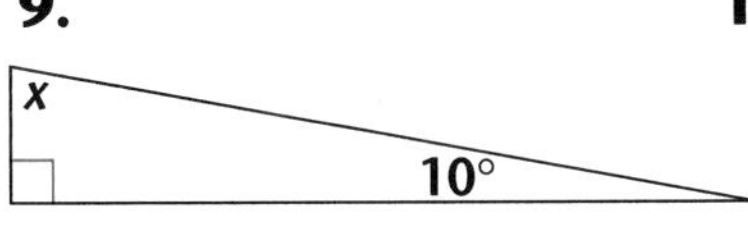

10.

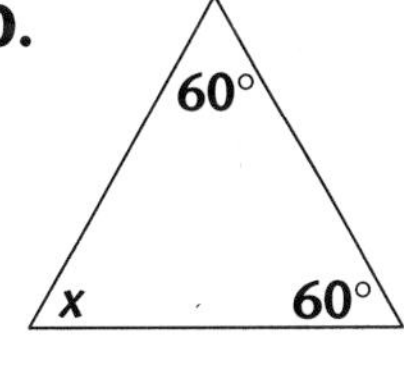

11.

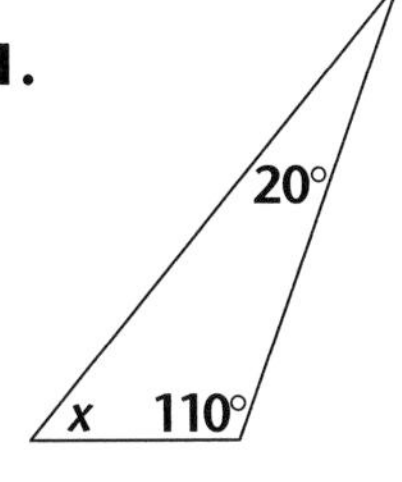

12.

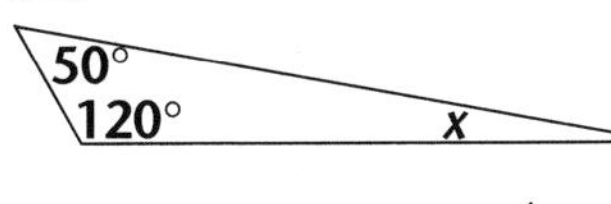

13.

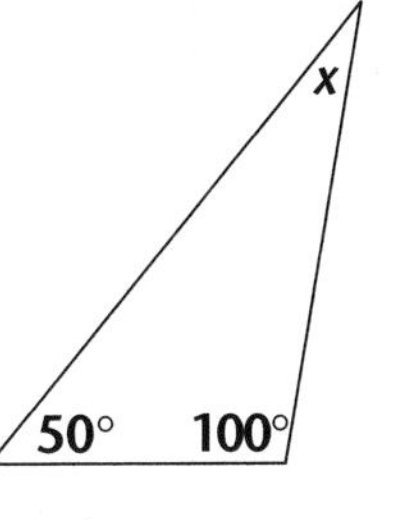

14.

15.

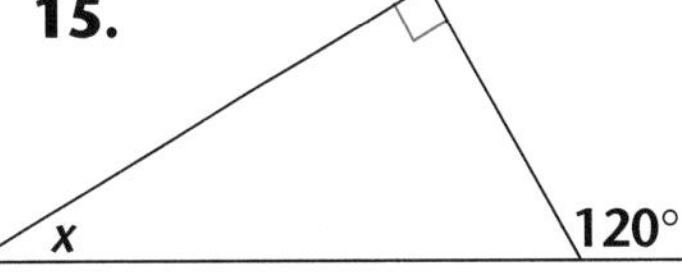

16.

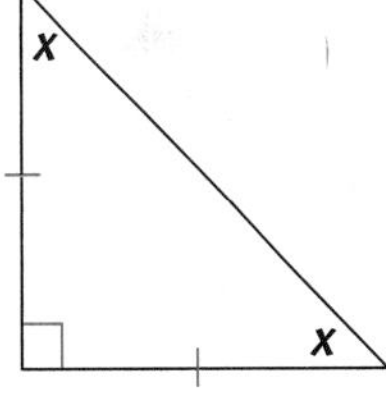

17.

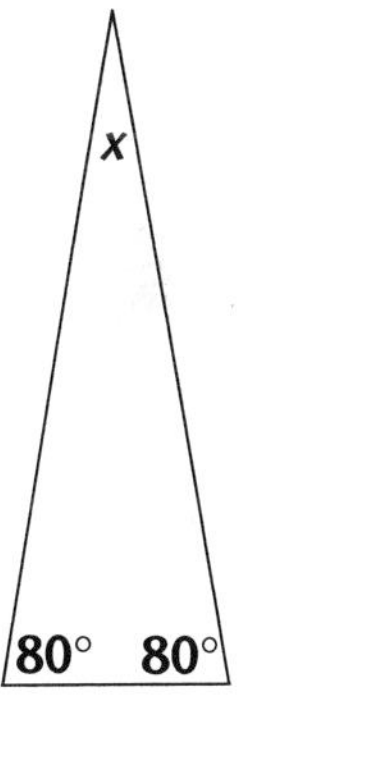

Exercise C Tell whether the following triangles are possible. Give reasons for your answer.

18. A right, obtuse triangle

19. An obtuse isosceles triangle

20. A right equilateral triangle

Lesson 6 Concave and Convex Polygons

Polygon
A closed, many-sided geometric figure

Regular polygon
A polygon with sides of equal length and angles of equal measure

Convex polygon
A polygon for which the line segment joining any two points in the interior lies entirely within the figure

Concave polygon
A polygon for which a segment joining any two points in the interior does not lie entirely within the figure

The word **polygon** means "many sided" and is used to describe geometric figures. A **regular polygon** has angles of equal measure and sides of equal length.

Most of the polygons you have studied had either three sides (triangle) or four sides (quadrilateral). In addition, most of the quadrilaterals you have studied have been **convex polygons.**

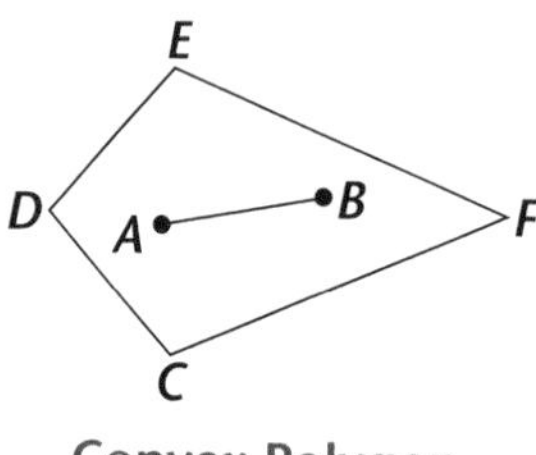

Convex Polygon

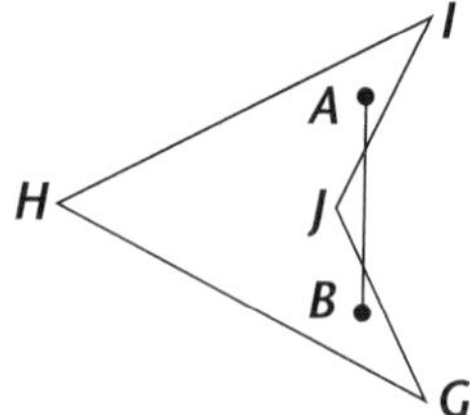

Concave Polygon

A figure is convex if, given any two points in the interior (inside), the segment joining the points lies wholly within the figure. The figure is nonconvex, or **concave,** if the segment does not necessarily lie wholly within the figure.

Another way to tell if a figure is concave or convex is to study the polygon's diagonals.

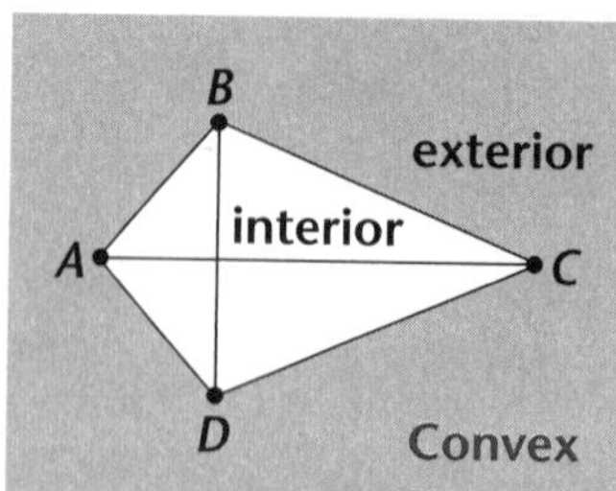

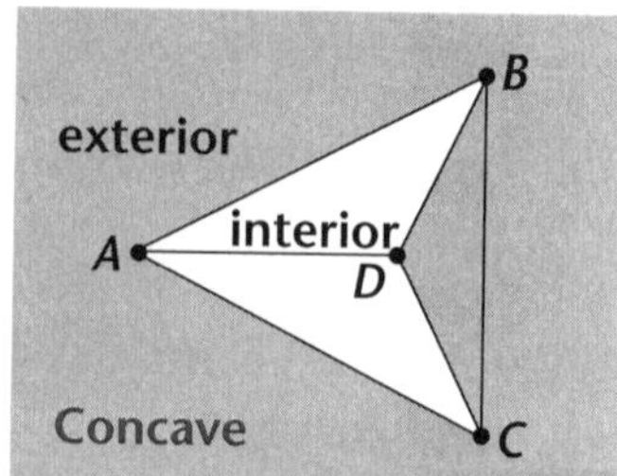

A concave polygon will have one or more diagonals that lie outside the figure.

Polygons are named by the number of sides that form the figure.

Polygon	Number of Sides	Regular Polygon (= sides, = angles)
Triangle	3	Equilateral Triangle
Quadrilateral	4	Square
Pentagon	5	Regular Pentagon
Hexagon	6	Regular Hexagon
Septagon	7	Regular Septagon
Octagon	8	Regular Octagon

As the number of sides, *n*, of a polygon increases, the number of diagonals also increases. Let's look for a pattern in how the numbers increase. Turn to the figures on the next page.

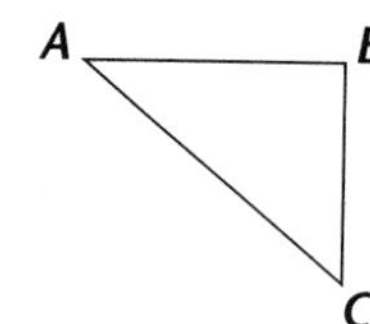

number of vertices = 3
number of diagonals = 0

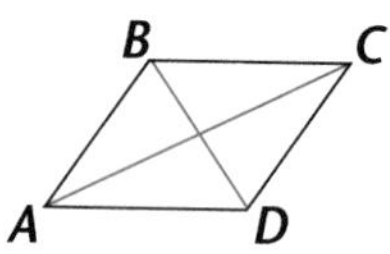

number of vertices = 4
number of diagonals = 2

There is one diagonal from each vertex. But each diagonal can be drawn twice:

$$A \text{ to } C = C \text{ to } A \text{ and } B \text{ to } D = D \text{ to } B$$

We can write this information as a formula:

Formula:
$$\frac{(\text{\# vertices}) \bullet (\text{\# diagonals from each vertex})}{2} = \text{total number of diagonals}$$

For the above quadrilateral this would be $\frac{4(1)}{2} = 2$ diagonals

Does the formula work for a pentagon?

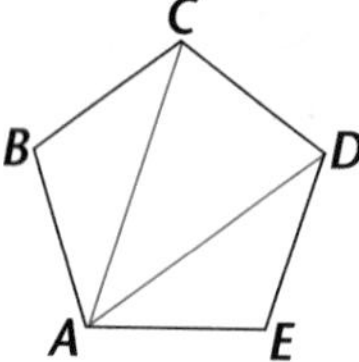

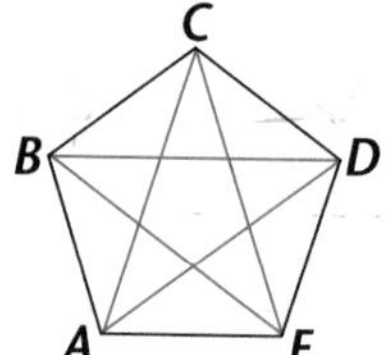

$$\frac{(\text{\# vertices}) \cdot (\text{\# diagonals from each})}{2} = \text{number of diagonals}$$

$$\frac{5(2)}{2} = 5$$

There is a pattern for finding the number of diagonals in a polygon.

Writing About Mathematics

What is the sum of the interior angle measures for a 4-sided convex polygon? Explain.

EXAMPLE 1

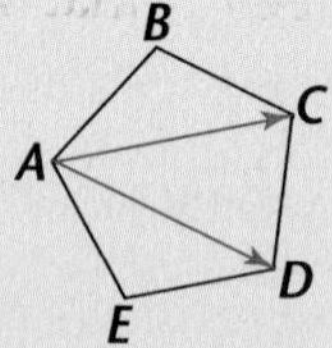

Step 1 Determine the number of diagonals that can be drawn from a single vertex.

Step 2 Multiply the number of diagonals for each vertex by *n*, the number of sides of the polygon.

Step 3 Divide the product by 2 to avoid counting any diagonal twice.

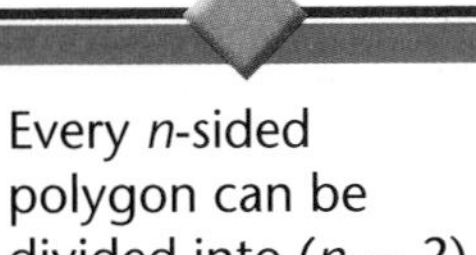

Every *n*-sided polygon can be divided into $(n - 2)$ triangles.

Remember, you can check your answer by drawing the polygon and all its diagonals.

As you draw all the possible diagonals from one vertex, if there is no overlap of areas or angles, you are dividing the polygon into triangles.

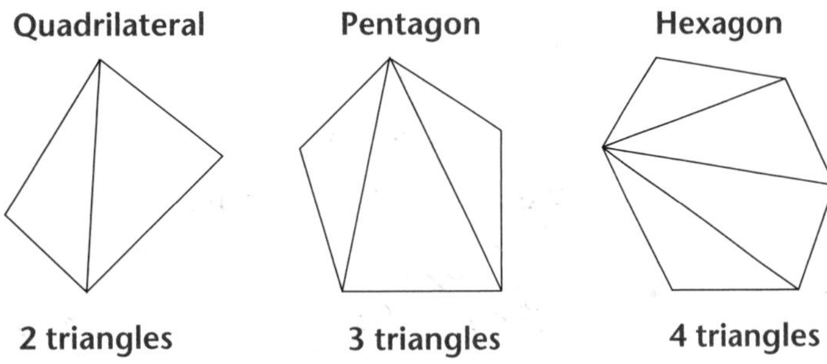

There is a pattern here as well.

Number of sides, *n*, for the polygon	Number of triangles formed by diagonals from one vertex	Difference between number of sides and number of triangles
3	1	$3 - 1 = 2$
4	2	$4 - 2 = 2$
5	3	$5 - 3 = 2$
6	4	$6 - 4 = 2$
....		
n	$(n - 2)$	2

The sum of the angles in a polygon, with number of sides $= n$, is $(n - 2)(180°)$.

Remember that the sum of the angles in any triangle is 180°.

Therefore, we can say that (the number of triangles) • (180°) = sum of the angles in the polygon.

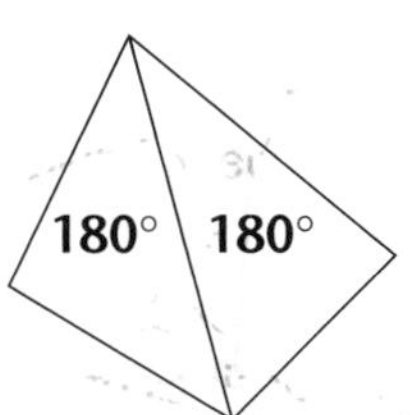

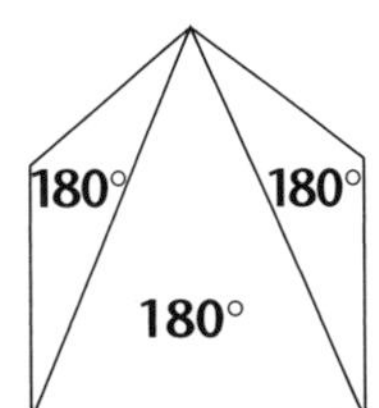

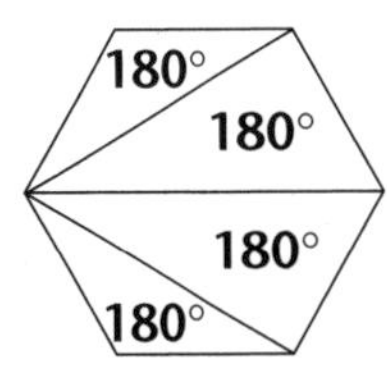

Because regular polygons have angles of equal measure, you can use this information to determine the measures of the angles in a regular polygon.

EXAMPLE 2 Square, $n = 4$

$(n - 2)(180°)$ = number of degrees in polygon

$2 \bullet 180° = 360°$

4 equal angles means each angle equals $360° \div 4 = 90°$

Each angle in a square measures 90°.

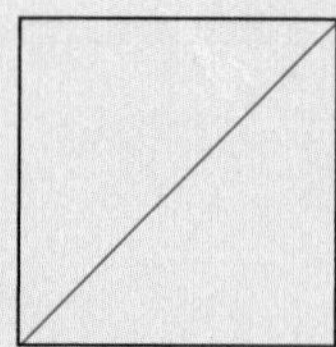

EXAMPLE 3 Pentagon, $n = 5$

$(n - 2)(180°)$ = number of degrees in polygon

$3 \bullet 180° = 540°$

5 equal angles means each angle equals $540° \div 5 = 108°$

Each angle in a regular pentagon measures 108°.

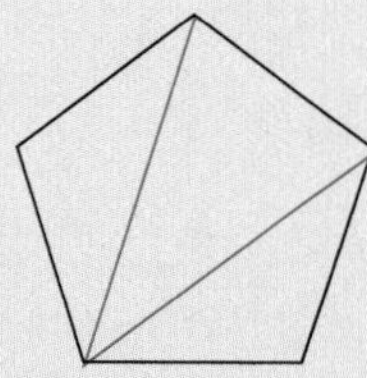

EXAMPLE 4 Hexagon, $n = 6$

$(n - 2)(180°)$ = number of degrees in polygon

$4 \bullet 180° = 720°$

6 equal angles means each angle equals $720° \div 6 = 120°$

Each angle in a regular hexagon measures 120°.

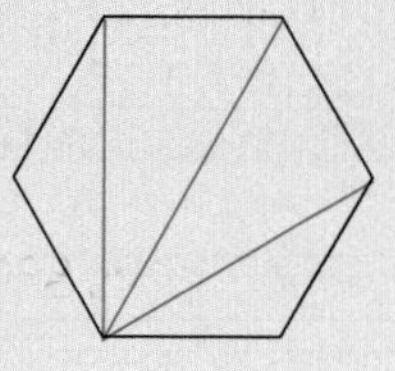

Exercise A Copy and complete this chart on a separate sheet of paper.

Polygon, n = number of sides	Number of diagonals from each vertex	Total number of diagonals	Number of triangles possible $(n - 2)$	Total number of degrees in polygon $(n - 2) \bullet (180°)$
$n = 8$	**1.** ______	**2.** ______	6	**3.** ______
$n = 9$	6	**4.** ______	**5.** ______	**6.** ______

Polygon, n = number of sides	Number of diagonals from each vertex	Total number of diagonals	Number of triangles possible $(n - 2)$	Total number of degrees in polygon $(n - 2) \cdot (180°)$
$n = 10$	**7.** _____	**8.** _____	**9.** _____	**10.** _____
$n = 11$	8	**11.** _____	**12.** _____	**13.** _____
$n = 12$	**14.** _____	**15.** _____	**16.** _____	1,800°

PROBLEM SOLVING

Exercise B Answer the following questions.

17. What polygon provides the outside shape for the snowflake shown? Is it regular? How many diagonals are shown? Explain your answer.

18. Is the figure shown a regular dodecagon (12-sided polygon)? Give reasons for your answer.

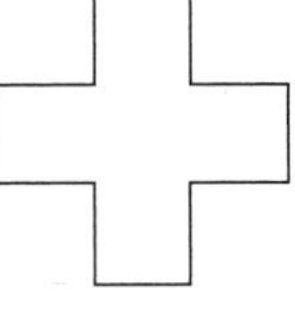

19. The object pictured to the right is called a *hex nut*. What is the sum of the interior angles for this nut?

20. This umbrella has eight equal sides, and eight equal angles. What is the measure of angle a? Explain.

Lesson 7 Constructing Perpendiculars

Perpendicular bisector

Line that bisects a given line segment and forms a right angle with it

Remember that in Chapter 4 you learned how to use a compass and a straightedge to find the midpoint of a line segment.

To find the midpoint of $\overline{AB}$, set your compass to about the length of $\overline{AB}$. Use A as a center and then B as a center to draw arcs above and below $\overline{AB}$. Connect the points where the arcs intersect by drawing line ℓ. The point, M, located where ℓ crosses $\overline{AB}$, is the midpoint of $\overline{AB}$.

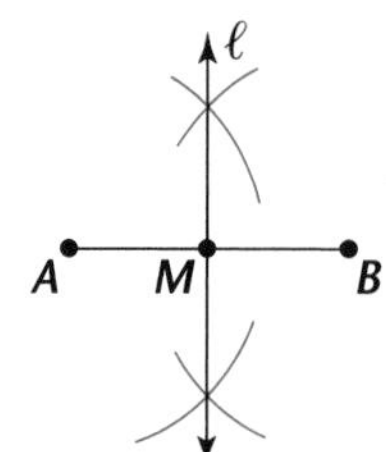

Line ℓ is also perpendicular to $\overline{AB}$ so we can say that ℓ is the **perpendicular bisector** of $\overline{AB}$. We will prove this in a later lesson.

CONSTRUCTION

Given: line ℓ and point P not on ℓ

Construct: a line perpendicular to ℓ from point P

Step 1 Open your compass to a distance somewhat greater than the distance from P to ℓ. Using P as the center of a circle, draw an arc that intersects ℓ in two places. Label the points A and B.

Step 2 Keeping your compass opening constant, and using A as the center of a circle, draw an arc below ℓ. Then, with the same compass opening, draw a second arc below ℓ using B as the center. Label the point where the arcs intersect C.

Step 3 Connect P and C. $\overline{PC} \perp \ell$.

You can use this construction to solve the following problem.

EXAMPLE 1 **Given:** $\triangle ABC$

Construct: a line $\perp$ from point B to $\overline{AC}$

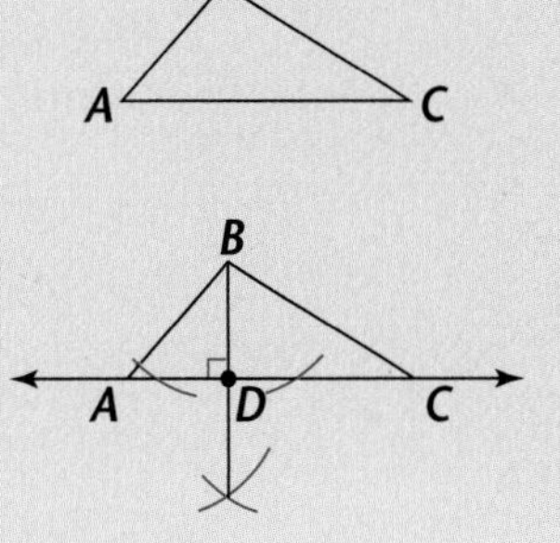

B is a point not on $\overline{AC}$.
Use the construction of a perpendicular from a point not on the line.

You may have to extend $\overline{AC}$ to $\overleftrightarrow{AC}$.
Note that $\overline{BD} \perp \overleftrightarrow{AC}$ and $\overline{BD} \perp \overline{AC}$.

In Chapter 1, Lesson 4, we demonstrated how to construct a line perpendicular to a given line and passing through a given point P on the line. You can use this same method to construct a perpendicular line through any point on a line, even if that line or line segment is part of a figure.

EXAMPLE 2 **Given:** $\triangle DEF$

Construct: a line $\perp$ to $\overline{DF}$ at point D

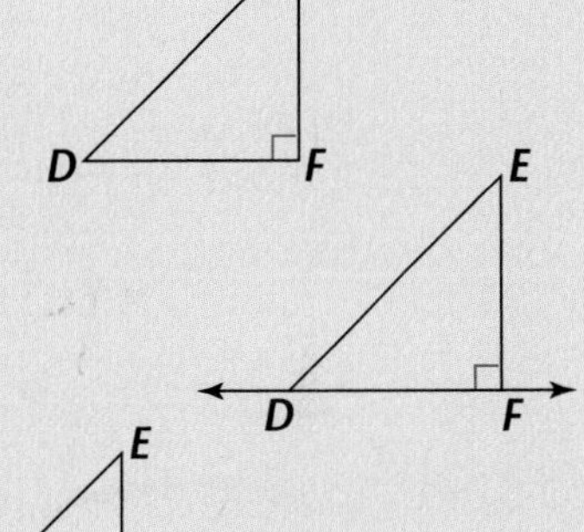

You may need to extend $\overline{DF}$. D is a point on $\overleftrightarrow{DF}$.
Use the construction of a perpendicular to a line through a point on the line.

Note that $\overline{GD} \perp \overleftrightarrow{DF}$ and $\overline{GD} \perp \overline{DF}$.

CONSTRUCTION

Exercise A Complete the following constructions on a separate sheet of paper. Use only a straightedge and a compass.

1. Draw a line ℓ and a point P not on ℓ. Construct a $\perp$ to ℓ through P.

2. Draw a line m and a point Q on m. Construct a $\perp$ to m at Q.

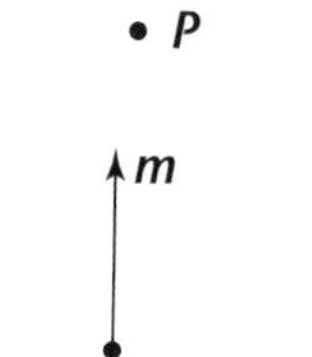

3. Construct any right triangle. Label the right angle R and the other two angles S and T. Construct a perpendicular to $\overline{ST}$ through the right angle vertex R.

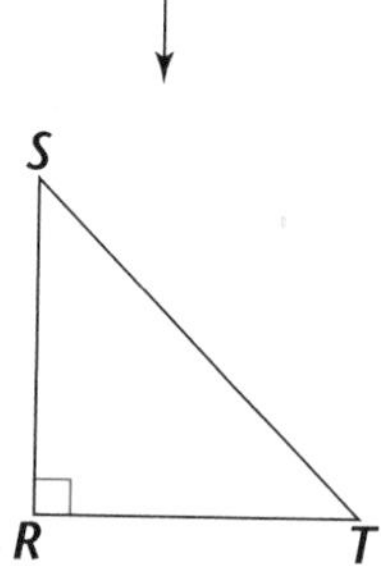

4. Draw a trapezoid $TRAP$ as shown. Construct a line $\perp$ to $\overline{TP}$ at point A.

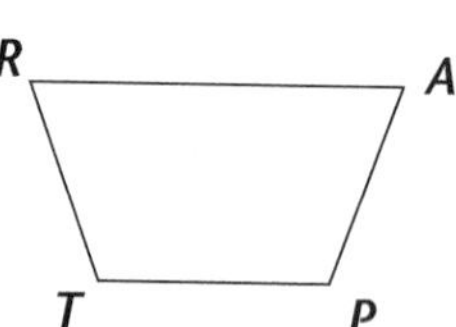

5. In the trapezoid $TRAP$ at right, $\overline{XT} \perp \overline{TP}$ by construction. Is $\overline{XT} \perp \overline{RA}$? Explain your answer.

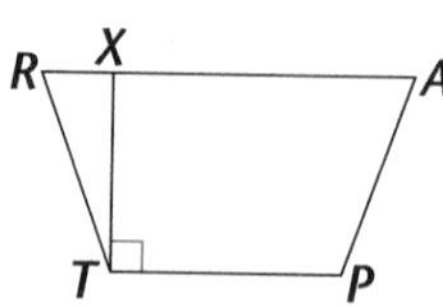

TRY THIS You can find triangles all around you—for example, a yield sign, a roof line, and a recycle symbol. Choose one and copy it on paper. Is the triangle acute, right, or obtuse? Then construct perpendicular bisectors through each vertex. Compare your triangles with those of your classmates. How are all perpendicular bisectors alike?

Lesson 8 Altitudes, Angle Bisectors, and Medians

Altitude

Line segment from the vertex of a triangle that is perpendicular to the opposite side

Orthocenter

The point where the altitudes of a triangle meet

Because triangles have three vertices, or angles, they have three **altitudes** and three angle bisectors.

A line from a vertex of a triangle that is perpendicular to the opposite side is the altitude of the triangle.

Acute Case

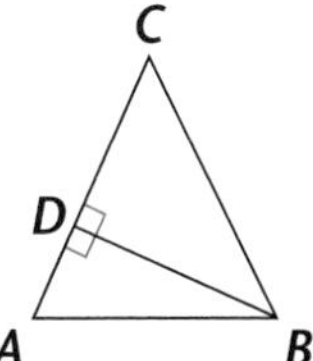

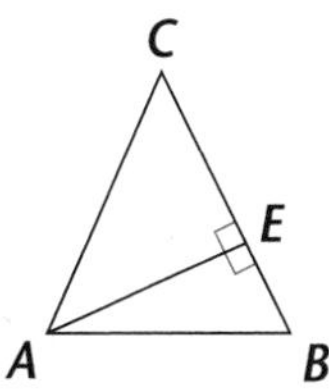

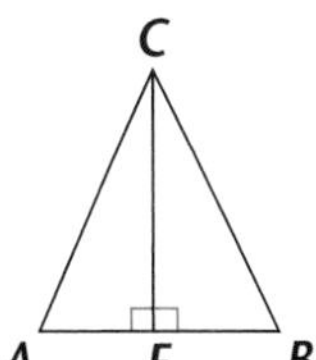

In an acute triangle, all the altitudes are internal. That is, they lie wholly within the triangle. The altitudes meet at one point called the **orthocenter.**

Review acute and obtuse triangles on page 149.

To construct an altitude, you can use the construction for constructing a perpendicular to a line from a point (vertex) not on the line. (See the construction in Lesson 7.)

Obtuse Case

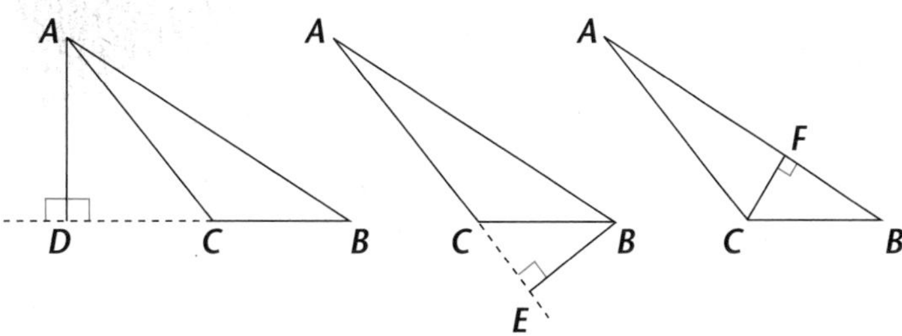

In the obtuse triangle *ABC* above, altitudes $\overline{AD}$ and $\overline{BE}$ are external while altitude $\overline{CF}$ is internal. Obtuse triangles have two external altitudes and one internal altitude. An external altitude is perpendicular to the line along the side opposite the vertex.

Triangles have three altitudes and they have three angle bisectors. This is a good time to review how to bisect an angle.

In-center

The point where the angle bisectors of the angles of a triangle intersect

Median

Line from a vertex of a triangle to the midpoint of the opposite side

Centroid

Point where the three medians of a triangle intersect

To bisect an angle, review Chapter 1, Lesson 3.

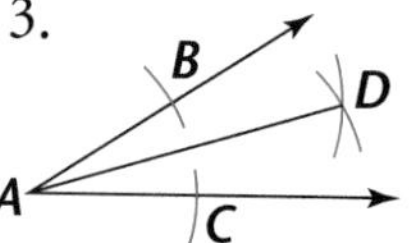

The angle bisectors of the angles of a triangle intersect at a point called the **in-center** of the triangle.

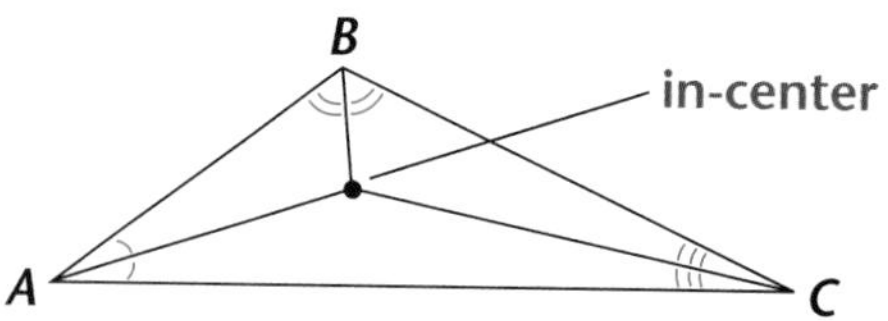

Because triangles have three sides, they have three **medians.** A line from a vertex of a triangle to the midpoint of the opposite side is a median of the triangle.

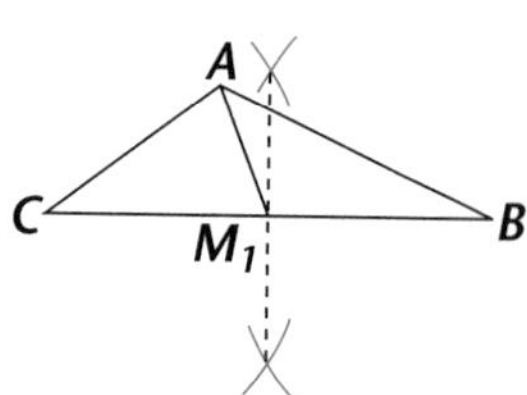

To construct the median from vertex A, find the midpoint, M_1, of $\overline{BC}$. To find the midpoint, construct the ⊥ bisector of $\overline{BC}$. Draw $\overline{AM_1}$, a median of ΔABC.

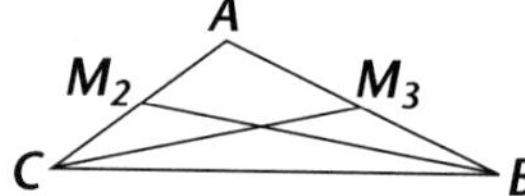

Repeat the steps to draw the other two medians, $\overline{BM_2}$ and $\overline{CM_3}$.

The point where the three medians of a triangle intersect is the **centroid.**

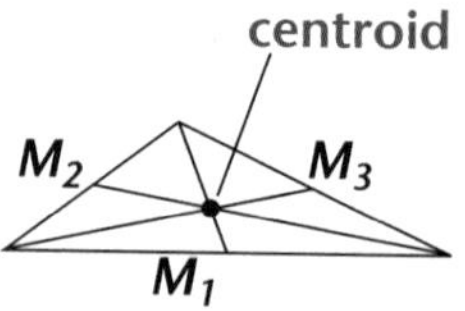

Altitudes intersect at the orthocenter
Angle bisectors intersect at the in-center
Medians intersect at the centroid

Acute triangles have three interior altitudes.

Obtuse triangles have two exterior altitudes and one interior altitude.

Estimation Activity

Estimate: Estimate the medians of a triangle before doing a construction.

Solution: Fold the triangle so that the endpoints of a side lie on top of each other. Make a crease in the paper. The point where the crease crosses the side is the median.

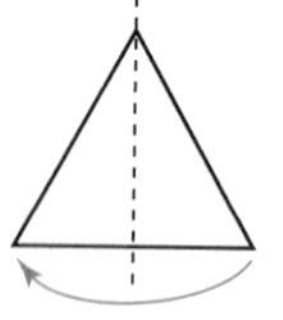

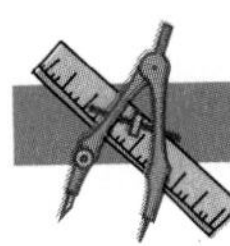

CONSTRUCTION

Exercise A Complete the following constructions on a separate sheet of paper. Use only a straightedge and a compass. (Note: You may find it easier to use large triangles for your constructions.)

1. Draw any acute triangle and label it ABC. Construct altitudes from A and C.

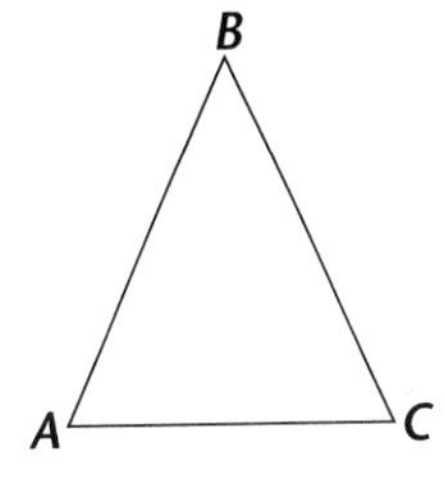

2. Draw any obtuse triangle and label the obtuse angle D and the triangle DEF. Construct the altitude from E to $\overline{DF}$.

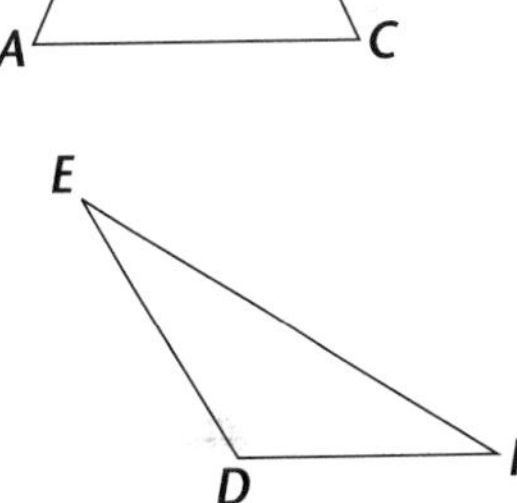

3. Draw any right triangle and label the right angle G and the triangle GHI. Construct the altitude from G to $\overline{HI}$.

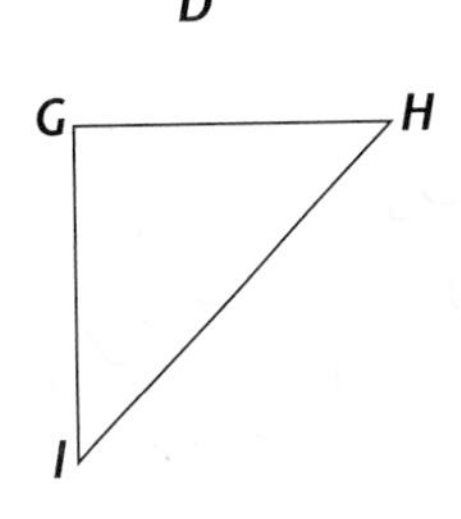

4. Draw an obtuse triangle like ΔJKL. Label the obtuse angle J. Construct all the medians of the triangle.

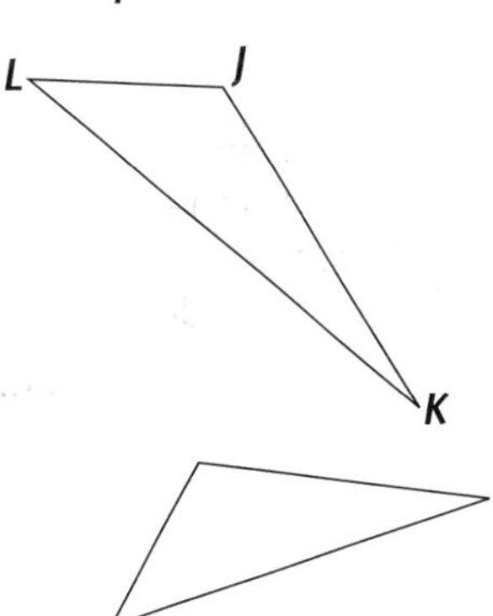

5. Draw any large scalene triangle. Construct the angle bisectors for each angle in the triangle.

6. Draw any isosceles triangle ABC with $AB = BC$. (You may need to review how to construct an isosceles triangle on page 146.) Construct the bisector of the vertex angle B.

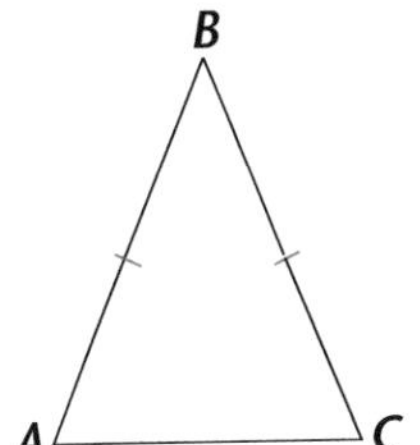

7. Using an isosceles triangle like the one in Problem 6, draw the median to the base, $\overline{AC}$, of the triangle.

8. Construct a large equilateral triangle. (You may need to review the directions on page 145.) Draw the perpendicular bisector from each vertex to the opposite side.

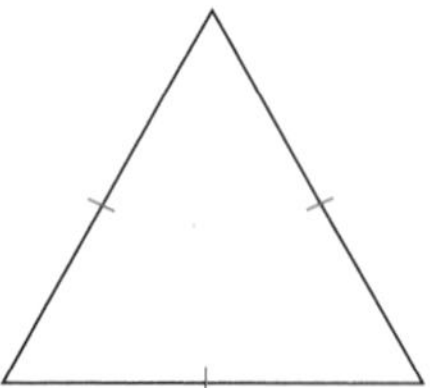

9. Using an equilateral triangle like the one in Problem 8, draw the angle bisector for each angle of the triangle.

10. Using an equilateral triangle like the one in Problem 8, draw the median to each side.

Exercise B Answer the following questions about your constructions.

11. For a right triangle like the triangle in Problem 3, what can you say about the altitudes from H to $\overline{GI}$ and from I to $\overline{HG}$?

12. At what point do the altitudes in a right triangle meet?

13. In the isosceles triangle used in Problems 6 and 7, what seems to be true about the bisector of the vertex angle and the median to the base?

14. For the equilateral triangle used in Problems 8, 9, and 10, what seems to be true about the perpendicular bisectors of the sides, the angle bisectors, and the medians to each side?

15. Look again at the bisectors for the angles in Problem 5. Label the point where the bisectors meet P. Draw a perpendicular line from P to each side of the triangle. Measure the length of each perpendicular line segment. What appears to be true about the segment lengths? What statement can you make about the point P where the angle bisectors meet and its distance from the sides of the triangle?

Lesson 9 Proof of the Angle Sum Theorem

In Lesson 5, you found that the sum of the measures of the angles in a triangle is 180°. Before we complete the formal proof of the theorem for all triangles, let's look at one more example.

Given: ΔABC with $m\angle A = 30°$ and $m\angle C = 50°$

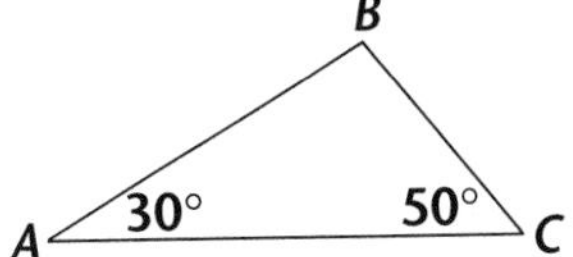

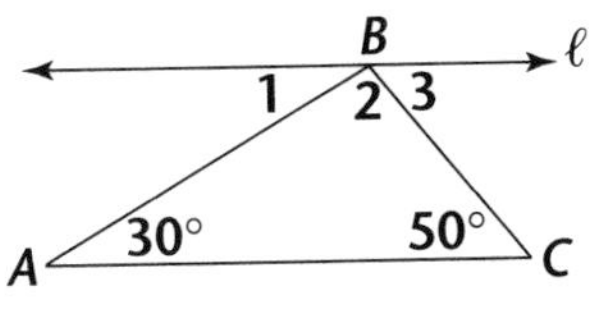

By the equivalent of Euclid's Parallel Postulate (Postulate 5), there is a unique line $\ell \parallel \overline{AC}$ passing through vertex B.

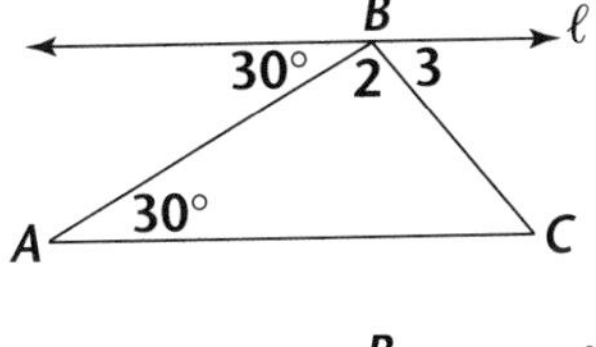

Think of $\overline{AB}$ as a transversal. Then $m\angle 1 = 30°$ by the alternate interior angles postulate.

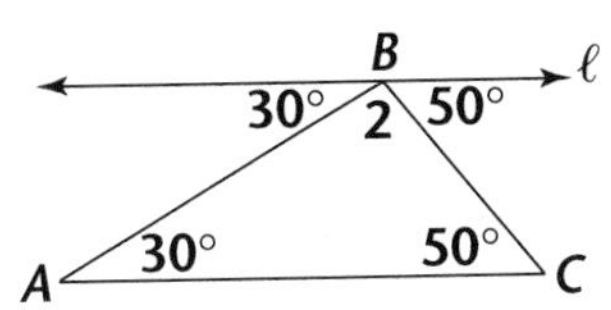

Think of $\overline{BC}$ as a transversal. Then $m\angle 3 = 50°$ by the alternate interior angles postulate.

ℓ is a straight line	$30° + m\angle 2 + 50° = 180°$
substitution	$m\angle A + m\angle 2 + m\angle C = 180°$
	$\therefore m\angle A + m\angle B + m\angle C = 180°$

Geometry in Your Life

Many builders use a *truss*, a framework of beams, when building a roof. If a builder knows the base angles of triangular truss, he can find the angle at the peak. To do this, he will use the Angle Sum Theorem. You can remember this theorem by doing the following activity. Draw any acute ΔABC on a sheet of paper. Cut out the triangle. Fold your triangle so that point B lies on $\overline{AC}$; the fold should be parallel to $\overline{AC}$. Then fold your triangle so that A and C are at B. Notice that $\angle A + \angle B + \angle C$ seem to make a straight angle. Try it again with another triangle. Does $\angle A + \angle B + \angle C$ still seem to make a straight angle? What does this tell you about the sum of the angles in any triangle? How can a builder use this to find the angle at the peak of the truss?

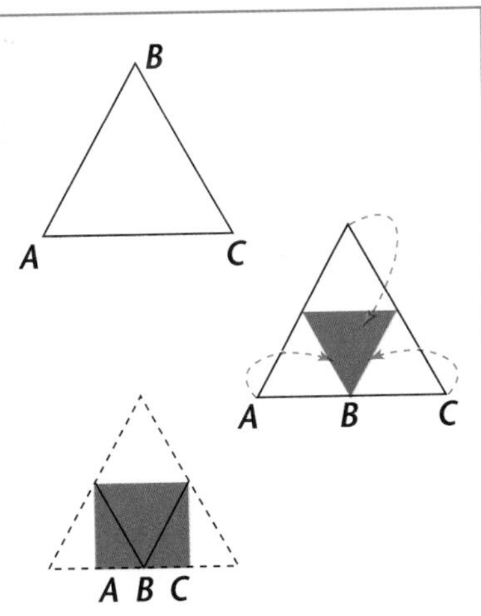

Corollary

A conclusion that follows easily from a given theorem

Exterior angle

Angle formed by extending one side of a triangle through any vertex

You can write a formal proof of the theorem in nearly the same manner. The only difference is that you may not specify the measure of any angle—you must prove the theorem is true for any triangle and its angles.

> **Angle Sum Theorem (5.9.1):**
> The sum of the angle measures in any triangle is 180°.

Given: any ΔABC

To Prove: $m\angle A + m\angle B + m\angle C = 180°$

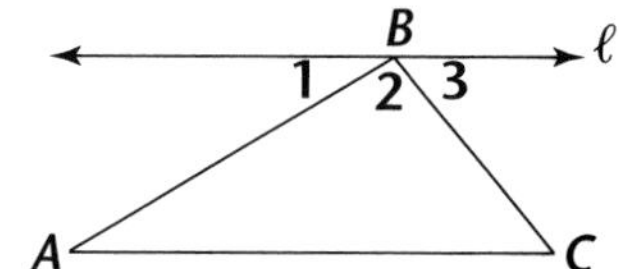

PROOF

Statement	Reason
1. ΔABC	**1.** Given.
2. Construct $\ell \parallel \overline{AC}$ through B	**2.** Equivalent of Euclid's Parallel Postulate.
3. $m\angle 1 + m\angle 2 + m\angle 3 = 180°$	**3.** Adjacent angles with exterior sides in a straight line form a straight angle; a straight angle measures 180°.
4. $m\angle 1 = m\angle A$, $m\angle 3 = m\angle C$	**4.** Alternate interior angles between parallel lines are equal.
5. $m\angle 2 = m\angle B$	**5.** Same angle.
6. $\therefore m\angle 1 + m\angle 2 + m\angle 3 = 180°$ becomes $m\angle A + m\angle B + m\angle C = 180°$	**6.** Substitution of equals for equals.

With this theorem, we can prove another related theorem. A conclusion that follows easily from a given theorem is often called a **corollary** to the original theorem.

> **Corollary to the Angle Sum Theorem (5.9.2):**
> If ΔABC is any triangle, then an exterior angle of ABC has the same measure as the sum of the measures of the two nonadjacent interior angles.

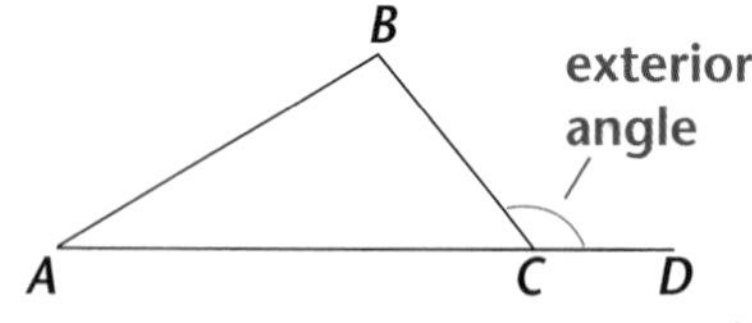

An **exterior angle** of a triangle is formed by extending one side of the triangle through any vertex. The extension forms an exterior angle with the adjacent side of the triangle.

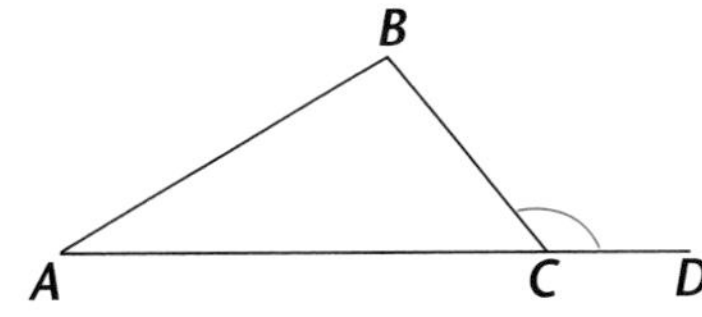

Let's prove the corollary.

Given: any ΔABC with exterior angle BCD
To Prove: $m\angle BCD = m\angle A + m\angle B$

PROOF

Statement	Reason
1. ΔABC with exterior angle BCD	1. Given.
2. $\angle C$ and $\angle BCD$ are adjacent angles	2. Definition of adjacent angles.
3. $m\angle BCD + m\angle C = 180°$	3. Adjacent angles with exterior sides in a straight line form a straight angle; a straight angle measures 180°.
4. $m\angle A + m\angle B + m\angle C = 180°$	4. Angle sum theorem.
5. $m\angle BCD + m\angle C = m\angle A + m\angle B + m\angle C$	5. Steps 3 and 4; quantities equal to the same quantity are equal to each other.
6. $\therefore m\angle BCD = m\angle A + m\angle B$	6. Subtracting equals from equals gives equal differences.

This corollary guarantees the following equalities.

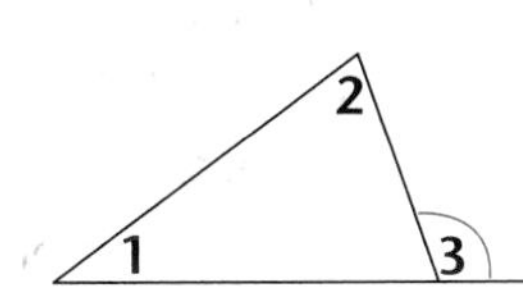

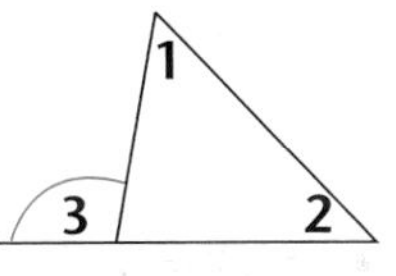

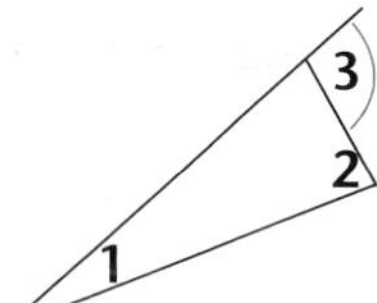

$m\angle 3 = m\angle 1 + m\angle 2$ in each triangle

The measure of an exterior angle equals the sum of the two nonadjacent interior angles.

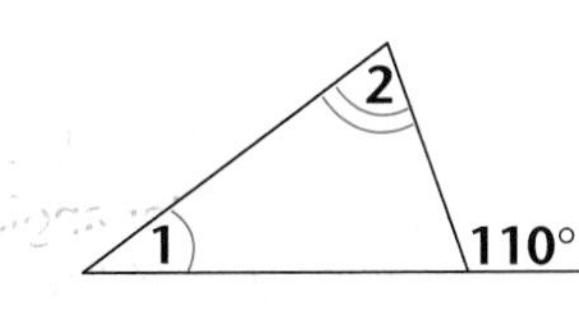

$m\angle 1 + m\angle 2 = 110°$

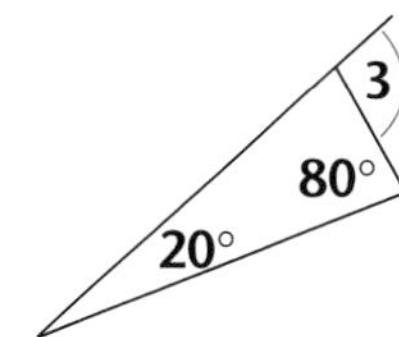

$m\angle 3 = 20° + 80° = 100°$

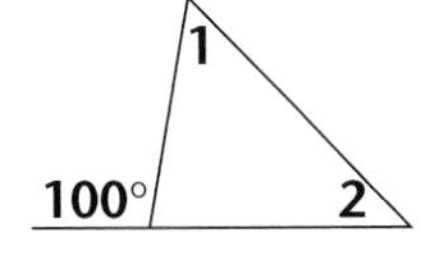

$m\angle 1 + m\angle 2 = 100°$

EXAMPLE 1 Solve for x.

$$x + 50° = 150° \text{ (by corollary)}$$
$$x = 100° \text{ (subtraction)}$$

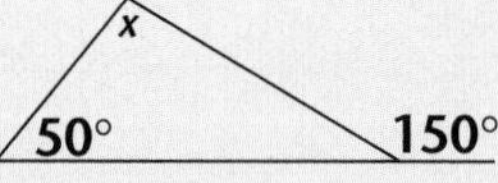

EXAMPLE 2 Solve for x.

$$70° + 70° + x = 180° \text{ (Angle Sum Theorem, definition of isosceles } \Delta)$$
$$x = 40° \text{ (subtraction)}$$

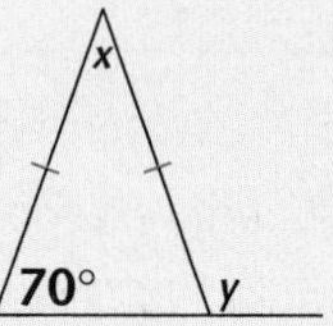

EXAMPLE 3 Solve for y.

$70° + 40° = y$ (by corollary) OR $70° + y = 180°$

$y = 110°$ (addition) $y = 110°$ (subtraction)

Exercise A Use the Angle Sum Theorem or its corollary to find the measures of the angles.

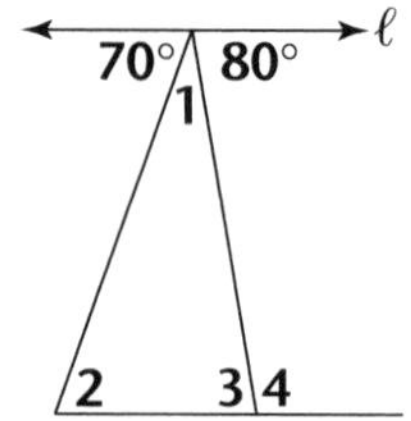

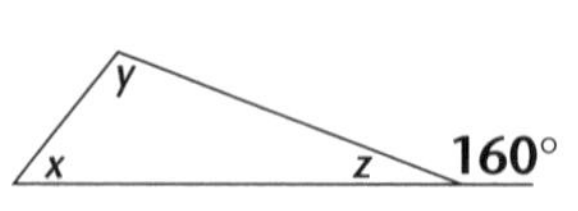

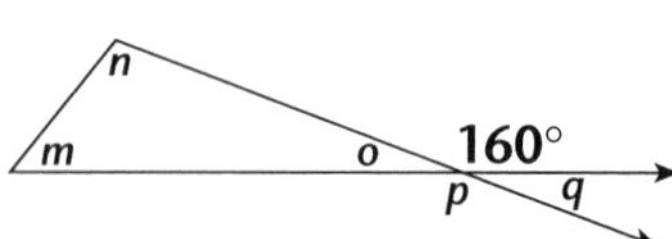

1. $\angle 1$
2. $\angle 2$
3. $\angle 3$
4. $\angle 4$
5. $m\angle x + m\angle y$
6. $m\angle z$
7. $m\angle x + m\angle y + m\angle z$
8. $m\angle o$
9. $m\angle p$
10. $m\angle q$
11. $m\angle m + m\angle n$
12. $m\angle m + m\angle n + m\angle o$

Exercise B Write *True* if the statement is true. Write *False* if the statement is false. Use the figure at the right.

13. $m\angle d = m\angle a + m\angle b$
14. $m\angle d = m\angle b + m\angle c$
15. $m\angle e = m\angle b + m\angle c$
16. $m\angle f = m\angle b + m\angle c$
17. $m\angle f = m\angle d$
18. $m\angle d + m\angle c = 180°$

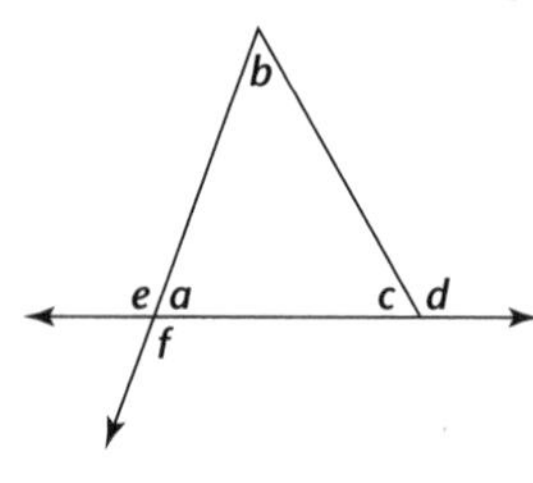

Exercise C Answer the following questions. Give reasons for each answer.

19. Suppose a triangle is equiangular. How many degrees are in each angle?

20. How many degrees are in each angle of a right isosceles triangle?

You can use your calculator to help find the missing angle measures.

EXAMPLE 4 $60° + 20° = y$
Press 60 [+] 20 [ENTER]. Display reads 80.

EXAMPLE 5 $80° + y = 180°$
Press 180 [−] 80 [ENTER]. Display reads 100.

Exercise D Find each unknown using a calculator.

21. $43° + 27° = y$

22. $92° + y = 180°$

23. $34° + 63° = y$

24. $21.5° + 34.5° = y$

25. $78° + y = 180°$

Polygons are everywhere. In a regular day, you see hundreds of polygons, probably without even realizing it. For example, traffic signs are often polygons. See the photograph for examples.

Lesson 10 Algebra Connection: Special Polynomial Products

Binomial

The sum or difference of two numbers or variables

You can picture the product of two factors as an area. You can picture the product of three factors as a volume. In this lesson, we will examine how to find products of two and three factors, and how to factor them. Factoring an expression can be helpful in finding the dimensions of a square or cube.

Remember: $ba = ab$

EXAMPLE 1 Find $(a + b)^2$.

$$
\begin{aligned}
(a + b)^2 &= (a + b)(a + b) \\
&= a(a + b) + b(a + b) \\
&= a^2 + ab + ba + b^2 \\
&= a^2 + 2ab + b^2
\end{aligned}
$$

	a	b
b	ab	b^2
a	a^2	ab

$(a + b)$ by $(a + b)$

Area = $(a + b)^2 = a^2 + 2ab + b^2$

A number or variable plus or minus another number or variable is a **binomial.**

You can use $(a + b)^2 = a^2 + 2ab + b^2$ as a model to square other binomials.

$$(n + 3)^2 = n^2 + 2(n)(3) + 3^2 = n^2 + 6n + 9$$

$$(x + 1)^2 = x^2 + 2(x)(1) + 1^2 = x^2 + 2x + 1$$

EXAMPLE 2 Find $(a + b)(a - b)$.

$$
\begin{aligned}
(a + b)(a - b) &= a(a - b) + b(a - b) \\
&= a^2 - ab + ab - b^2 \\
&= a^2 - b^2
\end{aligned}
$$

You can use $a^2 - b^2 = (a + b)(a - b)$ as a model to factor the difference of any two squares.

$x^2 - y^2 = (x + y)(x - y)$

$x^2 - 9 = (x + 3)(x - 3)$

	$(a - b)$	b
b	$b(a - b)$	b^2
$(a - b)$	$a(a - b)$	

Side lengths: a (left), a (bottom)

$a^2 - b^2$ = shaded area
$= a(a - b) + b(a - b)$
$= (a + b)(a - b)$

EXAMPLE 3 Find $(a + b)^3$.

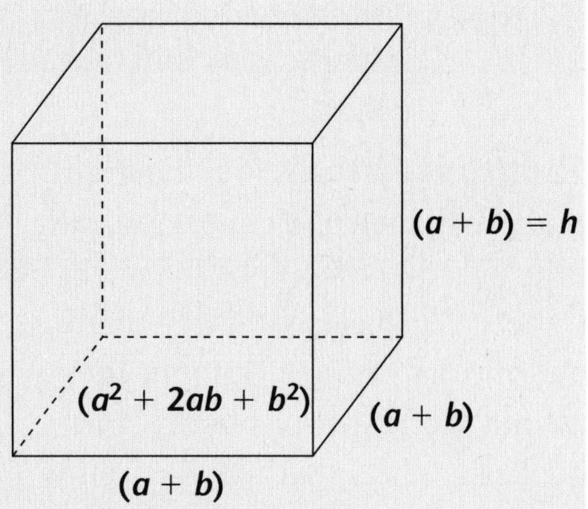

$$\begin{aligned}(a + b)^3 &= (a + b)[(a + b)(a + b)] \\ &= (a + b)(a^2 + 2ab + b^2) \\ &= a(a^2 + 2ab + b^2) + b(a^2 + 2ab + b^2) \\ &= a^3 + 2a^2b + ab^2 + a^2b + 2ab^2 + b^3 \\ &= a^3 + 3a^2b + 3ab^2 + b^3\end{aligned}$$

You can use $(a + b)^3 = a^3 + 3a^2b + 3ab^2 + b^3$ as a model for other cubes.

$(x + y)^3 = x^3 + 3x^2y + 3xy^2 + y^3$

$$\begin{aligned}(a + 2)^3 &= a^3 + 3a^2(2) + 3a(2)^2 + (2)^3 \\ &= a^3 + 6a^2 + 12a + 8\end{aligned}$$

$$\begin{aligned}\textbf{Vol.} &= (h)(\text{area of base}) \\ &= (a + b)(a^2 + 2ab + b^2) \\ &= a^3 + 3a^2b + 3ab^2 + b^3\end{aligned}$$

Exercise A Find each product. Compare your answer to the pattern in Example 1.

1. $(x + y)^2$ **2.** $(x + 3)^2$ **3.** $(5 + x)^2$ **4.** $(a + c)^2$

5. $(9 + y)^2$ **6.** $(c + d)^2$ **7.** $(a + 2)^2$ **8.** $(a - b)^2$

Exercise B Find each product. Compare your answer to the pattern in Example 2.

9. $(x + a)(x - a)$ **10.** $(3 + a)(3 - a)$

11. $(y - z)(y + z)$ **12.** $(x + 5)(x - 5)$

Exercise C Factor.

13. $c^2 - d^2$ **14.** $9 - x^2$ **15.** $w^2 - z^2$ **16.** $y^2 - 16$

Exercise D Find each product. Compare your answer to the pattern in Example 3.

17. $(c + d)^3$ **18.** $(w + z)^3$ **19.** $(x + 5)^3$ **20.** $(y + 4)^3$

TRY THIS What is the volume of a crate with dimensions $x + 1$, $x + 2$, and $x + 3$?

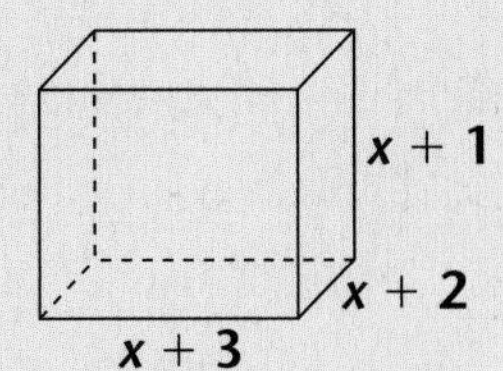

Application

Tangram Pictures The tangram puzzle originated in China and was introduced to the rest of the world by traders. The pieces were first made out of ivory or bone, but now they are made of paper or plastic. Many books have been written illustrating patterns that can be made with the seven pieces of a tangram. One book contains over six hundred patterns.

The tangram puzzle consists of seven shapes: five triangles, a square, and a parallelogram.

EXAMPLE 1 The seven shapes can be combined to form a variety of figures. One basic shape is a square, like the one shown at the right.

You can make your own set of tangrams by tracing and cutting out the shapes shown above.

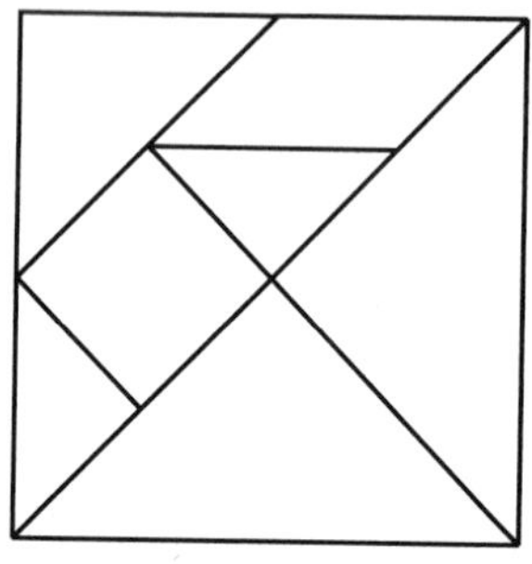

Exercise Form each of the following polygons using the tangram pieces. Sketch how you placed the shapes together. Compare your sketches with your classmates'. Find out if there was more than one way to form the polygon.

1. a rectangle using five shapes
2. a trapezoid using five shapes
3. a hexagon using six shapes
4. a pentagon using four shapes
5. Have some fun with tangrams! See if you can use all of seven shapes to form the cat, rabbit, and ship shown. Then see what other interesting figures you can form using all seven tangram shapes.

Chapter 5 REVIEW

Write the letter of the correct answer.

1. Given: ΔABC contains two equal sides. What type of triangle is ΔABC?

   A isosceles
   B equilateral
   C obtuse
   D right

2. ΔMNP contains a 60° and a 90° angle. What type of triangle is ΔMNP?

   A acute
   B equilateral
   C obtuse
   D right

3. *XYZW* is a rectangle. Which statement must be true?

   A *XYZW* is a parallelogram.
   B *XYZW* is a rhombus.
   C *XYZW* is a square.
   D *XYZW* is a trapezoid.

4. Which statement is false?

   A All squares are parallelograms.
   B All squares are rhombuses.
   C All parallelograms are rhombuses.
   D All rhombuses are parallelograms.

5. What is the measure of $\angle G$ in the triangle to the right?

   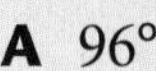

   A 96°
   B 108°
   C 118°
   D 138°

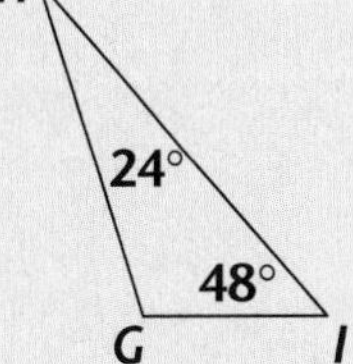

6. *ABCD* is a trapezoid with $\overline{AB} \parallel \overline{DC}$. Which statement must be true?

   A $m\angle A + m\angle B = 180°$
   B $m\angle A + m\angle D = 180°$
   C $m\angle A = m\angle B$
   D $m\angle A = m\angle C$

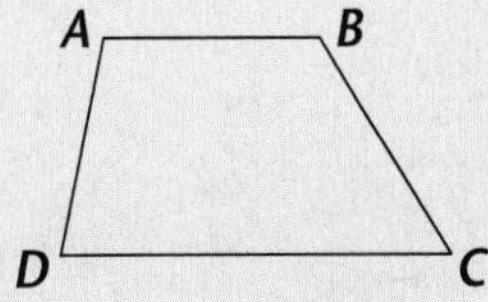

Use the information given to supply the angle measures.

Example: Find m∠z
Solution: $z + 170° = 180°$; $z = 10°$

Given: $ABCD$, a rectangle with diagonal $\overline{BD}$ and $m\angle 1 = 35°$

7. $m\angle 4$

8. $m\angle 1 + m\angle 2$

9. $m\angle 2$

10. $m\angle 3 + m\angle 4$

11. $m\angle 3$

12. $m\angle 4 + m\angle 2 + m\angle BAD$

13. $m\angle BCD + m\angle CDB + m\angle DBC$

Given: triangle XYZ, line $\ell \parallel m$

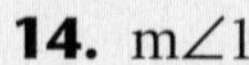

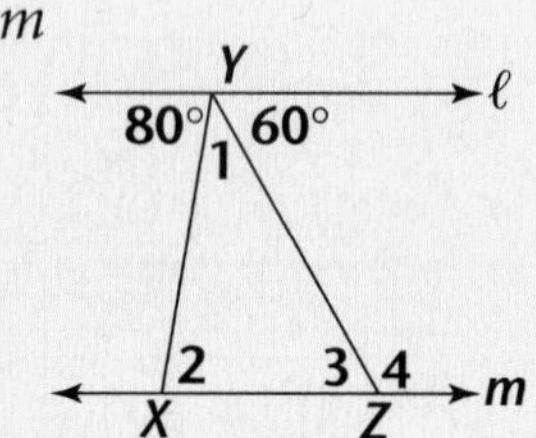

14. $m\angle 1$

15. $m\angle 2$

16. $m\angle 3$

17. $m\angle 4$

Use the Angle Sum Theorem or its corollary to find the measures.

Example: Find x.

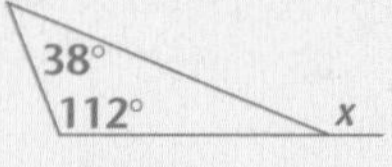

Solution: By the Corollary to the Angle Sum Theorem, $x = 38° + 112°$ So, $x = 150°$

18. Find $m\angle k$.

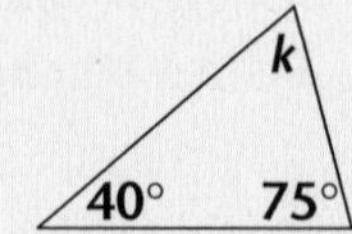

19. Find z.

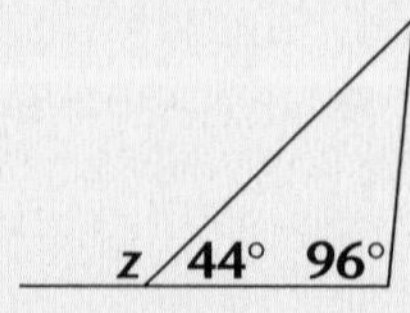

20. Find *x*.

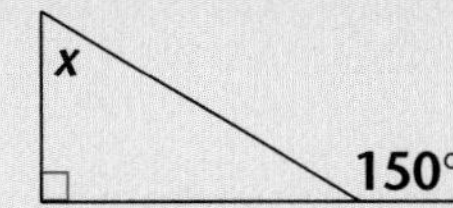

21. Find m∠1 + m∠2.

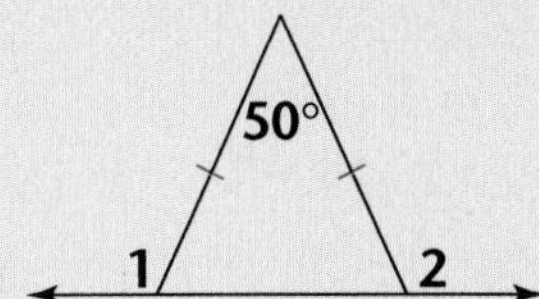

Complete the following constructions on a separate sheet of paper. Use only a straightedge and compass.

22. Construct equilateral triangle *ABC* in which each side has the length shown to the right.

23. Construct any right triangle. Label the right angle *R* and the other two angles *S* and *T*. Construct an angle bisector for angle *R*.

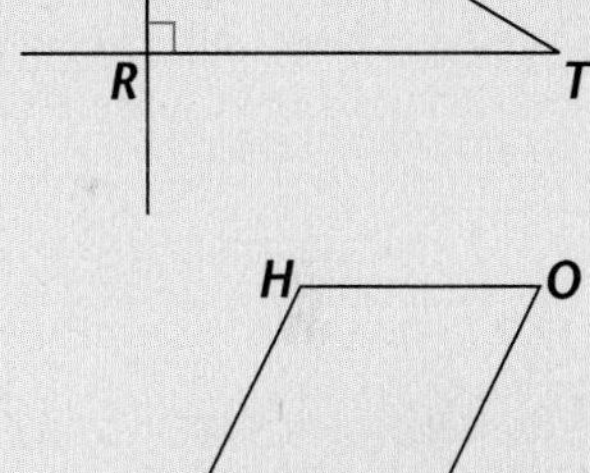

24. Draw a rhombus *RHOM* as shown. Construct an altitude from *O*.

25. Draw any obtuse triangle and label the obtuse angle *D* and the triangle *DEF*. Construct the three medians of the triangle.

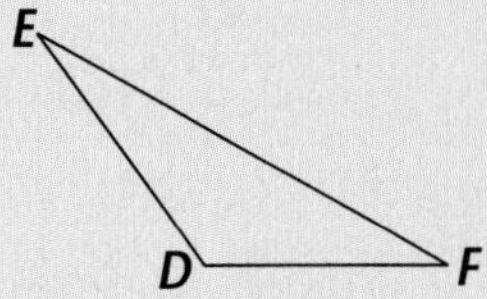

Test-Taking Tip

Before you begin a test, look it over quickly. Do the easier problems first to leave time for the more difficult ones. Try to set aside enough time to complete each section.

Chapter

Congruent Triangles and Transformations

The wind ceases to blow, and the ripples stop shaking the surface of the water. A still lake reflects the buildings on its shore like a mirror. Turn the photograph upside-down and you cannot tell the original barn and silos from their mirror images. A figure and its reflection match each other exactly. They have the same shape and are the same size. In geometry, this is called congruence.

In Chapter 6, you will learn about congruent triangles and transformations.

Goals for Learning

- To use the SAS Postulate to identify corresponding parts in triangles
- To construct triangles using SSS information
- To identify congruent triangles based on SSS and ASA structures
- To identify angle and side characteristics of congruent triangles
- To make generalizations about reflections and lines of reflection
- To identify lines of symmetry in reflections
- To map translations in a coordinate plane
- To describe and graph rotations

Lesson 1 Corresponding Parts: SAS Postulate

Congruent $\cong$

Having the exact same size and shape

Congruent angles

Angles that have equal measures

Congruent segments

Segments that have the same length

Congruent triangles

Triangles whose corresponding angles and sides are congruent

Corresponding angles

Pairs of angles in similar positions

The ' mark is used to show that two items are related. *A*' is read "*A* prime" and $\overline{A'B'}$ is read "segment *A* prime *B* prime."

In geometry, it is possible to know that one figure is equal to another without measuring either one. The word **congruent** is used to describe angles whose measures are equal, sides with equal lengths, and polygons whose angles and sides are equal to one another. The symbol for congruent is $\cong$.

Congruent angles have the same measure.

$\angle A$ and $\angle A'$ are congruent angles.

$\angle A \cong \angle A'$ and $m\angle A = m\angle A'$

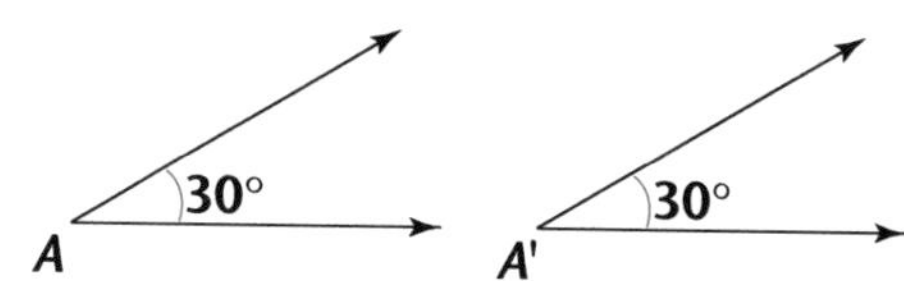

Congruent segments have the same length.

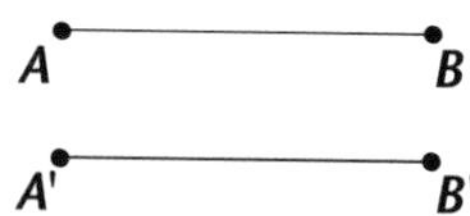

$\overline{AB}$ and $\overline{A'B'}$ are congruent; the length of $\overline{AB}$ equals the length of $\overline{A'B'}$. We can write this as $\overline{AB} \cong \overline{A'B'}$ and $AB = A'B'$.

Congruent triangles are triangles whose **corresponding angles** and sides are congruent. The symbol $\leftrightarrow$ means "corresponds to."

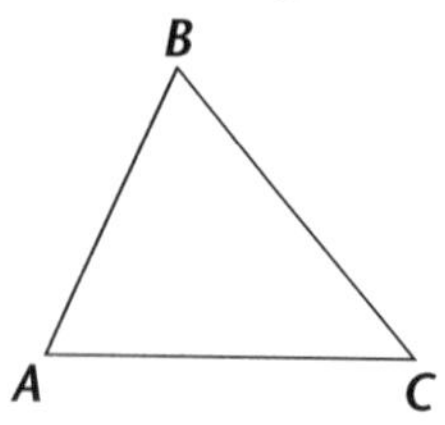

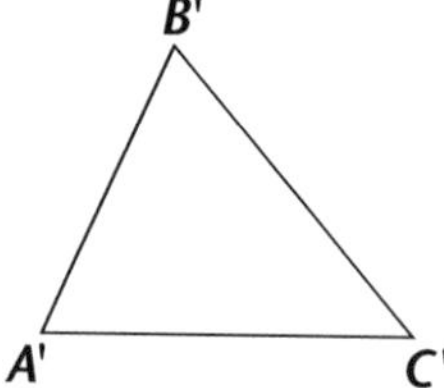

Corresponding Sides	Corresponding Angles
$\overline{AB} \leftrightarrow \overline{A'B'}$	$\angle A \leftrightarrow \angle A'$
$\overline{BC} \leftrightarrow \overline{B'C'}$	$\angle B \leftrightarrow \angle B'$
$\overline{AC} \leftrightarrow \overline{A'C'}$	$\angle C \leftrightarrow \angle C'$

$$\Delta ABC \cong \Delta A'B'C'$$

In congruent triangles, the corresponding angles have equal measures, and the corresponding sides have equal lengths.

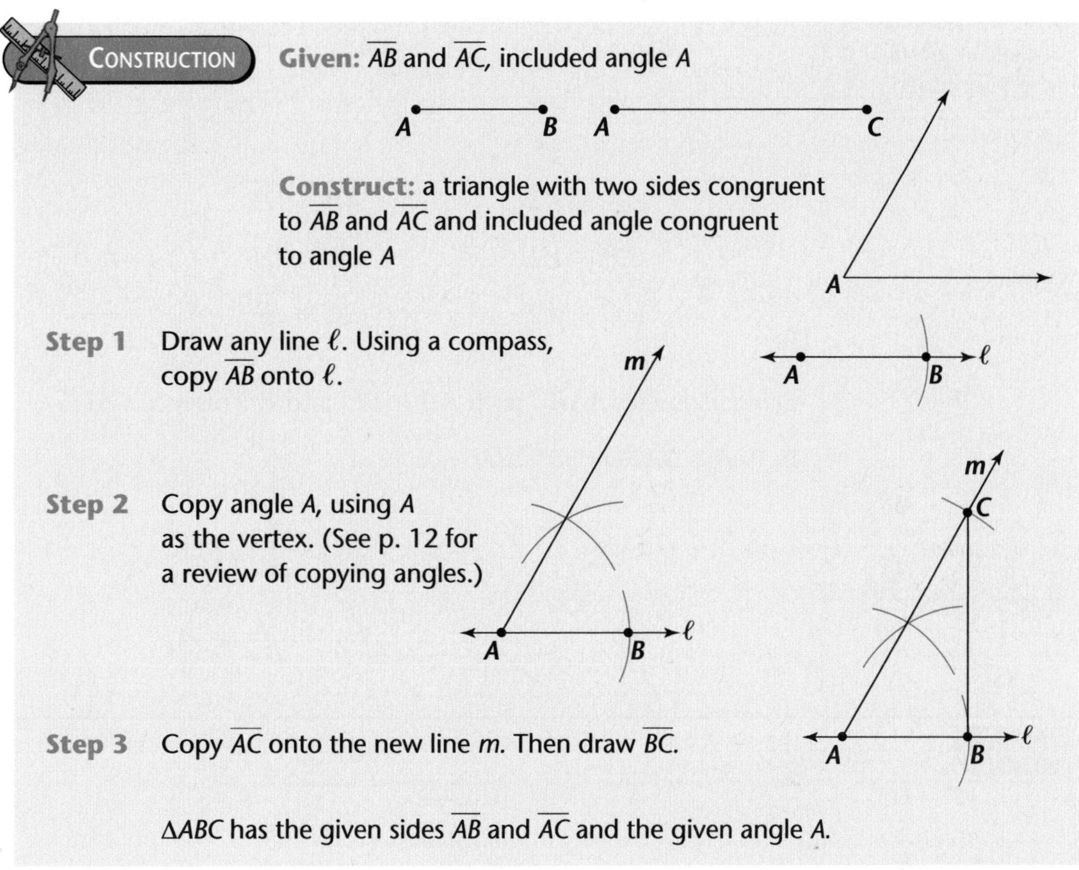

Note that ΔABC above is the only triangle you can construct using the given sides and the angle they form. If you are given a side of an angle, the angle, and the second side of the angle (abbreviated SAS) of a triangle, then there is only one possible construction for a triangle.

Because there is only one possible construction of a triangle given the SAS, all triangles using the same SAS will be congruent. This idea is expressed by the following postulate.

> **SAS (Side-Angle-Side) Postulate:**
> If two sides and the included angle of one triangle are congruent to the corresponding two sides and included angle of a second triangle, then the triangles are congruent.

Ticks (|) and arcs (◝) indicate which sides and angles are equal to one another.

If you know that $\Delta ABC \cong \Delta DEF$ by the SAS Postulate, then you can use the SAS Postulate, as well as the markings on the triangles, to identify which sides and angles are congruent.

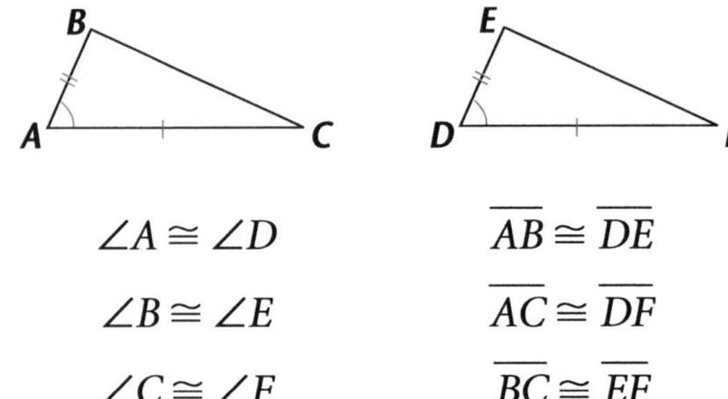

$\angle A \cong \angle D$	$\overline{AB} \cong \overline{DE}$
$\angle B \cong \angle E$	$\overline{AC} \cong \overline{DF}$
$\angle C \cong \angle F$	$\overline{BC} \cong \overline{EF}$

Given: isosceles ΔABC with $\overline{AB} \cong \overline{BC}$, and $\overline{BD}$ bisects $\angle ABC$

To Prove: $\Delta ABD \cong \Delta CBD$

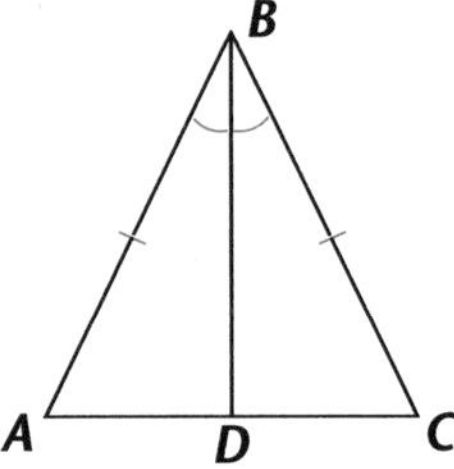

Proof

Statement	Reason
1. $\overline{AB} \cong \overline{BC}$	**1.** Given.
2. $\overline{BD}$ bisects $\angle ABC$	**2.** Given.
3. $\angle ABD \cong \angle DBC$	**3.** Definition of angle bisector.
4. $\overline{BD} \cong \overline{BD}$	**4.** Property of equality, any quantity is equal to itself.
5. $\therefore \Delta ABD \cong \Delta CBD$	**5.** SAS Postulate; side, angle, and side of $\Delta ABD \cong$ side, angle, and side of ΔCBD.

Given: G is the midpoint of $\overline{FI}$ and $\overline{EH}$

To Prove: $\Delta EFG \cong \Delta HIG$

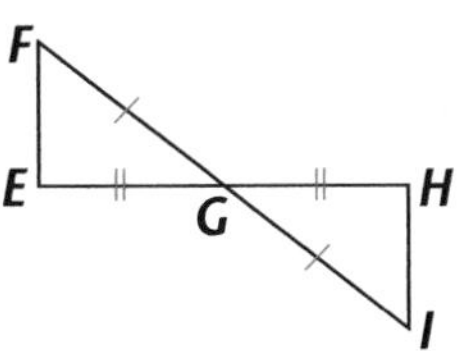

PROOF

Statement	Reason
1. G is the midpoint of $\overline{FI}$ and $\overline{EH}$	1. Given.
2. $\overline{EG} \cong \overline{GH}$ and $\overline{FG} \cong \overline{GI}$	2. Definition of midpoint.
3. $\angle EGF \cong \angle IGH$	3. Vertical angles are equal.
4. $\therefore \Delta EFG \cong \Delta HIG$	4. SAS Postulate; side, angle, and side of $\Delta EFG \cong$ side, angle, and side of ΔHIG.

EXAMPLE 1 $\Delta UVW \cong \Delta XYZ$ by SAS
Which sides of the given triangles are congruent?

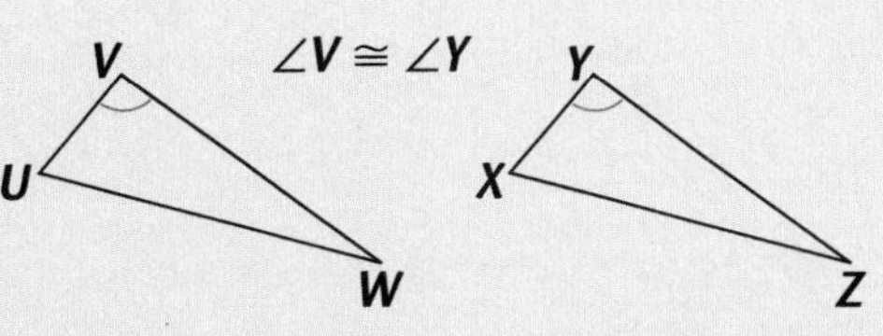

The segments that form the congruent angles are congruent.
$\overline{VU} \cong \overline{YX}$ and $\overline{VW} \cong \overline{YZ}$

EXAMPLE 2 $\Delta KLM \cong \Delta QRP$ by SAS
The markings show the congruent angles and one pair of congruent sides. What remaining pair of sides must be congruent to satisfy the SAS Postulate?

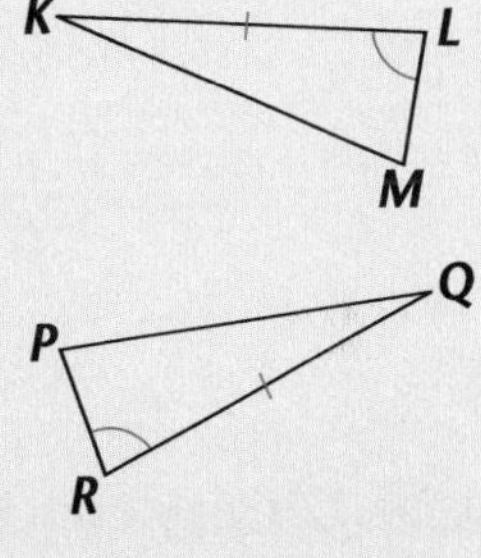

The congruent sides must be the second side of the congruent angles. Because $\angle L \cong \angle R$ and $\overline{KL} \cong \overline{QR}$, then $\overline{LM} \cong \overline{RP}$.

Geodesic domes, like the one at right, use congruent equilateral triangles to support their structure. This dome in the Science World Museum in Vancouver, Canada, is used as a large-screen theater. Geodesic domes are also used as greenhouses, aircraft hangers, and even homes.

Exercise A Each pair of triangles is congruent by SAS. List the given congruent angles and sides for each pair of triangles.

1.

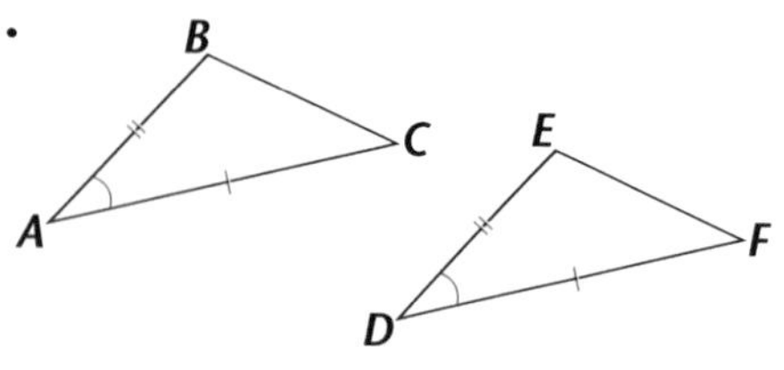

2.

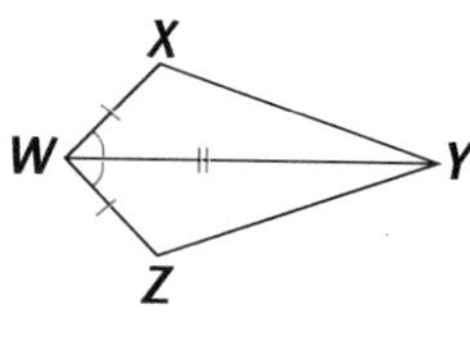

Exercise B Each pair of triangles has a pair of congruent angles. What pairs of sides must be congruent to satisfy the SAS Postulate?

3.

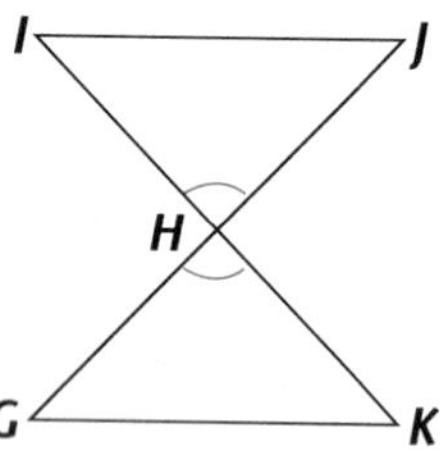

4.

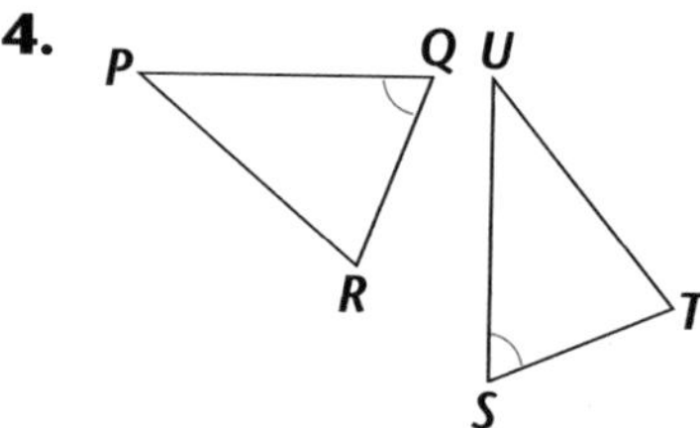

5.

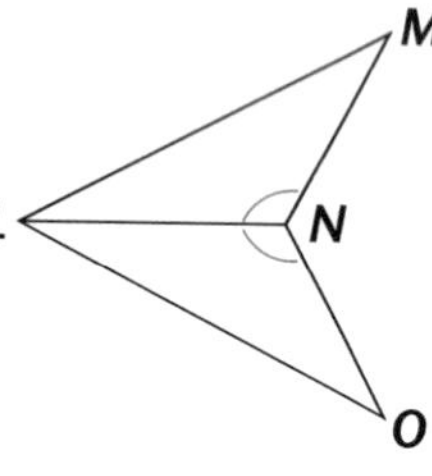

6.

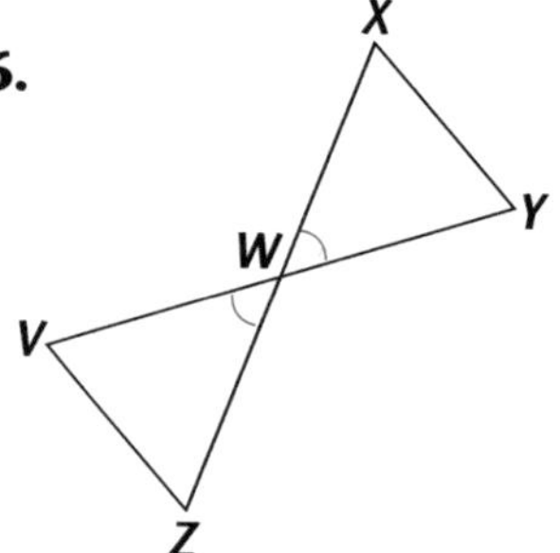

Exercise C Copy each proof. Fill in the missing steps.

Given: ΔABC, ΔADC, $\overline{AC}$ bisects $\angle BCD$, and $\overline{CD} \cong \overline{CB}$

To Prove: $\Delta ABC \cong \Delta ADC$

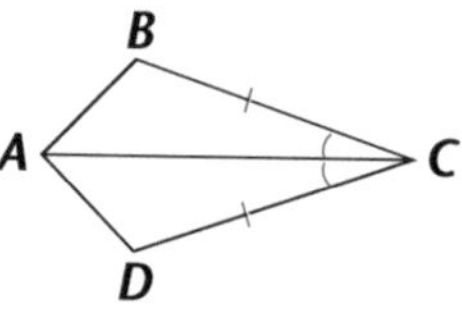

PROOF

Statement	Reason
1. $\overline{CD} \cong \overline{CB}$	1. **7.** ____
2. $\overline{AC}$ bisects $\angle BCD$	2. **8.** ____
3. $\angle ACD \cong$ **9.** ____	3. Definition of angle bisector.
4. $\overline{AC} \cong \overline{AC}$	4. **10.** ____
5. $\therefore \Delta ABC \cong \Delta ADC$	5. SAS Postulate; side, angle, and side of $\Delta ABC \cong$ side, angle, and side of ΔADC.

Given: right triangles ΔEFG and ΔHIK, $\overline{EF} \cong \overline{HI}$, and $\overline{FG} \cong \overline{IK}$

To Prove: $\Delta EFG \cong \Delta HIK$

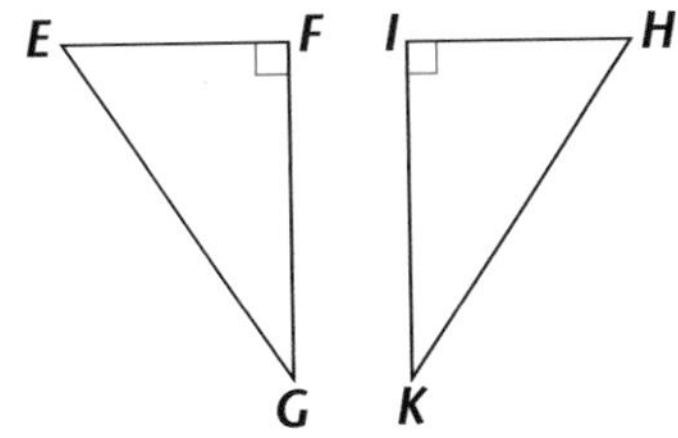

PROOF Statement	Reason
1. $\overline{EF} \cong \overline{HI}$ and $\overline{FG} \cong \overline{IK}$	1. **11.**
2. $m\angle EFG = 90°$, $m\angle HIK = 90°$	2. **12.**
3. **13.**	3. Things equal to the same thing are equal to each other.
4. $\therefore \Delta EFG \cong \Delta HIK$	4. **14.**

PROBLEM SOLVING

Exercise D Find the answer to the following problem.

15. Tamisha wants to swim across the widest part of the pond, but first she wants to know the distance she must swim. She places a marker at point *X*. She moves to point *A* and walks 25 paces in a straight line to *X*. At *X*, she continues in a straight line for another 25 paces. She marks that point *A*'.

Tamisha then moves to point *B*. Walking in a straight line, she takes 35 paces to reach point *X*. She walks an additional 35 paces in a straight line and marks the endpoint *B*'. She walks the distance from *B*' to *A*' and finds it is 40 paces. What is the distance across the pond from point *A* to point *B*? How do you know?

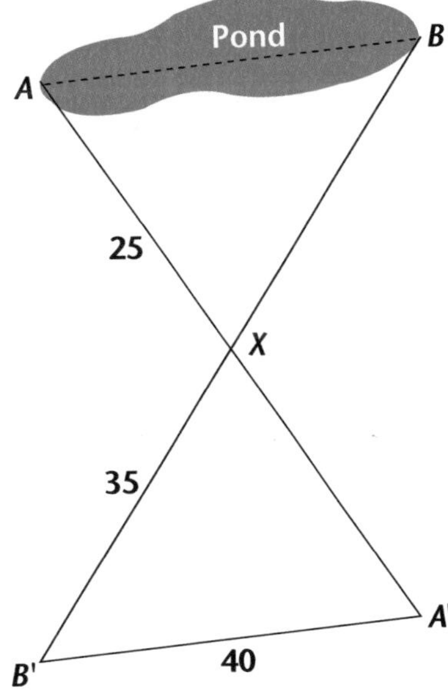

Lesson 2 SSS Construction and Triangle Inequality

Suppose you are given three sides of a triangle, *a*, *b*, and *c*. You can use a compass and a straightedge to construct the triangle. Because you are given three sides of the triangle, this construction is called the SSS construction.

Given: segments *a*, *b*, and *c*

Construct: a triangle with sides congruent to *a*, *b*, and *c*

a

b

c

Step 1 Draw any line ℓ. Using your compass, copy side *c* onto ℓ. Label the endpoints *A* and *B*.

Step 2 Draw an arc using *A* as the center and *b* as the radius.

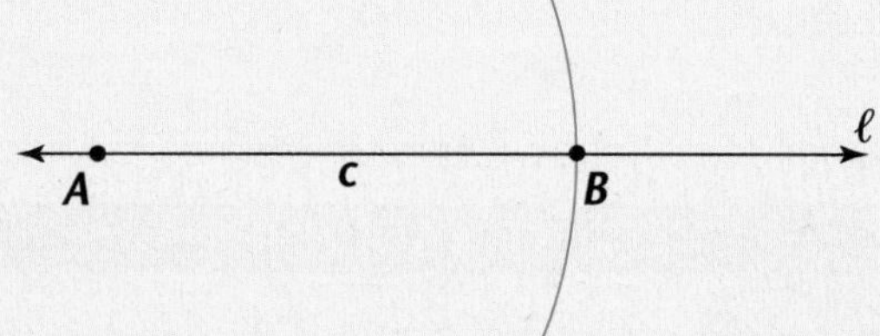

Step 3 Draw an arc using *B* as the center and *a* as the radius. Label the point where the arcs intersect *C*.

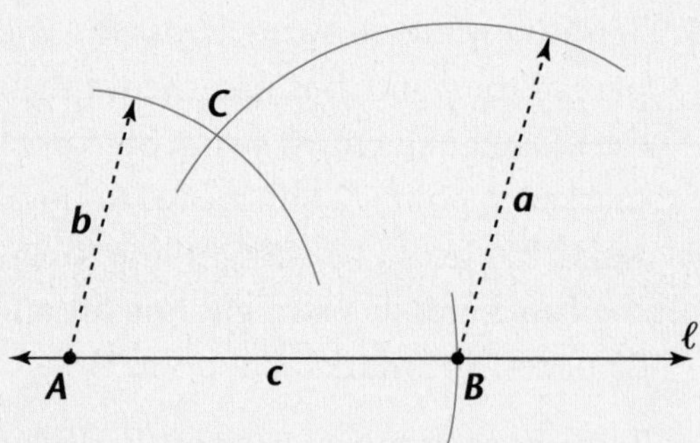

Step 4 Draw segments *AC* and *BC*.

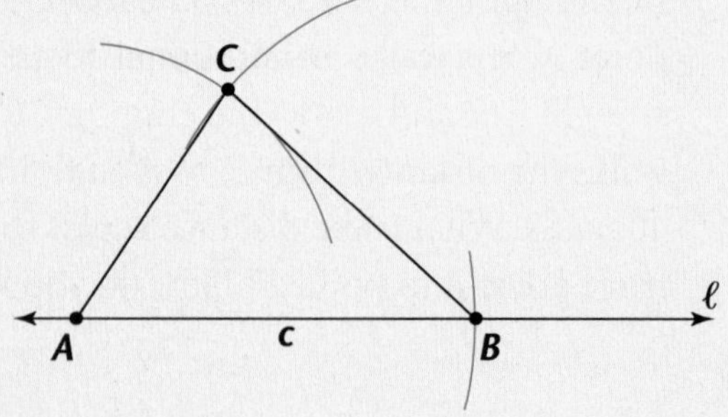

Triangle *ABC* has sides *a*, *b*, and *c* equal to the given segment lengths.

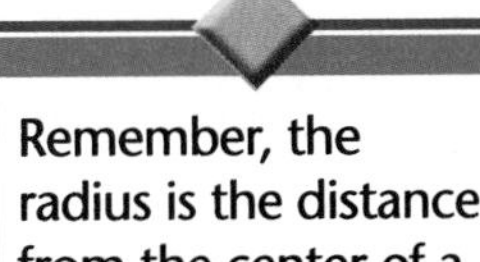

Remember, the radius is the distance from the center of a circle to the circle.

There is a general rule for naming the sides and angles of a triangle: side *a* is opposite angle *A*, side *b* is opposite angle *B*, and side *c* is opposite angle *C*.

Although you were able to use SSS to construct triangle *ABC* in the construction, you cannot use *any* three segments to construct a triangle.

EXAMPLE 1 **Given:** segments *a, b,* and *c*

Construct: a triangle with sides congruent to *a, b,* and *c*

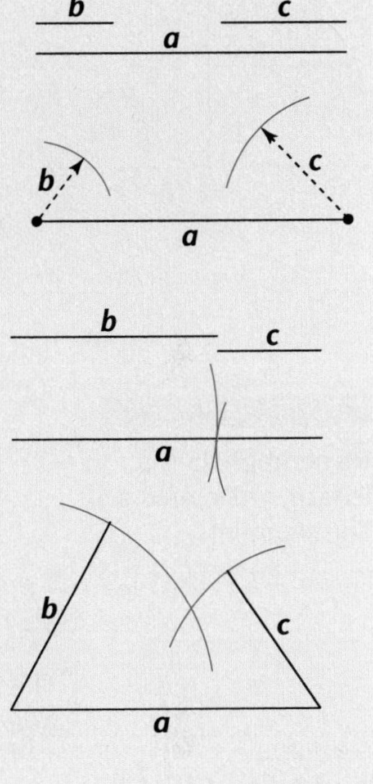

The arcs drawn from *A* and *B* do not intersect because the sum of the lengths of segments $b + c$ is less than the length of *a*. Therefore, no triangle can be constructed.

Suppose that $b + c = a$. In this case, shown at right, the arcs intersect on *a*, so again no triangle can be constructed.

Therefore, we can conclude that the sum of lengths $b + c$ must be greater than length *a* in order to construct a triangle.

Conclusion: The sum of the lengths of any two sides of a triangle must be greater than the length of the third side.

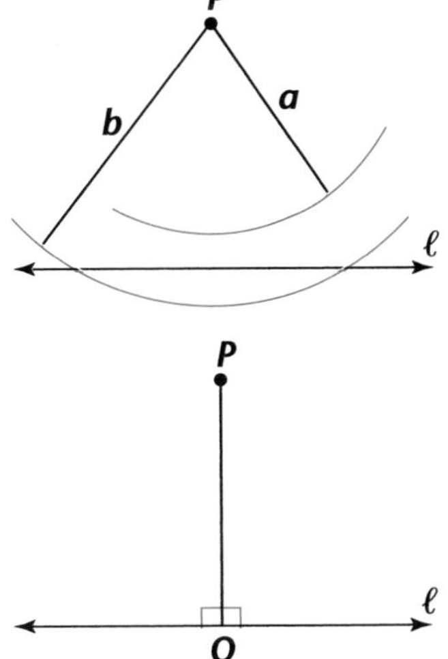

In order to formally prove this conclusion, we first need to learn about the shortest distance to a line.

Given a point *P* not on line ℓ, what is the shortest distance from *P* to ℓ?

Look at the first diagram of *P* and ℓ to the left. Radius *a* is too short, radius *b* is too long. The shortest distance is a perpendicular from *P* to ℓ. If $\overline{PQ} \perp \ell$, then *PQ* is the shortest distance from *P* to ℓ. This leads us to the Shortest Distance Theorem, which will be taken as true without proof.

Hypotenuse

The side opposite the right angle in a right triangle

Shortest Distance Theorem (6.2.1):

The perpendicular segment from a point to a line is the shortest segment from that point to the line. The length of the perpendicular segment is called the *distance* from the point to the line.

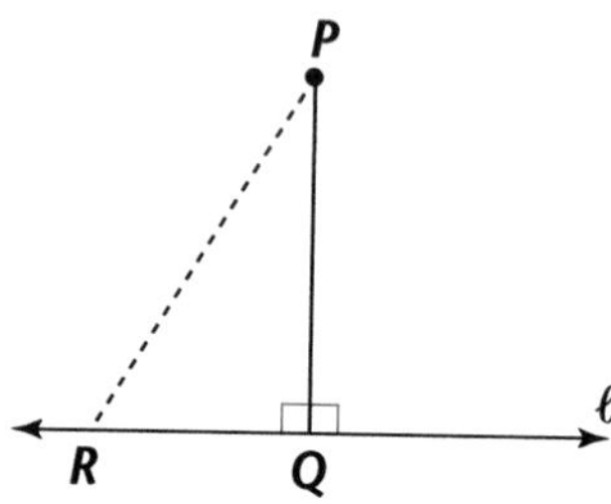

$PQ =$ shortest distance from P to ℓ.

$PR > PQ$, PR is *not* the shortest distance.

Likewise, $RQ =$ shortest distance from R to $\overline{PQ}$.

$PR > RQ$, PR is *not* the shortest distance.

Be sure you recognize that ΔPQR is a right triangle and that $\overline{PR}$, opposite the right angle, is the longest side of the triangle.

Remember, AB is a length, while $\overline{AB}$ is a line segment.

In a right triangle, the side opposite the right angle is the longest side of the triangle and is called the **hypotenuse.**

Now we have the tools we need to prove the Triangle Inequality Theorem.

Triangle Inequality Theorem (6.2.2):

The sum of the lengths of any two sides of a triangle must be greater than the length of the third side.

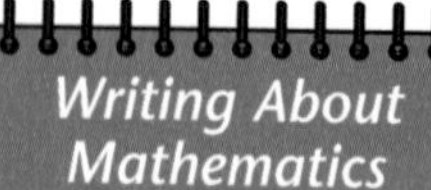

$\overline{BD}$ is an altitude from angle B to side $\overline{AC}$ of a triangle.
What can you say about $\overline{BD}$ and the distance to $\overline{AC}$?

Given: ΔABC, any triangle

To Prove: $AC + BC > BA$
$AB + AC > BC$
$AB + BC > AC$

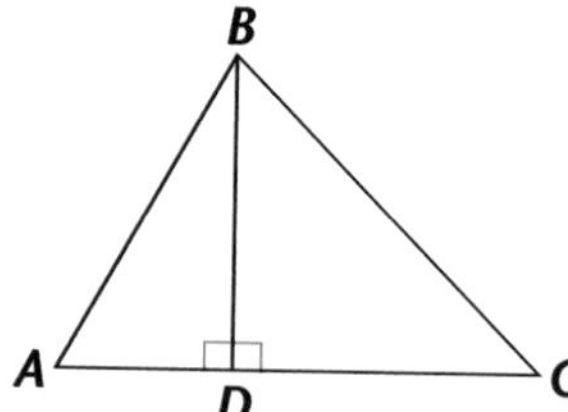

Statement	Reason
1. ΔABC	1. Given.
2. Construct $\overline{BD}$, a segment perpendicular to $\overline{AC}$ from B	2. Construction of a perpendicular to a line.
3. AD is the shortest distance from A to $\overline{BD}$, which means $AB > AD$ and CD is the shortest distance from C to $\overline{BD}$, which means $BC > DC$	3. Shortest Distance Theorem.
4. $AB > AD$ $BC > DC$ $AB + BC > AD + DC$	4. Addition.
5. $\therefore AB + BC > AC$.	5. Substitution.

Algebra Review

In the proof, Step 4 is related to Euclid's Axiom 2 (see Chapter 2, Lesson 4). Notice that Axiom 2 is a property of equations. The axiom used here is a property of inequalities.

Note that it is enough to prove $AB + BC > AC$. You can prove the other two cases by relabeling the vertices. You can use this theorem to help you determine if any three given sides can form a triangle.

Example 2 Can three segments of lengths 3 inches, 4 inches, and 5 inches form a triangle?

$3 + 4 > 5$ true

$3 + 5 > 4$ true

$4 + 5 > 3$ true

The segments satisfy the Triangle Inequality Theorem and so such a triangle exists.

Example 3 Can three segments of lengths 10 ft, 15 ft, and 4 ft form a triangle?

$10 + 4 > 15$ false

The segments do not satisfy the Triangle Inequality Theorem and so no such triangle exists.

Estimation Activity

Estimate: Could a triangle have sides 8, 10, and 6?

Solution: Add the smallest two lengths, 8 and 6, to see if their sum is larger that the length of the third side. If so, the lengths should be able to form a triangle. In this case, $8 + 6 = 14$, and $14 > 10$, so the lengths 8, 10, and 6 form a triangle.

Exercise A Tell whether you can construct a triangle with the given sides. Answer *yes* or *no*. Explain your answer.

1. a b c

2. a b c

3. a b c

4.

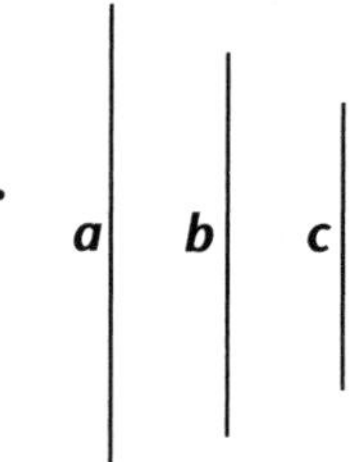

5. $a = 4, b = 7, c = 10$

6. $a = 8, b = 2, c = 5$

7. $a = 9, b = 11, c = 12$

8. $a = 9, b = 12, c = 15$

9. $a = 3, b = 3, c = 5$

10. $a = 6, b = 7, c = 14$

Exercise B Write >, <, or = to make each statement true. Refer to the figures below.

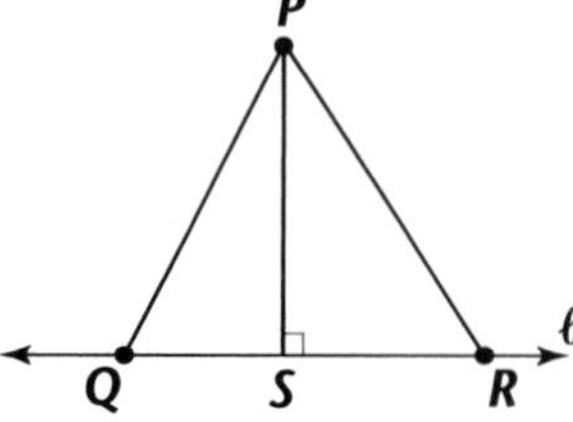

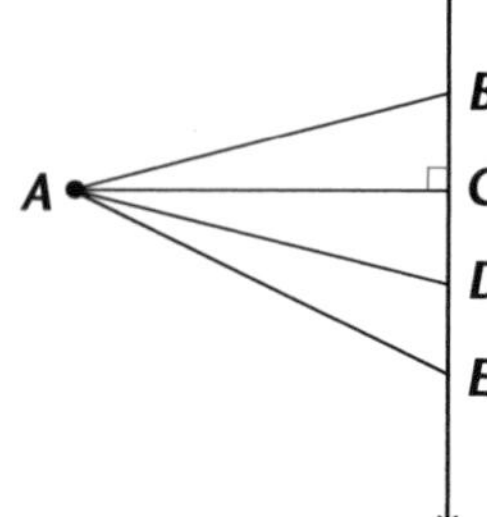

11. PQ ___ shortest distance from P to ℓ

12. PR ___ shortest distance from P to ℓ

13. PS ___ shortest distance from P to ℓ

14. AB ___ shortest distance from A to m

15. AC ___ shortest distance from A to m

16. AD ___ shortest distance from A to m

17. AE ___ shortest distance from A to m

CONSTRUCTION

Exercise C Construct each triangle using the given side lengths. Use only a compass and a straightedge.

18. a b c

19. p q r

20. x y z

Lesson 3 SSS and ASA Congruencies

You've shown that if you are given any three segments that satisfy the Triangle Inequality Theorem, you can construct a triangle whose sides are congruent to the segments. In addition, any other triangles that have those same sides are congruent to each other.

> **SSS (Side-Side-Side) Postulate:**
> If three sides of a triangle are congruent to three sides of a second triangle, then the triangles are congruent.

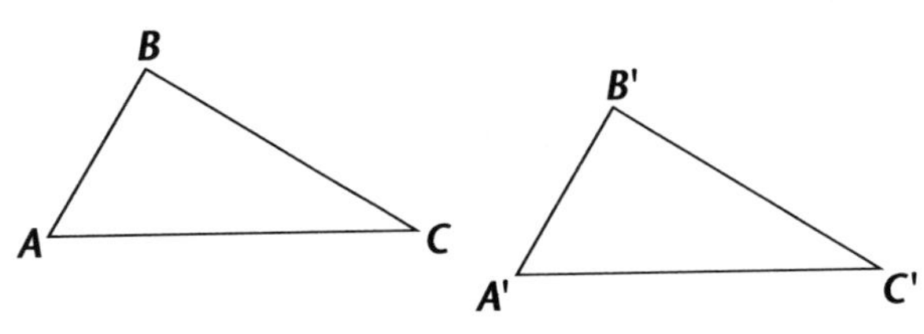

This means you now have two ways—SAS and SSS—to show that one triangle is congruent to another. There is a third way—angle-side-angle or ASA. The following construction is an example of ASA congruency.

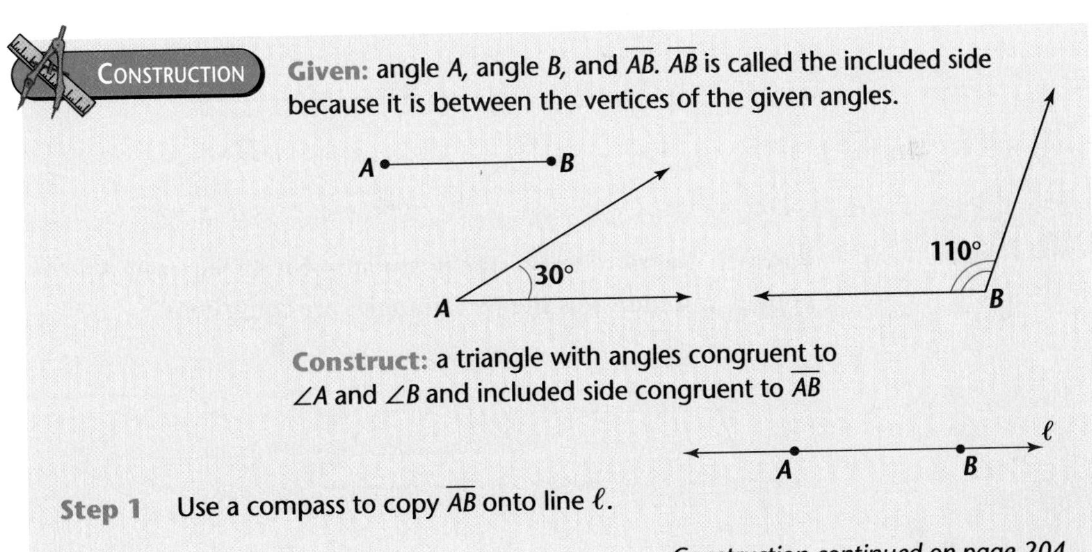

Construction

Given: angle A, angle B, and $\overline{AB}$. $\overline{AB}$ is called the included side because it is between the vertices of the given angles.

Construct: a triangle with angles congruent to $\angle A$ and $\angle B$ and included side congruent to $\overline{AB}$

Step 1 Use a compass to copy $\overline{AB}$ onto line ℓ.

Construction continued on page 204

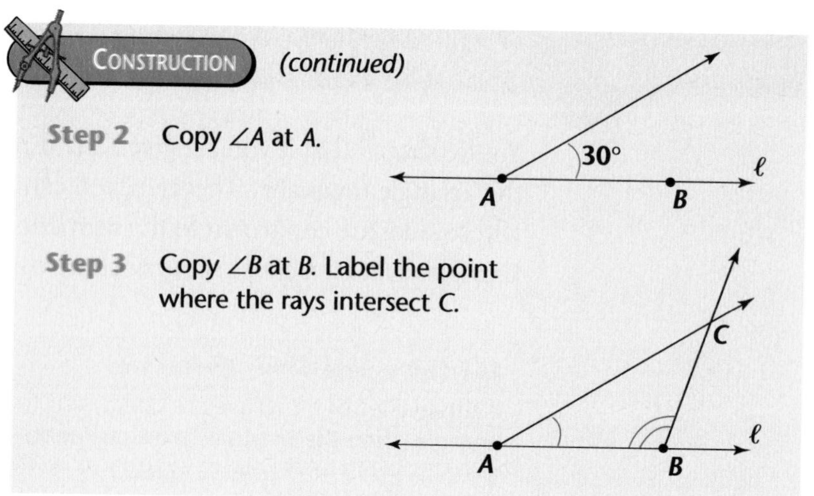

ΔABC has $\angle A$ and $\angle B$ as given and $\overline{AB}$, the included side, as its base. Any triangle using the same angle, side, and angle—ASA—will be congruent to ΔABC. This leads to the following postulate.

ASA (Angle-Side-Angle) Postulate:
If two angles and the included side of a triangle are congruent to the corresponding angles and included side of a second triangle, then the triangles are congruent.

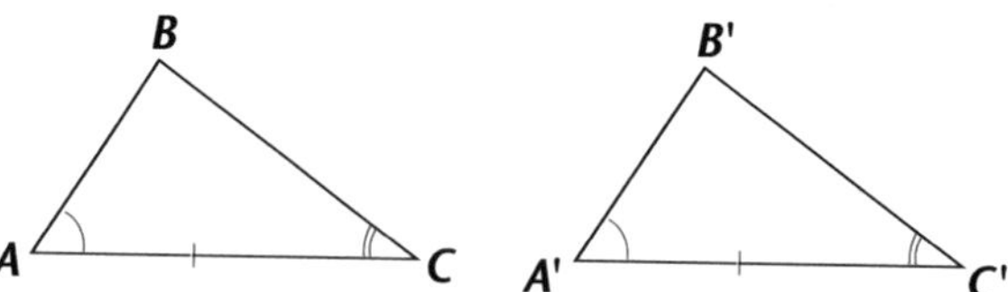

For each diagram below, one postulate—SAS, SSS, or ASA—applies and indicates the two triangles are congruent.

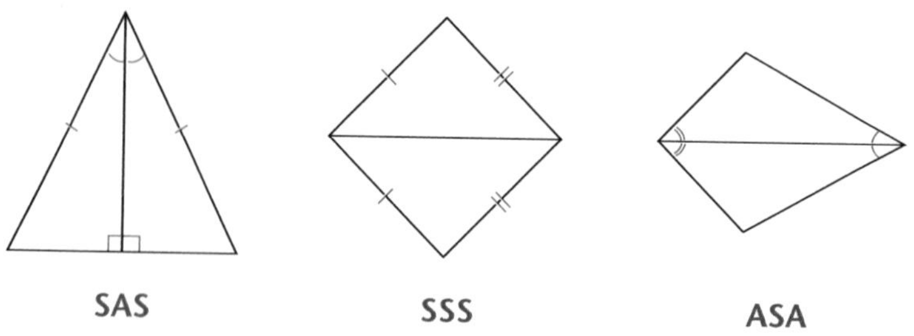

Given: quadrilateral $ABCD$ with diagonal $\overline{BD}$ that bisects angles B and D

To Prove: $\Delta ABD \cong \Delta CBD$

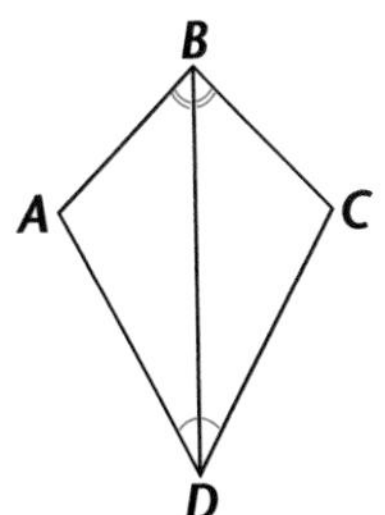

PROOF

Statement	Reason
1. $\overline{BD}$ bisects $\angle D$ $\overline{BD}$ bisects $\angle B$	1. Given.
2. $\angle ABD \cong \angle CBD$ $\angle ADB \cong \angle CDB$	2. Definition of angle bisector.
3. $\overline{BD} \cong \overline{BD}$	3. Property of equality, any quantity is equal to itself.
4. $\therefore \Delta ABD \cong \Delta CBD$	4. ASA Postulate; angle, side, and angle of ΔABD is congruent to an angle, side, and angle of ΔCBD.

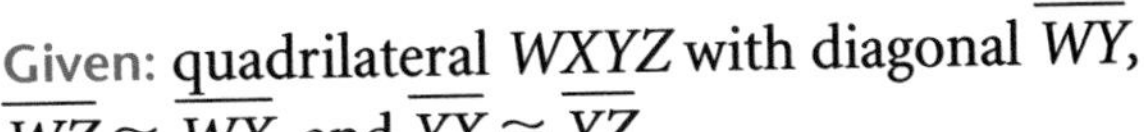

Given: quadrilateral $WXYZ$ with diagonal $\overline{WY}$, $\overline{WZ} \cong \overline{WX}$, and $\overline{YX} \cong \overline{YZ}$

To Prove: $\Delta WXY \cong \Delta WZY$

PROOF

Statement	Reason
1. $\overline{WZ} \cong \overline{WX}$ and $\overline{YX} \cong \overline{YZ}$	1. Given.
2. $\overline{WY} \cong \overline{WY}$	2. Property of equality, any quantity is equal to itself.
3. $\therefore \Delta WXY \cong \Delta WZY$	3. SSS Postulate.

In summary, you now have three ways to show that one triangle is congruent to another.

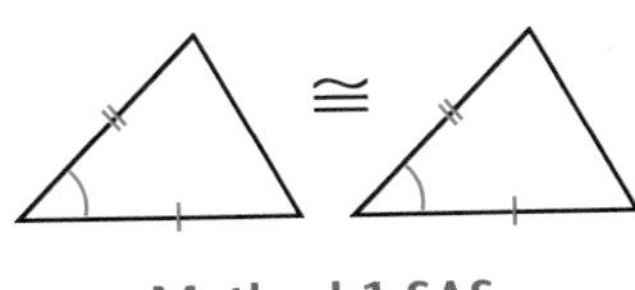

Method 1 SAS

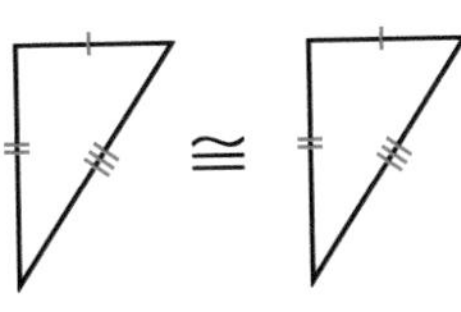

Method 2 SSS

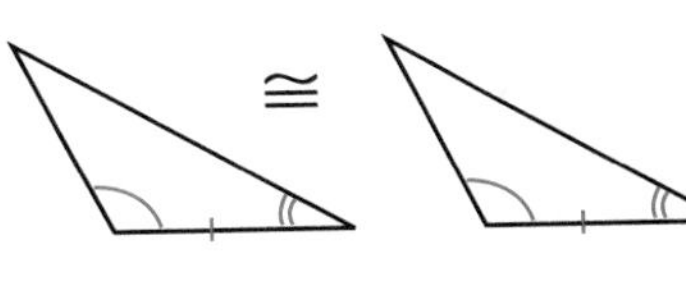

Method 3 ASA

Exercise A Tell whether the triangles in each pair are congruent. Write *yes* or *no.* If your answer is *yes,* give the postulate (SAS, SSS, or ASA) that explains why.

1.

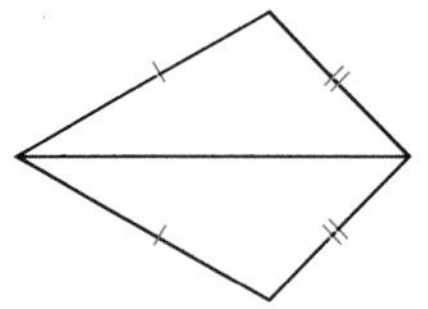

2.

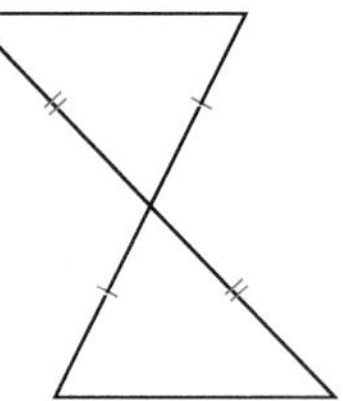

3.

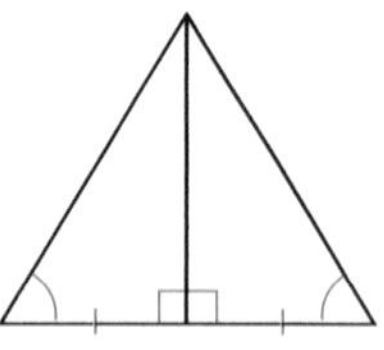

4.

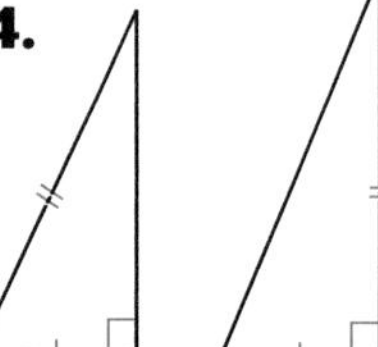

5.

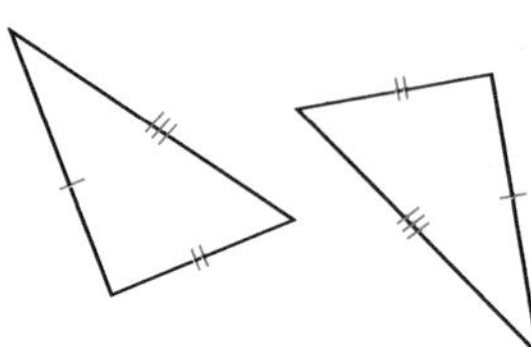

Exercise B Copy each proof. Fill in the missing steps.

Given: ΔABE and ΔDBC, $\overline{AD}$ and $\overline{CE}$ bisect each other at B

To Prove: $\Delta ABE \cong \Delta DBC$

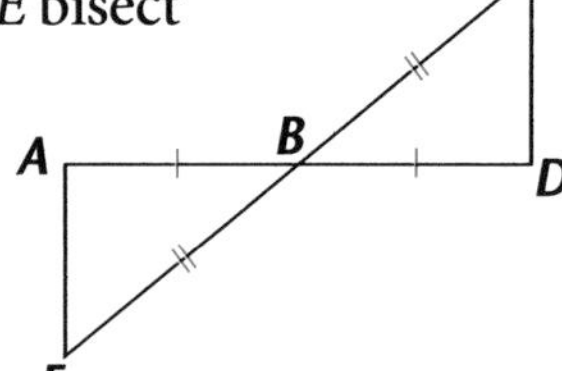

PROOF

Statement	Reason
1. ΔABE and ΔDBC	1. **6.**
2. $\overline{AD}$ bisects $\overline{EC}$ at B and $\overline{EC}$ bisects $\overline{AD}$ at B	2. **7.**
3. **8.**	3. Definition of bisector.
4. **9.**	4. Vertical angles are equal.
5. $\therefore \Delta ABE \cong \Delta DBC$	5. **10.**

Given: isosceles ΔFGH with perpendicular bisector $\overline{GI}$

To Prove: $\Delta FIG \cong \Delta HIG$

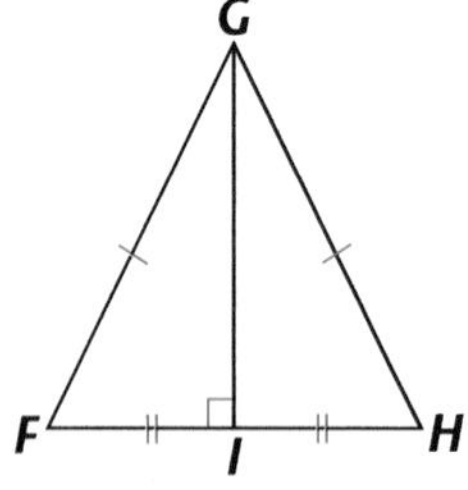

PROOF Statement	Reason
1. isosceles ΔFGH	1. **11.**
2. **12.**	2. Definition of isosceles.
3. $\overline{GI}$ bisects $\overline{FH}$	3. **13.**
4. **14.**	4. Definition of bisector.
5. **15.**	5. Property of equality, any quantity is equal to itself.
6. $\therefore \Delta FIG \cong \Delta HIG$	6. **16.**

CONSTRUCTION

Exercise C Complete the following constructions.

17. Draw any acute scalene triangle *ABC*. Draw a second triangle *A'B'C'* congruent to ΔABC using the SSS Postulate.

18. Draw any obtuse triangle. Label the obtuse angle *D* and the triangle *DEF*. Draw a second triangle *D'E'F'* congruent to ΔDEF using SAS where *D* is the included angle.

PROBLEM SOLVING

Exercise D Solve the following problems.

19. Triangle *ABC* has three equal sides and three equal angles. Triangle *DEF* has three equal sides and three equal angles, each equal to the angles of *ABC*. Is $\Delta ABC \cong \Delta DEF$? If yes, explain why. If no, give a counterexample.

20. At ten in the morning, a 30-foot flagpole casts a 10-foot shadow across the ground. A nearby tree casts a shadow of equal length. Rodney, a forester, drew the diagram at right. He assumed the $m\angle P = m\angle T$ because both are formed by the sun's rays as they reached the ground. How tall is the tree? How do you know?

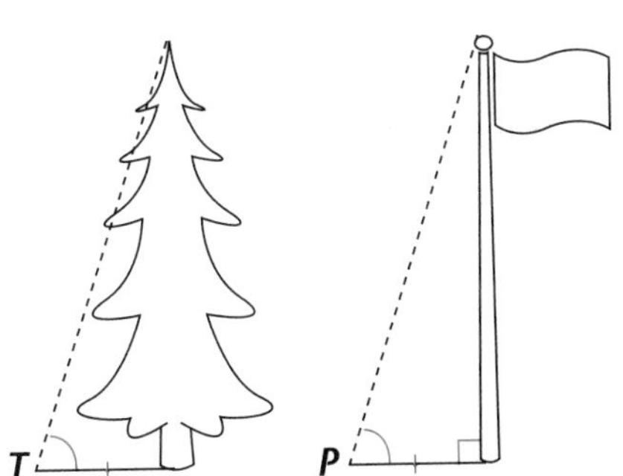

Lesson 4 Special Congruencies: Right Triangles

There is one more congruency theorem that can be applied to any triangle.

> **AAS (Angle-Angle-Side) Theorem (6.4.1):**
> If two angles in a triangle and one side not included between those angles are congruent to two angles and the corresponding side of a second triangle, then the two triangles are congruent.

You can prove this theorem using the Angle Sum Theorem for triangles.

PROOF

Given: $\triangle ABC$ and $\triangle A'B'C'$, where $\overline{AB} \cong \overline{A'B'}$, $\angle A \cong \angle A'$, and $\angle C \cong \angle C'$

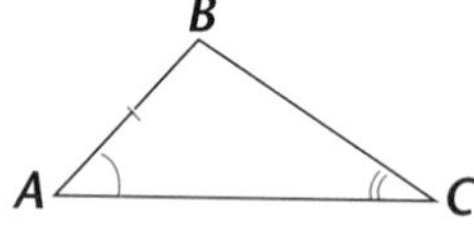

To Prove: $\triangle ABC \cong \triangle A'B'C'$

You already know that the sum of the measures of the three angles in any triangle is 180°. So you can write

$(m\angle A + m\angle C) + m\angle B = 180°$ and

$(m\angle A' + m\angle C') + m\angle B' = 180°$.

You can substitute equals for equals, and write

$(m\angle A + m\angle C) + m\angle B = (m\angle A' + m\angle C') + m\angle B'$.

By subtraction you get $m\angle B = m\angle B'$.
Therefore, by ASA, $\triangle ABC \cong \triangle A'B'C'$.

You already know that the right angles in any triangle are congruent to one another because the measure of all right angles equals 90°. There are other special conditions that apply only to right angles.

In a right triangle, you know that one angle must be 90°. Next we will prove that the sum of the remaining angles must also be 90°.

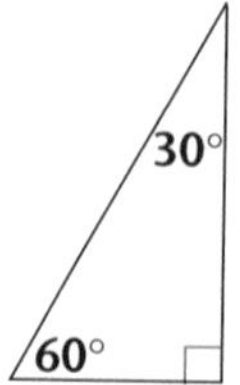

Theorem 6.4.2:
The acute angles in any right triangle are complementary.

PROOF

Given: right triangle ABC with $m\angle A = 90°$

To Prove: $m\angle B + m\angle C = 90°$

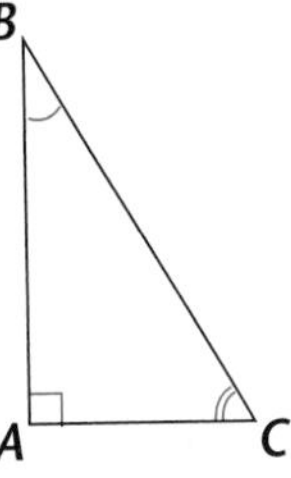

$m\angle A + m\angle B + m\angle C = 180°$	by the Angle Sum Theorem
$90° + m\angle B + m\angle C = 180°$	given $m\angle A = 90°$
$\therefore m\angle B + m\angle C = 90°$	subtraction

This theorem makes it possible for you to prove that right triangles are congruent using the congruency postulates for the following cases:

Case 1
Given: hypotenuse and one acute angle

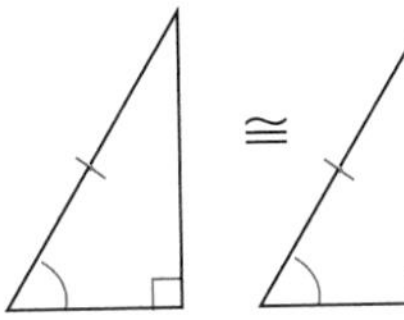

Congruent by ASA or AAS.

Case 2
Given: one leg and one acute angle

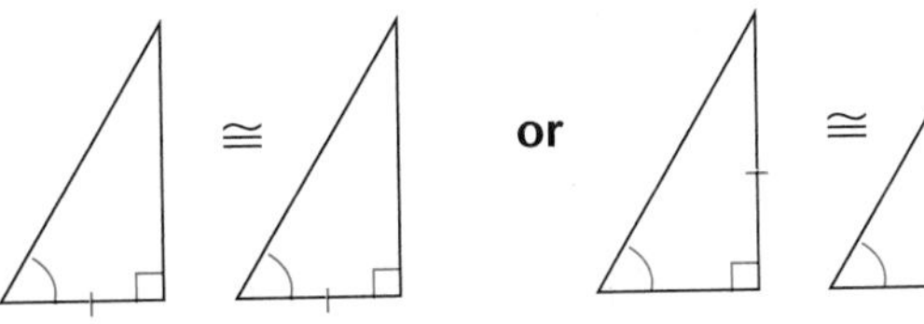

Congruent by ASA or AAS.

The leg of a right triangle is either one of the sides next to the right angle.

Case 3

Given: two legs

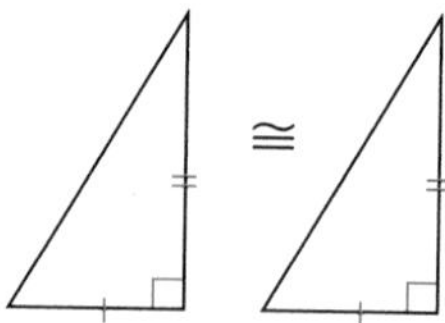

Congruent by SAS.

There is another way to prove the congruency of right triangles.

Case 4

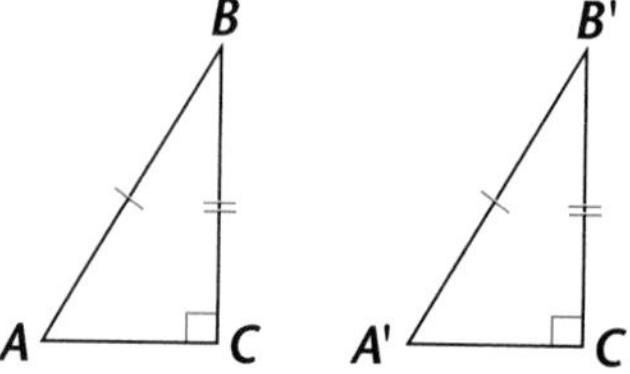

In this case, you are given that the hypotenuse and leg of one right triangle are congruent to the hypotenuse and corresponding leg of a second right triangle.

> **Hypotenuse-Leg (H-L) Theorem (6.4.3):**
> Two right triangles are congruent if the hypotenuse and leg of one triangle are congruent to the hypotenuse and corresponding leg of the second triangle.

This theorem is easily proven after the discussion of another theorem called the Pythagorean Theorem in Chapter 8. For now, we will take the theorem as true without proof.

Now you have all the information you need to prove right triangles congruent. What's more, you can use the fact that the acute angles in a right triangle are complementary to calculate angle measure.

EXAMPLE 1 **Given:** two right triangles with congruent parts as marked

Are these triangles congruent? Why?

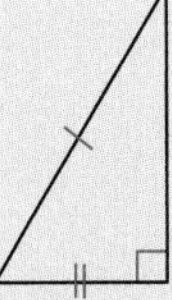

The hypotenuses and corresponding legs are congruent, so the triangles are congruent by the H-L Theorem.

EXAMPLE 2 **Given:** right triangles ABC and DEC, C is the midpoint of $\overline{BE}$

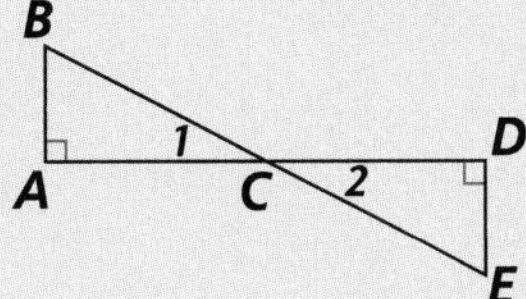

Are these triangles congruent? Why?

$\angle 1 \cong \angle 2$, vertical angles

$\overline{BC} \cong \overline{CE}$, definition of midpoint

$\therefore \triangle ABC \cong \triangle DEC$ by AAS of right triangles

EXAMPLE 3 **Given:** a right triangle with $m\angle 1 = 80°$

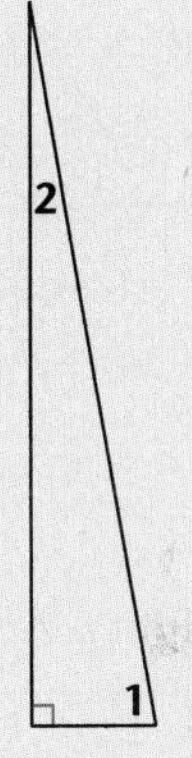

What is $m\angle 2$?

$m\angle 1 + m\angle 2 = 90°$	by theorem
$80° + m\angle 2 = 90°$	substitution
$m\angle 2 = 10°$	subtraction

EXAMPLE 4 **Given:** a right triangle in which $m\angle 1$ is three times $m\angle 2$

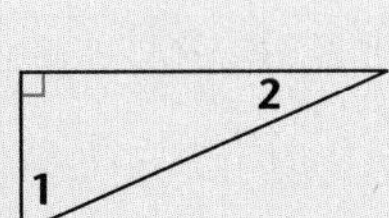

What is the measure of each angle?

Let $m\angle 2 = x$, $m\angle 1 = 3x$

$m\angle 1 + m\angle 2 = 90°$	by theorem
$3x + x = 90°$	by substitution
$4x = 90°$	addition
$x = 22.5°$	division
$m\angle 2 = 22.5°$, $m\angle 1 = 67.5°$	substitution for x and $3x$

Exercise A Give the reason for congruency for each pair of triangles.

1.

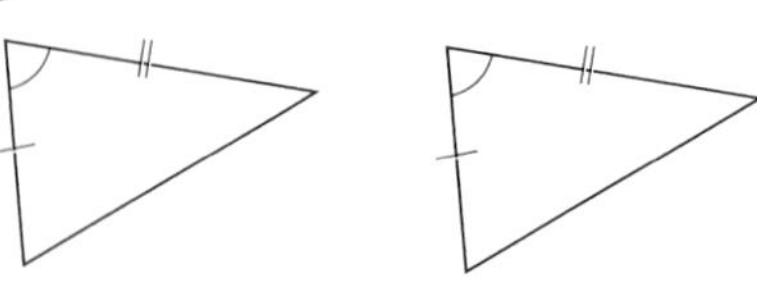

2.

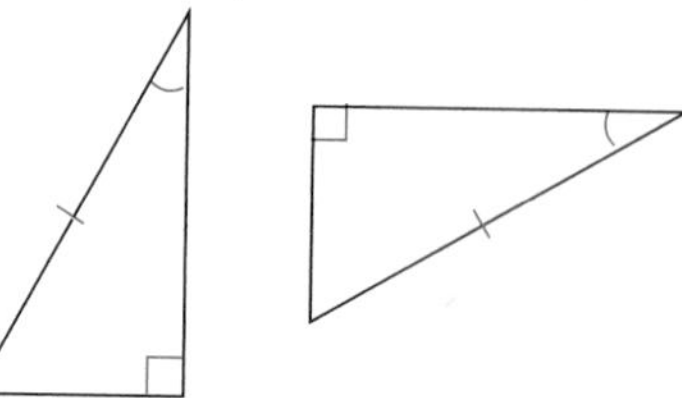

3.

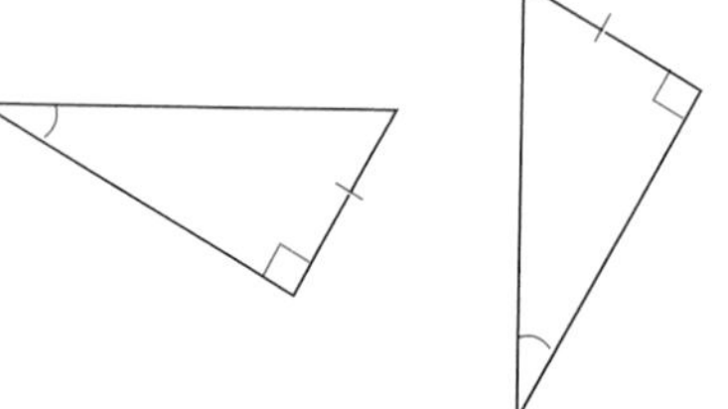

4.

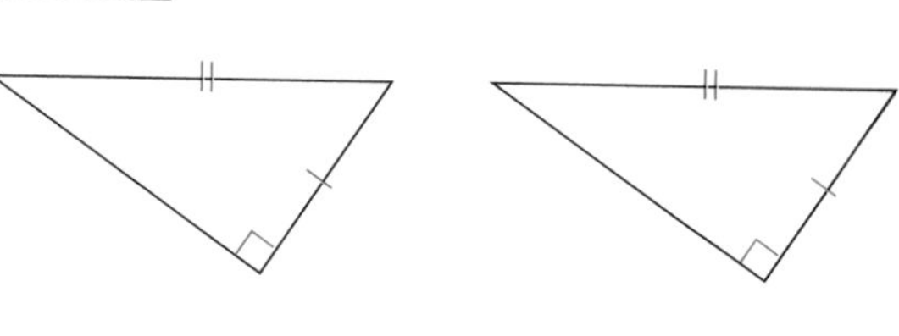

Exercise B Copy each proof. Fill in the missing steps.

Given: ΔABC, ΔEDC, C is the midpoint of $\overline{AE}$; $\overline{AB}$ and $\overline{DE} \perp \overline{AE}$; $\overline{BC} \cong \overline{DC}$

To Prove: $\Delta ABC \cong \Delta EDC$

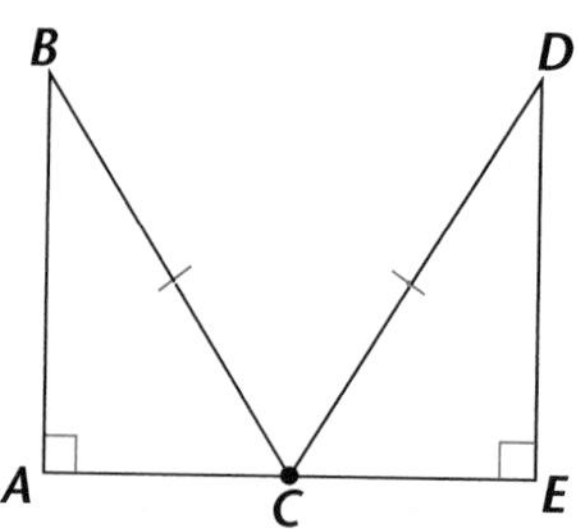

PROOF

Statement	Reason
1. $m\angle A = 90°$, $m\angle E = 90°$	1. **5.**
2. $\overline{AC} \cong \overline{CE}$	2. **6.**
3. $\overline{BC} \cong \overline{DC}$	3. Given.
4. $\therefore \Delta ABC \cong \Delta EDC$	4. **7.**

Given: ΔABC, ΔFED, $\overline{AC} \parallel \overleftrightarrow{DF}$

$\overline{AB}$ and $\overline{EF} \perp \overline{BE}$; $\overline{AB} \cong \overline{EF}$

To Prove: $\Delta ABC \cong \Delta FED$

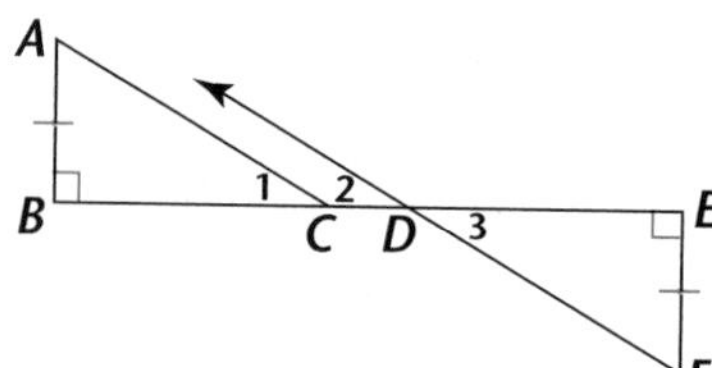

PROOF

Statement	Reason
1. $m\angle B = 90°$, $m\angle E = 90°$	1. **8.**
2. $m\angle 1 = m\angle 2$	2. **9.**
3. **10.**	3. Vertical angles are equal.
4. **11.**	4. Substitution of equals.
5. $\therefore \Delta ABC \cong \Delta FED$	5. **12.**

PROBLEM SOLVING

Exercise C Solve the following problems.

13. If m$\angle 2$ is twice m$\angle 1$, what is the measure of $\angle 1$? $\angle 2$?

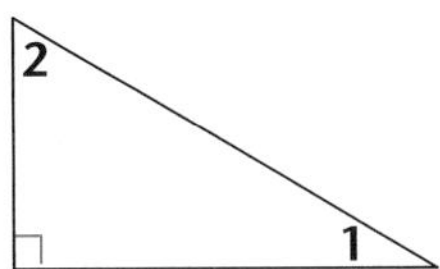

14. You plan to build a corner storage unit with four shelves. If you only measure two sides of each shelf, what postulates or theorems can you use to show that each shelf will be the same size and shape?

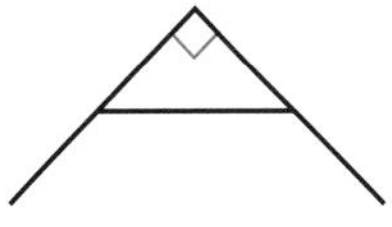

15. If m$\angle 3$ is ten degrees more than m$\angle 4$, what is the measure of $\angle 3$? $\angle 4$?

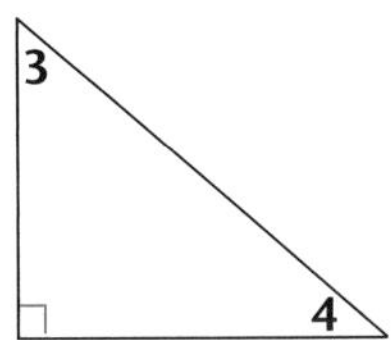

Calculator Practice

You can use your calculator to find the missing angle measures.

EXAMPLE 5 $\angle 1$ and $\angle 2$ are complementary angles.
m$\angle 1$ is twice m$\angle 2$. Let $x =$ m$\angle 2$, $2x =$ m$\angle 1$.
$2x + x = 90°$
$3x = 90°$
Press 90 ÷ 3 ENTER. Display reads 30.
m$\angle 2 = 30°$, m$\angle 1 = 60°$

Exercise D Find each unknown using a calculator.

16. $5x + x = 120°$

17. $3x + 2x = 100°$

18. $2x + 3x = 80°$

19. $2x + 3x = 120°$

20. $3x + 4x = 160°$

Writing About Mathematics

Suppose you have an isosceles triangle such as the one in the drawing below. What congruency theorem would you use to show $\triangle ADB \cong \triangle CDB$? Explain your choice.

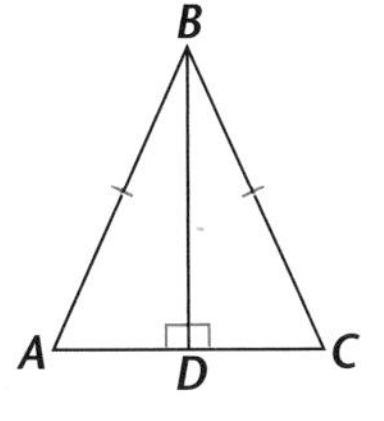

Lesson 5 Reflections in the Coordinate Plane

Image
Reflection of an object

Line of reflection
The line halfway between an object and its reflected image

You've probably noticed reflections of trees in a pond or lake or even reflections of buildings in puddles of water. In fact, you probably see a reflection of yourself every day when you look in a mirror. As you may already know, the reflection of an object is called its **image.**

In the picture, the object is the giraffe drinking at a watering hole. The image is the reflection of the giraffe on the water's surface.

As you work with objects and their reflections, or images, you will also work with the **line of reflection**. The object and its image are at equal distances from the line of reflection.

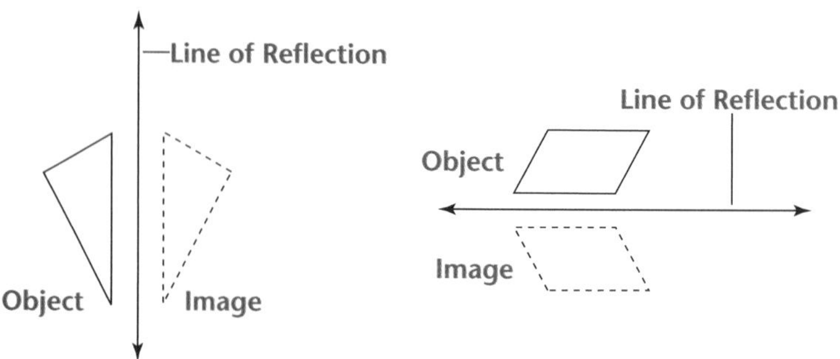

The distance between the object and its image can be shown and calculated if both are placed in a coordinate plane.

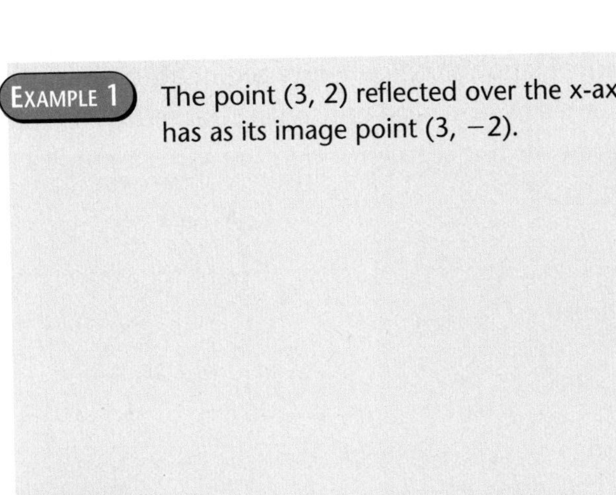

EXAMPLE 1 The point (3, 2) reflected over the x-axis has as its image point (3, −2).

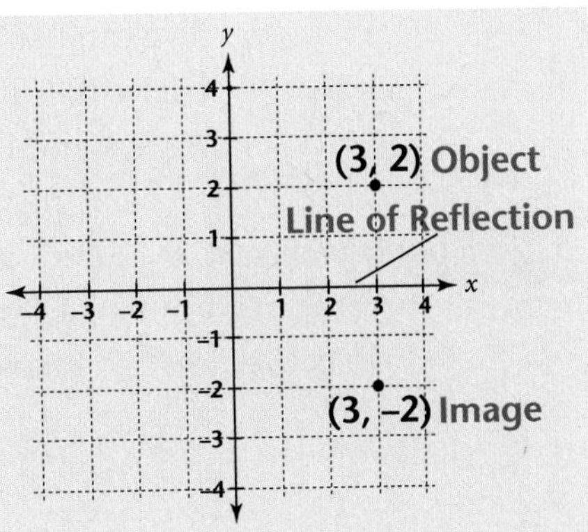

EXAMPLE 2 The same point, (3, 2), reflected over the y-axis has as its image point (−3, 2).

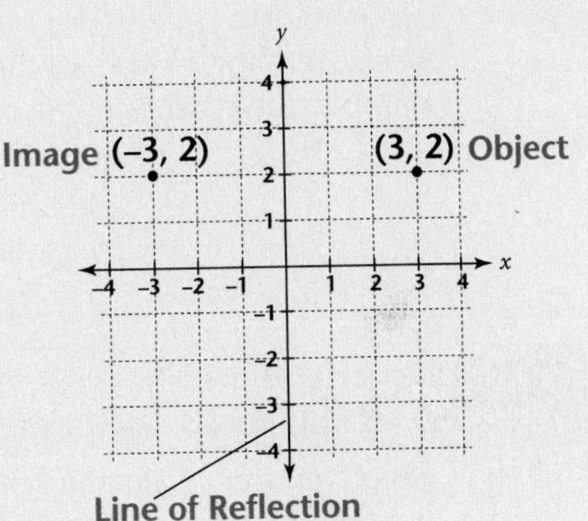

In fact, you can make the following generalizations or statements.

Reflection over *x*-axis

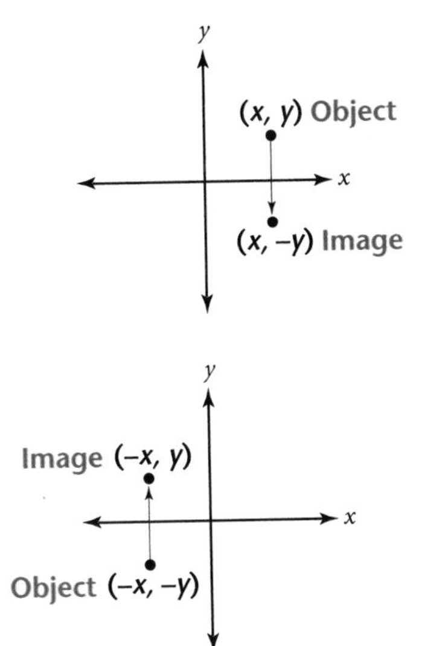

Image: *x*-value is the same
y-value has opposite sign

Reflection over *y*-axis

Image (−x, y) (x, y) Object

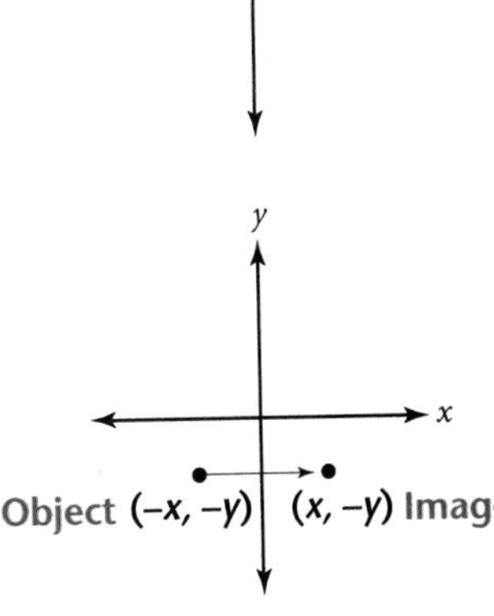

Image: *y*-value is the same
x-value has opposite sign

You can use this information to reflect entire geometric figures over either the x- or y-axis. You need only reflect the vertices of the figures and then draw the line segments. Here are some examples.

EXAMPLE 3 Reflect ΔABC over the x-axis.

$A = (2, 5)$, $B = (2, 2)$, $C = (5, 2)$

Object vertices	Image vertices
$A = (2, 5)$	$A' = (2, -5)$
$B = (2, 2)$	$B' = (2, -2)$
$C = (5, 2)$	$C' = (5, -2)$

Notice that the y-values of the image are opposite the y-values of the object.

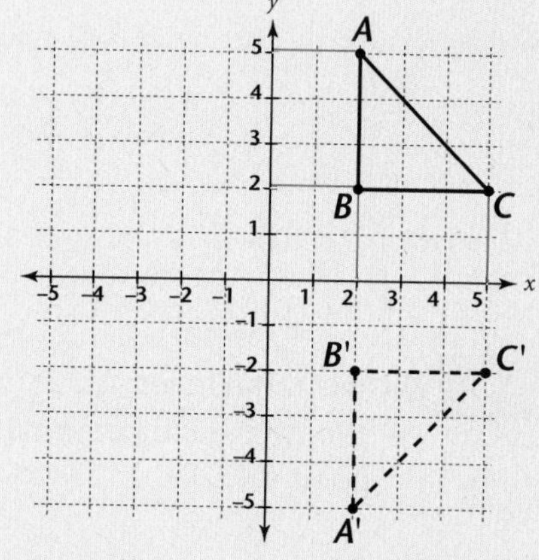

EXAMPLE 4 Reflect ΔDEF over the y-axis.

$D = (3, 2)$, $E = (5, 2)$, $F = (3, -1)$

Object vertices	Image vertices
$D = (3, 2)$	$D' = (-3, 2)$
$E = (5, 2)$	$E' = (-5, 2)$
$F = (3, -1)$	$F' = (-3, -1)$

Notice that the x-values of the image are opposite the x-values of the object.

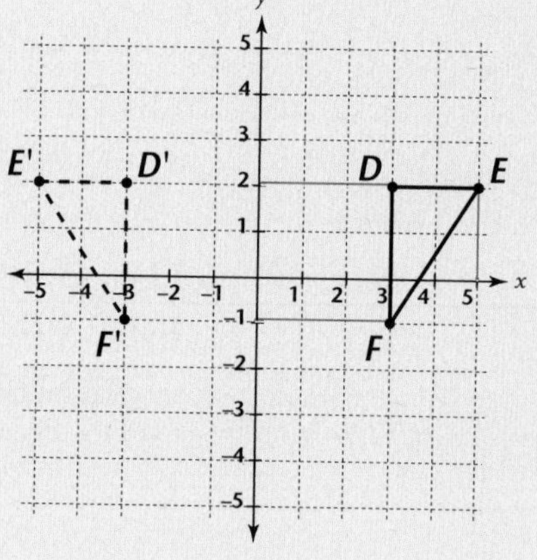

In each example above, you were able to find the coordinates of the image by finding the distance from the object points to the line of reflection and then using that same distance to place the image points.

You may, of course, use a line other than the x- or y-axis as the line of reflection. The geometry is still the same—the object points and their images are the same distance from the line of reflection.

EXAMPLE 5 Reflect ΔLMN over the line $y = 2$.
$L = (1, 5)$, $M = (5, 5)$, $N = (4, 3)$

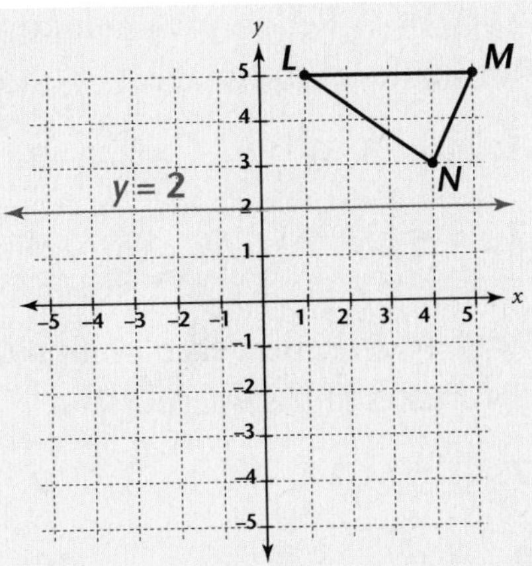

To locate the image, you need to find the distance of each object point to the line of reflection, $y = 2$. Then apply this same distance in the opposite direction from $y = 2$.

Object Point	Distance to Line of Reflection ($y = 2$)	Image Point
$L = (1, 5)$	$5 - 2 = 3$	$L' = (1, 2 - 3)$ $L' = (1, -1)$
$M = (5, 5)$	$5 - 2 = 3$	$M' = (5, 2 - 3)$ $M' = (5, -1)$
$N = (4, 3)$	$3 - 2 = 1$	$N' = (4, 2 - 1)$ $N' = (4, 1)$

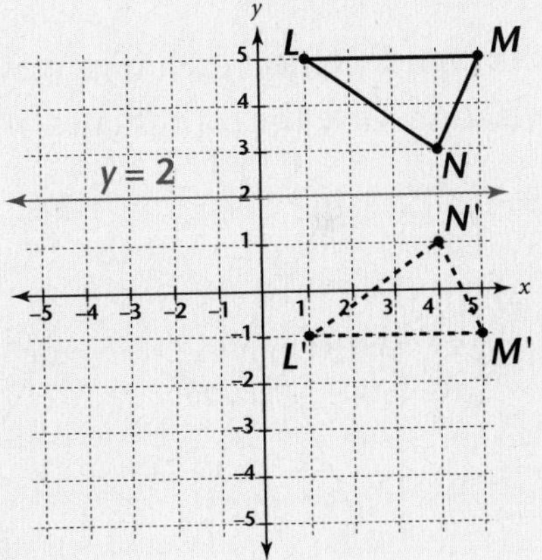

Vertices for object ΔLMN
(1, 5), (5, 5), (4, 3)

Vertices for image $\Delta L'M'N'$
(1, −1), (5, −1), (4, 1)

Geometry in Your Life

Choose a small photograph from a magazine. Trace the object onto a sheet of graph paper. Then hold the graph paper up to a mirror, making sure you're holding the paper flat. Ask yourself the following questions: How are the image in the mirror and the object alike? How are they different? Where is the line of reflection? How can you prove the object and the image are each the same distance from the line of reflection?

Exercise A Reflect each point over the x-axis. Give the coordinates of the image.

1. $A = (3, 5)$

2. $B = (3, -5)$

3. $C = (-3, 5)$

4. $D = (-3, -5)$

5. $E = (2, 0)$

6. $F = (0, 4)$

Exercise B Reflect each point over the y-axis. Give the coordinates of the image.

7. $G = (4, 2)$

8. $H = (4, -2)$

9. $I = (-4, 2)$

10. $J = (-4, -4)$

11. $K = (3, 0)$

12. $L = (0, 5)$

Exercise C Reflect each image over the specified line of reflection. Give the coordinates of the image vertices.

13. $x = 2$

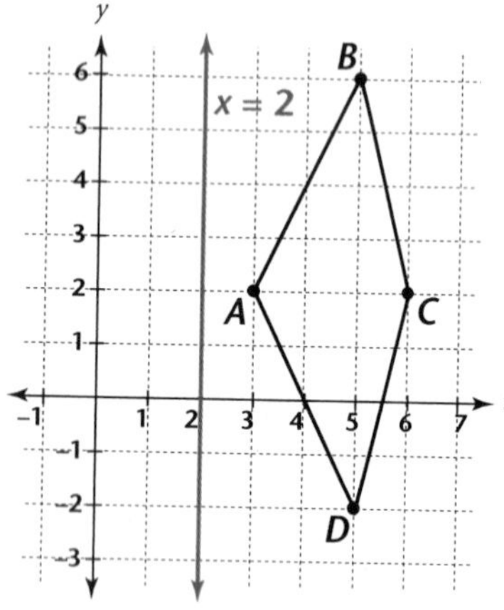

$A = (3, 2)$ $B = (5, 6)$
$C = (6, 2)$ $D = (5, -2)$

14. $y = -3$

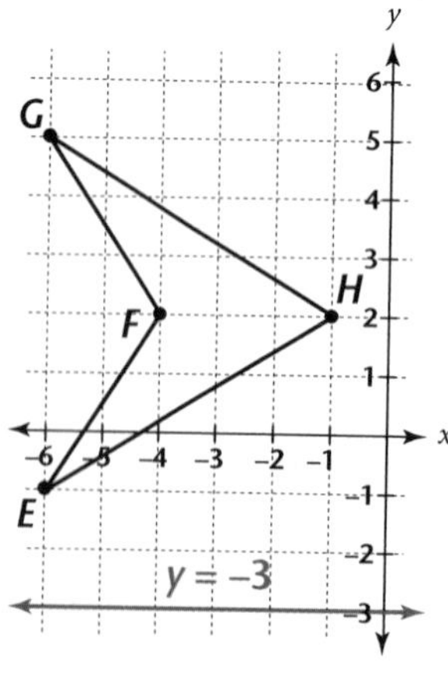

$E = (-6, -1)$ $F = (-4, 2)$
$G = (-6, 5)$ $H = (-1, 2)$

15. $x = 1$

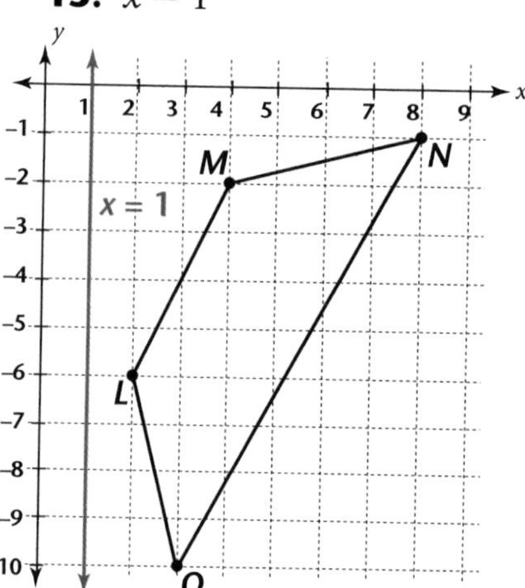

$L = (2, -6)$ $M = (4, -2)$
$N = (8, -1)$ $O = (3, -10)$

Technology Connection

Reflections play an important role in billiards and miniature golf. The angle at which the ball strikes a barrier and the angle at which it is reflected back onto the playing surface are related—in a specific and predictable way. This relationship holds true not just for games but also for sound, radio, and light waves. Knowing these reflection relationships has helped researchers determine what is inside an atom.

Lesson 6 Special Reflections: Symmetries

Line of symmetry

Reflection line of an object for which the object coincides with the image

A special class of geometric reflections leaves the object and image in the same location. That is, the object and its image appear as one. If you reflect a square over one of its diagonals, you get a triangle in which the object and image meet. The reflection line is called a **line of symmetry.** A figure with at least one line of symmetry is called *symmetric.*

EXAMPLE 1 A square has four lines of symmetry. Each diagonal is a line of symmetry. Each line connecting the midpoints of opposite sides of the square is also a line of symmetry.

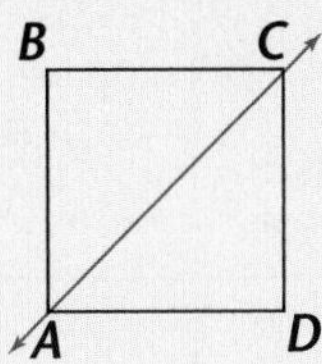

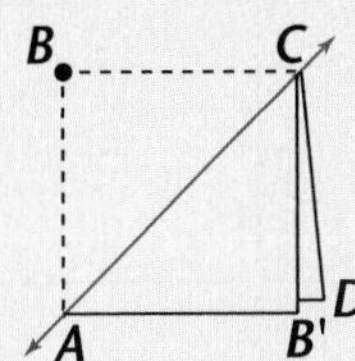

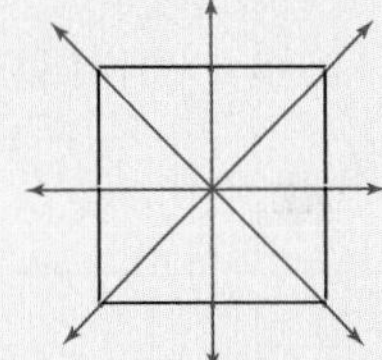

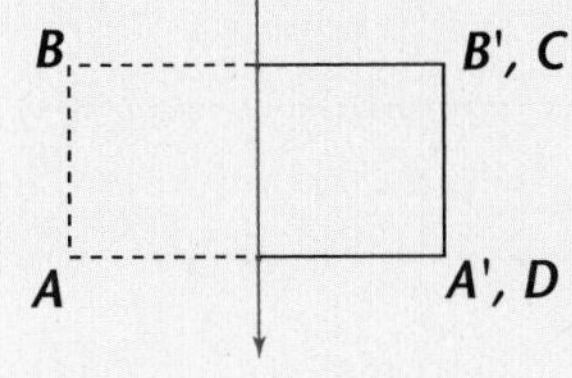

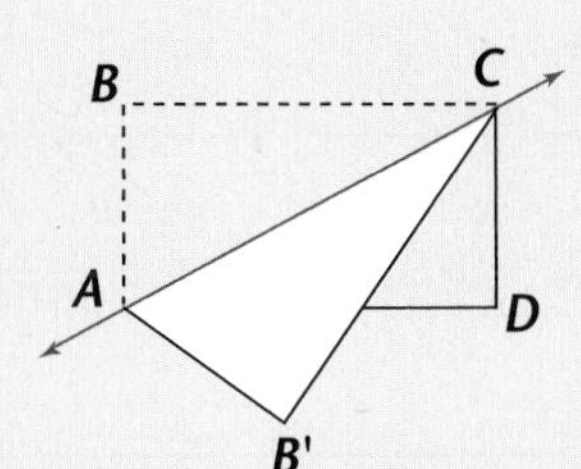

You can see that for rectangles, the lines connecting the midpoints of opposite sides are lines of symmetry.

However, unlike the square, the diagonals of a rectangle are not lines of symmetry.

An isosceles triangle has one line of symmetry. The line of symmetry is both the angle bisector and the perpendicular bisector of the base.

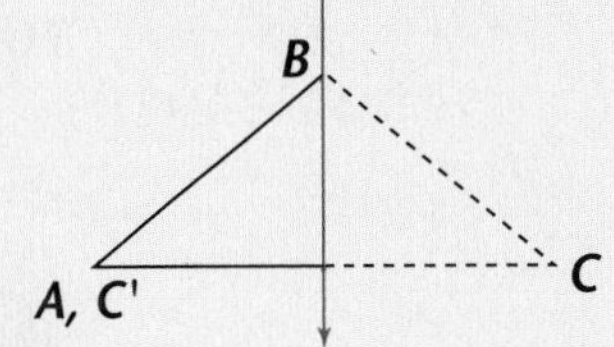

An equilateral triangle has three lines of symmetry. Each line of symmetry is the median of a side. It is also a bisector of the opposite angle.

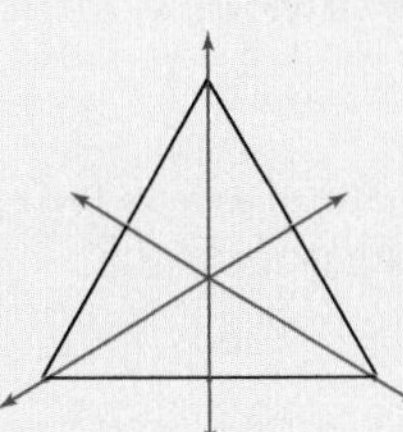

Sometimes you may meet the terms vertical symmetry or horizontal symmetry. The letter A, as printed to the left, has vertical symmetry. The letter E, as printed to the left, has horizontal symmetry.

Exercise A Decide if the given line of reflection is also a line of symmetry. Answer *yes* or *no.*

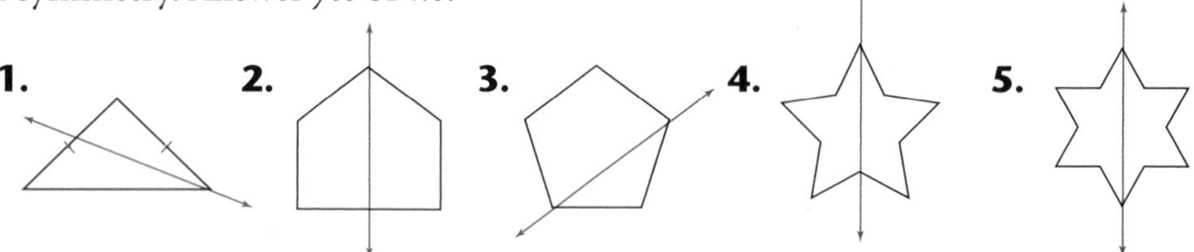

Exercise B Complete the following table. Then answer the questions.

Figure	Polygon	Number of Sides	Diagonals Acting as Lines of Symmetry	Total Number of Lines of Symmetry
6.	equilateral triangle	_____	none	3
7.	square	4	2	_____
8.	regular pentagon	_____	none	5

9. What appears to be necessary for a diagonal to be a line of symmetry?

10. What appears to be true about the perpendicular bisector of a side of a polygon and the polygon's lines of symmetry?

TRY THIS What do you think is the relationship between a diameter (distance across a circle through the center) of a circle and a circle's symmetry? How many lines of symmetry do you think a circle has?

Lesson 7 Slides and Translations

Transformation

Movement of a geometric figure from one location to another

Translation

Transformation in which a geometric figure slides from one location to another without affecting its size or shape

A **transformation** is the movement of a figure from one place to another. Reflections are one group of geometric transformations. A *slide*, or **translation,** is another example of a transformation. A slide is a transformation in which you "slide" the figure from one location to another. You do this without changing its size or shape. Sometimes this transformation is called *mapping;* you map point *A* onto point *A*'. A slide, or translation, leaves the object in one location and its image in another.

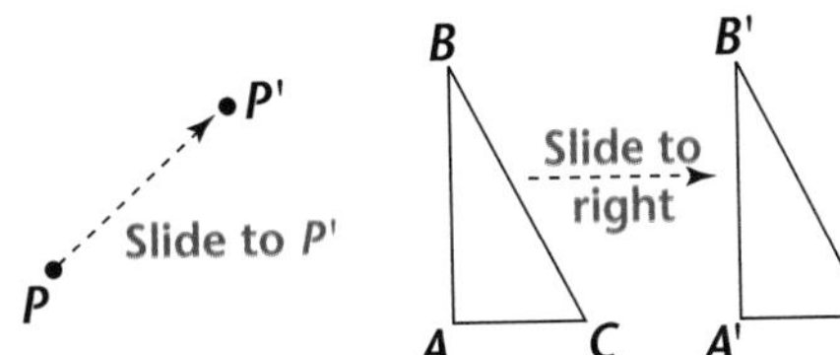

One way to study this kind of transformation is to look at slides or translations that occur in the coordinate plane.

EXAMPLE 1 Slide point $P(-1, -1)$ to location P'.

Looking at the grid you can see that to reach P' you need to move 4 units to the right $(x + 4)$ and 4 units up $(y + 4)$.

Here is how you can use the coordinates of P to find the coordinates of P'.

$P = (-1, -1)$

$P' = (x + 4, y + 4)$

$P' = (-1 + 4, -1 + 4) = (3, 3)$

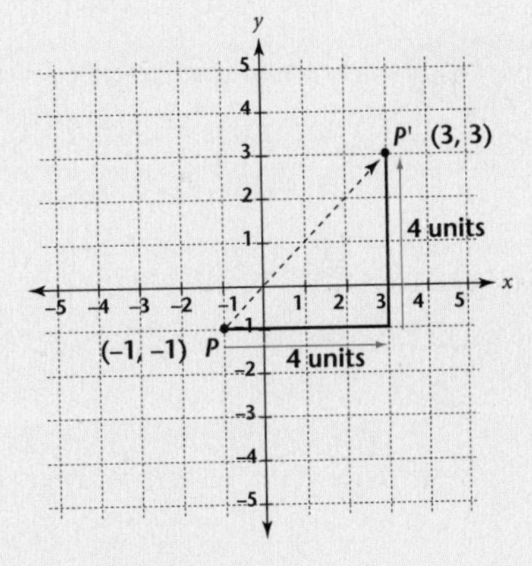

Formula:

To translate or slide point P a units horizontally (change in x) and b units vertically (change in y), you must change the x- and y-values of the coordinates of P.

$$P = (x, y) \text{ translates to } P' = (x + a, y + b)$$

Note that if $a > 0$, the image is to the right; if $a < 0$, the image is to the left. If $b > 0$, the image is above the object; if $b < 0$, the image is below the object.

EXAMPLE 2 Slide $\triangle ABC$ 4 units to the right and 3 units down.

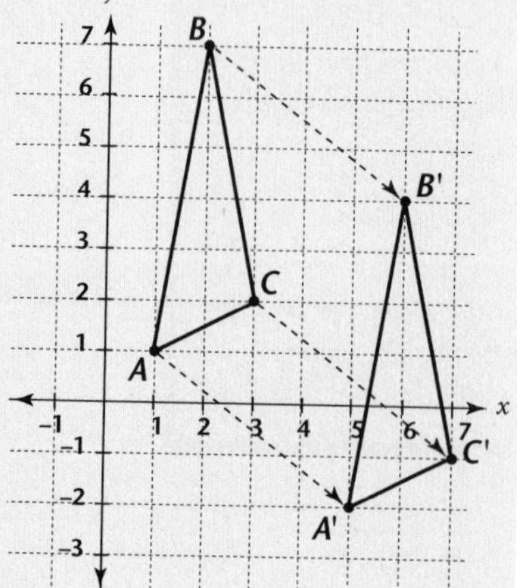

First slide each vertex.

$A = (1, 1)$, $B = (2, 7)$, and $C = (3, 2)$

$a = 4$ (4 units to the right)

$b = -3$ (3 units down)

$P = (x, y)$ translates to $P' = (x + a, y + b)$

$A = (1, 1)$ translates to $A' = (1 + 4, 1 + -3) = (5, -2)$

$B = (2, 7)$ translates to $B' = (2 + 4, 7 + -3) = (6, 4)$

$C = (3, 2)$ translates to $C' = (3 + 4, 2 + -3) = (7, -1)$

Once you have located each image vertex, draw $\triangle A'B'C'$.

EXAMPLE 3 A translation maps $(x, y) \rightarrow (x - 5, y + 3)$.

What are the coordinates of the image of $(-3, -7)$?

$$(x, y) \rightarrow (x - 5, y + 3)$$

$$(-3, -7) \rightarrow (-3 - 5, -7 + 3) = (-8, -4)$$

EXAMPLE 4 A translation maps $(4, -7) \rightarrow (0, 3)$.

What is the image of (x, y) under this translation?

$$(4, -7) \rightarrow (0, 3)$$

$$(4, -7) \rightarrow (x + a, y + b) = (4 + a, -7 + b)$$

$$0 = 4 + a \qquad 3 = -7 + b$$

$$a = -4 \qquad b = 10$$

The image of (x, y) is $(x - 4, y + 10)$.

A traditional Ferris wheel carries a seat high up in the air above the fair. Because of the way the seat is attached to the wheel, however, it doesn't rotate. If it did, the seat would turn upside down. The wheel is simply there to translate, or move, the seat from one position on the circle to the next.

Writing About Mathematics

Describe how you would slide a circle with a radius of 5 and center at (0, 0) 5 units to the left and 3 units up. What is the center of the image?

Exercise A Slide each point 3 units to the left and 2 units up. Graph the point and its image, naming the coordinates of the image.

1. $A = (3, 6)$

2. $B = (-3, 6)$

3. $C = (3, -6)$

4. $D = (-3, -6)$

5. $E = (0, 5)$

6. $F = (3, -2)$

7. $G = (0, 0)$

Exercise B Slide each triangle according to the given translation. Graph the image triangle and name the vertices of the image triangle.

8. ΔABC: $A = (-7, 3)$, $B = (-2, 1)$, $C = (4, 6)$; slide 4 right, 2 up

9. ΔEFG: $E = (-3, -2)$, $F = (2, 2)$, $G = (2, -3)$; slide 2 left, 3 up

10. ΔHIJ: $H = (2, 1)$, $I = (1, 4)$, $J = (5, 4)$; slide 6 left, 6 down

Exercise C Name the image point when the object point $(3, -1)$ is mapped by the following translations.

11. $(x, y) \rightarrow (x + 1, y + 5)$

12. $(x, y) \rightarrow (x + 3, y - 2)$

13. $(x, y) \rightarrow (x - 2, y - 4)$

14. $(x, y) \rightarrow (x, y - 3)$

15. $(x, y) \rightarrow (x + 4, y)$

Exercise D Identify the image of (x, y) under the following translations. Remember, the image takes the form $(x + a, y + b)$.

16. $(4, -1) \rightarrow (0, 3)$

17. $(6, 3) \rightarrow (9, 6)$

18. $(6, 3) \rightarrow (-3, -6)$

19. $(4, 2) \rightarrow (6, -2)$

20. $(1, 3) \rightarrow (-3, 5)$

Lesson 8 Rotations

Rotation

Transformation in which a geometric figure turns around a center point without affecting its size or shape

Remember, an object that moves *clockwise* moves in the same direction as the hands on a clock move. An object that moves *counterclockwise* moves in the direction opposite to the direction the hands on a clock move.

The final group of transformations you will study are called **rotations.** You see and use rotations every day. Wheels on a bus, door knobs, and swivel chairs are examples of objects that turn, or rotate.

Below are diagrams of the rotations of some common geometric figures. Notice that each diagram shows an *O*, the center of rotation. This is the point that remains in place as the geometric figure turns around it. It is rather like the needle of a drawing compass.

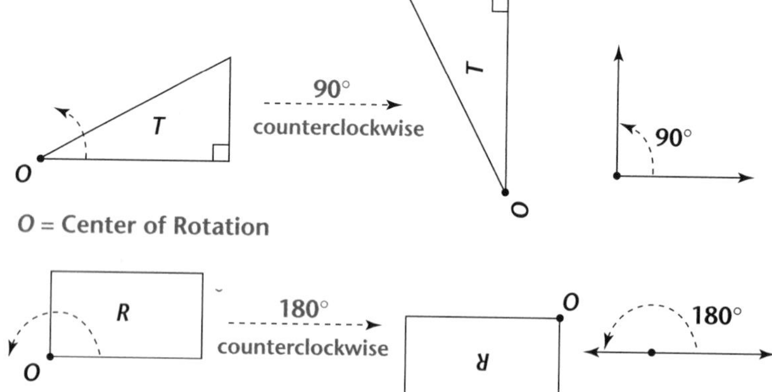

As with other transformations, you can specify a rotation by placing the figure on a coordinate plane.

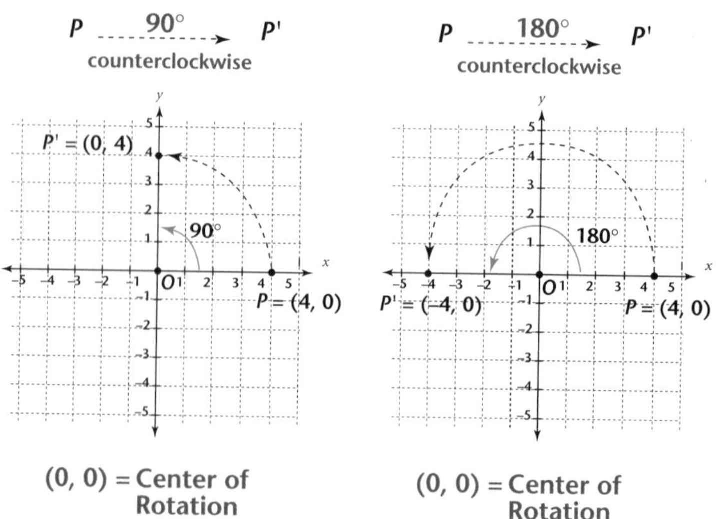

These examples show that knowing the location of the center of rotation, *O*, is key to making the transformation. Without knowing the center of rotation, you have no way of knowing how the object figure is transformed.

Object

90° counterclockwise

Image

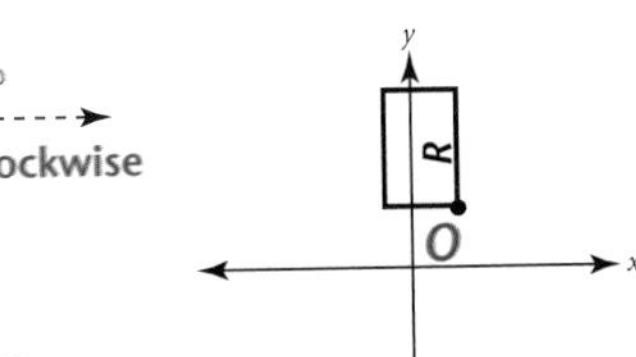

Center of Rotation (0, 0)

Object

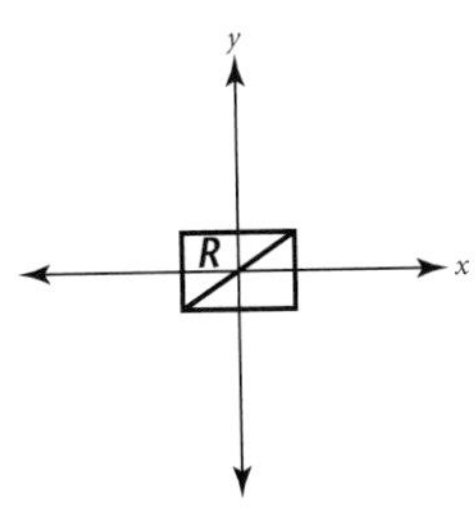

Image

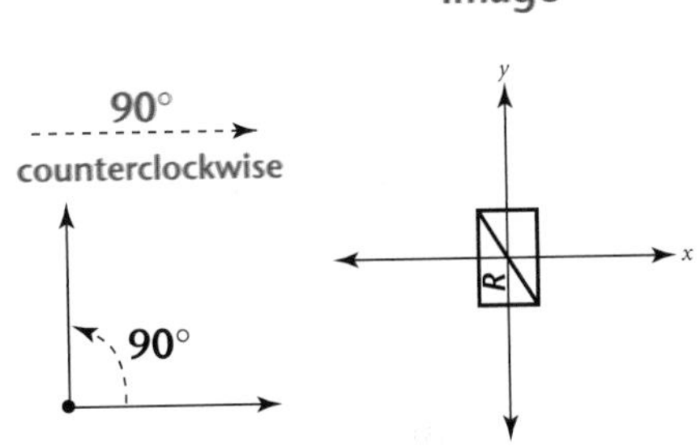

Center of Rotation (0, 0)

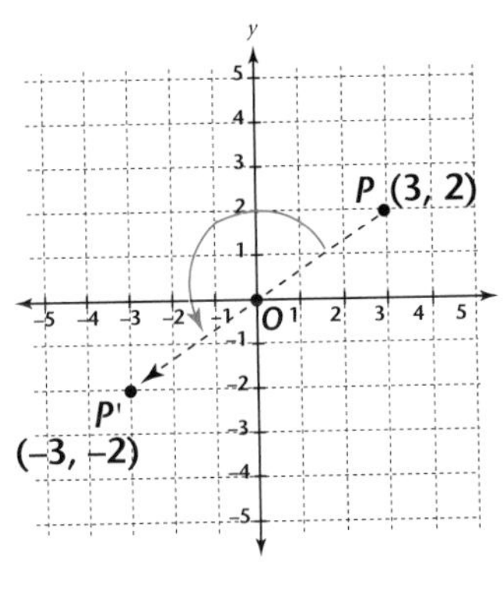

(3, 2) —180° counterclockwise→ (–3, –2)

(x, y) —180° counterclockwise→ $(-x, -y)$

Center of Rotation (0, 0)

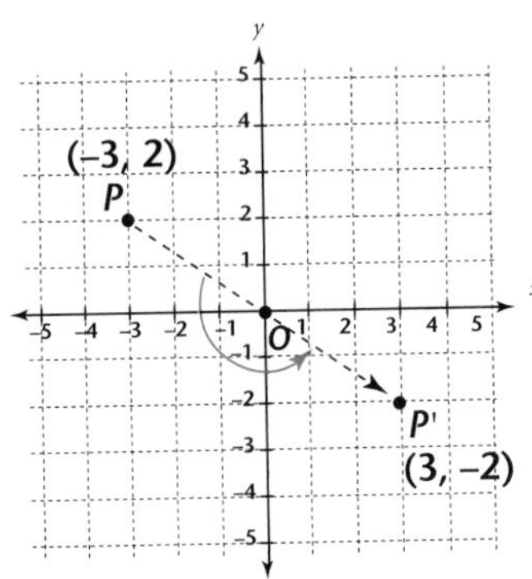

(–3, 2) —180° counterclockwise→ (3, –2)

$(-x, y)$ —180° counterclockwise→ $(x, -y)$

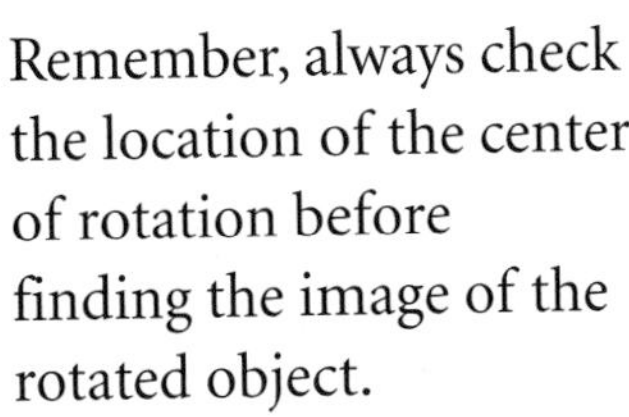

Remember, always check the location of the center of rotation before finding the image of the rotated object.

Exercise A Copy the given figure onto graph paper. Then rotate the object 90° counterclockwise to produce an image. Draw the image. (Remember, O is the center of rotation.)

1.

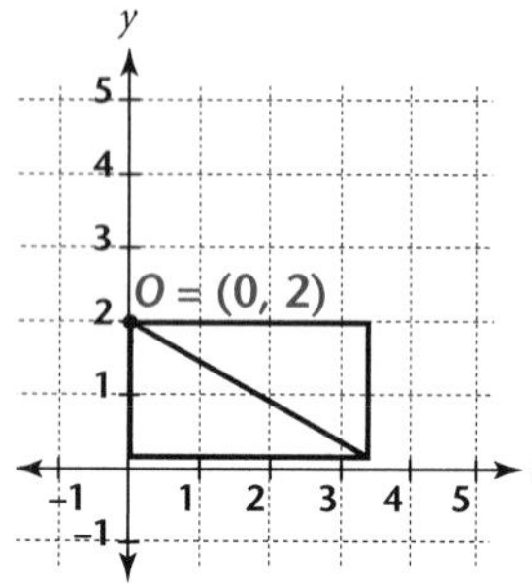

2.

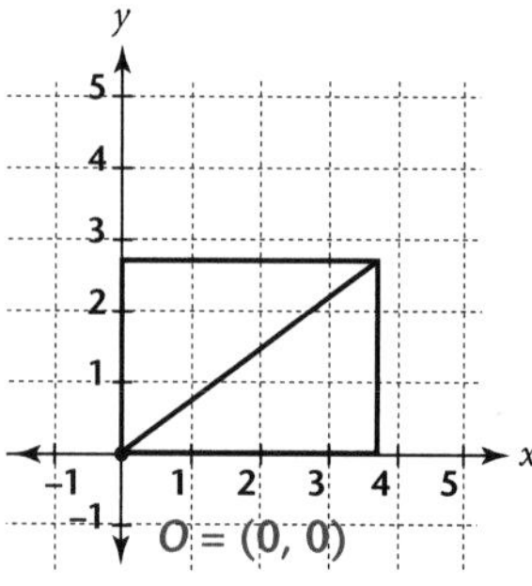

3.

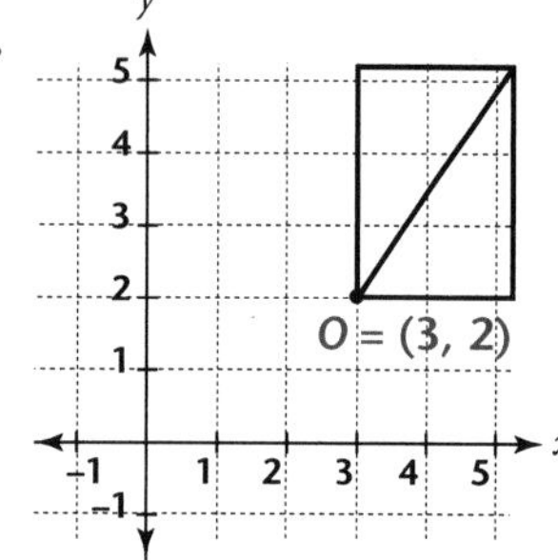

4.

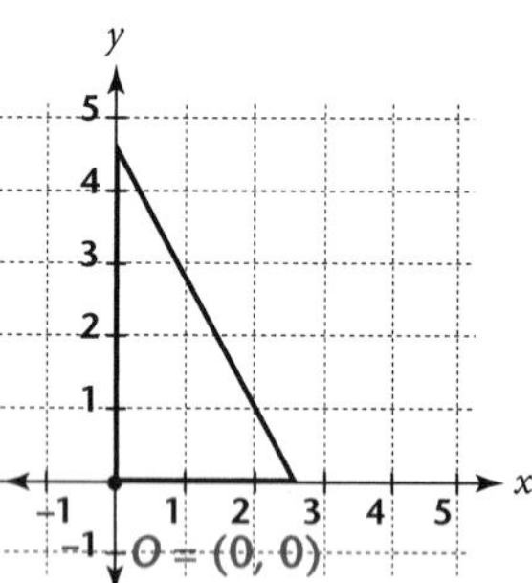

5.

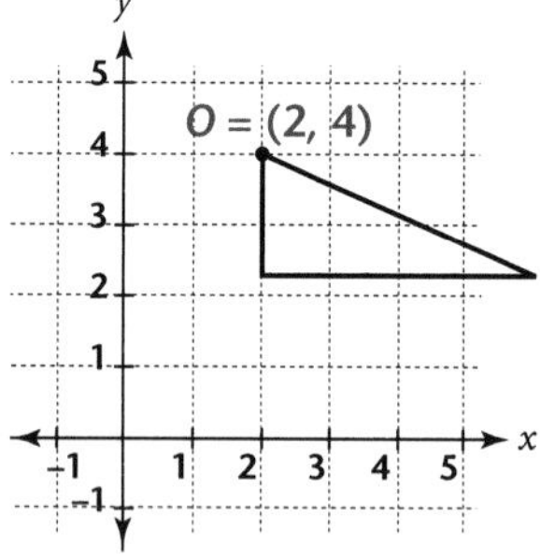

6.

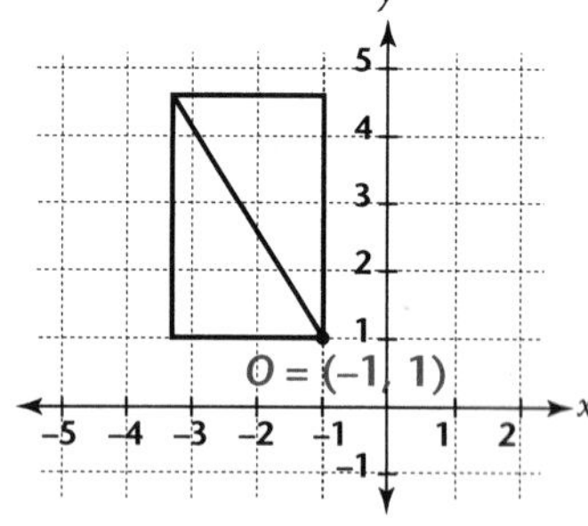

7.

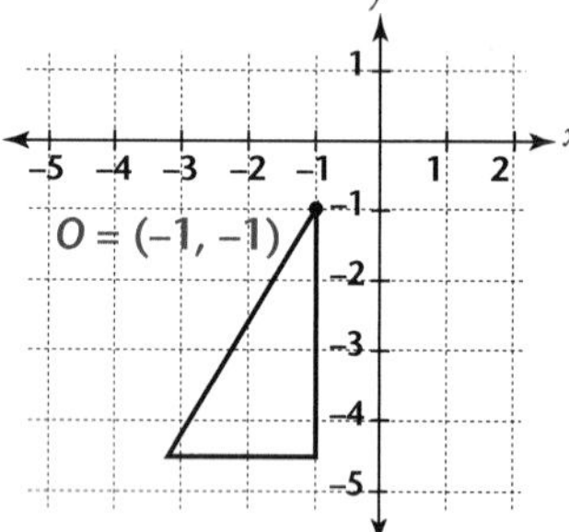

Exercise B Copy the given figure onto graph paper. Then rotate the object 180° counterclockwise to produce an image. Draw the image. (Remember, O is the center of rotation.)

8.

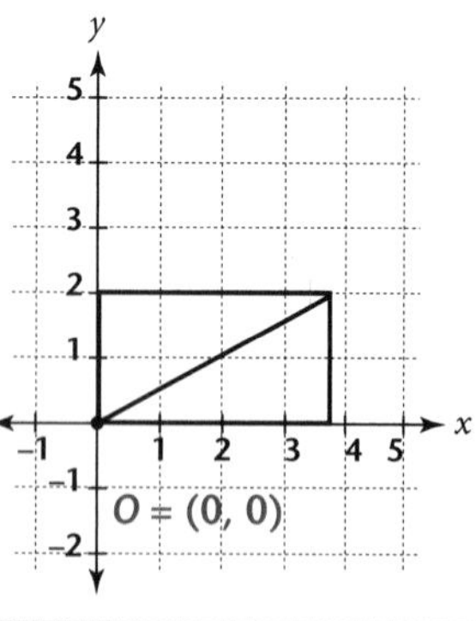

9.

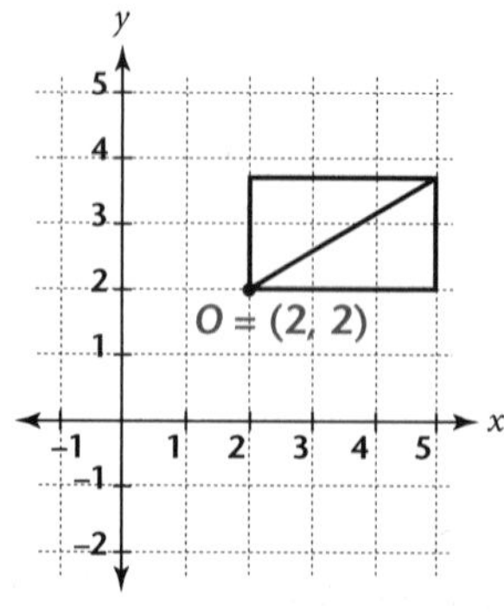

10.

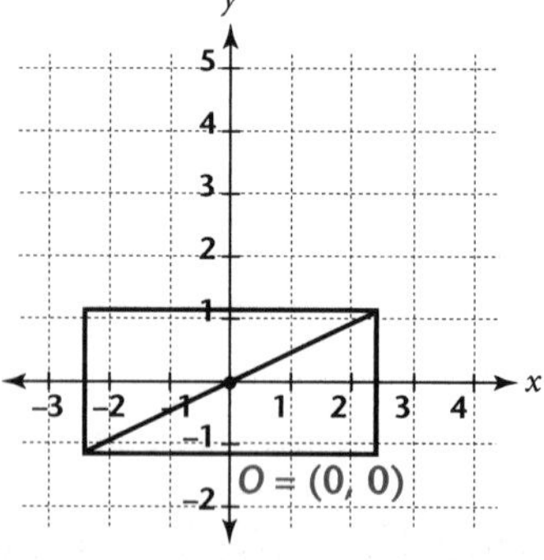

Writing About Mathematics

Describe the image of the circle in the diagram if the circle is rotated 90° or rotated 180° with a center of rotation at (0, 0).

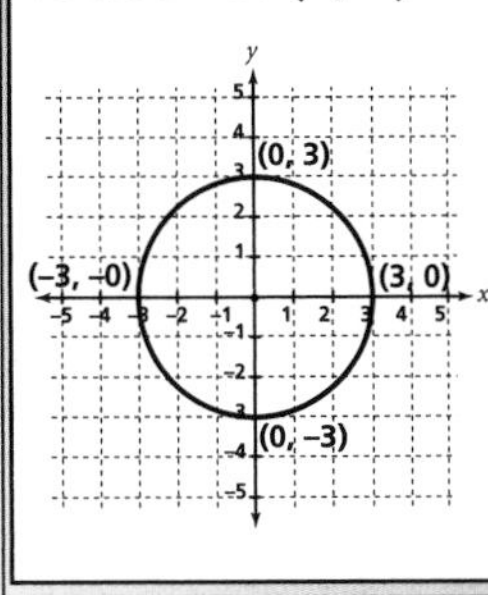

11.

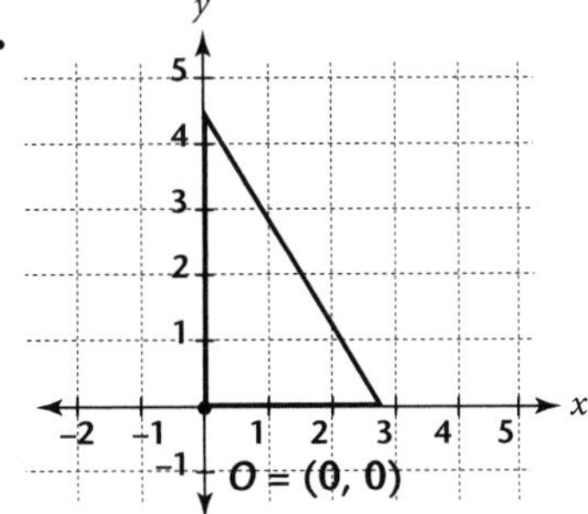

12.

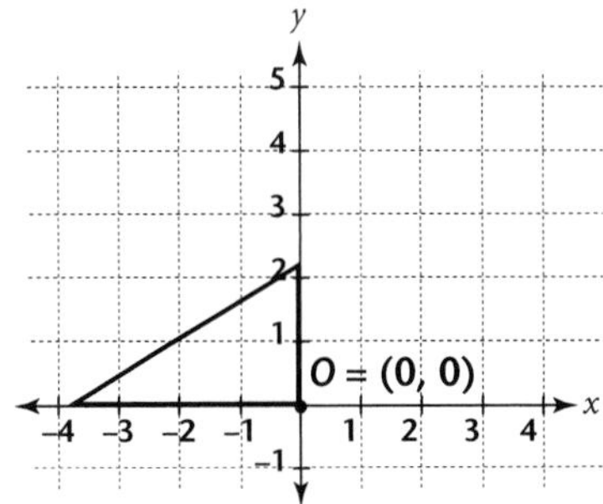

13.

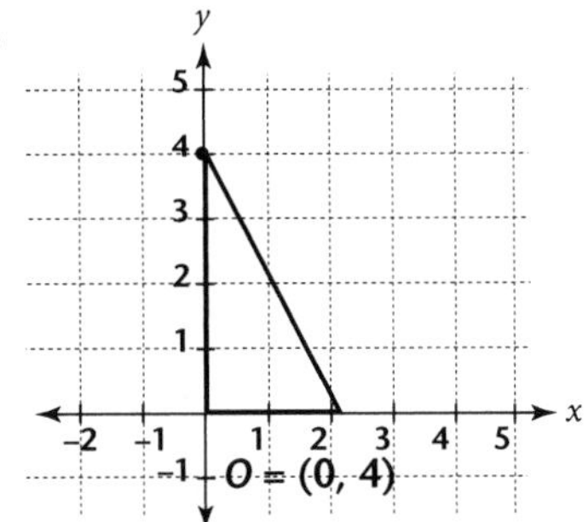

14.

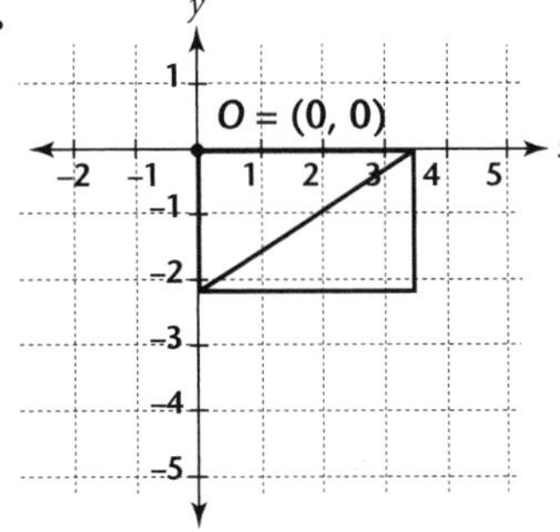

Exercise C Rotate each of the following points 180° counterclockwise around the origin. Give the coordinates of the image point.

15. $(4, -5)$

16. $(5, 5)$

17. $(7, 1)$

18. $(-8, 3)$

19. $(8, -3)$

20. $(4, -6)$

Geometry in Your Life

Skateboarders and bicycle riders do tricks that include rotations about a point. They use front or rear wheel or the middle of the bike or board as the center of rotation. These rotations do not affect the size or shape of the vehicle. To illustrate a rotation, start by cutting a triangle, square, and rectangle from heavy construction paper. Mark a center of rotation at one vertex on each shape. Then, using your compass needle to anchor the center of rotation, turn each shape first 90° clockwise and then 180° counterclockwise.

Lesson 9 Algebra Connection: Quadratic Equations

Quadratic equation

An equation in which the highest power of the variable is the second power

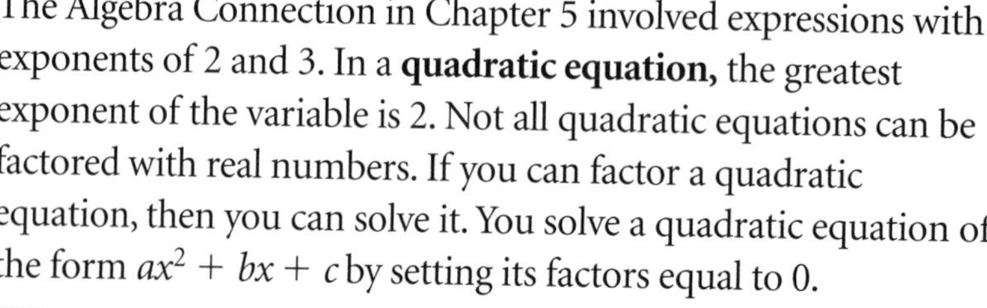

The Algebra Connection in Chapter 5 involved expressions with exponents of 2 and 3. In a **quadratic equation,** the greatest exponent of the variable is 2. Not all quadratic equations can be factored with real numbers. If you can factor a quadratic equation, then you can solve it. You solve a quadratic equation of the form $ax^2 + bx + c$ by setting its factors equal to 0.

Remember:
If $ab = 0$, then $a = 0$, $b = 0$, or $a = b = 0$.

EXAMPLE 1 Solve for x: $x^2 + x - 2 = 0$

Step 1 Make sure that one side is 0. Then factor the other side.

Think: $(x + 2)(x - 1) = x(x - 1) + 2(x - 1)$
$= x^2 - x + 2x - 2$
$= x^2 + x - 2$

So, we can write $x^2 + x - 2 = 0$ as $(x + 2)(x - 1) = 0$.

Step 2 Set *each* factor equal to 0.
$x + 2 = 0$ or $x - 1 = 0$

Step 3 Solve. There are two equations, so, there are two solutions.

$x + 2 = 0 \rightarrow x = -2$ $\quad$ $x - 1 = 0 \rightarrow x = 1$

One solution is $x = -2$. The other solution is $x = 1$.

Step 4 Check $x = -2$: $x^2 + x - 2 = (-2)^2 + (-2) - 2$
$= 4 - 2 - 2 = 0$

Check $x = 1$: $x^2 + x - 2 = (1)^2 + (1) - 2$
$= 1 + 1 - 2 = 0$

EXAMPLE 2 Solve for x: $x^2 + 5x + 6 = 0$

Step 1 Factor. Think $6 = 2 \bullet 3$ and $2 + 3 = 5$.

$x^2 + 5x + 6 = (x + 2)(x + 3)$

So, $(x + 2)(x + 3) = 0$

Step 2 Set each factor equal to 0.
$x + 2 = 0$ or $x + 3 = 0$

Step 3 Solve for each x.

$x + 2 = 0 \rightarrow x = -2$ $\quad$ $x + 3 = 0 \rightarrow x = -3$

Step 4 Check $x = -2$: $x^2 + 5x + 6 = (-2)^2 + 5 \bullet (-2) + 6$
$= 4 - 10 + 6 = 0$

Check $x = -3$: $x^2 + 5x + 6 = (-3)^2 + 5 \bullet (-3) + 6$
$= 9 - 15 + 6 = 0$

TRY THIS

The area of a rectangle is given by the formula $3x^2 + 16x + 5$. What are the dimensions of the rectangle? What is the perimeter? **Hint:** The length, width, and perimeter are algebraic expressions.

$w = \blacksquare$ | $3x^2 + 16x + 5$ | $l = \blacksquare$

EXAMPLE 3 Solve for x: $2x^2 + 13x + 15 = 0$

Step 1 Factor.

Try $(2x + 3)(x + 5)$, $(2x + 5)(x + 3)$, $(2x + 1)(x + 15)$, and $(2x + 15)(x + 1)$. Multiply each to find the correct factors.

$2x^2 + 13x + 15 = (2x + 3)(x + 5)$

Step 2 Set each factor equal to 0.

$2x + 3 = 0$ or $x + 5 = 0$

Step 3 Solve for each x.

$$2x + 3 = 0 \qquad x + 5 = 0$$
$$2x = -3 \qquad x = -5$$
$$x = -\frac{3}{2}$$

Step 4 Check $x = -\frac{3}{2}$: $2x^2 + 13x + 15 =$

$$2\left(-\frac{3}{2}\right)^2 + 13\left(-\frac{3}{2}\right) + 15 =$$
$$\frac{9}{2} - \frac{39}{2} + \frac{30}{2} = 0$$

Check $x = -5$: $2x^2 + 13x + 15 =$

$$2(-5)^2 + 13(-5) + 15 =$$
$$50 - 65 + 15 = 0$$

Exercise A Solve for each unknown. Check your answers.

1. $x^2 + 7x + 12 = 0$
2. $y^2 - y - 30 = 0$
3. $m^2 - 4m - 5 = 0$
4. $a^2 + 3a - 18 = 0$
5. $z^2 + z - 6 = 0$
6. $n^2 + 9n + 14 = 0$
7. $c^2 - 5c - 24 = 0$
8. $x^2 + 3x - 10 = 0$
9. $a^2 - 6a + 8 = 0$
10. $b^2 + 2b - 8 = 0$

Exercise B Solve for each unknown. Check your answers.

11. $3x^2 + 12x - 36 = 0$
12. $2y^2 - 16y + 30 = 0$
13. $2z^2 + 13z + 15 = 0$
14. $4w^2 - 42w + 20 = 0$
15. $2x^2 - x - 3 = 0$

Application

Tessellations Look at your classroom floor or ceiling. Is either covered by a series of rectangles or squares placed one next to the other?

Each of these is an example of a *tessellation.* A tessellation is an arrangement of shapes that cover a plane surface without overlapping and without leaving gaps between the shapes. Not all regular polygons tessellate. More complex tessellations use other shapes, a combination of shapes, or a regular shape that has been altered in a special way. Artists make elaborate designs and pictures using tessellations.

EXAMPLE 1 Make a tessellation using the shape at the right.

To make the tessellation you may have to turn, rotate, slide, or flip the basic shape as needed. The only rules are (1) there can be no gaps, and (2) the shapes cannot overlap.

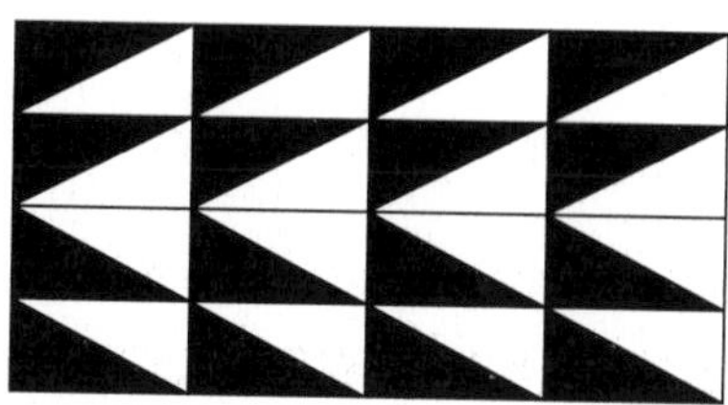

Exercise Test whether shapes tessellate and create your own tessellations by following the directions below.

1. Test which of these shapes can tessellate. Draw each tessellation on a sheet of paper. When you are finished, compare your tessellations with those your classmates found.

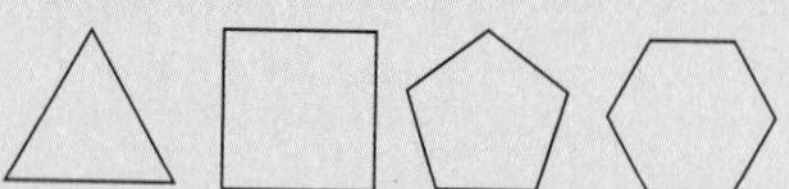

2. Draw a tessellation using regular octagons and squares.

3. Determine if you can make a tessellation using the octagon shown.

4. Draw a tessellation using triangles and rectangles.

5. Draw a tessellation using triangles and squares.

Chapter 6 REVIEW

Write the letter of the correct answer.

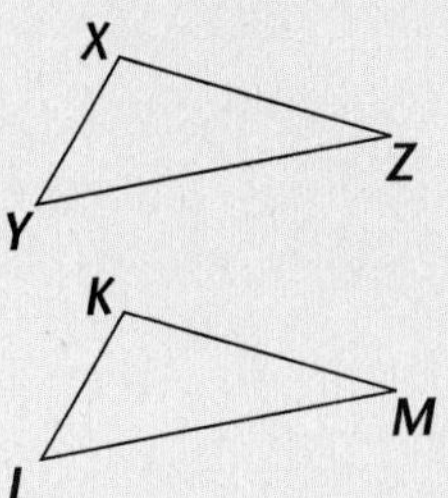

1. $\Delta XYZ \cong \Delta KLM$. Which statement must be true?

   A $\angle K \cong \angle Z$ **C** $\overline{XZ} \cong \overline{KM}$
   B $\angle Y \cong \angle Z$ **D** $\overline{YZ} \cong \overline{KM}$

2. A triangle has sides of length *a*, *b*, and *c*. Which of the following *could not* be possible values for *a*, *b*, and *c*?

   A $a = 6, b = 6, c = 6$ **C** $a = 6, b = 30, c = 30$
   B $a = 6, b = 8, c = 10$ **D** $a = 6, b = 40, c = 50$

3. How many lines of symmetry does the square shown here have?

   A 1 **B** 2 **C** 4 **D** 8

4. The point (3, 6) is reflected over the *y*-axis. What are the coordinates of its image?

   A $(-3, 6)$ **B** $(-3, -6)$ **C** $(3, -6)$ **D** $(6, 3)$

5. The point $(-1, 7)$ is translated using the rule $(x, y) \rightarrow (x - 5, y - 3)$. What is the image of $(-1, 7)$?

   A $(-5, 3)$ **B** $(-6, 4)$ **C** $(-4, 4)$ **D** $(4, 10)$

6. Which theorem or postulate allows you to prove that the two triangles shown are congruent?

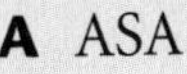

   A ASA **C** SSS
   B SAS **D** H-L

7. In the figure to the right, $\overline{AB}$ and $\overline{CD}$ intersect at point *X*. Which theorem or postulate allows you to prove that $\Delta AXC \cong \Delta BXD$?

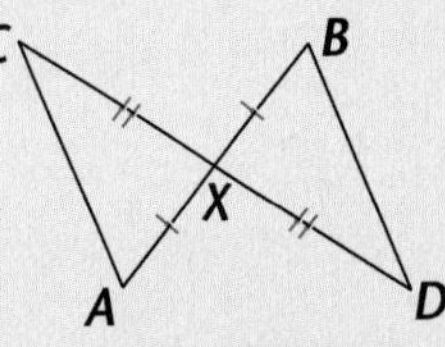

   A ASA **B** SAS **C** SSS **D** H-L

Complete the following constructions on a separate sheet of paper.

Example: Draw acute ΔABC. Then use SSS to construct ΔXYZ such that $\Delta XYZ \cong \Delta ABC$.

Solution:

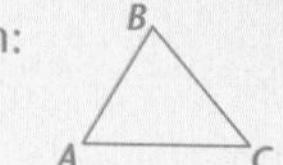

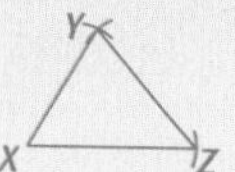

8. Draw obtuse ΔABC. Then use SAS to construct ΔXYZ such that $\Delta XYZ \cong \Delta ABC$.

9. Draw acute ΔABC. Then use ASA to construct ΔXYZ such that $\Delta XYZ \cong \Delta ABC$.

Find the measurement for each angle listed. Write the measurement.

Example:

Given: $m\angle 1$ is twice $m\angle 2$

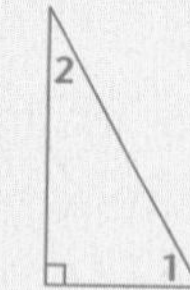

Solution: $m\angle 2 = 30°$; $m\angle 1 = 60°$
let $x = m\angle 2$, $2x = m\angle 1$
$x + 2x + 90° = 180°$ sum of angles in triangle
$3x = 180° - 90° = 90°$
$x = 30°$ $m\angle 2 = 30°$ $m\angle 1 = 2(30°) = 60°$

10. $m\angle e = m\angle f$
$m\angle f =$ ___

11. $m\angle g$ is 10° greater than $m\angle h$
$m\angle g =$ ___
$m\angle h =$ ___
$m\angle i =$ ___

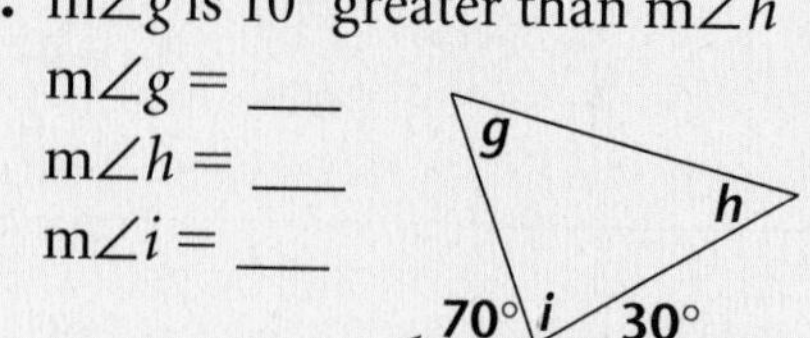

Tell whether the given line of reflection is also a line of symmetry. Write *yes* or *no*.

Example:

Solution: Yes, the image and object will coincide.

12.

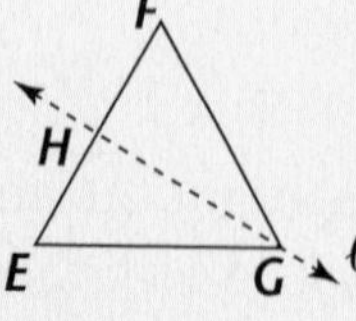

13.

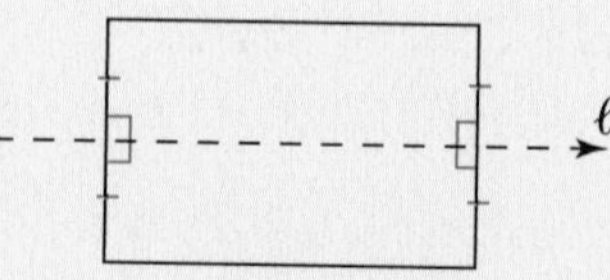

14.

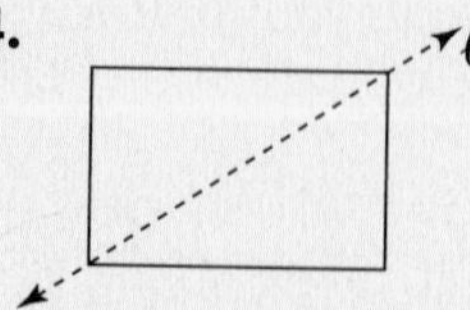

15.

Tell whether the image (blue) is a slide, reflection, or rotation of the object.

Example: 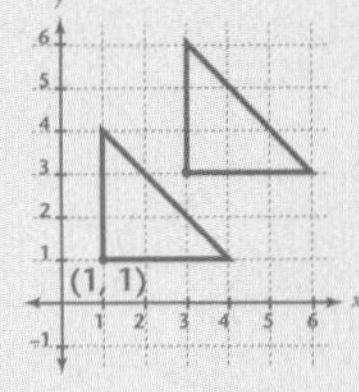

Solution: Slide; the image is above and to the right of the object.

16. 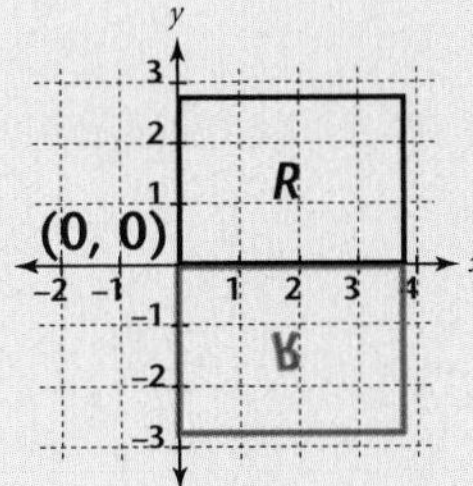

17. 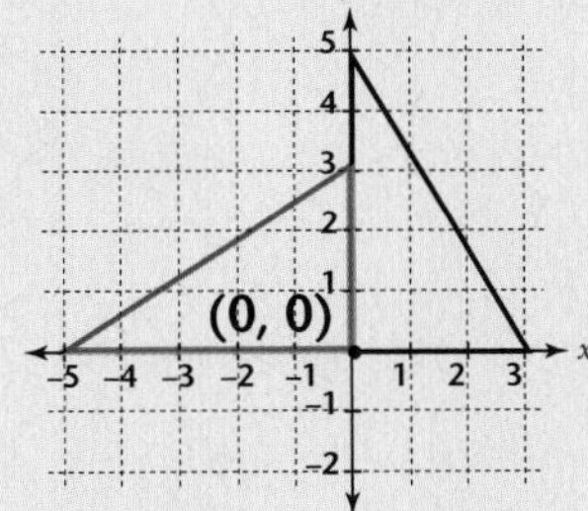

18. 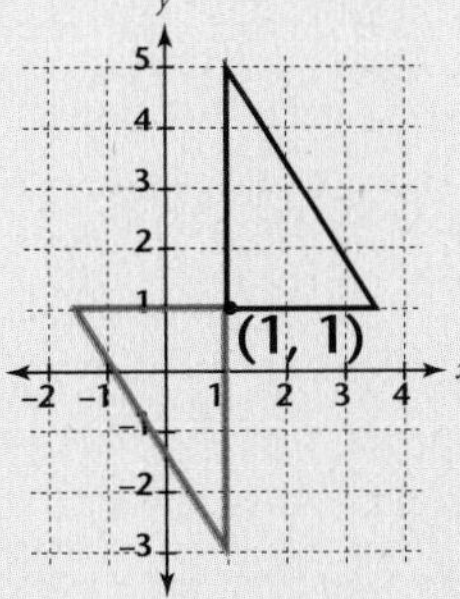

19. 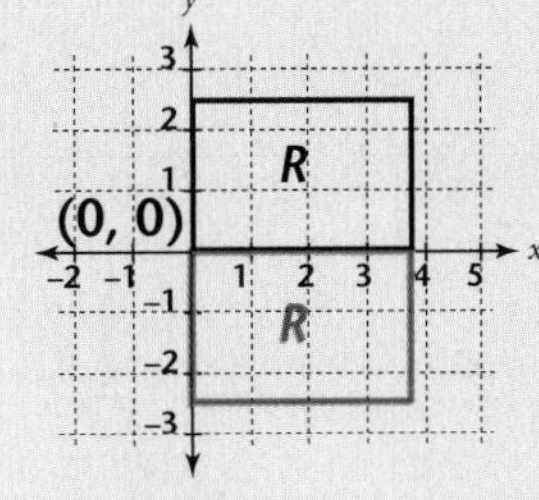

Find the coordinates of each image point.

Example: (2, 4) is reflected across the x-axis.
Solution: When (x, y) is reflected across the x-axis, its image is $(x, -y)$.
So, (2, 4) has image (2, −4).

20. $(-5, -8)$ is reflected across the y-axis.

21. $(0, 6)$ is translated 4 units to the left and 4 units down.

22. $(1, 3)$ is rotated 180° clockwise around the origin.

23. $(0, -10)$ is rotated 180° around the origin counterclockwise.

24. $(-1, -2)$ is mapped by the translation $(x, y) \rightarrow (x + 1, y - 1)$.

25. $(7, 7)$ is reflected across the line $x = 5$.

Test-Taking Tip

When studying for a test, review any tests or quizzes you took earlier that cover the same information. Make sure you have the correct answers for any items you missed.

Chapter

Proportion and Similarity

Russian *matushka* or stacking dolls have been popular toys for more than one hundred years. They come in styles and designs from animals to celebrities. Each doll but the smallest splits in half at its middle. The largest can hold all the others inside.

We would not say that the dolls pictured here are *the same* because they vary in size. But we might say that the dolls are *similar* because they seem to have the same shape and appearance. In geometry, the word *similar* is used to describe figures that have the same shape but not necessarily the same size.

In Chapter 7, you will learn about similarities and proportions in geometric shapes.

Goals for Learning

- To identify equal proportions
- To understand that the product of the extremes equals the product of the means and to use this theorem to solve problems
- To solve for the missing sides of similar triangles
- To construct regular polygons and demonstrate their similarity
- To give coordinates of dilations

Lesson 1 Similar Figures and Proportions

Similar

Having the same shape

Ratio

Comparison of two like quantities

$\frac{a}{b}$ *or* a:b

Diameter

Distance across a circle through the center

Ratio of similarity

A ratio comparing the relative sizes of similar figures

Look around and you may notice that many things are the same shape but are very different sizes. For example, these three models are all trains. The trains have the same basic shape but different sizes.

In geometry, **similar** figures are figures that have the same shape. They do not need to be the same size. The different sizes can be compared using a **ratio**, a fraction that represents the relative sizes.

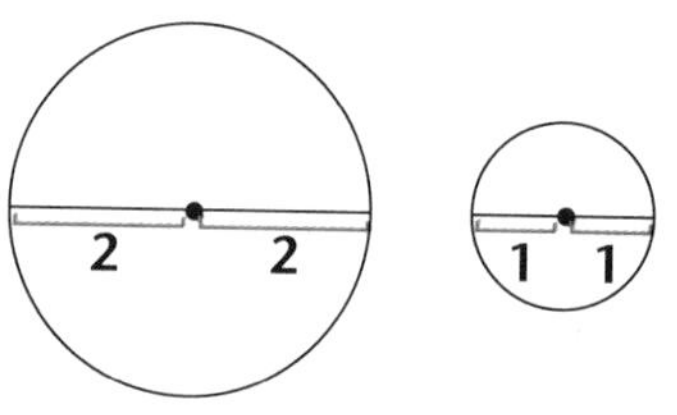

For the circles above, the ratio of **diameters** is 4 to 2. We can write this as 4:2 or $\frac{4}{2}$. We can also state that the **ratio of similarity** between the two circles is $\frac{4}{2}$ or $\frac{2}{1}$.

You already know that all squares are similar. All squares have the same shape and all have four right angles. The squares below have sides measuring 2 to 6 units long.

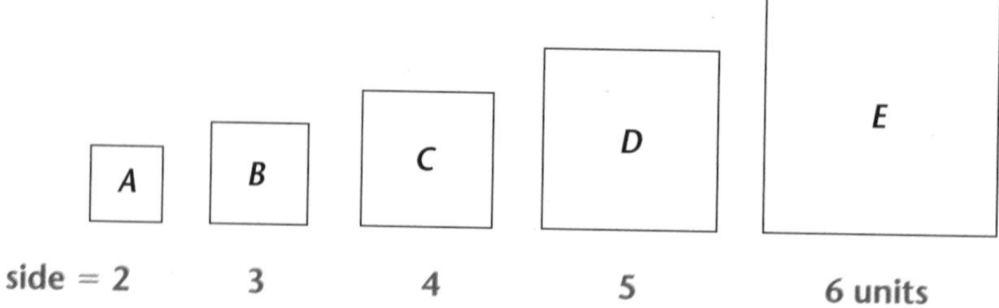

The ratio of similarity between the sides of *A* and *B* is 2 to 3 or $\frac{2}{3}$. The ratio of similarity between the sides of *A* and *E* is 2 to 6 or $\frac{2}{6} = \frac{1}{3}$.

The symbol $\sim$ is used to show that two geometric figures are similar. Read it as "is similar to."

In the same way, you can see that all equilateral triangles have the same shape. Each angle measures 60°. The sides of the triangles below are 1, 2, or 3 units long.

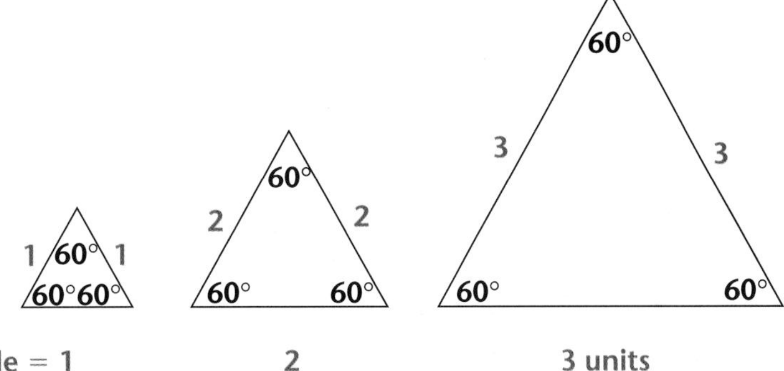

The ratio of similarity between the smallest and largest triangles is 1 to 3 or $\frac{1}{3}$.

The ratio of similarity between the largest and middle triangles is 3 to 2 or $\frac{3}{2}$.

Triangles need not be equilateral to be similar. Any two triangles can be similar if certain conditions are present.

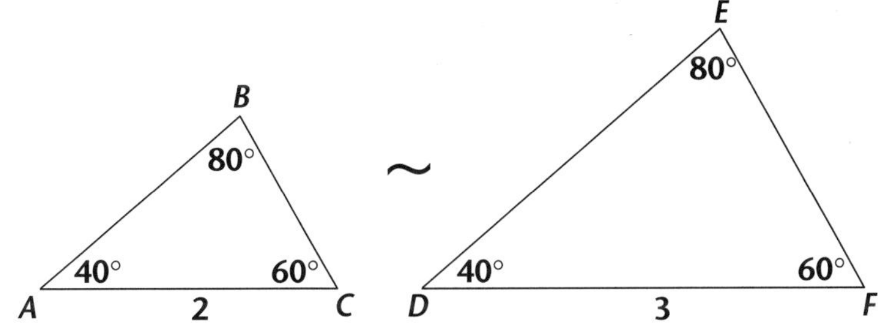

ΔABC is similar to ΔDEF if the corresponding angles of the triangles are equal and the corresponding pairs of sides have the same ratio of similarity.

Because the corresponding sides of the triangles have the same ratio of similarity, we know that

$$\frac{AB}{DE} = \frac{BC}{EF} = \frac{AC}{DF}$$

The ratio $\frac{AC}{DF}$ is given as 2 to 3 or $\frac{2}{3}$.

Therefore, the ratios $\frac{AB}{DE}$ and $\frac{BC}{EF}$ are also equal to $\frac{2}{3}$.

As we learned in Chapter 6, congruent triangles have equal sides, so the ratio of similarity is 1 to 1 or $\frac{1}{1}$. Congruent shapes are a special case of similar figures.

Proportion

The equality of two ratios

$\frac{a}{b} = \frac{c}{d}$

An example of a ratio you can form with right triangles is the ratio of the hypotenuse of one triangle to the hypotenuse of a second triangle. Another ratio is the shortest side of one triangle to the shortest side of a second triangle, and so on. You can write these ratios as fractions such as

$$\frac{\text{hypotenuse}_1}{\text{hypotenuse}_2} \qquad \frac{\text{base}_1}{\text{base}_2} \qquad \frac{\text{shortest side of } \Delta_1}{\text{shortest side of } \Delta_2}$$

Remember, the hypotenuse is the longest side in a right triangle.

If two ratios are equal, we can write them as a **proportion.** A proportion, written $\frac{a}{b} = \frac{c}{d}$, is the equality of two ratios.

In a proportion, terms a and d are called the *extremes* while terms b and c are called the *means.*

Note that $\frac{a}{b} = \frac{c}{d}$ can also be written as $a{:}b{::}c{:}d$ (read "a is to b as c is to d"). This form may help you to tell the means from the extremes.

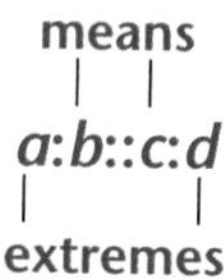

Theorem 7.1.1: In any proportion, the product of the extremes equals the product of the means.

Here's the proof of this theorem.

Given: any proportion $\frac{a}{b} = \frac{c}{d}$

To Prove: $ad = bc$

PROOF

Statement	Reason
1. $\frac{a}{b} = \frac{c}{d}$	1. Given.
2. $\frac{a}{b}(b)(d) = \frac{c}{d}(b)(d)$	2. Multiply by equals.
3. $ad = cb$	3. Simplify.

Example 1 **Given:** ΔABC is similar to ΔDEF

Find: length of $\overline{DE}$

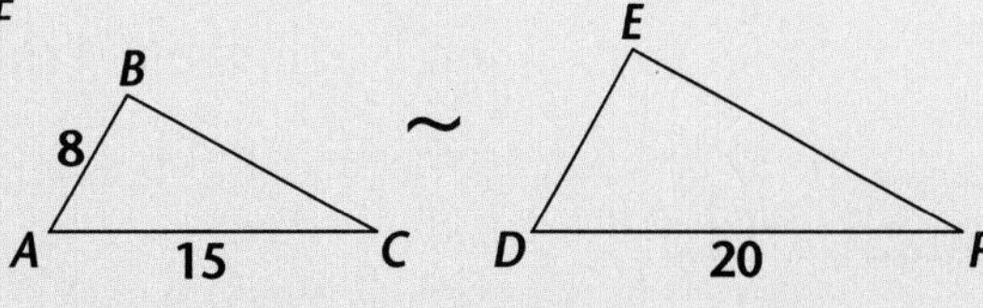

Because the triangles are similar, their corresponding sides are in proportion. This means

$\frac{AC}{DF} = \frac{15}{20}$, which can be reduced to $\frac{3}{4}$.

Therefore, $\frac{3}{4} = \frac{AB}{DE}$

or $\frac{3}{4} = \frac{8}{DE}$

Using product of the means = product of the extremes,

$$\frac{8}{DE} \times \frac{3}{4}$$

so $3(DE) = 8 \bullet 4$

and $3(DE) = 32$

so $DE = \frac{32}{3} = 10\frac{2}{3}$

The length of $\overline{DE}$ is $10\frac{2}{3}$.

Example 2 **Given:** ΔABC is similar to ΔDEF

Find: length of leg $\overline{DE}$ and length of hypotenuse $\overline{EF}$

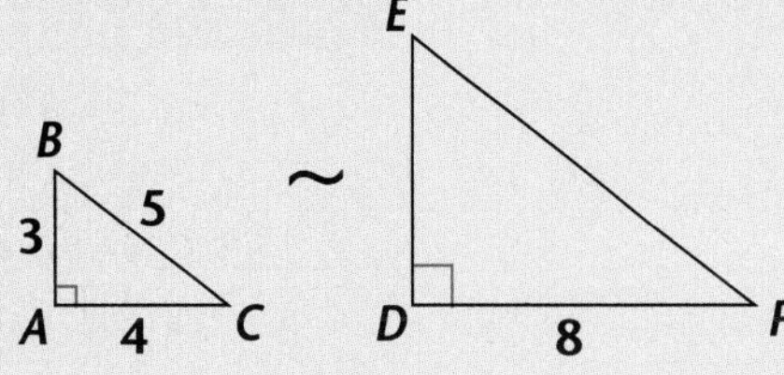

Because the triangles are similar, their corresponding sides are in proportion. This means

$\frac{AC}{DF} = \frac{4}{8} = \frac{1}{2}$

Therefore, $\frac{1}{2} = \frac{AB}{DE}$

or $\frac{1}{2} = \frac{3}{DE}$

Using product of the extremes = product of the means,

$DE = 2 \bullet 3 = 6$ The length of $\overline{DE}$ is 6.

Also, $\frac{1}{2} = \frac{BC}{EF}$

or $\frac{1}{2} = \frac{5}{EF}$

Using product of the extremes = product of the means,

$EF = 2 \bullet 5 = 10$ The length of $\overline{EF}$ is 10.

To find out if $\Delta ABC \sim \Delta DEF$, we need to look at the ratios $\frac{3}{6}$ and $\frac{5}{9}$ to find out if they are equal.

EXAMPLE 3 Are the ratios $\frac{3}{6}$ and $\frac{5}{9}$ equal?

If the ratios are equal, then they form a proportion. In a proportion, the product of the extremes equals the product of the means.

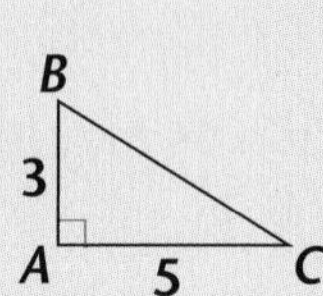

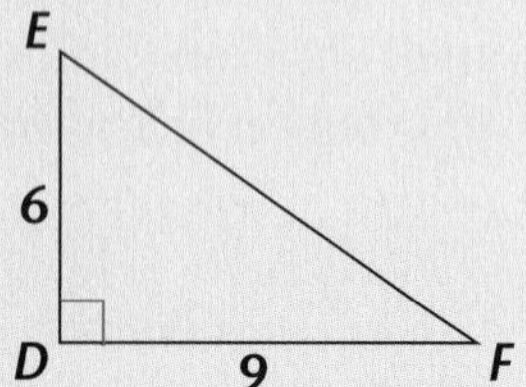

$$\frac{3}{6} = \frac{5}{9}$$

(extremes) $3 \bullet 9 = 5 \bullet 6$ (means)

$27 = 30$ False. The ratios are not equal and the triangles are not similar.

Calculator Practice

You can use your calculator to find the missing value in a proportion.

EXAMPLE 4 $\frac{3}{5} = \frac{6}{x}$

(extremes) $3 \bullet x = 5 \bullet 6$ (means)

$$x = \frac{(5 \bullet 6)}{3}$$

Press 5 [×] 6 [÷] 3 [ENTER]. Display shows 10.

Exercise A Find the missing value in each proportion.

1. $\frac{2}{3} = \frac{x}{9}$

2. $\frac{3}{5} = \frac{6}{y}$

3. $\frac{7}{8} = \frac{z}{4}$

4. $\frac{3}{4} = \frac{a}{12}$

5. $\frac{5}{4} = \frac{b}{32}$

6. $\frac{c}{49} = \frac{4}{28}$

7. $\frac{21}{e} = \frac{7}{3}$

8. $\frac{f}{33} = \frac{11}{121}$

9. $\frac{h}{2} = \frac{42}{6}$

10. $\frac{2}{j} = \frac{12.5}{25}$

Exercise B Solve for the lengths of the missing sides in each pair of similar triangles. Round to the nearest tenth if necessary.

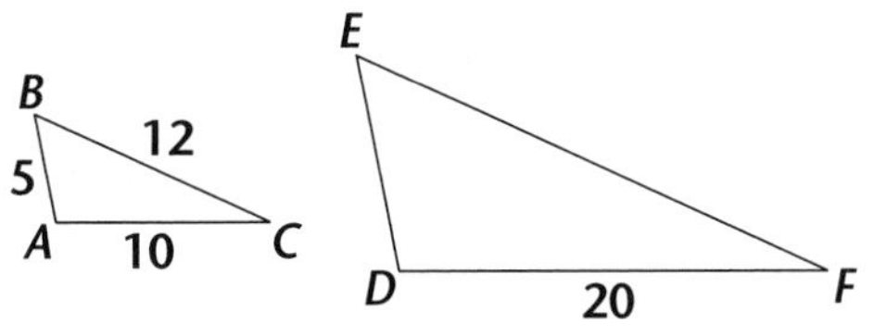

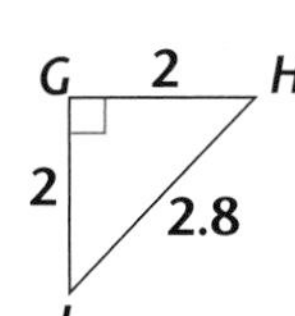

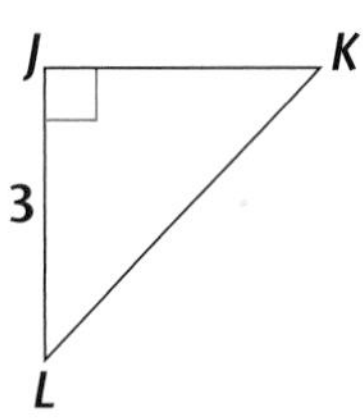

11. $\overline{DE}$

12. $\overline{EF}$

13. $\overline{JK}$

14. $\overline{KL}$

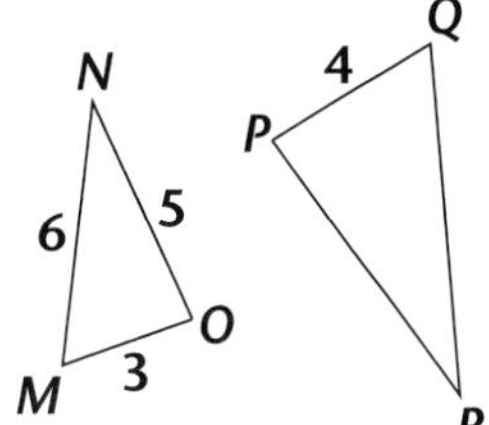

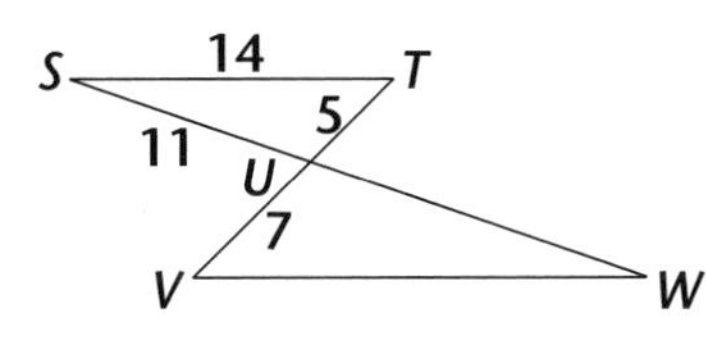

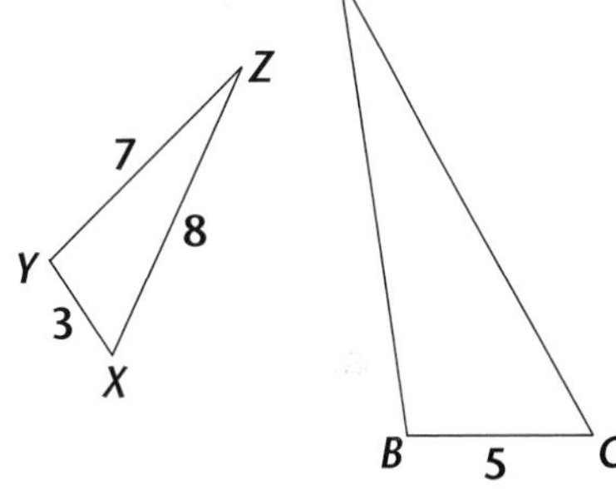

15. $\overline{PR}$

16. $\overline{RQ}$

17. $\overline{VW}$

18. $\overline{WU}$

19. $\overline{AB}$

20. $\overline{CA}$

Exercise C Are the following ratios equal? Write *yes* or *no.* Use the theorem that the product of the extremes equals the product of the means.

21. $\frac{3}{5}$ and $\frac{10}{16}$

22. $\frac{3}{7}$ and $\frac{5}{8}$

23. $\frac{1}{3}$ and $\frac{7}{21}$

24. $\frac{4}{9}$ and $\frac{28}{63}$

25. $\frac{6}{13}$ and $\frac{12}{29}$

26. $\frac{7}{9}$ and $\frac{49}{81}$

27. $\frac{6}{17}$ and $\frac{18}{51}$

28. $\frac{3}{23}$ and $\frac{27}{21}$

29. $\frac{6}{11}$ and $\frac{16}{61}$

30. $\frac{7}{21}$ and $\frac{12}{36}$

TRY THIS You know all equilateral triangles are similar. Is the same true for all isosceles triangles? Give reasons or an example to support your answer.

Lesson 2 Similar Triangles

Similar triangles

Triangles whose corresponding angles are equal and whose corresponding sides are in proportion

In the last lesson, you looked at several groups of similar geometric figures such as squares, circles, and equilateral triangles. You even worked with triangles that were not equilateral but were similar.

Similar triangles are triangles whose corresponding angles are equal and whose corresponding sides are proportional.

The following two triangles illustrate the definition of similar.

Corresponding angles are equal:

$m\angle A = m\angle D$

$m\angle B = m\angle E$

$m\angle C = m\angle F$

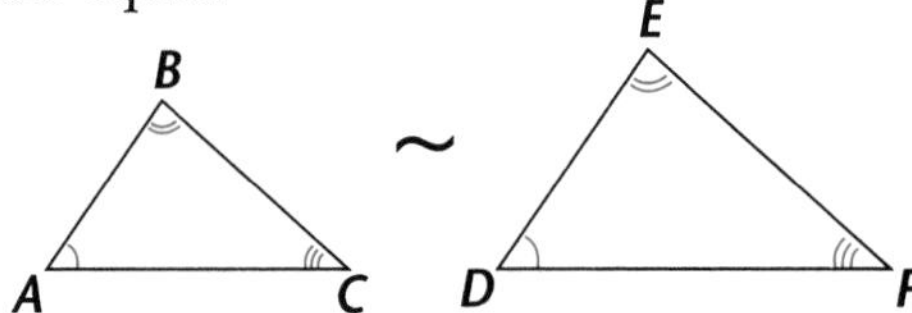

Opposite each pair of equal angles is a pair of corresponding sides that are proportional:

$\frac{BC}{EF}$	=	$\frac{AC}{DF}$	=	$\frac{AB}{DE}$
sides opposite $\angle A$ and $\angle D$		sides opposite $\angle B$ and $\angle E$		sides opposite $\angle C$ and $\angle F$

If two triangles are similar, you can calculate the length of an unknown side of one triangle using the lengths of known corresponding sides. Given any three sides in a proportion, you can always solve for the fourth side.

EXAMPLE 1 **Given:** $\Delta ABC \sim \Delta DFE$, $AB = 10$, $DF = 5$, $AC = 8$, $EF = 7$

Find: values for x and y

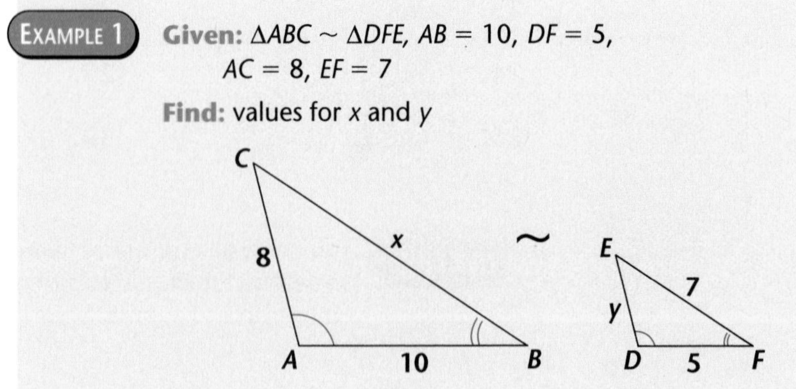

EXAMPLE 1 *(continued)*

For similar triangles, pairs of corresponding sides have the same ratio of similarity.

Because $\frac{AB}{DF} = \frac{10}{5} = \frac{2}{1}$, we know all other pairs of corresponding sides are in the ratio 2:1.

You can use the products of the means and the extremes to find the values for x and y.

$\frac{x}{7} = \frac{2}{1}$ becomes $(x \bullet 1) = (7 \bullet 2)$; $x = 14$

Check: $\frac{14}{7} = \frac{2}{1}$ True

$\frac{8}{y} = \frac{2}{1}$ becomes $(8 \bullet 1) = (y \bullet 2)$; $y = 4$

Check: $\frac{8}{4} = \frac{2}{1}$ True

EXAMPLE 2 **Given:** right $\triangle ABC \sim$ right $\triangle DEC$, $AC = 15$, $DC = 5$

Find: the ratio of AB to DE or $\frac{AB}{DE}$

$$\frac{AB}{DE} = \frac{\text{larger altitude}}{\text{smaller altitude}} = \frac{\text{larger base}}{\text{smaller base}} = \frac{15}{5} = \frac{3}{1}$$

Therefore, $\frac{AB}{DE} = \frac{3}{1}$

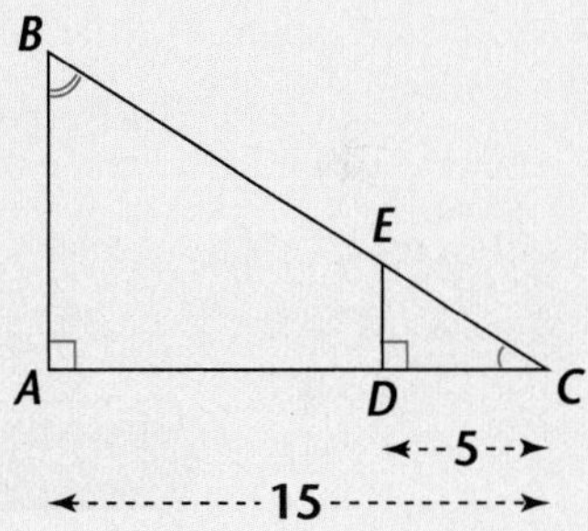

One way to show that two triangles are similar is to show that two angles of one triangle are equal to two angles of a second triangle.

Because every triangle has 180° as its angle sum, if two angles in one triangle equal two angles in the second triangle, then the third angles must also be equal. If the triangles have three pairs of corresponding equal angles, the triangles are similar. Examples of similar triangles follow.

Writing About Mathematics

Are the nested triangles shown in the diagram below similar? Why or why not?

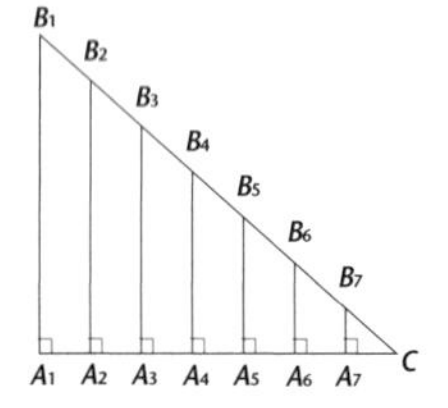

The following statement is assumed to be true without proof.

AA Similarity Postulate:
If two angles of a triangle have the same measures as two angles of a second triangle, then the two triangles are similar.

You can use this postulate to prove the following theorem.

Theorem 7.2.1:
If one acute angle of a right triangle has the same measure as one acute angle of a second right triangle, then the two right triangles are similar.

Given: right ΔABC and right ΔDEF with $m\angle C = m\angle F$

To Prove: $\Delta ABC \sim \Delta DEF$

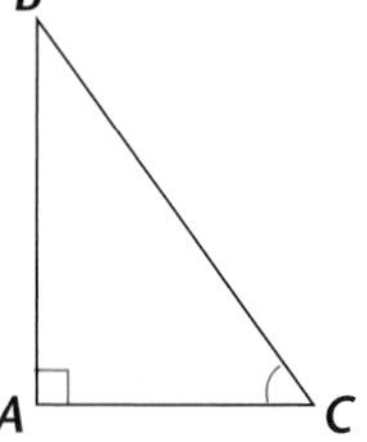

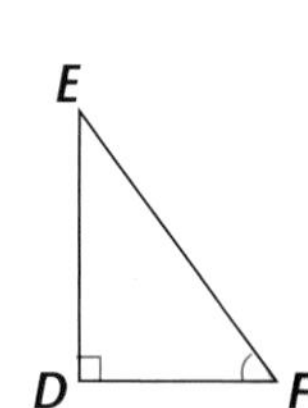

PROOF

Statement	Reason
1. $m\angle A = m\angle D$	1. All right angles are equal.
2. $m\angle C = m\angle F$	2. Given.
3. $\therefore$ right $\Delta ABC \sim$ right ΔDEF	3. AA Similarity Postulate.

Using the AA Similarity Postulate, we can show $\Delta ABC \sim \Delta EDC$ as shown below.

EXAMPLE 3 **Given:** $\overline{AB} \parallel \overline{DE}$, $AB = 10$, $DE = 5$, $BC = 7$

Find: the value of x

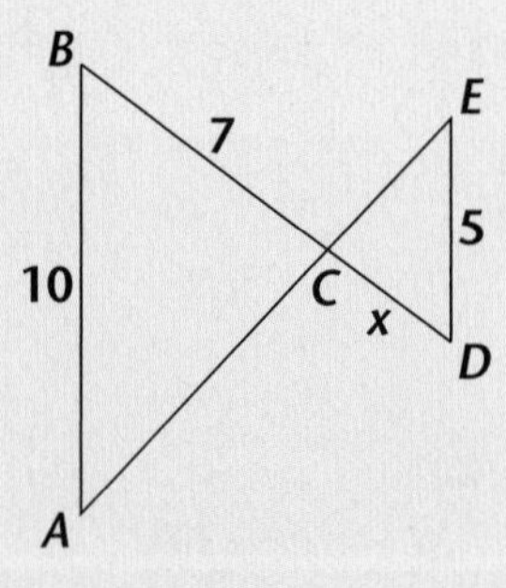

$m\angle ACB = m\angle DCE$
Vertical angles are equal.

$m\angle A = m\angle E$
$\overline{AB} \parallel \overline{DE}$ (given) and alternate interior angles are equal.

$\therefore$ $\Delta ABC \sim \Delta EDC$ by AA Similarity Postulate.

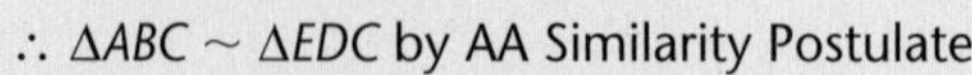

$\Delta ABC \sim \Delta EDC$ so $\frac{AB}{DE} = \frac{BC}{DC}$

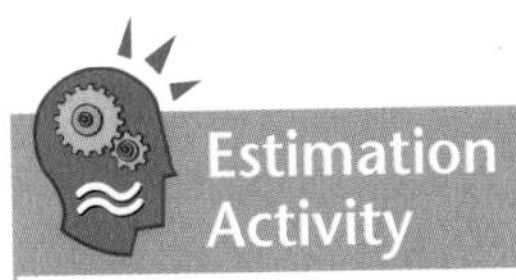

Estimation Activity

Estimate: Estimate the length of side x.

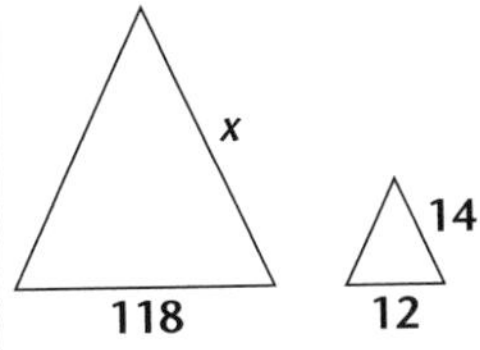

Solution:
Select a pair of corresponding sides. 118 and 12

Round the lengths of the sides.
$118 \approx 100$; $12 \approx 10$

Find the ratio of similarity.
$\frac{100}{10} = \frac{10}{1}$

Multiply the ratio by the given side.
$14(\frac{10}{1}) = 140$

The missing length is about 140.

Example 3 *(continued)*

$$\text{and } \frac{10}{5} = \frac{7}{x}$$
$$10x = 35$$
$$x = 3.5 \text{ The value of } x \text{ is } 3.5.$$

Check: $\frac{10}{5} = \frac{7}{3.5}$
$35 = 35$ True

Exercise A Tell whether each pair of triangles is similar. Answer *yes* or *no*. Give reasons for your answer.

1.
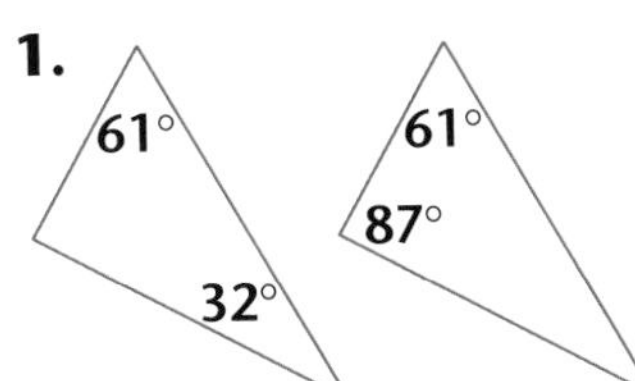

2.
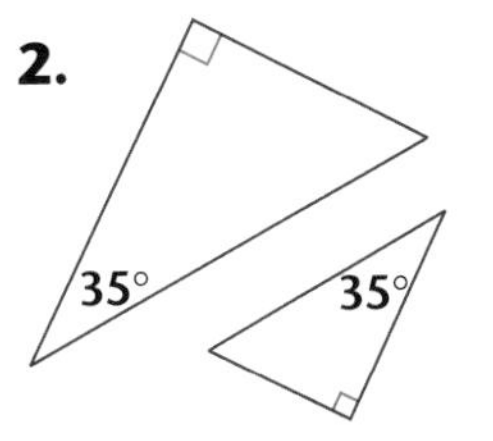

3.
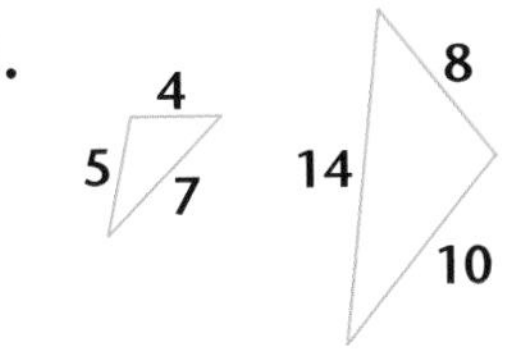

4.
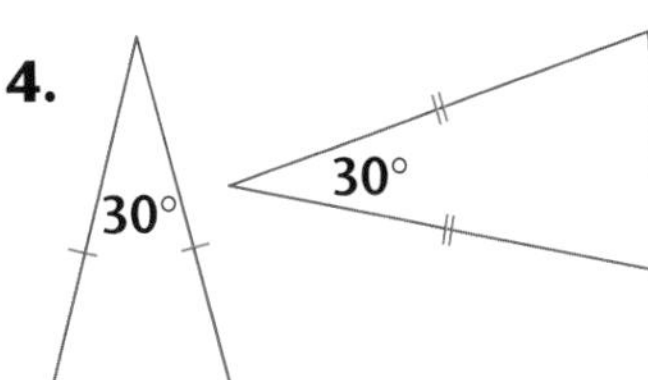

5.
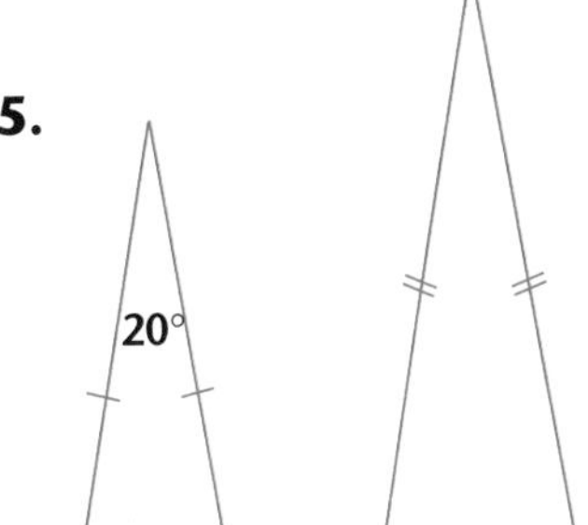

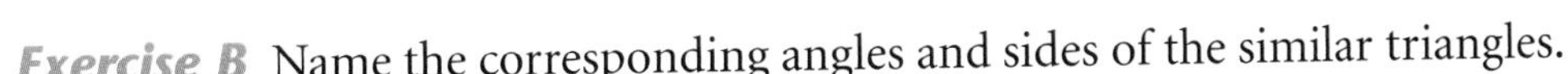

Exercise B Name the corresponding angles and sides of the similar triangles.

6. $m\angle A = \blacksquare$

7. $m\angle B = \blacksquare$

8. $m\angle ACB = \blacksquare$

9. $\frac{AB}{\blacksquare} = \frac{AC}{\blacksquare}$

10. $\frac{AC}{\blacksquare} = \frac{BC}{\blacksquare}$

11. $m\angle QPS = \blacksquare$

12. $m\angle PQR = \blacksquare$

13. $m\angle PSQ = \blacksquare$

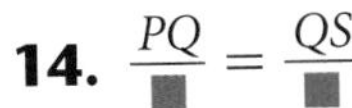

14. $\frac{PQ}{\blacksquare} = \frac{QS}{\blacksquare}$

15. $\frac{QS}{\blacksquare} = \frac{PS}{\blacksquare}$

Exercise C Each pair of triangles is similar. Solve for the values of the unknowns.

16. x

17. y

8 6 11 x y 22

20. s

21. t

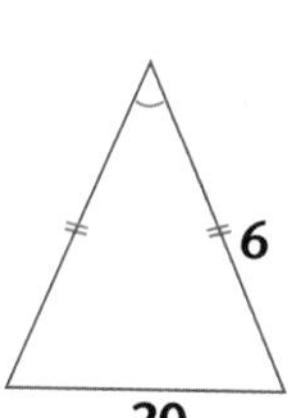

18. a

19. b

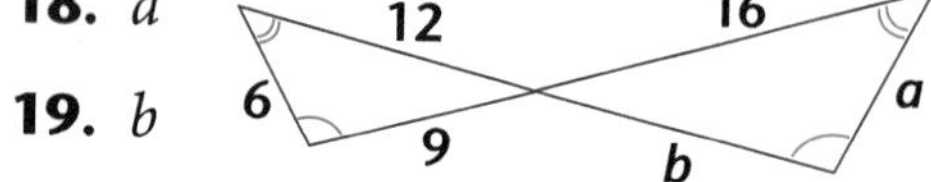

22. m

23. n

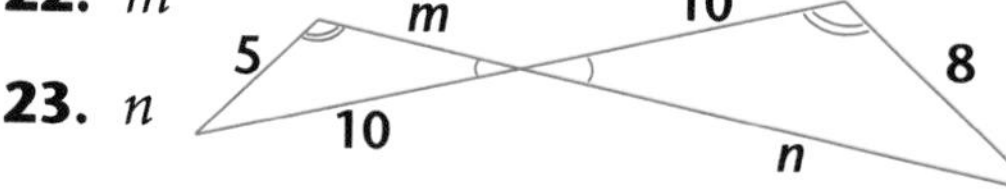

PROBLEM SOLVING

Exercise D Find the answer to each of the following problems.

24. A landscape planner used similar triangles and the shadow of a tree to draw the diagram shown. What is the height of the tree?

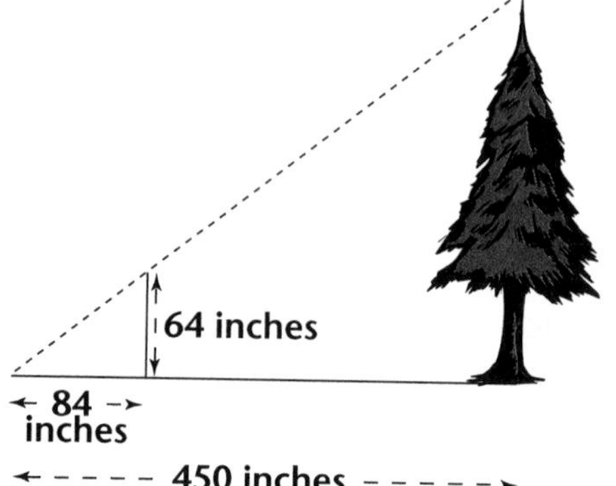

25. A surveyor needs to estimate the width of a pond. She has made the measurements shown in the diagram. How wide is the pond?

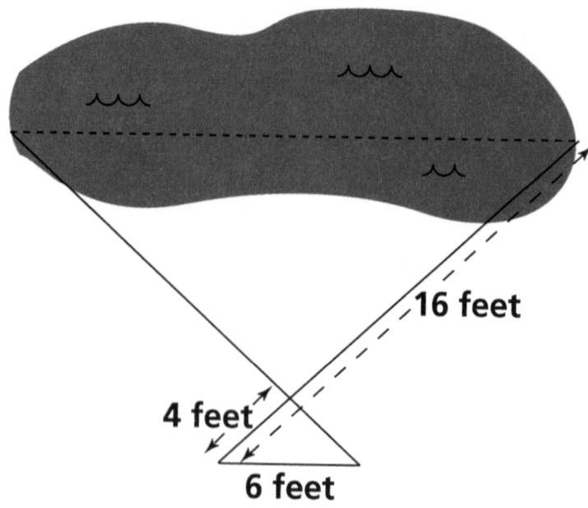

Lesson 3 Angle Measure in Regular Polygons

> ***Radius***
>
> *The distance from the center of a circle to the circle*

From your work with polygons you already know that regular polygons are polygons that have angles of equal measure and sides of equal length. Because regular polygons have equal angles, regular polygons with the same number of sides are similar. You are already familiar with some regular polygons.

All equilateral triangles are similar.

n = number of sides

$n = 3$

All squares are similar.

$n = 4$

A five-sided regular polygon is called a pentagon. All regular pentagons are similar.

$n = 5$

What is the angle measure of each of the five equal angles? We can reason out the answer for one pentagon and know that it will apply to all pentagons because they are similar figures.

Draw a circle around a regular pentagon. Each angle at the center—each central angle—measures $\frac{360°}{5} = 72°$.

The triangles forming the pentagon are each isosceles. Can you tell why? Each is formed using a **radius** of the circle. Each radius of a circle is equal to the others.

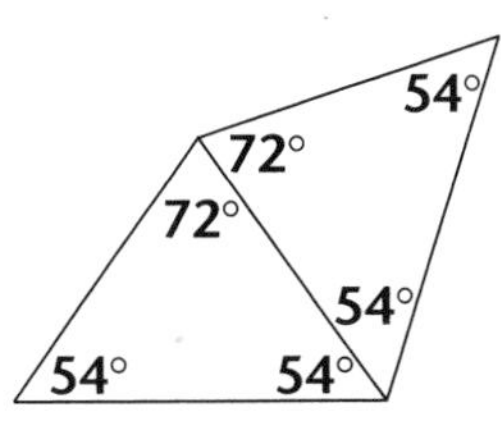

To find the measure of each base angle (x),

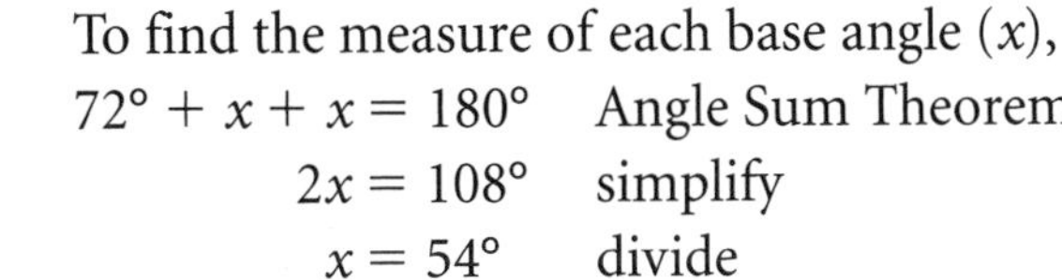

$72° + x + x = 180°$	Angle Sum Theorem
$2x = 108°$	simplify
$x = 54°$	divide

But two angles of 54° make up one interior angle of a regular pentagon.

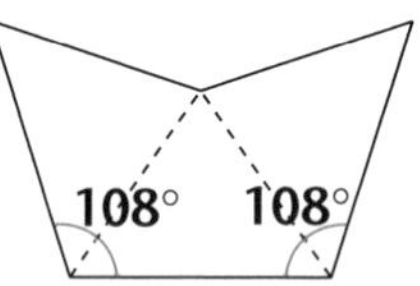

$\therefore 2(x) = \text{interior angle}$

$2(54°) = 108°$ the measure of each interior angle of a regular pentagon

You can also use algebra to find the angle measure.
Let n = number of equal sides, x = the base angle of the triangle.

$$\text{Then} \quad \frac{360°}{n} + 2x = 180°$$

$$2x = 180° - \frac{360°}{n}$$

Formula:
The measure of an interior angle of a regular polygon $= 180° - \frac{360°}{n}$, where n = number of sides.

EXAMPLE 1 **Given:** regular hexagon ($n = 6$)
Find: the size of the interior angles

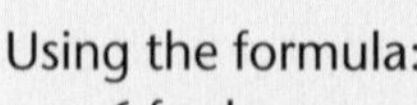

Using the formula:
$n = 6$ for hexagon
angle measure =
$180° - \frac{360°}{6} = 180° - 60° = 120°$

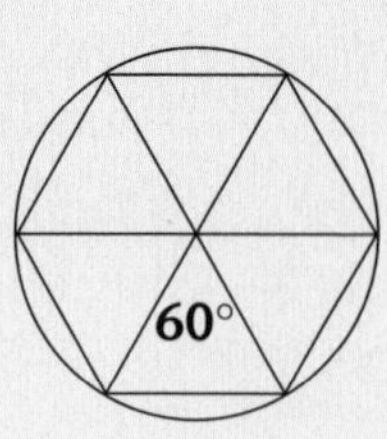

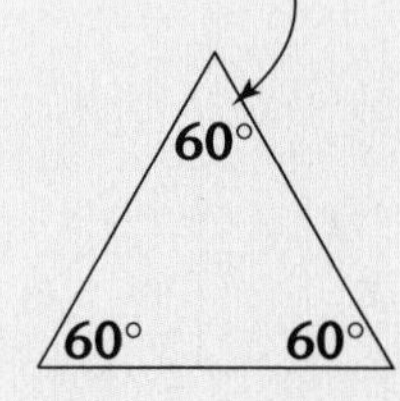

Using reasoning:
central angle measures $\frac{360°}{6} = 60°$
$180° - 60° = 120°$, $120° \div 2 = 60°$

But the triangle is isosceles.
(In fact, it's equilateral for $n = 6$.)

measure of the angle of a regular hexagon =
$2 \bullet 60° = 120°$

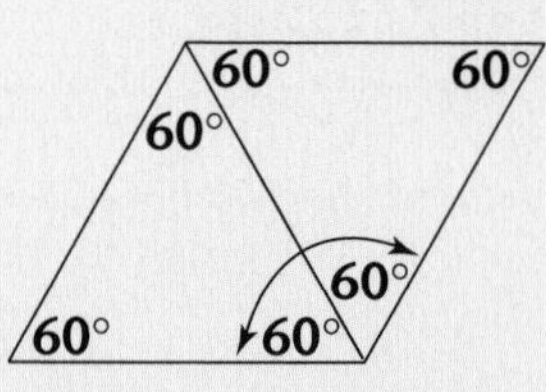

Of course, all regular hexagons are similar.

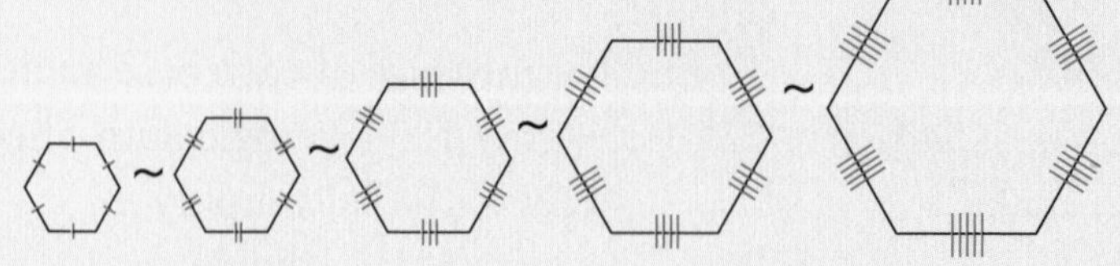

Writing About Mathematics

Use reasoning, rather than the formula, to find the measure of each interior angle of a regular octagon ($n = 8$).

Perimeter

The distance around the outside of a shape

Example 2 **Given:** two regular hexagons, $AB = 5$, and the ratio of similarity is 5:8

Find: the perimeter of the larger hexagon

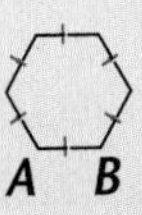

Perimeter of (distance around) smaller hexagon is $5 + 5 + 5 + 5 + 5 + 5 = 5 \bullet 6 = 30$.

A′ B′

The ratio of similarity is $\frac{AB}{A'B'} = \frac{5}{8}$.

$$\frac{\text{smaller}}{\text{larger}} = \frac{5}{8} = \frac{30}{x} = \frac{\text{perimeter of smaller}}{\text{perimeter of larger}}$$

$5x = 8(30)$	product of extremes = product of means
$5x = 240$	simplify
$x = 48$	

You can use the fact that regular hexagons contain six equilateral triangles to construct a regular hexagon.

Construction **Given:** circle with center O and radius r

Construct: a regular hexagon

Step 1 Draw a circle with center O and radius r.

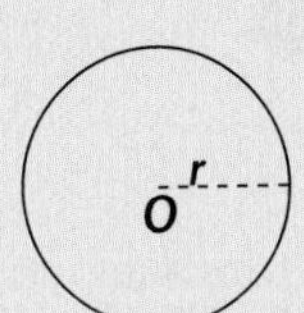

Step 2 With your compass open to the radius, mark off 6 arcs on the circumference. You can use any point on the circle as the center of the first arc.

Then use each intersection of an arc and the circle as the next center.

Step 3 Connect the 6 points where the arcs intersect the circle. You constructed a regular hexagon.

You can bisect angles to construct a regular octagon.

Given: circle with center O

Construct: a regular octagon

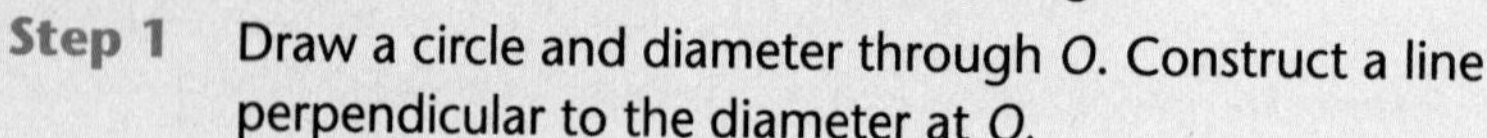

Step 1 Draw a circle and diameter through O. Construct a line perpendicular to the diameter at O.

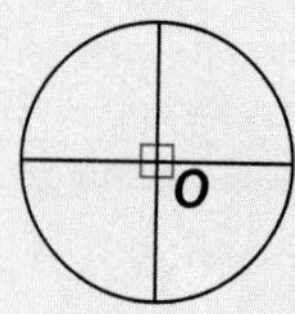

Step 2 Bisect two 90° angles. Draw two diameters.

Think: I need to bisect only two angles to make four points on the circle.

Step 3 Connect the endpoints of the 4 diameters. You have constructed a regular octagon.

You can use a graphing calculator to write a program that uses the formula for finding the measure of each interior angle for a regular polygon.

EXAMPLE 3

Step 1 Press [PRGM] [▶] [▶]. This displays the PRGM NEW menu.

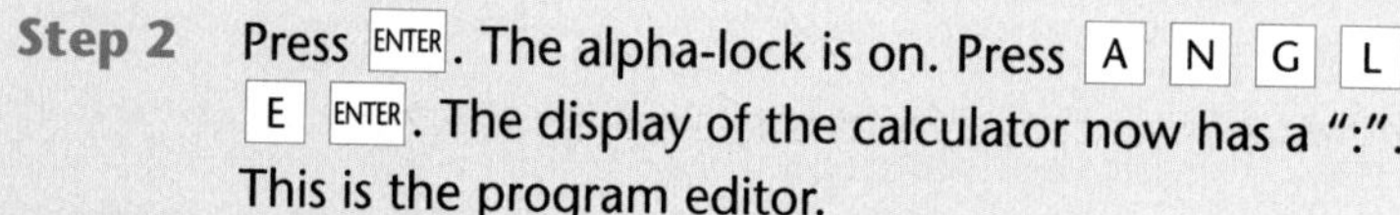

Step 2 Press [ENTER]. The alpha-lock is on. Press [A] [N] [G] [L] [E] [ENTER]. The display of the calculator now has a ":". This is the program editor.

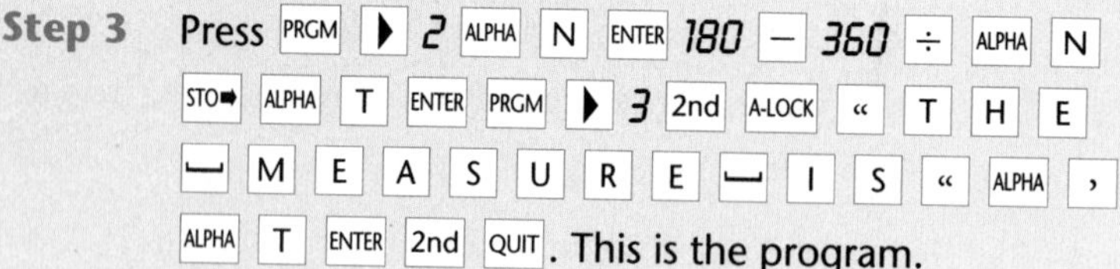

Step 3 Press [PRGM] [▶] *2* [ALPHA] [N] [ENTER] *180* [−] *360* [÷] [ALPHA] [N] [STO➡] [ALPHA] [T] [ENTER] [PRGM] [▶] *3* [2nd] [A-LOCK] [«] [T] [H] [E] [␣] [M] [E] [A] [S] [U] [R] [E] [␣] [I] [S] [«] [ALPHA] [,] [ALPHA] [T] [ENTER] [2nd] [QUIT]. This is the program.

Step 4 Press [PRGM] [ENTER] [ENTER]. The display shows a "?" asking for the number of sides, n.

Step 5 Press 6 [ENTER]. The display shows that the measure of each interior angle for a regular polygon with 6 sides is 120°. Press [ENTER] to clear the field and enter another number of sides.

Exercise A Find the measure of each interior angle for a regular polygon with the given number of sides. Use the formula to calculate the measure. Use your calculator to check your answers.

1. $n = 3$

2. $n = 4$

3. $n = 5$

4. $n = 6$

5. $n = 8$

6. $n = 10$

7. $n = 12$

8. $n = 20$

9. $n = 30$

10. $n = 40$

Exercise B Use the ratio of similarity to find the perimeter of the larger polygon.

11. The perimeter of the smaller triangle is 6; the ratio of similarity is 3:5.

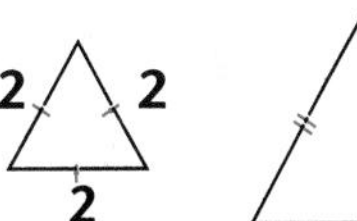

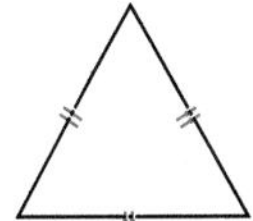

12. The perimeter of the smaller square is 16; the ratio of similarity is 2:3.

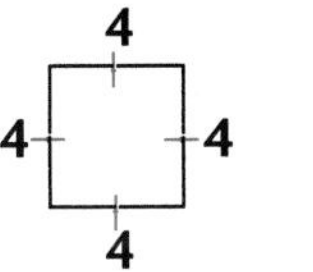

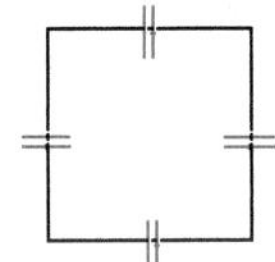

13. One side of the smaller pentagon measures 5; the ratio of similarity is 1:3.

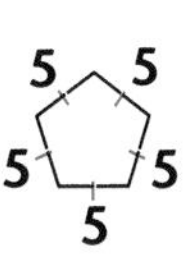

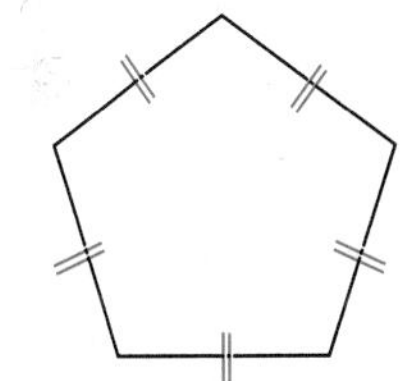

14. One side of the smaller hexagon measures 4; the ratio of similarity is 4:7.

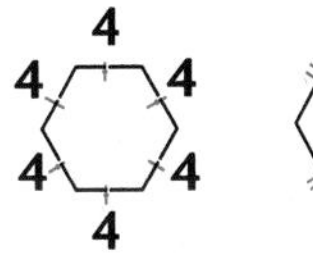

15. One side of the smaller octagon measures 3; the ratio of similarity is 3:7.

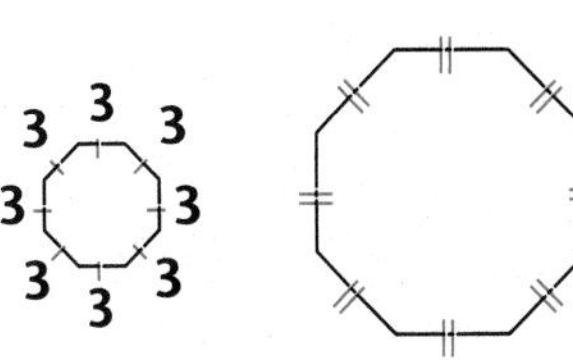

CONSTRUCTION

Exercise C Complete the construction or answer the question.

16. On a separate sheet of paper, construct a regular hexagon. Use only a straightedge and a compass.

17. How could you use the construction in exercise 16 to create an equilateral triangle in the circle? a regular dodecagon (12-sided figure)?

18. On a separate sheet of paper, construct a regular octagon. Use only a straightedge and a compass.

19. How could you use the construction in exercise 18 to create a regular polygon with 16 sides?

20. How could the constructions in exercises 16 and 18 help you construct an angle that measures 15°?

Geometry in Your Life

You can find ratios and proportions anywhere, including in your kitchen. Packaged foods often have directions such as "use $\frac{1}{2}$ cup of cereal for every cup of water" or "mix 1 cup rice with 2 cups water." Rewrite any ratios you find in the form $x{:}y$ or $\frac{x}{y}$.

Lesson 4 Enlarging Geometric Figures

Dilation

Process by which a geometric figure is enlarged or shrunk

During business presentations, graphs and charts may be projected on a screen and enlarged so everyone can see them. If a group of people had to look at a small computer screen or slide, it would be difficult for everyone to see.

You can use the fact that similar geometric figures have the same shape but different sizes to understand how to make geometric figures larger (or smaller).

In the diagram you can see that $\Delta A'B'C'$ is a larger version of ΔABC. Each of the sides of the smaller triangle has been multiplied by a factor of 2 to produce the larger triangle. The triangles are similar; the ratio of similarity of $\Delta A'B'C'$ to ΔABC is 2 to 1.

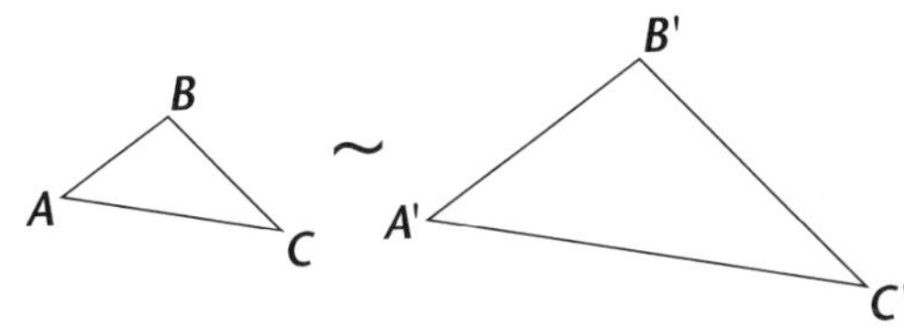

Rule:
If the ratio of similarity between a resulting figure and the original is greater than one, then the resulting figure is enlarged.

The number used to produce the second figure—the multiplier—is equal to the ratio of similarity of the second figure to the first figure. Multiplication by a number greater than one will produce an image that is larger than the original figure. The process is called **dilation.**

One way to illustrate enlargements, or dilations, is to place the figures in the coordinate plane. The ordered pairs of the vertices provide a way to read or record the original lengths as well as the dilations.

EXAMPLE 1 **Given:** ΔABC with $A = (1, 1)$, $B = (2, 4)$, and $C = (2, 1)$

Enlarge: ΔABC by a factor of 3

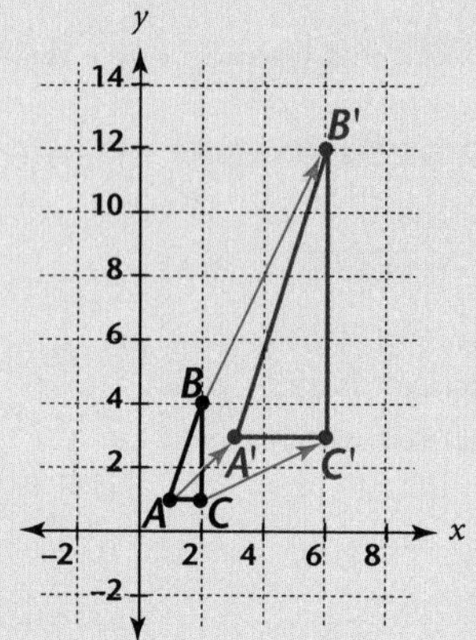

To enlarge ΔABC using a ratio of similarity of $\frac{3}{1}$, multiply each coordinate by 3 or $\frac{3}{1}$.

$A = (1, 1) \rightarrow A' = (1 \bullet 3, 1 \bullet 3) = (3, 3)$

$B = (2, 4) \rightarrow B' = (2 \bullet 3, 4 \bullet 3) = (6, 12)$

$C = (2, 1) \rightarrow C' = (2 \bullet 3, 1 \bullet 3) = (6, 3)$

This will give the coordinates of the image $\Delta A'B'C'$.

An arrow → can be used to show the movement of points to new coordinates.

Transform

To change the size or shape of a figure

Center of the dilation

The origin of the rays passing through the vertices of the dilated images

Below is a diagram of two dilations. ΔABC has been **transformed** into two larger triangles.

Note that all the triangles are similar to ΔABC and that each triangle has its vertices on $\overrightarrow{OA}$, $\overrightarrow{OB}$, and $\overrightarrow{OC}$. The point O, (0, 0), is called the **center of the dilation.** Each of the enlarged triangles was formed by multiplying the coordinates by the ratio of similarity.

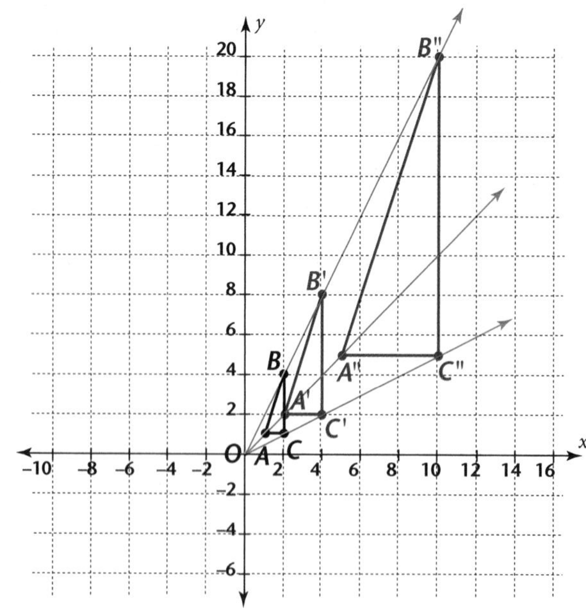

EXAMPLE 2 **Given:** $D = (-2, -1)$, $E = (6, 5)$, and $F = (6, 1)$

Find: the coordinates of the image of ΔDEF, $\Delta D'E'F'$, under a dilation of 4 or $\frac{4}{1}$. Use (0, 0) as the center of the dilation. Graph both triangles.

To enlarge ΔDEF using a ratio of similarity of $\frac{4}{1}$, multiply each coordinate by $\frac{4}{1}$.

$D = (-2, -1) \rightarrow D' = (-2 \bullet 4, -1 \bullet 4) = (-8, -4)$

$E = (6, 5) \rightarrow E' = (6 \bullet 4, 5 \bullet 4) = (24, 20)$

$F = (6, 1) \rightarrow F' = (6 \bullet 4, 1 \bullet 4) = (24, 4)$

Again, note that $\Delta DEF \sim \Delta D'E'F'$.

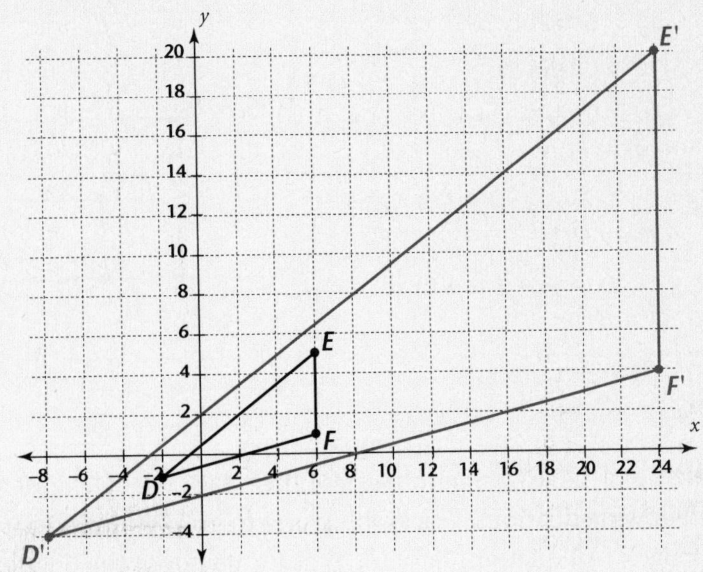

EXAMPLE 3 **Given:** square $KLMN$ with coordinates $(-1, -1)$, $(-1, 1)$, $(1, 1)$, and $(1, -1)$

Find: the coordinates of a similar square under a dilation of $\frac{5}{1}$, with (0, 0) as the center of the dilation. Graph both squares.

To enlarge the square using a ratio of similarity of $\frac{5}{1}$, multiply each coordinate by $\frac{5}{1}$. The squares—like all squares—are similar to one another.

$K = (-1, -1) \rightarrow (-1 \bullet 5, -1 \bullet 5) = (-5, -5) = K'$

$L = (-1, 1) \rightarrow (-1 \bullet 5, 1 \bullet 5) = (-5, 5) = L'$

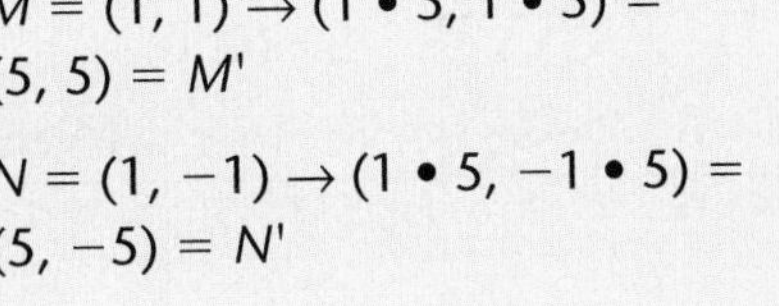

$M = (1, 1) \rightarrow (1 \bullet 5, 1 \bullet 5) = (5, 5) = M'$

$N = (1, -1) \rightarrow (1 \bullet 5, -1 \bullet 5) = (5, -5) = N'$

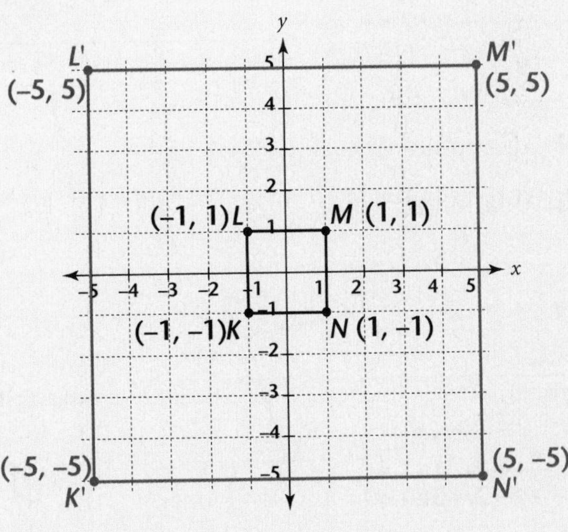

EXAMPLE 4 **Given:** rectangle $PQRS$ with coordinates $(-2, 0)$, $(-2, 2)$, $(3, 2)$, and $(3, 0)$

Find: the coordinates of a similar rectangle under a dilation of 2 or $\frac{2}{1}$, with (0, 0) as the center of the dilation. Graph both rectangles.

To enlarge the rectangle, using a ratio of similarity of $\frac{2}{1}$, multiply each coordinate by $\frac{2}{1}$.

$P = (-2, 0) \rightarrow (-2 \bullet 2, 0 \bullet 2) = (-4, 0) = P'$

$Q = (-2, 2) \rightarrow (-2 \bullet 2, 2 \bullet 2) = (-4, 4) = Q'$

$R = (3, 2) \rightarrow (3 \bullet 2, 2 \bullet 2) = (6, 4) = R'$

$S = (3, 0) \rightarrow (3 \bullet 2, 0 \bullet 2) = (6, 0) = S'$

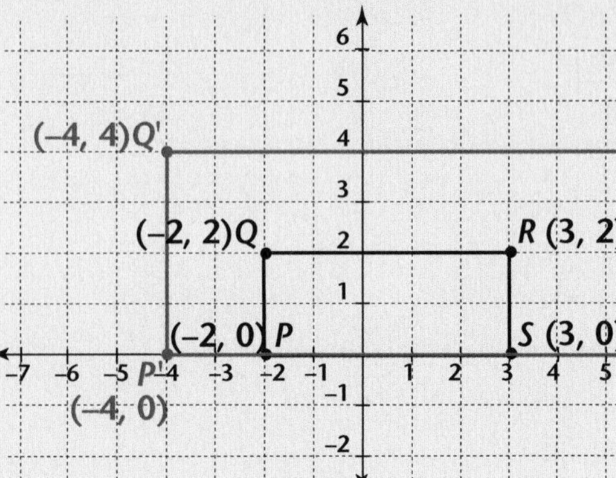

Exercise A Give the coordinates of the image triangle under the following dilations. Use graph paper to graph the object and its images. (All dilations have (0, 0) as the center of the dilation.)

1. dilation of 2

2. dilation of 3

3. dilation of 4

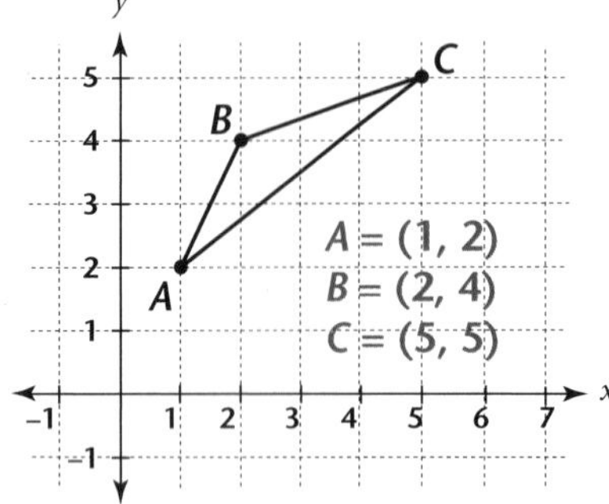

4. dilation of 2

5. dilation of 3

6. dilation of 4

7. dilation of 3

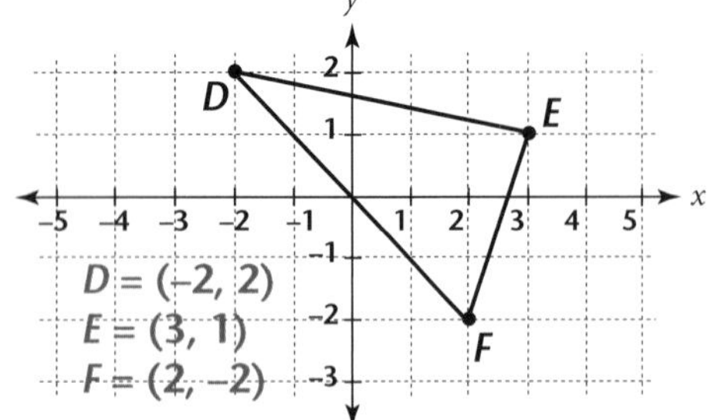

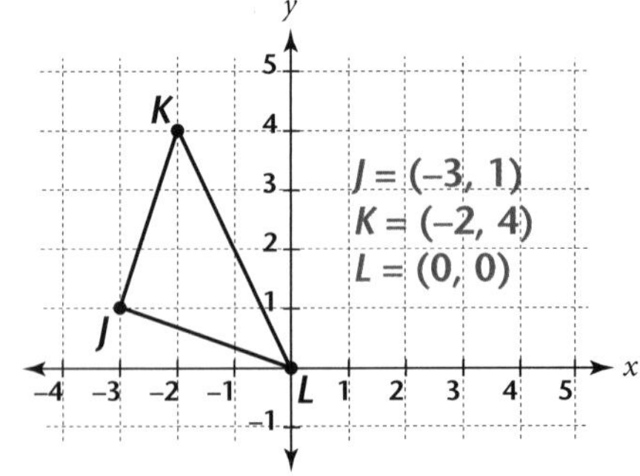

Exercise B Give the coordinates of the image under the following dilations. Use graph paper to graph the object and its images. (All dilations have (0, 0) as the center of the dilation.)

8. dilation of 2

9. dilation of 3

10. dilation of 4

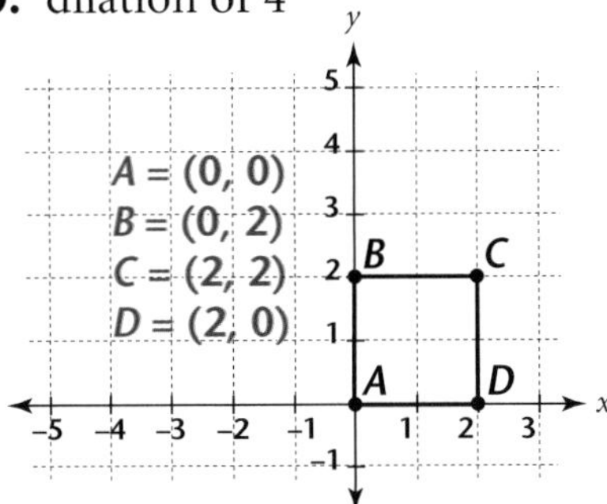

11. dilation of 2

12. dilation of 3

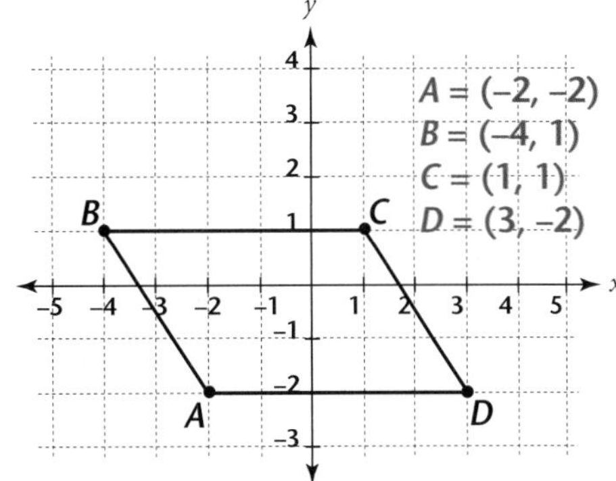

PROBLEM SOLVING

Exercise C Solve the following problems.

13. Haley is in charge of making flyers and posters announcing a swim meet at her school. She wants the posters to be three times as large as the flyers. She drew the size of the flyers, 6 inches by 4 inches, on a grid. What will be the size of the posters?

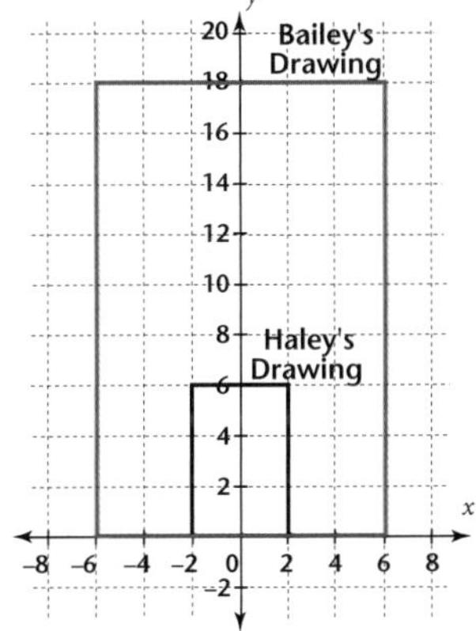

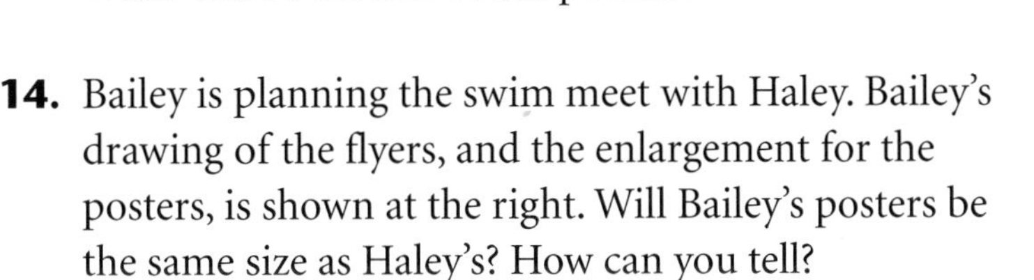

14. Bailey is planning the swim meet with Haley. Bailey's drawing of the flyers, and the enlargement for the posters, is shown at the right. Will Bailey's posters be the same size as Haley's? How can you tell?

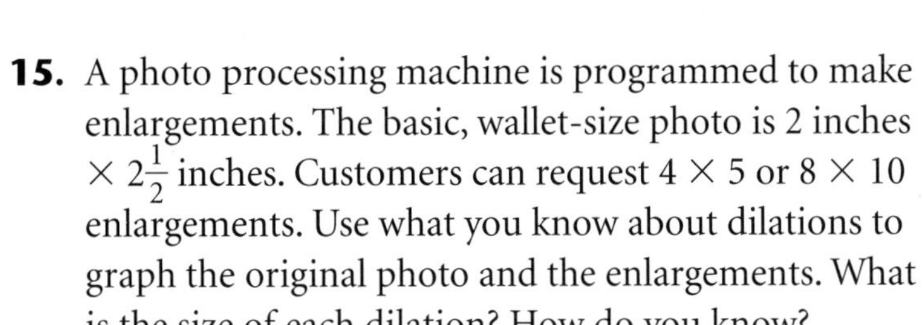

15. A photo processing machine is programmed to make enlargements. The basic, wallet-size photo is 2 inches $\times 2\frac{1}{2}$ inches. Customers can request 4×5 or 8×10 enlargements. Use what you know about dilations to graph the original photo and the enlargements. What is the size of each dilation? How do you know?

Lesson 5 Shrinking Geometric Figures

In the last lesson, you enlarged geometric figures while keeping their shapes. To enlarge the figures, you multiplied by the ratio of similarity, which was greater than one. In this lesson, you will learn how to shrink geometric figures by multiplying by a ratio of similarity *less than one.*

Rule:

If the ratio of similarity comparing a resulting figure to the original is less than one, then the resulting figure is shrunk.

EXAMPLE 1 **Given:** ΔABC with $A = (4, 2)$, $B = (10, 8)$ and $C = (10, 2)$

Find: the coordinates of the image of ΔABC under a dilation of $\frac{1}{2}$. Use (0, 0) as the center of the dilation.

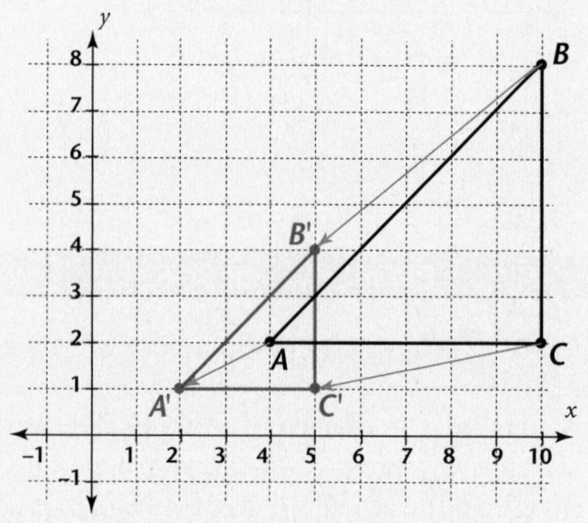

Shrinking a geometric figure is similar to enlarging the figure—you multiply each coordinate by the ratio of similarity, in this case, $\frac{1}{2}$. Your work will be easier if you use graph paper.

$A = (4, 2) \rightarrow (4 \bullet \frac{1}{2}, 2 \bullet \frac{1}{2}) = (2, 1) = A'$

$B = (10, 8) \rightarrow (10 \bullet \frac{1}{2}, 8 \bullet \frac{1}{2}) = (5, 4) = B'$

$C = (10, 2) \rightarrow (10 \bullet \frac{1}{2}, 2 \bullet \frac{1}{2}) = (5, 1) = C'$

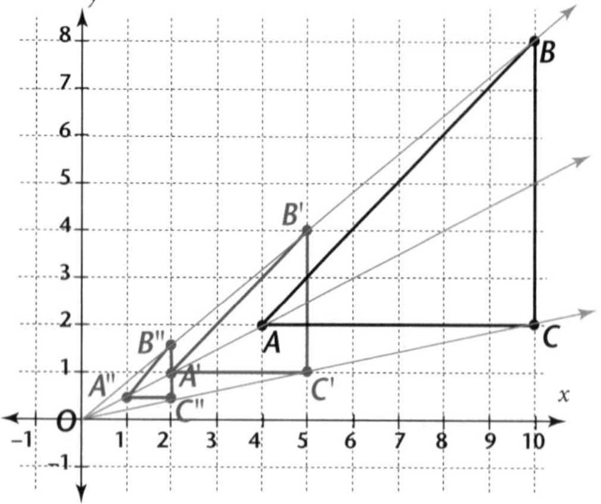

You now have the coordinates of the image $\Delta A'B'C'$. Note that ΔABC and $\Delta A'B'C'$ are similar.

As you can see, when the ratio of similarity is less than one, the figure shrinks. However, like the enlargement, the figure's vertices remain in the rays $\overrightarrow{OA}$, $\overrightarrow{OB}$, and $\overrightarrow{OC}$. All the triangles similar to ΔABC, whether larger or smaller, have their vertices on these three rays.

EXAMPLE 2 **Given:** $D = (-2, -2)$, $E = (6, 12)$, and $F = (6, -2)$

Find: the coordinates of the image of ΔDEF, $\Delta D'E'F'$, under a dilation of $\frac{1}{3}$

Use (0, 0) as the center of the dilation. Graph both triangles.

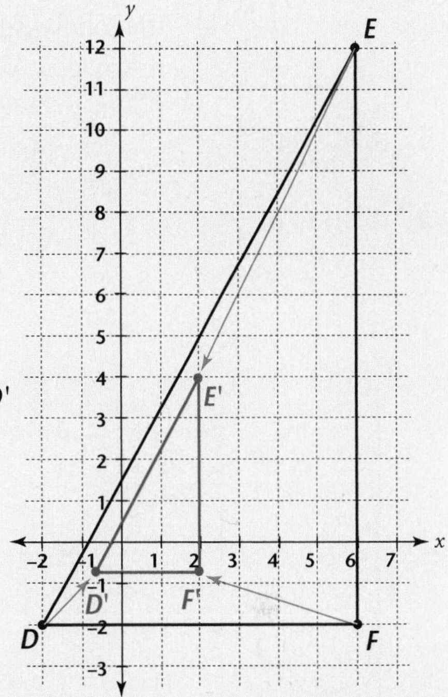

To shrink ΔDEF using a ratio of similarity of $\frac{1}{3}$, multiply each coordinate by $\frac{1}{3}$.

$D = (-2, -2) \rightarrow (-2 \bullet \frac{1}{3}, -2 \bullet \frac{1}{3}) = (-\frac{2}{3}, -\frac{2}{3}) = D'$

$E = (6, 12) \rightarrow (6 \bullet \frac{1}{3}, 12 \bullet \frac{1}{3}) = (2, 4) = E'$

$F = (6, -2) \rightarrow (6 \bullet \frac{1}{3}, -2 \bullet \frac{1}{3}) = (2, -\frac{2}{3}) = F'$

Again, note that $\Delta DEF \sim \Delta D'E'F'$.

EXAMPLE 3 **Given:** square *SQAR* with coordinates $(-5, -5)$, $(-5, 5)$, $(5, 5)$, and $(5, -5)$

Find: the coordinates of a similar square under a dilation of $\frac{1}{5}$, with (0, 0) as the center of the dilation. Graph both squares.

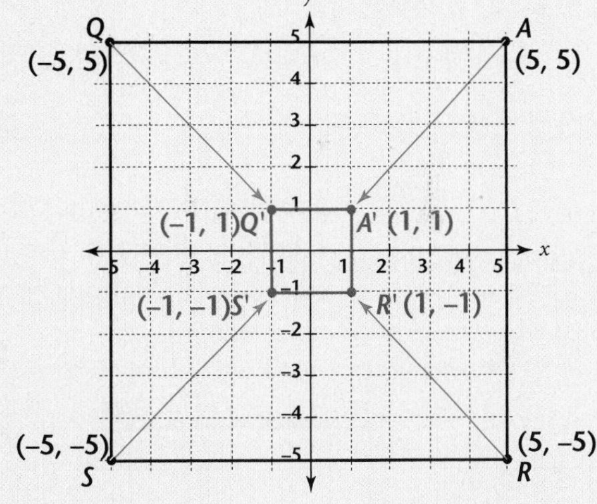

To shrink the square using a ratio of similarity of $\frac{1}{5}$, multiply each coordinate by $\frac{1}{5}$. The squares—like all squares—are similar to one another.

$S = (-5, -5) \rightarrow (-5 \bullet \frac{1}{5}, -5 \bullet \frac{1}{5}) = (-1, -1) = S'$

$Q = (-5, 5) \rightarrow (-5 \bullet \frac{1}{5}, 5 \bullet \frac{1}{5}) = (-1, 1) = Q'$

$A = (5, 5) \rightarrow (5 \bullet \frac{1}{5}, 5 \bullet \frac{1}{5}) = (1, 1) = A'$

$R = (5, -5) \rightarrow (5 \bullet \frac{1}{5}, -5 \bullet \frac{1}{5}) = (1, -1) = R'$

Exercise A Give the coordinates of the image triangle under the following dilations. Use graph paper to graph the object and its images. All dilations have (0, 0) as the center of the dilation.

1. dilation of $\frac{1}{2}$

2. dilation of $\frac{1}{4}$

3. dilation of $\frac{1}{3}$

4. dilation of $\frac{2}{3}$

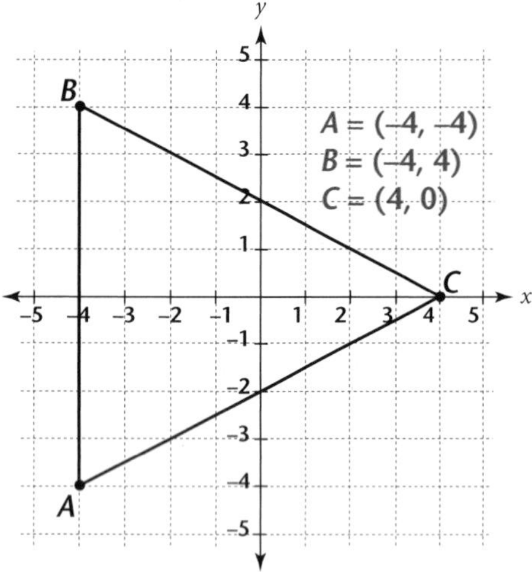

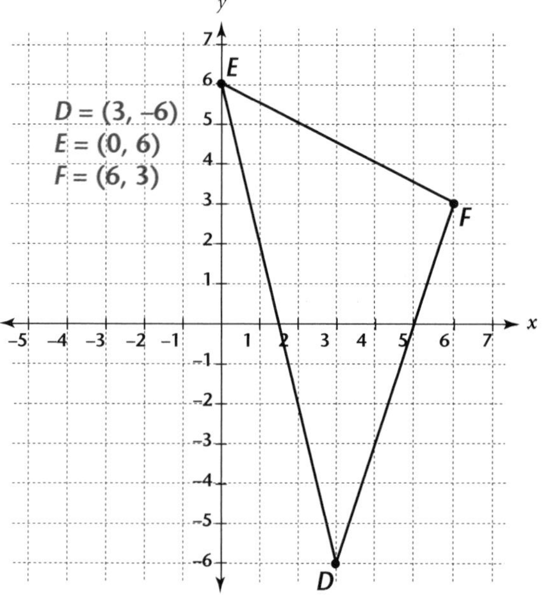

Exercise B Give the coordinates of the image under the following dilations. Use graph paper to graph the object and its images. (All dilations have (0, 0) as the center of the dilation.)

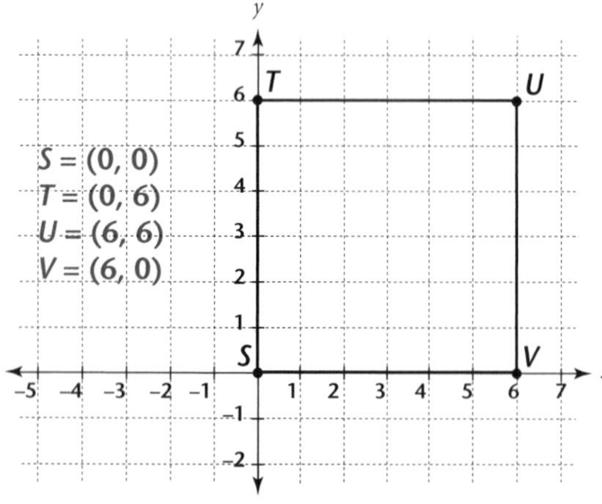

5. dilation of $\frac{1}{6}$

6. dilation of $\frac{1}{3}$

7. dilation of $\frac{2}{3}$

8. dilation of $\frac{5}{6}$

9. dilation of $\frac{1}{2}$

10. dilation of $\frac{1}{4}$

PROBLEM SOLVING

Exercise C Use what you know about proportions and ratios of similarity to solve the following problems.

11. The cars for a model railroad are built in proportion to actual railroad cars. HO models represent actual dimensions with a ratio of similarity of 1:80. If an HO-scale freight car is 14 cm long, what is the approximate length of the actual railroad car?

12. For N-scale model trains, the ratio of similarity is 1:160. If an N-scale freight car is 7 cm, what is the approximate length of the actual railroad car?

13. Shenequa wants to make a model of her favorite dinosaur. She will use a ratio of similarity of 1 in.:1 ft or, in other words, 1 inch of the model represents 1 foot (12 in.) of dinosaur. She knows that the dinosaur was about 45 feet from snout to tail. What will her model measure from snout to tail?

14. Raphael's miniature racer collection has several cars made with a ratio of similarity of 1:60. If the Red Menace car measures $1\frac{1}{4}$ inches, what is the measurement of the actual Red Menace racer?

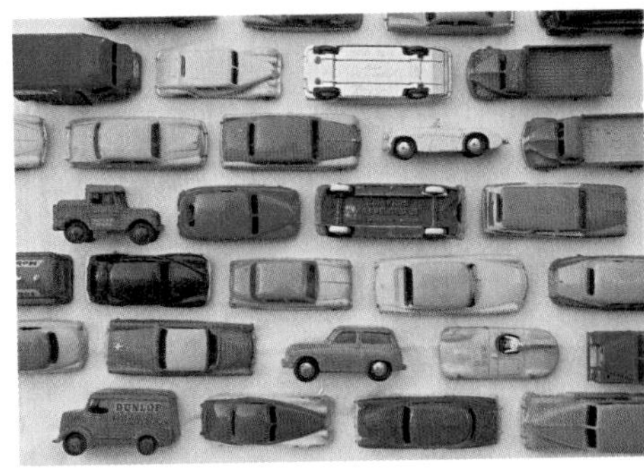

15. A working model of a pump delivers 1 gallon of water every 10 minutes. The model's output has a ratio of similarity with the actual pump of $\frac{1}{2,750}$. How much water does the actual pump deliver in 10 minutes? in an hour?

Technology Connection

You can explore similar figures with any computer program that lets you draw or insert pictures into it. Start by drawing an object or inserting a picture. You can shrink or enlarge it by changing the image size. You can either change the measurements (in pixels, inches, or centimeters) or the enlargement/reduction percent (greater than 100% increases the size, less than 100% decreases the size).

Lesson 6 Algebra Connection: The Counting Principle

Fundamental counting principle

A rule that states if one task can be done p different ways and another can be done q different ways, then both can be done pq different ways

How many different outfits can you make with three shirts and three pairs of pants?

The **fundamental counting principle** states that you *multiply* the number of choices for each task to find the total number of choices.

EXAMPLE 1 Suppose three different roads go from A to B and four different roads go from B to C. In how many different ways can you go from A to C?

Solution: $A_1 \rightarrow B$: 4 ways to C
$A_2 \rightarrow B$: 4 ways to C
$A_3 \rightarrow B$: 4 ways to C
12 ways

A —1, 2, 3→ B —1, 2, 3, 4→ C

3 ways • 4 ways = 12 ways

You can go from A to C in 12 different ways.

EXAMPLE 2 A test has five true/false questions. How many arrangements of answers are possible?

Solution: Each choice can be made in two ways.

Question	1		2		3		4		5		
Answers	T, F		T, F		T, F		T, F		T, F		
Arrangements:	2	•	2	•	2	•	2	•	2	=	32

There are 32 possible arrangements of answers.

EXAMPLE 3 Hanna has three winter hats, four scarves, and three pairs of mittens. How many different combinations of one hat, one scarf, and one pair of mittens can she wear?

Solution:

3 • 4 • 3 = 36

Hanna can wear 36 different combinations.

EXAMPLE 4 Sam, Maria, LaVerne, John, and Carlos line up for a picture. In how many different orders can the five friends line up?

Solution: Let the first letter of each name represent the person.

TRY THIS

A license plate can have 3 letters followed by three digits. Letters and digits may be repeated. How many different license plates are possible?

EXAMPLE 4 *(continued)*

Step 1 There are 5 choices for first place: S, M, L, J, or C. Suppose Carlos is in first place.

Step 2 Now there are 4 choices for second place: S, M, L, or J. Suppose LaVerne is in second place.

Step 3 Now there are 3 choices for third place: S, M, or J. Suppose Sam is in third place.

Step 4 Now there are 2 choices for fourth place: M or J. Suppose Maria is in fourth place.

Step 5 There is 1 choice for fifth place: J.

This is the order above:	C		L		S		M		J		
Place in line:	1		2		3		4		5		
Number of choices:	5		4		3		2		1		
Total number of choices:	5	•	4	•	3	•	2	•	1	=	120

The five friends can line up in 120 different ways.

A short way to write 5 • 4 • 3 • 2 • 1 is "5!" This is called "5 **factorial**."

Factorial **!**

The product of all positive integers from 1 to n

EXAMPLE 5

$3! = 3 \bullet 2 \bullet 1 = 6$

$4! = 4 \bullet 3 \bullet 2 \bullet 1 = 24$

$5! = 5 \bullet 4 \bullet 3 \bullet 2 \bullet 1 = 120$

$n! = n(n - 1)(n - 2)(n - 3) \ldots 2 \bullet 1$, n = positive integer.

Exercise A Write each factorial as a product of its factors, then find the product. You may use a calculator.

1. 10! **2.** 15!

Exercise B Solve the following problems.

3. In how many different orders can you read three books?

4. You can go from point *A* to point *B* in 5 different ways and from point *B* to point *C* in 3 different ways. In how many different ways can you go from point *A* to point *C*?

5. In how many different orders can 6 people line up for a picture?

Application

Gearing Up A unicycle, a bicycle built for two, and a penny farthing (like the one pictured here) all work in the same way: you pedal to move forward. The size of the gears, how fast you pedal, and the size of your tires all affect your speed.

The ratio of the numbers of teeth in the two gears (pedal and rear wheel) determines how many pedal strokes (revolutions) you must make for your wheels to turn all the way around. By changing the combination of gears you use, you can change the ease of pedaling and the speed you're traveling.

EXAMPLE 1 Say your bike is using a front gear with 30 teeth and a rear gear with 15 teeth. If you pedal at the rate of 60 rpm (revolutions per minute) how far will you travel in one minute?

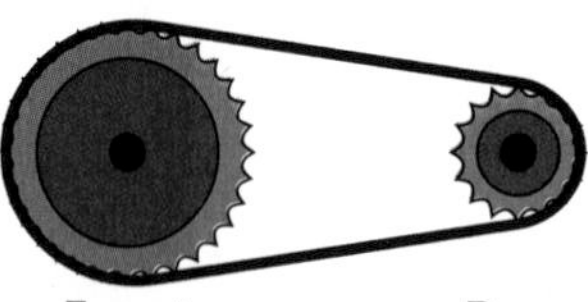

Gear ratio: 30 to 15 or $\frac{30}{15} = \frac{2}{1}$ The rear wheel turns twice with each pedal stroke.

Multiply the gear ratio by the pedal rate to find how often the rear wheel will turn.

$\frac{2}{1} \times \frac{60}{1} = \frac{120}{1}$ The rear wheel will turn 120 times in 1 minute.

Most bicycle tires measure about 82 inches around. Multiply the circumference of the tire by the number of times it turns. 82 inches $\times$ 120 = 9,840 inches or $\frac{9{,}840}{12} =$ 820 feet. You would travel 820 feet in one minute.

Exercise For each problem, use a tire that is 82 inches around.

1. How far would you travel in 3 minutes using a front gear with 30 teeth and a rear gear with 10 teeth, pedaling at 60 rpm?

2. How far would you travel in one minute using a front gear with 40 teeth and a rear gear with 8 teeth, pedaling at 60 rpm?

3. How far would you travel in 3 minutes using a front gear with 40 teeth and a rear gear with 10 teeth, pedaling at 60 rpm?

Chapter 7 REVIEW

Write the letter of the correct answer.

1. Which of the following proportions is true?

A $\frac{3}{4} = \frac{4}{5}$ **C** $\frac{2}{8} = \frac{12}{18}$

B $\frac{3}{7} = \frac{9}{27}$ **D** $\frac{9}{12} = \frac{6}{8}$

2. What value of x makes the proportion $\frac{2}{3} = \frac{x}{9}$ true?

A 6 **C** 13.5

B 8 **D** 54

3. ΔDEF is similar to ΔUGR, as shown in the diagram below. What is $m\angle R$?

A 19° **C** 42°

B 38° **D** 76°

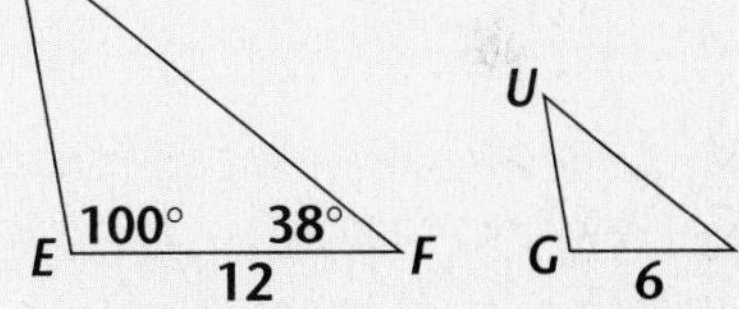

4. In the diagram below, a building casts a 60-ft shadow and a man casts a 10-ft shadow. If the man is 6 ft tall, how tall is the building?

A 24 ft **C** 36 ft

B 30 ft **D** 54 ft

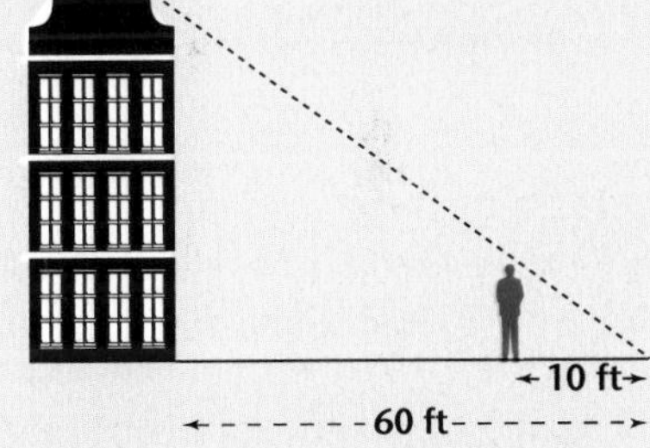

5. Rectangle $RSTU$ has vertices $R(0, 0)$, $S(0, 5)$, $T(-5, -5)$, and $U(-5, 0)$. If $RSTU$ is dilated by a factor of 5, which coordinate has an image that stays at its original location?

A R **C** T

B S **D** U

Find the missing value in each proportion.

Example: $\frac{2}{3} = \frac{y}{18}$ Solution: product of extremes = product of means so $2 \cdot 18 = 3y$ $36 = 3y$ $12 = y$

6. $\frac{3}{5} = \frac{12}{y}$

7. $\frac{8}{9} = \frac{z}{18}$

8. $\frac{3}{4} = \frac{a}{12}$

9. $\frac{2}{5} = \frac{12}{x}$

10. $\frac{9}{n} = \frac{12}{20}$

11. $\frac{z}{30} = \frac{30}{36}$

Solve for the length of the missing sides in each pair of similar triangles.

Example: Find x.

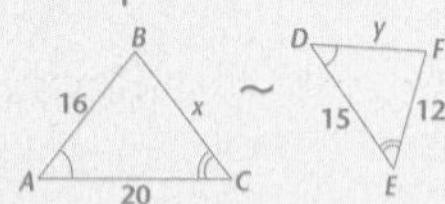

Solution: $\frac{AB}{DF} = \frac{BC}{FE} = \frac{AC}{DE}$
corresponding sides of similar triangles have the same ratio

$\frac{AC}{DE} = \frac{20}{15} = \frac{4}{3}$ so $\frac{BC}{FE} = \frac{4}{3}$

Let $x = BC$ and substitute 12 for FE: $\frac{x}{12} = \frac{4}{3}$

$3x = 48$ product of extremes = product of means
$x = 16$ divide

12. $\overline{BC}$

13. $\overline{EF}$

14. $\overline{JL}$

15. $\overline{KJ}$

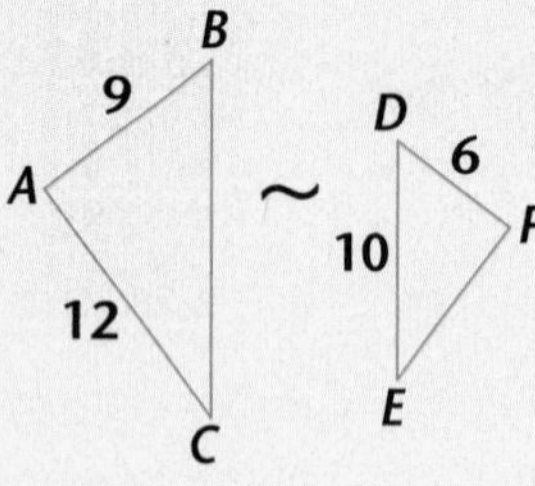

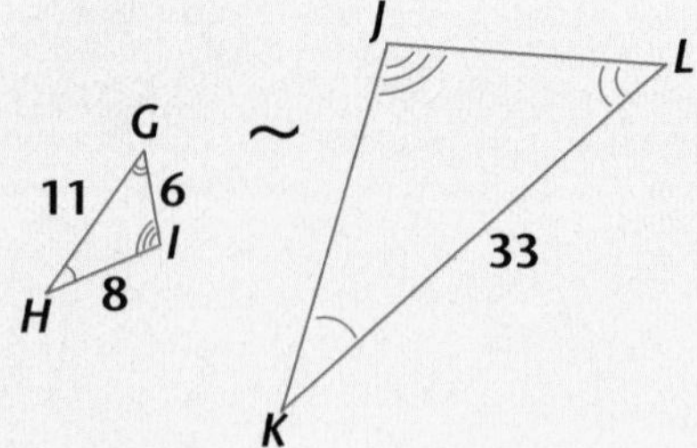

16. $\overline{AB}$

17. $\overline{CD}$

18. $\overline{HJ}$

19. $\overline{HI}$

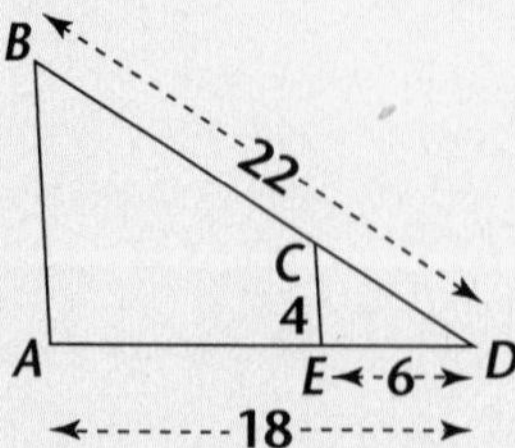

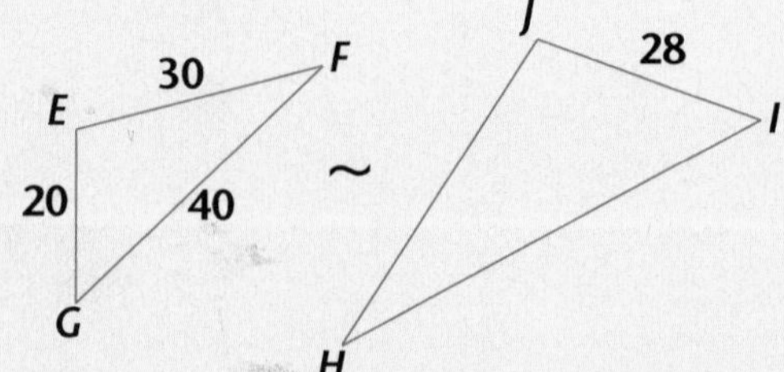

Give the coordinates of the image under the following dilations. Use graph paper to graph the object and its images. All dilations have (0, 0) as the center of the dilation.

Example: enlarge ΔABC using a dilation of $\frac{2}{1}$

Solution: to enlarge ΔABC, multiply the coordinates of each vertex by the ratio of similarity $\frac{2}{1}$

$A = (-2, -1) \rightarrow (-2 \bullet \frac{2}{1}, -1 \bullet \frac{2}{1})$
$= (-4, -2) = A'$

$B = (0, 1) \rightarrow (0 \bullet \frac{2}{1}, 1 \bullet \frac{2}{1}) = (0, 2) = B'$

$C = (2, -1) \rightarrow (2 \bullet \frac{2}{1}, -1 \bullet \frac{2}{1}) = (4, -2) = C'$

A' = (–4, –2)
B' = (0, 2)
C' = (4, –2)

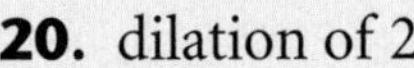

20. dilation of 2

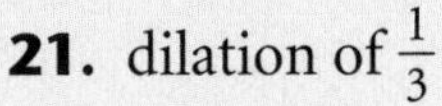

21. dilation of $\frac{1}{3}$

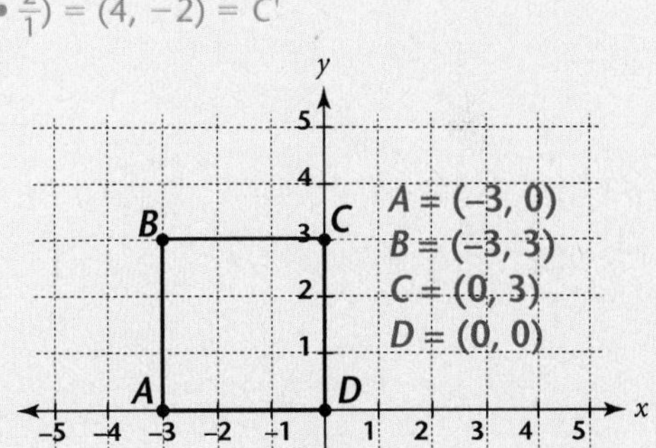

22. dilation of $\frac{1}{2}$

23. dilation of 2

24. dilation of $\frac{1}{4}$

25. dilation of 3

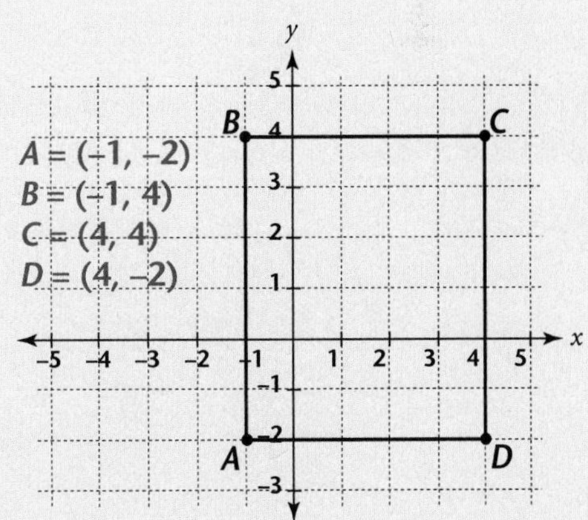

Test-Taking Tip

Review for tests by studying together in small groups and asking each other questions about the material.

Chapter

The Pythagorean Theorem

The Manhattan Bridge in New York is one of three bridges connecting Brooklyn to downtown Manhattan. It opened in 1909, twenty-six years after the Brooklyn Bridge. The Manhattan Bridge lets pedestrians, bicyclists, cars, and even subway trains cross the East River. 78,000 vehicles and 350,000 people use the bridge's roadways and subway tracks each day.

Do you see the right triangles in the bridge's design? These are trusses, or beams, that connect and support its two decks. The design uses right triangles, so engineers probably used the Pythagorean Theorem to make sure all the trusses were the correct length.

In Chapter 8, you will learn how to prove and apply the Pythagorean Theorem.

Goals for Learning

- ◆ To identify Pythagorean Triples
- ◆ To use the Pythagorean Theorem to determine the length of an unknown side of a right triangle
- ◆ To use the ratios of sides of special triangles to find an unknown side
- ◆ To determine the area of a trapezoid
- ◆ To find the distance between points, using the distance formula

Lesson 1 Pythagorean Triples

Integer

One of the set of positive and negative whole numbers including zero

An ancient Greek mathematician, Pythagoras, became famous for his theorems and thought that all things were based in numbers. We use numbers to describe geometric figures. Sometimes the numbers occur in patterns. These patterns can help us learn even more about the figures they describe. One of the most useful number patterns includes positive **integers** and their squares.

N:	1	2	3	4	5	6	7	8	9	10	11	12	13	14	15…
N^2:	1	4	9	16	25	36	49	64	81	100	121	144	169	196	225...

Let's look at three squares: 9, 16, and 25. Note that $9 + 16 = 25$ or $3^2 + 4^2 = 5^2$.

Can we find other numbers among the squared integers such that the sum of the two smaller squares is equal to the largest square?

You know that $3^2 + 4^2 = 5^2$ is an equation. So you know that you can multiply each side of the equation by the same number and you will have another equation.

EXAMPLE 1 **Given:** a right triangle with sides equal to 3, 4, and 5

Will the sides of a similar triangle, dilated by a factor of 2, still make a true equation?

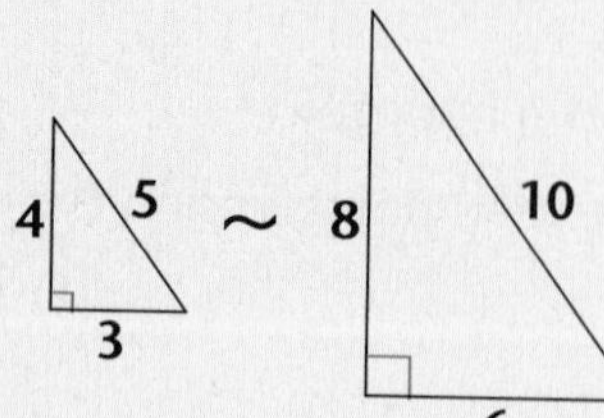

$$3^2 + 4^2 = 5^2$$
$$(3 \bullet 2)^2 + (4 \bullet 2)^2 = (5 \bullet 2)^2$$
$$6^2 + 8^2 = 10^2$$
$$36 + 64 = 100$$

True

(3, 4, 5)
↓
(6, 8, 10)

Example 2 **Given:** a right triangle with sides equal to 3, 4, and 5

Will the sides of a similar triangle, dilated by a factor of 3, still make a true equation?

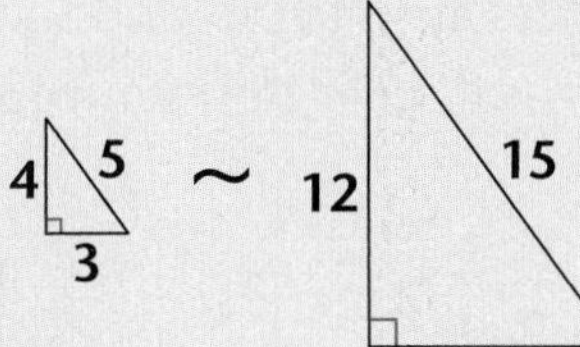

$$3^2 + 4^2 = 5^2 \qquad (3, 4, 5)$$
$$(3 \cdot 3)^2 + (4 \cdot 3)^2 = (5 \cdot 3)^2 \qquad \downarrow$$
$$9^2 + 12^2 = 15^2 \qquad (9, 12, 15)$$
$$81 + 144 = 225$$

True

Example 3 **Given:** a right triangle with sides equal to 3, 4, and 5

Will the sides of a similar triangle, dilated by a factor of 10, still make a true equation?

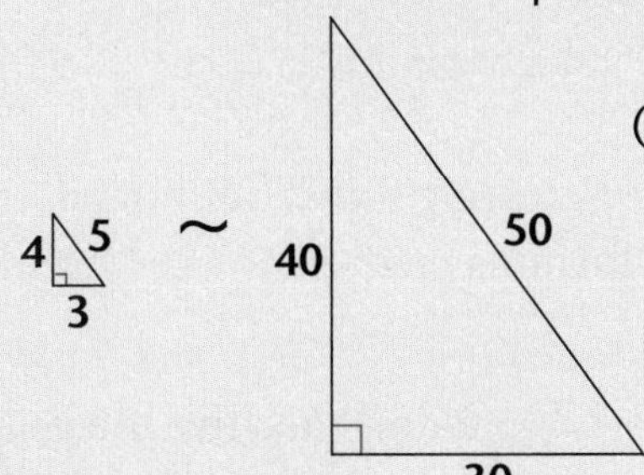

$$3^2 + 4^2 = 5^2 \qquad (3, 4, 5)$$
$$(3 \cdot 10)^2 + (4 \cdot 10)^2 = (5 \cdot 10)^2 \qquad \downarrow$$
$$30^2 + 40^2 = 50^2 \qquad (30, 40, 50)$$
$$900 + 1{,}600 = 2{,}500$$

True

> ***Pythagorean Triple***
>
> *Integers* a, b, c *such that* $a^2 + b^2 = c^2$

The integers *a, b, c* form a **Pythagorean Triple** if $a^2 + b^2 = c^2$.

Another Pythagorean Triple is 5, 12, 13:

$$5^2 + 12^2 = 13^2$$
$$25 + 144 = 169$$

Again, you can create more triples by multiplying 5, 12, and 13 by the same factor. (Use a calculator.)

Example 4 **Given:** Pythagorean Triple (5, 12, 13)

Will a triple multiplied by a factor of 2 still make a true equation?

$$5^2 + 12^2 = 13^2 \qquad (5, 12, 13)$$
$$(5 \cdot 2)^2 + (12 \cdot 2)^2 = (13 \cdot 2)^2 \qquad \downarrow$$
$$10^2 + 24^2 = 26^2 \qquad (10, 24, 26)$$
$$100 + 576 = 676 \qquad \text{True}$$

Example 5 **Given:** Pythagorean Triple (5, 12, 13)

Will a triple multiplied by a factor of 3 still make a true equation?

$$5^2 + 12^2 = 13^2 \qquad (5, 12, 13)$$
$$(5 \cdot 3)^2 + (12 \cdot 3)^2 = (13 \cdot 3)^2 \qquad \downarrow$$
$$15^2 + 36^2 = 39^2 \qquad (15, 36, 39)$$
$$225 + 1{,}296 = 1{,}521 \qquad \text{True}$$

Following this model, you can show that (10, 24, 26) and (15, 36, 39) are also Pythagorean Triples.

Of course, not all triples of positive integers are Pythagorean Triples. To determine if three numbers are a triple, add the squares of the two smaller numbers and see if the sum equals the square of the largest number.

EXAMPLE 6 Is (4, 5, 6) a Pythagorean Triple?

Check: 4, 5 are the smaller, 6 is the largest

$4^2 + 5^2 = 6^2$

$16 + 25 = 36$ False

$\therefore$ (4, 5, 6) is not a Pythagorean Triple.

Choose any two different whole numbers m and n. Then the three numbers $2mn$, $m^2 - n^2$, and $m^2 + n^2$ must be a Pythagorean Triple. For example, $m = 10$ and $n = 3$ give you the triple (60, 91, 109). Plato's Formula is a special case of this.

There are algebraic formulas for creating some, but not all, Pythagorean Triples. Here is a formula credited to the Greek philosopher Plato:

$$(2m)^2 + (m^2 - 1)^2 = (m^2 + 1)^2 \quad \text{for any positive integer } m$$

EXAMPLE 7 Use Plato's Formula for $m = 2$. Check if the results are a Pythagorean Triple.

for $m = 2$: $2m = 4$, $m^2 - 1 = 3$ and $m^2 + 1 = 5$

$(2m)^2 + (m^2 - 1)^2 = (m^2 + 1)^2$

$4^2 + 3^2 = 5^2$

$16 + 9 = 25$ True

$\therefore$ Plato's Formula shows that (3, 4, 5) is a Pythagorean Triple.

TRY THIS Suggest a formula to create triples that would produce right triangles similar to ΔABC shown at the right with leg 3, leg 4, and hypotenuse 5.

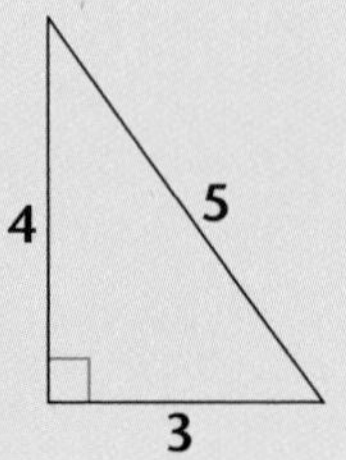

You can use x^2 on your calculator to find the sum of the squares of two numbers.

EXAMPLE 8 **Find:** $3^2 + 4^2$

Press 3 x^2 + 4 x^2 ENTER. Display reads 25.

Exercise A Find the sum of the squares of the following numbers.

1. 5 and 12

2. 9 and 12

3. 12 and 16

4. 6 and 7

5. 6 and 8

Exercise B Find additional triples using the given triples and multipliers. Use a calculator.

6. triple (3, 4, 5) by 4

7. triple (3, 4, 5) by 5

8. triple (3, 4, 5) by 6

9. triple (3, 4, 5) by 7

10. triple (3, 4, 5) by 20

11. triple (5, 12, 13) by 4

12. triple (5, 12, 13) by 5

13. triple (5, 12, 13) by 6

14. triple (5, 12, 13) by 7

15. triple (5, 12, 13) by 20

Exercise C Check if the given sets of numbers are Pythagorean Triples. Use a calculator.

16. (3, 6, 9)

17. (65, 72, 97)

18. (119, 120, 169)

19. (10, 20, 30)

20. (56, 90, 106)

Exercise D Use Plato's Formula to find Pythagorean Triples for the given integers. Use a calculator.

21. $m = 3$

22. $m = 6$

23. $m = 10$

24. $m = 15$

25. $m = 20$

Lesson 2 Pythagorean Triples and a Proof

> ***Area***
> *The number of square units inside a closed region*

We can use a Pythagorean Triple to illustrate one of the more famous theorems in history. First, let's look at a specific case.

We can form a square that is 5 units on a side by placing four 3, 4, 5 right triangles in the arrangement shown at the right. Notice that the arrangement leaves a 1×1 "window" at the center of the square.

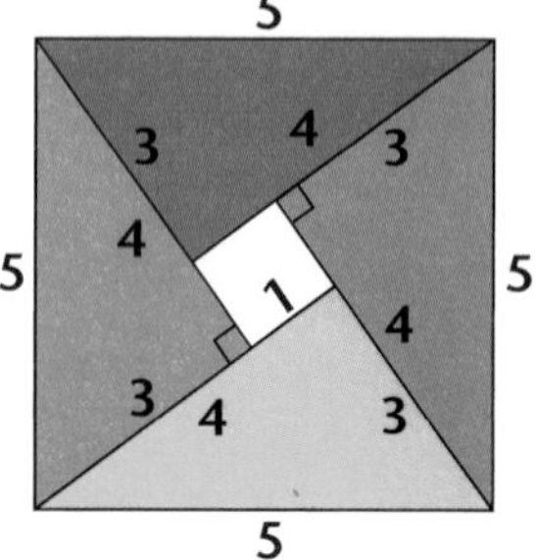

> Remember, the area of a triangle is $\frac{1}{2}$ (base • height).

We know that the **area** of the larger square is $5 \times 5 = 25$. But we can think of the area in another way. The areas of the four right triangles plus the area of the center square equal the area of the larger square. Let's add the areas inside the larger square.

$1 \times 1 = 1$	area of center square
$\frac{1}{2}(3 \cdot 4) = 6$	area of red triangle
$\frac{1}{2}(3 \cdot 4) = 6$	area of blue triangle
$\frac{1}{2}(3 \cdot 4) = 6$	area of green triangle
$\frac{1}{2}(3 \cdot 4) = 6$	area of yellow triangle

Total area = 25 square units = area of large square

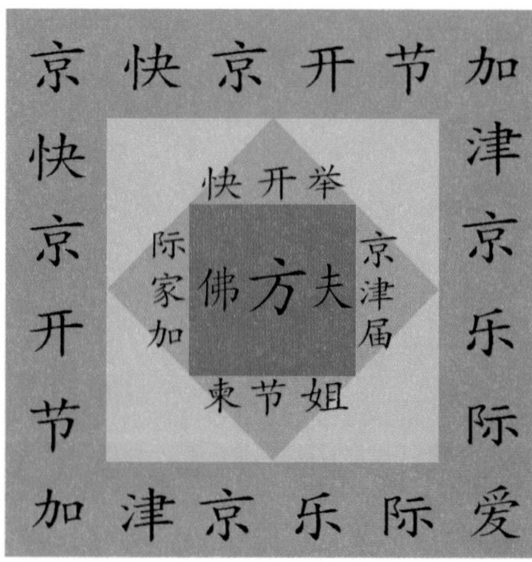

This illustration of a Chinese block print shows a series of triangles within a larger square. How many squares and triangle sets can you find?

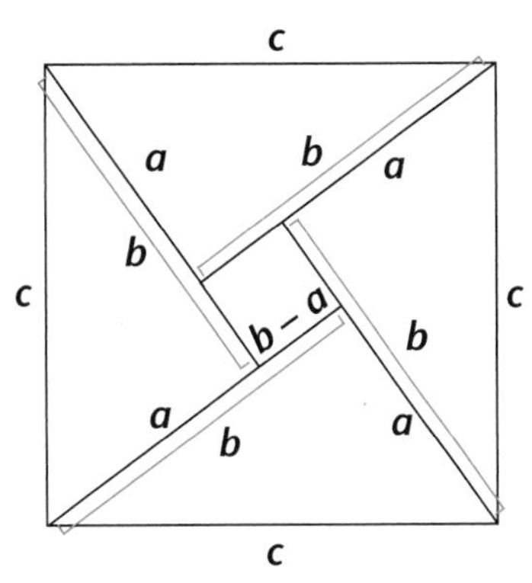

Now suppose the right triangles have legs a and b and a hypotenuse c. We can use this arrangement to prove the theorem $a^2 + b^2 = c^2$.

Pythagorean Theorem (8.2.1)
If a triangle is a right triangle with legs a and b and hypotenuse c, then $a^2 + b^2 = c^2$.

Given: area of large square $= c^2$
area of inner square $= (b - a)^2$
area of each right triangle $= \frac{1}{2}ab$

To Prove: $a^2 + b^2 = c^2$

PROOF

Statement	Reason
1. Area of 4 right triangles + area of inner square = area of larger square	1. By construction.
2. $4(\frac{1}{2}ab) + (b - a)^2 = c^2$	2. Whole is equal to sum of its parts.
3. $2ab + b^2 - 2ab + a^2 = c^2$	3. Simplify.
4. $2ab - 2ab + a^2 + b^2 = c^2$	4. Rearrange terms.
5. $\therefore a^2 + b^2 = c^2$	5. Simplify.

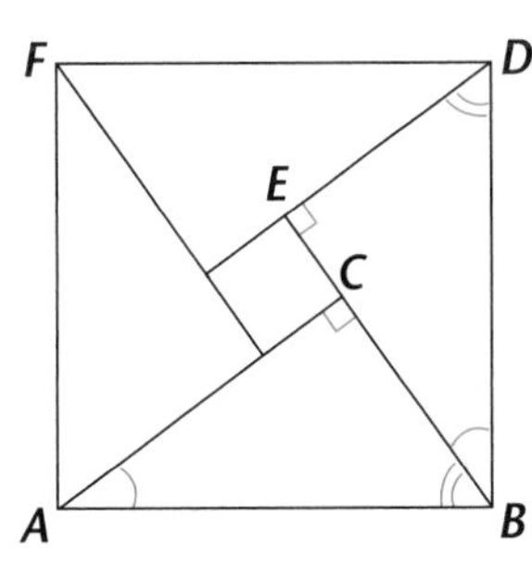

This equality is known as the Pythagorean Theorem. The method of this proof is based on Bhāskara, a leading Indian mathematician who lived in the 12th century. Note that in the diagram, the right triangles can be shown to be congruent.

Technology Connection

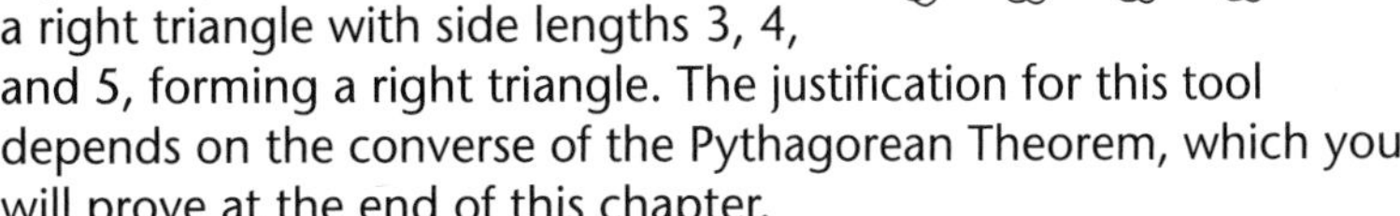

The ancient Egyptians developed a simple technology in which they used the Pythagorean Theorem to survey land. They positioned 12 equally spaced knots in a rope. They then bent the rope to form a right triangle with side lengths 3, 4, and 5, forming a right triangle. The justification for this tool depends on the converse of the Pythagorean Theorem, which you will prove at the end of this chapter.

Given: square $ABDF$ (on page 275)
To Prove: $\Delta ABC \cong \Delta BDE$

PROOF

Statement	Reason
1. *ABDF* is a square.	1. Given.
2. $AB = BD$	2. Definition of square; sides of a square are equal.
3. $m\angle ABC + m\angle DBE = m\angle ABD = 90°$	3. Given; definition of square.
4. $m\angle BAC + m\angle ABC = 90°$	4. Acute angles of a right triangle are complementary.
5. $m\angle ABC + m\angle DBE = m\angle ABC + m\angle BAC$	5. Quantities equal to the same quantity are equal to each other.
6. $m\angle DBE = m\angle BAC$	6. Subtraction.
7. $\therefore m\angle BDE = m\angle ABC$	7. Complements of equal angles are equal.
8. $\therefore \Delta ABC \cong \Delta BDE$	8. Angle-Side-Angle.

Exercise A Use the figure to find the following quantities.

1. Area of large square
2. Area of each right triangle
3. Side length and area of the small square
4. Sum of the areas that make up the large square
5. Does the area of the large square equal the sum of the areas of the four triangles plus the area of the small square?

Exercise B Use the figure to answer the questions.

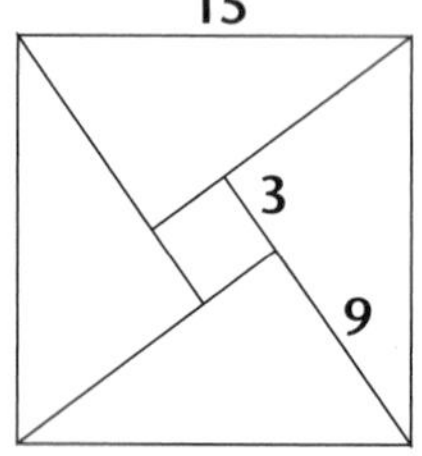

6. What are the side lengths of the right triangles?
7. What is the area of each right triangle?
8. What is the area of the center square?
9. How can you use the area of the large square to find the area of one of the right triangles? Find the area.
10. Describe another way to find the areas of the four triangles.

Lesson 3 Pythagorean Demonstration

Pythagoras lived in ancient Greece about 540 B.C. He developed a "demonstration," or proof, of what we now call the Pythagorean Theorem. The following is believed to be the demonstration he developed.

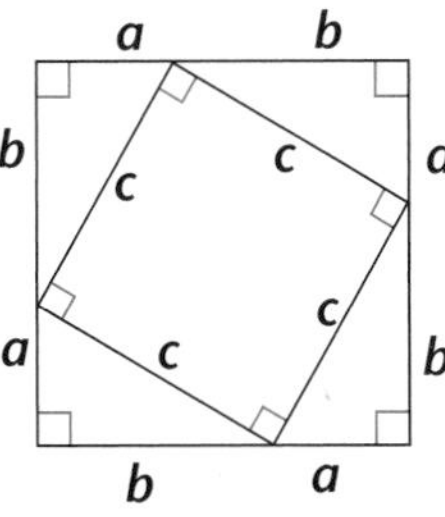

$\cong$

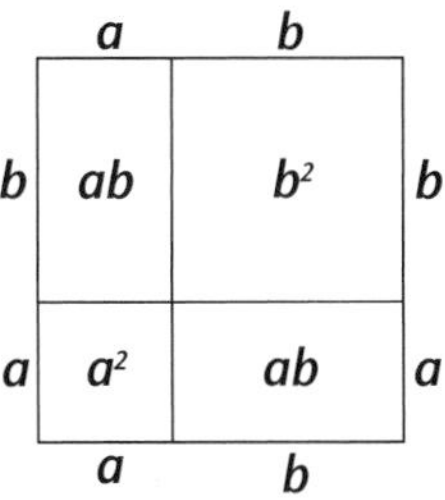

Area of large square = **Area of large square**

$$c^2 + \frac{1}{2}ab + \frac{1}{2}ab + \frac{1}{2}ab + \frac{1}{2}ab = a^2 + b^2 + ab + ab$$

$$c^2 + 2ab = a^2 + b^2 + 2ab$$

Algebra Review

To simplify complicated expressions, you combine like terms. In the expression above, the terms containing *ab* are like terms. So, you can combine them:

$\frac{1}{2}ab + \frac{1}{2}ab + \frac{1}{2}ab + \frac{1}{2}ab = 2ab$

since $\frac{1}{2} + \frac{1}{2} + \frac{1}{2} + \frac{1}{2} = 2$.

Subtract four right triangles

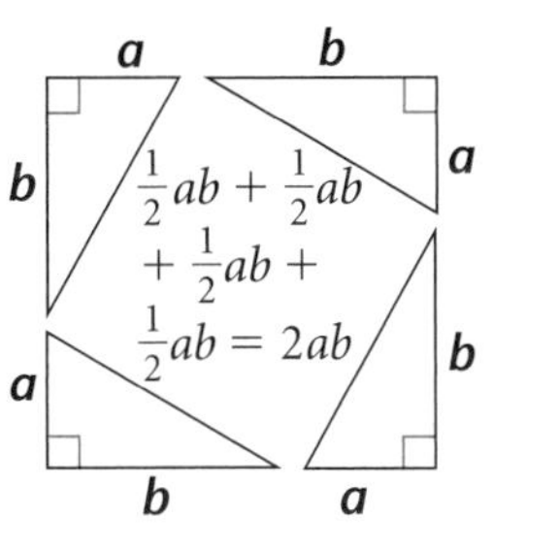
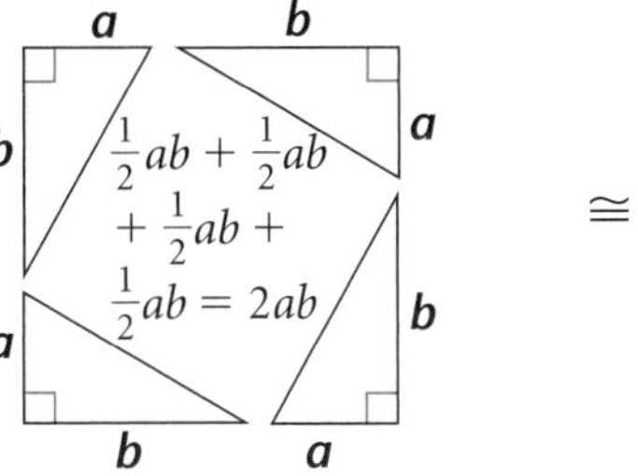

$\cong$

Subtract two rectangles

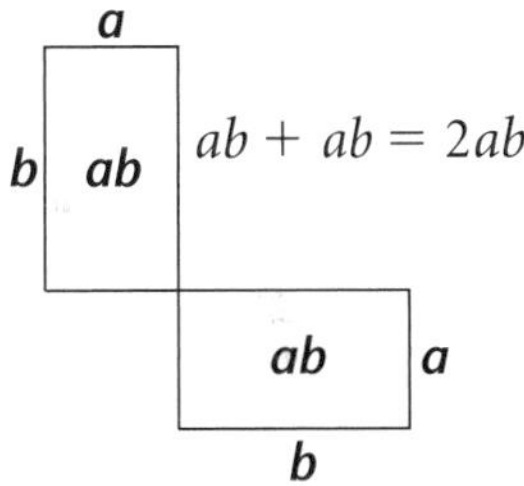

$$c^2 + 2ab - 2ab = a^2 + b^2 + 2ab - 2ab$$

$$c^2 = a^2 + b^2$$

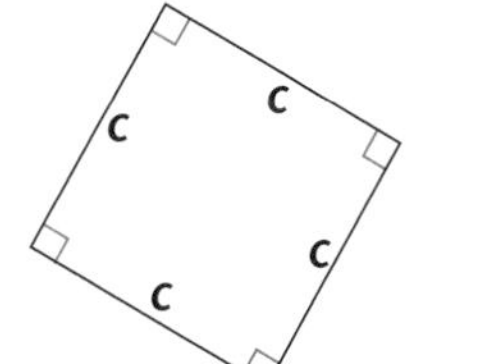

$\cong$

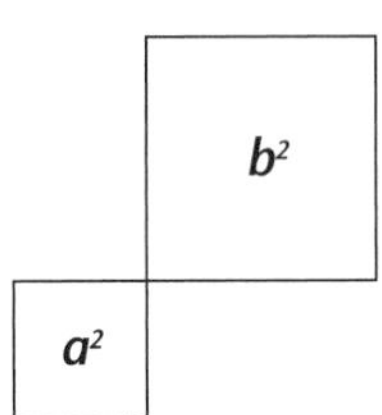

For the above demonstration to be valid, the center portion of the original diagram must be a square. Here is that proof.

Given: *ACEG* a square with equal segments as marked

To Prove: *BDFH* is a square

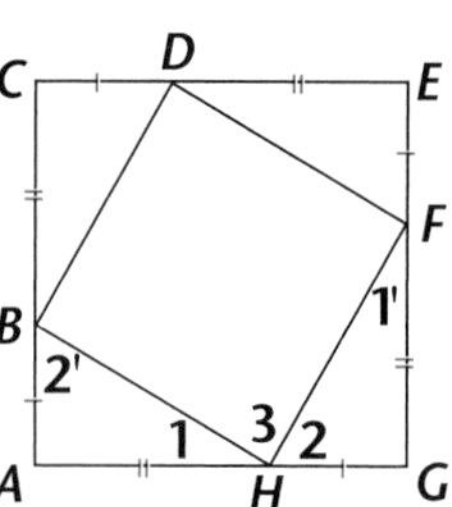

PROOF

Statement	Reason
1. *ACEG* is a square	1. Given.
2. $\angle A$, $\angle C$, $\angle E$, and $\angle G$ are right angles	2. Definition of square.
3. $m\angle 1 + m\angle 2 + m\angle 3 = 180°$	3. Adjacent angles with exterior sides in a straight line are supplementary.
4. $\Delta ABH \cong \Delta CDB \cong \Delta EFD \cong \Delta GHF$	4. SAS, sides are given as equal.
5. $HB = BD = DF = FH$ and $m\angle 2 = m\angle 2'$	5. Corresponding parts of congruent triangles are equal.
6. $m\angle 1 + m\angle 2' = 90°$	6. Acute angles of right triangles are complementary.
7. $m\angle 1 + m\angle 2 = 90°$	7. Substitution using Step 5.
8. $90° + m\angle 3 = 180°$	8. Substitution using Steps 3 and 7.
9. $\therefore m\angle 3 = 90°$	9. Subtraction.
10. Argument holds for angles at *D, F,* and *B*	10. Same argument applies.
11. $\therefore$ *BDFH* is a square	11. Definition of a square is satisfied.

We can use specific dimensions to illustrate the proof.

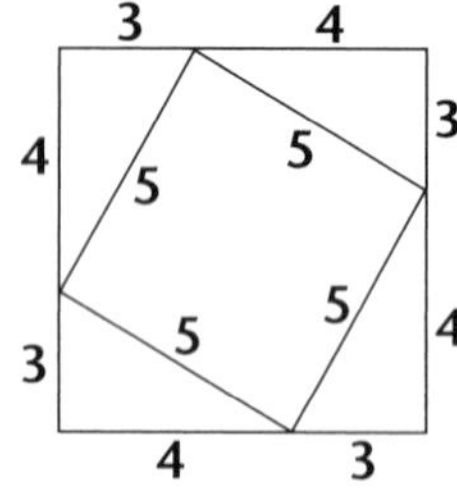

$\cong$

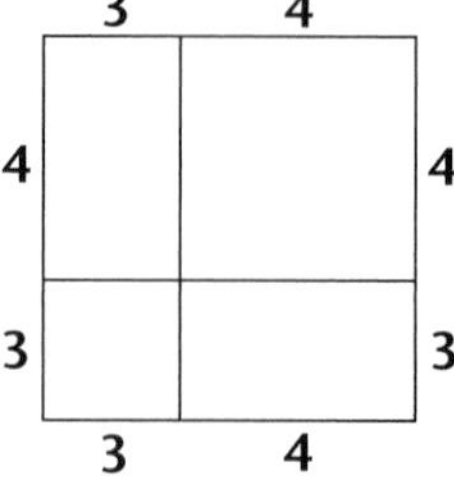

Area of large square	=	Area of large square
$25 + 4[\frac{1}{2}(3 \cdot 4)]$	=	$9 + 16 + 12 + 12$
49	=	49 True

You can use the equation $a^2 + b^2 = c^2$ to check if three given side lengths satisfy this formula for a right triangle. This is similar to checking for Pythagorean Triples, except in this case, a, b, and c can be any real numbers, not just integers. You can also use $a^2 + b^2 = c^2$ if you are given two side lengths of a right triangle and you wish to find the length of the third side. Use a calculator.

EXAMPLE 1 Do 3.1, 7.2, and 8.4 satisfy the formula $a^2 + b^2 = c^2$? Round to the nearest tenth.

Let $a = 3.1$, $b = 7.2$, and $c = 8.4$

$a^2 + b^2 = c^2$

$(3.1)^2 + (7.2)^2 = (8.4)^2$

$9.6 + 51.8 = 70.6$ False

$\therefore$ The given sides do not satisfy the formula.

EXAMPLE 2 The legs of a right triangle are 8.1 and 6.7.

What is the length, to the nearest tenth, of the hypotenuse?

8.1
c
6.7

Let $a = 8.1$, $b = 6.7$

$a^2 + b^2 = c^2$

$(8.1)^2 + (6.7)^2 = c^2$

$65.6 + 44.9 = c^2$

$110.5 = c^2$ simplify

$10.5 \approx c$ take the square root of both sides; round to the nearest tenth

Estimation Activity

Estimate: What is the value of b in the equation $2.3^2 + b^2 = 4.2^2$?

Solution: $2.3^2 + b^2 = 4.2^2$

$2^2 + b^2 = 4^2$ Round the numbers.

$4 + b^2 = 16$ Solve.

$b^2 = 12$

$b \approx 3.5$

Approximate the square root. $\sqrt{12}$ is between $\sqrt{9}$ and $\sqrt{16}$. So, b is between 3 and 4. $\sqrt{12}$ is about halfway between $\sqrt{9}$ and $\sqrt{16}$, so 3.5 is a reasonable estimate.

EXAMPLE 3 **Given:** right triangle with one leg = 31, hypotenuse = 70

Find: the length of the second leg

Let x = length of the second leg

$x^2 + 31^2 = 70^2$

$x^2 + 961 = 4{,}900$

$x^2 = 3{,}939$ simplify

$x \approx 62.8$ take the square root of both sides; round to the nearest tenth

x 70 31

EXAMPLE 4 **Given:** isosceles right Δ with a hypotenuse of 10

Find: the length of the legs

Let x = length of each leg

$x^2 + x^2 = 10^2$

$2x^2 = 100$

$x^2 = 50$ simplify

$x \approx 7.1$ take the square root of both sides; round to the nearest tenth

x 10 x

You can use 2nd x^2 on your graphing or scientific calculator to find the square root of a number.

EXAMPLE 5 Find the square root of 225.

Press 2nd x^2 225 ENTER, or, on a scientific calculator, 225 2nd x^2.

The square root of 225 is 15.

Exercise A Find the square root of each number.

1. 625 **2.** 169 **3.** 3,969 **4.** 2,209

Exercise B Use the figures to answer the questions.

Square I

5 12 5 12 13 13 13 13 12 5 12 5

5. What is the area of each right triangle in Square I?

6. What is the area of the inner square in Square I?

7. What is the total area of Square I?

8. What is the sum of the areas of the four right triangles plus the area of the inner square?

Square II

5 12 12 12 5 5 5 12

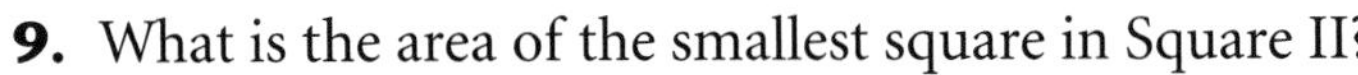

9. What is the area of the smallest square in Square II?

10. What is the area of the larger inside square?

11. What is the area of each rectangle in Square II?

12. What is the sum of the areas of the squares plus the areas of the rectangles?

13. How does the area of Square I compare to the area of Square II?

Exercise C Find the length of the unknown side of each right triangle.

14.

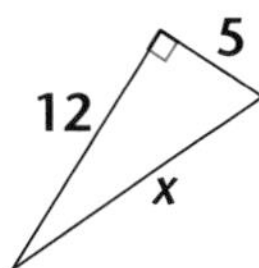

15.

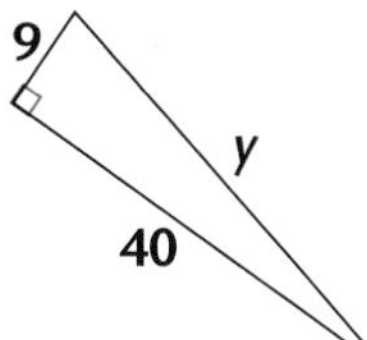

16.

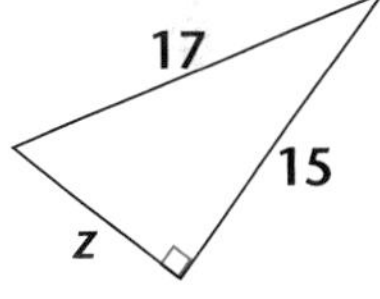

17.

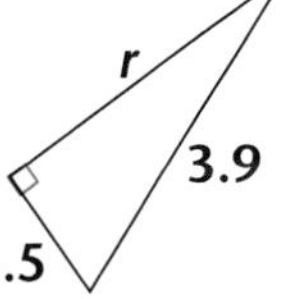

18.

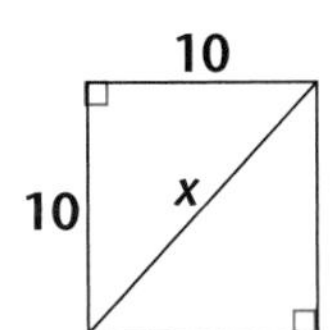
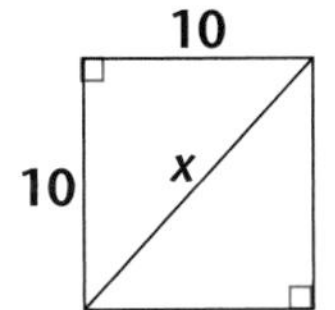

19.

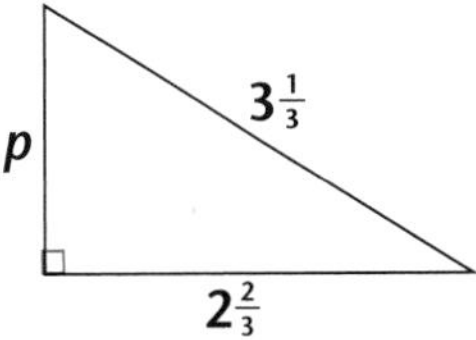

20.

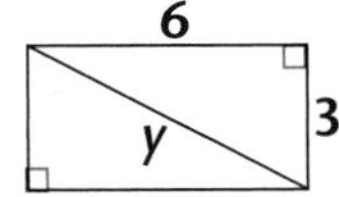

Lesson 4 Pythagorean Theorem and Similar Triangles

One of the interesting facts about the Pythagorean Theorem, as well as other theorems, is that there are a number of ways to prove the theorem true. In this lesson, you will "make the case" using similar triangles.

You already know that the corresponding angles of similar triangles are equal. One way to produce similar triangles is to take any right triangle and draw a line perpendicular to the hypotenuse from the right angle vertex.

Given: right ΔABC, $\overline{BD} \perp \overline{AC}$

To Prove: $\Delta ADB \sim \Delta BDC \sim \Delta ABC$

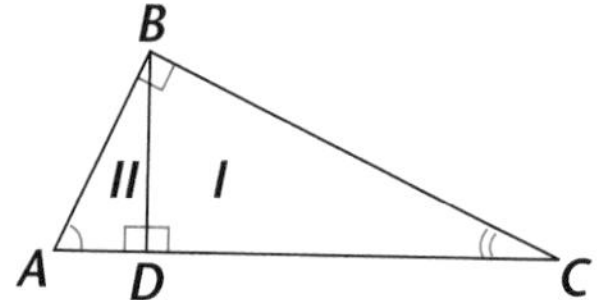

Split the given figure into two separate triangles.

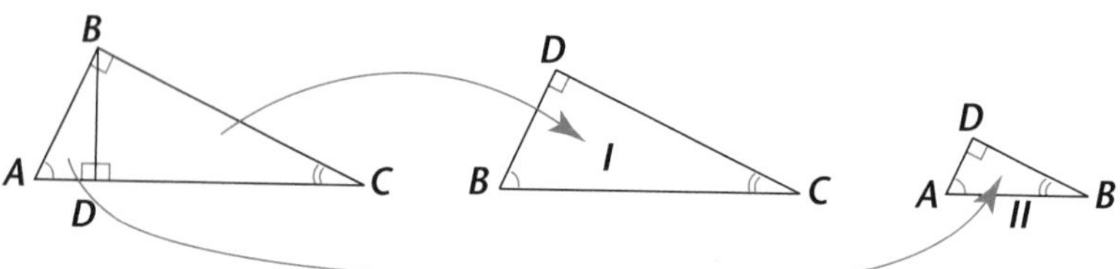

Because the acute angles of a right triangle are complementary, the corresponding angles of all three triangles are equal.

right angle:	$m\angle B$	=	$m\angle BDC$	=	$m\angle BDA$
$m\angle A$:	$m\angle A$	=	$m\angle DBC$	=	$m\angle DAB$
$m\angle C$:	$m\angle C$	=	$m\angle DCB$	=	$m\angle ABD$

By the AA Similarity Postulate, these three triangles are similar.

Remember that AB is a distance written as a number, while $\overline{AB}$ is a line segment.

Pythagorean Theorem (8.4.1):
In any right triangle ABC, with hypotenuse $\overline{AC}$, $(AC)^2 = (AB)^2 + (BC)^2$.

The Pythagorean Theorem can be proven using the similar triangles above.

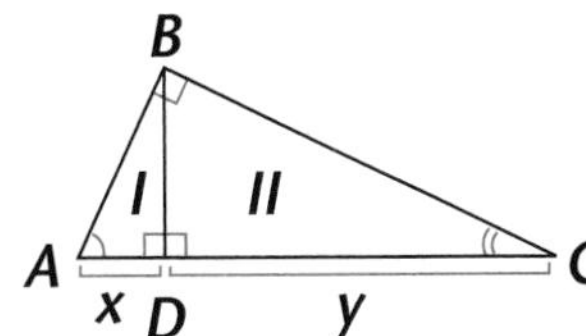

Given: ΔABC, right angle at B, and $\overline{BD} \perp \overline{AC}$

To Prove: $(AC)^2 = (AB)^2 + (BC)^2$

PROOF

Statement	Reason
1. ΔABC, right angle at B, and $\overline{BD} \perp \overline{AC}$	1. Given.
2. $\Delta ABC \sim \Delta I \sim \Delta II$	2. By above discussion.
3. Let $x = AD$ and $y = CD$	3. Substitution.
4. $\frac{x}{AB} = \frac{AB}{AC}$	4. $\Delta I \sim \Delta ABC$; $\frac{\text{small leg}}{\text{small leg}} = \frac{\text{hypotenuse}}{\text{hypotenuse}}$
5. $x \bullet AC = (AB)^2$	5. Product of means = product of extremes.
6. $x = \frac{(AB)^2}{AC}$	6. Division by equals.
7. $\frac{y}{BC} = \frac{BC}{AC}$	7. $\Delta II \sim \Delta ABC$; $\frac{\text{large leg}}{\text{large leg}} = \frac{\text{hypotenuse}}{\text{hypotenuse}}$
8. $y \bullet AC = (BC)^2$	8. Product of means = product of extremes.
9. $y = \frac{(BC)^2}{AC}$	9. Division by equals.
10. $x + y = \frac{(AB)^2 + (BC)^2}{AC}$	10. Addition of equals, and Steps 6 and 9.
11. $x + y = AD + DC = AC$	11. Substitution, Step 3.
12. $AC = \frac{(AB)^2 + (BC)^2}{AC}$	12. Substitution for $x + y$ from Step 10.
13. $\therefore (AC)^2 = (AB)^2 + (BC)^2$	13. Multiplication by equals.

The Pythagorean Theorem is one of the most useful theorems in geometry. It offers a way to solve many practical problems.

EXAMPLE 1 **Given:** a 40-ft flagpole casts a 60-ft shadow

Find: length of $\overline{AB}$ to the nearest hundredth (Use a calculator.)

$40^2 + 60^2 = (AB)^2$	substitute in formula
$1{,}600 + 3{,}600 = (AB)^2$	square
$5{,}200 = (AB)^2$	simplify
$72.11 \text{ ft} \approx AB$	take square root of each side

B
40′
A
60′

EXAMPLE 2 **Given:** a 100-ft-long ramp is to be constructed from the top of a 20-ft wall to ground level

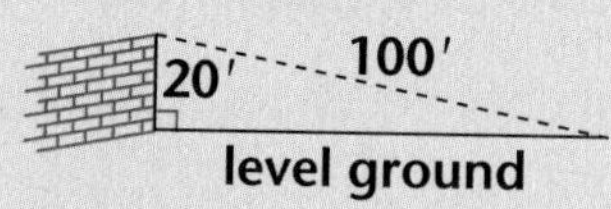

Find: the distance along the ground from the wall to the end of the ramp. (Use a calculator. Compute to the nearest hundredth.)

Let x equal distance from wall.

$20^2 + x^2 = 100^2$	substitute in formula
$400 + x^2 = 10{,}000$	square
$x^2 = 9{,}600$	subtract
$x \approx 97.98$ ft	take square root of each side

EXAMPLE 3 **Given:** $AB = 100$ km, $AC = 300$ km, $\overline{AC} \perp \overline{AB}$

Find: the shortest distance between B and C. (Use a calculator. Compute to the nearest hundredth.)

BC is the shortest distance. $\overline{BC}$ is also the hypotenuse of right ΔABC.

$(AB)^2 + (AC)^2 = (BC)^2$	theorem
$100^2 + 300^2 = (BC)^2$	substitution
$10{,}000 + 90{,}000 = (BC)^2$	square
$100{,}000 = (BC)^2$	simplify
$316.23 \text{ km} \approx BC$	take square root of each side round to the nearest hundredth

Exercise A Answer the following questions. Use the figure.

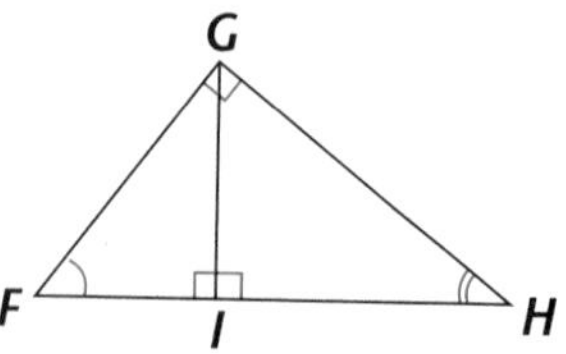

1. Name the three similar triangles.
2. Which angles in ΔFIG correspond to which angles in ΔFGH? $\angle F =$ __, $\angle I =$ __, $\angle FGI =$ __

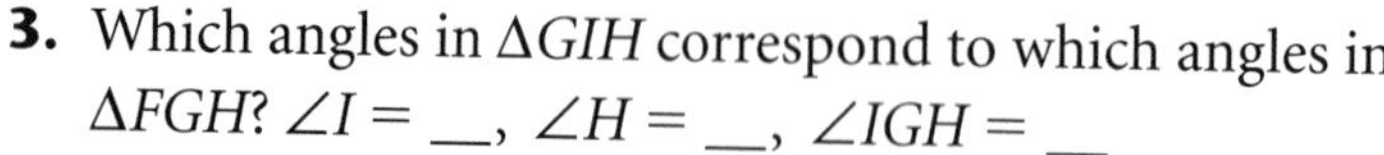

3. Which angles in ΔGIH correspond to which angles in ΔFGH? $\angle I =$ __, $\angle H =$ __, $\angle IGH =$ __

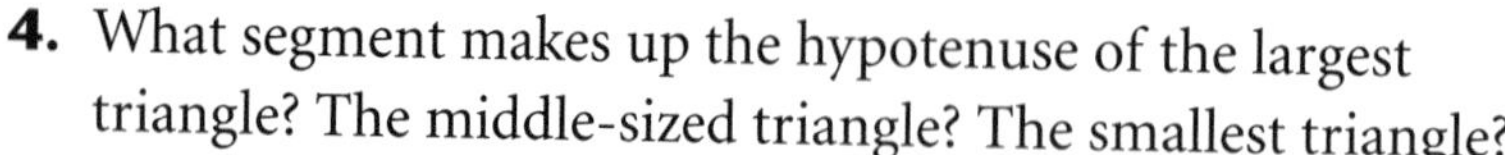

4. What segment makes up the hypotenuse of the largest triangle? The middle-sized triangle? The smallest triangle?
5. Is $\Delta FGI \sim \Delta GHI$? Why?

PROBLEM SOLVING

Exercise B Solve the following problems. Note the right angles in the diagrams. Use a calculator. Round answers to the nearest hundredth.

6. The minute hand of a clock is 14 cm long; the hour hand is 9 cm long. What is the distance between their tips when it is 9 A.M.?

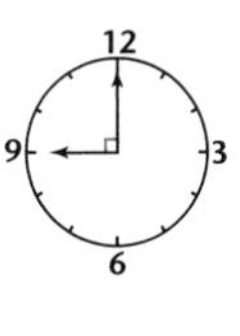

7. A corner of a park has been set aside for dogs. The park fencing along the shorter leg is 27 ft. The length along the longer leg is 36 ft. How much more fencing will be needed to close in the doggie corner?

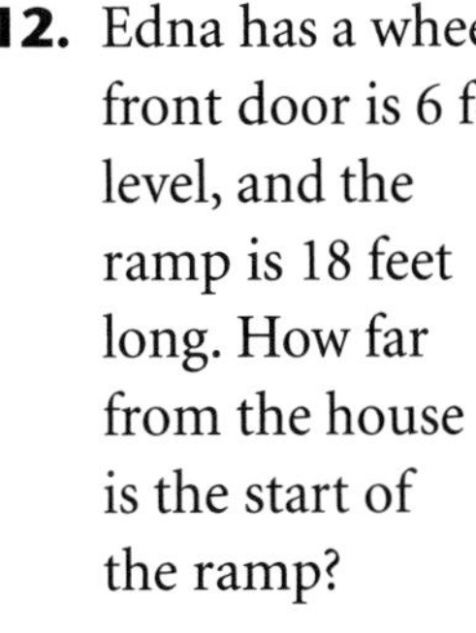

8. The base of a 10-foot ladder is placed 2 feet away from a wall. Will the ladder touch a window sill that is 9.9 feet above ground? Why or why not?

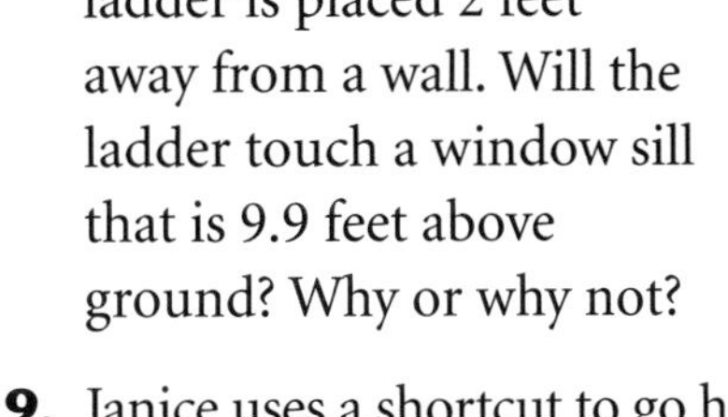

9. Janice uses a shortcut to go home from school. She knows that she walks 100 paces across the playground. She also knows that her house is 30 paces from corner *A*. What is the distance, in paces, from corner *A* to the school?

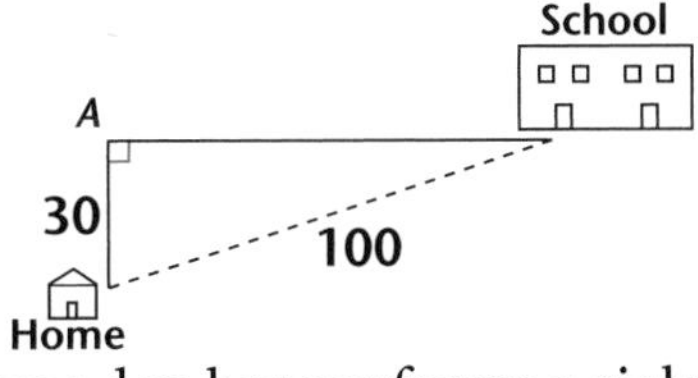

10. A wooden hanger forms a right triangle with legs equal to 12 inches each. How wide is the bottom?

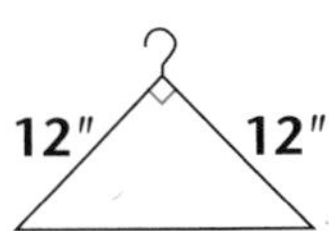

11. Ephraim is making a corner shelf. One edge will be 8 inches; the second edge will be 12 inches. How long will the front edge of the shelf be?

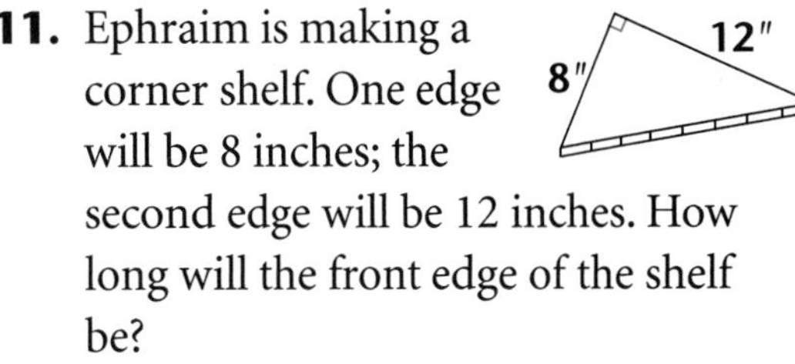

12. Edna has a wheelchair ramp. Her front door is 6 feet above ground level, and the ramp is 18 feet long. How far from the house is the start of the ramp?

13. A piece of wallboard is 4 feet wide and 6 feet long. The opening in Ken's van is 3 feet tall by 4 feet wide. Will the wallboard fit in Ken's van? Why or why not?

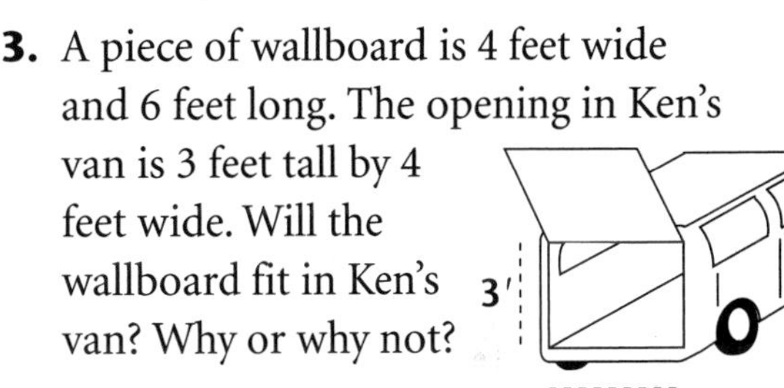

14. A transmission tower stands 22 feet tall. It will be secured by a wire attached 4 feet from the base of the tower. How long will the wire need to be?

15. The sailboat is 400 m from a lighthouse. The cruise ship is 600 m from it. How far apart are the boats?

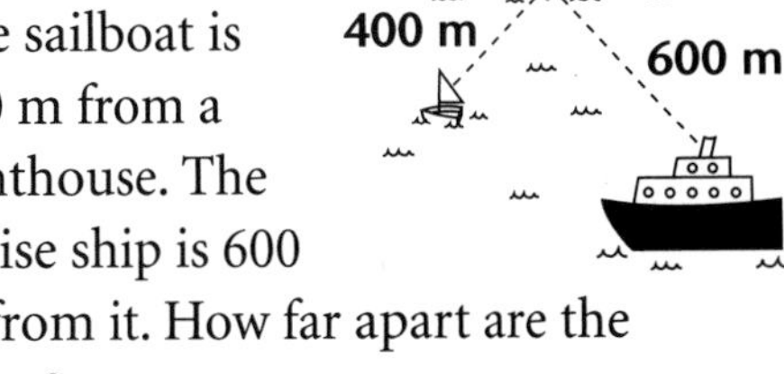

Lesson 5 Special Triangles

Equiangular triangle
A triangle with three equal angles

In Chapter 7 you learned that similar triangles have corresponding angles that are equal. Also, their corresponding sides are proportional.

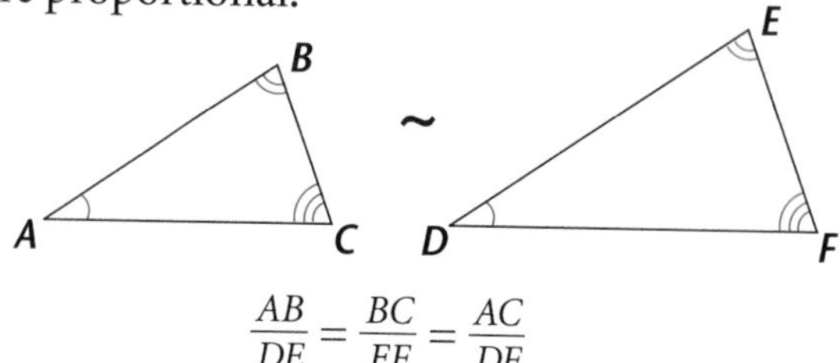

$$\frac{AB}{DE} = \frac{BC}{EF} = \frac{AC}{DF}$$

Determine whether the ratios of the sides of similar triangles, $AB:BC:AC$ and $DE:EF:DF$, are equal.

$(AB)(EF) = (BC)(DE)$	Multiply the means and extremes of the first two ratios.
$\frac{AB}{BC} = \frac{DE}{EF}$	Divide both sides by EF and BC.
$(BC)(DF) = (AC)(EF)$	Multiply the means and extremes of the second two ratios.
$\frac{BC}{AC} = \frac{EF}{DF}$	Divide both sides by DF and AC.
$AB:BC = DE:EF$	Rewrite the ratios.
$BC:AC = EF:DF$	
$AB:BC:AC = DE:EF:DF$	Combine the ratios.

So we see that the ratios of the sides of similar triangles are equal. We will look at these ratios for equilateral triangles and for two special right triangles.

> **Theorem 8.5.1:** The angles opposite equal sides in a triangle are equal.

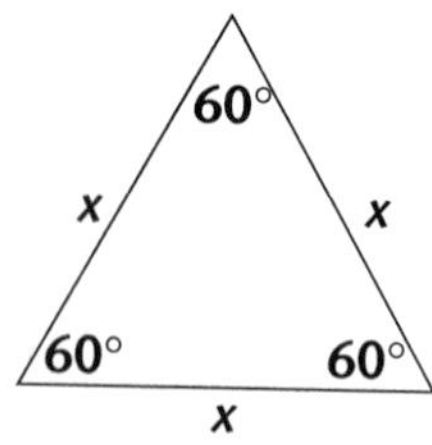

Equilateral triangles have three equal sides. Therefore, by theorem, equilateral triangles also have three equal angles. Each equal angle is $180° \div 3 = 60°$. So, equilateral triangles are also **equiangular triangles.** All equilateral, equiangular triangles are similar. So the ratio of the sides of equilateral triangles is 1:1:1.

EXAMPLE 1 If one side of an equilateral triangle is 7, what are the other two sides?

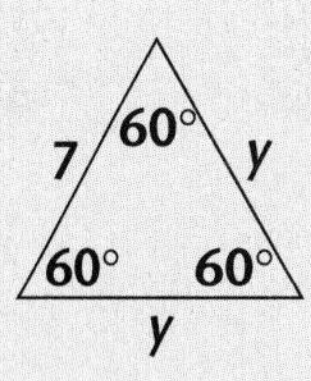

Solution: The ratio of sides is 1:1:1. Multiply each number by 7. The ratio of sides is 7:7:7. The unknown sides are both 7.

ΔABC is an isosceles right triangle with 45°, 45°, and 90° angles. Another name for an isosceles right triangle is a 45°-45°-90° triangle.

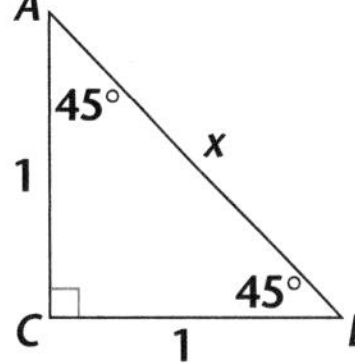

Let $AC = BC = 1$.
Call the unknown side x.

Then $1^2 + 1^2 = x^2$	by the Pythagorean Theorem
$2 = x^2$	by simplification
$\sqrt{2} = x$	

So, the ratio of the sides of an isosceles right triangle is $1:1:\sqrt{2}$. We can use this ratio to find an unknown side of any isosceles right triangle.

EXAMPLE 2 If each equal side is 5 units, what is the hypotenuse?

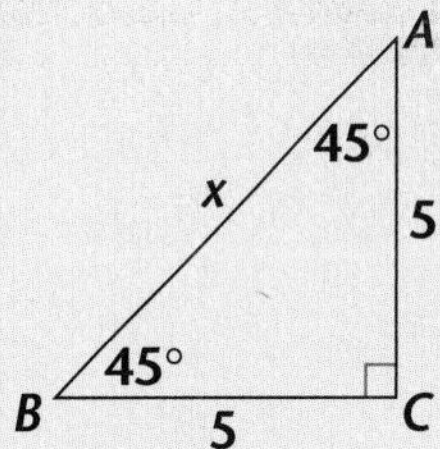

Solution 1

The ratio of sides is $1:1:\sqrt{2}$.

Multiply each number by 5.

The ratio of sides is $5:5:5\sqrt{2}$.

The hypotenuse is $5\sqrt{2}$.

Solution 2

Use the Pythagorean Theorem.

$5^2 + 5^2 = x^2$

$25 + 25 = x^2$

$\sqrt{2 \bullet 25} = x$ or $x = 5\sqrt{2}$

ΔABC is a 30°-60° right triangle. Another name for a 30°-60° right triangle is a 30°-60°-90° triangle.

> **Theorem 8.5.2:** In a 30°-60° right triangle, the side opposite the 30° angle is one-half the length of the hypotenuse.

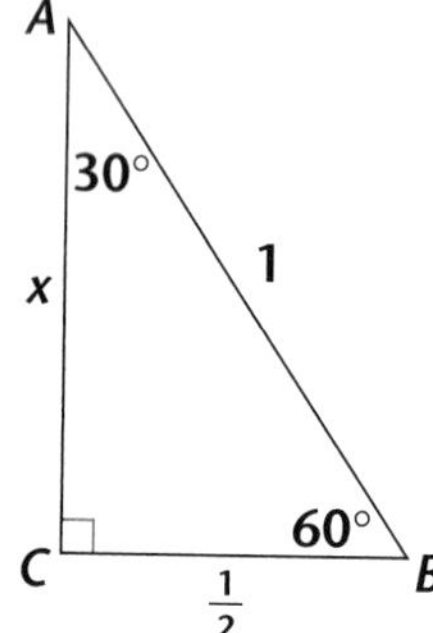

We can use this theorem to find the value of x in the diagram at the left.

Let $AB = 1$ and $BC = \frac{1}{2}$.

$$\text{Then } x^2 + \left(\frac{1}{2}\right)^2 = 1^2 \quad \text{by the Pythagorean Theorem}$$

$$x^2 + \frac{1}{4} = 1$$

$$x^2 = \frac{3}{4}$$

$$x = \frac{\sqrt{3}}{2}$$

So, the ratio of the sides of a 30°-60° right triangle is $1:\frac{1}{2}:\frac{\sqrt{3}}{2}$.

EXAMPLE 3 If the hypotenuse of a 30°-60° right triangle is 10 units, what are the lengths of the two legs?

Solution 1

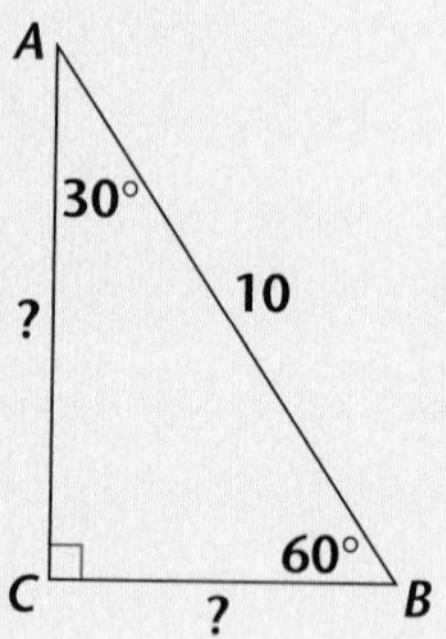

The ratio of the sides is $1:\frac{1}{2}:\frac{\sqrt{3}}{2}$.

Multiply the ratio by 10.

$$1 \bullet 10 : \frac{1}{2} \bullet 10 : \frac{\sqrt{3}}{2} \bullet 10$$

$$\downarrow \qquad \downarrow \qquad \downarrow$$

$$10 \qquad 5 \qquad 5\sqrt{3}$$

The legs are 5 and $5\sqrt{3}$.

Solution 2

Use the theorem above.

$BC = \frac{1}{2} \bullet 10 = 5$

Use the Pythagorean Theorem.

$(AC)^2 + 5^2 = 10^2$

$AC = \sqrt{75} = \sqrt{3 \bullet 25} = 5\sqrt{3}$

Exercise A One side of an equilateral triangle is given. Solve for the measures of the other sides.

1. 17 in.

2. 31 ft

3. 4.5 mi

Exercise B One leg of an isosceles right triangle is given. Solve for the hypotenuse.

4. 6 units

5. 10 units

6. 20 cm

7. 25 in.

8. 3 m

9. 13 ft

Exercise C The hypotenuse of a 30°-60° right triangle is given. Solve for both legs.

10. 5 units

11. 15 units

12. 30 cm

13. 16 m

14. 25 cm

15. 12 in.

TRY THIS The side opposite the 30° angle in a 30°-60° right triangle is 6 m. Solve for the other two sides.

Geometry in Your Life

30°-60° right triangles can be used to demonstrate the AA Similarity Postulate. Cut two large congruent 30°-60° right triangles from construction paper. On one, draw a line from the right angle perpendicular to the hypotenuse at *D*. Now cut along the perpendicular line to make two triangles. Compare all three triangles. See which of these angles correspond by placing the smaller triangles on top of the larger triangle. Line up the right angle, then the smallest angle, then the remaining angle. Do they all seem to match up?

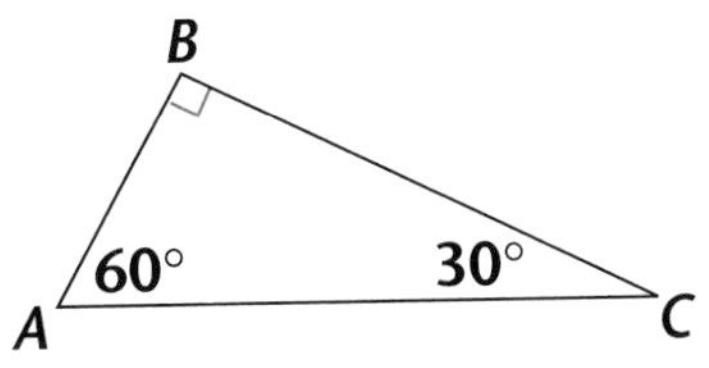

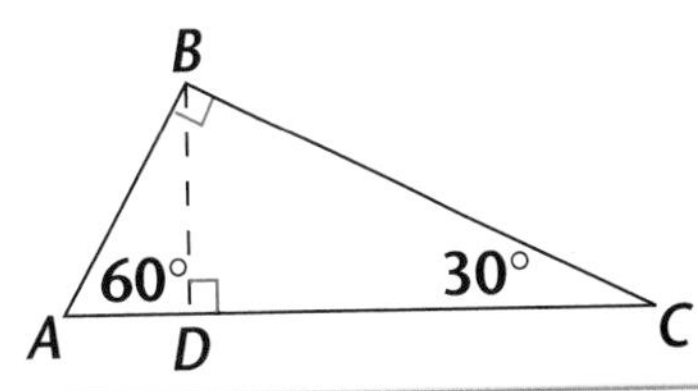

Lesson 6 Pythagorean Proof and Trapezoids

> ***Average***
>
> *A number found by dividing the sum of all the quantities by the number of quantities*

There is yet another way to prove the Pythagorean Theorem. This proof, which relies on the characteristics of a trapezoid, was developed by James Garfield, the 20th president of the United States!

Before we begin the proof, we need to review the steps used to find the area of a trapezoid. Recall that the area of a rectangle is the product of its base and its height.

Area = base × height

$A = b \bullet h$

h = height

b = base

While a rectangle has two pairs of parallel sides, a trapezoid has only one pair of parallel sides. Usually the parallel sides of a trapezoid are called the *bases*. In this diagram, the bases are *a* and *b*.

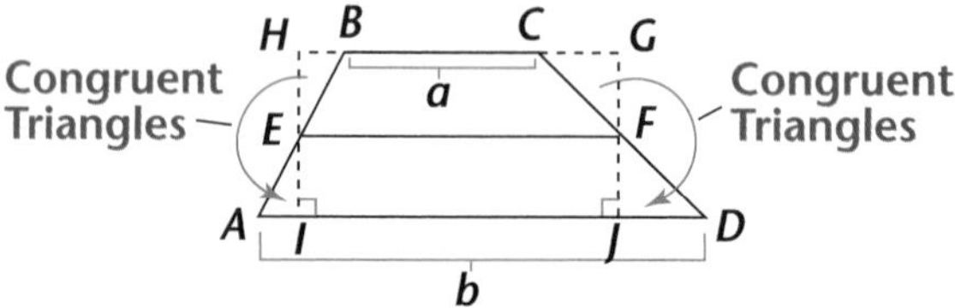

We can find the length of $\overline{EF}$ by finding the **average** of the lengths of *a* and *b*.

$EF = \frac{(a + b)}{2}$ = **average of two bases**

Note that $\overline{EF}$ joins the midpoints of the nonparallel sides. Also note that $\overline{HI}$ and $\overline{GJ}$ are perpendicular to the bases, so the pair of triangles formed at either edge of the trapezoid are congruent—here $\Delta BHE \cong \Delta AIE$ and $\Delta CGF \cong \Delta DJF$. Therefore, the rectangle *GHIJ* has the same area as the trapezoid.

Area of trapezoid = (average of bases)(height) $= \frac{(a + b)}{2}h$

Once you know how to find the area of a trapezoid, you can solve problems similar to these below.

EXAMPLE 1

Given: trapezoid with dimensions as marked

Find: area of the trapezoid

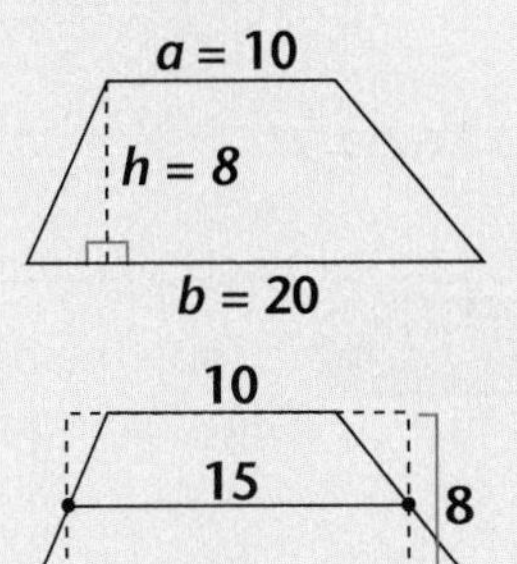

Area of trapezoid $= \left(\frac{a + b}{2}\right)h$

$= \left(\frac{10 + 20}{2}\right)8$

$= \left(\frac{30}{2}\right)8$

$= 15 \bullet 8 = 120$

Note that the formula actually calculates the area of the rectangle, $15 \bullet 8 = 120$.

EXAMPLE 2

Given: trapezoid with dimensions as marked

Find: area of the trapezoid

Area of trapezoid $= \left(\frac{a + b}{2}\right)h$

$= \left(\frac{22 + 32}{2}\right)10$

$= \left(\frac{54}{2}\right)10$

$= 27 \bullet 10 = 270$

Again, the formula actually calculates the area of the rectangle, $27 \bullet 10 = 270$.

Geometry in Your Life

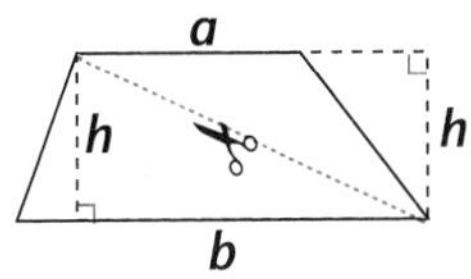

Say you want to design a room that is hexagonal or an irregular shape. How do you find the area of the room? One way is to cut it up into other shapes and find their areas. The area of any triangle is given by the formula $A = \frac{1}{2}bh$ where b is the base and h is the height. You can find the area of a trapezoid using this formula. Start with a construction paper trapezoid. Label the trapezoid bases a and b. Cut the trapezoid into two triangles as shown. Write algebraic expressions for the areas of both triangles and add them together. Then write the algebraic expression for the area of the trapezoid. Simplify the expressions. Are they equal?

Now that we can compute the area of a trapezoid, we can continue with Garfield's proof of the Pythagorean Theorem.

Given: ΔABC, $m\angle C = 90°$,
legs a and b, hypotenuse c

To Prove: $a^2 + b^2 = c^2$

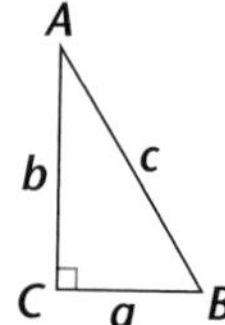

PROOF

Copy the given triangle so that a and b form a straight line as shown at the right.

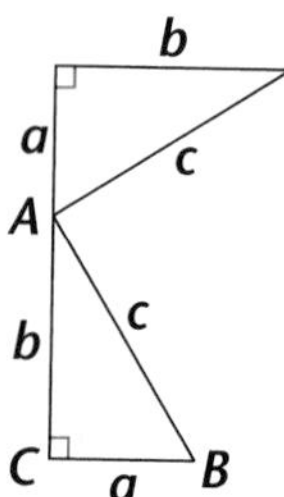

Connect the endpoints to form a trapezoid as shown. The angles at A must equal 180°. The acute angles ($\angle 2$ and $\angle 1$) are complementary because the given triangle is a right triangle. So the middle angle, $\angle 3$, must be 90°.

The height (h) of this trapezoid is $a + b$, so

Area of trapezoid $= \left(\frac{a+b}{2}\right)h$ becomes

$\left(\frac{a+b}{2}\right)(a+b)$ by substitution

Area of three triangles = Area of trapezoid

$$\Delta I + \Delta II + \Delta III = \text{Area of trapezoid}$$

$$\frac{1}{2}ab + \frac{1}{2}ab + \frac{1}{2}c^2 = \left(\frac{a+b}{2}\right)(a+b)$$

$$ab + \left(\frac{1}{2}\right)c^2 = \left(\frac{a+b}{2}\right)(a+b) \qquad \text{simplify}$$

$$2ab + c^2 = (a+b)^2 \qquad \text{multiply by 2}$$

$$2ab + c^2 = a^2 + 2ab + b^2 \qquad \text{square of quantity } (a+b)$$

$$c^2 = a^2 + b^2 \qquad \text{subtract } 2ab$$

This completes the fourth proof of the Pythagorean Theorem.

Exercise A Calculate the area of each trapezoid.

1.

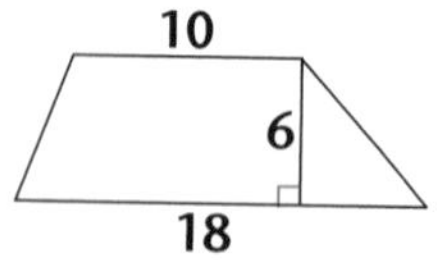

2.

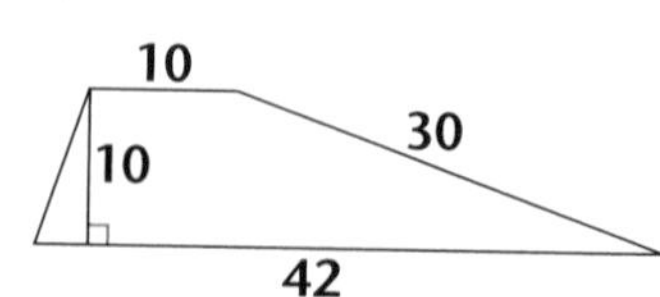

3.

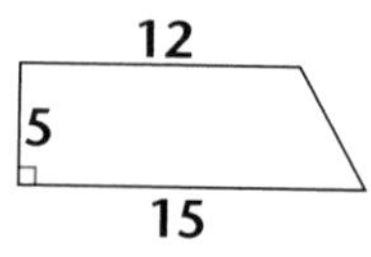

4.

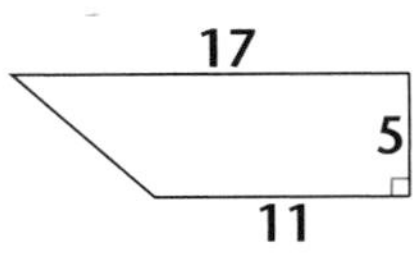

5.

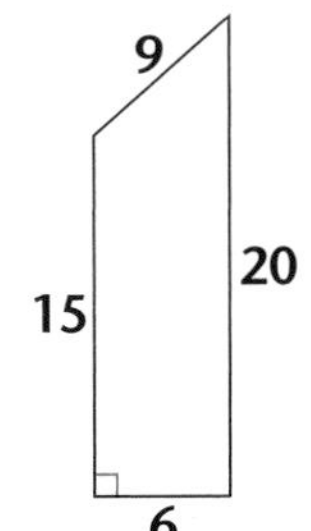

6.

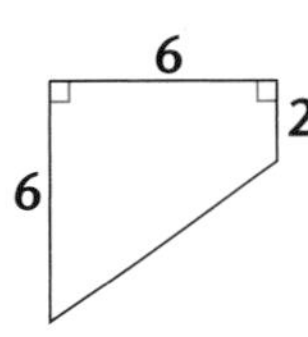

7.

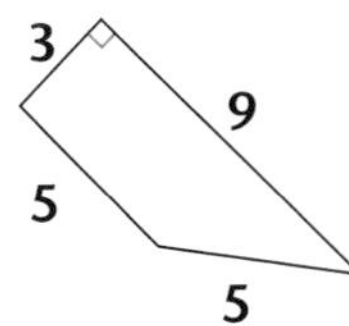

8.

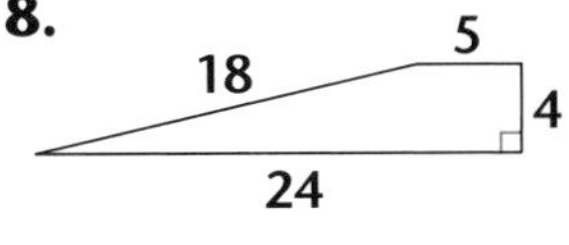

9.

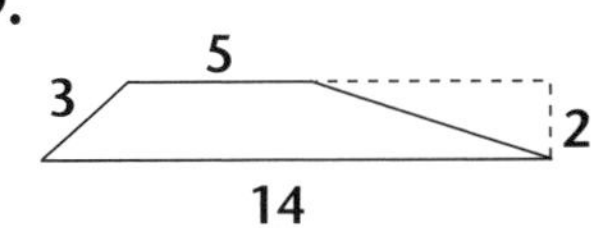

Exercise B Copy and complete the chart by calculating the areas for the given side lengths.

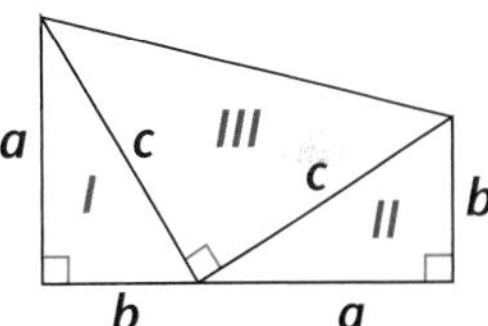

Side Lengths	Area Δ *I*	Area Δ *II*	Area Δ *III.*	Trapezoid Area
$a = 4, b = 3,$ $c = 5$	**10.** ______	**11.** ______	**12.** ______	**13.** ______
$a = 5, b = 12,$ $c = 13$	**14.** ______	**15.** ______	**16.** ______	**17.** ______
$a = 8, b = 6,$ $c = 10$	**18.** ______	**19.** ______	**20.** ______	**21.** ______
$a = 20, b = 48,$ $c = 52$	**22.** ______	**23.** ______	**24.** ______	**25.** ______

Lesson 7 Distance Formula: Pythagorean Theorem

One of the most useful applications of the Pythagorean Theorem is finding the distance between any two points in the coordinate plane.

Find the distance between points A and B in the coordinate plane.

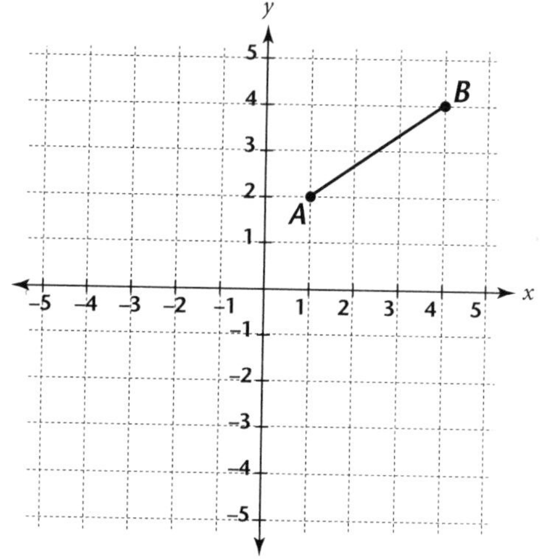

The axes form a right angle at their intersection, so it is possible to form a right triangle with hypotenuse $\overline{AB}$. If you know the coordinates of A and B, then you can use the Pythagorean Theorem to find the distance that separates them.

EXAMPLE 1 **Given:** $A = (2, 3)$ and $B = (6, 6)$

Find: the distance AB

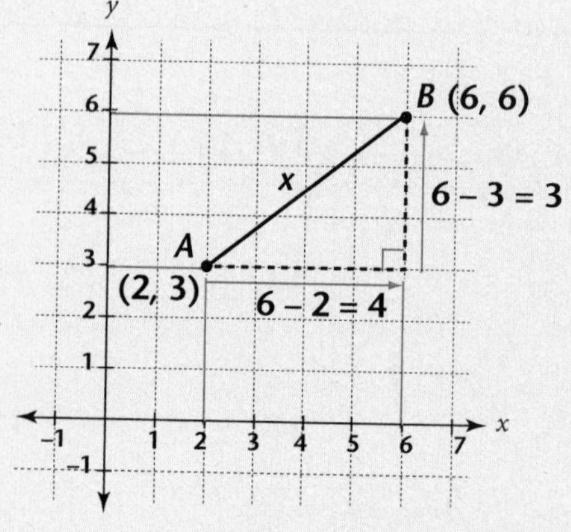

Complete the right triangle. The length of the leg || to the x-axis is $6 - 2 = 4$ and the leg || to the y-axis is $6 - 3 = 3$.

$x^2 = 3^2 + 4^2$ by Pythagorean Theorem

$x^2 = 9 + 16$

$x^2 = 25$

$x = 5$

The distance between (2, 3) and (6, 6) is 5.

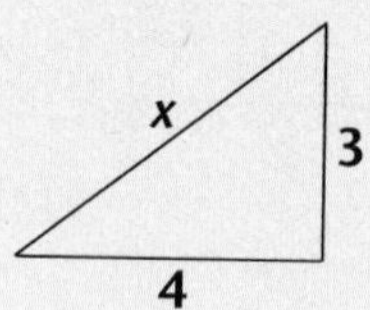

EXAMPLE 2 **Given:** $D = (-2, -3)$ and $C = (1, 4)$

Find: the distance CD

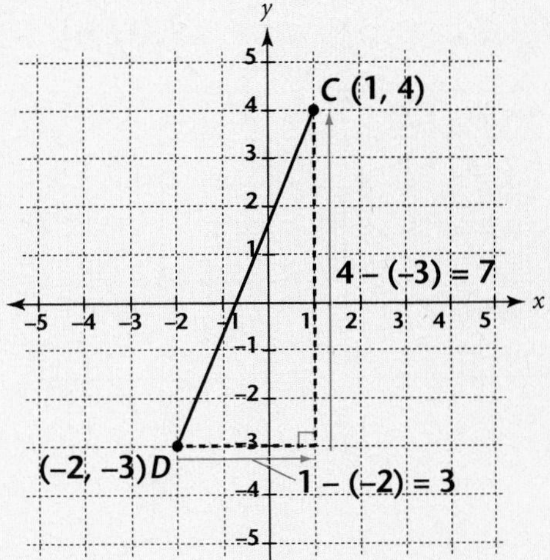

Complete the right triangle.
Let x = the distance CD.

$x^2 = 7^2 + 3^2$ by Pythagorean Theorem

$x^2 = 49 + 9$

$x^2 = 58$

$x = \sqrt{58}$

The distance between $(-2, -3)$ and $(1, 4)$ is $\sqrt{58}$.

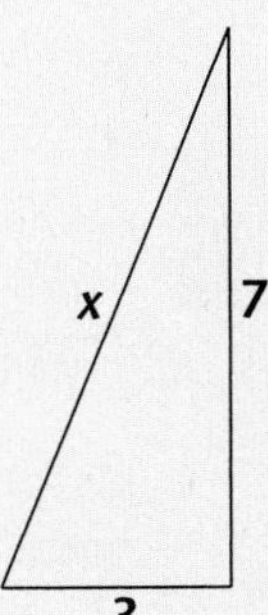

EXAMPLE 3 **Given:** $E = (-2, 5)$ and $F = (3, -4)$

Find: the distance EF

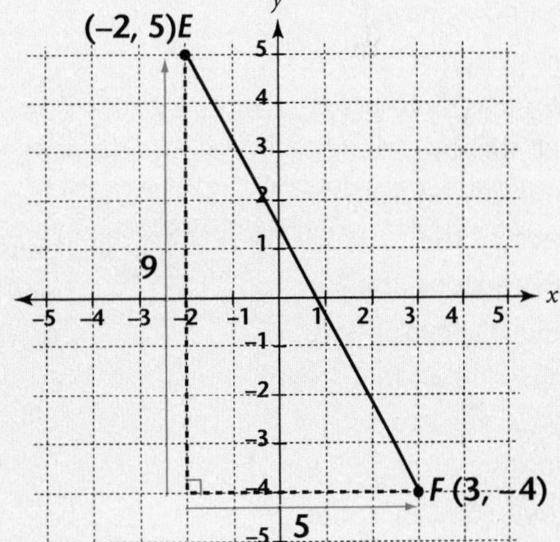

Complete the right triangle and use the Pythagorean Theorem. Let x = the distance EF.

The length of the leg parallel to the x-axis is $-2 - 3 = -5$. You will need to use the absolute value of -5 or $|-5| = 5$.

The length of the leg parallel to the y-axis is $5-(-4) = 9$.

$x^2 = 9^2 + 5^2$

$x^2 = 81 + 25$

$x^2 = 106$

$x = \sqrt{106}$

The distance between $(-2, 5)$ and $(3, -4)$ is $\sqrt{106}$.

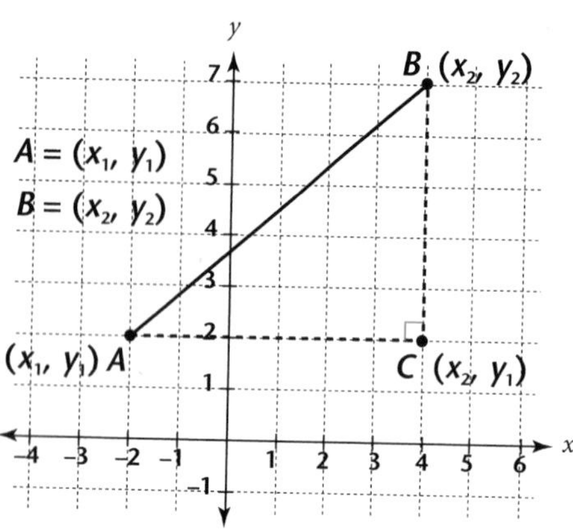

All of these kinds of problems can be solved using the formula below, which comes from the Pythagorean Theorem. Because we need the distances to be positive, we will use absolute values for the lengths of the legs.

$AC = |\text{difference in } x\text{-values}| = |x_2 - x_1|$

$BC = |\text{difference in } y\text{-values}| = |y_2 - y_1|$

ΔABC is a right triangle because the coordinate axes form a right angle.

Let $d = AB$, then by the Pythagorean Theorem,

$$d^2 = (AC)^2 + (BC)^2$$

$$d^2 = (x_2 - x_1)^2 + (y_2 - y_1)^2$$

In the distance formula, it does not matter whether you write $(x_2 - x_1)^2$ or $(x_1 - x_2)^2$. No matter what values x_1 and x_2 have, $(x_2 - x_1)^2 = (x_1 - x_2)^2$. You can see this by multiplying out each of the expressions. It also doesn't matter if $(x_2 - x_1)$ and $(y_2 - y_1)$ are positive or negative. Their squares in the formula are always positive.

Distance Formula:
$d^2 = (x_2 - x_1)^2 + (y_2 - y_1)^2$ or $d = \sqrt{(x_2 - x_1)^2 + (y_2 - y_1)^2}$

EXAMPLE 4 Use the distance formula to find the distance between (3, 4) and (6, 10). You may leave the answer in the square root form.

$d = \sqrt{(x_2 - x_1)^2 + (y_2 - y_1)^2}$

let $(x_1, y_1) = (3, 4)$, $(x_2, y_2) = (6, 10)$

$d = \sqrt{(6 - 3)^2 + (10 - 4)^2}$

$d = \sqrt{9 + 36} = \sqrt{45}$

EXAMPLE 5 Use the distance formula to find the distance between (−2, 3) and (−5, −7). You may leave the answer in the square root form.

$d = \sqrt{(x_2 - x_1)^2 + (y_2 - y_1)^2}$

let $(x_1, y_1) = (-2, 3)$, $(x_2, y_2) = (-5, -7)$

$d = \sqrt{(-5 - (-2))^2 + (-7 - 3)^2}$

$d = \sqrt{(-3)^2 + (-10)^2}$

$d = \sqrt{9 + 100} = \sqrt{109}$

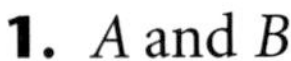
Exercise A Complete the right triangle to find the distance between the named points. Use graph paper. You may leave the distance in square root form.

1. A and B
2. B and C
3. D and E
4. C and E
5. B and D

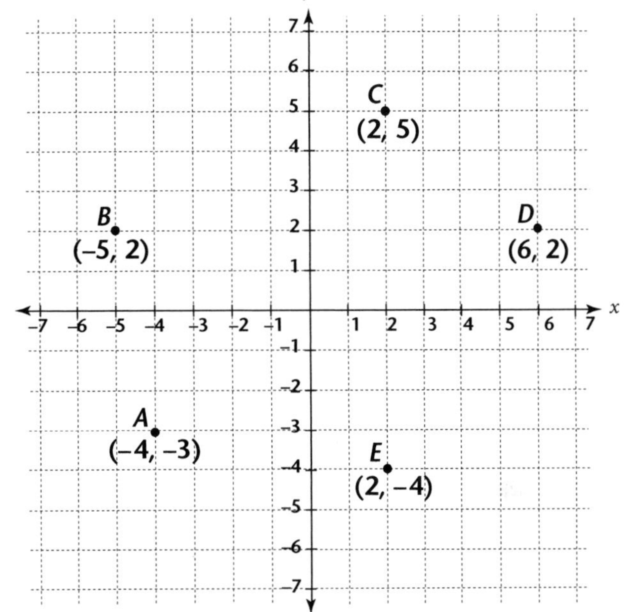

6. $(8, 9)$ and $(5, 6)$
7. $(-12, 1)$ and $(6, 9)$
8. $(6, -2)$ and $(-3, -6)$
9. $(-13, 7)$ and $(5, 6)$

10. $(-30, -25)$ and $(-20, -15)$

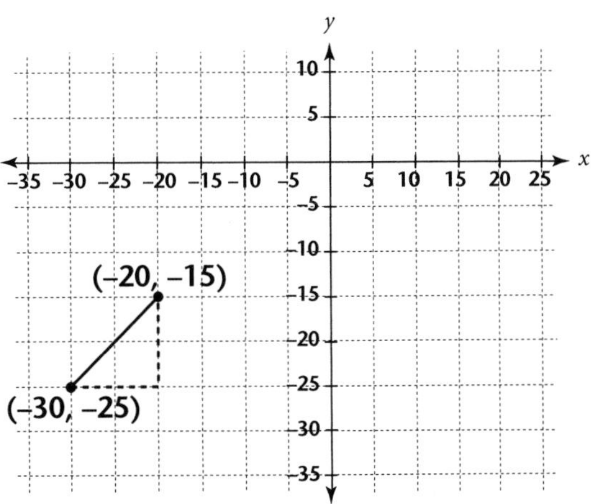

Writing About Mathematics

Which method of finding distance do you prefer—completing the triangle or using the distance formula? Explain why.

Exercise B Use the distance formula to find the distances between the given points. You may leave the distance in square root form.

11. $(-2, -3)$ and $(4, 5)$

12. $(2, 3)$ and $(0, 0)$

13. $(6, 4)$ and $(4, 9)$

14. $(2, 5)$ and $(6, -3)$

15. $(-6, -2)$ and $(-7, -9)$

Calculator Practice

EXAMPLE 6 Find the distance between (4, 6) and (2, 3).

$d = \sqrt{(x_2 - x_1)^2 + (y_2 - y_1)^2}$

Let $(x_1, y_1) = (4, 6)$, $(x_2, y_2) = (2, 3)$.

To find d, press 2nd x^2 (2 − 4) x^2 + (3 − 6) x^2) ENTER. The display gives $\sqrt{13}$ as a decimal, 3.605551275.

To see the number before the square root is taken, press x^2 ENTER. This gives the value of the radicand before the square root is taken, 13.

Exercise C Use the distance formula and your calculator to find the distances between the points. Write the distance in square root and decimal form. Round to the nearest hundredth if necessary.

16. $(-8, 50)$ and $(30, -11)$

17. $(-10, 15)$ and $(-20, 20)$

18. $(9, 16)$ and $(25, 36)$

19. $(17, 16)$ and $(21, 19)$

20. $(21, 20)$ and $(20, 12)$

Lesson 8 Converse of the Pythagorean Theorem

Remember, in a converse, the "If" and "then" terms of a conditional are reversed.

Example:
Conditional
If *A*, then *B*.
Converse
If *B*, then *A*.

The Pythagorean Theorem tells us that $a^2 + b^2 = c^2$ for right triangles. Does that also mean that if you have a triangle such that $a^2 + b^2 = c^2$ you can be sure it is a right triangle? Let's look at a specific case: $3^2 + 4^2 = 5^2$ because $9 + 16 = 25$ is a true statement. You might think you have a right triangle, but can you be sure? To be sure you have to prove the following.

Converse of the Pythagorean Theorem (8.8.1)
If for ΔABC, $(AC)^2 = (AB)^2 + (BC)^2$, then ΔABC is a right triangle.

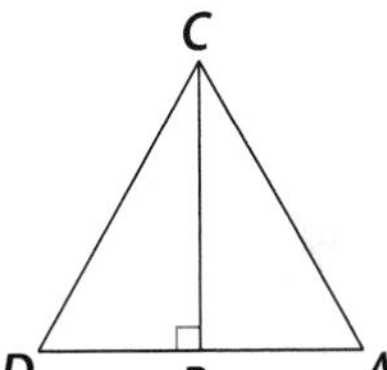

Given: ΔABC, $(AC)^2 = (AB)^2 + (BC)^2$
To Prove: ΔABC is a right triangle

PROOF

Statement	Reason
1. ΔABC with $(AC)^2 = (AB)^2 + (BC)^2$	1. Given.
2. Draw $\overline{BD}$ at right angles to $\overline{BC}$ so that $BD = BA$.	2. Construction of perpendiculars and copy line segments.
3. Draw $\overline{DC}$.	3. Postulate 1, two points determine a line.
4. $(BD)^2 = (BA)^2$	4. Square both sides from Step 2.
5. $(BD)^2 + (BC)^2 = (BA)^2 + (BC)^2$	5. Equals added to equals.
6. $(DC)^2 = (BD)^2 + (BC)^2$	6. Pythagorean Theorem for ΔBCD.
7. $\therefore (DC)^2 = (AC)^2$	7. Steps 1, 4, and 6 and substitution.
8. $DC = AC$	8. Take square root of each side of Step 7.
9. $BC = BC$	9. A quantity is equal to itself.
10. $\therefore \Delta BCD \cong \Delta ABC$	10. SSS Postulate.
11. $m\angle DBC \cong m\angle BCA$	11. Corresponding parts of congruent triangles are equal.
12. $m\angle ABC$ is a right angle and ΔABC is a right triangle.	12. All right angles are equal.

Now that you have proved this converse of the Pythagorean Theorem, you know that anytime the sum of the squares of two sides of a triangle equals the square of the third side of the triangle, the triangle must be a right triangle.

Pythagorean Theorem

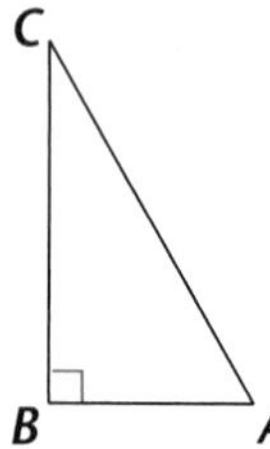

If ΔABC is a right triangle, then $(AC)^2 = (AB)^2 + (BC)^2$.

Converse of Pythagorean Theorem

If $(AC)^2 = (AB)^2 + (BC)^2$, then ΔABC is a right triangle.

EXAMPLE 1 The sides of a triangle are 6, 8, and 12. Is the triangle a right triangle?

If it is a right triangle, then $a^2 + b^2 = c^2$. Substitute the triangle lengths for *a, b,* and *c.*

$$a^2 + b^2 = c^2$$
$$6^2 + 8^2 = 12^2$$
$$36 + 64 = 144$$
$$100 \neq 144$$ The triangle is not a right triangle.

EXAMPLE 2 The sides of a triangle are 5, 12, and 13. Is the triangle a right triangle?

Substitute the triangle lengths for *a, b,* and *c.*

$$a^2 + b^2 = c^2$$
$$5^2 + 12^2 = 13^2$$
$$25 + 144 = 169$$
$$169 = 169$$ The triangle is a right triangle.

> **Writing About Mathematics**
>
> Use algebra to show why multiples of a triple such as 3, 4, 5 correspond to similar right triangles.

Exercise A Use the converse of the Pythagorean Theorem to test whether these triples are sides of a right triangle. Answer *yes* or *no.*

1. 3, 4, 5

2. 9, 10, 11

3. 7, 8, 10

4. 6, 8, 10

5. 10, 25, 36

6. 9, 12, 15

7. 10, 20, 30

8. 7, 6, 5

9. 11, 12, 13

10. 17, 60, 70

Exercise B Answer the following questions about isosceles ΔABC.

11. What is the length of $\overline{BD}$?

12. How long is $\overline{AB}$?

13. Why must $AD = CD$?

14. What do you know about $\angle DAB$ and $\angle DCB$?

15. Why must $\angle ADB \cong \angle CDB$?

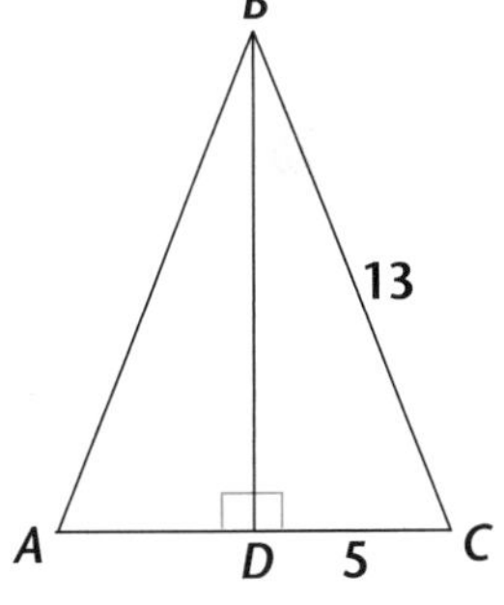

You can find several examples of triangles in nature—the arms of a starfish or the points in a star fruit (called a carambola). How would you determine if these triangles were right triangles?

Lesson 9 Algebra Connection: Denominators and Zero

Rational number

An integer a divided by another integer b where b ≠ 0

Numbers such as $\frac{3}{4}$, $\frac{12}{4}$, and $\frac{0}{-5}$ are examples of rational numbers. In general, a **rational number** is of the form $\frac{a}{b}$, where $b \neq 0$ and a and b are integers.

This means that $\frac{1}{0}$ and $\frac{x}{0}$ for $x \neq 0$ are not rational numbers. Here is why.

EXAMPLE 1 We know that $\frac{12}{4} = 3$ is true because $12 = 4 \bullet 3$ is true.

In general, $\frac{a}{b} = c$ because $a = b \bullet c$.

Assume that $\frac{12}{0}$ = some number. Then $12 = 0 \bullet$ some number.

This means that $12 = 0$.

But $12 = 0$ is false. Therefore, $\frac{12}{0}$ = some number is also false.

So, 0 is never a denominator in algebraic expressions.

Rule:
$\frac{1}{0}$ and $\frac{x}{0}$ for $x \neq 0$ are undefined because division by 0 is not defined.

EXAMPLE 2 For what value of x is $\frac{1}{x + \frac{3}{4}}$ undefined?

Solution: When $x + \frac{3}{4} = 0$, the fraction is undefined.

Solve $x + \frac{3}{4} = 0$ for x.

$x + \frac{3}{4} - \frac{3}{4} = 0 - \frac{3}{4}$

$x = -\frac{3}{4}$ makes the fraction undefined.

Check: For $x = -\frac{3}{4}$, $\frac{1}{x + \frac{3}{4}} = \frac{1}{-\frac{3}{4} + \frac{3}{4}} = \frac{1}{0}$, and $\frac{1}{0}$ is undefined.

EXAMPLE 3 For what values of y is $\frac{1}{y^2 - 9}$ undefined?

Solution: When $y^2 - 9 = 0$, the fraction is undefined.

Solve $y^2 - 9 = 0$ for y.

$(y + 3)(y - 3) = 0$

$y + 3 = 0$ or $y - 3 = 0$

$y = -3$ or $y = 3$

We can write $y = -3$ or $y = 3$ as $y = \pm 3$.

For $y = \pm 3$, the fraction is undefined.

Check: For $y = 3$, $\frac{1}{y^2 - 9} = \frac{1}{3^2 - 9} = \frac{1}{9 - 9} = \frac{1}{0}$

For $y = -3$, $\frac{1}{y^2 - 9} = \frac{1}{(-3)^2 - 9} = \frac{1}{9 - 9} = \frac{1}{0}$

EXAMPLE 4 For what values of x is $\frac{x - 4}{x(x + 1)}$ undefined?

Solution: When $x(x + 1) = 0$, the fraction is undefined.

Solve $x(x + 1) = 0$ for x.

$x = 0$ or $x + 1 = 0$

$x = 0$ or $x = -1$

For $x = 0$ or $x = -1$, the fraction is undefined.

Check: For $x = 0$, $\frac{x - 4}{x(x + 1)} = \frac{0 - 4}{0(0 + 1)} = \frac{-4}{0}$

For $x = -1$, $\frac{x - 4}{x(x + 1)} = \frac{-1 - 4}{(-1)(-1 + 1)} = \frac{-5}{(-1)(0)} = \frac{-5}{0}$

$\frac{-4}{0}$ and $\frac{-5}{0}$ are undefined.

Exercise A Find the value for which each fraction is undefined.

1. $\frac{1}{x + 10}$ **2.** $\frac{5}{y - 4}$ **3.** $\frac{-15}{c + 3}$ **4.** $\frac{4x}{-7y}$

Exercise B Find the values for which each fraction is undefined.

5. $\frac{-2}{9w^2}$ **6.** $\frac{-20x}{5x^2}$ **7.** $\frac{13}{m^2 - 16}$ **8.** $\frac{4a}{y^2 - 49}$

9. $\frac{4}{b^2 - 100}$ **10.** $\frac{-12}{c^2 - 81}$ **11.** $\frac{2z}{4 - z^2}$ **12.** $\frac{0}{a^2 - 25}$

Exercise C Find the values for which each fraction is undefined.

13. $\frac{x - 3}{(9 - x^2)(x + 5)}$ **14.** $\frac{2y + 7}{2y^2 - y - 1}$ **15.** $\frac{w + 7}{w^2 + 5w + 4}$

Application

Architecture and Geometric Shapes Triangles play an important role in architecture, but one that is usually hidden. In the roof of a house, triangles are used to distribute the weight of the roof to the outside walls. Most skyscrapers are supported by steel frameworks. Usually these supports can't be seen. But in the 100-story John Hancock tower in Chicago, the architect left the triangular bracing exposed. These triangles are used to stabilize the building against wind and its own weight.

EXAMPLE 1 Name a geometric shape that is used in the design of the Air Force Academy Chapel shown at the right.

One shape is a tetrahedron. A tetrahedron is a three-dimensional shape with four triangular faces.

Exercise Follow the directions below to examine geometric shapes in architecture.

1. Find several photographs of large structures such as the buildings pictured here, the bridge shown at the beginning of this chapter, or the geodesic dome in Chapter 6.

2. Examine each photograph and determine how triangles were used in the structure. Identify any triangles that may be similar to one another and any that may be congruent.

3. List three examples in which a triangle shape (perhaps in the form of a cross brace) is used to strengthen an object.

4. Review the pictures. Look for other geometric shapes. Identify each shape and tell how you identified it.

5. Make a sketch of a building, using triangles in your design as well as other geometric shapes.

Chapter 8 REVIEW

Write the letter of the correct answer.

1. A right triangle has legs of lengths 5 and 12. What is the length of its hypotenuse?

A $\sqrt{119}$ **C** 17

B 13 **D** 19

2. A right triangle has a hypotenuse of length 10 and a leg of length 5. To the nearest tenth, what is the length of the other leg?

A 5.0 **C** 8.7

B 7.5 **D** 11.2

3. What is the ratio of the lengths of sides in a 30°-60° right triangle?

A $1:1:\sqrt{2}$ **C** $1:\frac{1}{2}:\frac{\sqrt{3}}{2}$

B 1:2:3 **D** $1:\frac{\sqrt{2}}{2}:\frac{\sqrt{3}}{2}$

4. What is the distance between the points $(-3, 4)$ and $(7, -7)$?

A 5 **C** $\sqrt{137}$

B $\sqrt{109}$ **D** $\sqrt{221}$

5. Which of the following is not a Pythagorean Triple?

A (3, 4, 5) **C** (30, 40, 50)

B (4, 5, 6) **D** (39, 52, 65)

Find the length of the unknown side of each right triangle. Use a calculator and round your answer to the nearest hundredth.

Example:

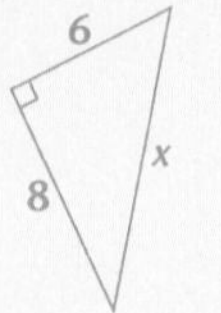

Solution: In a right triangle, $a^2 + b^2 = c^2$
Substitute the values for a and b.
$8^2 + 6^2 = x^2$
$64 + 36 = x^2$
$100 = x^2$
$\sqrt{100} = 10 = x$

6.

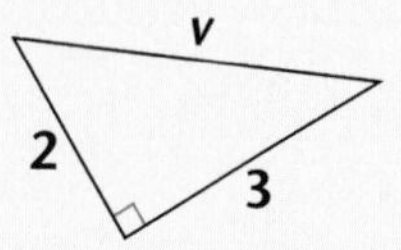

7.

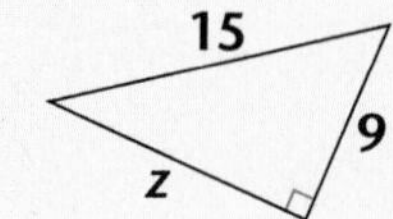

Find the missing lengths asked for in each triangle. Write your answers as whole numbers or in square root form.

Example:

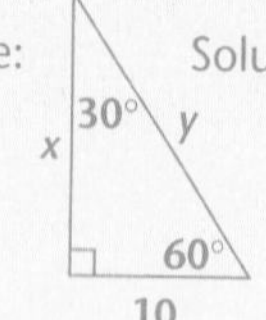

Solution: The sides of a 30°-60° right triangle have lengths in ratio $1:\frac{1}{2}:\frac{\sqrt{3}}{2}$. So, $x = 10 \bullet \sqrt{3} = 10\sqrt{3}$ and $y = 10 \bullet 2 = 20$

8.

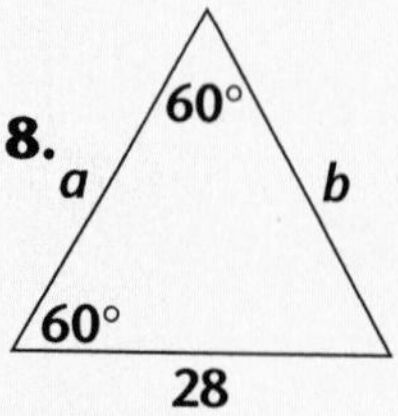

9.

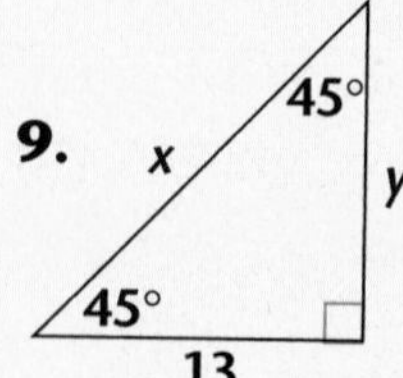

10.

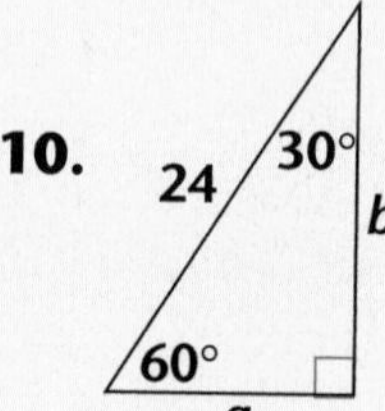

Calculate the area of each trapezoid.

Example:

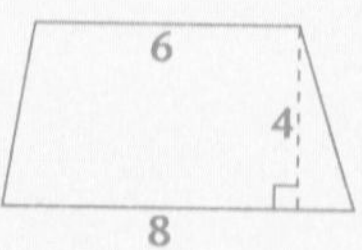

Solution: Area of a trapezoid $= h\frac{(a + b)}{2}$ where h is the height and a and b are the parallel sides. Substitute the given values in the formula, $h = 4$, $a = 6$, $b = 8$.

area $= 4\frac{(6 + 8)}{2} = 4\left(\frac{14}{2}\right) = 4 \bullet 7$
area $= 28$

11.

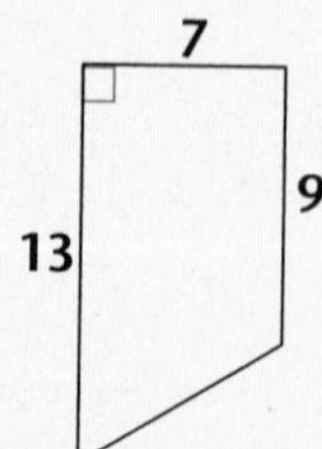

12.

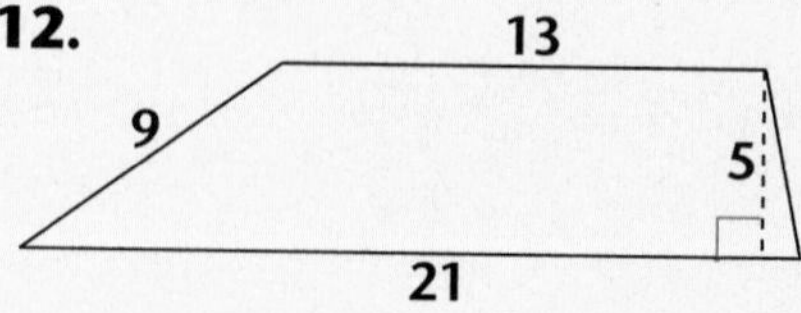

Find the distance between the named points. Use the distance formula. You may leave the distance in square root form.

Example: A and B

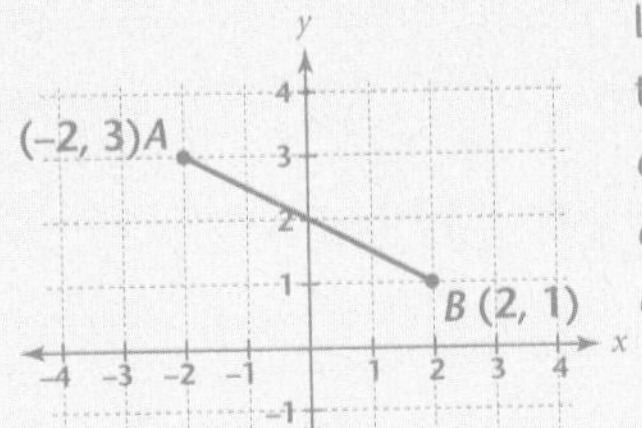

Solution: distance $= \sqrt{(x_2 - x_1)^2 + (y_2 - y_1)^2}$
Let $(-2, 3) = (x_1, y_1)$ and let $(2, 1) = (x_2, y_2)$
then $d = \sqrt{(2 - (-2))^2 + (1 - 3)^2}$
$d = \sqrt{(4)^2 + (-2)^2}$
$d = \sqrt{16 + 4}$
$d = \sqrt{20} = 2\sqrt{5}$

13. C and D

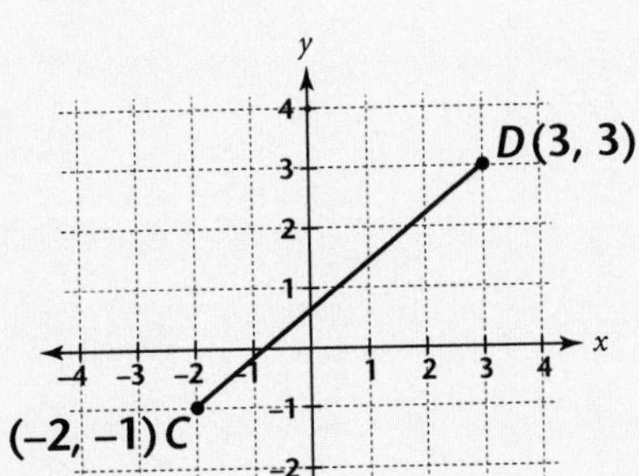

14. E and F

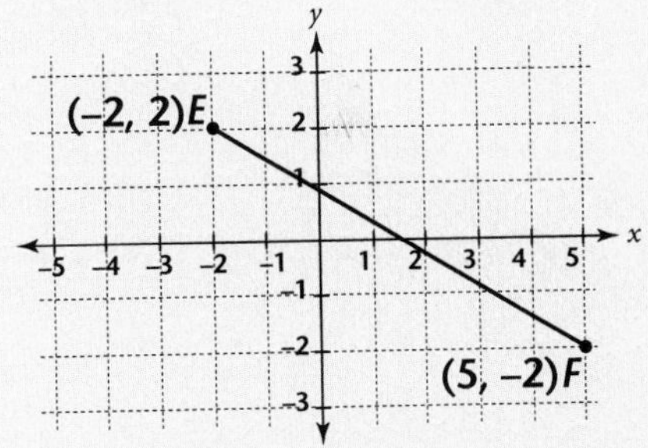

Tell whether these triples are sides of a right triangle. Answer *yes* or *no*.

Example: 25, 60, 65
Solution: Use the formula: $a^2 + b^2 = c^2$.
Substitute the given values in the equation.
$25^2 + 60^2 = 65^2$ $\quad$ $625 + 3{,}600 = 4{,}225$
$4{,}225 = 4{,}225$ $\quad$ Yes, the triple forms a right triangle.

15. 9, 12, 15

16. 7, 8, 11

17. 12, 35, 37

18. 35, 84, 91

19. 40, 400, 401

20. 20, 99, 101

Test-Taking Tip

It is a good idea to double check the location of numbers or letters that help label a diagram or figure.

FRONT ELEVATION
3600
3275
BED 4
ROOF LIGHT
ROOF LIGHT
2210
MAIN BEDROOM
HW
BATH
4395
BED 2
BED 3
2470

Chapter

Perimeter and Area

A house plan is a drawing that shows the size and location of each room in a house. It may also show the design of the exterior. A builder uses the drawing to decide how much to charge for construction of the house.

How much will it cost to build a fence around a property? The material is sold by the foot, so the builder must measure the perimeter, or distance around the lot. And how much will it cost to build the house? Builders find the area of the house, the total number of square feet in all the rooms. That number is multiplied by a dollar amount to find the total cost of construction.

In Chapter 9, you will learn how to use formulas to calculate the perimeters and areas of polygons.

Goals for Learning

- To identify formulas for finding the perimeters of polygons
- To use the distance formula for finding perimeter
- To use the Pythagorean Theorem to determine perimeter and area
- To identify formulas for finding the areas of polygons
- To use formulas to find the perimeters and areas of polygons

Lesson 1 Perimeters of Polygons

Perimeter of a polygon

Sum of the lengths of all the sides of a polygon

A common way to think about perimeter is to picture it as the distance around a figure. This picture matches the more formal definition.

The **perimeter of a polygon** is the sum of the lengths of all the sides of the polygon.

EXAMPLE 1 Perimeter = 5 + 6 + 7 = 18

Formula: $P = a + b + c$

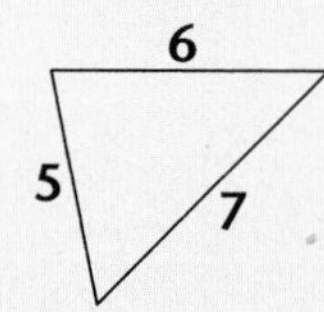

EXAMPLE 2 Perimeter = 10 + 15 + 13 + 20 = 58

Formula: $P = a + b + c + d$

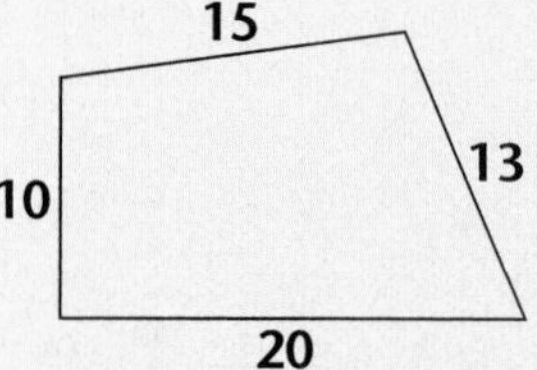

EXAMPLE 3 Perimeter = 10 + 30 + 20 + 8 + 15 = 83

Formula: $P = a + b + c + d + e$

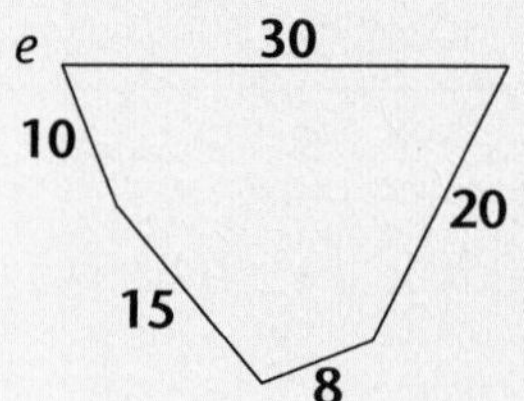

When a polygon has no equal sides, like those in the examples above, there is no formula or "shortcut" for finding the perimeter. The length of each side must be known.

If you know the perimeter of a polygon, then you can use algebra to find the length of one missing side.

EXAMPLE 4 A quadrilateral has a perimeter of 60 ft. If three of its sides are 10 ft, 12 ft, and 15 ft long, what is the length of the fourth side?

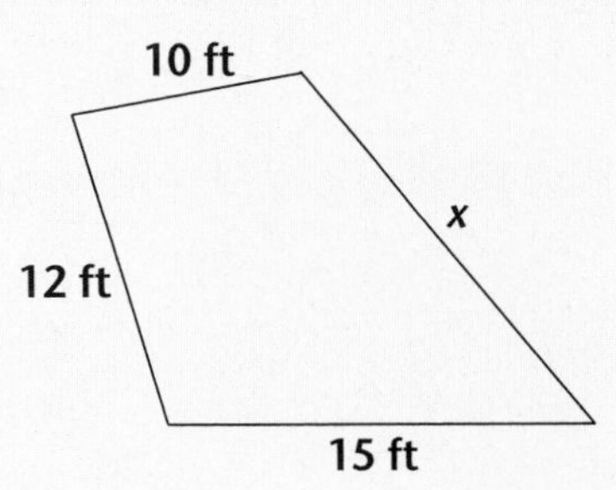

Draw a picture to help you solve the problem.

Let x = length of missing side.

$10 + 12 + 15 + x = 60$

$37 + x = 60$

$x = 60 - 37$

$x = 23$ The missing side is 23 ft long.

EXAMPLE 5 The short side of a rectangular garden is 10 m; the long side is 15 m. What is the perimeter of the garden?

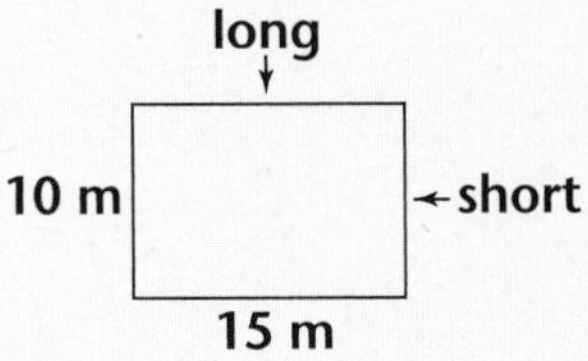

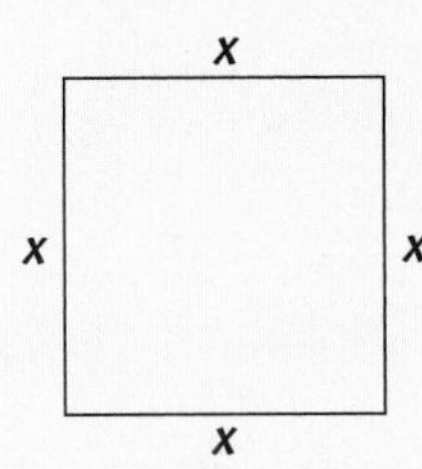

Draw a picture to help you solve the problem.

Perimeter = 2 short sides + 2 long sides

$P = 2(10) + 2(15)$

$P = 20 + 30 = 50$ The perimeter of the garden is 50 m.

EXAMPLE 6 Suppose you have 100 ft of wire fencing to make a square enclosure for your dog. How long will each side of the square be?

Draw a picture to help you solve the problem.

$P = 100$

$P = x + x + x + x = 4x$

$P = 4x = 100$

$x = 25$ Each side is 25 ft.

How would you find the distance you have to walk to make it through this hedge maze? Being able to find the perimeter of geometric figures will allow you to measure distances. You can use this knowledge to figure out how far you will need to walk to navigate the maze.

Exercise A Find the perimeter of each polygon.

1.

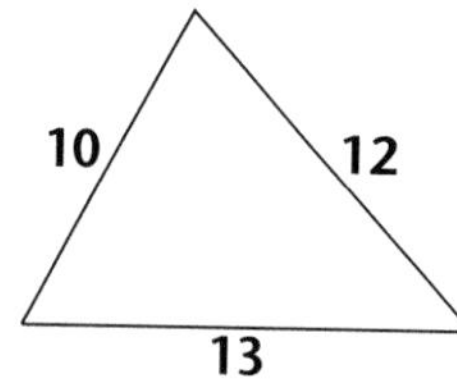

2.

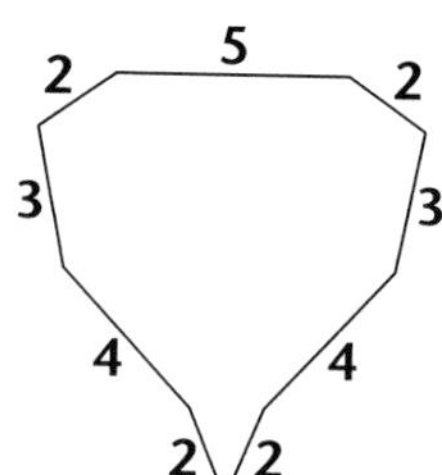

3.

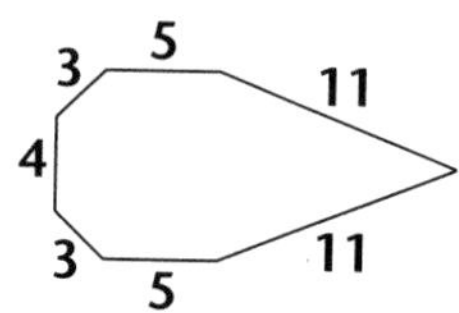

Exercise B Solve for the missing side. The perimeter is given.

4.

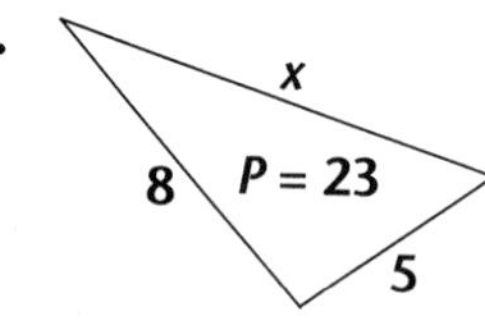

5.

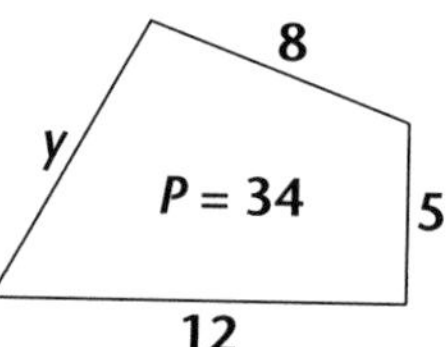

6.

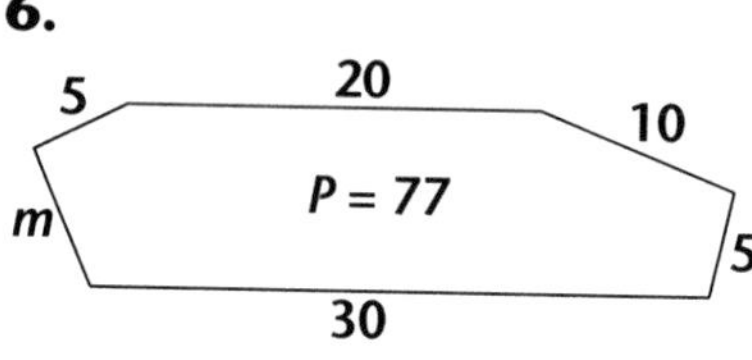

7.

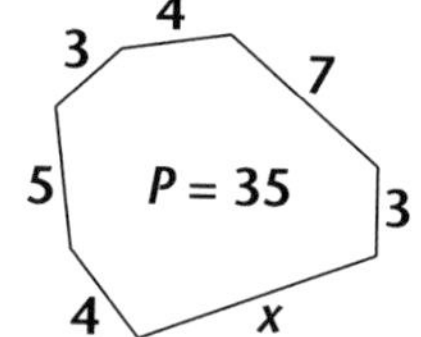

Exercise C Find the perimeter for each item.

8. A rectangle has a short side of 15 m and a long side of 25 m. What is the perimeter of the rectangle?

9. The short side of a rectangle is 23 ft; the long side of the same rectangle is 32 ft. What is the perimeter of the rectangle?

10. The long side of a rectangle is 11 inches; the short side is 10 inches. What is the perimeter of the rectangle?

Lesson 2 Perimeter Formulas

If a polygon has equal sides and equal angles, the polygon is a regular polygon. You can use a formula to find the perimeter. In the table below, s = the length of one side of a regular polygon.

Formulas for Perimeter	Examples
Equilateral Triangle $P = s + s + s$ $P = 3s$ 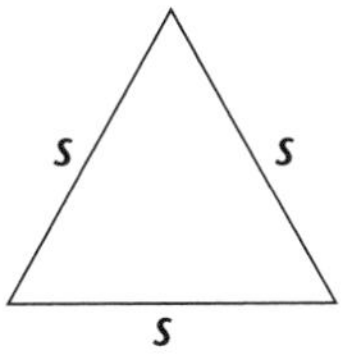	$P = 6 + 6 + 6$ $P = 3 \cdot 6 = 18$ 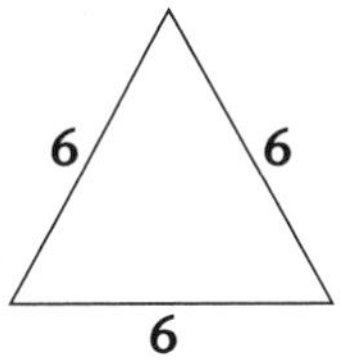
Rhombus $P = s + s + s + s$ $P = 4s$ 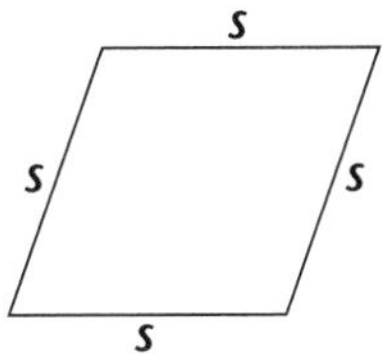	$P = 5 + 5 + 5 + 5$ $P = 4 \cdot 5 = 20$ 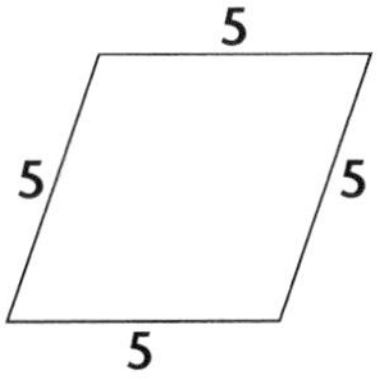
Square $P = s + s + s + s$ $P = 4s$ 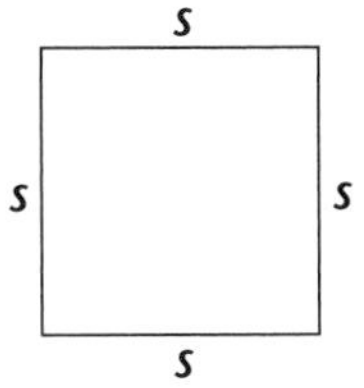	$P = 5 + 5 + 5 + 5$ $P = 4 \cdot 5 = 20$ 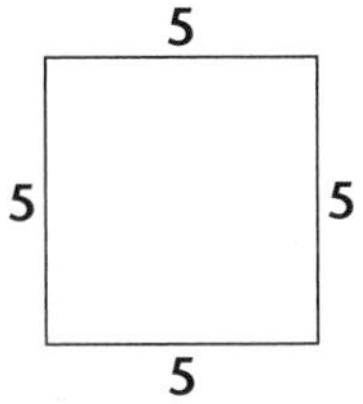
Regular Pentagon $P = s + s + s + s + s$ $P = 5s$ 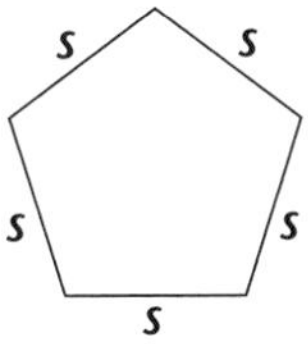	$P = 10 + 10 + 10 + 10 + 10$ $P = 5 \cdot 10 = 50$ 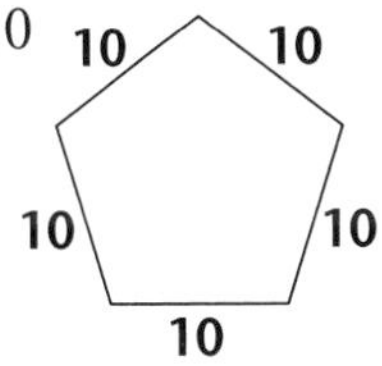
Regular Hexagon $P = s + s + s + s + s + s$ $P = 6s$ 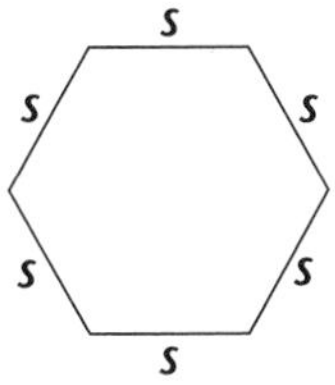	$P = 4 + 4 + 4 + 4 + 4 + 4$ $P = 6 \cdot 4 = 24$ 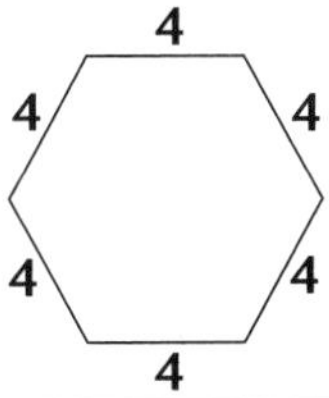
Regular n-sided Polygon $P = s + \ldots + s$ $P = ns$	$P =$ (number of sides)(length of one side) $P = n \cdot s$

The perimeter of a rectangle presents a special case. There are two pairs of equal sides, called the *length* and the *width*, or the *base* and the *height.*

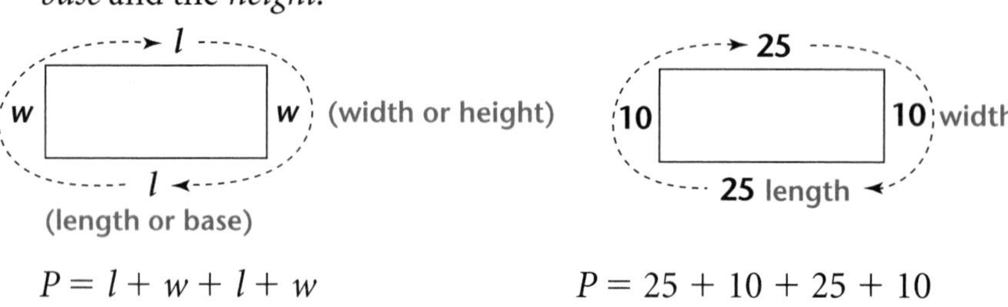

$P = l + w + l + w$
$P = l + l + w + w$
$P = 2l + 2w$
$P = 2(l + w)$

OR

$P = b + h + b + h$
$P = b + b + h + h$
$P = 2b + 2h$
$P = 2(b + h)$

$P = 25 + 10 + 25 + 10$
$P = 25 + 25 + 10 + 10$
$P = 2 \cdot 25 + 2 \cdot 10$
$P = 2(25 + 10) = 70$

Each of the formulas for perimeter is written in two different ways. Those two ways of writing each formula are related by the distributive property of multiplication.

Perimeter Formula for Rectangles:

$P = 2l + 2w$ or $P = 2(l + w)$

$P = 2b + 2h$ or $P = 2(b + h)$

The formula for the perimeter of a parallelogram is the same as for the rectangle, except the terms used are *base* and *side.*

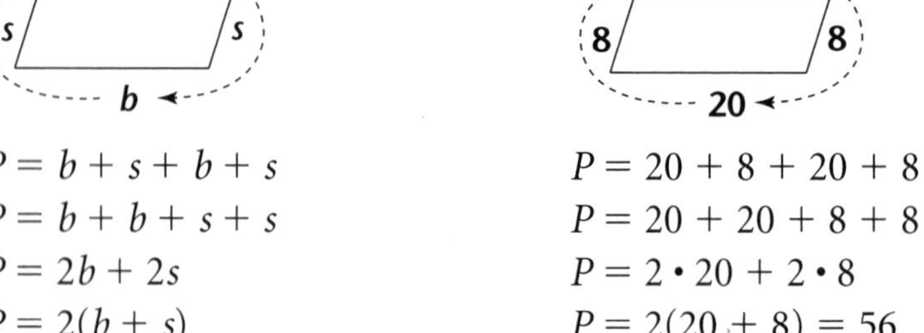

$P = b + s + b + s$
$P = b + b + s + s$
$P = 2b + 2s$
$P = 2(b + s)$

$P = 20 + 8 + 20 + 8$
$P = 20 + 20 + 8 + 8$
$P = 2 \cdot 20 + 2 \cdot 8$
$P = 2(20 + 8) = 56$

Perimeter Formula for Parallelograms:

$P = 2b + 2s$ or $P = 2(b + s)$

You can use these formulas to solve for a missing term.

EXAMPLE 1 The perimeter of a rectangle is 200. Its length is 60. What is its width?

Substitute for P and l in the formula. Then solve for w, the unknown.

$$P = 2(l + w)$$
$$200 = 2(60 + w)$$
$$100 = 60 + w$$
$$40 = w$$

EXAMPLE 2 The perimeter of a rectangle is 600. The length of the rectangle is twice the width. How long is each side of the rectangle?

Let x = width and $2x$ = length. Substitute in the formula. Then solve for x.

$$P = 2(l + w)$$
$$600 = 2(2x + x)$$
$$600 = 2(3x)$$
$$600 = 6x$$
$100 = x$ The width is 100, the length is 200.

Exercise A Use the formulas on page 313 to find the perimeter for each polygon.

1. equilateral triangle, $s = 10$

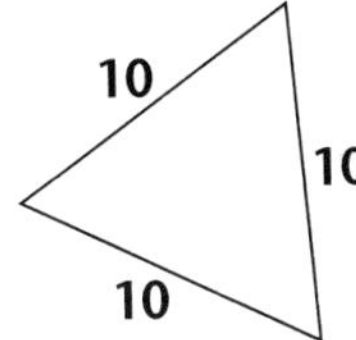

2. rhombus, $s = 17$

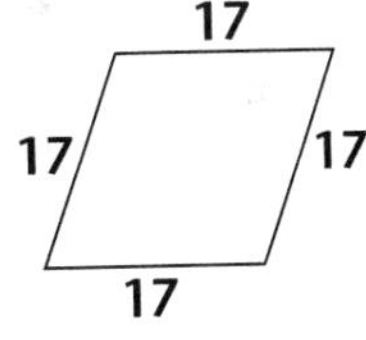

3. square, $s = 14$

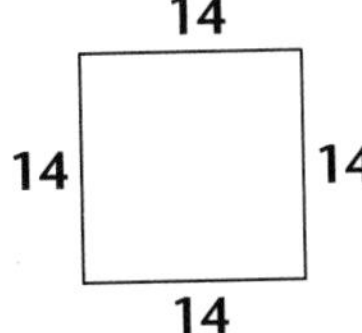

4. regular pentagon, $s = 7$

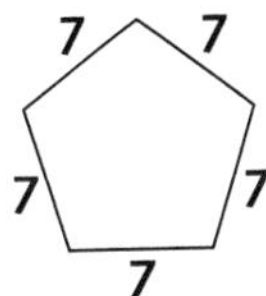

5. regular hexagon, $s = 8$

6. regular 10-sided polygon, $s = 12$

7. regular 20-sided polygon, $s = 4$

8. regular octagon, $s = 12$

Writing About Mathematics

Suppose a rectangle and a square each have a perimeter of 120 ft. Which figure has the greater area? (Hint: Choose a rectangle where $P = 120$ and compare it to the area of the square.)

Exercise B Use the formulas on page 314 to calculate the rectangle or parallelogram perimeters.

9. $l = 5, w = 2$

10. $l = 8, w = 4$

11. $l = 6, w = 3$

12. $l = 11, w = 4$

Exercise C Use what you know about perimeters to solve the following problems.

13. What is the length and width of a rectangle that has a perimeter of 160 and a length 3 times the width?

14. What are the side lengths of a rectangle whose length is 3 more than its width and whose perimeter is 84?

15. Two times the base of a parallelogram is equal to 3 times the side. The parallelogram has a perimeter of 800. What is its base? Side?

16. The side of a parallelogram is $\frac{1}{4}$ the length of its base. The parallelogram's perimeter is 125. What is the base and the side of the parallelogram?

17. The length of a rectangle is 6 times the width. The perimeter of the rectangle is 105. What is the length and width of the rectangle?

PROBLEM SOLVING

Exercise D Solve the following problems.

18. Delma is making a picture frame. She wants to glue gold braid around the edge of the frame. The frame is 9 in. × 14 in. What is the least amount of braid Delma will need? If the braid is sold by the yard and fractions of a yard, how much should Delma buy?

19. The El Sol community garden is in the shape of a regular octagon, 12 ft on a side. How much fencing is needed to enclose the garden?

20. Rhonda found 45 feet of fencing at a flea market. She wants to use the fencing to enclose her rectangular vegetable garden, which is 15 ft long. How wide can she make the garden and still be able to fence it in? Explain.

Lesson 3 Perimeters and Diagonals

Remember ≈ means "approximately equal to."

You'll find the Pythagorean Theorem is an important tool in finding the lengths of perimeters and diagonals.

EXAMPLE 1 **Given:** a right-angled trapezoid with the measurements shown

Find: the perimeter

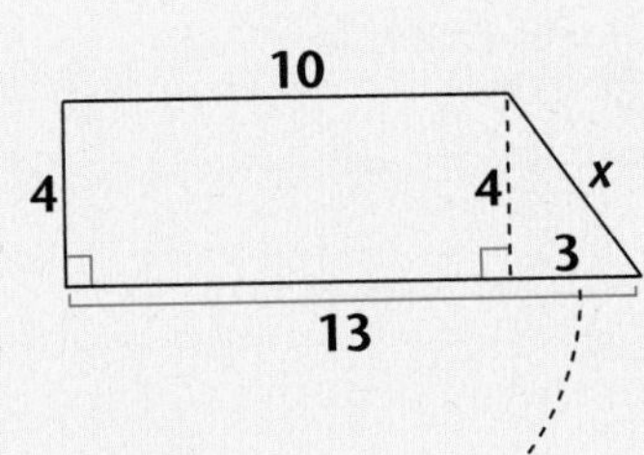

To find the perimeter, you'll need to add all the side lengths, including length x. To find x, you can use the Pythagorean Theorem.

$P = 13 + x + 10 + 4$

$P = 27 + x$

$x^2 = 4^2 + 3^2$

$x^2 = 16 + 9 = 25$

$x = \sqrt{25} = 5$

$\therefore P = 27 + 5 = 32$

EXAMPLE 2 **Given:** rectangle $ABCD$ with $AD = 15$ and $DC = 10$

Find: the perimeter of ΔADC

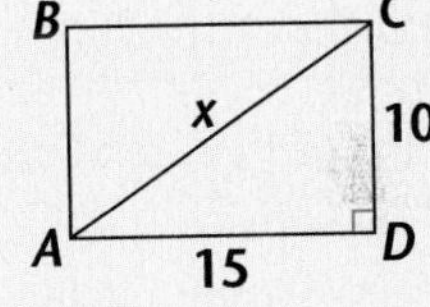

To find the perimeter of the triangle, you will need to add the side lengths together, including the diagonal x ($\overline{AC}$), which is the hypotenuse of the right ΔADC. To find x, use the Pythagorean Theorem.

$P = 15 + 10 + x$

$x^2 = 10^2 + 15^2$

$x^2 = 100 + 225 = 325$

$x = \sqrt{325} \approx 18.0$

$\therefore P \approx 15 + 10 + 18 = 43$

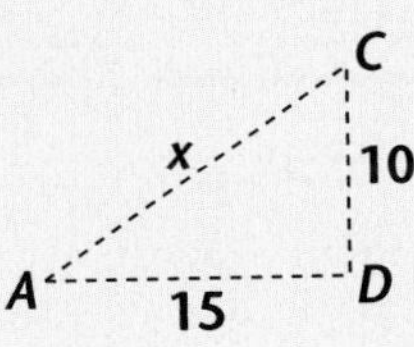

Remember that the absolute value of a number is equivalent to its distance from zero on the number line. $|n|$ is the symbol for the absolute value of n. For example, $|-3| = 3$.

EXAMPLE 3 Calculate the perimeter of the triangle with these vertices in the coordinate plane.

$A = (1, 2)$

$B = (10, 2)$

$C = (1, 8)$

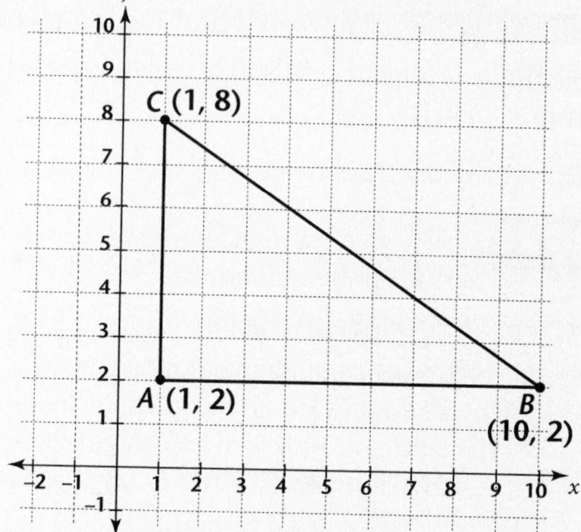

To find the perimeter, you will need to find the length of each side. You can use the Pythagorean Theorem to find the length of $\overline{BC}$. (Use a calculator and round this length to the nearest tenth.)

$$P = AC + AB + BC$$

$$AC = |\text{difference in the } y\text{-values}|$$

$$= |2 - 8| = 6 \text{ or } |8 - 2| = 6$$

$$AB = |\text{difference in the } x\text{-values}|$$

$$= |1 - 10| = 9 \text{ or } |10 - 1| = 9$$

$$(BC)^2 = 6^2 + 9^2$$

$$= 36 + 81$$

$$= 117$$

$$BC = \sqrt{117} \approx 10.8$$

$$\therefore P \approx 6 + 9 + 10.8 = 25.8$$

Algebra Review

Keep in mind that the length of $\overline{BC}$ is exactly $\sqrt{117}$ and only ≈ 10.8. When you apply mathematics, you often use approximations of lengths, such as 10.8. But there are times when it is preferable to leave a length in a form such as $\sqrt{117}$.

EXAMPLE 4 Calculate the perimeter of ΔDEF whose vertices are

$D = (-2, 3)$

$E = (1, 6)$

$F = (3, 4)$

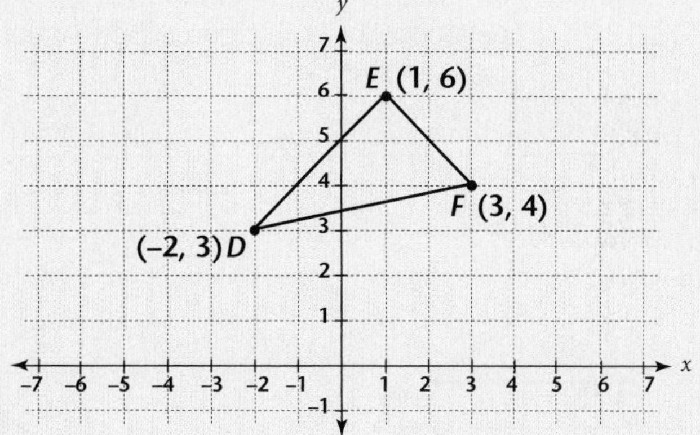

Use the distance formula you learned in Chapter 8 ($d = \sqrt{(x_2 - x_1)^2 + (y_2 - y_1)^2}$) to find the length of each of the three sides. Then add the lengths to find the perimeter. (Use a calculator and round to the nearest tenth.)

$P = DE$	+ EF	+ FD
$D = (-2, 3), E = (1, 6)$	$E = (1, 6), F = (3, 4)$	$D = (-2, 3), F = (3, 4)$
$d = \sqrt{(-2 - 1)^2 + (3 - 6)^2}$	$d = \sqrt{(1 - 3)^2 + (6 - 4)^2}$	$d = \sqrt{(-2 - 3)^2 + (3 - 4)^2}$
$d = \sqrt{9 + 9} = \sqrt{18}$	$d = \sqrt{4 + 4} = \sqrt{8}$	$d = \sqrt{25 + 1} = \sqrt{26}$
$d \approx 4.2$	$d \approx 2.8$	$d \approx 5.1$

$\therefore P \approx 4.2 + 2.8 + 5.1 = 12.1$

Exercise A Use the Pythagorean Theorem to find the missing side. Then calculate the perimeter. (Use a calculator and round to the nearest tenth.)

1.

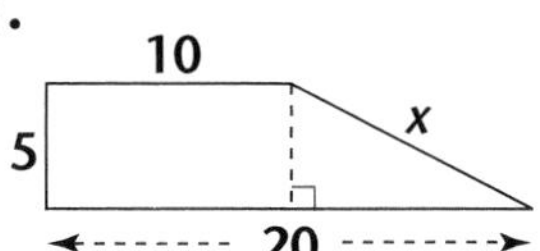

2.

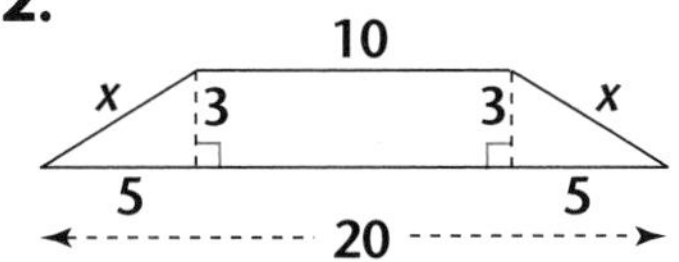

3.

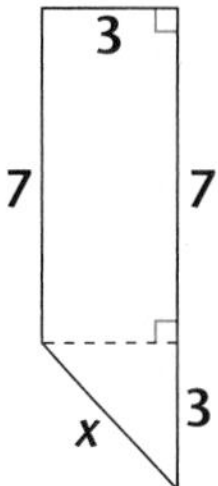

4. $P\Delta WYZ$

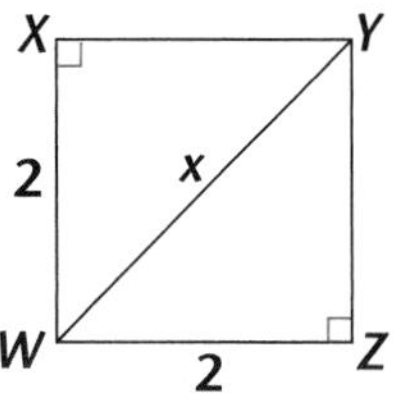

5. $P\Delta ABC$

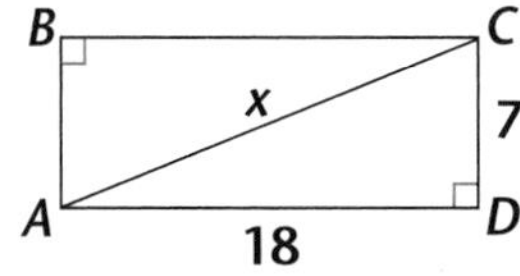

Exercise B Find the perimeters of the following figures. Use the distance formula to find side lengths, then calculate the perimeter of each figure. (Use a calculator and round to the nearest tenth.)

6.

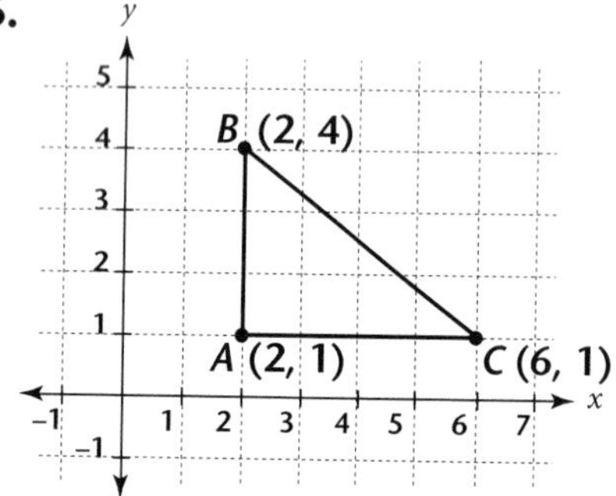

7.

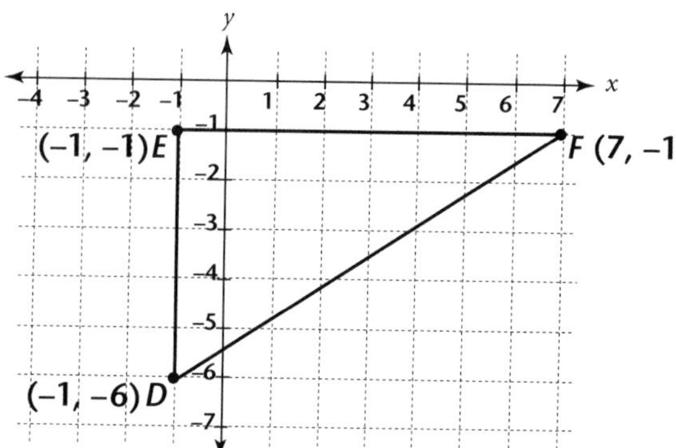

8.

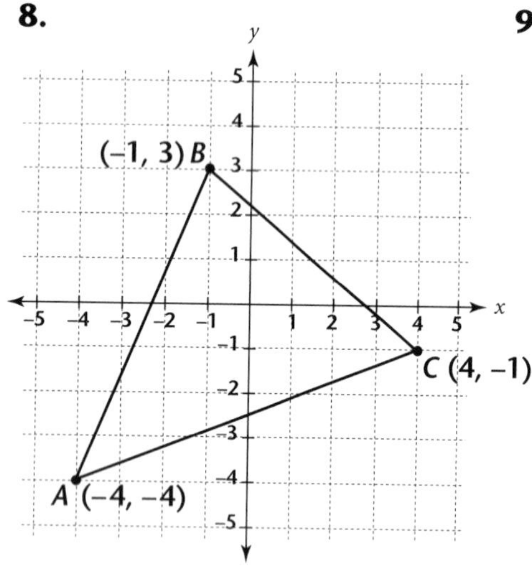

9.

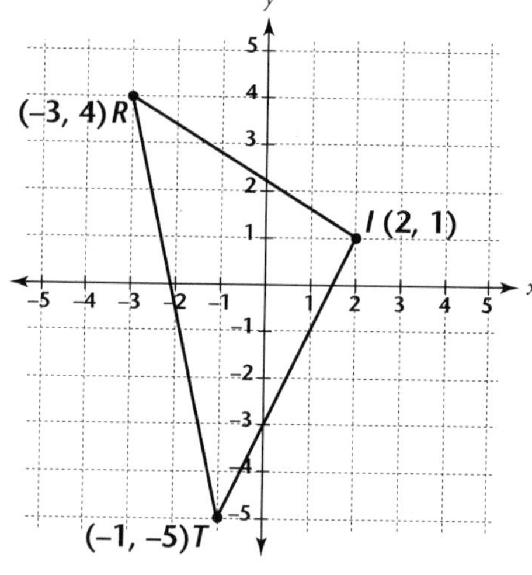

10.

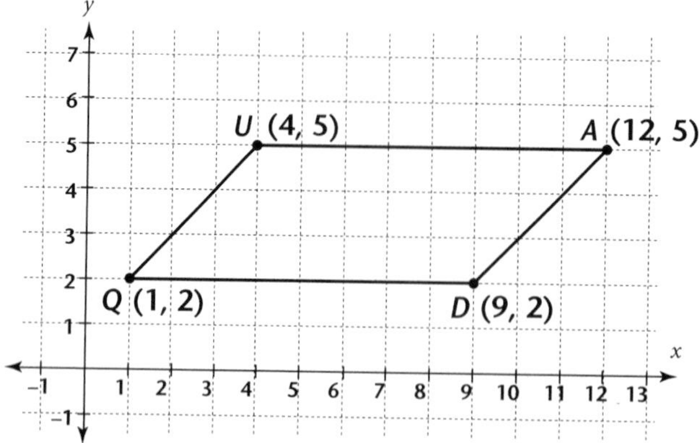

Lesson 4 Area: Squares, Rectangles, Parallelograms

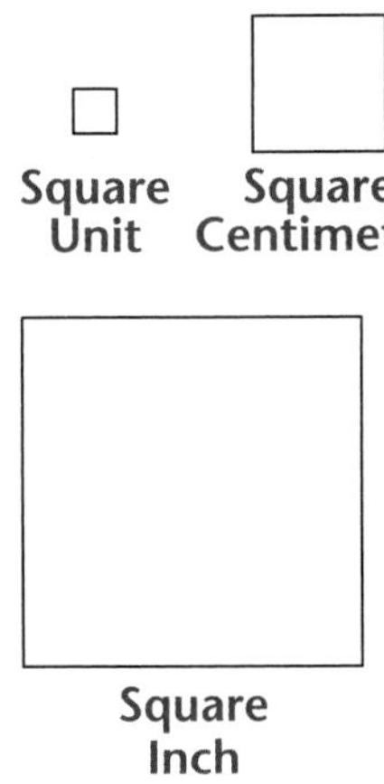

Area is a measure of the region enclosed by a polygon. The basic unit of measurement is a square. Any square can be used. To the left are some common examples.

ABCD is a square with a side length equal to 10 units. The area of *ABCD* is measured in square units. Each unit is a square with a side length of 1. These units are called square units and can be written as units^2.

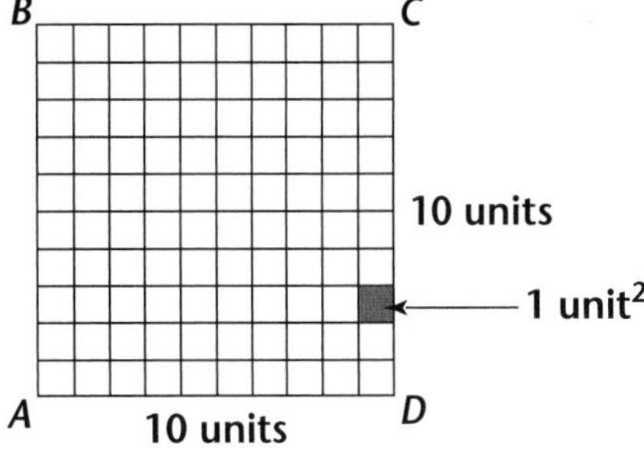

100 squares cover the entire area

You can count the number of square units in square *ABCD* to find that its area is 100 square units. You can also calculate the area by multiplying the side length by the side width.

Area = (10 units)(10 units) = 100 units^2

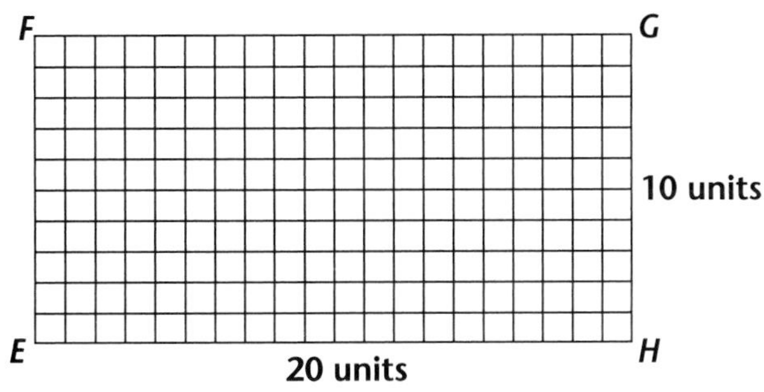

200 squares cover the entire area

EFGH is a rectangle with a width of 10 units and a length of 20 units.

You can count the number of square units in the rectangle—200 square units—or you can calculate the area by multiplying the length of the base by the length of the height.

Area = (20 units)(10 units) = 200 units^2

Area of a Square:
s^2, where s = length of a side

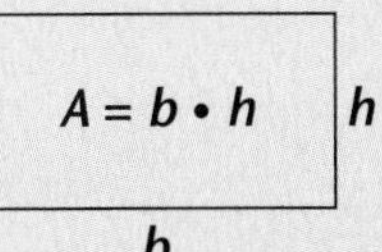

Area of a Rectangle:
$b \cdot h$, where b = base and h = height
Special case
When $b = h$, the rectangle is a square.

$A = b \cdot h$ h b

As you work with the areas of polygons, you will meet these abbreviations:

sq = square
in. = inch
in.^{2} = square inch
ft = foot
ft^2 = square foot
cm = centimeter
cm^2 = square centimeter

The area of a parallelogram is also $b \cdot h$. However, in this case, h is not the length of a side of the parallelogram but the length of the altitude of the parallelogram.

Area of a Parallelogram:
$b \cdot h$, where b = base and
h = height or altitude

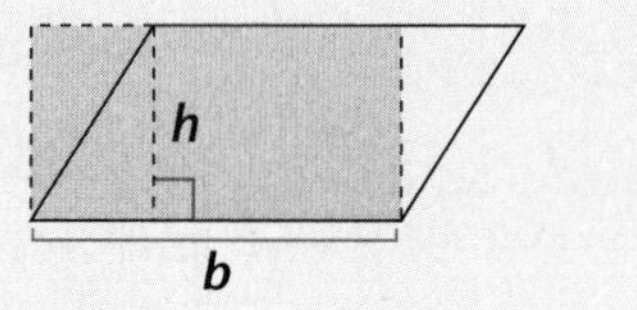

$b \cdot h$ calculates the area of the shaded rectangle. The triangles on the left and the right of the parallelogram are congruent. Therefore, the area of the shaded rectangle = the area of the parallelogram.

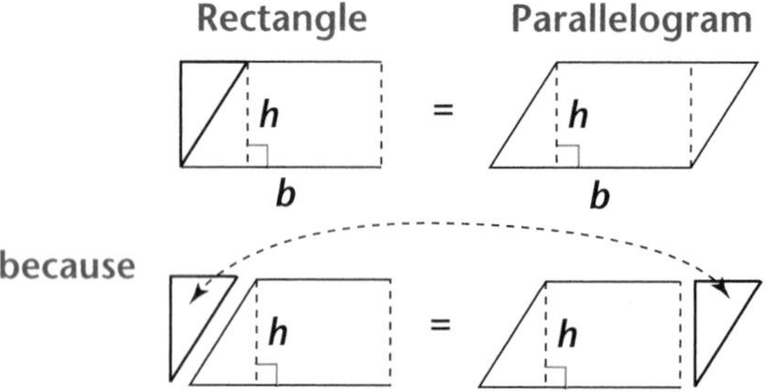

Geometry in Your Life

You can prove this to yourself by starting with a construction-paper rectangle. Mark the rectangle with a dotted line. Label it h as shown in the diagram. Next, cut the left triangle from the rectangle as shown. Place it along the right side of your figure—the result is a parallelogram.

You can use these formulas to solve several different kinds of problems.

EXAMPLE 1 The side of a square is 3 in. What is its area?

Area of square = s^2 = (3 in.)^2 = 9 sq in.

You can use the same formula, $A = s^2$, to find the side of a square if you know its area. You take the square root of each side of the equation.

$\sqrt{A} = s$

Example 2 The area of a square is 100 cm^2. What is the side length of the square?

$$\sqrt{A} = s$$
$$\sqrt{100} = s$$
$$10 = s \qquad \text{Each side is 10 cm.}$$

Example 3 1 foot = 12 inches. How many square inches in a square foot?

$$1 \text{ foot} = 12 \text{ inches}$$
$$(1 \text{ foot})(1 \text{ foot}) = (12 \text{ in.})(12 \text{ in.}) \qquad \text{square both sides}$$
$$1 \text{ sq ft} = 144 \text{ sq in.}$$

Example 4 The height of a rectangle is 5 cm; its base is 10 cm. What is its area?

$$A = b \bullet h$$
$$= (10 \text{ cm})(5 \text{ cm})$$
$$A = 50 \text{ cm}^2$$

You can solve the formula $A = b \bullet h$ for either b or h.

$A = b \bullet h$ and $A = b \bullet h$

$\frac{A}{h} = b$ $\frac{A}{b} = h$

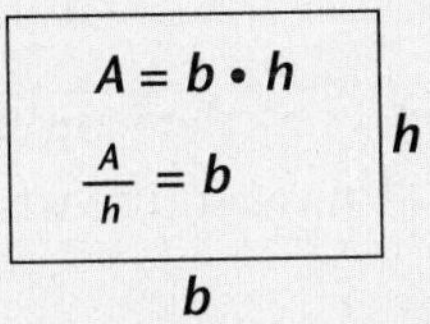

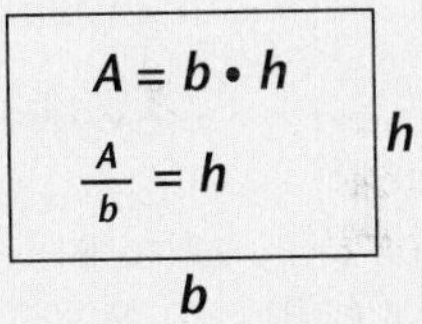

Example 5 The area of a rectangle is 120 sq units; the base is 30 units. What is the height of the rectangle?

$$A = b \bullet h$$
$$\frac{A}{b} = h$$
$$\frac{120}{30} = h$$
$$4 = h \qquad \text{The height of the rectangle is 4 units.}$$

Writing About Mathematics

Do these quadrilaterals have the same area? Explain.

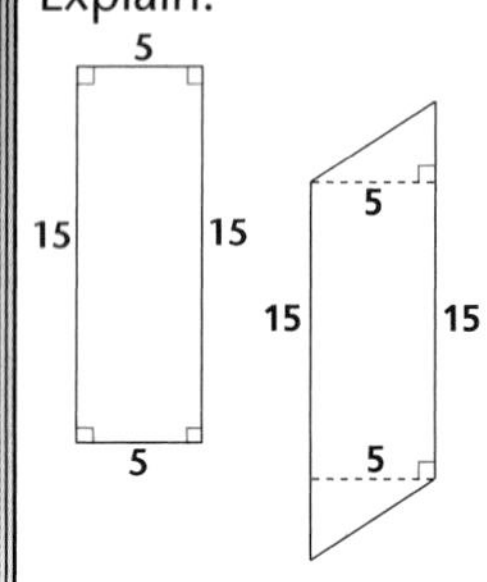

EXAMPLE 6 Find the area of this parallelogram.

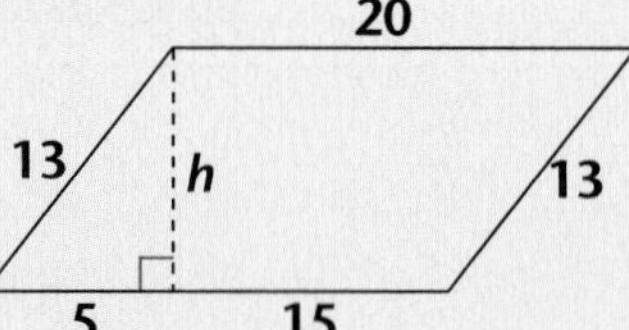

First you will need to use the Pythagorean Theorem to find the value of h.

$$A = b \bullet h$$
$$5^2 + h^2 = 13^2$$
$$25 + h^2 = 169$$
$$h^2 = 169 - 25$$
$$h^2 = 144$$
$$h = 12$$
$$A = 20 \bullet 12$$
$$A = 240 \text{ sq units}$$

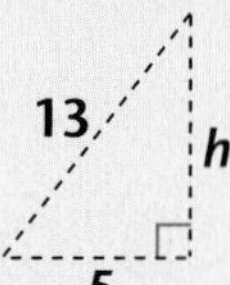

Exercise A Find the area of the square or rectangle with the given side lengths.

1. $s = 15$ cm

2. $s = 20$ ft

3. $s = 9$ in.

4. $s = 3$ km

5. $b = 8$ cm, $h = 6$ cm

6. $b = 3$ in., $h = 4$ in.

7. $b = 12$ km, $h = 5$ km

8. $b = 40$ m, $h = 15$ m

Exercise B Find the length of one side of a square with the given area. Round to the nearest tenth.

9. 81 cm^2

10. 121 m^2

11. 49 sq in.

12. 60 sq ft

Exercise C Find the missing dimension, either h or b, for rectangles with these areas.

13. $A = 110 \text{ mi}^2$, $h = 10$ mi

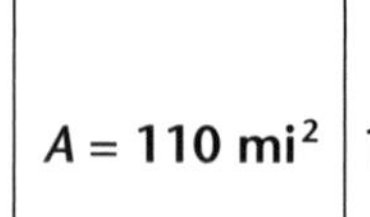

14. $A = 180 \text{ km}^2$, $b = 60$ km

A = 180 km²

60 km

15. $A = 825 \text{ m}^2$, $b = 25$ m

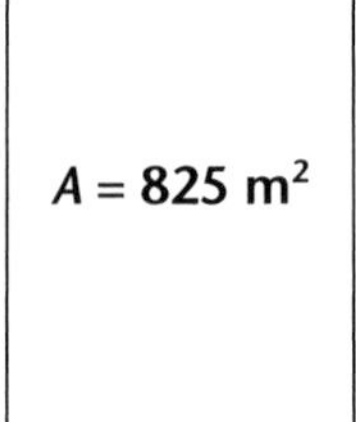

Exercise D Find the area of each parallelogram.

16.

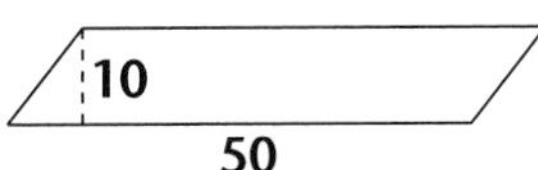

17.

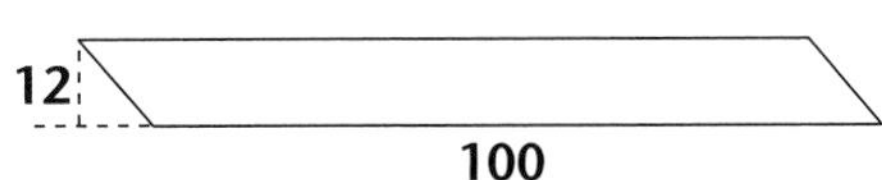

18.

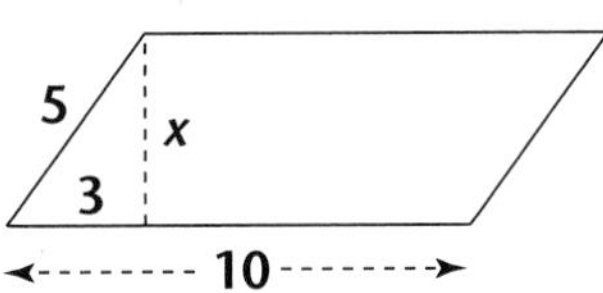

19.

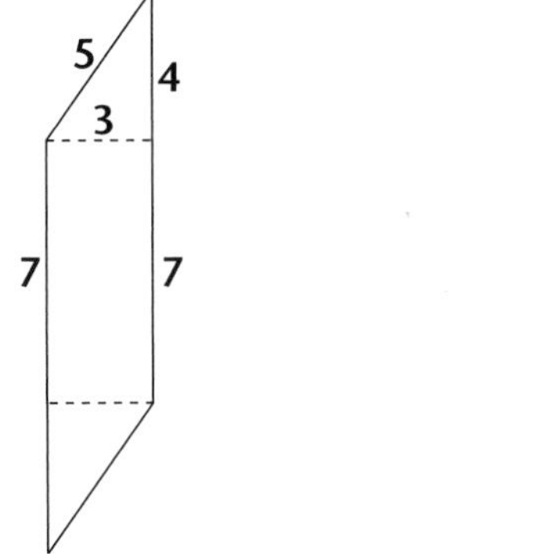

20.

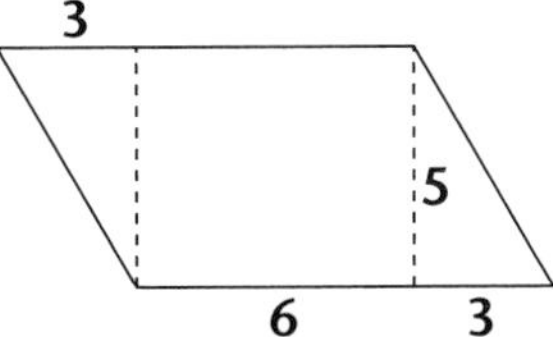

21.

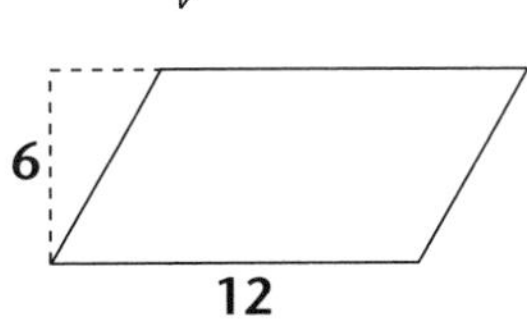

PROBLEM SOLVING

Exercise E Solve the following problems.

22. The Lugo family is tiling their kitchen floor. How many square feet of tile will they need?

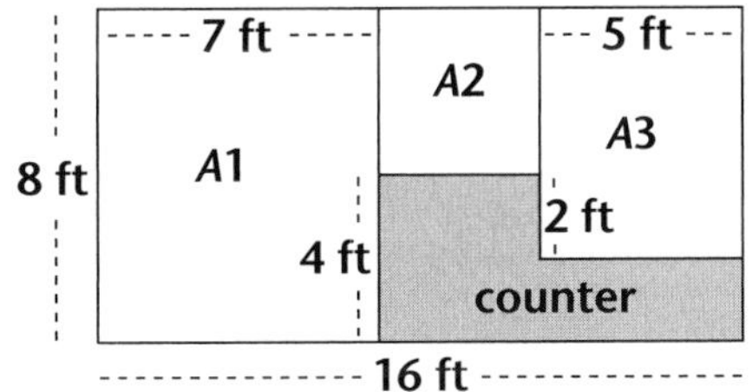

23. Dharma purchased a bag of lawn food that covers 5,000 square feet. Her yard is 75 ft × 30 ft. How many complete applications does she have? Explain.

24. Raul plans to paint his room. There are four walls, each 10 ft high and 12 ft wide. The paint can says the paint will cover 500 square feet. Will he have enough paint to finish the job?

25. How many square feet are in one square yard? (Hint: Draw a picture.)

Lesson 5 Areas of Trapezoids

Average base

The line that connects the midpoints of the nonparallel sides of a trapezoid

You can also think of the area of a trapezoid as the sum of the area of two triangles.

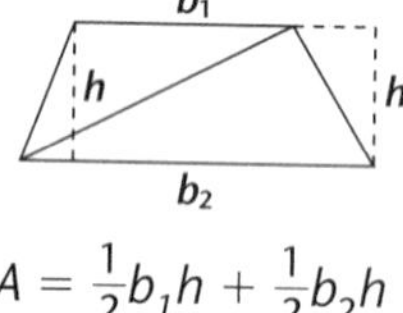

$A = \frac{1}{2}b_1h + \frac{1}{2}b_2h$

$= \frac{1}{2}(b_1 + b_2)h$

$= \frac{b_1 + b_2}{2}h$

In Chapter 8, you used the formula for the area of a trapezoid to prove the Pythagorean Theorem. In this lesson, you will see how that formula came from that theorem.

Suppose you have a right-angled trapezoid and you want to know its area. You can think through a way to find the area using diagrams like these.

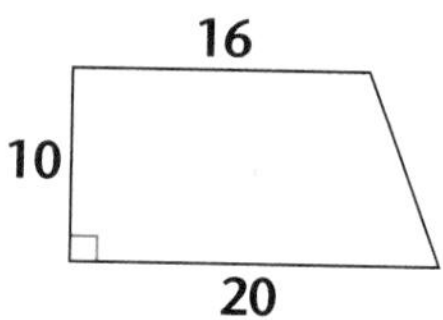

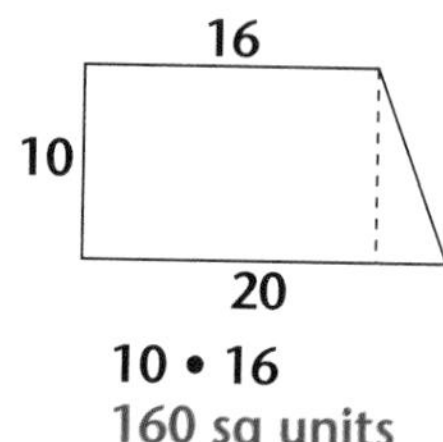

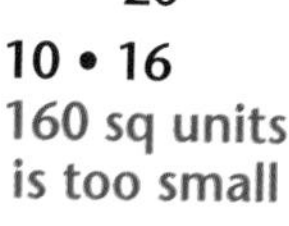

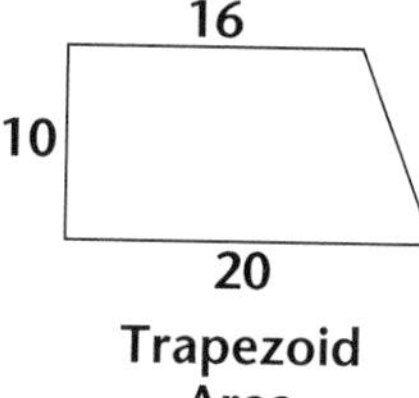

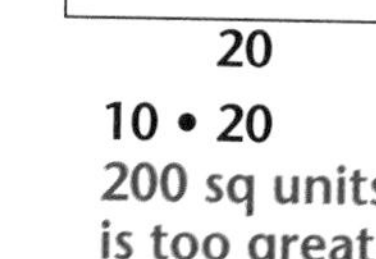

Based on the information in the diagram, you might decide to use the **average base** length.

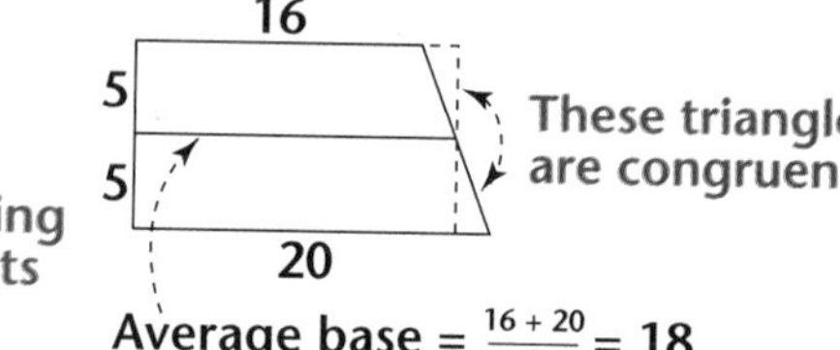

In this case you would find

$A = 10 \cdot 18$

$A = 180$ square units

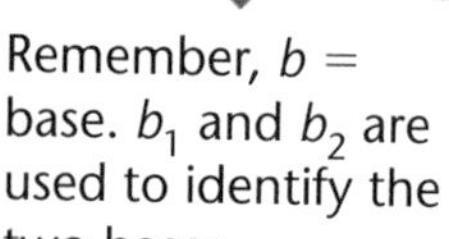

Remember, b = base. b_1 and b_2 are used to identify the two bases.

Let's see if we can apply this to finding the area of any trapezoid. Remember, the average base connects the midpoints of the nonparallel sides.

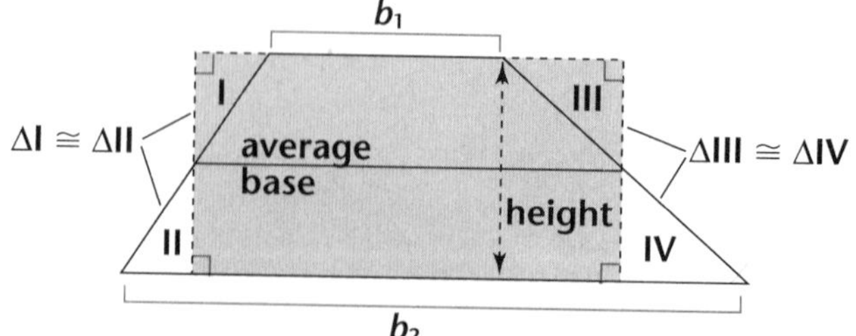

Shaded area = area of trapezoid

Area of a Trapezoid:
(average base) • (height) $= \frac{b_1 + b_2}{2}h$

You can use this formula to solve problems involving the areas of trapezoids.

EXAMPLE 1 Calculate the area of the trapezoid shown.

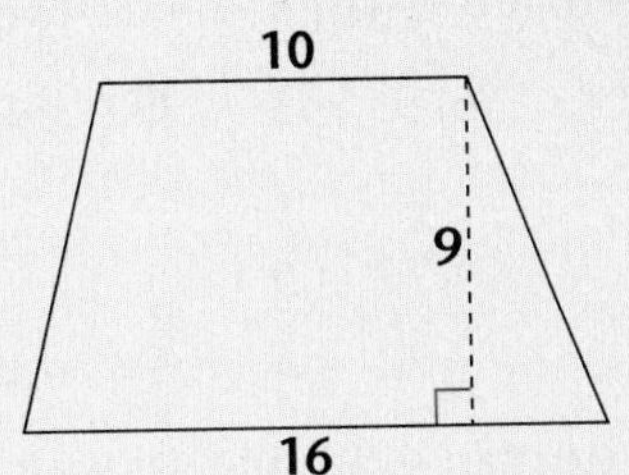

Use the formula $A = \frac{b_1 + b_2}{2}h$

Substitute the values from the diagram.

$b_1 = 10$, $b_2 = 16$, $h = 9$

$$A = \frac{10 + 16}{2}9$$

$$= 13 \bullet 9 = 117 \text{ square units}$$

EXAMPLE 2 The area of a trapezoid is 120 square units and the average base is 10. What is the height of the trapezoid?

Solve the area formula for h. $A = (\text{average base}) \bullet (\text{height})$

$$\frac{A}{\text{average base}} = h$$

$$\frac{120}{10} = h$$

$$12 = h$$

EXAMPLE 3 The area of trapezoid $ABCD$ is 300 sq units and its height is 10. The lower base is twice as long as the upper base. How long is each base?

Draw a picture to help you.

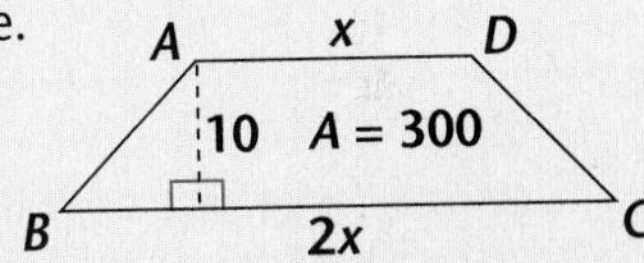

Let $b_1 = x$ and $b_2 = 2x$, then substitute in the formula.

$$A = \frac{b_1 + b_2}{2}h$$

$$300 = \left(\frac{x + 2x}{2}\right)10$$

$$300 = \left(\frac{3x}{2}\right)10 \quad \text{simplify}$$

$$600 = (3x)(10) \quad \text{multiply by 2}$$

$$60 = 3x \quad \text{divide by 10}$$

$$20 = x \quad \text{divide by 3}$$

$\therefore$ Upper base = 20, lower base = 40

EXAMPLE 4 Calculate the area of the isosceles trapezoid *ISOL*.

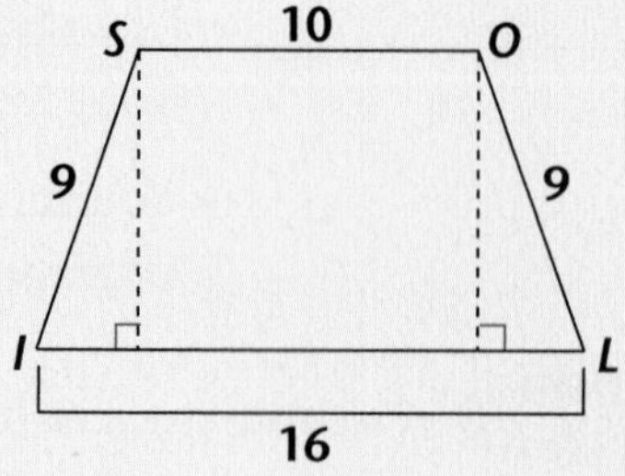

To be able to use the area formula, you must first find the height of *ISOL*.

Draw two perpendiculars from the upper base.

This shows you that the two right triangles formed must have short legs equal to $(16 - 10) \div 2 = 3$.

So, $9^2 = 3^2 + h^2$ by the Pythagorean Theorem

$81 = 9 + h^2$

$72 = h^2$

$\sqrt{72} = h \approx 8.5$ rounded to nearest tenth

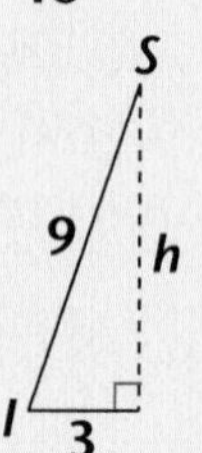

Now you can substitute values in the area formula:

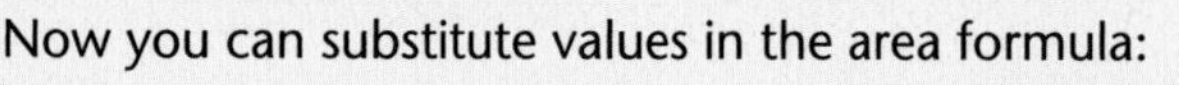

$$A = \frac{b_1 + b_2}{2} h \approx \frac{10 + 16}{2} 8.5 = (13)(8.5) = 110.5 \text{ sq units}$$

Exercise A Find the areas of these trapezoids.

1. 15, 10, 25

2. 21, 3, 25

3. 18, 12, 14

4.

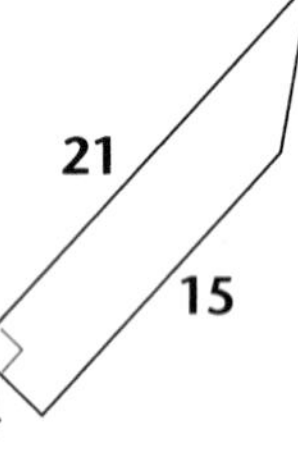

5.

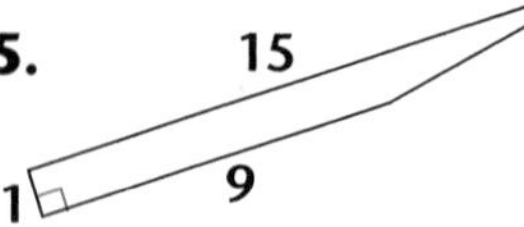

6.

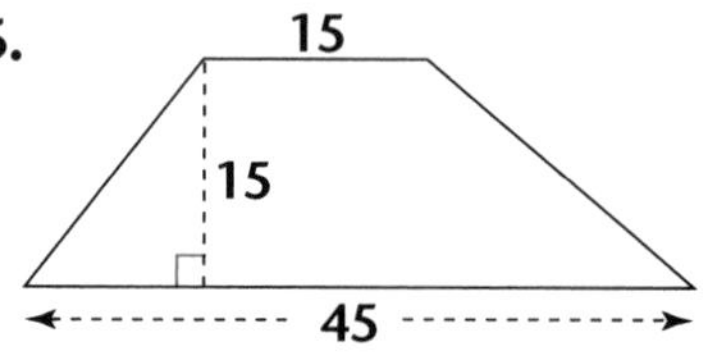

Estimation Activity

Estimate: What is the area of the trapezoid?

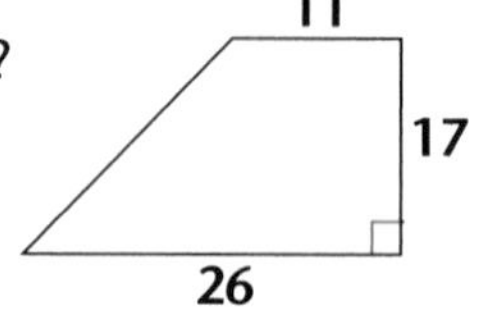

Solution: $11 \approx 10$ and $26 \approx 30$ Round the lengths of the bases.

$(10 + 30) \div 2 = 20$ Find the average length.

$20 \times 17 = 340$ Multiply the height by the average.

So, the area is about 340 sq units.

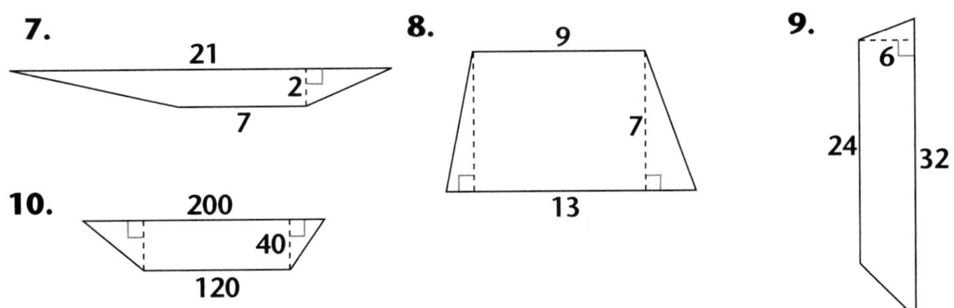

Exercise B Use what you know about the area of a trapezoid to find the values of the following unknowns.

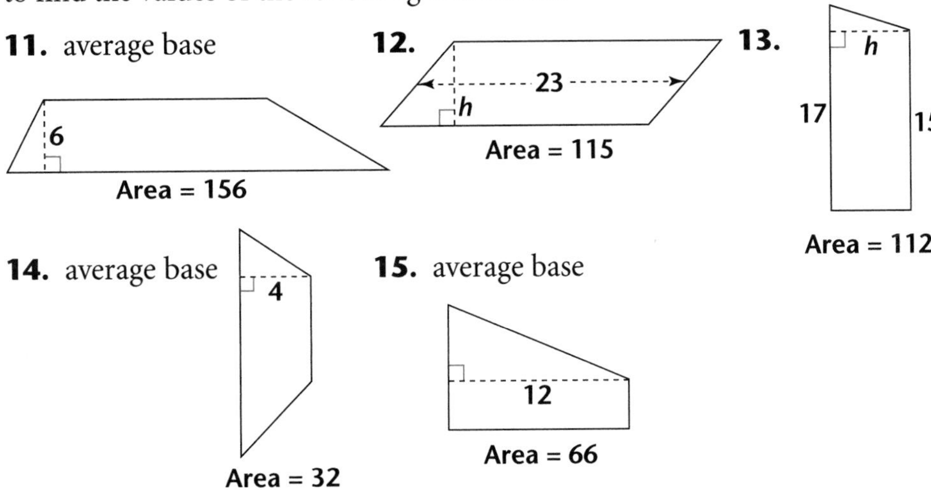

Exercise C Find the areas of these isosceles trapezoids. You may use a calculator. Round to the nearest tenth.

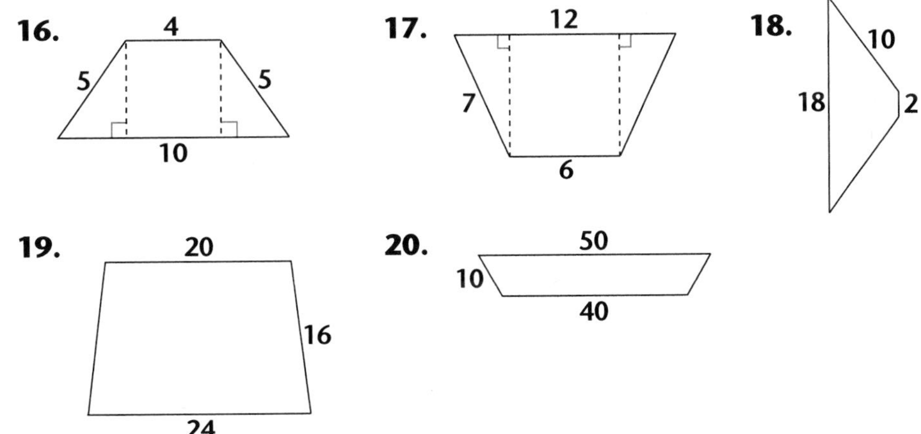

TRY THIS Can you use the trapezoid area formula to calculate the area of a rectangle? Try it and describe the results.

Lesson 6 Areas of Triangles

If you look closely at the areas of squares and rectangles, you may see a pattern for finding the areas of triangles.

Given a square

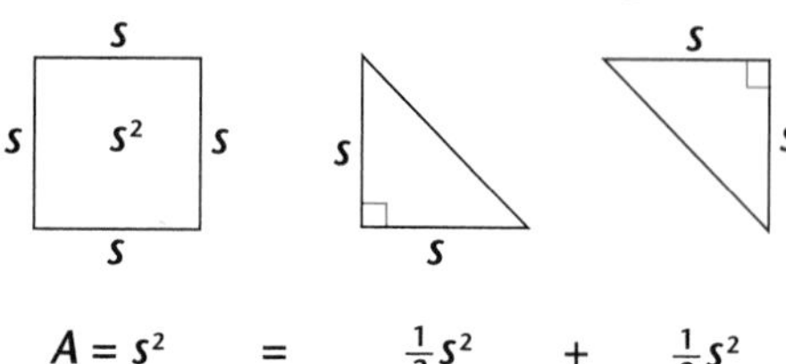

$A = s^2 \quad = \quad \frac{1}{2}s^2 \quad + \quad \frac{1}{2}s^2$

$\therefore$ Area of an isosceles right triangle with side $s = \frac{1}{2}s^2$

EXAMPLE 1 Square Area of each right triangle $= \frac{1}{2}(5)^2 = \frac{1}{2}(25)$

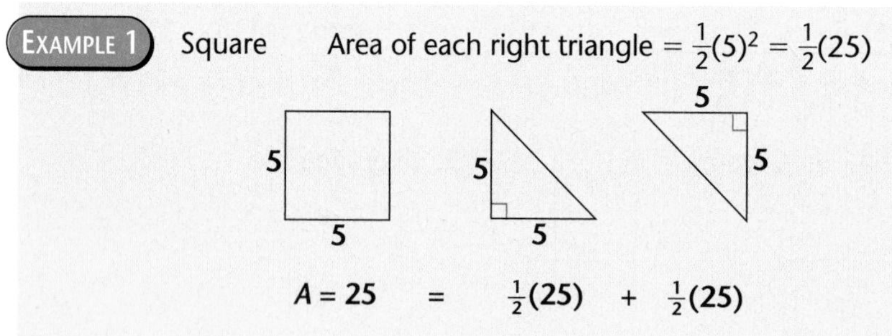

$A = 25 \quad = \quad \frac{1}{2}(25) \quad + \quad \frac{1}{2}(25)$

Given a rectangle

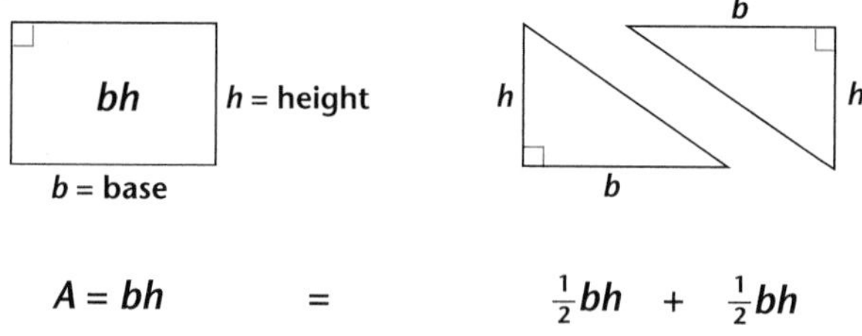

$A = bh \quad = \quad \frac{1}{2}bh \quad + \quad \frac{1}{2}bh$

$\therefore$ Area of any right triangle $= \frac{1}{2}bh$.

EXAMPLE 2 Rectangle

Area of right triangles $= \frac{1}{2}(10 \bullet 30) = 150$

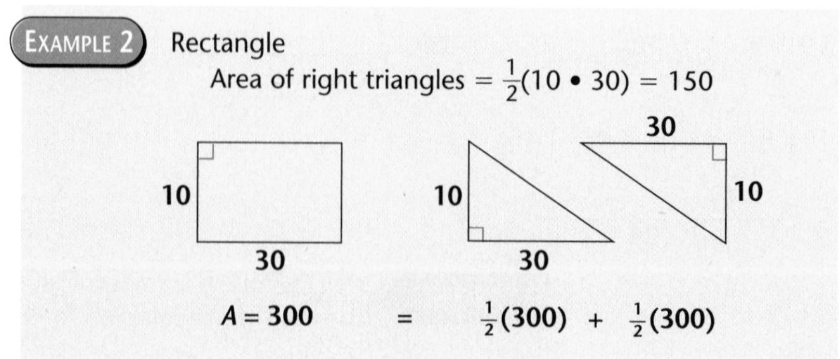

$A = 300 \quad = \quad \frac{1}{2}(300) \quad + \quad \frac{1}{2}(300)$

Now we need to find the formula for the area of any triangle. We can start with the construction of a scalene triangle *ABC*.

EXAMPLE 3 Let ΔABC be any scalene triangle with altitude $\overline{BD}$. The height of ΔABC equals *BD*.

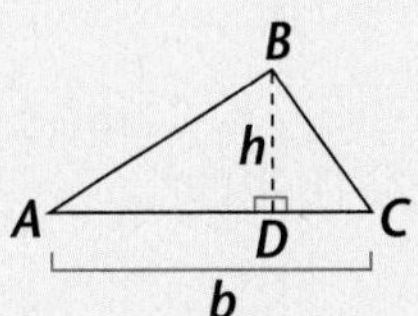

Construct a rectangle *AFEC* with $b = AC$ and $h = BD$ on $\overline{AC}$. The area of rectangle $AFEC = b \bullet h$.

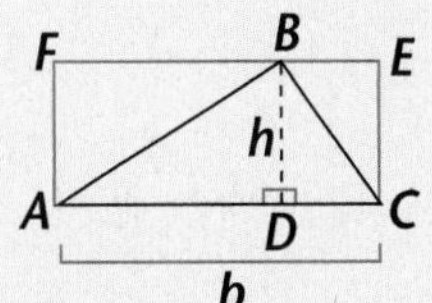

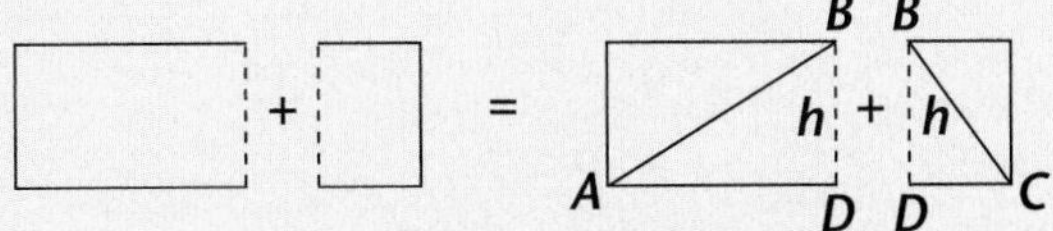

The whole is equal to the sum of its parts.

+ = A B B h + h D D C

Draw diagonals to create right triangles.

Areas of right triangles

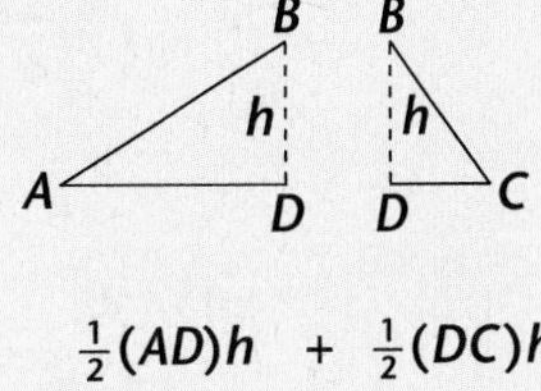

$\frac{1}{2}(AD)h \ + \ \frac{1}{2}(DC)h$

The whole equals the sum of its parts.

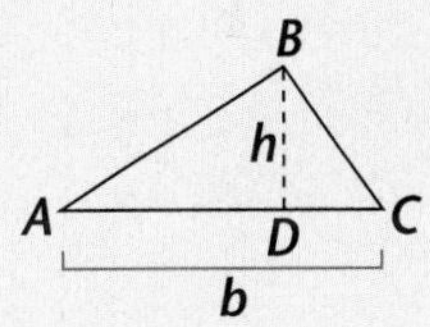

Remember that for multiplication of real numbers, $x(a + b) = xa + xb$.

Area of scalene ΔABC

$= \frac{1}{2}(AD)h + \frac{1}{2}(DC)h$	Whole equals sum of its parts
$= \frac{1}{2}h(AD + DC)$	Distributive property
$= \frac{1}{2}(hb)$	Substitution $b = AD + DC$

Area of a Triangle:
$A = \frac{1}{2}(\text{base})(\text{height})$

You can use this formula to calculate the area of any triangle—all you need to know is the base and the height. Remember, the height of a triangle equals the height of the altitude to the side used as the base.

For ΔABC, the area can be calculated in three different ways.

Using $\overline{AC}$ as the base, $A = \frac{1}{2}(AC)h_1$.

Using $\overline{BC}$ as the base, $A = \frac{1}{2}(BC)h_2$.

Using $\overline{AB}$ as the base, $A = \frac{1}{2}(AB)h_3$.

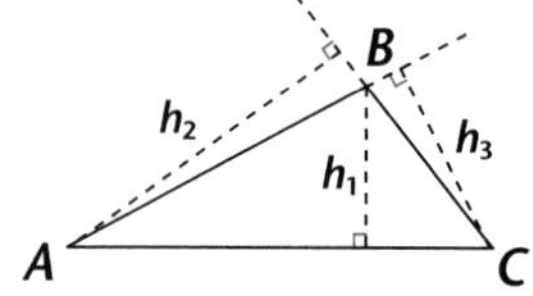

EXAMPLE 4 Calculate the area of ΔABC.

Area of triangle $= \frac{1}{2}bh$

$\frac{1}{2}(15)(8) = 60$ sq units

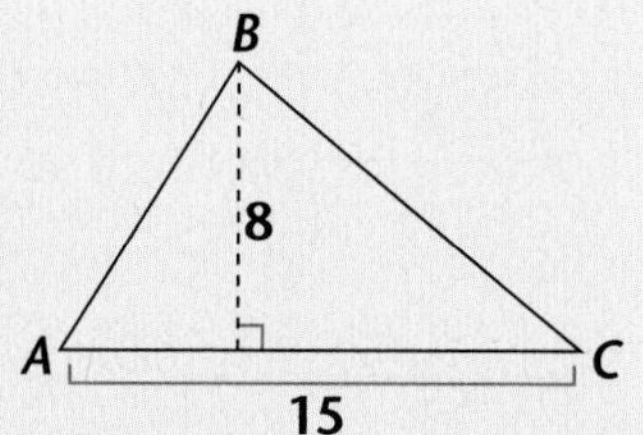

EXAMPLE 5 Calculate the area of ΔDEF.

Area of triangle $= \frac{1}{2}bh$

$\frac{1}{2}(25)(10) = 125$ sq units

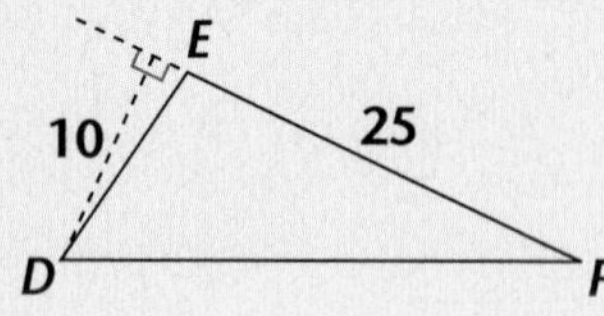

EXAMPLE 6 Calculate the area of ΔGHI.

Area of triangle $= \frac{1}{2}bh$

$\frac{1}{2}(12)(20) = 120$ sq units

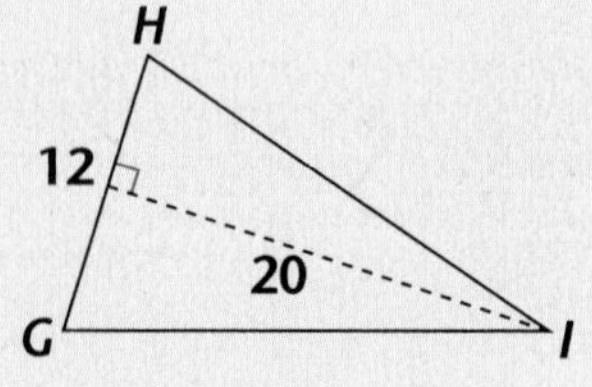

There is a way to find the area of a triangle even if the only information you have about the triangle is its sides.
This method for finding the area of a triangle was developed two thousand years ago by the Greek mathematician Heron of Alexandria.

Heron's Formula:

Area of a triangle $= \sqrt{s(s-a)(s-b)(s-c)}$

where a, b, and c are the sides of the triangle and $s = \frac{1}{2}(a + b + c)$.

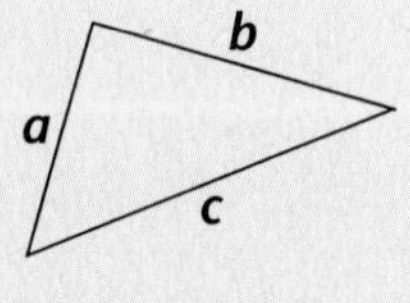

EXAMPLE 7 Use Heron's Formula to find the area of a triangle whose side lengths are 3, 4, and 5.

Area of triangle $= \sqrt{s(s-a)(s-b)(s-c)}$

Let $a = 3$, $b = 4$, $c = 5$

$s = \frac{(3 + 4 + 5)}{2} = 6$

$s - a = 6 - 3 = 3$; $s - b = 6 - 4 = 2$; $s - c = 6 - 5 = 1$

Area of triangle $= \sqrt{6(3)(2)(1)}$

$= \sqrt{36} = 6$

EXAMPLE 8 Use Heron's Formula to find the area of this triangle. (Use a calculator and round to the nearest tenth.)

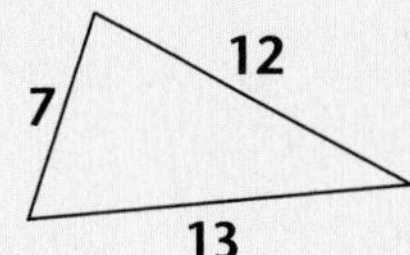

Area of triangle $= \sqrt{s(s-a)(s-b)(s-c)}$

Let $a = 7$, $b = 12$, $c = 13$

$s = \frac{(7 + 12 + 13)}{2} = \frac{32}{2} = 16$

$s - a = 16 - 7 = 9$; $s - b = 16 - 12 = 4$; $s - c = 16 - 13 = 3$

Area of triangle $= \sqrt{16(9)(4)(3)}$

$= \sqrt{1{,}728} \approx 41.6$ sq units

EXAMPLE 9 **Find:** square root of 6 • 7 • 8 and round to the nearest tenth.

On a graphing calculator, press MODE ▼ ▶ ▶ ENTER CLEAR. Now the calculator will automatically round to the nearest tenth.

2nd x^2 6 × 7 × 8 ENTER. Display reads 18.3.

Exercise A Use a calculator to find the square roots of these products. Round each answer to the nearest tenth.

1. 3 • 4 • 5

2. 12 • 13 • 7

3. 9 • 11 • 13

4. 6 • 8 • 9

5. 5 • 8 • 12

Exercise B Use the formula for the area of a triangle to find the areas of the following triangles.

6.

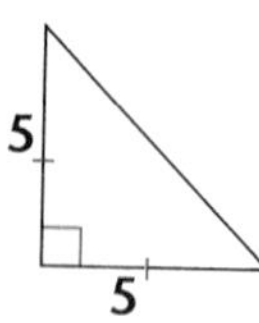

7.

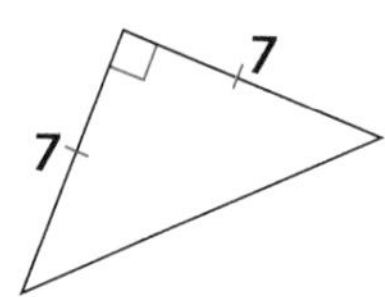

8.

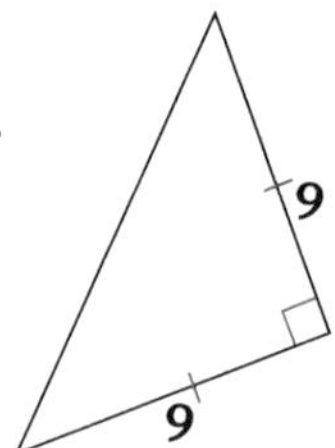

9. An isosceles right triangle with legs = 12

10. An isosceles right triangle with legs = 20

11.

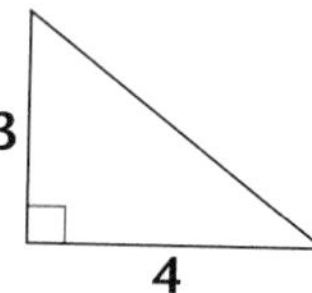

12.

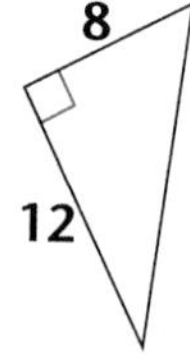

13.

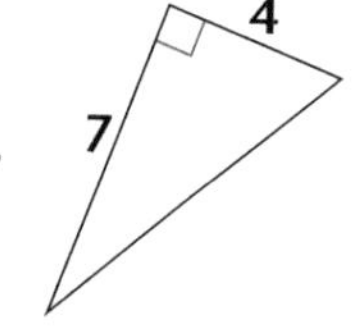

14. A right triangle with perpendicular sides of 10 and 20

15. A right triangle with perpendicular sides of 30 and 15

16.

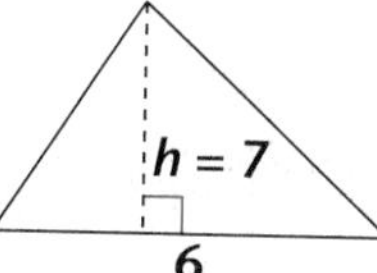

17.

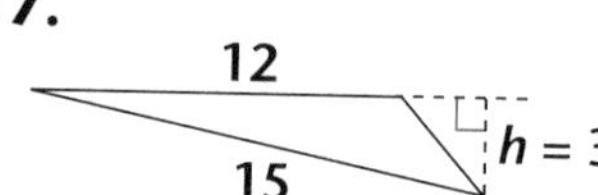

18.

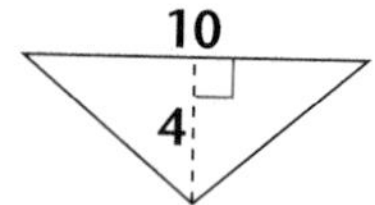

19. A scalene triangle with a base of 9 and a height of 5

20. A scalene triangle with a base of 15 and a height of 32

Technology Connection

Laser beams can be used to level everything from the land a house is built on to the cabinets in the new kitchen. Lasers can also be used to find the distance between objects. There is a degree of accuracy associated with each laser. The error is how far the laser measurement is off at a given distance, such as $\pm \frac{1}{8}$ inch at 100 feet. You can verify the accuracy of the laser by having it measure known distances. Then compare the results with the actual measurements.

Exercise C Use Heron's Formula to find the areas of the triangles with the given side lengths. Use a calculator and round to the nearest tenth.

21. 6, 7, 8

22. 10, 15, 20

23. 11, 13, 16

24. 5, 6, 7

25. 10, 14, 22

TRY THIS Use Heron's Formula to find the area of an equilateral triangle whose sides measure x units.

A bee's honeycomb is an example of hexagons in nature. Each cell is composed as a double layer of beeswax hexagons—polygons with six equal sides. Note that the hexagons fit closely together so that the honeycomb has no spaces between the cells of honey.

Lesson 7 Algebra Connection: Graphing Inequalities

Linear equation

An equation whose graph is a straight line
$y = mx + b$

Inequality

The state of being unequal; shown by the less than, greater than, and not equal to signs

If the graph of an equation is a straight line, the equation is a **linear equation.** The formula for all linear equations is: $y = mx + b$, where m = slope and b = y-intercept. This equation should be familiar from Chapter 4. But what if you are given an **inequality,** such as $y < mx + b$, $y > mx + b$, $y \leq mx + b$, or $y \geq mx + b$? How do you graph an inequality?

A line in a plane divides a plane into three parts: the points on the line, the points on one side of the line, and the points on the other side the line. Whenever you graph inequalities, begin by drawing the equality, then decide whether you need to shade the region above or below the line.

EXAMPLE 1 Graph the region represented by $y > 2x - 5$

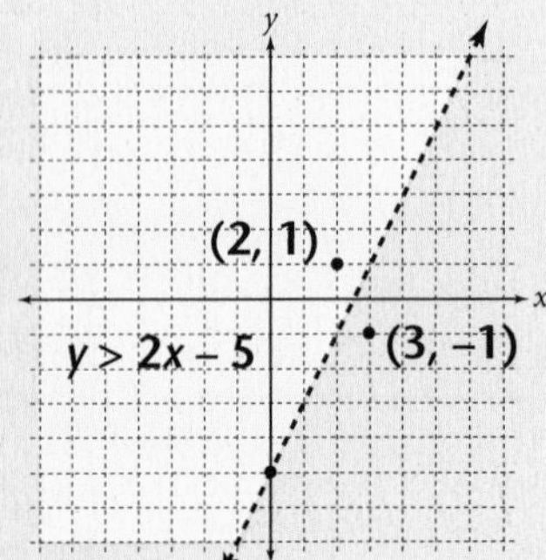

Step 1 Use $y = 2x - 5$ and substitution to find two points on the line. Plot the points and then draw a broken line between them. A broken line means that none of the points on the line are included in the graph.

Step 2 Choose two points, one above and one below the line, to see which fulfills the inequality.

$y > 2x - 5$	$y > 2x - 5$
$(x, y) = (3, -1)$	$(x, y) = (2, 1)$
$-1 > 2(3) - 5$	$1 > 2(2) - 5$
$-1 > 1$ False	$1 > -1$ True

Step 3 Shade the region above the broken line, not including the broken line. Label the graph $y > 2x - 5$.

EXAMPLE 2 Graph the region represented by $x < -3$

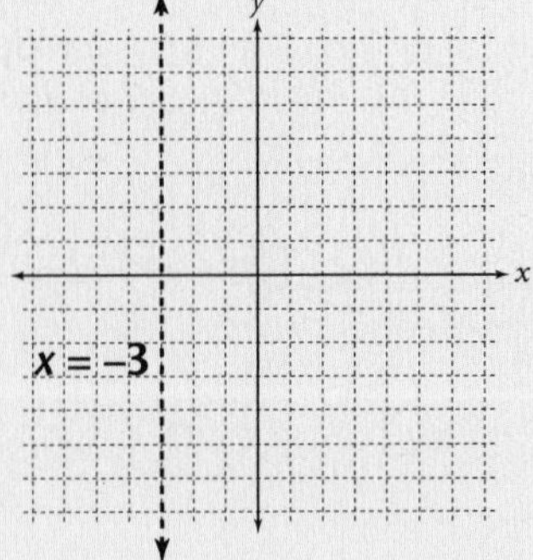

Step 1 All ordered pairs with an x-value of -3 are on the vertical line $x = -3$ that is parallel to the y-axis. Draw this as a broken line.

15.

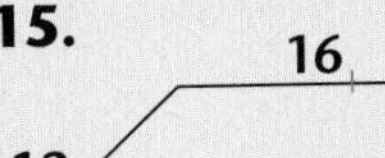

16.

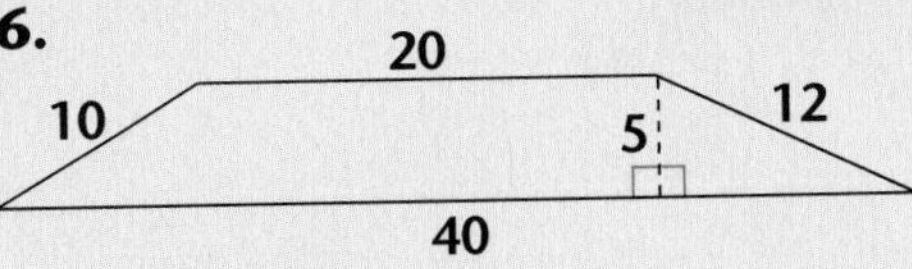

Use the Pythagorean Theorem to find the missing side, *x*. Then calculate the perimeter and the area of the shaded portion of each figure. (Use a calculator and round to the nearest tenth.)

Example:

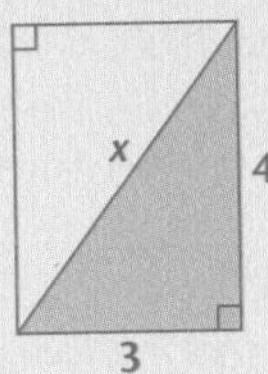

Solution: Let x = the missing side, then $P = 3 + 4 + x$.
$x^2 = 3^2 + 4^2 = 25$; $x = \sqrt{25} = 5$
substituting, $P = 3 + 4 + 5 = 12$ units
$A = \frac{1}{2}(bh) = \frac{1}{2}(3 \bullet 4) = \frac{1}{2}(12) = 6$ sq units

17.

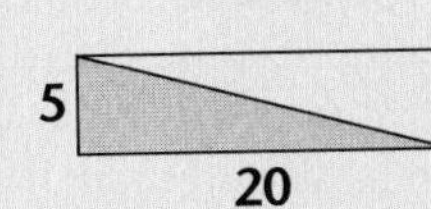

18.

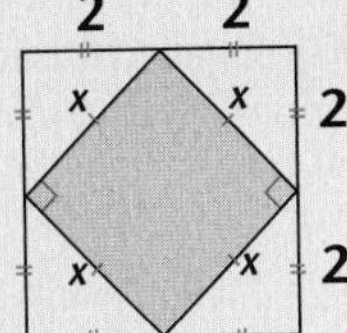

19.

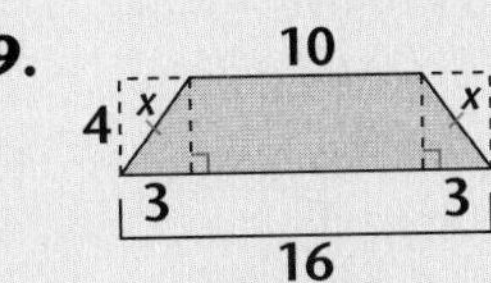

20.

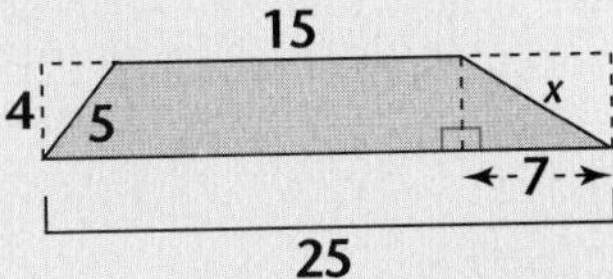

Test-Taking Tip

When several geometry concepts are put together in one problem, it can look complicated. Stop and think about what you already know. Break the problem down into smaller parts.

Chapter

Circles and Spheres

Circles and spheres are everywhere. You can find them at a Saturday afternoon baseball game, for example. The pitcher stands on the mound, a raised circle of dirt cut out of the infield grass. The pitcher throws a sphere-shaped ball to a batter. The batter hits the ball with a bat that has a circular cross-section. An outfielder catches the ball while shading his eyes from the sun. The sun looks circular in the afternoon sky, but it is actually a sphere, like the ball.

How much leather is needed to cover the baseball? How much dirt is used for the pitcher's mound? How far around is the fattest part of the bat? How big is the sun? All of these questions can be answered using geometry.

In Chapter 10, you will learn and use formulas for circles and spheres, including an introduction to trigonometry.

Goals for Learning

- To identify formulas for the radius, diameter, circumference, and area of a circle
- To find the circumference, diameter, and radius of a circle
- To solve problems involving area and probability
- To determine the area of a circle
- To construct circles
- To define trigonometric ratios and use them to find the missing side of a right triangle
- To determine the volume and surface area of a sphere

Lesson 1 Definition of a Circle

Circle

Set of points at the same distance from a given point

Radius *r*

Distance between the center of a circle and any point on the circle

Chord

Line segment joining two points on a circle

Diameter *d*

A chord that passes through the center of a circle

Circumference

The complete length around a circle

If asked to point out a circle, you would not have a problem pointing to items such as dinner plates, compact disks, or some clock faces. The outline of each item is a circle. But suppose someone asked you for a formal definition of a circle. You would need to provide a definition of a set of points that satisfies certain conditions.

A **circle** is the locus set points equidistant (at the same distance) from a given point, called the center.

distance
center
circle

Remember that Euclid's Postulate 3 states that a circle may be drawn using any point as a center and any distance as a **radius.**

O = center
r = radius

The radius, *r*, of a circle is the distance between the center, *O*, and any point on the circle.

A **chord** of a circle is any line segment joining two points on the circle.

$\overline{AB}$ = chord

The plural of *radius* is *radii.*

The **diameter**, *d*, of a circle is a chord that passes through the center of a circle. The diameter of a circle is twice as long as a radius of the same circle. A diameter divides a circle into two equal parts called *semicircles.*

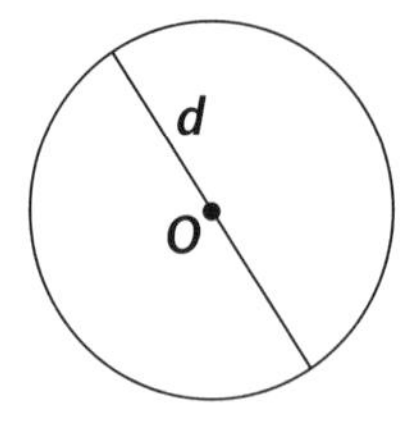

d = diameter

The **circumference** of a circle is the complete length around the circle. The circumference is $2\pi r$, where r is the radius of the circle. (The symbol π is the Greek letter *pi* and is pronounced "pie.") π is a real number whose value is approximately 3.14. You will learn more about π in the next lesson.

Quadrant
One-fourth of a circle

The circumference of a circle is divided into 360°. Each circle can be divided into fourths of 90° each.

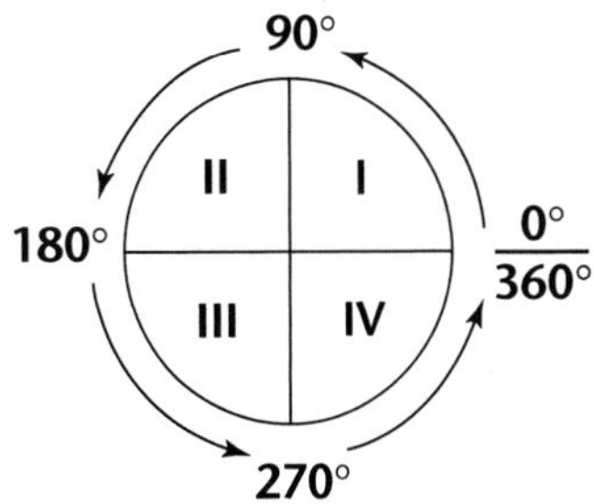

A **quadrant** of a circle is one-fourth of the circle. Quadrants of the circle are numbered from I to IV in a counterclockwise direction.

You can use these definitions to solve problems involving circles.

EXAMPLE 1 Name the parts of the circle represented by O, $\overline{AB}$, $\overline{CD}$, $\overline{OE}$.

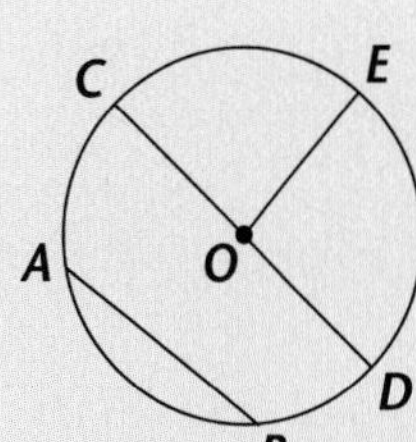

O = center
$\overline{AB}$ = chord
$\overline{CD}$ = diameter
$\overline{OE}$ = radius

EXAMPLE 2 The radius of a circle is 10 units long. How long is the diameter of the circle? How long is the circumference?

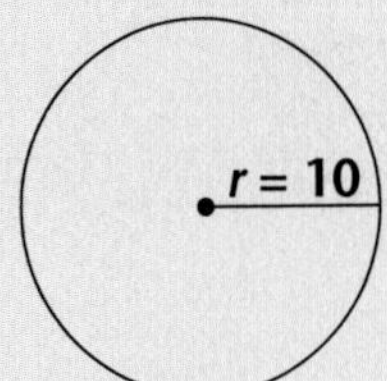

diameter = 2(radius) $\qquad d$ = diameter

or $\quad d = 2r \qquad r$ = radius

$d = 2(10) = 20$ units

The symbol $\approx$ means "approximately equal to."

circumference $= 2\pi r$ $\qquad$ (π approximately equal to 3.14)

$= 20\pi \approx 20(3.14) = 62.8$ units

EXAMPLE 3 The earth has a diameter of approximately 8,000 miles at the equator. Estimate the distance around the world.

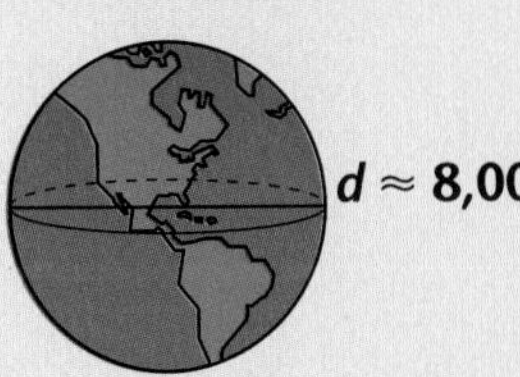

diameter = 2(radius) = $2r$

= 8,000 mi

circumference $= 2\pi r = (2r)\pi = d\pi$

$= 8{,}000\pi \approx 25{,}120$ miles

Exercise A Give the name or the symbol for each part of the circle.

1. O

2. $\overline{XY}$

3. $\overline{LM}$

4. $\overline{OZ}$

5. $\overline{OX}$

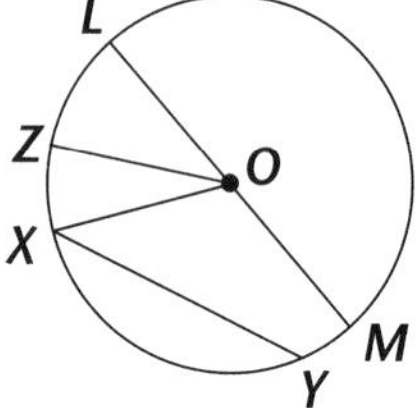

6. radius

7. diameter

8. chord

9. circumference

10. center

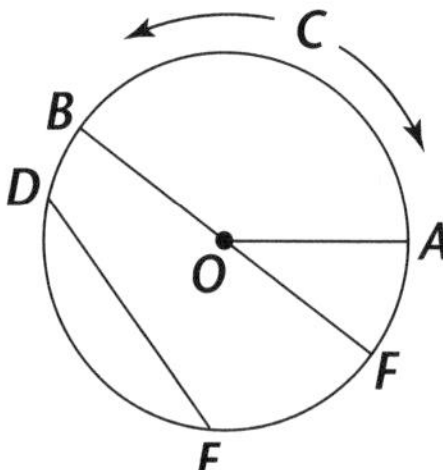

Exercise B Use the information about radius, diameter, and circumference to answer the following questions.

11. What is the diameter of the circle with center P?

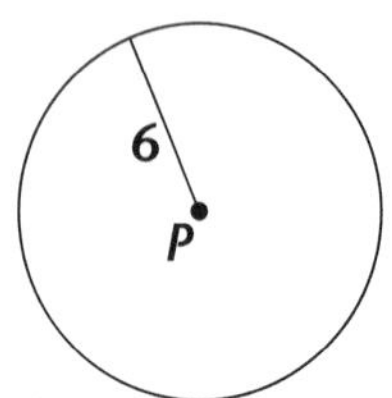

12. What is the circumference of the circle with center Q?

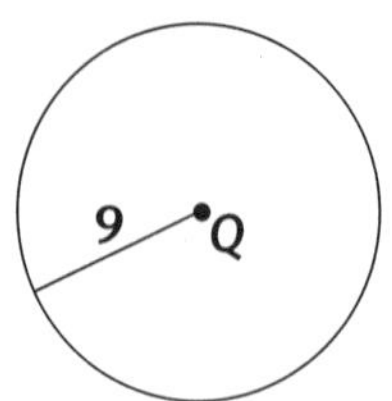

13. The circumference of a circle is 14π. What is the radius of the circle?

14. The diameter of a circle is 12. What is the radius of the circle?

15. The diameter of a circle equals 12 units. What is the exact circumference of the circle? What is the approximate circumference?

Lesson 2 The Ratio π

Pi π

Ratio of the circumference of a circle to its diameter

You have learned that triangles that have the same shape but are different sizes are similar.

Because the right triangles shown are similar, the corresponding sides are in proportion:

$$\frac{\text{altitude}}{\text{base}} = \frac{a}{b} = \frac{c}{d} = \frac{e}{f} \text{ and so on.}$$

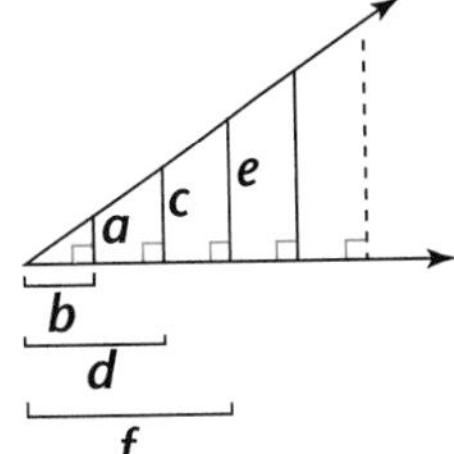

The same reasoning applies to circles. Although they may be different sizes, all circles are the same shape. This means that all circles are similar to one another. Because they are similar—

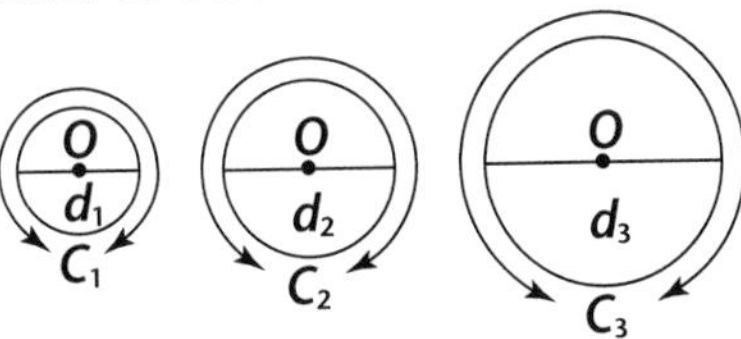

$$\frac{\text{circumference}}{\text{diameter}} = \frac{C_1}{d_1} = \frac{C_2}{d_2} = \frac{C_3}{d_3} \text{ and so on.}$$

These ratios always equal a single real number, **pi** or π.

$$\frac{\text{circumference}}{\text{diameter}} = \frac{C_1}{d_1} = \frac{C_2}{d_2} = \frac{C_3}{d_3} = \pi \text{ is true for any circle.}$$

π is a real irrational number and can be placed on the real number line.

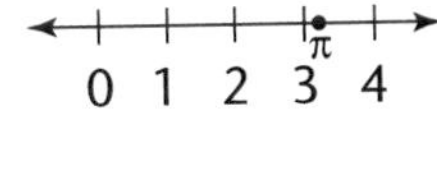

As an irrational number, π can never be written out with all of its decimals. The first ten digits of π are 3.141592654.

Because it is important in many formulas, π often has its own key on calculators. However, you can usually use algebra to work with formulas that include π without evaluating it or using a calculator.

Pi Day takes place each year on March 14th. This date in numbers, 3/14, is the first three digits of pi. Throughout the world, people come together on this day to explore the many uses of pi. Festivities include games, art projects, and contests. What could you do at your school to celebrate Pi Day?

The ratio of the circumference of any circle to its diameter is called pi. In formula form:

$$\pi = \frac{\text{circumference}}{\text{diameter}} = \frac{C}{d}$$

Because $\pi = \frac{C}{d}$

$\pi d = C$ multiply both sides by d

and $d = \frac{C}{\pi}$ divide both sides by π

Also, because $d = 2r$, where r = radius:

$$\pi d = C$$

$$2\pi r = C$$

EXAMPLE 1 Calculate the circumference of a circle whose diameter is 100 cm.

Use the formula $C = \pi d$

$C = \pi(100 \text{ cm}) = 100\pi \text{ cm}$

EXAMPLE 2 Calculate the circumference of a circle whose radius is 25 in.

$C = \pi d = 2\pi r$ substitute $d = 2r$

$C = 2\pi(25 \text{ in.})$ substitute $r = 25$

$= 50\pi$ in.

EXAMPLE 3 Find the radius of a circle whose circumference is 50π in.

$C = \pi d$

$C = 2\pi r$ substitute $d = 2r$

$r = \frac{C}{2\pi}$ divide both sides by 2π

$r = \frac{50\pi}{2\pi}$ substitute $C = 50\pi$

$= 25$ in.

EXAMPLE 4 A circle has a circumference of 42π. Its diameter is 42. What is the ratio of the diameter to the circumference?

$\frac{42\pi}{42} = \pi$

EXAMPLE 5 The circumference of circle 1 is four times the circumference of circle 2. The diameter of circle 1 is 28. What is the diameter of circle 2?

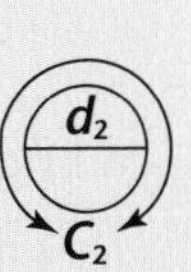

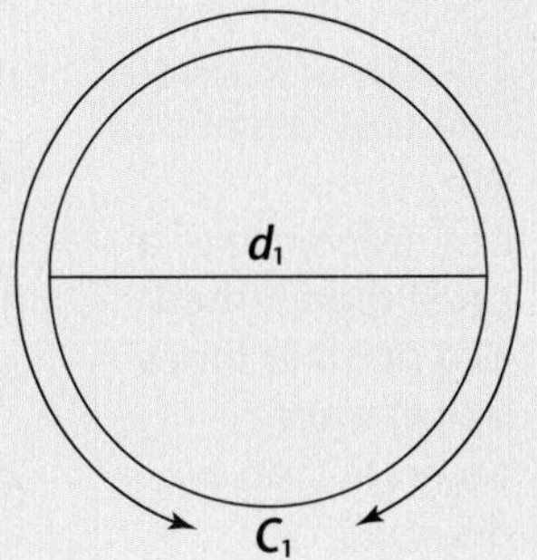

All circles are similar, so:

$\frac{\text{circumference circle 1}}{\text{diameter circle 1}} = \frac{\text{circumference circle 2}}{\text{diameter circle 2}}$ or $\frac{C_1}{d_1} = \frac{C_2}{d_2}$

$\frac{C_1}{d_1} = \frac{C_2}{x}$	let x = diameter of circle 2
$\frac{4C_2}{28} = \frac{C_2}{x}$	substitute $d_1 = 28$, $C_1 = 4C_2$
$(28)(C_2) = (4C_2)x$	product of means = product of extremes
$\frac{(28)(C_2)}{(4C_2)} = x$	divide by $4C_2$
$\frac{28}{4} = x$	simplify
$7 = x$	The diameter of circle 2 = 7 units.

Geometry in Your Life

Painting a circle on a basketball court, finding the distance traveled with one turn of a bicycle wheel, or measuring material for a circular bracelet all involve pi. Since pi is an irrational number, it cannot be expressed as a terminating or repeating decimal. Like other irrational numbers, such as $\sqrt{2}$ and $\sqrt{3}$, you can find an *approximate* value for pi.

Follow these steps to find an approximate value of π.

1. Collect a number of circular objects, such as a water glass, bucket, soda can, and dinner plate.
2. Use a string or flexible tape measure to measure each object's circumference.
3. Use a ruler to measure each circle's diameter (longest distance across). Be sure that measurements for a single object are in the same units.
4. Divide *C* by *d*.
5. Record your measurements in a table like the one below.

Object	Circumference, *C*	diameter, *d*	$\frac{C}{d}$

You should find the values of $\frac{C}{d}$ are slightly greater than 3.

Writing About Mathematics

Why is the circumference of a circle represented as a number times π ($n\pi$) more accurate than a decimal?

Exercise A Find the circumference of a circle with the given radius or diameter. Express your answer in terms of π.

1. $d = 12$ units

2. $r = 3$ units

3. $r = 15.5$ m

4. $d = 8$ cm

5. $r = 10$ in.

6. $d = 9$ ft

7. $r = 9$ ft

8. $r = 33$ m

Exercise B Find the diameter and radius of a circle with the given circumference.

9. $C = 44\pi$ ft

10. $C = 96\pi$ m

11. $C = 12\pi$ in.

12. $C = 24\pi$ cm

13. $C = 15\pi$ ft

14. $C = 43\pi$ mm

15. $C = 22\pi$ cm

16. $C = \pi$ in.

PROBLEM SOLVING

Exercise C Use what you know about similar circles, radius, diameter, and circumference to solve the following problems.

17. Kris used 23π feet of fencing to enclose his circular garden. How wide is the garden at its widest?

18. Katja's trampoline has a diameter of 10 ft. Its circumference is twice as great as the circumference of Nelida's trampoline. What is the diameter of Nelida's trampoline?

19. One sprinkler makes a circle with a diameter of 12 m. Another makes a circle with a diameter of 24 m. What is the ratio of the circumferences of the first circle to the second?

20. The circumference of a circle is 13π. What is the ratio of its circumference to its diameter? Explain.

Lesson 3 Approximating the Area of a Circle

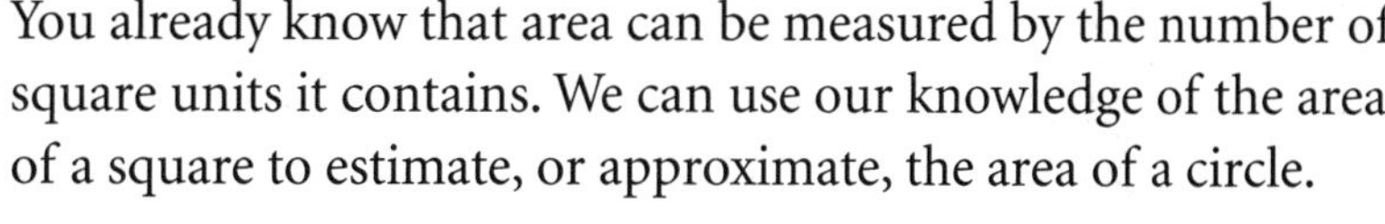

You already know that area can be measured by the number of square units it contains. We can use our knowledge of the area of a square to estimate, or approximate, the area of a circle.

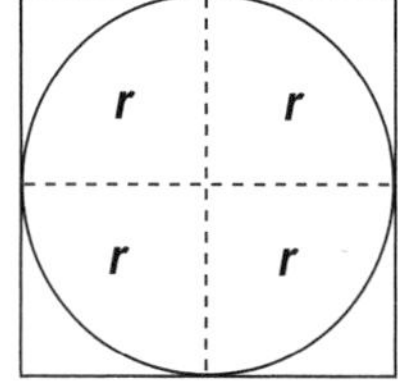

Draw any circle, radius r. Draw a square, side length $2r$, around the circle. Be sure the square's sides touch the circle. You can see that

the area of the circle $<$ the area of the square, or

the area of the circle $< 4r^2$.

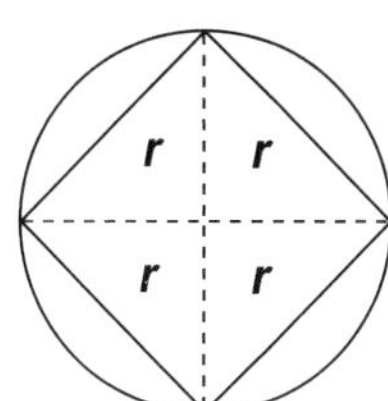

Now, draw a square inside the circle.

area of the small square $<$ area of the circle, or

$\frac{1}{2}r^2 + \frac{1}{2}r^2 + \frac{1}{2}r^2 + \frac{1}{2}r^2 <$ area of the circle, or

$2r^2 <$ area of the circle

The large square at the top of this page has area of $4r^2$ because $2r \bullet 2r = 2 \bullet 2 \bullet r \bullet r = 4r^2$. And each of the small right triangles in the second figure has area of $\frac{1}{2}r^2$ because each has base of r and height of r.

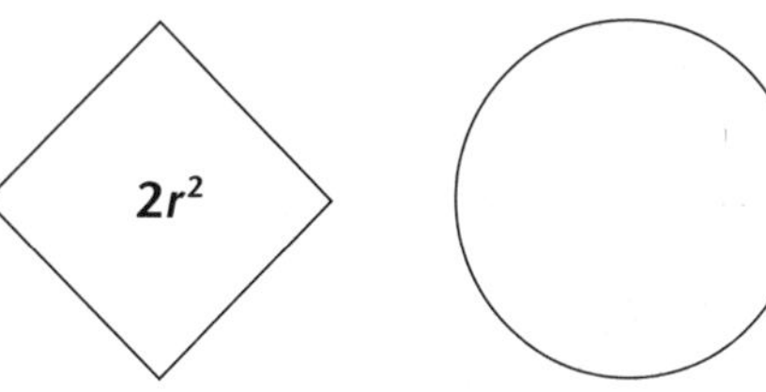

$4r^2$

If we take the average of $2r^2$ and $4r^2$, we get $\frac{(2r^2 + 4r^2)}{2} = 3r^2$

$2r^2 < 3r^2 < 4r^2$

Area Estimation Formula:
Area of a circle $\approx 3r^2$, where r = radius and $\approx$ means "approximately equal to."

The examples on the following page use the Area Estimation Formula.

Example 1 Estimate the area of a circle with a radius of 5 cm.

Use the Area Estimation Formula.
area $\approx 3r^2$
$3(5)^2 = 3(25) = 75 \text{ cm}^2$

Here is a way to check the estimate:
Area of large square $= 4r^2 = 4(5)^2 = 4(25) = 100 \text{ cm}^2$
Area of small square $= 2r^2 = 2(5)^2 = 2(25) = 50 \text{ cm}^2$
Average of areas $= \frac{(100 + 50)}{2} = \frac{150}{2} = 75 \text{ cm}^2$

Estimate the area of a circle whose radius is 7 units.
Use the Area Estimation Formula.
area $\approx 3r^2$
$3(7)^2 = 3(49) = 147$ sq units

Example 3

The diameter of a circle is 20 in. Estimate the area of the circle.
First, find the radius: $d = 2r = 20$ in., $r = 10$ in.
Use the Area Estimation Formula.
area $\approx 3r^2$
$3(10)^2 = 3(100) = 300$ sq in.

If you are given the area of a circle, you can use the Area Estimation Formula to estimate the length of the circle's radius.

The area of a circle is 75 sq units. Estimate its radius.
Use the Area Estimation Formula.
area $\approx 3r^2$

$$75 = 3r^2$$
$$25 = r^2$$
$$\sqrt{25} = r$$
$$5 = r$$

Exercise A For each item, find the area of each square and estimate the area of the circle.

1.

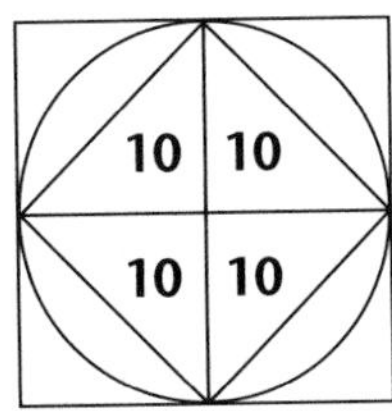

2.

9 9
9 9

3.

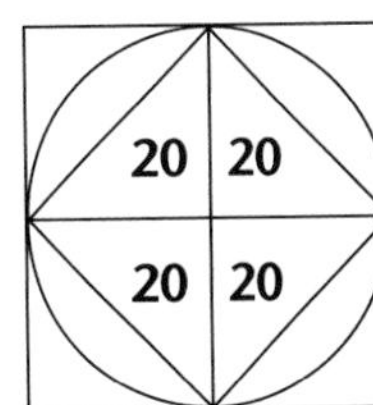

4.

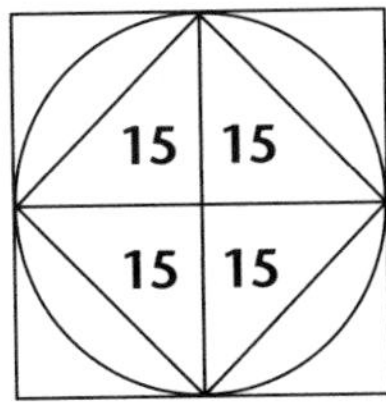

5.

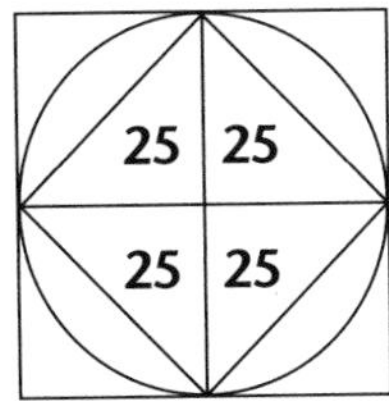

Writing About Mathematics

In your own words, explain why the area of the smaller square is half the area of the larger square.

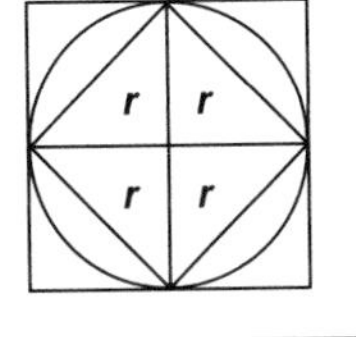

Exercise B Use the Area Estimation Formula to estimate the area of a circle with each diameter or radius.

6. $r = 4$

7. $r = 6$

8. $r = 9$

9. $r = 17$

10. $d = 14$

11. $d = 24$

12. $d = 36$

13. $d = 18$

14. $d = 30$

15. $d = 42$

Exercise C Estimate the radius of a circle with each given area. Use the Area Estimation Formula.

16. $A = 48$

17. $A = 108$

18. $A = 192$

19. $A = 300$

20. $A = 147$

Lesson 4 Area and Probability

Probability

The chance or likelihood of an event occurring

Suppose you pick any point, at random, inside the circle on the right. What is the **probability** of picking a point in the top semicircle?

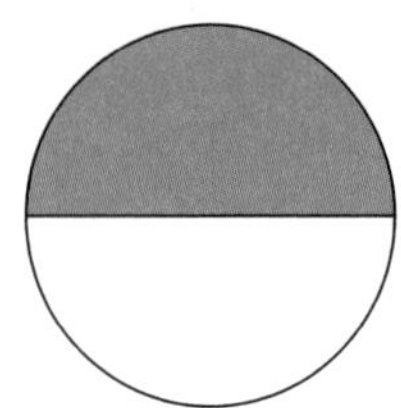

Since $\frac{\text{area of semicircle}}{\text{area of circle}} = \frac{1}{2}$,

you can conclude that the probability is $\frac{1}{2}$ or 50% by comparing the area of the desired outcome (top semicircle) to the whole circle.

$$\text{Probability} = \frac{\text{area of desired outcome}}{\text{total area}}$$

Algebra Review

The probability of an event is always a number between 0% and 100%. If an event can never occur, its probability is 0%. If an event must occur, its probability is 100%. If the probability of an event occurring is *p*, the probability of that event *not* occurring is 100% − *p*.

EXAMPLE 1 Points are chosen at random from the circle. The four quadrants are equal.

What is the probability of picking a point in Quadrant I (QI)?

II I III IV

$P(QI) = ■$

$\frac{\text{area of QI}}{\text{area of circle}} = \frac{1}{4}$ $\frac{1}{4}$ of 100% = 25%

Suppose the given area is a square.

EXAMPLE 2 The square is divided into three equal regions.

What is the probability of picking a point in the shaded region?

$P(\text{Shaded Region}) = ■$

$\frac{\text{shaded region}}{\text{area of square}} = \frac{1}{3}$ $\frac{1}{3}$ of 100% = $33\frac{1}{3}\%$

What is the probability of picking a point in the unshaded region?

$P(\text{Unshaded Region}) = ■$

$\frac{\text{unshaded region}}{\text{area of square}} = \frac{2}{3}$ $\frac{2}{3}$ of 100% = $66\frac{2}{3}\%$

or $P(\text{Unshaded Region}) = 100\% - 33\frac{1}{3}\% = 66\frac{2}{3}\%$

Exercise A Find the probability for picking a point in the shaded regions. Write your answer as a percentage.

1. P(QI or QII) = ■

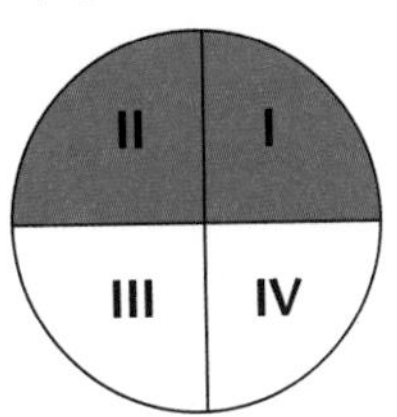

2. P(Shaded Region) = ■

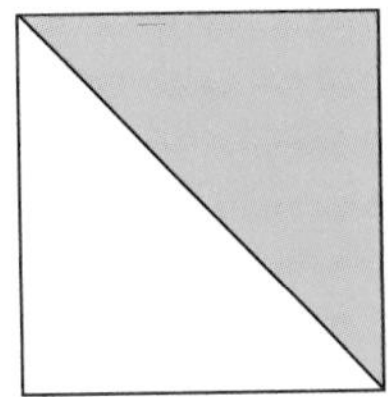

3. P(QI or QII or QIII) = ■

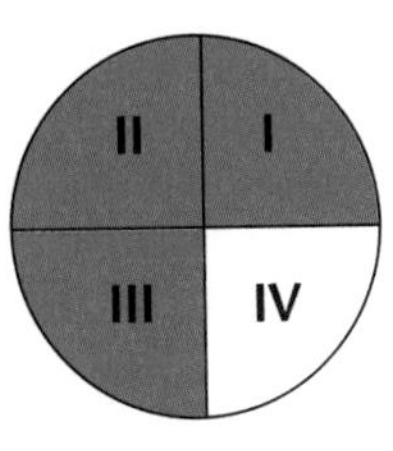

4. P(Shaded Region) = ■

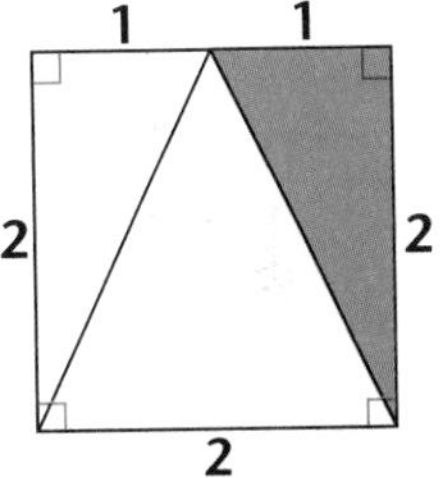

5. P(Isosceles Triangle) = ■

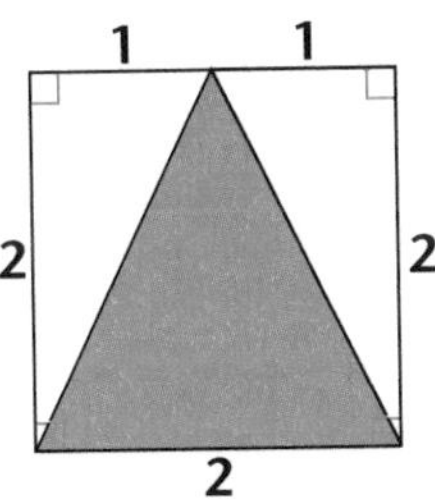

TRY THIS Say you lost your watch and don't know what time it is. What is the probability that it's between 4 and 5 o'clock?

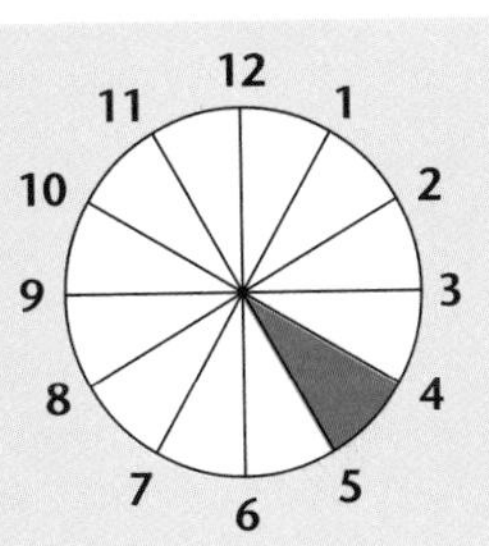

Lesson 5 Formula for the Area of a Circle

In Lesson 3, you used a formula for estimating the area of a circle. The exact area of a circle is given by the following formula.

> **Area of a Circle:**
> πr^2, where r is the radius of the circle.

The formula $A = \pi r^2$ gives a value slightly greater than that given by the Area Estimation Formula,

Area of circle $\approx 3r^2$.

Here is the reason for the formula. Suppose a circle were cut into many equal parts, as shown. As the number of parts increases, each part looks more and more like an isosceles triangle.

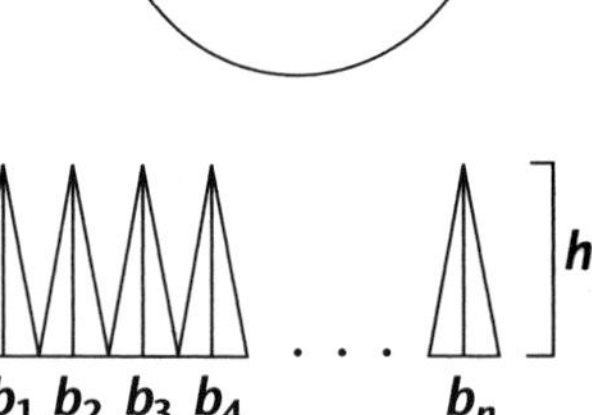

The height of each triangle begins to approximate the radius of the circle. At the same time, the sum of the bases of the triangles begins to approximate the circumference of the circle.

$$\begin{aligned}
\text{Area of circle} = \text{total area} &= \tfrac{1}{2}b_1r + \tfrac{1}{2}b_2r + \tfrac{1}{2}b_3r + \tfrac{1}{2}b_4r + \ldots + \tfrac{1}{2}b_nr \\
&= \tfrac{1}{2}r(b_1 + b_2 + b_3 + b_4 + \ldots + b_n) \\
&= \left(\tfrac{1}{2}r\right)(\text{circumference}) \\
&= \left(\tfrac{1}{2}r\right)(2\pi r) = \pi r^2
\end{aligned}$$

$\therefore$ The formula for the area of any circle $= \pi r^2$, where r is the radius of the circle.

Because $2r = d$ $\qquad d =$ diameter

$r = \frac{d}{2}$ $\qquad$ can be substituted in the formula, giving

$$\text{Area of circle} = \pi\left(\frac{d}{2}\right)^2 = \pi\frac{d^2}{4} = \frac{1}{4}\pi d^2$$

> **Area of a Circle:**
> $\frac{1}{4}\pi d^2$, where d is the diameter of the circle.

You can use these formulas to solve for the areas, radii, or diameters of circles.

EXAMPLE 1 Find the area of a circle whose radius is 12 units. Give the answer in terms of π.

$$\begin{aligned}\text{Area of circle} &= \pi r^2 \\ &= \pi(12)^2 \\ &= 144\pi \text{ sq units}\end{aligned}$$

EXAMPLE 2 Find the area of a circle whose radius is 1.2 cm. Give the answer to the nearest tenth.

$$\begin{aligned}\text{Area of circle} &= \pi r^2 \\ &= \pi(1.2)^2 \\ &= \pi(1.44) \text{ cm}^2 \\ &\approx 4.5 \text{ cm}^2\end{aligned}$$

EXAMPLE 3 Find the area of a circle whose diameter is 15 in. Calculate the answer to the nearest hundredth.

$$\begin{aligned}\text{Area of circle} &= \tfrac{1}{4}\pi d^2 \\ &= \left(\tfrac{1}{4}\right)\pi(15)^2 \\ &= \left(\tfrac{1}{4}\right)\pi(225) \text{ sq in.} \\ &\approx 176.71 \text{ sq in.}\end{aligned}$$

EXAMPLE 4 The area of a circle is 200 sq units. Calculate the circle's radius to the nearest hundredth.

$$\begin{aligned}\text{Area of circle} &= \pi r^2 \\ 200 &= \pi r^2 \\ \frac{200}{\pi} &= r^2 \\ \sqrt{\frac{200}{\pi}} &= r \\ 7.98 \text{ units} &\approx r\end{aligned}$$

Some problems will require you to calculate an answer using a value for π. On your graphing calculator, you will need to press 2nd and ^ to use the number π. Using these special keys will help you calculate the areas of circles.

EXAMPLE 5 Find the product of $5^2\pi$.

Press 5 x^2 × 2nd ^ ENTER. The display reads 78.53981634.

Often you will be instructed to give the answer to the nearest hundredth, 78.54, or to the nearest tenth, 78.5. To set a graphing calculator to round to a given number of decimal places, press MODE ▼ ▶ ▶ ENTER before making your calculations.

EXAMPLE 6 Find the square root of 2,209.

Press 2nd x^2 2209 ENTER. The display reads 47.00. The two zeros after the decimal point are because the calculator was set to round to and display two decimal places.

Exercise A Find the product or the square root. Use your calculator. Give the answer to the nearest hundredth.

1. $7^2\pi$

2. $15^2\pi$

3. $4^2\pi$

4. $25^2\pi$

5. $9^2\pi$

6. $\sqrt{2,704}$

7. $\sqrt{625}$

8. $\sqrt{12,321}$

9. $\sqrt{1,234,321}$

10. $\sqrt{10,201}$

Exercise B Find the area of a circle with the given radius. Give your answer in terms of π.

11. $r = 3$ in.

12. $r = 23$ cm

13. $r = 9$ m

14. $r = 40$ mi

15. $r = 15$ km

Exercise C Find the area of a circle with the given radius or diameter. Use a calculator and give your answer to the nearest tenth.

16. $r = 12$ in.

17. $r = 6$ ft

18. $r = 13$ cm

19. $r = 17$ mm

20. $r = 20$ m

21. $d = 24$ km

22. $d = 100$ mi

23. $d = 14$ ft

24. $d = 40$ m

25. $d = 90$ mi

Exercise D Find the radius of a circle with the given area. Use a calculator and give your answer to the nearest tenth.

26. $A = 210$ cm^2

27. $A = 400$ sq in.

28. $A = 1{,}000$ m^2

29. $A = 314$ km^2

30. $A = 65$ mi^2

Lesson 6 Circles and Their Angles and Sectors

> ### *Sector*
> *The area enclosed within a central angle of a circle*
>
> ### *Central angle*
> *An angle with its vertex at the center of a circle and the circle's radii as its sides*
>
> ### *Arc* $\overset{\frown}{AB}$
> *A portion of a circle bounded by two distinct points on the circle*

You are familiar with the shape of a slice of pizza or apple pie.

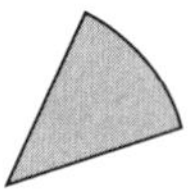

This shape is a part of a circle called a **sector.** A sector is contained in a **central angle** and its **arc.**

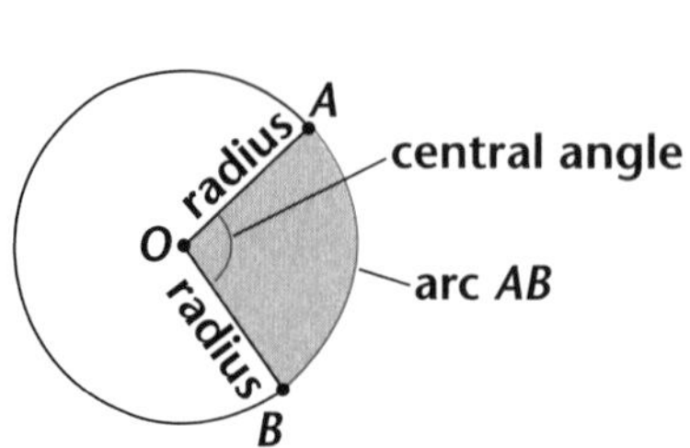

A segment of a circle bounded by two endpoints is called an arc.

The symbol for the arc between points *A* and *B* is $\overset{\frown}{AB}$. The shorter length is called the *minor arc,* the greater distance is the *major arc.* In this book, the symbol $\overset{\frown}{AB}$ refers to the minor arc.

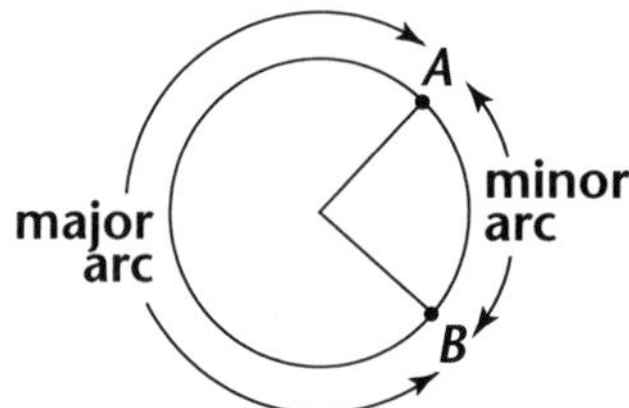

Arcs of a circle are measured in degrees. For example, for the circle above, $\overset{\frown}{AB} = 90°$. You can write "arc *AB* is 90°" in symbols as $\overset{\circ}{\overset{\frown}{AB}} = 90$.

A central angle of a circle has its vertex at the center of the circle and has sides formed by radii of the circle. Note that the central angle is always taken to be less than 180°. A sector of a circle is the area enclosed within a central angle of the circle.

You can form a central angle by drawing radii from the endpoints of an arc to the center of the circle. If you know the number of degrees in a circular arc, you automatically know the size of the central angle.

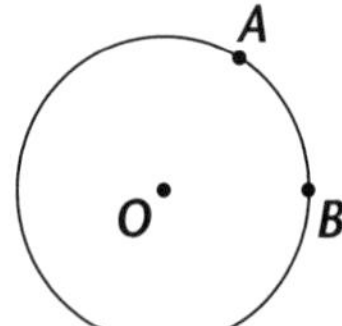

Given: $\overset{\frown}{AB} = 60°$

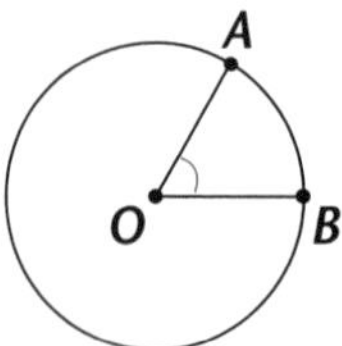

Draw radii $\overline{AO}$ and $\overline{BO}$, forming central angle *AOB*. $m\angle AOB = 60°$

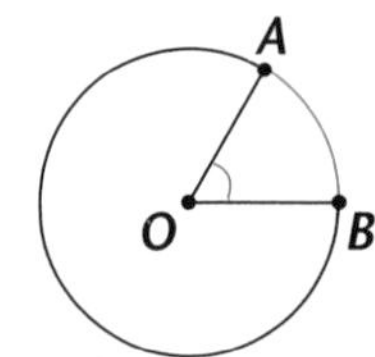

$\overset{\frown}{AB} = m\angle AOB$, or arc degrees = central angle measure

EXAMPLE 1 **Given:** $\overset{\circ}{\widehat{AB}} = 30$, $\overset{\circ}{\widehat{AC}} = 130$

Find: $\overset{\circ}{\widehat{BC}}$, $m\angle AOB$, $m\angle AOC$, $m\angle BOC$

$$\overset{\circ}{\widehat{AC}} - \overset{\circ}{\widehat{AB}} = \overset{\circ}{\widehat{BC}}$$

$$130 - 30 = 100 \qquad \therefore\ \overset{\circ}{\widehat{BC}} = 100$$

m(central angle) = degrees in arc with radii as angle sides

$\overset{\circ}{\widehat{AB}} = 30$, so $m\angle AOB = 30°$

$\overset{\circ}{\widehat{AC}} = 130$, so $m\angle AOC = 130°$

$\overset{\circ}{\widehat{BC}} = 100$, so $m\angle BOC = 100°$

If you know the measure of the central angle, you can use the following ratio to determine what part of the circle's area is covered by the sector:

$$\frac{\text{central angle}}{360°} = \text{fraction of the circle's area covered by the sector}$$

With this information, you can then calculate the area of a sector.

EXAMPLE 2 A circle has a radius of 5 units. What is the area of a sector whose central angle is 90°?

First, find the fraction of the circle's area covered by the sector: $\frac{90°}{360°} = \frac{1}{4}$ of the circle

$$\text{Area of circle} = \pi r^2 = 25\pi \text{ sq units}$$

$$\text{Area of sector} = \frac{1}{4}\text{ Area of circle} = \frac{1}{4}(25\pi)$$

$$= \frac{25}{4}\pi \text{ sq units}$$

This picture of the Sky Dome in Ontario, Canada, shows several examples of sectors. The line separating the infield from the outfield is an arc, while the first base and third base foul lines are radii. A larger arc is made by the outfield wall. Both of these sectors have the same central angle at home plate. What is its measure?

Inscribed angle

An angle formed by two chords that intersect on the circle

Intercepted arc

The arc of a circle within an inscribed angle

EXAMPLE 3 A circle has a radius of 6 units, m(central angle) = 30°. Calculate the area of the sector.

First, find the fraction of the circle's area covered by the sector.

$\frac{30°}{360°} = \frac{1}{12}$ of the circle

Area of circle $= \pi r^2$

$= \pi(6)^2 = 36\pi$ sq units

Area of sector $= \frac{1}{12}$ Area of circle

$= \frac{1}{12}(36\pi)$

$= 3\pi$ sq units

EXAMPLE 4 A circle has a radius of 10 units, m(central angle) = 60°. What is the area of the circle not covered by the sector?

First, find the fraction of the circle's area covered by the sector.

$\frac{60°}{360°} = \frac{1}{6}$ of the circle is covered by the sector, so $\frac{5}{6}$ is not covered.

Area of circle $= \pi r^2$

$= \pi(10)^2 = 100\pi$

Area of circle not covered by sector $= \frac{5}{6}$ Area of circle

$= \frac{5}{6}(100\pi)$

$= \frac{250}{3}\pi$ sq units

In addition to a central angle, there can be another type of angle in a circle, an **inscribed angle**.

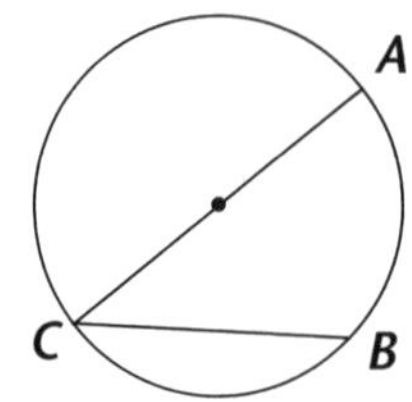

$\angle ACB$ is an example of an inscribed angle. Its sides, $\overline{AC}$ and $\overline{CB}$, are chords of the circle.

An inscribed angle has its vertex on the circle; its sides are chords of the circle. $\overset{\frown}{AB}$ is called the **intercepted arc**. We will assume the following theorem without proof.

Theorem 10.6.1:

The measure of an inscribed angle is half the measure of its intercepted arc.

Writing About Mathematics

Describe what you need to know in order to find the area bounded by chord $\overline{AB}$ and arc AB.

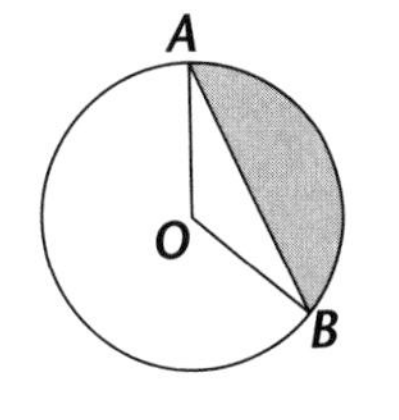

EXAMPLE 5 An inscribed angle has an intercepted arc of 60°. What is the measure of the angle?

$m\angle C = \left(\frac{1}{2}\right)60° = 30°$

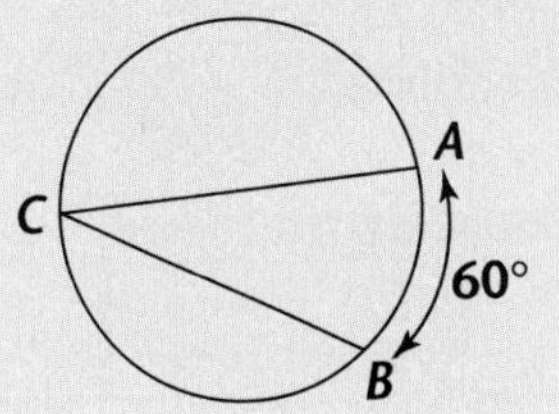

Exercise A Find the value for each of the circle components.

1. $m\angle ACB$
2. $\overset{\frown}{ED}$
3. $\overset{\frown}{BD}$
4. $m\angle FCA$
5. $\overset{\frown}{FE}$

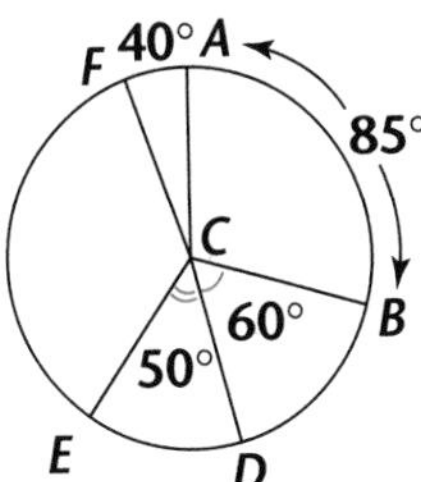

Exercise B Find the area of the shaded sector. Give your answer in terms of π.

6.

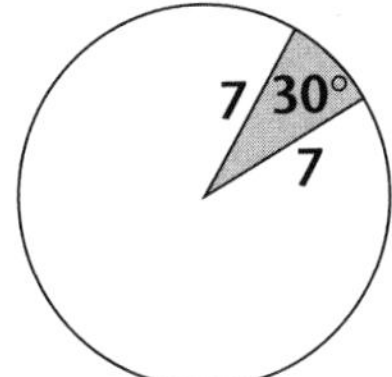

7.

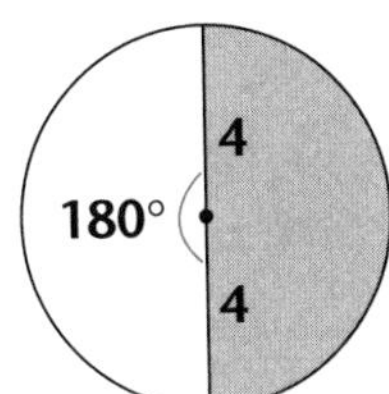

8.

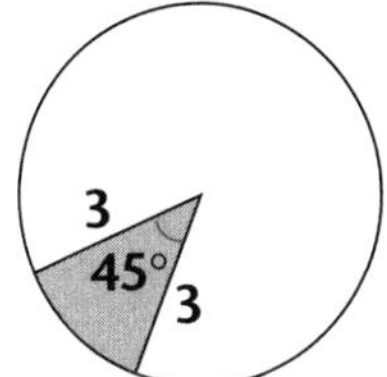

Exercise C Find the value of the unknown.

9. inscribed angle

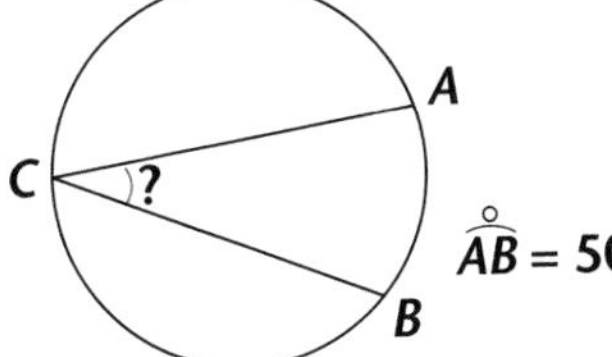

10. arc MN

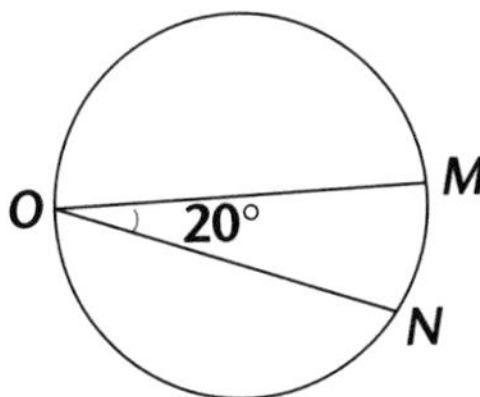

TRY THIS What is the size of any inscribed angle whose intercepted arc is 180°?

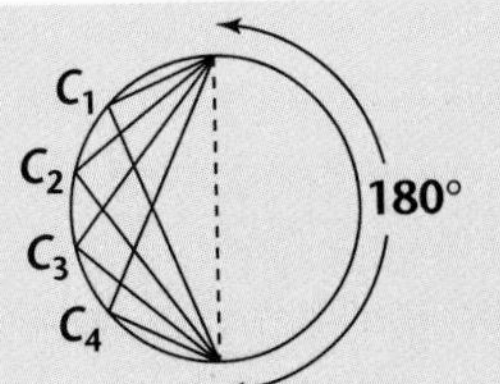

Lesson 7 Tangents, Circumcircles, and Incircles

Tangent

Line that touches but does not intersect a circle

Point of tangency

The point when the tangent touches the circle

You now know from Lesson 6 that the measure of an inscribed angle is equal to half its intercepted arc. Look at $\angle ABC$ and $\overset{\frown}{AC}$ below.

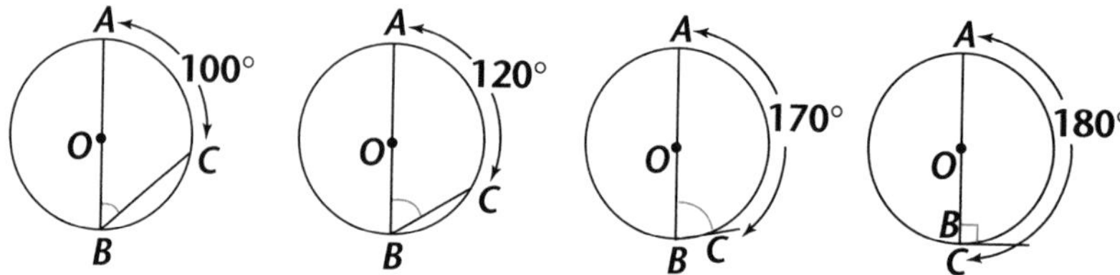

Arc $AC \to 180°$ as
Inscribed angle $ABC \to 90°$

By studying the diagrams above, you can see that as point C moves closer to point B, the value of the intercepted arc moves toward 180°. The value of the inscribed angle moves toward 90°. When the arc is equal to 180°, the inscribed angle is 90°. Side $\overline{BC}$ is no longer a chord—it is now outside the circle and touches the circle only at point B.

In this case, $\overleftrightarrow{BC}$ is called a **tangent** to the circle. A tangent to a circle is a line that touches the circle at only one point. The point at which the tangent touches the circle is called the **point of tangency**.

In the diagram below, $\overline{OB}$ is a radius, B is the point of tangency, and $\overleftrightarrow{BD}$ is tangent to the circle. A radius drawn to the point of tangency is perpendicular to the tangent line.

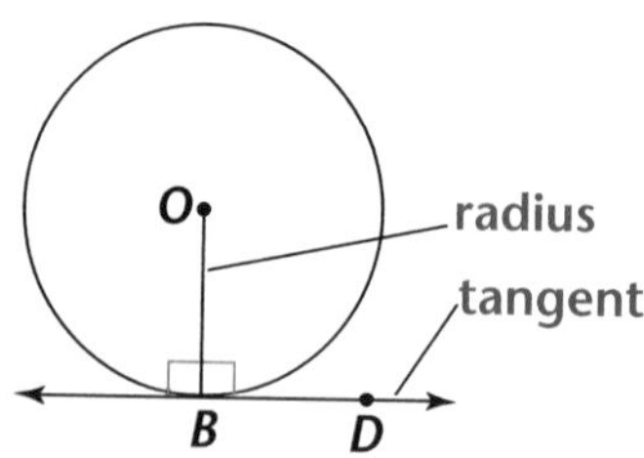

Perpendicular bisector

Set of points equidistant from two given points

Locus of points

A set of points that satisfy a certain condition

Equidistant

At an equal distance

Think back to the steps you used to construct a **perpendicular bisector** of any segment.

$\overleftrightarrow{CD} = \perp$ bisector of $\overline{AB}$

M = midpoint of $\overline{AB}$

Also, any point X on $\overleftrightarrow{CD}$ is an equal distance from both point A and point B. We can indicate this by writing:

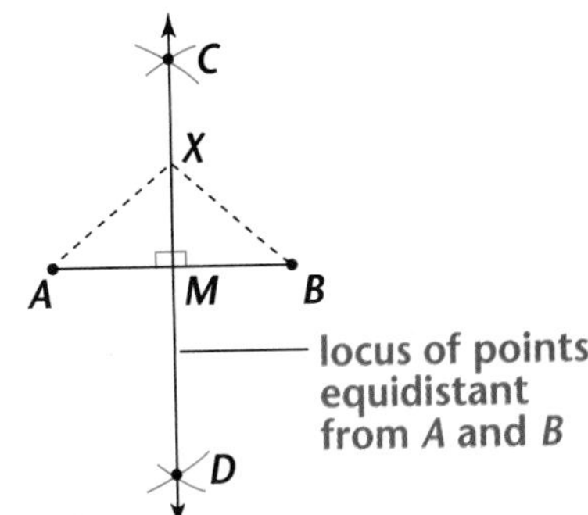

$\Delta AXM \cong \Delta BXM$ Why? SAS Postulate

$\therefore\ AX = XB$ Why? Corresponding sides

Because this will be true for any point on $\overleftrightarrow{CD}$, we can form the following definition.

The **locus of points equidistant** from two given points is the perpendicular bisector of the segment that joins the two points.

This definition is useful for finding a point equidistant from three noncollinear (not on the same line) points.

Given: points A, B, and C not on the same line

The locus of points equidistant from points A and B intersects the locus of points equidistant from points A and C at point D. Therefore, point D is equidistant from A, B, and C. Because of this, D can serve as the center of a circle that passes through points A, B, and C.

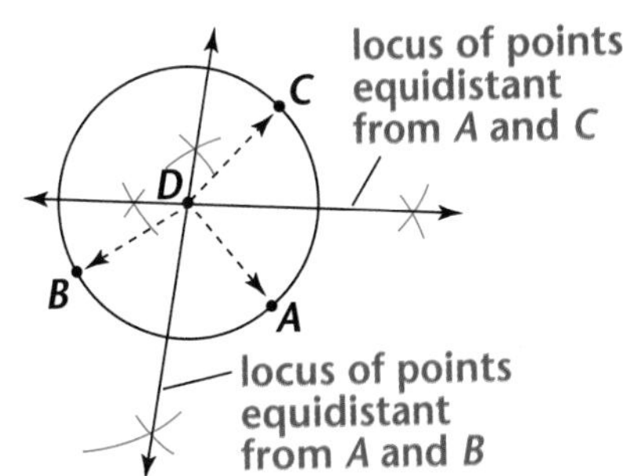

Circumcircle
Circle that passes through the three vertices of a triangle

Circumcenter
Center of a circumcircle and located at the intersection of the perpendicular bisectors of any two sides of a triangle

Angle bisector
Locus of points equidistant from the sides of an angle

Incircle
Circle inside a triangle and tangent to each of the triangle's sides

You already know that any three noncollinear points determine a triangle. And so, the construction on the previous page results in a circle that passes through each of the three vertices of a triangle. This circle is called the *circumscribed circle* or **circumcircle.**

The circumcircle of a triangle is the circle that passes through the three vertices of the triangle. The center of this circle, called the **circumcenter,** is at the intersection of the perpendicular bisectors of any two sides of the triangle.

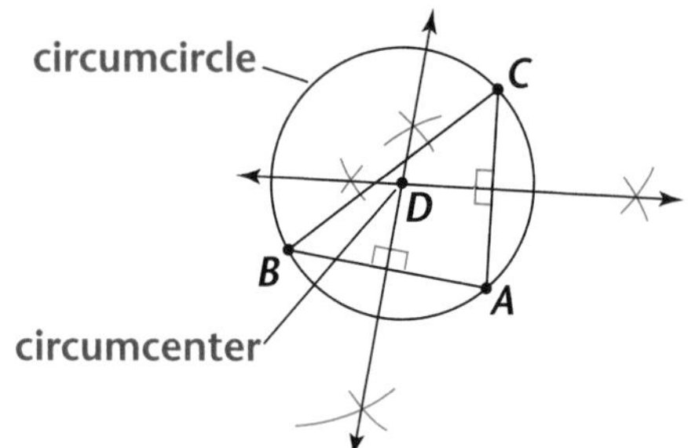

We have shown that a perpendicular bisector is the locus of points equidistant from two points. We can develop a similar definition for an **angle bisector.** The locus of points equidistant from the sides of an angle is the angle bisector.

EXAMPLE 1 **Given:** any $\angle ABC$ with bisector $\overrightarrow{BD}$

Let X be any point on $\overrightarrow{BD}$. Draw a perpendicular from X to each side of angle ABC.

right $\Delta FXB \cong$ right ΔEXB
Why? AAS Theorem
$\therefore\ FX = EX$

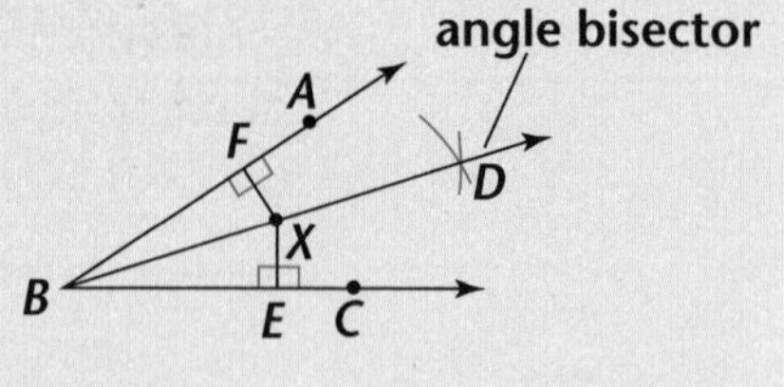

This definition is useful for finding the center of a circle inside a triangle that is tangent to each side of the triangle.

Look at ΔABC. Construct angle bisectors of $\angle A$ and $\angle B$. The point where the bisectors intersect is the center of the circle that touches each side of the triangle at one point. This circle is the *inscribed circle* or **incircle.**

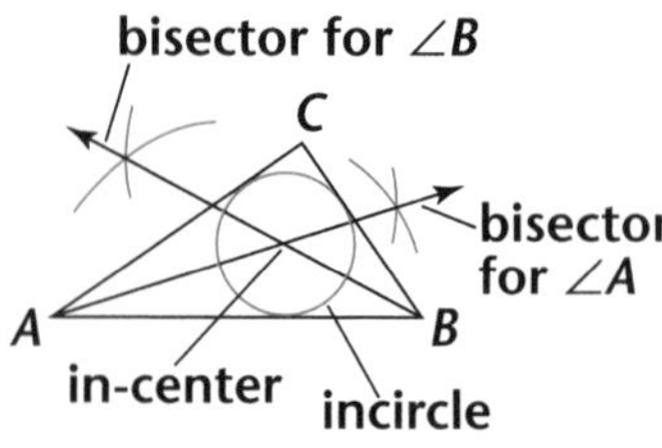

The incircle is a circle inside a triangle that is tangent to each of the triangle's sides. The center of the circle, called the *incenter,* is the intersection of any two angle bisectors. The incenter is also the point that is the shortest distance from all three sides of the triangle.

Problem: What is the largest circle you can fit inside $\triangle ABC$?

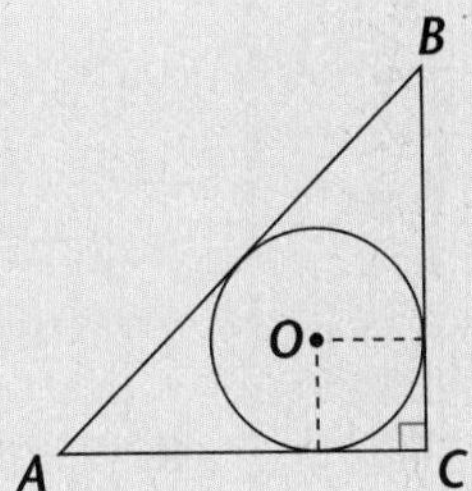

Construct the incircle for the triangle. The circle will touch every side of the triangle. A larger circle would extend outside the triangle.

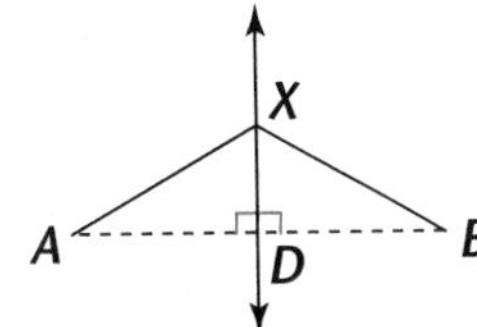

Exercise A Copy and complete the following proof.

Given: X, a point on $\overleftrightarrow{XD}$, the perpendicular bisector of $\overline{AB}$

To Prove: $AX = BX$

PROOF

Statement	Reason
1. X, a point on $\overleftrightarrow{XD}$	1. **1.**
2. D is the midpoint of **2.**	2. Given; definition of bisector.
3. $AD = DB$	3. **3.**
4. **4.**	4. A quantity is equal to itself.
5. **5.**	5. Given $\overleftrightarrow{XD}$ is $\perp$ to $\overline{AB}$; all right angles are equal to each other.
6. $\triangle ADX \cong \triangle BDX$	6. **6.**
7. $\therefore AX = BX$	7. **7.**

CONSTRUCTION

Exercise B Complete the following constructions.

8. Construct any $\angle EDF$. Then construct a locus of points equidistant from $\overrightarrow{DE}$ and $\overrightarrow{DF}$.

9. Construct the circumcircle for any obtuse triangle.

10. Construct the incircle for any scalene triangle.

Lesson 8 Sine, Cosine, and Tangent

Unit circle

Circle whose radius is one

Sine (sin)

For an angle of a right triangle (not the right angle), the ratio of the length of the opposite leg to the length of the hypotenuse

Cosine (cos)

For an angle of a right triangle (not the right angle), the ratio of the length of its adjacent leg to the length of the hypotenuse

Tangent (tan)

For an angle of a right triangle (not the right angle), the ratio of the length of the opposite leg to the length of the adjacent leg

You can use a **unit circle,** a circle with radius = 1, to develop three important ratios for right triangles.

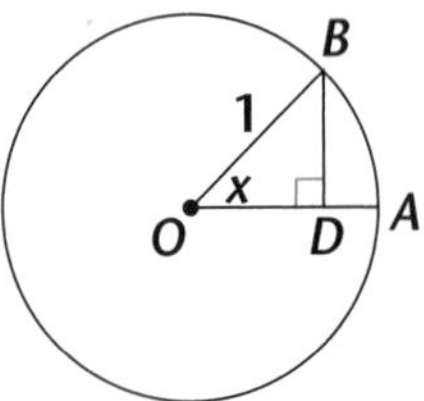

We can draw a central angle, $\angle x$, in the circle. We can then construct $\overline{BD}$ perpendicular to $\overline{OA}$. The result is right triangle ODB. Note that $\overline{OA}$ and $\overline{OB}$ both equal 1, the radius of the circle.

EXAMPLE 1 Form the ratio $\frac{BD}{OB}$, which is the side opposite $\angle x$ divided by the hypotenuse of the right triangle.

$$\frac{BD}{OB} = \frac{BD}{\text{radius}} = \frac{BD}{1} = BD$$

This ratio is called the **sine** ratio of $\angle x$. It is abbreviated as sin x. For the unit circle,

$$\sin x = \frac{BD}{1} = BD.$$

In general, $\sin x = \frac{\text{side opposite } \angle x}{\text{hypotenuse}}$.

Note that any time you change the size of the central angle you also change the lengths of the sides and the ratios. This means that for every different angle x, there is a unique set of ratios.

EXAMPLE 2 Form the ratio $\frac{OD}{OB}$, which is the side adjacent $\angle x$ divided by the hypotenuse of the right triangle.

$$\frac{OD}{OB} = \frac{OD}{\text{radius}} = \frac{OD}{1} = OD$$

This ratio is called the **cosine** ratio of $\angle x$.
It is abbreviated as cos x. For the unit circle,

$$\cos x = \frac{OD}{1} = OD.$$

In general, $\cos x = \frac{\text{side adjacent } \angle x}{\text{hypotenuse}}$.

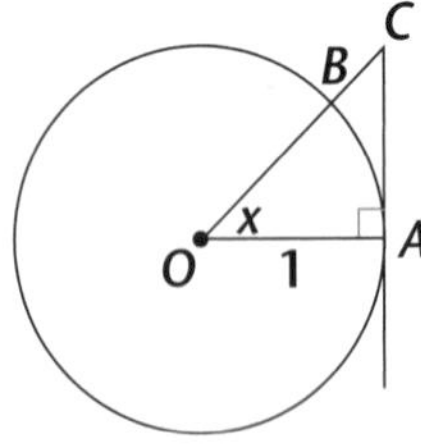

Using the unit circle, we can construct a tangent to the circle at point A. $\overline{OB}$ has been extended to meet the tangent at C. The result is right triangle OAC. Note that OA and OB both equal 1, the radius of the circle. Right triangle OAC will be used for the **tangent** ratio.

EXAMPLE 3 Form the ratio $\frac{AC}{OA}$, which is the side opposite $\angle x$ divided by the side adjacent $\angle x$.

$\frac{AC}{OA} = \frac{AC}{\text{radius}} = \frac{AC}{1} = AC$

This ratio is called the tangent ratio of $\angle x$. It is abbreviated as tan x.

For the unit circle, $\tan x = \frac{AC}{1} = AC$.

In general, $\tan x = \frac{\text{side opposite } \angle x}{\text{side adjacent } \angle x}$.

Trigonometry

Branch of mathematics dealing with relations between the sides and angles of triangles

The sine, cosine, and tangent ratios are the basis of the branch of mathematics called **trigonometry**. These ratios provide values necessary to solve many different types of problems.

EXAMPLE 4 Given an isosceles right triangle, find the sine, cosine, and tangent ratios of 45°.

Use the unit circle and the fact that the legs of the triangle are equal.

$\sin 45° = \frac{\text{side opposite}}{\text{hypotenuse}} = \frac{BD}{OB} = \frac{x}{1} = x \approx 0.71$ (To find x, see below.)

$\cos 45° = \frac{\text{side adjacent}}{\text{hypotenuse}} = \frac{OD}{OB} = \frac{x}{1} = x \approx 0.71$

$\tan 45° = \frac{\text{side opposite}}{\text{side adjacent}} = \frac{AC}{OA} = \frac{1}{1} = 1$

To find x: $x^2 + x^2 = 1$ Pythagorean Theorem

$2x^2 = 1$ $x^2 = \frac{1}{2}$

$x = \sqrt{\frac{1}{2}} \approx 0.71$ Use a calculator and round to the nearest hundredth.

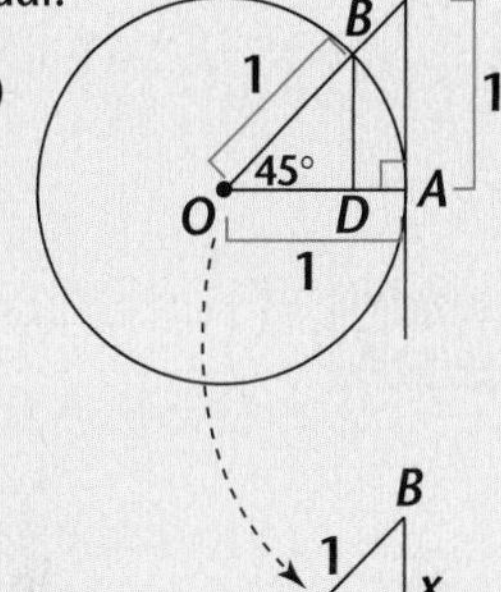

EXAMPLE 5 Find the sine, cosine, and tangent for 22°. Round to the nearest hundredth.

Step 1 Press SIN 22 ENTER. The display reads *0.37*.

Step 2 Press COS 22 ENTER. The display reads *0.93*.

Step 3 Press TAN 22 ENTER. The display reads *0.40*.

Exercise A Use your calculator to find the sine, cosine, and tangent for each angle. Round to the nearest hundredth.

1. 0°

2. 30°

3. 45°

4. 60°

5. 90°

Lesson 9 Solving Triangles Using Trigonometry

You can find the length of an unknown side of a right triangle if you know the value of the sine, cosine, or tangent of one acute angle and the length of one side.

Use the trigonometric ratios introduced in the previous lesson to set up and solve equations for the unknown side.

EXAMPLE 1

Given: right ΔABC, $m\angle A = 35°$, $AB = 15$

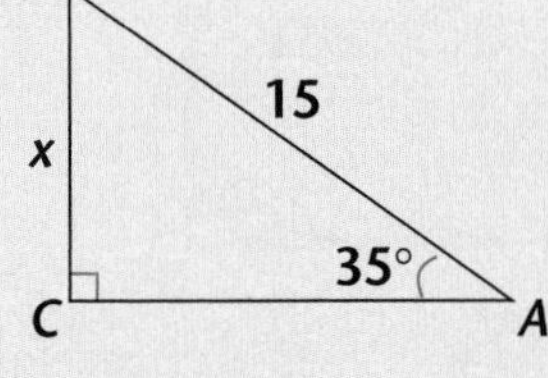

Find: the value of x

Solution: We need a function involving $\angle A$, x, and 15.

$$\sin A = \frac{\text{side opposite}}{\text{hypotenuse}} = \frac{x}{15}$$

$$\sin 35° = \frac{x}{15}$$

$15 \bullet \sin 35° = x$ → Using a calculator, multiply the sine of 35° by 15, then round your answer to the nearest hundredth.

$x \approx 8.60$

So, $x = BC \approx 8.60$

EXAMPLE 2

Given: right ΔDEF, $m\angle D = 65°$, $DF = 20$

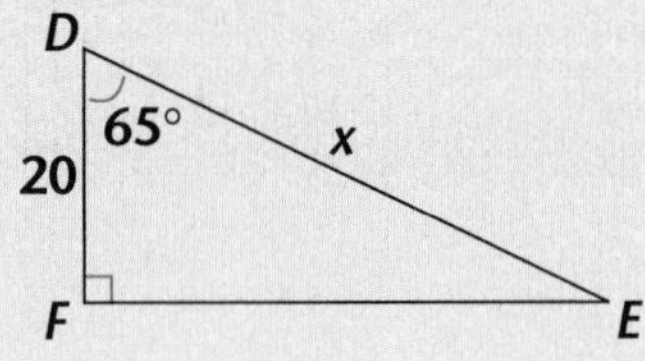

Find: the value of x

Solution: We need a function involving $\angle D$, x, and 20.

$$\cos D = \frac{\text{side adjacent}}{\text{hypotenuse}} = \frac{20}{x}$$

$$\cos 65° = \frac{20}{x}$$

$$x \bullet \cos 65° = 20$$

$x = \frac{20}{\cos 65°}$ → Using a calculator, divide 20 by the cosine of 65°, then round your answer to the nearest hundredth.

$x \approx 47.32$

So, $x = DE \approx 47.32$

Example 3 **Given:** right ΔGHJ, $m\angle G = 21°$, $HJ = 18$

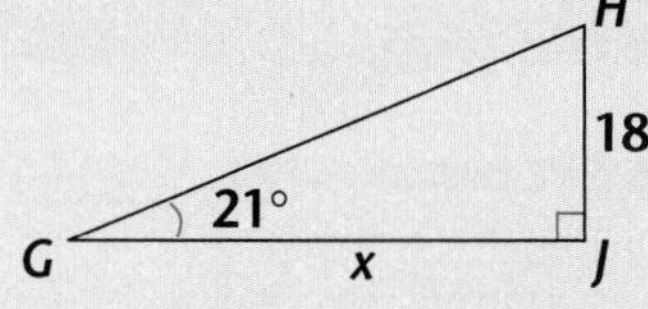

Find: the value of x

Solution: You need a function involving $\angle G$, 18, and x.

$$\tan G = \frac{\text{side opposite}}{\text{side adjacent}} = \frac{18}{x}$$

$$\tan 21° = \frac{18}{x}$$

$$x \bullet \tan 21° = 18$$

$$x = \frac{18}{\tan 21°}$$ → Using a calculator, divide 18 by the tangent of 21°, then round your answer to the nearest hundredth.

$$x \approx 46.89$$

So, $x = GJ \approx 46.89$

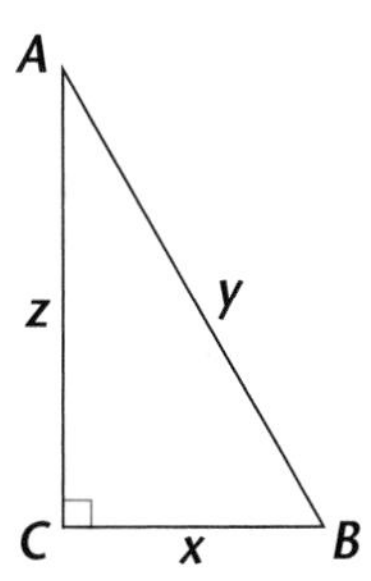

Exercise A For right ΔABC, find x to the nearest hundredth.

1. $m\angle A = 30°$, $AB = 12$

2. $m\angle A = 40°$, $AB = 5$

3. $m\angle A = 33°$, $AB = 9$

4. $m\angle A = 26°$, $AB = 25$

Exercise B For right ΔABC, find y to the nearest hundredth.

5. $m\angle B = 60°$, $BC = 15$

6. $m\angle B = 50°$, $BC = 8$

7. $m\angle B = 53°$, $BC = 20$

Exercise C For right ΔABC, find z to the nearest hundredth.

8. $m\angle A = 3°$, $BC = 1$

9. $m\angle A = 40°$, $BC = 21$

10. $m\angle A = 24°$, $BC = 18$

TRY THIS **Given:** right ΔWXY, $m\angle X = 17°$, $XY = 30$

Find: $\angle W$, $\angle Y$, WY, WX

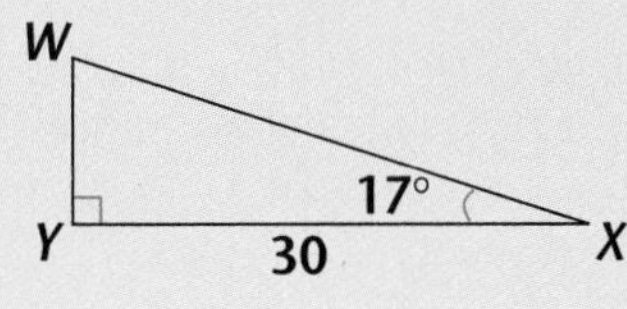

Lesson 10 Spheres

> ***Sphere***
> *Locus of points in space equidistant from a fixed point*
>
> ***Great circle***
> *Circle on a sphere whose center is the center of the sphere and whose radius equals the radius of the sphere*

Circles and **spheres** are closely related.

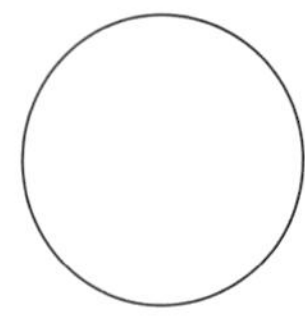

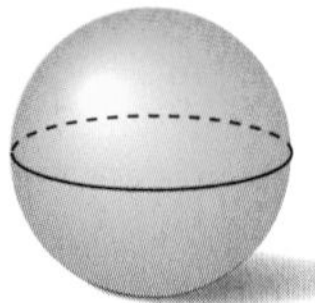

You can think of a sphere as the result of a circle spinning around one of its diameters.

A sphere is the locus of points in space that are at a given distance from a fixed point called the *center of the sphere.* The given distance is the *radius* of the sphere.

The diameter of a sphere is twice the radius, $d = 2r$, just like the diameter of a circle.

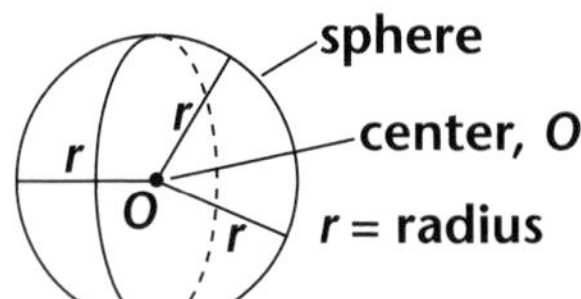

A **great circle** of a sphere is a circle on the sphere whose center is the center of the sphere and whose radius is equal to the radius of the sphere.

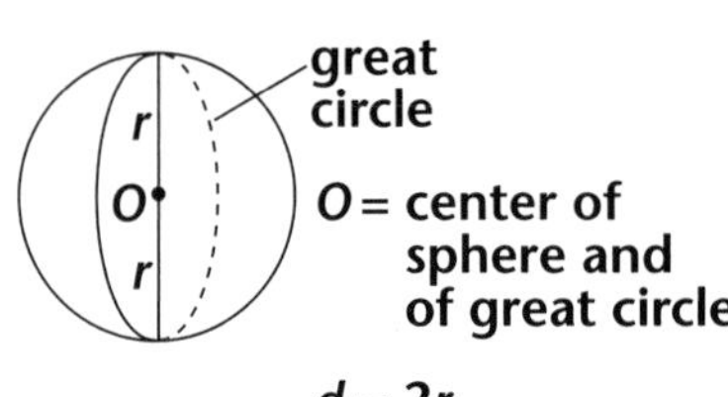

Geometry in Your Life

Spinning disks are used as lawn ornaments, mobiles for babies, and toys for birds. As the disks spin, they give the illusion of a solid sphere. You can create your own spinning disk. First, cut out two one-inch diameter paper circles. Draw a diameter on each. Place a toothpick along the diameter of one circle. Make sure it extends past each end of the diameter. Glue the toothpick in place, then place a few drops of glue on the toothpick. Position the second circle's diameter so it also lies along the toothpick. Allow the glue on your paper-and-toothpick sandwich to dry. Hold one end of the toothpick between your thumb and forefinger, and roll it back and forth between your fingers. See if you can visualize the sphere the circle forms as it spins.

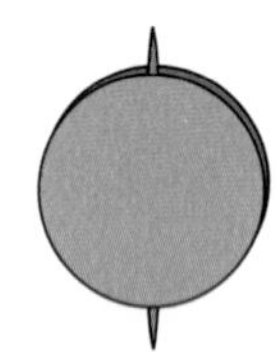

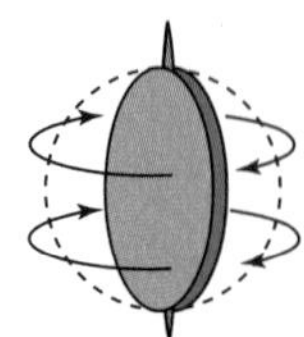

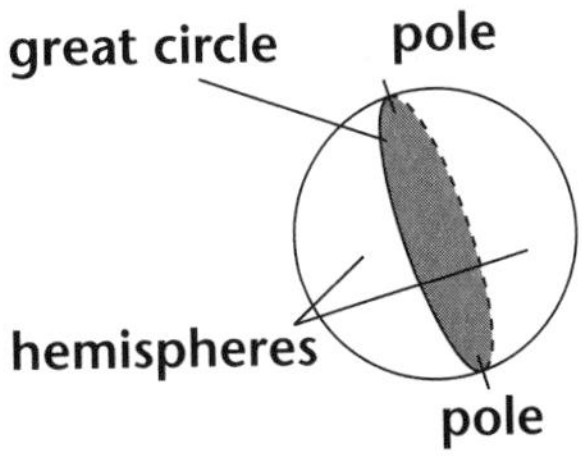

One way to picture a great circle is to picture the circle that divides the sphere into two equal halves called **hemispheres**.

The endpoints of the diameter of a sphere are called **poles.**

The surface area of a sphere is equal to the area of four great circles, $4\pi r^2$. The volume of a sphere is $\frac{4}{3}\pi r^3$.

Formulas:
S = Surface area of a sphere = $4\pi r^2$
V = Volume of a sphere = $\frac{4}{3}\pi r^3$

Hemisphere
Half of a sphere

Poles
Endpoints of the diameter of a sphere

EXAMPLE 1 What is the surface area of a sphere whose radius is 10 cm? Give your answer in terms of π.

S = surface area of sphere = $4\pi r^2$
Substitute the given radius.

$S = 4\pi(10 \text{ cm})^2 = 400\pi \text{ cm}^2$

EXAMPLE 2 A sphere has a radius of 9 in. What is its volume? Use 3.14 for π.

V = volume of sphere = $\frac{4}{3}\pi r^3$
Substitute the given values.

$V = \frac{4}{3}(3.14)(9 \text{ in.})^3$

$= \frac{4}{3}(3.14)(729 \text{ in.}^3)$ divide 729 by 3

$= 4(3.14)(243) \text{ in.}^3$

$= 3{,}052.08 \text{ in.}^3$

The planet Earth is often represented by a sphere. Which of the following correspond to great circles—lines of longitude, lines of latitude, the equator, or the prime meridian? Which poles are used on the geographic sphere?

EXAMPLE 3 A sphere has a radius of 10. What happens to the surface area and the volume of the sphere if its radius is doubled to 20?

Find the surface area and volume with radius 10, then with radius 20. Compare your results.

S = surface area of sphere = $4\pi r^2$
Substitute the given radius.

$r = 10$	$r = 20$
$S = 4\pi(10)^2$	$S = 4\pi(20)^2$
$= 4\pi(400)$	$= 4\pi(100)$
$= 400\pi$	$= 1{,}600\pi$

$$\frac{1{,}600}{400} = \frac{4}{1}$$

$\therefore$ Doubling the radius gives four times the surface area.

V = volume of sphere = $\frac{4}{3}\pi r^3$
Substitute the given radius.

$r = 10$	$r = 20$
$V = \frac{4}{3}\pi(10)^3$	$V = \frac{4}{3}\pi(20)^3$
$= \frac{4}{3}\pi(1{,}000)$	$= \frac{4}{3}\pi(8{,}000)$
$= \frac{(4{,}000)}{3}\pi$	$= \frac{(32{,}000)}{3}\pi$

$$\frac{32{,}000}{4{,}000} = \frac{8}{1}$$

$\therefore$ Doubling the radius gives eight times the volume.

Exercise A Find the surface area and the volume of a sphere with the given radius or diameter. Give your answer in terms of π.

1. $r = 3$ units

2. $r = 7$ units

3. $r = 4$ units

4. $d = 10$ units

5. $d = 12$ units

6. $d = 11$ units

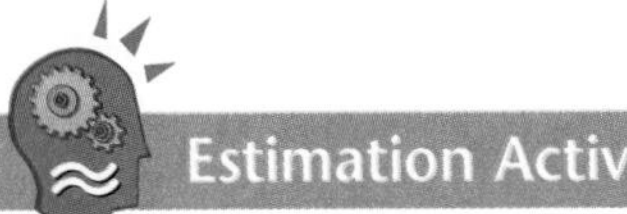

Estimation Activity

Estimate: What is the volume of a sphere with a radius of 4 units?

Solution: Use 3 to estimate π in the formula.

$$r = 4 \qquad V = \tfrac{4}{3}(3)(4 \text{ units})^3$$
$$= 4(64 \text{ units}^3)$$
$$= 256 \text{ units}^3$$

So, the volume is about 256 units^3.

Exercise B Find the surface area and the volume of a sphere with the given radius or diameter. Use the pi function on a calculator and give your answer to the nearest hundredth.

7. $r = 2$ units

8. $r = 8$ units

9. $r = 11$ units

10. $d = 7$ units

11. $d = 20$ units

12. $d = 50$ units

Writing About Mathematics

Review problems 13, 14, and 15. Write a rule that describes what happens to the surface area and volume of a sphere when its radius is doubled.

Exercise C Copy the chart. Find the surface area and the volume of a sphere with the given radius. Fill in the blanks. Give your answer in terms of π.

Radius	$S = 4\pi r^2$	$V = \frac{4}{3}\pi r^3$
13. 3	____	____
14. 6	____	____
15. 12	____	____

Technology Connection

Ball bearings are found inside of many devices from hard drives to inline skates. They help individual parts (such as a wheel) to spin smoothly. The bearings are housed between two rings. Only a small amount of friction (force caused by contact between two surfaces) is produced because the bearings only touch the inner and outer ring at one point at any time. That means that less energy is wasted, and there is less wear on the parts.

Lesson 11 Algebra Connection: Systems of Linear Equations

System of linear equations

A system of equations for two or more straight lines

When we graph a **system of linear equations,** the straight lines may intersect at a point.

The coordinates of that point are the common solution to the system of linear equations.

If the lines are parallel, they will not intersect, and there is no common solution.

The two methods of solving linear equations are *substitution* and *elimination.*

EXAMPLE 1 Using the *substitution* method, find the common solution for $y = 2x + 1$ and $y = x - 4$.

Step 1 In the second equation $y = x - 4$, y is expressed in terms of x.
So, we can substitute $x - 4$ for y in the first equation to get a new equation with only one variable.

$$y = 2x + 1$$
$$x - 4 = 2x + 1$$

Step 2 Solve for x.

$$-4 = x + 1$$
$$-5 = x$$

Step 3 Substitute -5 for x in either equation. Solve for y.

$$x = -5$$

$y = 2x + 1$	$y = x - 4$
$y = 2(-5) + 1 = -10 + 1$	$y = (-5) - 4$
$y = -9$	$y = -9$

The common solution is the ordered pair $(-5, -9)$.

Check: Substitute $(-5, -9)$ in both equations.

$y = 2x + 1$	$y = x - 4$
$-9 = 2(-5) + 1$	$-9 = (-5) - 4$
$-9 = -9$ True	$-9 = -9$ True

If you graphed the lines $y = 2x + 1$ and $y = x - 4$, they would intersect at the point named by the common solution, $(-5, -9)$.

By Euclid's Axiom 2, you can add equals to equals and the sums are equal. The same is true for multiplication. If you multiply equals by the same number, the products are equal.

Example 2 Using the *elimination* method, find the common solution for $x + 3y = 6$ and $-x + y = 10$.

Step 1 Add the equations to eliminate x. Then solve for x.

$$\begin{array}{r} x + 3y = 6 \\ + \quad -x + y = 10 \\ \hline 0 + 4y = 16 \rightarrow y = 4 \end{array}$$

Step 2 Substitute 4 for y in both equations. Solve for x.

$$y = 4$$

$$\begin{array}{ll} x + 3y = 6 & -x + y = 10 \\ x + 3(4) = 6 & -x + 4 = 10 \\ x + 12 = 6 \rightarrow x = -6 & -x = 6 \rightarrow x = -6 \end{array}$$

The common solution is the ordered pair $(-6, 4)$.

Check: $(-6) + 3(4) = -6 + 12 = 6$
and $-(-6) + 4 = 6 + 4 = 10$

Example 3 Find the common solution for $2x + 5y = 10$ and $-x + y = 2$.

Step 1 Multiply $-x + y = 2$ by 2. Then eliminate x.

$$\begin{array}{lr} 2(-x + y) = 2(2) & 2x + 5y = 10 \\ -2x + 2y = 4 \quad \rightarrow & + \quad -2x + 2y = 4 \\ \hline & 0 + 7y = 14 \rightarrow y = 2 \end{array}$$

Step 2 Substitute 2 for y in either equation. Solve for x.

$$\begin{array}{ll} 2x + 5y = 10 & -x + y = 2 \\ 2x + 5(2) = 10 & -x + 2 = 2 \\ 2x + 10 = 10 \rightarrow x = 0 & -x = 0 \rightarrow x = 0 \end{array}$$

The common solution is the ordered pair $(0, 2)$.

Check: $2(0) + 5(2) = 0 + 10 = 10$ and $-(0) + (2) = 2$

Exercise A Use either method to find a common solution. Check your solution.

1. $2x + y = 4$ and $3x - y = 6$
2. $3x + 2y = 7$ and $2x + 3y = 3$
3. $2x + y = 2$ and $-x - y = -3$
4. $4x - 2y = -8$ and $-3x + 2y = 5$
5. $4x - 3y = 1$ and $2x + 3y = 2$
6. $4x - 4y = 1$ and $-2x + 8y = -5$
7. $x + 4y = 5$ and $3x + 3y = 10\frac{1}{2}$
8. $4x + 2y = 1$ and $-2x + y = -2$
9. $x + 3y = \frac{1}{2}$ and $-2x + y = 3\frac{2}{3}$
10. $x + 5y = 10$ and $-2x + y = 3$

Application

Statistics You are constantly exposed to information. More and more, that information is in the form of *statistics*—numerical facts about people, places, or things. Statistics are the result of carefully collecting information by survey or research. School districts track their enrollments, or the number of students in each grade, from year to year in order to make decisions. The data is entered into a table, like the one below, or displayed as a circle graph, like the one shown at the table's right.

Students in Grades 9–12

	2002	2003	2004	2005
Grade 9	3,056	3,169	3,352	3,604
Grade 10	2,945	2,868	3,027	3,131
Grade 11	2,749	2,629	2,656	2,748
Grade 12	2,650	2,473	2,431	2,843
Total	11,400	11,139	11,466	12,326

Students in Grades 9–12, 2005

Grade 12 23%
Grade 9 29%
Grade 11 22%
Grade 10 26%

EXAMPLE 1 What percentage of the students were in grade 9 in 2004? How many degrees of the circle graph would represent the students? Round to the nearest whole percent or degree.

$3{,}352 \div 11{,}466 \approx 0.29$ or 29% Divide and round to the nearest percent.

The grade 9 students were 29% of the total student population.

$0.29 \times 360^\circ = 104.4^\circ \approx 104^\circ$ Multiply and round to the nearest degree.

The sector representing grade 9 students in 2004 would measure 104°.

Exercises Complete the table. Round each answer to the nearest whole number.

		2002	2003	2004
Grade 9	Percentage	**1.**	**2.**	29%
Grade 9	Number of Degrees	**3.**	**4.**	104°
Grade 10	Percentage	**5.**	**6.**	**7.**
Grade 10	Number of Degrees	**8.**	**9.**	**10.**

Chapter 10 REVIEW

Write the letter of the correct answer.

1. A circle has a circumference of 64π feet. What is its diameter?

A 8 feet
B 16 feet
C 32 feet
D 64 feet

2. If a circle has an area of A, which expression represents the radius of that circle?

A πA^2
B $\frac{A}{\pi}$
C $\frac{\sqrt{A}}{\pi}$
D $\sqrt{\frac{A}{\pi}}$

3. A point is chosen at random inside the square shown to the left. What is the probability that the point lies in the shaded region?

A 50%
B $33\frac{1}{3}\%$
C $66\frac{2}{3}\%$
D $42\frac{6}{7}\%$

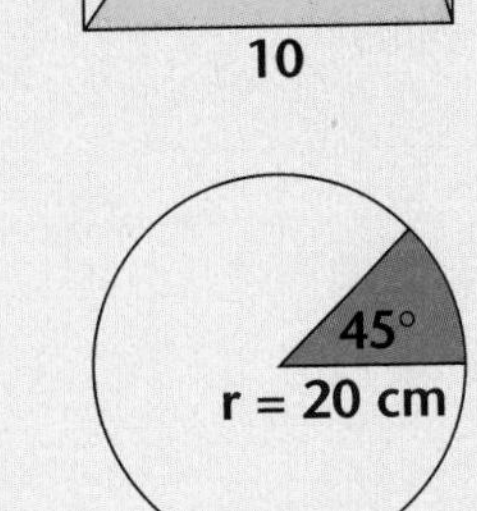

4. What is the area of the shaded part of the circle shown to the left?

A 5π sq cm
B 18π sq cm
C 50π sq cm
D 180π sq cm

5. A circle has circumference of 100π meters. What is its radius?

A 10 meters
B 20 meters
C 50 meters
D 100 meters

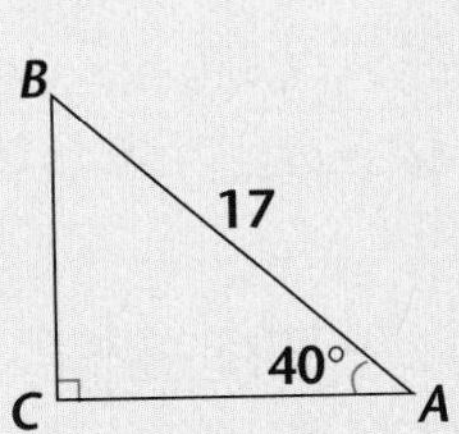

6. Which expression represents the length of $\overline{AC}$ in the right triangle to the left?

A $17 \sin(40°)$
B $17 \cos(40°)$
C $\frac{17}{\sin(40°)}$
D $\frac{17}{\cos(40°)}$

Find the circumference and the area of each circle. Use the pi function on a calculator and round your answer to the nearest tenth.

Example:

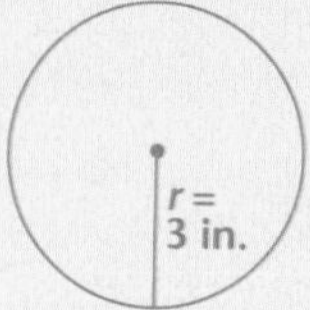

Solution: $C = 2\pi r$, substitute for r.
$C = 2\pi(r) = 2\pi(3) \approx 18.8$ in.
Use the formula for area,
$A = \pi r^2$. Substitute for r.
$A = \pi(3)^2 = 9\pi \approx 28.3$ sq in.

7.

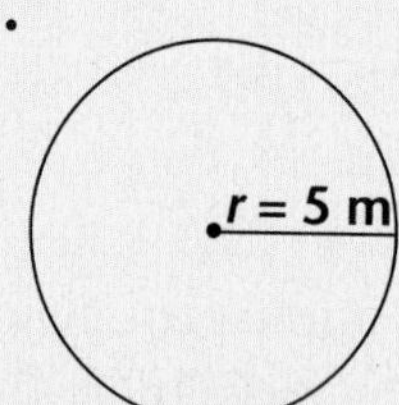

8.

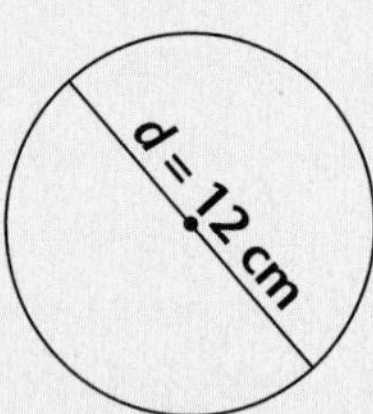

9.

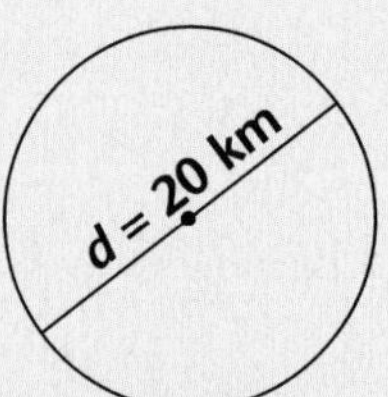

Find the probability of randomly choosing a point inside the given region. Express your answer as a percentage.

Example: P(Unshaded Region)

Solution: $P = \frac{\text{unshaded region}}{\text{area of circle}}$
$= \frac{1}{2}$ of 100% = 50%

10. P(Shaded Region)

11. P(Unshaded Region)

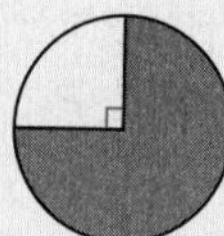

Complete the following constructions.

Example: Construct the angle bisector for an acute angle.

Solution:

12. Construct the circumcircle for a scalene triangle.

13. Construct the incircle for an isosceles triangle.

Use your calculator to find the sine, cosine, and tangent for each angle. Round to the nearest hundredth.

Example: 60° Solution: Press SIN 60 ENTER, 0.87; Press COS 60 ENTER, 0.5;
Press TAN 60 ENTER, 1.73

14. 33° **15.** 46°

Find the value of x in each right triangle below. Use your calculator. Round your answers to the nearest hundredth.

Example:

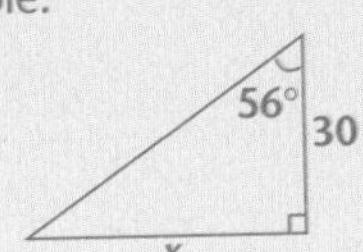

Solution: $\tan(56°) = \frac{\text{side opposite}}{\text{side adjacent}} = \frac{x}{30}$

So, $x = 30 \bullet \tan(56°)$

$x \approx 44.47$

16.

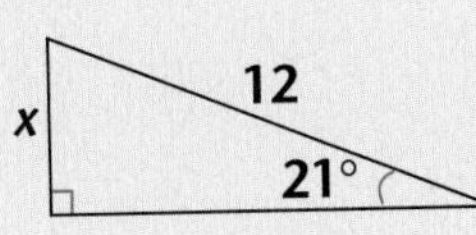

17.

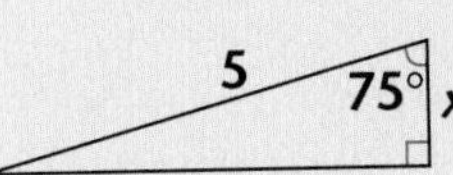

18.

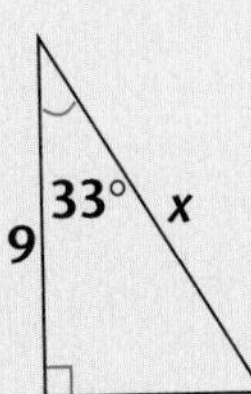

19.

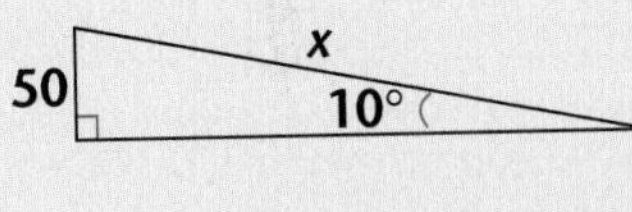

Find the surface area and the volume of each sphere. Give your answer in terms of π.

Example: $r = 3$ in. Solution: Use the formula for surface area,

$S = 4\pi r^2$. Substitute for r.

$S = 4\pi(3)^2 = 36\pi$ sq in.

Use the formula for volume,

$V = \frac{4}{3}\pi r^3$. Substitute for r.

$V = \frac{4}{3}\pi(3)^3 = (\frac{4}{3})\pi(27) = 36\pi$ cu in.

20. $r = 6$ in.

21. $r = 10$

22. $r = 5$ m

23. $r = 7$

24. $r = 4$ km

25. $d = 6$

Test-Taking Tip

If time allows, read over all of your answers. Make sure you have answered the question that was asked.

Chapter

Solid Geometric Figures and Their Measures

A rainbow appears—but there's no rain! Like raindrops, crystal prisms can be used to separate light into a spectrum of colors. Though raindrops and prisms are clear, the spectrum is every color from red to violet. Decorations called sun catchers have many prisms that create rainbows in sunlight. Even this is an application of geometry.

Prisms are geometric solids, or three-dimensional shapes. The crystal solids pictured here include prisms, spheres, cylinders, and pyramids. These geometric shapes are used in art and architecture to create pleasing designs. How many can you find in your classroom? In your home? In your neighborhood?

In Chapter 11, you will learn and use formulas to find the volume and surface area of geometric solids.

Goals for Learning

- To identify formulas for determining the volume of solids
- To determine the volume of solids
- To find the surface area of solids
- To use formulas to determine a missing dimension of a solid given its surface area or volume
- To use customary and metric units of measurement

Lesson 1 Basic Volume Formulas

Volume

The measure of the number of unit cubes in a solid figure

Prism

A three-dimensional figure that has congruent polygons as bases in parallel planes and whose sides are parallelograms

In the last chapter, you created a sphere by spinning a circular area around its diameter. In fact, you can create any **volume** by moving an area through space.

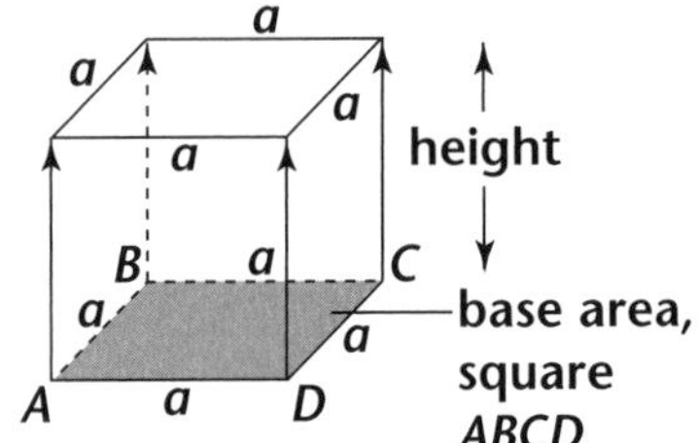

Look at square *ABCD*. Picture what would happen if you moved the square straight up. You could call the distance you moved the square the *height*. You will have created a volume that has a base congruent to the original square *ABCD*. In addition, the figure now has some height, *h*, the distance you moved the square. You have now created a **prism.** The size of the volume is calculated by multiplying the area of the base by the height the base moved.

Start with any area as a base, and the same formula will apply.

Rectangular Box

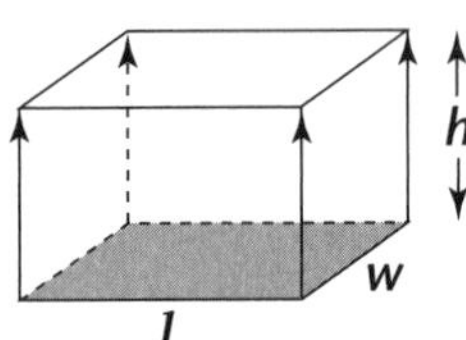

V = (area of base)(height)
$V = (l \bullet w) \bullet h$

Triangular Prism

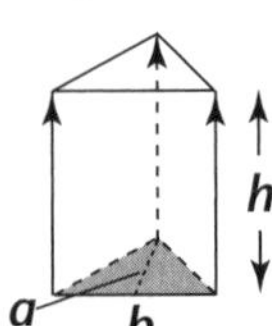

V = (area of base Δ)(height)
$V = (\frac{1}{2}ba)(h)$ where a = altitude of the base Δ

Cylinder

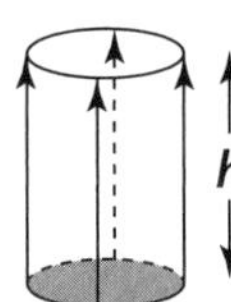

V = (area of base circle)(height)
$V = (\pi r^2)(h)$ when r = radius of the base circle

> **Volume of a solid:**
> V = (area of the base) • (the height)

EXAMPLE 1 What is the volume of a cube with a side of 10 units?

Volume = area of base • height
= area of a square • height
Substitute values:
= (10 • 10)10
= 1,000 cubic units

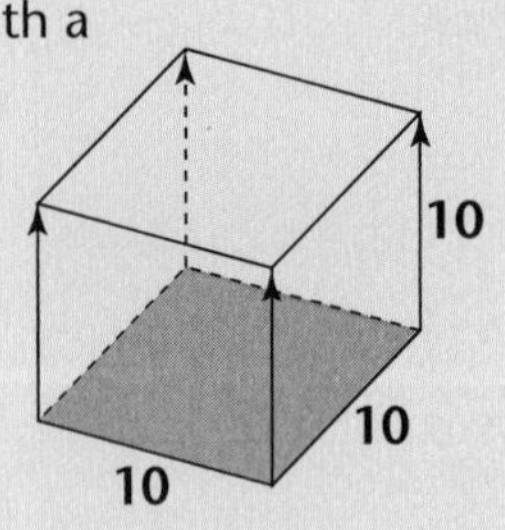

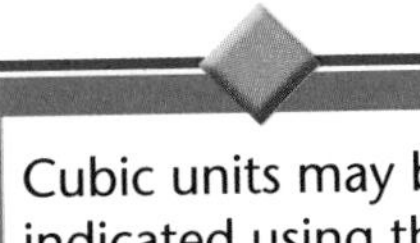

Cubic units may be indicated using the abbreviation *cu*, as in *cu units*, or using the exponent 3, as in $unit^3$.

For three-dimensional measures, the word *cubic* means the basic measure is a unit cube. The cube in Example 1 contains 1,000 of these cubes, so its volume is 1,000 cubic units.

Volume is the measure of the number of unit cubes contained in a solid figure. The figure at the right has a 10×10 base area and height of 1. Its volume is $10 \times 10 \times 1$ or 100 cubic units.

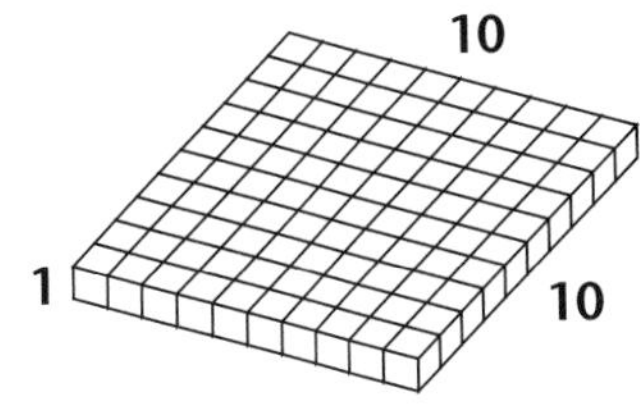

EXAMPLE 2 What is the volume of a rectangular box whose base measures 3 units by 10 units and whose height is 20 units?

V = area of base • height

Substitute values:

= (3 • 10)20

= 600 cubic units

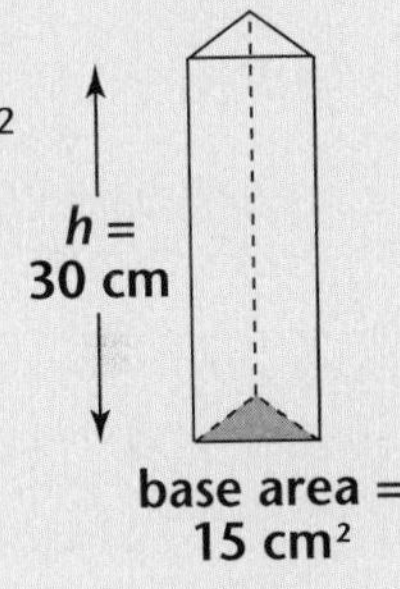

EXAMPLE 3 A triangular prism is a solid whose base is a triangle. For the prism at right, the area of the base is 15 cm^2 and the height is 30 cm. What is the volume of the prism?

V = area of base • height

Substitute values:

= (15 cm^2)30 cm

= 450 cm^3

EXAMPLE 4 A cylindrical tank has a radius of 10 ft and a height of 25 ft. What is its volume? Give your answer in terms of π.

V = area of base • height

Substitute values:

= $(\pi r^2)h$

= $\pi(10^2)(25)$

= 2,500π cu ft

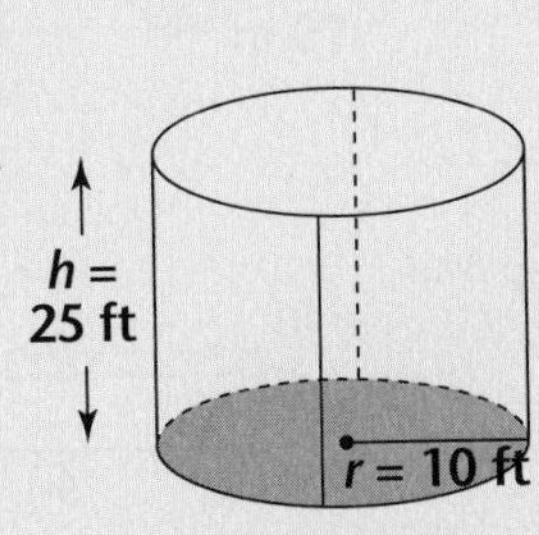

If you do not want your answer in terms of π, substitute an approximation for π. If your answer needs to be accurate to the nearest hundred, you might choose $\pi \approx 3$. If you need an answer to the nearest tenth, you might choose $\pi \approx 3.14$. If you need a more accurate answer, you might choose $\pi \approx 3.1416$. Consider the answer from Example 4, 2,500π cu ft.

Let $\pi \approx 3$	Let $\pi \approx 3.14$	Let $\pi \approx 3.1416$
$V = 2{,}500 \cdot 3$	$V = 2{,}500 \cdot 3.14$	$V = 2{,}500 \cdot 3.1416$
$V = 7{,}500$ cu ft	$V = 7{,}850$ cu ft	$V = 7{,}854$ cu ft

EXAMPLE 5 The volume of a rectangular box is 2,400 cu units. The measurements of the base are 60 × 20. What is the height of the box?

First, draw a sketch. Include the information that is given. Let h be the unknown. Substitute the given values and solve the formula for h.

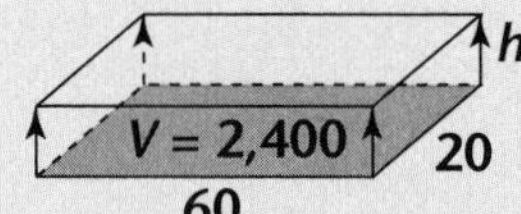

V = area of base • height

$2{,}400 = (60)(20)h$

$2{,}400 = 1{,}200h$

$2 = h$ The height of the box is 2 units.

Exercise A Find the volume of each rectangular solid.

1.

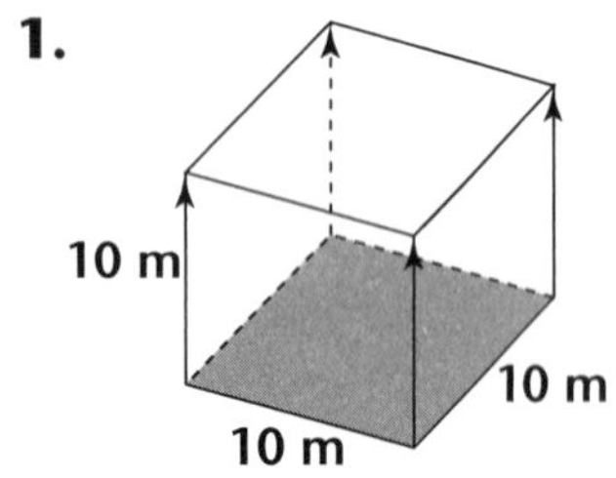

2.

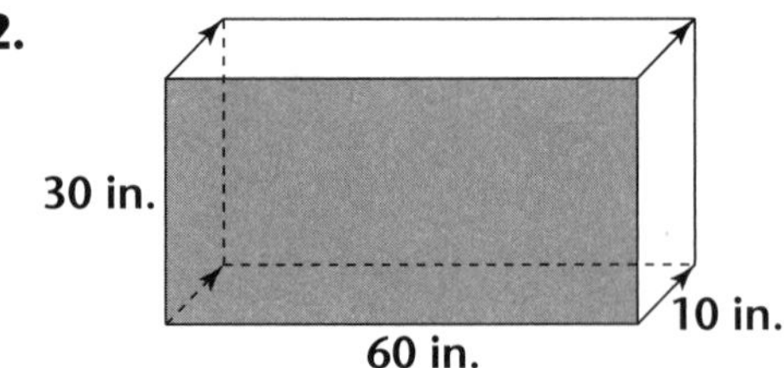

3.

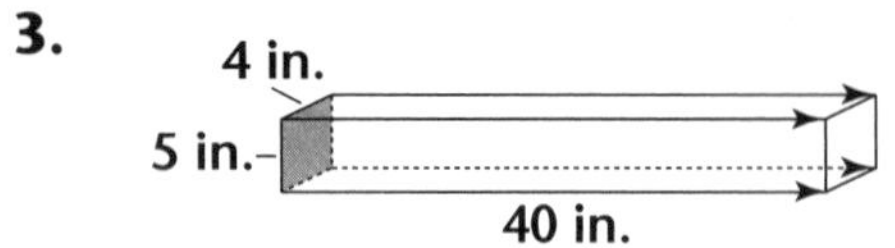

4.

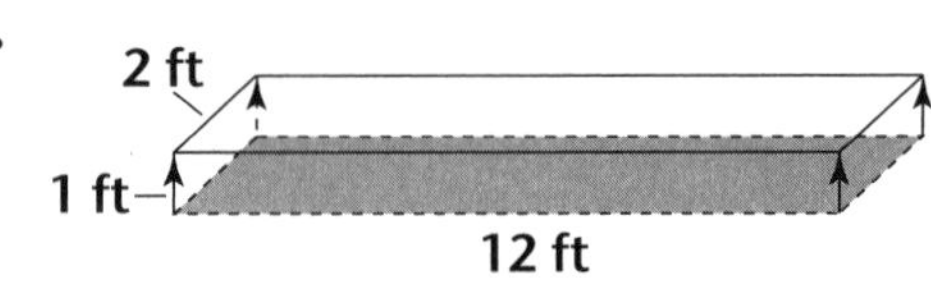

Exercise B Find the volume of each triangular prism.

5. 6 in.

Base area = 24 sq in.

6.

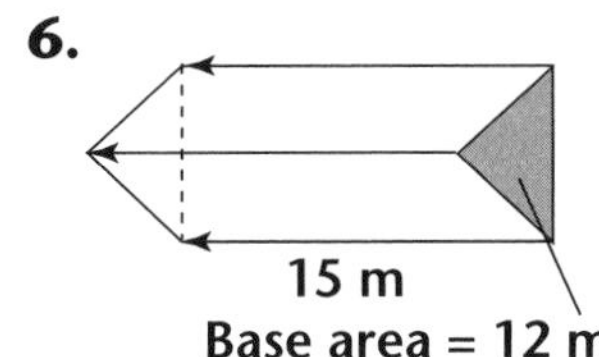

Base area = 12 m^2

7.

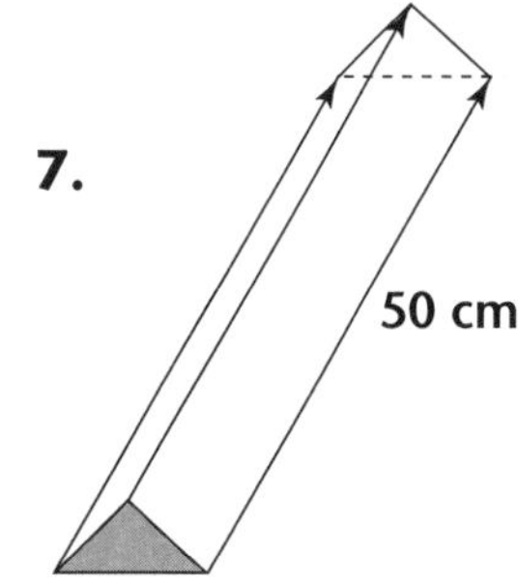

Base area = 30 cm^2

Exercise C Find the volume of each cylinder. Give your answer in terms of π. Then use 3, 3.1, and 3.14 as approximations for π.

Cylinder measurements	V in terms of π	π ≈ 3	π ≈ 3.1	π ≈ 3.14
$r = 10$, 10	**8.** ______	**9.** ______	**10.** ______	**11.** ______
5, $r = 5$	**12.** ______	**13.** ______	**14.** ______	**15.** ______

PROBLEM SOLVING

Exercise D Use what you know about volumes to find the unknown in each item.

16. $h =$ ___

$V = 250$, h

Base area = 25

17. $r =$ ___

r, $h = 30$, $V = 1{,}470\pi$

18. $l =$ ___

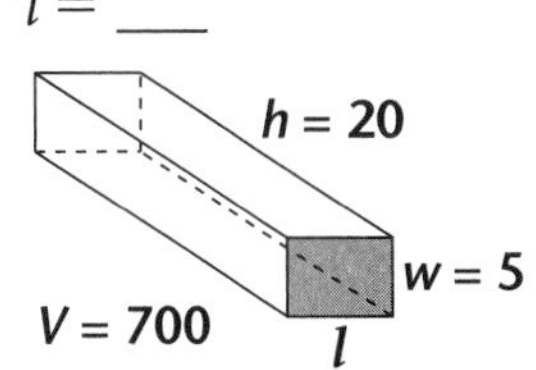

19. $s =$ ___

10, s, $V = 640$, s

20. $s =$ ___

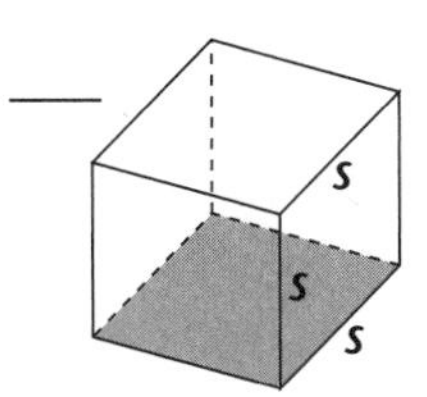

$V = 125$

Lesson 2 Volumes of Pyramids and Cones

Pyramid

A three-dimensional figure with a single base and sides that are triangles

Cone

A three-dimensional figure whose base is a circle and all segments that join the circle to a vertex, V, not in the plane of the circle

A **pyramid** is a three-dimensional figure with a single base and sides that are triangles. The sides of a pyramid meet at a vertex opposite the base. A pyramid can be named by the shape of its base.

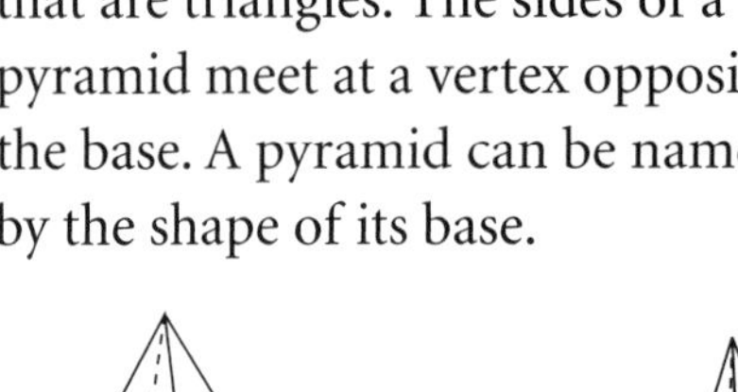

Triangular Pyramid

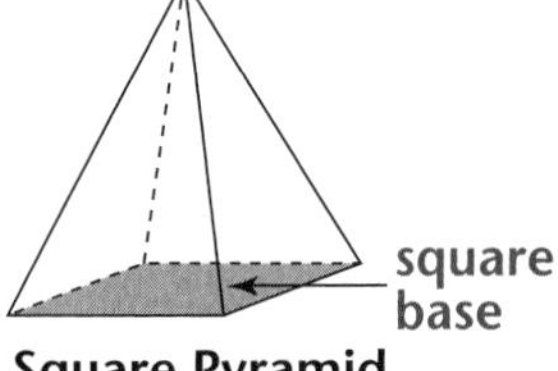

Square Pyramid

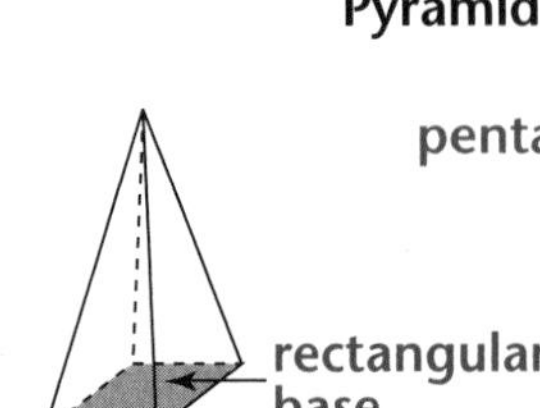

Rectangular Pyramid

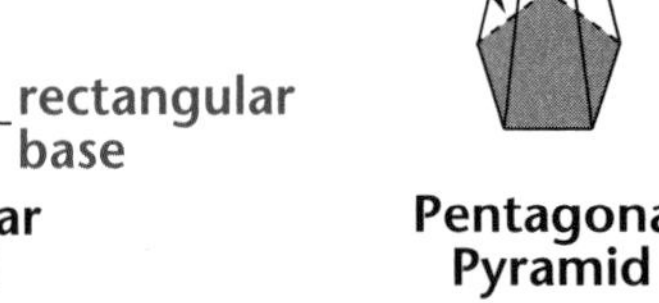

Pentagonal Pyramid

If the base of a pyramid is a circle, the pyramid is called a **cone.**

Cone

Remember, you found the volume of a rectangular prism and a cylinder. How do you think the volume of a pyramid might compare to the volume of a cylinder of similar height?

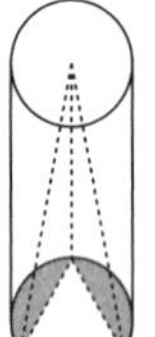

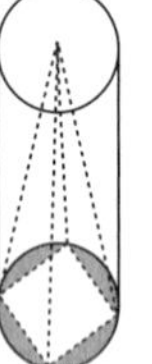

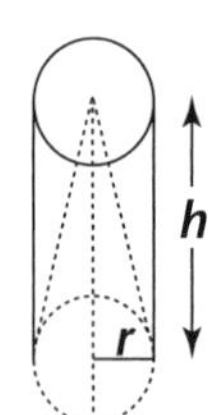

Look at the illustrations. The volumes of the pyramids are completely contained inside the cylinders. The same is true for the volume of the cone—it can be completely contained in a cylinder. The volume of a cone with height h and radius r is less than the volume of a cylinder with the same height and radius. Use this experiment to figure out how the volumes of cones and cylinders are related.

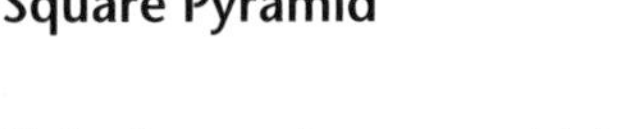

Geometry in Your Life

Would you rather have an ice cream cone or an ice cream cylinder? You can see which can hold the most ice cream by conducting an experiment. You will need a cone and a cylinder with the same radius and height. You may want to choose a cylindrical drinking glass, can, or plastic container and then roll a sheet of paper into a cone shape with the same radius and height. Fill the cone with rice or small beans. Empty the cone into the cylinder. Find how many cones full of rice or beans it takes to fill the cylinder.

From your experiment, you can conclude that the volume of the cone is about one-third of the volume of the cylinder. The correct formula is given here.

Volume of a Cone: $\frac{1}{3}$(area of base)(height) $= \frac{1}{3}\pi r^2 h$

EXAMPLE 1 What is the volume of a cone whose height is 10 units and whose base has radius 5? Express your answer in terms of π.

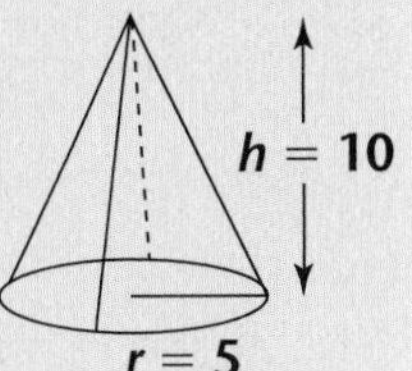

First, make a sketch that shows the given information. Then use the formula.

Volume of cone $= \frac{1}{3}\pi r^2 h$ Substitute values for r and h:

$= \left(\frac{1}{3}\right)(\pi 5^2)(10)$

$= \frac{1}{3}(25\pi)(10)$

$= \left(\frac{250}{3}\right)\pi$ cubic units

Once you have this value, you can use an approximation of π to obtain a decimal value. You can let $\pi = 3$, $\pi = 3.14$, or $\pi = 3.1416$.

Because you already know that a cone is a pyramid with a circular base, you can reason that the formula for the volume of a pyramid will be much like the formula for the volume of a cone.

Volume of a Pyramid: $\frac{1}{3}$(area of base)(height)

EXAMPLE 2 What is the volume of a square pyramid whose height is 15 units and whose base sides are each 5 units?

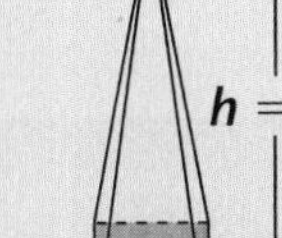

Make a sketch that shows the given information.

Volume of pyramid $= \frac{1}{3}$(area of base)(height)

area of base $= 5^2 = 25$

Volume of pyramid $= \frac{1}{3}$(area of base)(height)

Substitute values for area and h:

$= \frac{1}{3}(25)(15)$

$= (25)(5)$

$= 125$ cubic units

EXAMPLE 3 What is the volume of a triangular pyramid whose base is a 3, 4, 5 right triangle and whose height is 20 units?

Make a sketch.

Volume of pyramid $= \frac{1}{3}$(area of base)(height)

area of base $= \frac{1}{2}bh = \frac{1}{2}(3)(4)$

$= 6$ sq units

Volume of pyramid $= \frac{1}{3}$(area of base)(height)

Substitute values for area and h:

$= \left(\frac{1}{3}\right)(6)(20)$

$= (2)(20)$

$= 40$ cubic units

EXAMPLE 4 What is the height of a cone whose volume is 120 cubic units and whose base radius is 5? Use $\pi = 3.14$.

Make a sketch.

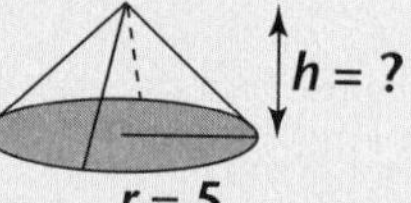

Volume of cone $= \frac{1}{3}$(area of base)(height)

Substitute values in the formula:

$120 = \frac{1}{3}\pi(25)h$

$120 = (\frac{25}{3})\pi h$ multiply

$120 = \frac{25}{3}(3.14)h$ use $\pi \approx 3.14$

$120 \approx 26.17h$ solve for h

$h \approx 4.59$

Exercise A Find the volume of each cone. Give your answer in terms of π. Then use 3, 3.1, and 3.14 as approximations for π.

Measurements	V in terms of π	$\pi \approx 3$	$\pi \approx 3.1$	$\pi \approx 3.14$
$r = 10, h = 10$	**1.** ______	**2.** ______	**3.** ______	**4.** ______
$r = 6, h = 12$	**5.** ______	**6.** ______	**7.** ______	**8.** ______
$r = 3, h = 4$	**9.** ______	**10.** ______	**11.** ______	**12.** ______

Exercise B Find the volume of each pyramid. Be sure to make and label a sketch for each.

13. $s = 10$ in.,
$h = 10$ in.

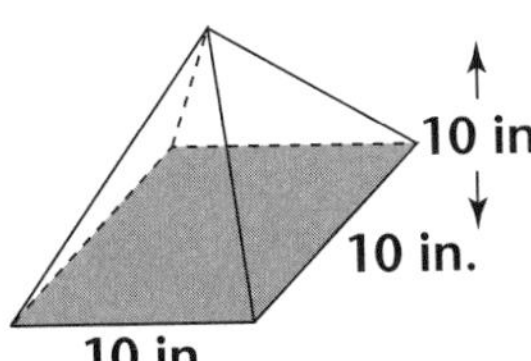

14. $l = 8$ ft,
$w = 5$ ft,
$h = 15$ ft

15 ft
5 ft
8 ft

15. base area = 20 cm^2,
$h = 12$ cm

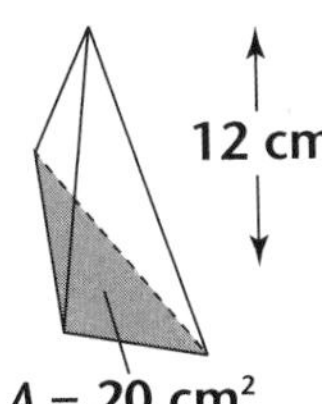

16. Square pyramid: $s = 5$ in., $h = 50$ in.

17. Triangular pyramid: base area = 15 m^2, $h = 20$ m

Exercise C Use the formula for the volume of a pyramid or cone to find the value of the unknown. Use $\pi = 3.1$.

18. $V = 80$ cm^3, $w =$ ___

19. $V = 8{,}906.3$ cu in., $r =$ ___

20. $V = 700$ cu ft, $w =$ ___

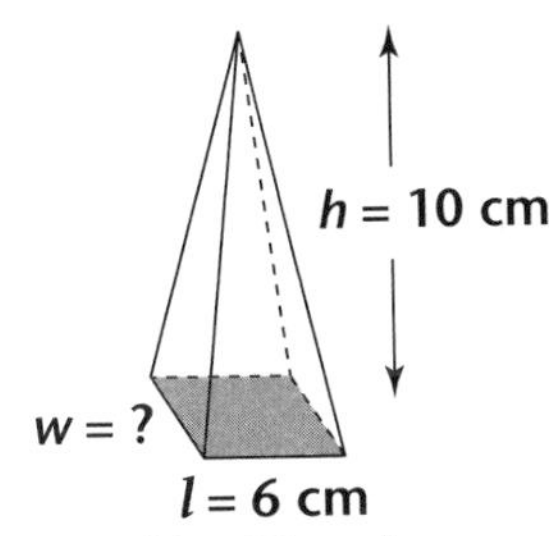

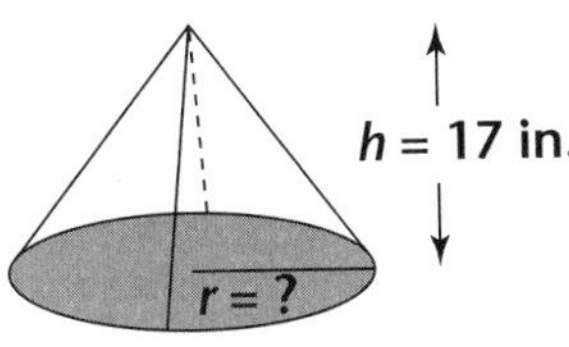

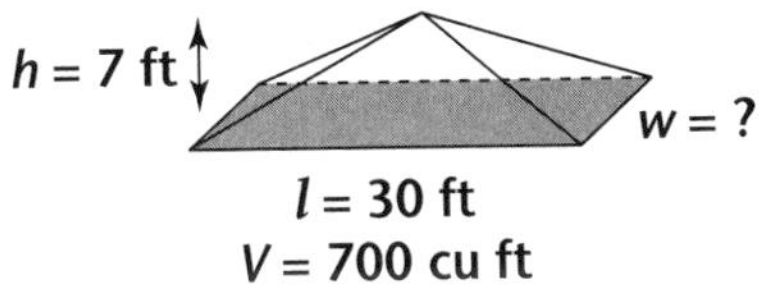

Estimation Activity

Estimate: What is the approximate volume of a square pyramid with $s = 11$ cm, and $h = 14$ cm?

Solution: 10 cm × 10 cm = 100 cm^2 — Round the side length and find the area of the base.

14 cm ≈ 15 cm — Round the height to the nearest multiple of 3

15 cm ÷ 3 = 5 cm — and divide by 3.

(100 cm^2)(5 cm) = 500 cm^3 — Multiply.

So, the volume is about 500 cm^3.

Lesson 3 Surface Areas of Prisms and Cylinders

Net

The two-dimensional representation of the surface of a three-dimensional figure

In addition to volume, three-dimensional figures also have another measurable characteristic—surface area. The surface area of a three-dimensional geometric figure can be computed by adding the areas of its faces. We can see this more easily with all of the faces in the same plane. If the surfaces are connected so the figure can be folded up into the three-dimensional solid, then the figure is called a **net**.

Technology Connection

Musicians record music in sound-proof rooms so no external sound is accidentally recorded. These rooms may be lined with foam padding or embedded with foam pyramids. The pyramid shape aids in the disruption of sound waves and allows the padding to absorb the sound more easily.

Cube

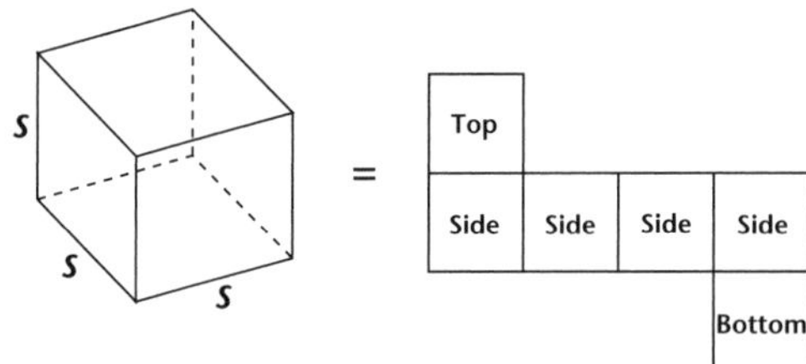

Total surface area of cube = area of 6 squares

Total surface area = 2(area of base) + 4(area of a side)

Surface Area of a Cube:

Surface area = $6s^2$

Rectangular Prism

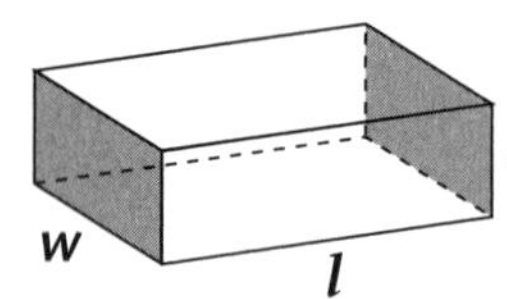

$$
\begin{aligned}
\text{Area} &= 2(lw) + h(l + w + l + w)\\
&= 2(lw) + h(2l + 2w)\\
&= 2lw + 2hl + 2hw\\
\text{Area} &= \text{base and top} + \text{two larger sides} + \text{two smaller sides}
\end{aligned}
$$

Surface Area of a Rectangular Prism:

Surface area = $2(lw + hl + hw)$

Right prism

Prism in which the base and the sides are at right angles

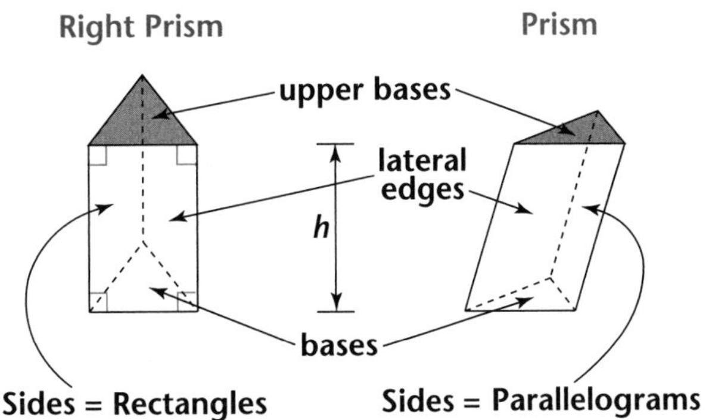

Cubes and rectangular prisms can be grouped as **right prisms.** In a right prism, the side surfaces are perpendicular to the base and the upper surface. The total surface area is the sum of the areas of the base, the upper surface (top), and the sides. The side surfaces are rectangles. In prisms that are not right prisms, the sides are parallelograms.

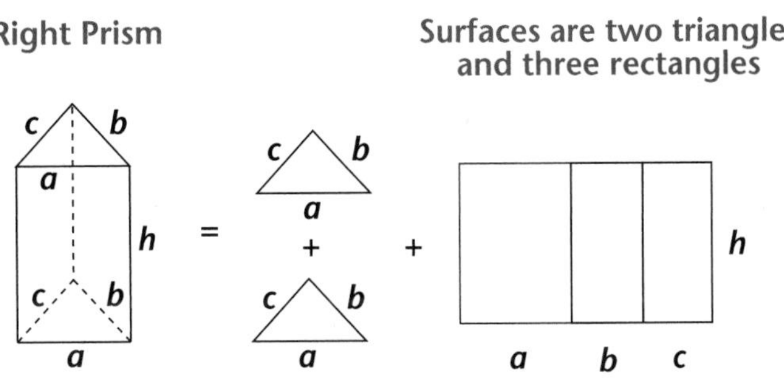

Surface Area of a Right Prism:

Surface area = 2(area of triangle) + $h(a + b + c)$

If the side surfaces of a prism are not perpendicular to the base and top, the sides are parallelograms.

Triangular Prism

Surfaces are two triangles and three parallelograms

c b a h = + + a b c

A cylinder whose parallel bases are circles requires a special formula.

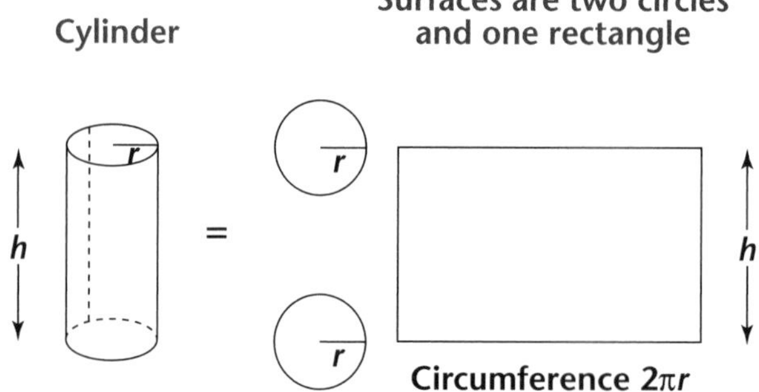

The formula for a cylinder's surface area can be rewritten as $2\pi r(r + h)$. This form may be easier to use when you have to do the calculation by hand.

Surface Area of a Cylinder:
Surface area $= 2\pi r^2 + (2\pi r)h$

You can use these formulas to calculate the surface areas of some of the most common three-dimensional objects.

EXAMPLE 1 What is the total surface area of a cube whose side is 5 units long?

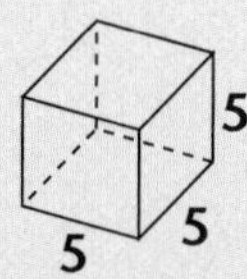

Sketch the net including all the surfaces of the cube.

Surface area of cube $= 6s^2$

$= 6(5^2) = 6(25)$

$= 150$ sq units

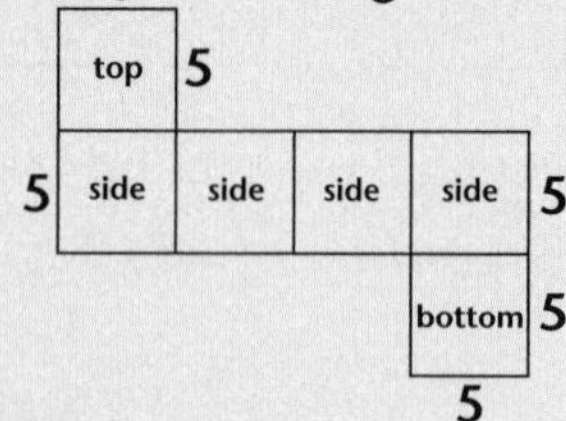

EXAMPLE 2 What is the total surface area of a box that is 10 in. on a side and has no lid?

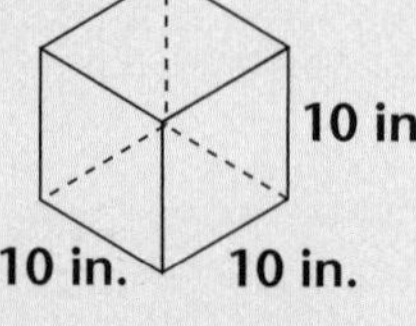

Sketch the net including all the surfaces of the box.

Surface area of cube $= 5s^2$

$= 5(10^2) = 5(100)$

$= 500$ sq in.

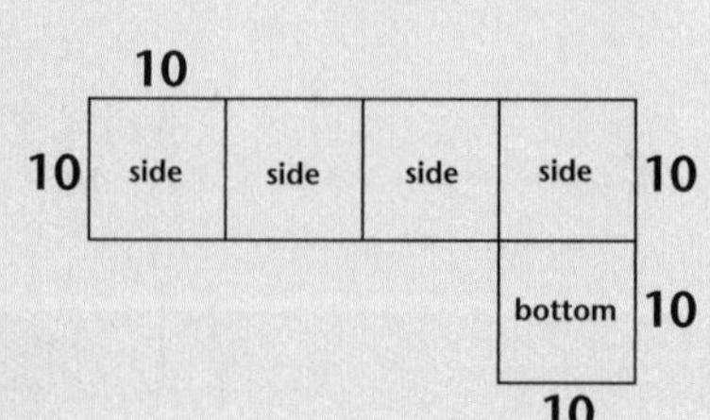

EXAMPLE 3 Calculate the total surface area of a rectangular box whose dimensions are 10 • 8 • 5.

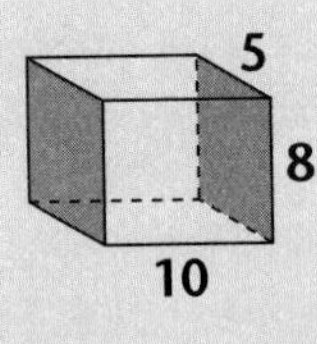

Sketch the net including all the surfaces of the box.

Surface area of rectangular prism = $2(lw + hl + hw)$

let $l = 10$, $w = 5$, $h = 8$

Surface area $= 2[(8 \bullet 10) + (5 \bullet 10) + (8 \bullet 5)]$

$= 160 + 100 + 80$

$= 340$ sq units

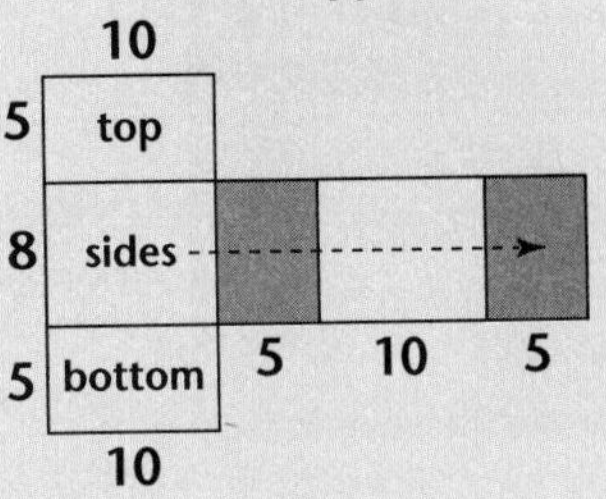

EXAMPLE 4 What size label is needed to cover only the sides of a can whose radius is 2 in. and whose height is 7 in.?

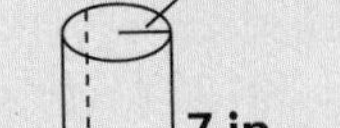

Sketch each surface of the cylinder.

surface area $= l \bullet w$

$w = 7$

l = circumference $= 2\pi r$

$= 2\pi 2 = 4\pi$

surface area $= 7(4\pi)$

$= 28\pi$ sq in.

Exercise A Find the surface area of each of the following three-dimensional figures. Some answers may include square roots or π.

1.

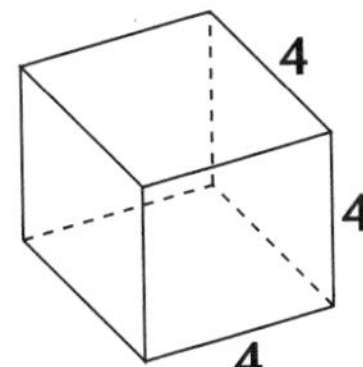

2.

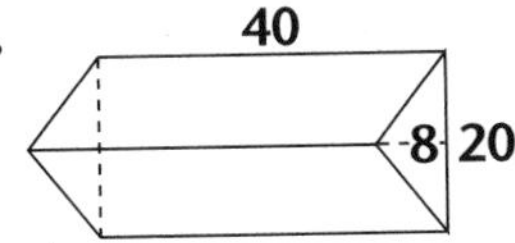

3.

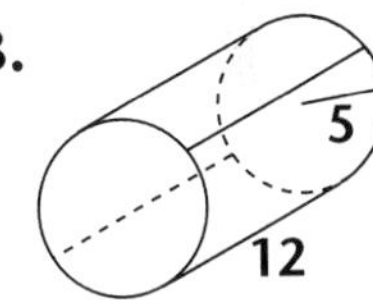

Exercise B Solve the following problems. You may leave some answers in terms of radicals or π.

4. What is the surface area of a 12-in.-tall cylindrical vase whose radius is 4 in.?

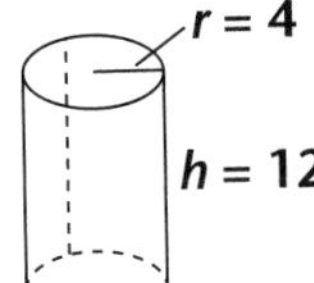

5. Juanita plans to paint the walls and ceiling of a room bright green. The room is 10 ft wide and 12 ft long. The ceilings are 9 ft above the floor. She has one can of paint that covers 500 sq ft. Will it be enough? Why?

Lesson 4 Surface Areas of Pyramids and Cones

Slant height l

Distance from the base of a cone to the vertex or from the midpoint of a base side to the vertex of a pyramid

In the previous lesson, you found the area of each side of a three-dimensional figure and then added the areas. You can use the same method to find the surface areas of pyramids and cones. First, separate the base of the pyramid (a polygon) from its sides (triangles). Here is an example using a square pyramid.

The area of each of the four side triangles is found using the base of the triangle and a measurement called the **slant height** of the pyramid. Think of the slant height as the straight-line distance you would have to climb from the midpoint of a base to the top of the pyramid. The symbol for slant height is l.

$$\text{Surface area of square pyramid} = s \cdot s + \tfrac{1}{2}sl + \tfrac{1}{2}sl + \tfrac{1}{2}sl + \tfrac{1}{2}sl$$
$$= s^2 + 2sl$$

Surface Area of a Square Pyramid:

Surface area = area of base + areas of four triangles
$= s^2 + 2sl$

The surface area of a cone is found in much the same way. Think of cutting the surface of the cone from the base to the vertex. Then flatten the surface. You will see that the surface of the cone is made up of the surfaces of two areas. One is a circle with radius r. The other is much like a triangle with a base that is equal to the circumference of the circle and a height that is the slant height of the cone.

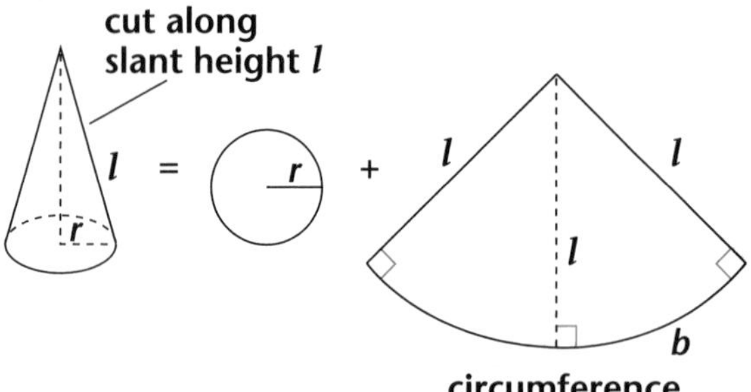

Surface area of a cone $= \pi r^2 + \frac{1}{2}bl$

In this case, the base of the triangle, b, equals the circumference of the circle. The height of the triangle is the slant height, l, of the cone.

$$= \pi r^2 \quad + \quad \frac{1}{2}(2\pi r \cdot l)$$
$$= \pi r^2 \quad + \quad \pi r l$$
$$= \pi r(r + l)$$

> **Surface Area of a Cone:**
> Surface area = area of base + area of sides
> $= \pi r(r + l) = \pi r^2 + \frac{1}{2}bl$

Each of these formulas can be used to find the total surface areas of square pyramids and cones.

EXAMPLE 1 Find the areas of the sides and then the total surface area of the square pyramid with the given dimensions.

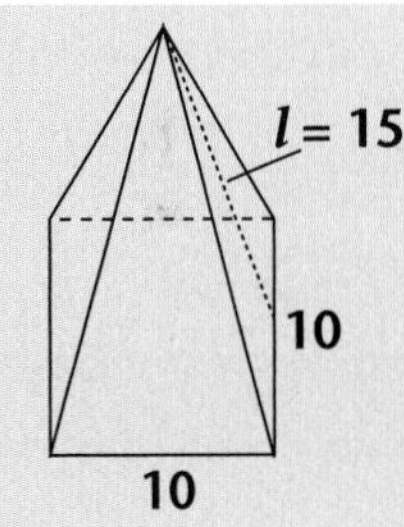

Sketch all the surfaces of the pyramid.
Surface area of pyramid = area of base + areas of four triangles
Surface area of base = 10 • 10 = 100 sq units
Surface area of pyramid sides = areas of four triangles

Surface area of pyramid sides $= 4\left(\frac{1}{2}\right)(sl)$ $s = 10, l = 15$

$= 4\left(\frac{1}{2}\right)(10)(15) = 2(150)$

= 300 sq units

10 + 15 + 15 + 15 + 15
10 10 10 10 10

Surface area of pyramid = 100 sq units + 300 sq units = 400 sq units

EXAMPLE 2 What is the surface area of a cone whose radius is 5 and whose slant height is 10?

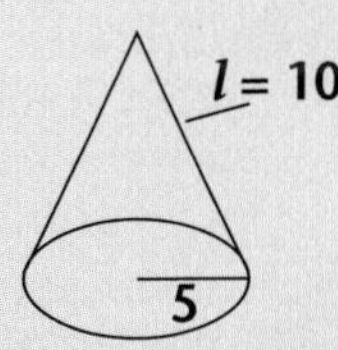

Sketch the surface.
Surface area of cone = area of circular base + area of triangle

$= \pi r^2 + \frac{1}{2}bl$

b = the circumference of the circle $= 2\pi r = 2\pi 5$, $l = 10$

Surface area of cone $= \pi 5^2 + \frac{1}{2}(2\pi 5)(10)$

$= \pi 25 + \pi 50$

$= 75\pi$ sq units

5

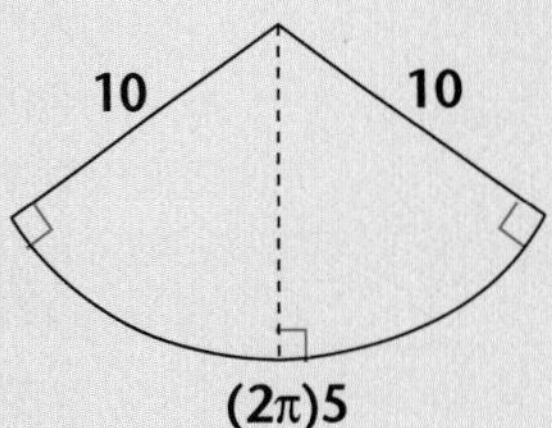

As with cylinders, you can substitute 3, 3.1, 3.14, or another approximation for π.

EXAMPLE 3 Find the total surface area of the triangular pyramid whose base measures 10 units on a side and whose slant height is 25 units.

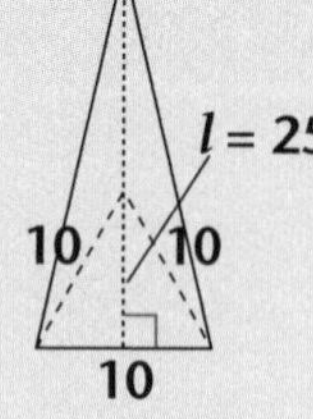

Sketch all the surfaces of the pyramid.

Surface area of pyramid = area of base + areas of three triangles

Surface area of pyramid sides = areas of three triangles

$= 3(\frac{1}{2})(sl) \qquad s = 10, l = 25$

$= 3(\frac{1}{2})(10)(25) = 3(5 \bullet 25) = 375$ sq units

Surface area of base $= \frac{1}{2}(sh)$

$s = 10$ but you must find the value of h:

Using the Pythagorean Theorem:

$10^2 = 5^2 + h^2$

$100 = 25 + h^2$

$75 = h^2$

$\sqrt{3 \bullet 25} = h$

$5\sqrt{3} = h$

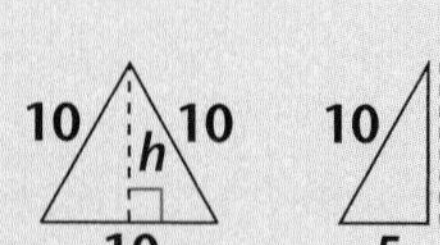

Surface area of base $= \frac{1}{2}(sh) = \frac{1}{2}(10)(5\sqrt{3}) = 25\sqrt{3}$

Surface area of pyramid = area of base + areas of three triangles $= 25\sqrt{3} + 375$ sq units

Exercise A Find the surface areas of these pyramids and cones.

1.

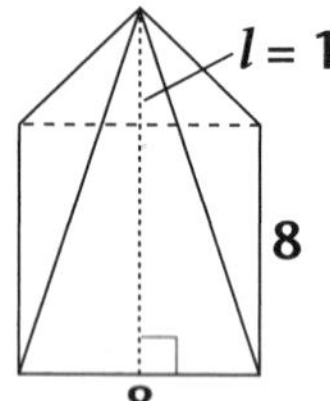

2.

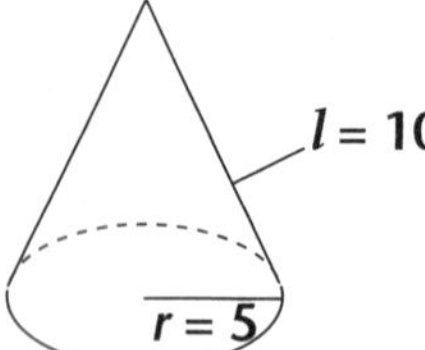

3. $l = 10$, 8, 8, 8

Calculator Practice

You can use your calculator to find the missing value in a proportion.

Exercise B Find the squares and square roots of the following numbers. Use a calculator and round to the nearest hundredth if necessary.

4. 16

5. 18

6. 24

7. 23

8. 19

PROBLEM SOLVING

Exercise C Solve the following problems.

9. Roger has to make a model tepee for social studies class. He has a triangle with the dimensions shown. Can he make a wigwam whose base radius is 8 ft? Explain.

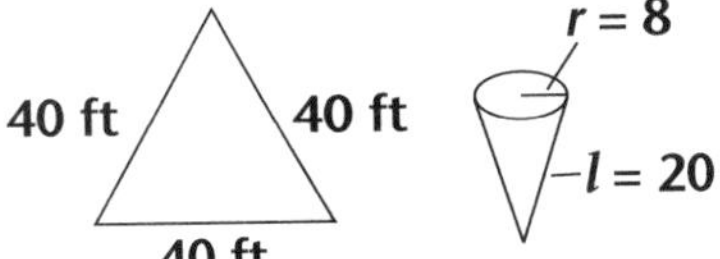

10. The largest of the Egyptian pyramids, built for Pharaoh Khufu, is a square pyramid with the dimensions shown. What is the surface area of the sides of Khufu's pyramid?

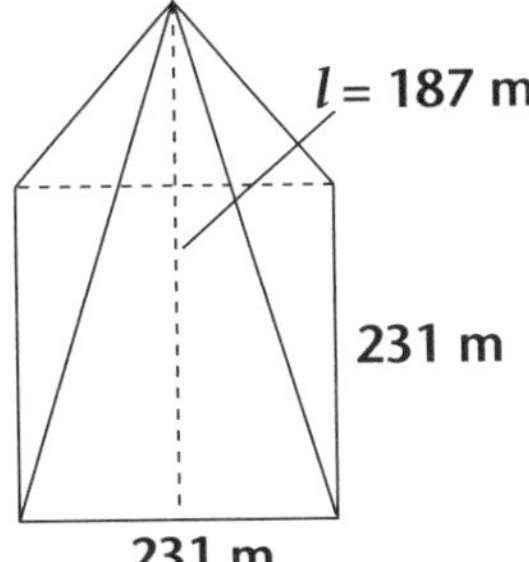

Writing About Mathematics

Are the areas of the sides of these two pyramids equal? Explain. (Hint: You may use numbers to test your idea. Do not include the area of the base.)

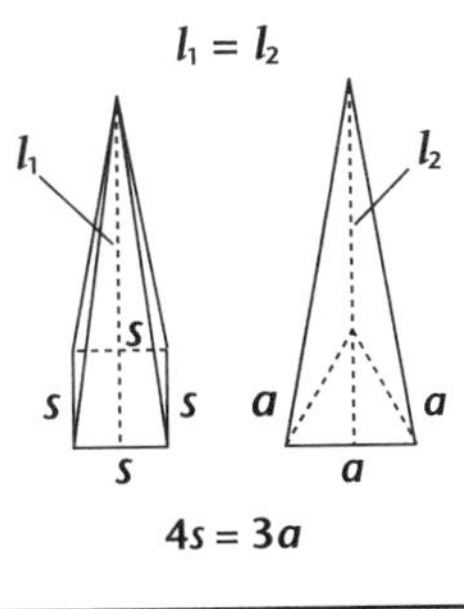

TRY THIS Find the surface area of a pyramid whose sides have a slant height of 20 units and whose base is a rectangle 10 units long and 5 units wide.

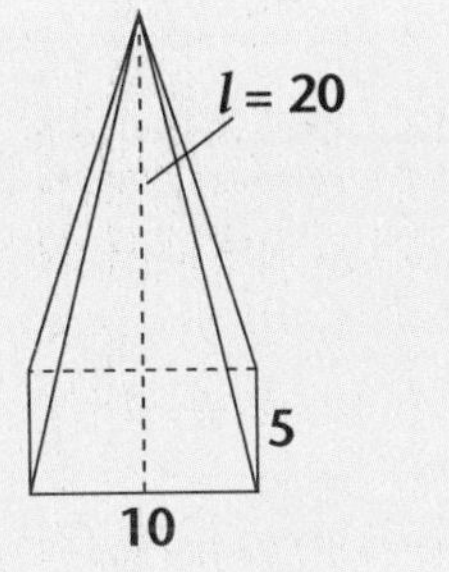

The ancient Egyptians weren't the only ones to use pyramids in their architecture. You can see the shape of a pyramid in the traditional Chinese bell tower as well as these modern skylights.

Lesson 5 Measurements

Customary

Usual or common, ordinary; system of measurement used mostly in the United States; inches and cups are basic units

Capacity

The amount a container will hold when full

Metric

System of measurement based on powers of ten; grams and meters are basic units

In your study of surface areas and volumes, you used measurements from two different systems. In the United States, most measurements are given in **customary** units—the units of length are inch (in.), foot (ft), yard (yd), and mile (mi).

To convert one measurement unit to another, you need to know the relationship between the units.

1 ft = 12 in.	1 yd = 3 ft	1 mi = 1,760 yd
	1 yd = 36 in.	1 mi = 5,280 ft

The customary system has a special unit for area, the acre.

1 sq yd = 9 sq ft

1 acre = 43,560 sq ft = 4,840 sq yd

There are customary units for **capacity** and weight as well.

Capacity	1 cup = 8 fluid ounces	2 pints = 1 quart
	2 cups = 1 pint	4 quarts = 1 gallon
Weight	1 pound = 16 ounces	2,000 pounds = 1 ton

You can use these relationships to change one unit of measurement to another.

A centimeter is about the width of your little finger.

EXAMPLE 1 A car has a total length of 2 yd 1 ft. How many feet long is the car? How many inches?

2 yd = 2 • 3 ft = 6 ft   so 2 yd 1 ft = 7 ft

7 ft = 7 • 12 in. = 84 in.

Most of the world uses the **metric** measurement system. In the metric system, the basic unit of length is the meter (m). Other units in the metric system are formed by multiplying the meter by positive or negative powers of ten. Some of the other units of length are centimeter (cm), decimeter (dm), and kilometer (km).

To convert one measurement to another, you need to know the relationship between the measurements.

10 cm = 1 dm	10 dm = 1 m	1,000 m = 1 km
	100 cm = 1 m	

The metric system also has a basic unit for capacity—the liter—and for mass—the gram. (Mass is the amount of matter in an object.)

With customary units, you need to remember many different ratios for units of length, capacity, and weight. In the metric system, you need to remember the prefix that names the power of ten used in the unit.

Prefix	milli-	centi-	deci-	Basic Unit	kilo-
Power of ten	10^{-3} 0.001	10^{-2} 0.01	10^{-1} 0.1	10^{0} 1	10^{3} 1,000
Length	millimeter (mm)	centimeter (cm)	decimeter (dm)	meter (m)	kilometer (km)
Capacity	milliliter (ml)	centiliter (cl)	deciliter (dl)	liter (l)	kiloliter (kl)
Mass	milligram (mg)	centigram (cg)	decigram (dg)	gram (g)	kilogram (kg)

Algebra Review

The use of a negative exponent has a special meaning: $a^{-x} = \frac{1}{a^x}$. For example, $10^{-3} = \frac{1}{1,000} = 0.001$.

A list of measurement conversion factors can be found on pages 514–515 of this textbook. These tables can also be used to change measurements from customary to metric units or from metric to customary units.

EXAMPLE 2 A fund-raising race is advertised as a 5K race. The K stands for kilometers (usually abbreviated km). How many meters long is the race? How many centimeters?

1 km = 1,000 m, so 5 km = 5 • 1,000 m = 5,000 m

1 m = 100 cm, so 5,000 m = 5,000 • 100 cm = 500,000 cm

Exercise A Complete each statement.

1. 12 yd = ___ in.
2. 14 pounds = ___ ounces
3. 1 mi = ___ in.
4. 8 pints = ___ gal
5. 1 sq yd = ___ sq ft
6. 13 cm = ___ mm
7. 15 kg = ___ g
8. 22 l = ___ ml
9. 10 km = ___ cm
10. 12.5 cm = ___ mm

Lesson 6 Algebra Connection: Radicals in Equations

> **Radical**
> *An expression written with a radical sign, such as $\sqrt{2}$*
>
> **Radicand**
> *Expression inside a radical sign; example: in $\sqrt{a + b}$, $a + b$ is the radicand*

Suppose the area of a square is 100 square units. How long is each side of the square?

$(10)^2 = 10 \cdot 10 = 100$

$(\sqrt{100})^2 = \sqrt{100} \cdot \sqrt{100}$
$= 100$

Area = 100 $\sqrt{100} = 10$

$\sqrt{100} = 10$

In general, $(\sqrt{A})(\sqrt{A}) = (\sqrt{A})^2$
$= A.$

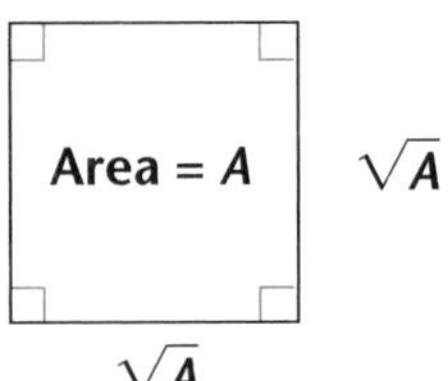

$\sqrt{A}$ and $\sqrt{100}$ are called **radicals,** and A and 100 under the square root sign are called **radicands.**

We can use the fact that $(\sqrt{x})^2 = x$ to solve equations with radicals.

Example 1 Solve for x when $\sqrt{2x} = 4$.

Step 1 Square both sides of the equation. Then solve.

$(\sqrt{2x})^2 = 4^2$
$2x = 16$
$x = 8$

Step 2 Check: Substitute 8 for x in $\sqrt{2x} = 4$.

$\sqrt{2(8)} = 4$
$\sqrt{16} = 4$ True

Example 2 Find x when $\sqrt{x - 1} = 7$.

Step 1 Square both sides of the equation. Then solve.

$(\sqrt{x - 1})^2 = 7^2$
$x - 1 = 49$
$x = 50$

Step 2 Check: Substitute 50 for x in $\sqrt{x - 1} = 7$.

$\sqrt{50 - 1} = 7$
$\sqrt{49} = 7$ True

Remember:

$(-) \bullet (-) = (+)$

$(-) \bullet (+) = (-)$

$(+) \bullet (-) = (-)$

$(+) \bullet (+) = (+)$

And:

$(-\sqrt{x})^2 = x$, since $(-\sqrt{x})^2 = (-\sqrt{x})(-\sqrt{x})$ and $(-) \bullet (-) = (+)$

EXAMPLE 3 Find x when $10 - \sqrt{5x} = 6$

Step 1 Get the term with the variable by itself.

$$10 - \sqrt{5x} = 6$$
$$-\sqrt{5x} = 6 - 10$$
$$-\sqrt{5x} = -4$$

Step 2 Square both sides of the equation. Then solve.

$$(-\sqrt{5x})^2 = (-4)^2$$
$$5x = 16$$
$$x = \frac{16}{5}$$

Step 3 Check: Substitute $\frac{16}{5}$ for x in $10 - \sqrt{5x} = 6$.

$$10 - \sqrt{5\left(\frac{16}{5}\right)} = 6$$
$$10 - \sqrt{16} = 6$$
$$10 - 4 = 6 \rightarrow \quad 6 = 6 \quad \text{True}$$

Exercise A Solve for x. Check your work.

1. $\sqrt{3x} = 6$
2. $\sqrt{2x} = 5$
3. $\sqrt{7x} = 5$
4. $-\sqrt{5x} = -10$
5. $-\sqrt{10x} = -20$
6. $\sqrt{x - 2} = 5$
7. $\sqrt{x - 3} = 9$
8. $\sqrt{x + 3} = 10$
9. $\sqrt{x + 5} = 9$
10. $-\sqrt{x + 2} = -12$

Exercise B Solve for x. Check your work.

11. $5 - \sqrt{x} = 1$
12. $9 - \sqrt{2x} = 6$
13. $\sqrt{3x} + 1 = 10$
14. $-\sqrt{2x} + 12 = -4$
15. $4 + \sqrt{6x} = 10$
16. $\sqrt{x + 5} + 4 = 11$
17. $15 - \sqrt{6x + 3} = 6$
18. $3\sqrt{2x} = 36$
19. $2\sqrt{3x - 2} = 10$
20. $4\sqrt{12 - x} = 16$

Application

Origami You already know that you can bend a sheet of paper to form a three-dimensional surface such as a cylinder or cone. You probably also realize that you can fold paper to make many geometric as well as fanciful three-dimensional figures. The Japanese art of paper folding, often called *origami*, offers a way to make hundreds of different figures. Each uses only a single sheet of paper.

EXAMPLE 1 Make a rectangular box following these eight steps.

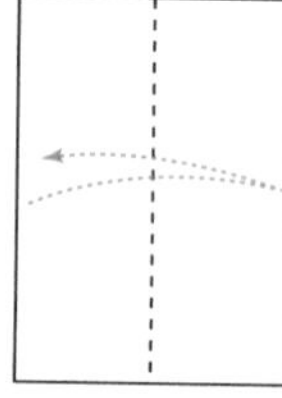

1. Fold paper in half, crease, and open.

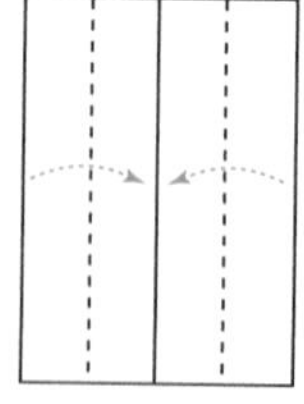

2. Fold each edge to meet center crease.

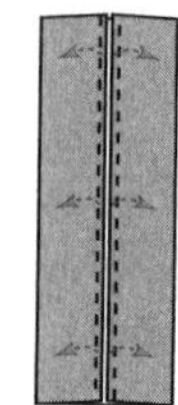

3. Make a small outward fold along long edges. Crease.

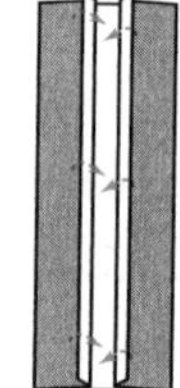

4. Undo fold from Step 3.

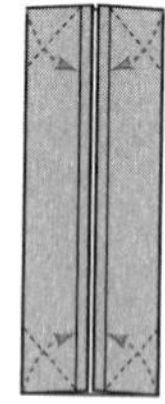

5. Make 45° fold at each corner.

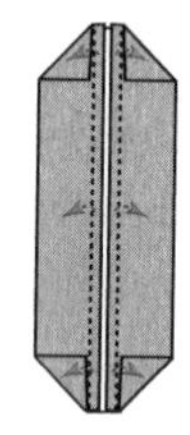

6. Open fold from Step 3.

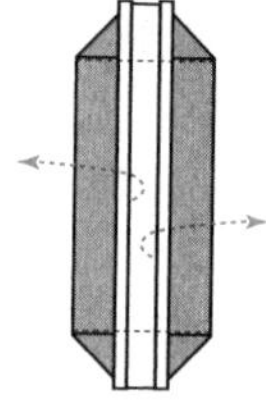

7. Lift flaps and form box.

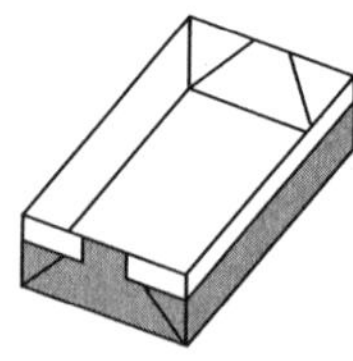

8. You may need to square the corners.

Exercise Construct another rectangular box.

1. Find the area of the sheet of paper you plan to use for your box.

2. Fold the paper to make the box.

3. Find the outside surface area of your completed box.

4. Find the ratio of the surface area of the completed box to the surface area of the original sheet of paper.

5. Compare results with your classmates.

Chapter 11 REVIEW

Write the letter of the correct answer.

1. The volume of a square prism equals ___ .

A (base area)(area of sides) **C** $\frac{1}{3}$(base)(height)

B (base area)(height) **D** $\frac{1}{2}$(base)(height)

2. The surface area of a cylinder equals ___ .

A $\pi r^2 h$

B $2\pi r^2 h$

C $2\pi r^2 + 2\pi rh$

D $2\pi r^2 + 2\pi r^2 h$

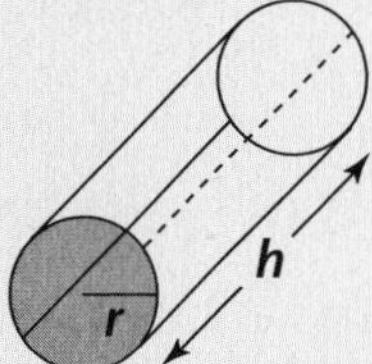

3. What is the volume of the triangular prism below?

A 12,600 cm^3

B 16,800 cm^3

C 25,200 cm^3

D 50,400 cm^3

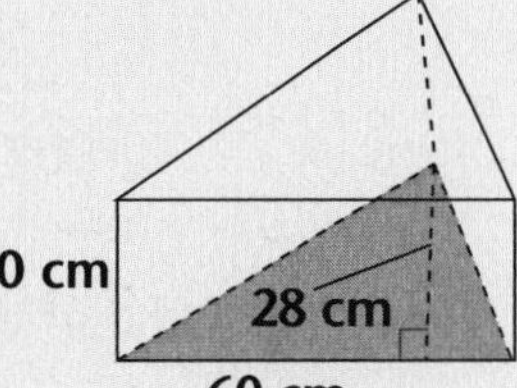

4. Each edge of a cube has a length of 9 inches. What is the surface area of this cube?

A 324 sq in. **C** 648 sq in.

B 486 sq in. **D** 729 sq in.

5. How many milligrams are there in 1 kilogram?

A 1,000,000 **C** 10,000

B 100,000 **D** 1,000

State the formula.

Example: What is the volume of the rectangular solid shown below?
Solution: *lwh*

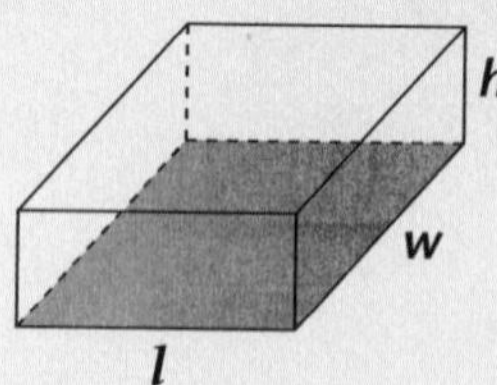

6. What is the surface area of the rectangular solid shown above?

7. What is the volume of a cube in which each edge has length *s*?

8. What is the volume of the square pyramid shown to the right?

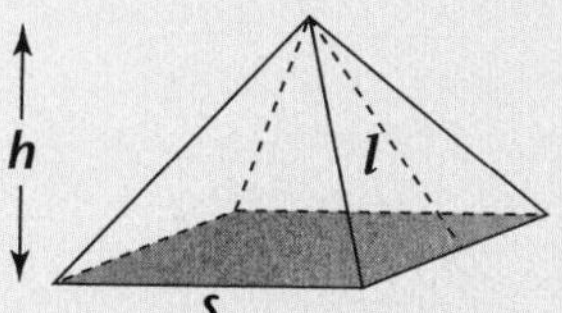

9. What is the surface area of the square pyramid shown in problem 8?

Find the volume and total surface area for each figure. You may give your answers in terms of π.

Example:

12 in.
2 in.
10 in.

Solution: Volume
$l \bullet w \bullet h = 12 \bullet 10 \bullet 2 = 240$ cu in.
Total Surface Area
$2(lw + hl + hw) = 2(10 \bullet 12 + 2 \bullet 12 + 2 \bullet 10)$
$2(120 + 24 + 20) = 2(164) = 328$ sq in.

10. Volume

11. Total Surface Area

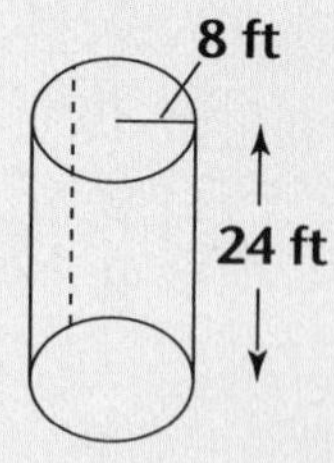

12. Volume

13. Total Surface Area

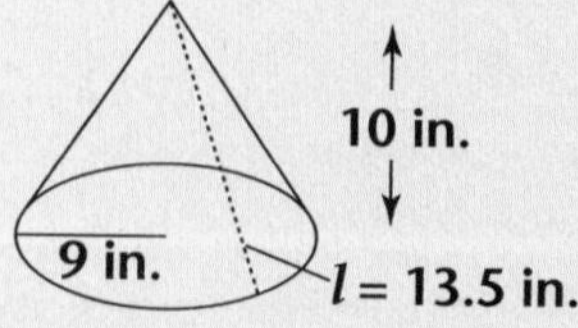

Use what you know about surface areas and volumes to find the unknowns.

Example: The topless box has a surface area of 125 sq in. What is the length of a side, s, of the box?

Solution: The topless box has 5 sides. Divide the area by 5. $125 \div 5 = 25$. Take the square root of 25 to find the length of side s. $\sqrt{25} = 5$ in.

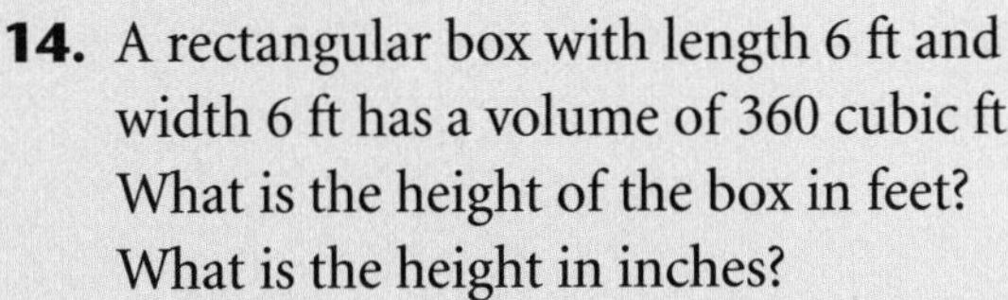

14. A rectangular box with length 6 ft and width 6 ft has a volume of 360 cubic ft. What is the height of the box in feet? What is the height in inches?

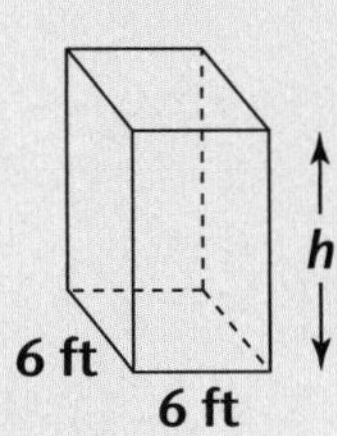

15. The volume of a cylinder is 600π cm^3, and its height is 18 cm. What is the approximate radius of the cylinder?

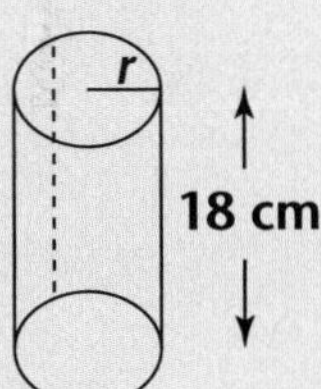

16. The volume of a cone is 600π cm^3, and its height is 18 cm. What is the radius of the cone in cm? What is the radius in dm?

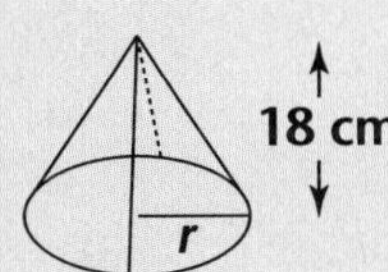

Find the equivalent measurement.

Example: How many ounces are equal to 8 pounds?
Solution: Since 1 pound equals 16 ounces,
8 pounds equals $8 \times 16 = 128$ ounces.

17. How many grams are equal to 12 kilograms?

18. How many pints are equal to 7 gallons?

19. How many centimeters are equal to 500 millimeters?

20. How many yards are equal to $\frac{1}{4}$ mile?

Test-Taking Tip

Read each test question twice. Read first to get the big idea. Then read again to gather specific numbers and other information needed to solve the problem.

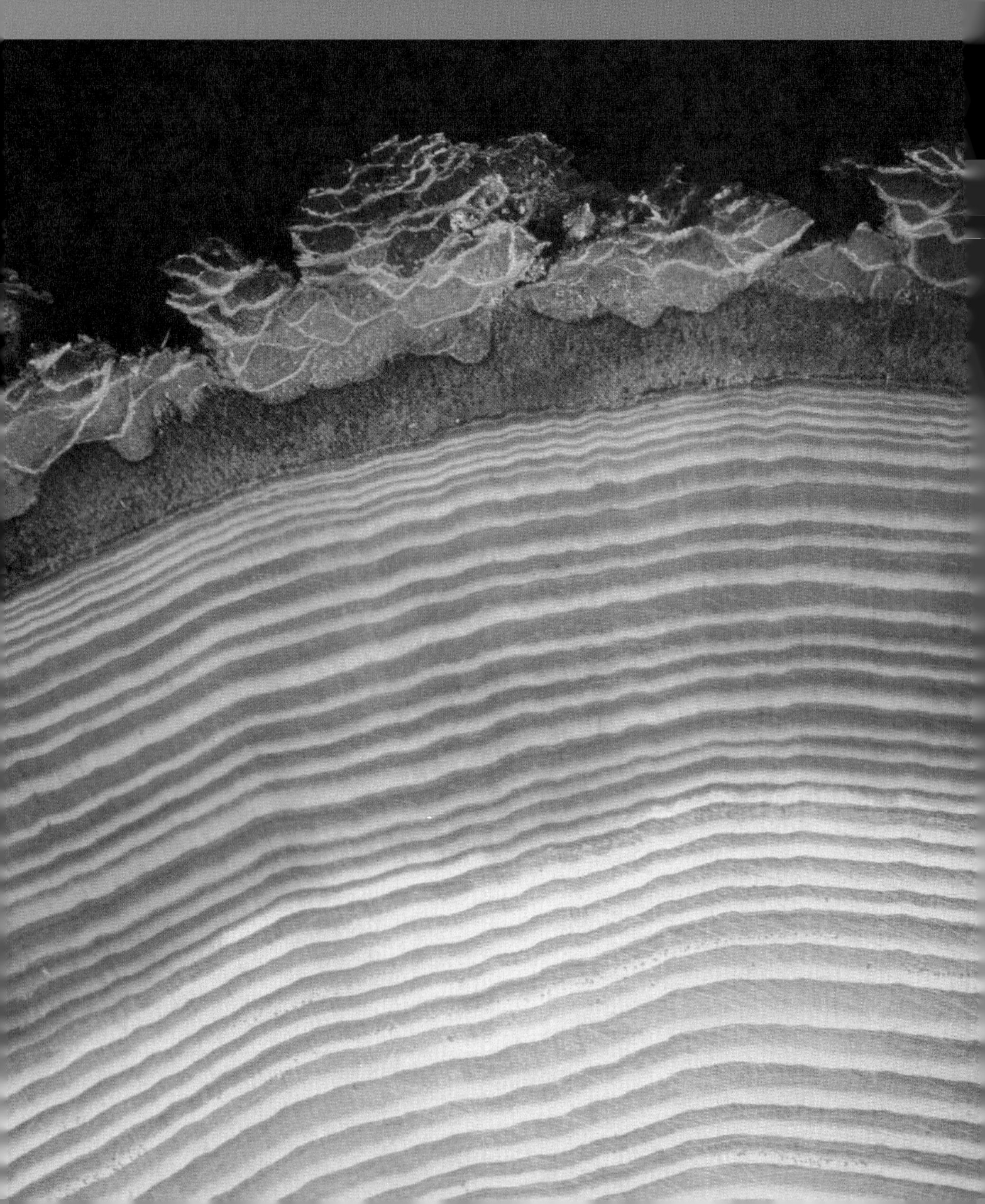

Chapter

Geometry and Imagination

From the outside, a tree trunk shows only bark, without a hint of what is inside. This cross section shows a very different view of the tree. A tree's growth rings can be read like a book. The rings can show the age of the tree and much more, such as whether there was a fire one year, or if the tree was sick or injured at one time.

This cross section gives you a clear sense of one way in which a plane (the saw) can intersect a cylinder (the trunk). This chapter deals with ways of visualizing intersections in space.

In Chapter 12, you will apply the concept of locus to geometric figures in two and three dimensions, and write equations for loci.

Goals for Learning

- ◆ To identify how geometric figures intersect in space
- ◆ To write equations for loci
- ◆ To construct simple and compound loci
- ◆ To describe compound loci

Lesson 1 Lines and Planes in Space

You may find it easy to draw geometric figures in a plane. However, it is more difficult to show three-dimensional figures with a drawing on a flat sheet of paper. To understand some geometric figures you need to be able to imagine how those figures look and how they act in space.

Remember from Chapter 10 that the *locus of points* describes the location of points. The plural of *locus* is *loci.*

In the Plane

Recall that the *locus of points* at equal distances from a given point is a *circle.* The center is the given point; *r,* the radius, is the given distance.

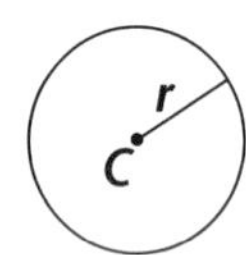

Circle

In Space

The locus of points in space at equal distances from a given point is a *sphere.* The center is the given point; *r,* the radius, is the given distance.

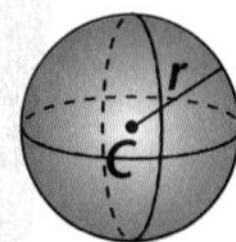

Sphere

Now, think about any line. In how many ways can the circle—or the sphere—and the line relate to one another?

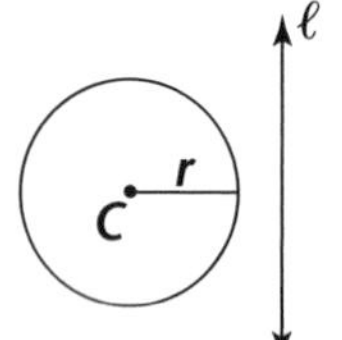

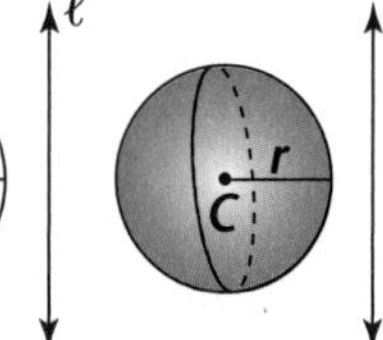

No intersection

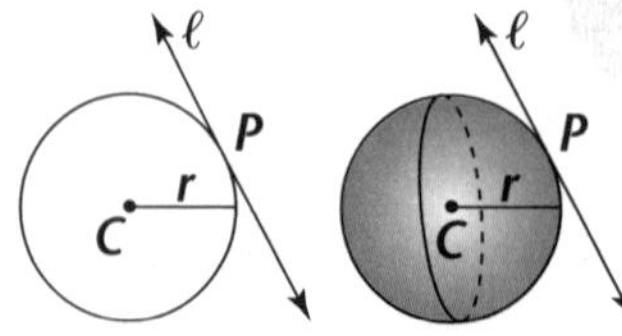

Tangent at a single point

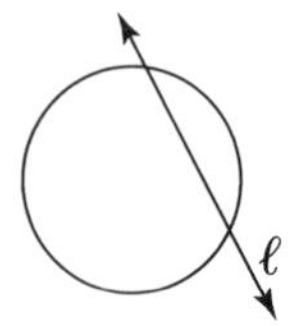

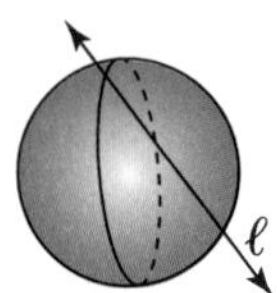

Intersects at two points, forming a chord between the points

If a circle in the coordinate plane has center (a, b) and radius r, its equation is $(x - a)^2 + (y - b)^2 = r^2$. This formula is really just the distance formula that you learned in Chapter 8.

If the chord formed equals the diameter of the circle, you know the line must pass through the center of the circle.

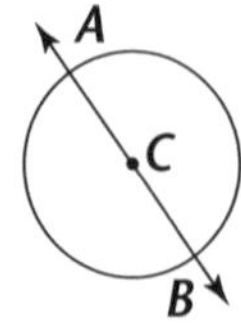

$\overline{AB}$ = diameter

If the chord formed equals the diameter of the sphere, you know the line must pass through the center of the sphere.

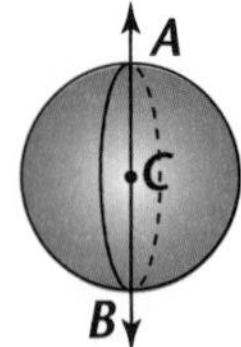

$\overline{AB}$ = diameter
A and *B* are poles.

Remember that a sphere is the locus of points, in space, at equal distances from a given point.

You have visualized how a line and a circle or a sphere might intersect. Now, try to imagine, or visualize, how a plane and a sphere might intersect.

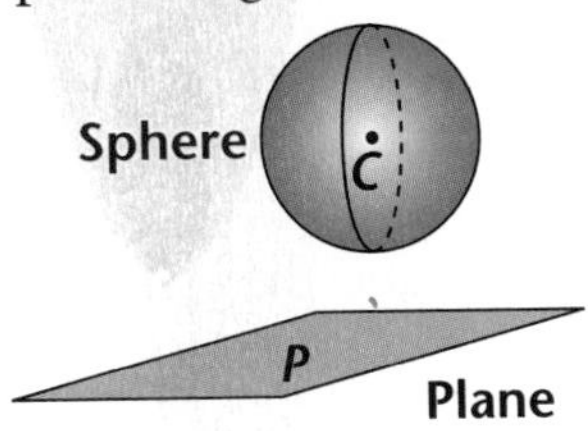

No intersection

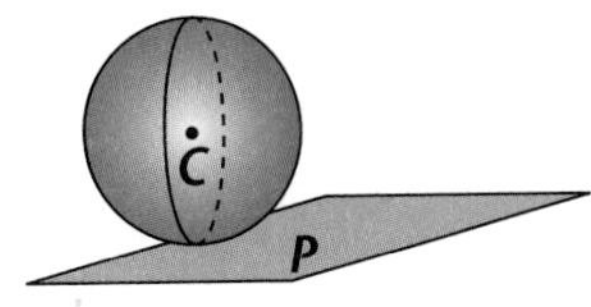

Tangent at a single point

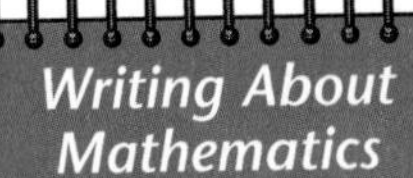

Writing About Mathematics

An arrow hits a circular target at a single point. Is this an example of a line tangent to a circle? Explain why or why not.

A plane passing through a sphere intersects in a circle. The center of the circle of intersection is not the center of the sphere, so the circle is not a great circle.

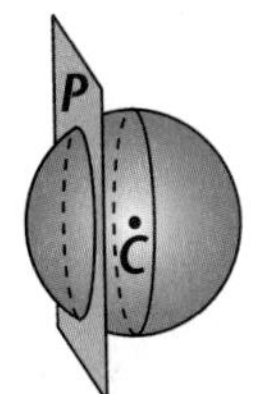

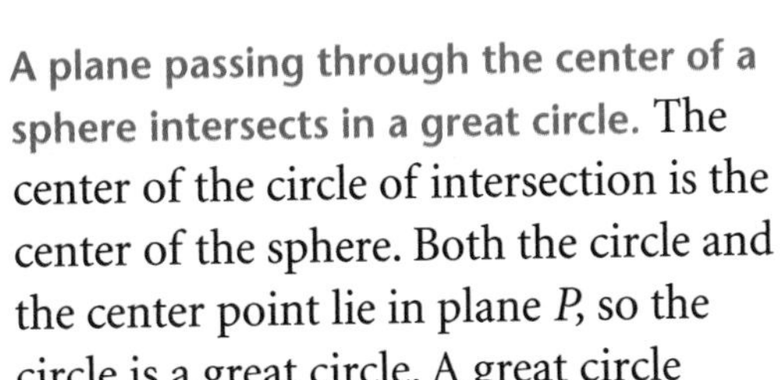

A plane passing through the center of a sphere intersects in a great circle. The center of the circle of intersection is the center of the sphere. Both the circle and the center point lie in plane *P*, so the circle is a great circle. A great circle divides the sphere into two hemispheres.

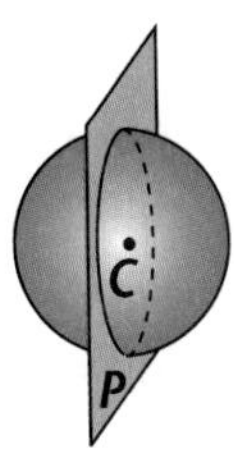

Exercise A Given a cylinder and a line in space, draw a sketch and then describe the following. (You may wish to use an empty can and a pencil to model each item.)

1. The line and the cylinder have one point in common.
2. The line and the cylinder have two points in common.
3. The line is part of the cylinder.
4. The line is at a fixed distance from the cylinder. The distance is larger than the radius of the cylinder.

Exercise B Given a cylinder and a plane in space, draw a sketch and then describe the following. (You may wish to use an empty can and a sheet of paper to model each item.)

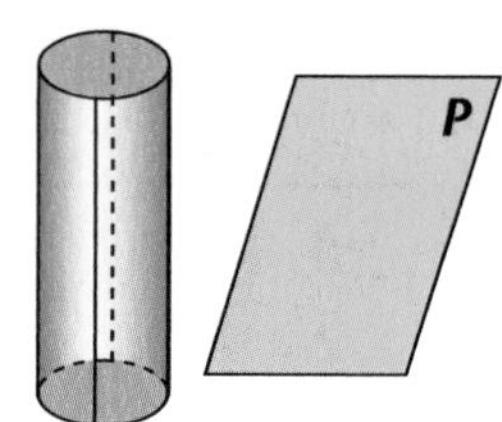

5. Describe how the intersection can be a pair of parallel line segments.

6. How can the plane and the cylinder intersect to form a circle?

7. How can the plane and the cylinder meet to form a single straight line segment?

8. If the cylinder is infinitely long, can the cylinder and the plane ever meet in just one point? Explain.

PROBLEM SOLVING

Exercise C Solve the following problems.

9. A violent tornado sends a two-by-four board through a tree trunk. If the board were a line, describe the situation using geometric terms.

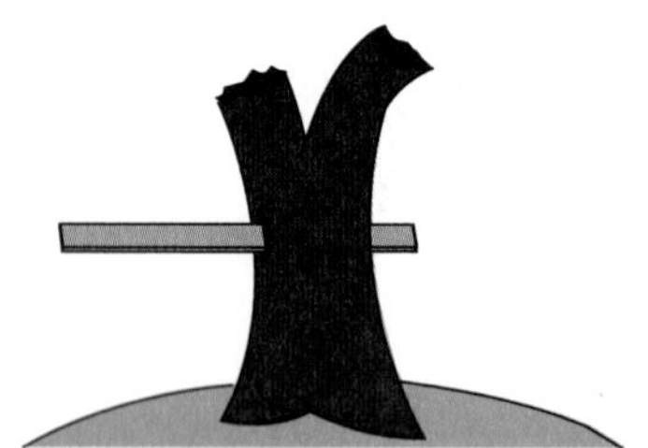

10. The illustration shows several beads strung on a wire. What geometric figures can be used to describe the illustration? Where are the holes for the wire located?

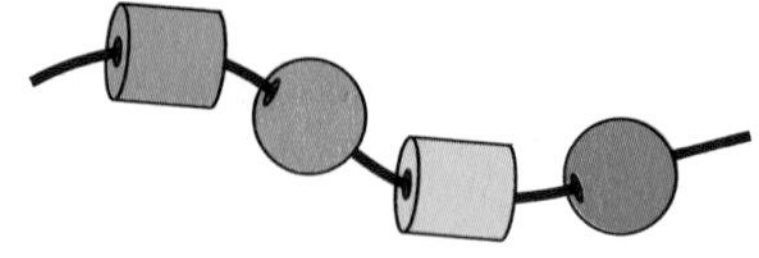

Geometry in Your Life

If you have trouble visualizing intersections of a plane with a sphere, you can model them. You will need a round ball of soft clay for the sphere. You can use a piece of cardboard as the plane. Use your sphere and plane to model each of these possibilities: not touching, tangent, intersecting to form a circle, and intersecting to form a great circle.

Lesson 2 Loci in the Coordinate Plane

You can use the idea of loci, the locations of points, to solve many problems in algebra. Here are some examples.

Example 1 **Given:** line $y = 3$

Find: the locus of points one unit away from $y = 3$

The locus will be two parallel lines. Each line will be a distance of 1 unit from $y = 3$. The equations of the lines are $y = 4$ and $y = 2$.

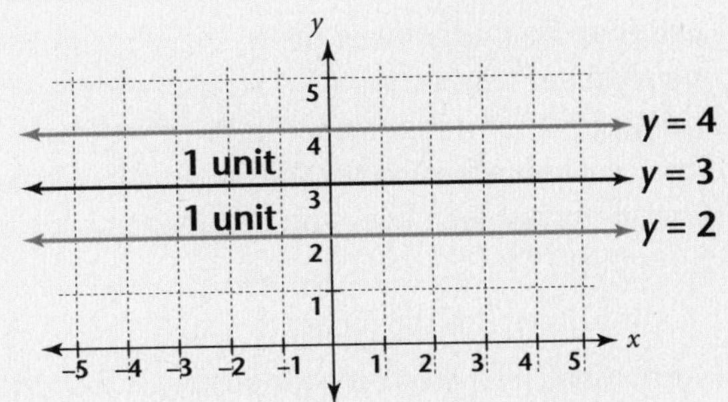

Example 2 **Given:** line $y = -x + 4$

Find: the locus of points equidistant from the given line and passing through (0, 3) and (0, 5)

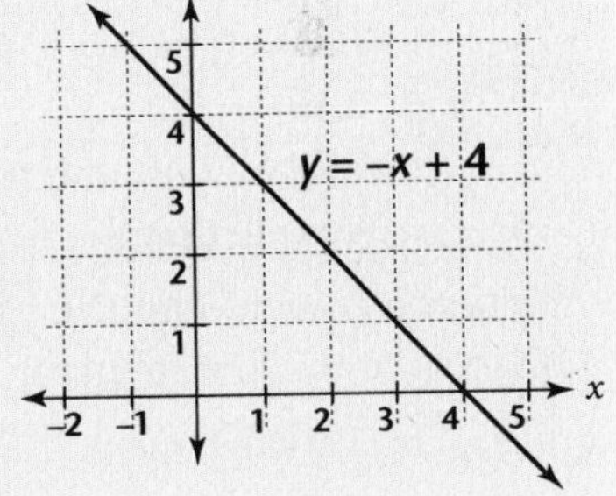

The locus will be two parallel lines—one passing through a point one unit above the y-intercept of 4 and one passing one unit below the y-intercept of 4. Because the lines are parallel, they have equal slope. Therefore, the lines are

$y = -x + 5$ one unit above the given line

$y = -x + 4$ the given line

$y = -x + 3$ one unit below the given line

Make a sketch to help you check whether your answer is reasonable.

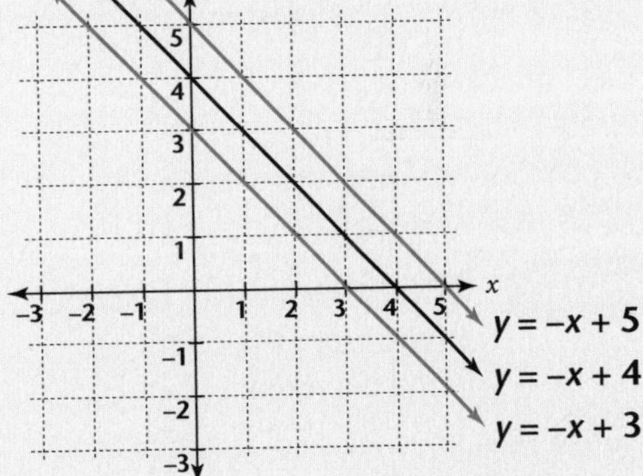

Algebra Review

Remember that a line can be graphed quickly if its equation is written in slope-intercept form. An equation of the form $y = mx + b$ has slope of m and y-intercept at the point $(0, b)$.

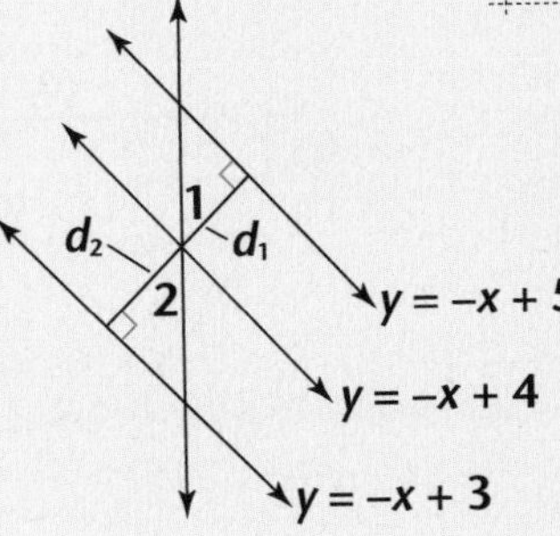

Note: The perpendicular distances, d_1 and d_2, are equal because the two right triangles formed are congruent. (AAS: right angles are equal; vertical angles 1 and 2 are equal; distances along y-axis are equal.)

You can use the information in the note on page 413 to solve a related problem.

EXAMPLE 3 **Given:** two parallel lines: $y = 2x + 1$ and $y = 2x + 5$

Find: the locus of points equidistant from the two lines

First, find the midpoint of the line segment connecting (0, 1) and (0, 5). That midpoint is (0, 3). Then write an equation for the line parallel to the given lines and passing through (0, 3)

$y = 2x + 3$ is the locus.

Make a sketch to check if your answer is reasonable.

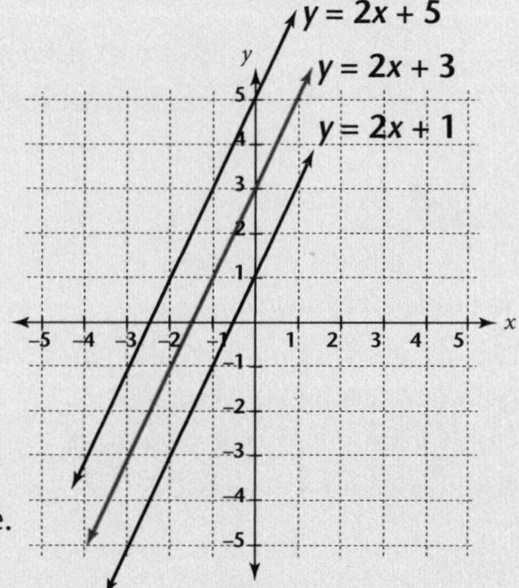

EXAMPLE 4 **Given:** the pair of points (3, 4) and (−2, 4) and the line segment connecting the two points

Write the equation for the perpendicular bisector to the line segment.

$x = \frac{1}{2}$ is the locus.

Make a sketch to check if your answer is reasonable.

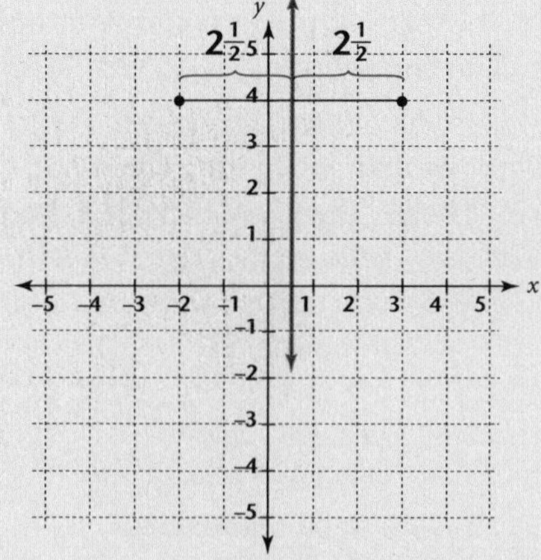

EXAMPLE 5 What is the locus of points 5 units from the origin in the coordinate plane?

From your knowledge of geometric definitions, you know that the locus is a circle with center (0, 0) and a radius of 5. You can find the equation for the circle using algebra.

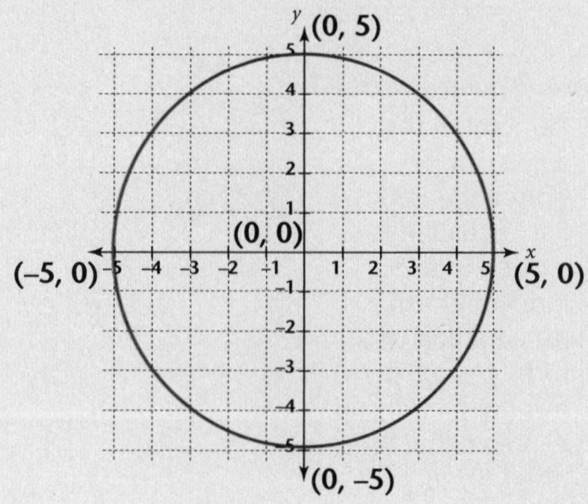

EXAMPLE 5 *(continued)*

Let (x, y) be any point on the circle. Using the Pythagorean Theorem, you know that $5^2 = x^2 + y^2$. This is the equation of the locus, a circle with radius 5 and a center at (0, 0). In general, the equation for a circle with radius r and center (0, 0) is $r^2 = x^2 + y^2$.

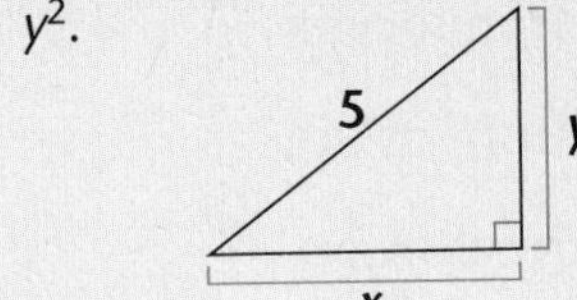

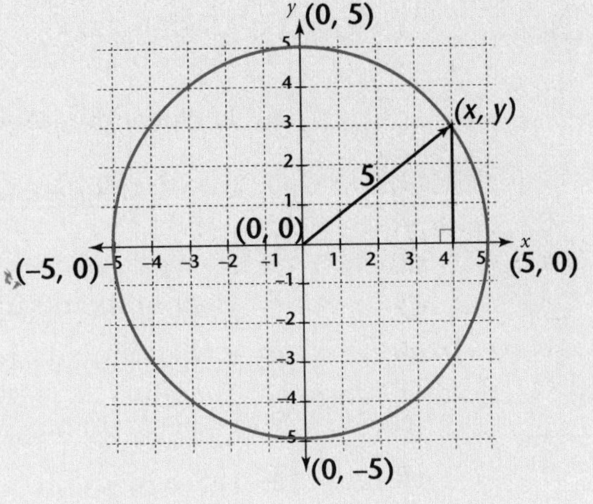

Estimation Activity

Estimate: Estimate whether the two lines in the graph are parallel.

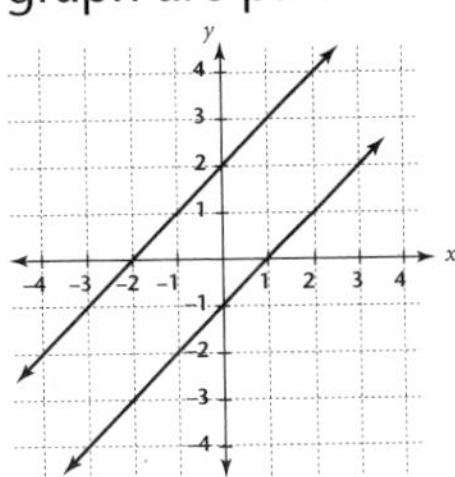

Solution: Hold your pencil so that the tip is on one line and the shaft is perpendicular to the other line. Hold your finger where the second line crosses the pencil. Slide the pencil tip along the line up or down. Keep the shaft perpendicular to the line. If the distance between them remains the same, the lines are parallel.

Exercise A Find each locus. Draw a sketch and write the equation.

1. Locus of points 3 units away from $y = 5$

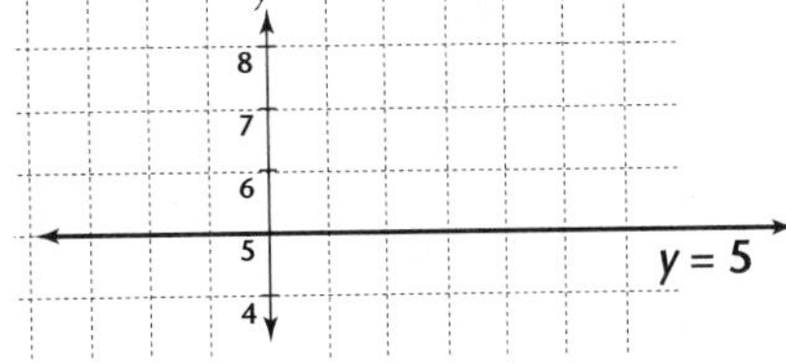

2. Locus of points equidistant from $y = x + 3$ and passing through (0, 1) and (0, 5)

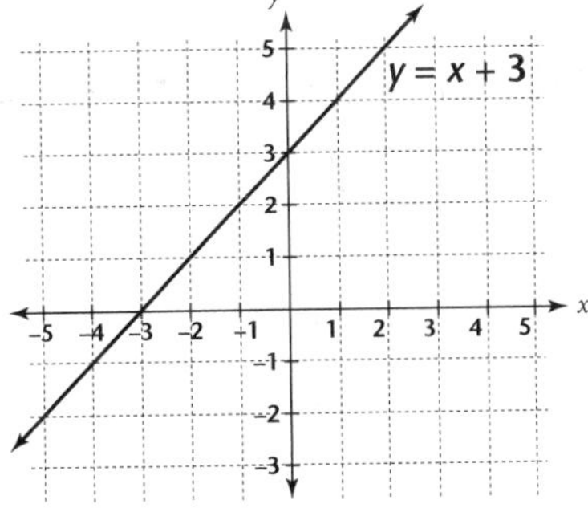

3. Locus of points equidistant from $y = -\frac{1}{2}x + 2$ and passing through (0, 1) and (0, 3)

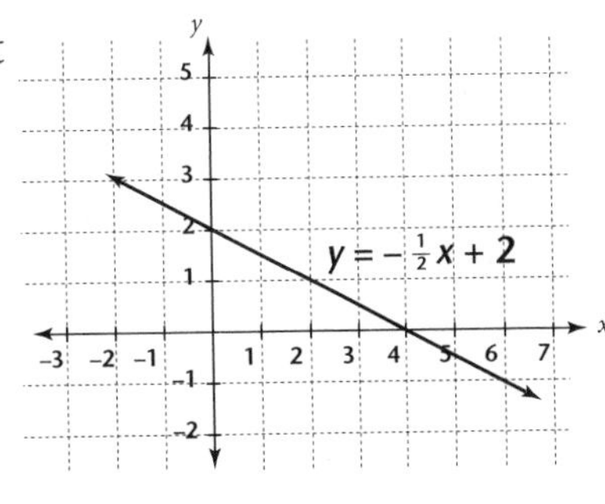

4. Locus of points equidistant from $x = 2$ and $x = -3$

5. Locus of points equidistant from $y = 3$ and $y = -5$

6. Locus of points equidistant from $(3, 2)$ and $(-4, 2)$

Exercise B Find each locus. Draw a sketch and write the equation.

7. Locus of points 6 units from origin

8. Locus of points 4 units from origin

9. Locus of points $\frac{1}{2}$ unit from origin

10. Locus of points 3 units from origin

Exercise C Describe the following loci in the coordinate plane.

11. Loci of points $2\frac{1}{2}$ units from $x = \frac{1}{2}$

12. Locus of points equidistant from $y = -3x + 1$ and $y = -3x + 2$

13. Locus of points 0 units from the origin

14. Locus of points 5 units from $(-3, -2)$

15. Locus of points equidistant from $x^2 + y^2 = 49$

Technology Connection

The Computerized Axial Tomography, or CAT scan, is one of many tools doctors use to learn about a person's health. A CAT scan produces a series of x-ray pictures. Each picture shows a "slice" of a person's body as if a plane were passed through it. Doctors can study the pictures to learn the location of a tumor or other abnormalities.

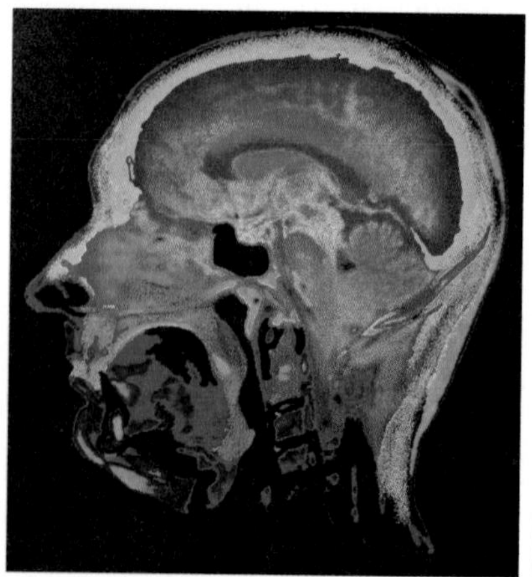

Lesson 3 Compound Loci

Compound locus
A set of points satisfying more than one condition at a time.

You've learned how to visualize loci and how to use the idea of loci to solve many problems in algebra. In this lesson, you will be looking for points, or loci, that satisfy more than one condition at a time. Such loci are called **compound loci**. Here are some examples.

EXAMPLE 1 **Given:** lines ℓ and m, points A and B

What is the locus of points equidistant from A and B and equidistant from the parallel lines ℓ and m?

You will need to find each locus separately and then determine their intersection, which will be the compound locus.

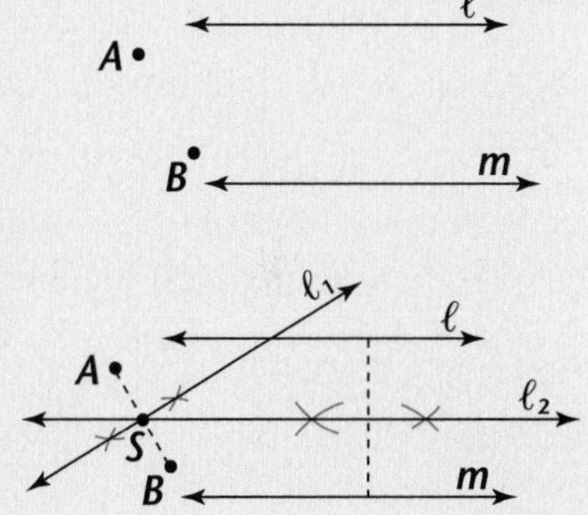

First, find the locus of points equidistant from A and B by finding the perpendicular bisector of $\overline{AB}$. Label this line ℓ_1.

Next, find the locus of points equidistant from ℓ and m. Label this line ℓ_2.

The two loci, ℓ_1 and ℓ_2, intersect at S. Therefore, S is both equidistant from A and B and equidistant to the parallel lines ℓ and m. Point S is the compound locus.

EXAMPLE 2 **Given:** line ℓ, $\overline{AB}$, and point C

Find: the locus of points at a distance AB from C and a distance AB from ℓ.

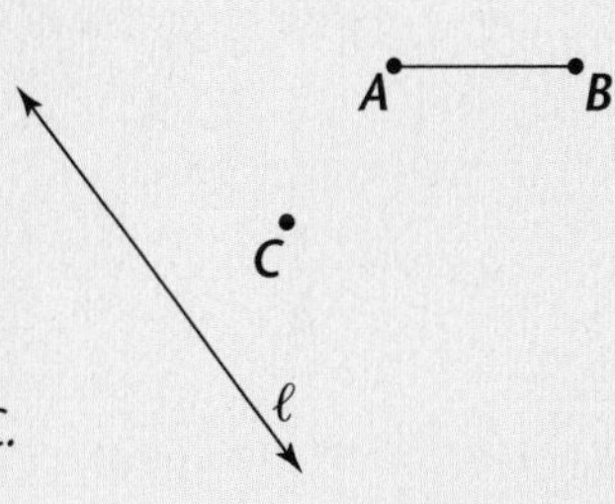

First, find the locus of points a distance AB from C. This is a circle with radius $\overline{AB}$ and center C.

Next, draw two lines, each parallel to ℓ and each a distance AB from ℓ.

EXAMPLE 2 *(continued)*

Find where the two loci intersect and label these points *S* and *T*.

S and *T* are the only two points that are a distance *AB* both from point *C* and from line ℓ.

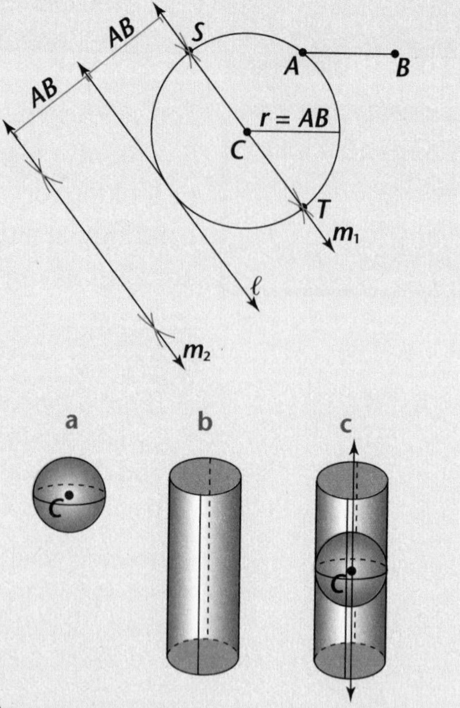

EXAMPLE 3 Describe and then sketch the following loci in space.

a. points equidistant from a given point *C*

b. points equidistant from a given line

c. points equidistant from a point *C* and a line, with *C* being on the line

The compound locus is a great circle where the sphere touches the cylinder.

Exercise A Construct and then describe the following compound loci.

1. The locus of points equidistant from the parallel lines ℓ and *m* and at a distance of *AB* from *C*.

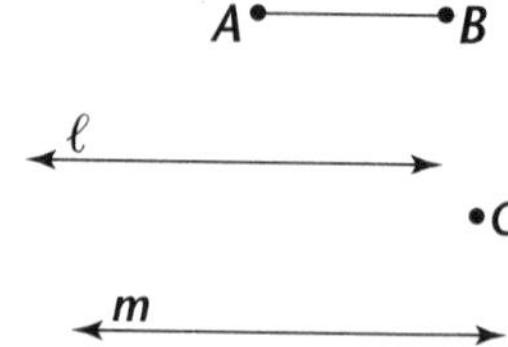

2. The locus of points equidistant from $\overrightarrow{AB}$ and $\overrightarrow{AC}$ and at a distance of *EF* from *A*.

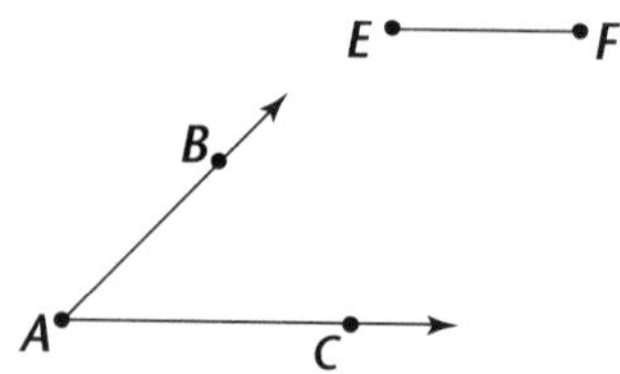

3. The locus of points equidistant from vertices *A*, *B*, and *C*.

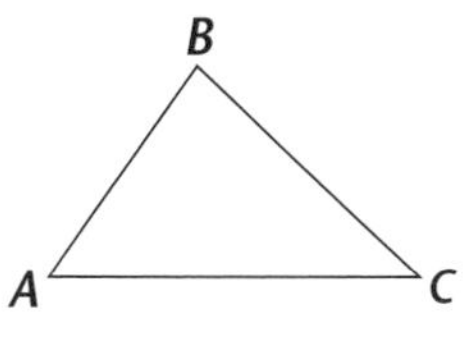

4. The locus of points equidistant from $\angle E$ and $\angle F$.

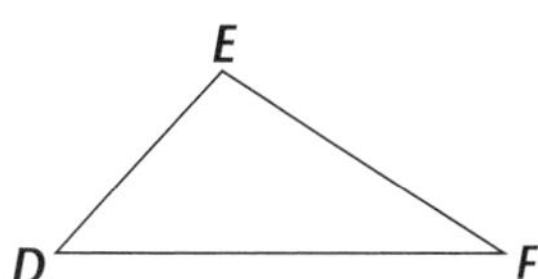

TRY THIS

Make a rectangular prism 2 in. wide by 2 in. high by 8 in. long from clay. Use a piece of cardboard to act as a plane. Form the following figures, by intersecting a plane and the prism: a square, a rectangle, and a triangle.

Exercise B Sketch and then describe the following compound loci.

5. The intersection of a line with a plane.

6. The intersection of a plane with a sphere.

7. The intersection of a plane and a square pyramid in which the plane is parallel to the base of the pyramid.

8. The intersection of a plane and a square pyramid in which the plane is not parallel to the base but does intersect the base.

9. The intersection of a plane and a cone in which the plane is parallel to the base of the cone.

10. The intersection of a plane and a cone in which the plane is not parallel to the base.

Look around for examples of the interaction of geometric figures. For instance, a knife (plane) is used to cut a grapefruit (sphere) to form slices (circles).

Lesson 4 Algebra Connection: The Quadratic Formula

Quadratic formula

Formula that can provide roots of any quadratic equation

Root

A value of x that satisfies the equation $ax^2 + bx + c = 0$

Quadratic functions have the form $y = ax^2 + bx + c$. Their graphs are a curved shape called a parabola. If you set y equal to 0, you can find where the graph crosses the x-axis.

Use the **quadratic formula** to find the solution to any quadratic equation of the form $ax^2 + bx + c = 0$. The solution is

$$x = \frac{-b \pm \sqrt{b^2 - 4ac}}{2a}$$

The $\pm$ sign means x has two values. These are the solutions, or **roots**, of the quadratic equation.

This formula gives us three pieces of information.

1. Equation for the axis of symmetry: $x = \frac{-b}{2a}$
2. Two real solutions if the radicand $(b^2 - 4ac)$ is positive
3. Two complex solutions if the radicand is negative (The graph does not cross the x-axis.)

To find the radicand, substitute values into the expression.

$b^2 - 4ac > 0$ means two real roots.

$b^2 - 4ac < 0$ means two complex roots.

$b^2 - 4ac = 0$ means one real root.

3.

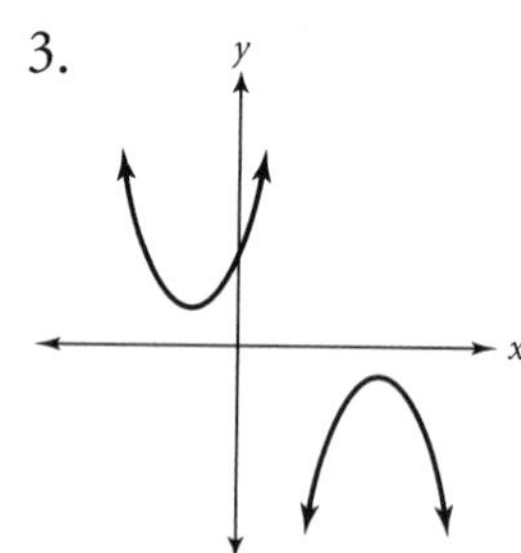

graph of $y = ax^2 + bx + c$

1. $x = \frac{-b}{2a}$ axis of symmetry

2. root $x_1 = \frac{-b - \sqrt{b^2 - 4ac}}{2a}$

2. root $x_2 = \frac{-b + \sqrt{b^2 - 4ac}}{2a}$

Example 1 For $3x^2 + 4x - 3 = 0$

a. Write the equation of the axis of symmetry.

b. Are the roots real or complex?

Step 1 Identify a, b, and c: $a = 3$, $b = 4$, $c = -3$

Step 2 Find the axis of symmetry. $\frac{-b}{2a} = \frac{-4}{2(3)} = -\frac{4}{6} = -\frac{2}{3}$

The equation of the axis of symmetry is $x = -\frac{2}{3}$.

Step 3 radicand $= b^2 - 4ac = (4)^2 - 4(3)(-3) = 16 + 36 = 52$

Since the radicand > 0, there are two real roots.

EXAMPLE 2 Find the roots of the equation $2x^2 = -3x + 5$.

Step 1 Rewrite in standard form.

$$2x^2 + 3x - 5 = 0$$
$$\downarrow \quad \downarrow \quad \downarrow$$
$$ax^2 + bx + c = 0$$

Step 2 Identify a, b, and c: $a = 2$, $b = 3$, $c = -5$

Step 3 Substitute $a = 2$, $b = 3$, and $c = -5$ into the formula. Solve.

$$x = \frac{-b \pm \sqrt{b^2 - 4ac}}{2a} = \frac{-3 \pm \sqrt{3^2 - 4(2)(-5)}}{2(2)} = \frac{-3 \pm \sqrt{9 + 40}}{4}$$

$$= \frac{-3 \pm \sqrt{49}}{4} = \frac{-3 \pm 7}{4}$$

$$x = \frac{-3 + 7}{4} = \frac{4}{4} = 1 \quad \text{or} \quad x = \frac{-3 - 7}{4} = \frac{-10}{4} = -\frac{5}{2}$$

Step 4 Check $x = 1$:

$$2(1)^2 = -3(1) + 5$$
$$2(1) = -3 + 5 \rightarrow 2 = 2$$

Check $x = -\frac{5}{2}$:

$$2\left(-\frac{5}{2}\right)^2 = -3\left(-\frac{5}{2}\right) + 5$$
$$2\left(\frac{25}{4}\right) = \frac{15}{2} + 5 \rightarrow \frac{25}{2} = \frac{15}{2} + \frac{10}{2} = \frac{25}{2}$$

EXAMPLE 3 Find the roots of $3x^2 + x + 5 = 0$.

Step 1 Identify a, b, and c: $a = 3$, $b = 1$, $c = 5$

Step 2 Substitute $a = 3$, $b = 1$, and $c = 5$ into the formula. Solve.

$$x = \frac{-b \pm \sqrt{b^2 - 4ac}}{2a} = \frac{-1 \pm \sqrt{1^2 - 4(3)(5)}}{2(3)} = \frac{-1 \pm \sqrt{1 - 60}}{6} = \frac{-1 \pm \sqrt{-59}}{6}$$

Since the radicand < 0, there are two complex roots: $x = \frac{-1 + \sqrt{-59}}{6}$ or $x = \frac{-1 - \sqrt{-59}}{6}$

Exercise A Write the equation of the axis of symmetry. Are the roots real or complex?

1. $x^2 + x + 3 = 0$

2. $2x^2 + x - 4 = 0$

3. $-3x^2 + 2x = -1$

4. $5x^2 = -x + 6$

5. $-3x^2 + 9x = 3$

Exercise B Solve for x. Check your answers.

6. $x^2 - 8x = -15$

7. $x^2 + 2x - 8 = 0$

8. $5x^2 - 8x + 3 = 0$

9. $x^2 = 25$

10. $x^2 - 10x + 3 = 0$

Application

Conic Sections An hourglass is an example of two cones joined together. Two cones in this position can be used to generate *conic sections.* The conic sections are the circle, ellipse, parabola, and hyperbola. Each is shown below.

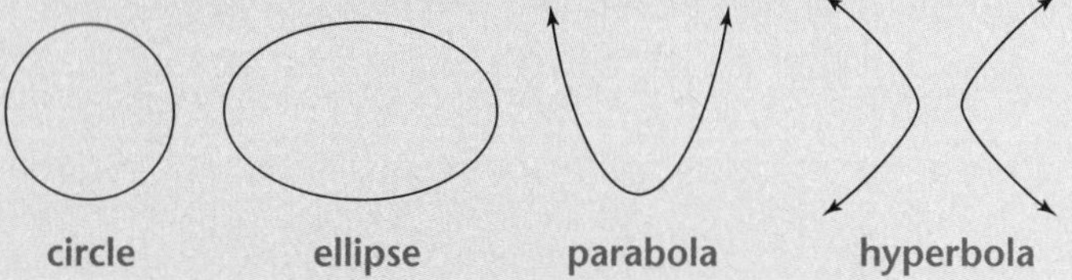

A conic section can be described as a locus of points. The locus is the path of points where the ratio of its distance from a fixed point to the distance from a fixed line is a constant. Varying values of the constant, or eccentricity of the locus, generate the different conic sections.

Another way to obtain these shapes is by looking at the intersection of a plane with a pair of cones in the hourglass position.

EXAMPLE 1 How could you intersect the double cones with a plane to form a parabola?

The plane is parallel to the edge of the top cone and passes through the bottom cone.

Exercises Describe how to intersect the double cones with a plane to get each of the following geometric figures.

1. circle **2.** ellipse **3.** hyperbola **4.** point **5.** line

Chapter 12 REVIEW

Write the letter of the correct answer.

1. Which of the following is a possible intersection for a sphere and a plane?

A a circle
B a line
C a line segment
D a ray

2. What is the equation for the locus of points that are equidistant from the lines $x = 5$ and $x = -3$?

A $x = 2$
B $x = 1$
C $x = -1$
D $x = -2$

3. What is the locus of points equidistant from the vertices of ΔABC?

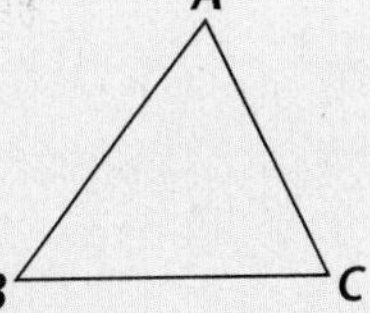

A a line
B a line segment
C a point
D a set of three lines

4. What is the locus of points equidistant from the parallel lines ℓ and m?

A a line
B a set of two parallel lines
C a point
D a set of three parallel lines

5. Which statement is false?

A A line and a circle can have no intersection.
B A line and a circle can touch at one point.
C A line and a circle can intersect at two points.
D A line and a circle can intersect in a line segment.

Sketch and describe the following.

Example: A line and a circle have one point in common.

Solution: The line is tangent to the circle.

6. A line and a sphere have one point in common.

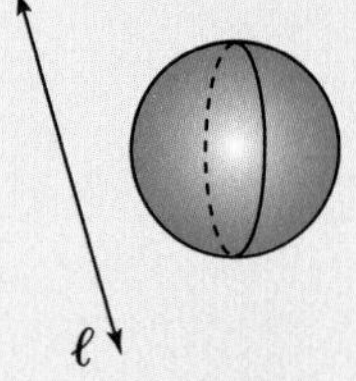

7. A line and a sphere have two points in common.

8. A line and a cylinder have one point in common.

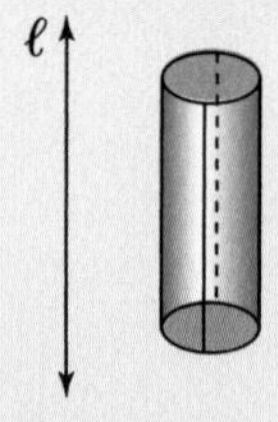

9. A line and a cylinder have infinitely many points in common.

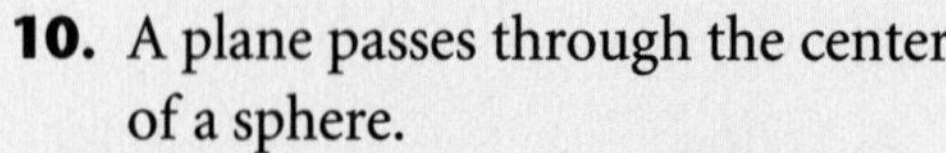

10. A plane passes through the center of a sphere.

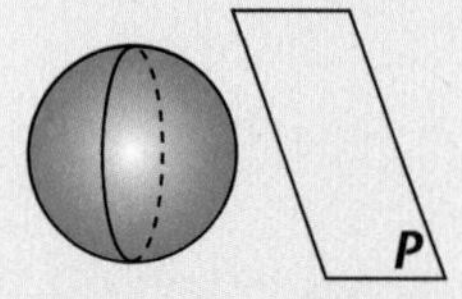

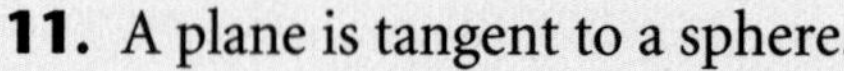

11. A plane is tangent to a sphere.

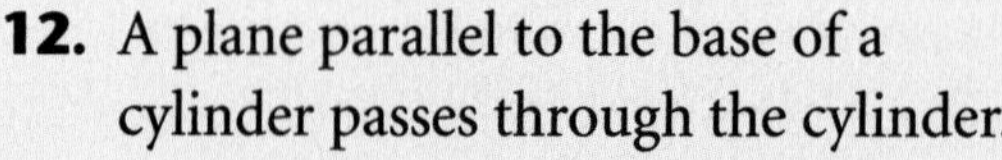

12. A plane parallel to the base of a cylinder passes through the cylinder.

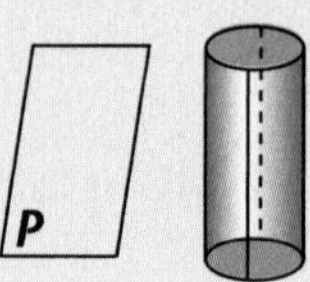

Draw a sketch and write the equation for each locus.

Example: Locus of points 2 units away from $y = 4$.

Solution: The locus is two lines parallel to $y = 4$ and two units away from $y = 4$. The equations are $y = 2$ and $y = 6$.

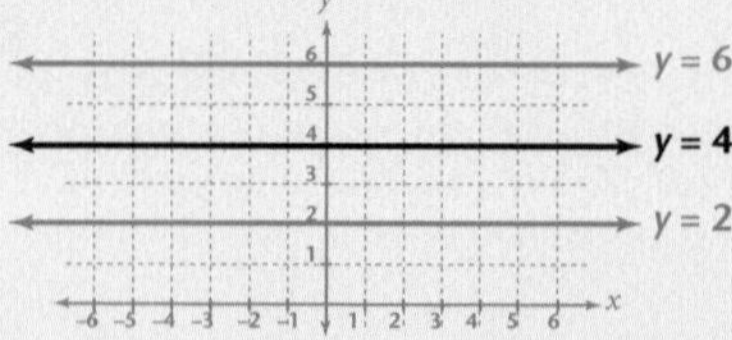

13. Locus of points equidistant from $y = 2$ and $y = -4$

14. Locus of points equidistant from $(3, 4)$ and $(3, -2)$

15. Locus of points 5 units from origin

16. Locus of points 2 units from origin

17. Locus of points 3 units from origin

Construct and describe the following compound loci.

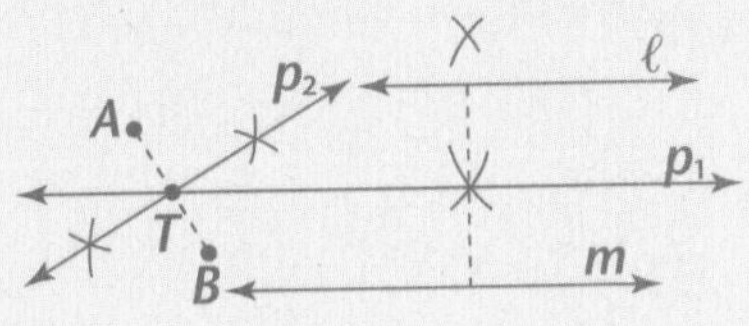

Example: The locus of points equidistant from parallel lines ℓ and m and equidistant from A and B

Solution: Find each locus separately. Every point on line p_1 is equidistant from both ℓ and m. Every point on line p_2 is equidistant from A and B. p_1 and p_2 intersect at T. Therefore, T is equidistant from ℓ and m and equidistant from A and B.

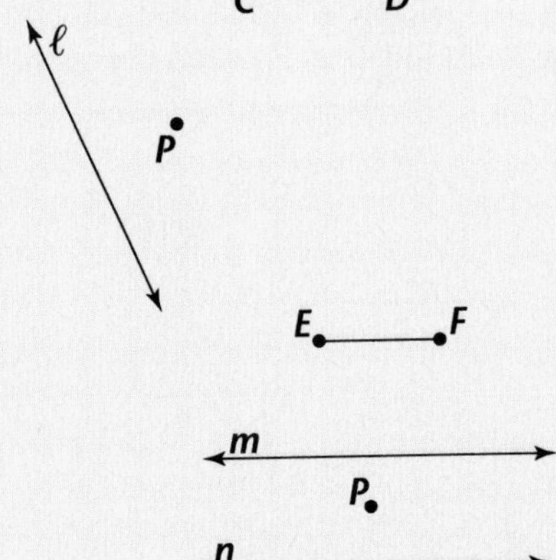

18. The locus of points at a distance CD from P and at a distance CD from line ℓ.

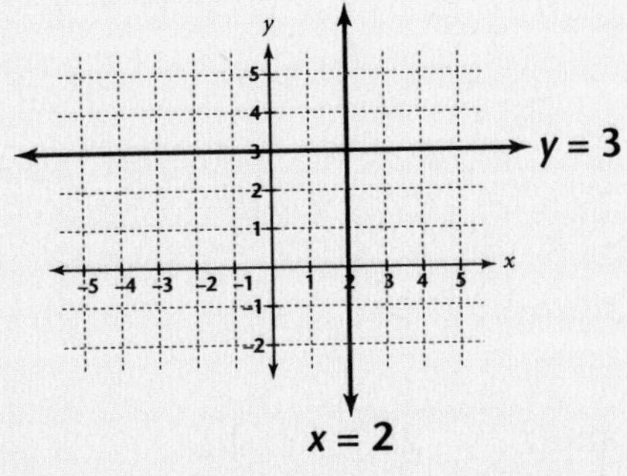

19. The locus of points equidistant from the parallel lines m and n and a distance EF from a point, P.

20. The locus of points 3 units from the line $x = 2$ and 2 units from the line $y = 3$.

y = 3

x = 2

Test-Taking Tip

When answering multiple-choice questions, read every choice before you choose an answer. Put a line through choices you know are wrong. Then choose the best answer from the remaining choices.

Chapter 1 Supplementary Problems

Tell whether each figure is a point, a line, a line segment, or a ray. Then use symbols to name each figure.

1. 

2. 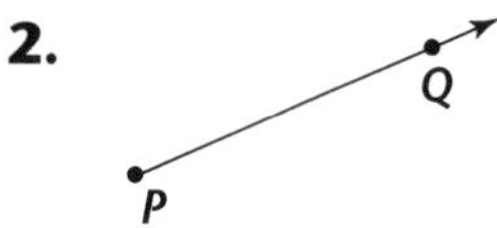

3. m

4. B

5. 

6. y

Use the Ruler Postulate to name the real number or letter corresponding to the point named.

A B C D E F G H I J

–3 $-2\frac{1}{2}$ –2 $-1\frac{1}{2}$ –1 $-\frac{1}{2}$ 0 $\frac{1}{2}$ 1 $1\frac{1}{2}$ 2 $2\frac{1}{2}$ 3

7. *A*

8. -2

9. *H*

10. $2\frac{1}{2}$

11. $-1\frac{1}{2}$

12. *J*

13. 1

14. *E*

15. *G*

16. -1

Find the distance between the points.

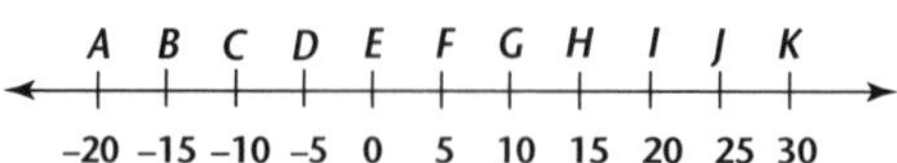

17. *B* and *E*

18. *G* and *I*

19. *E* and *F*

20. *F* and *H*

21. *C* and *D*

22. *D* and *F*

23. *C* and *E*

24. *B* and *G*

25. *A* and *D*

26. *B* and *I*

Chapter 1 Supplementary Problems

Write the letter of the answer to each question.

27. How many points are used to name a line?

A none **B** one **C** two

28. How many dimensions does a plane have?

A none **B** one **C** two

29. What geometric term can you use to describe beads on a string?

A points on a ray **B** points on a line segment **C** points on a line

30. What are points on the same line called?

A collinear points **B** parallel points **C** endpoints

Name each figure in another way.

31. $\overleftrightarrow{AC}$

32. $\overrightarrow{XZ}$

33. $\overline{QR}$

34. $\angle E$

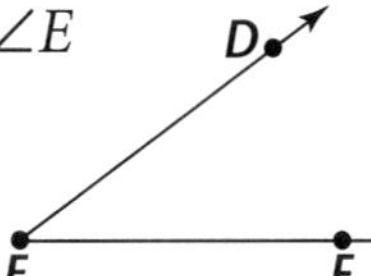

Copy each angle. Then bisect each angle using a compass and straightedge.

35.

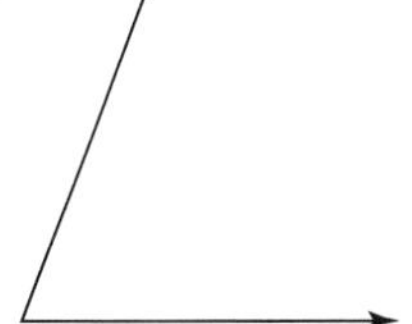

36.

Chapter 1 Supplementary Problems

Classify each angle. Write *acute, right, obtuse,* or *straight.*

37. m∠$DEF = 90°$

38. m∠$XYZ < 90°$

39.

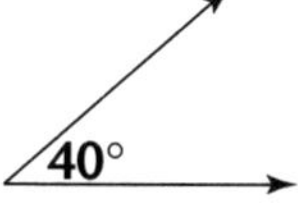

40. m∠$Q = 120°$

41. m∠$2 = 180°$

42.

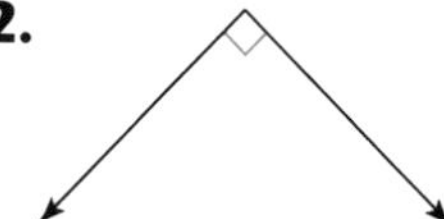

Find the measure of each angle.

43. m∠2

44. m∠6

45. m∠4

46. m∠3

47. m∠VXS

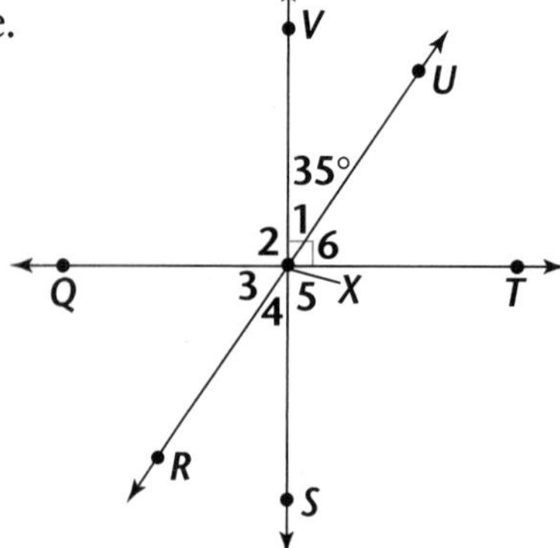

Solve for the missing angle(s).

48.

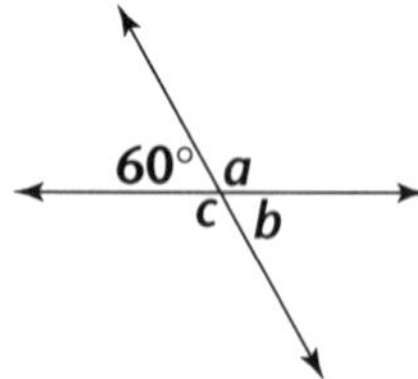

49.

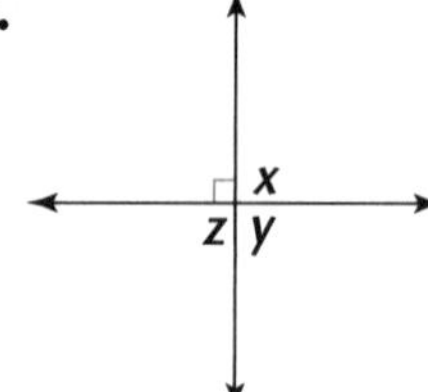

50.

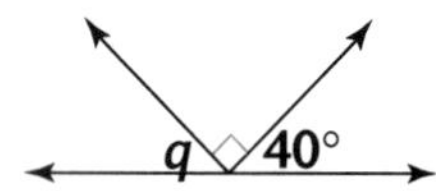

Chapter 2 Supplementary Problems

Copy each statement. Draw one line under the hypothesis. Circle the conclusion.

1. If an angle is a right angle, then its measure is 90°.
2. If an angle is a straight angle, then its measure is 180°.
3. If a figure is a quadrilateral, then it has 4 sides.
4. If two angles have equal measures, then they are congruent.
5. If an animal is an insect, then it has 6 legs.

Write the converse of each conditional and tell whether it is true or false.

6. If a figure has three sides, then it is a triangle.
7. If two angles are supplementary, then the sum of their measures is 180°.
8. If it is raining, then the sun is not shining.
9. If you are a citizen of the United States, then you must pay taxes.

Decide which postulate allows the construction.

10. Connect the points with line segments to form a rectangle.

11. Draw circle P with radius 4.

R

4

P

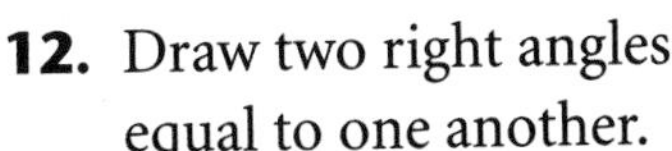

12. Draw two right angles equal to one another.

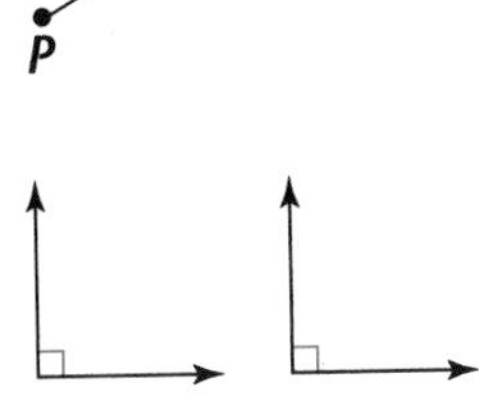

Chapter 2 Supplementary Problems

Decide which postulate allows the conclusion to be made.

13. Conclusion: Line m is the only line that passes through point X and is parallel to line ℓ.

14. 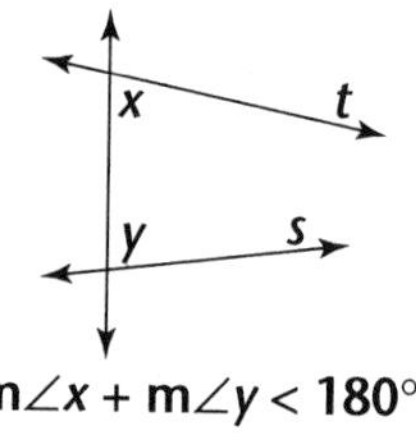

Conclusion: Lines t and s are intersecting lines.

15. 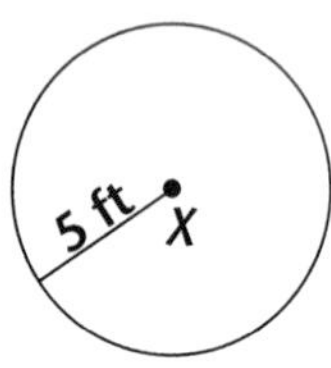

Conclusion: Circle X is shown with a radius of 5 feet.

Answer each question. Tell which postulate or axiom you used.

16. Is $m\angle A = m\angle E$?

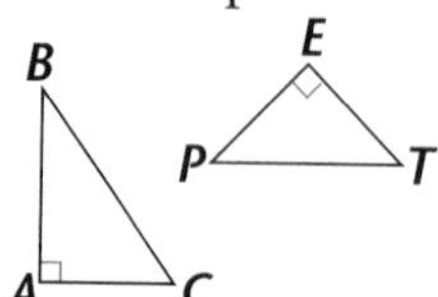

17. What is the measure of $\angle A$?

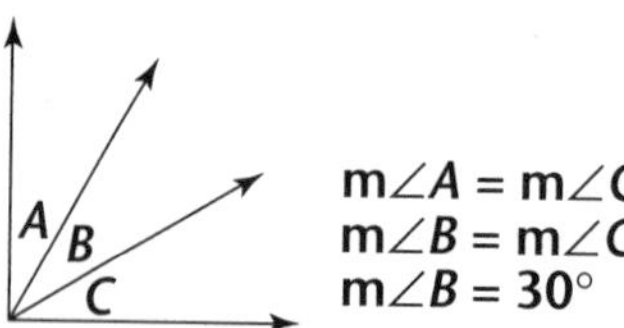

18. Which angles, or sum of angles, have a measure less than 90°?

Chapter 2 Supplementary Problems

19. If $m\angle a + m\angle b = m\angle b + m\angle c$, does $m\angle a = m\angle c$?

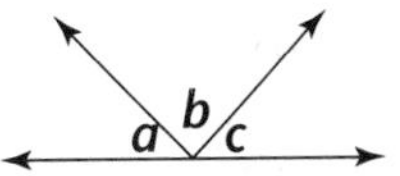

20. If $4x + 16 = 56$, does $4x = 40$?

Find the measures of angles Q, R, and S.

21.

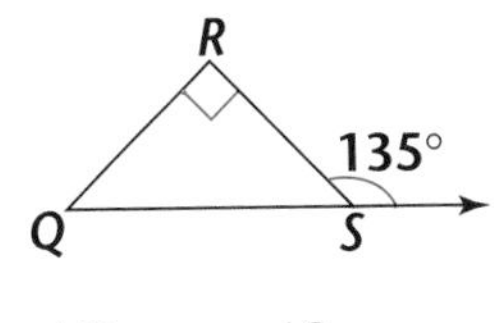

$m\angle Q = m\angle S$

22.

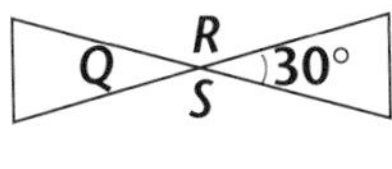

23.

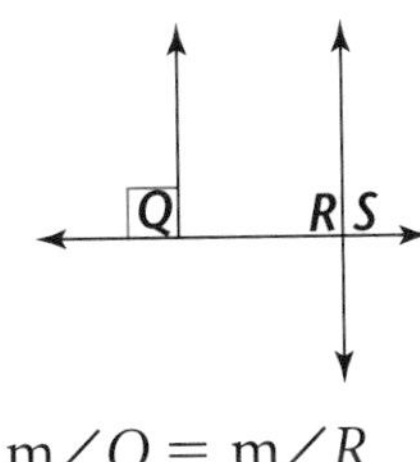

$m\angle Q = m\angle R$

Give a reason for each of the following statements. Use the diagram at the right.

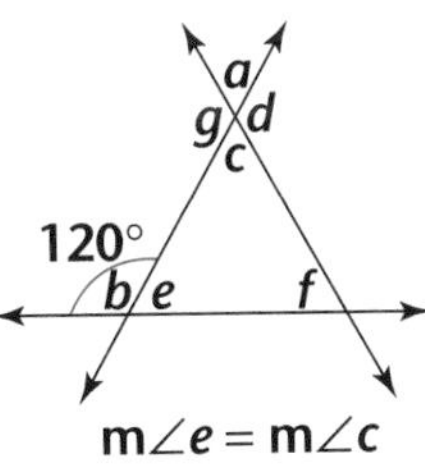

24. $m\angle e = m\angle c$

25. $m\angle a = m\angle c$

26. $m\angle e = 60°$

27. $m\angle b - m\angle c = m\angle b - m\angle a$

28. $m\angle f < 180°$

29. $m\angle c + m\angle d = 180°$

30. $m\angle e + m\angle f < 180°$

Chapter 3 Supplementary Problems

Use the figure to identify lines or angles as described below.

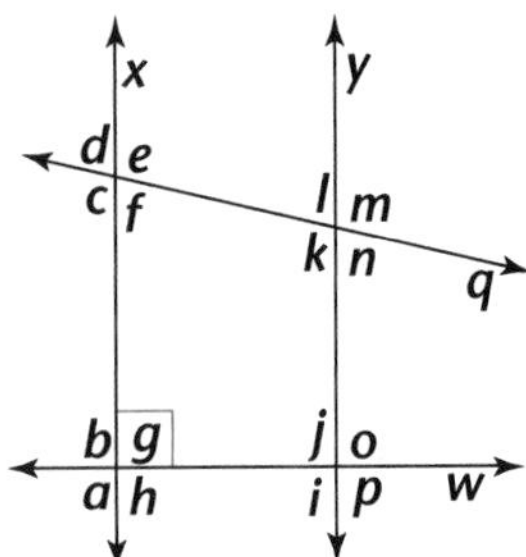

1. parallel line

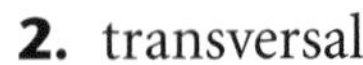

2. transversal

3. a pair of acute, vertical angles

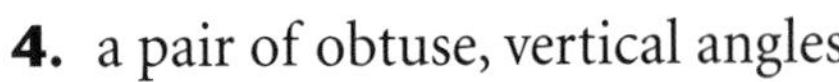

4. a pair of obtuse, vertical angles

5. intersecting lines

6. a pair of acute, alternate interior angles

Classify each pair of angles. Write *alternate interior, alternate exterior, corresponding,* or *supplementary.*

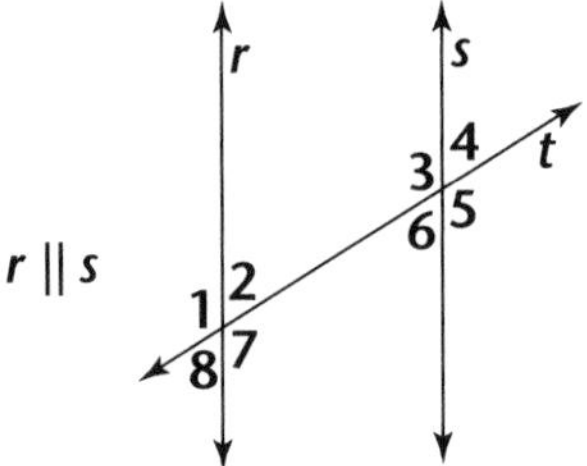

7. $\angle 1$ and $\angle 2$

8. $\angle 3$ and $\angle 7$

9. $\angle 4$ and $\angle 8$

10. $\angle 2$ and $\angle 6$

11. $\angle 6$ and $\angle 7$

12. $\angle 1$ and $\angle 5$

13. $\angle 6$ and $\angle 8$

14. $\angle 2$ and $\angle 3$

15. $\angle 1$ and $\angle 3$

16. $\angle 1$ and $\angle 4$

Chapter 3 Supplementary Problems

Find the measure of each angle.

17. $\angle 2$

18. $\angle 9$

19. $\angle 4$

20. $\angle 6$

21. $\angle 11$

22. $\angle 12$

23. $\angle 16$

24. $\angle 13$

25. $\angle 8$

26. $\angle 10$

27. $\angle 3$

28. $\angle 14$

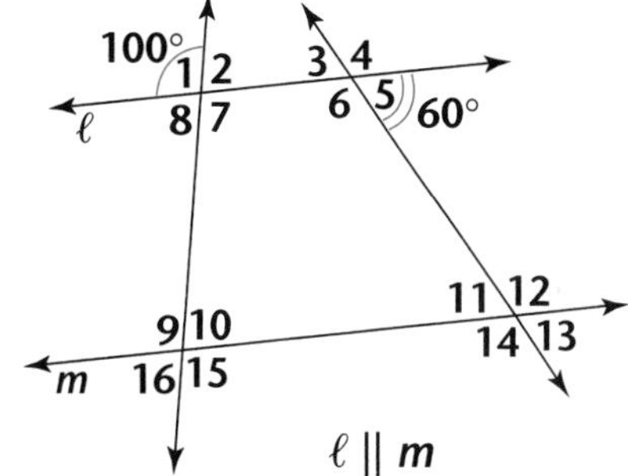

Use the theorems about parallel lines to find the measure of each angle.

29. The measure of $\angle b$ is twice that of $\angle c$.

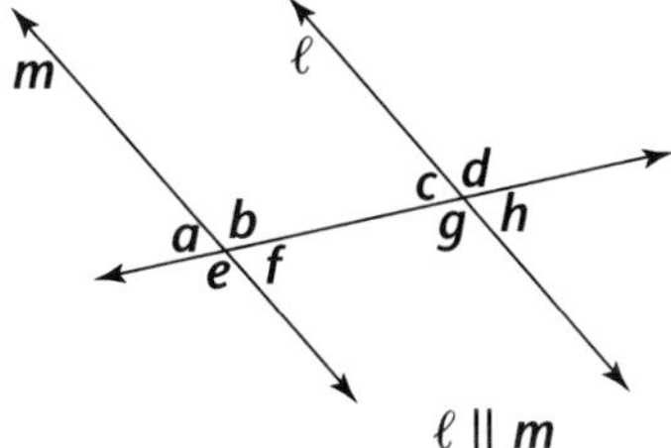

$m\angle b =$ ____

$m\angle c =$ ____

30. The measure of $\angle w$ is $\frac{1}{3}$ that of $\angle y$.

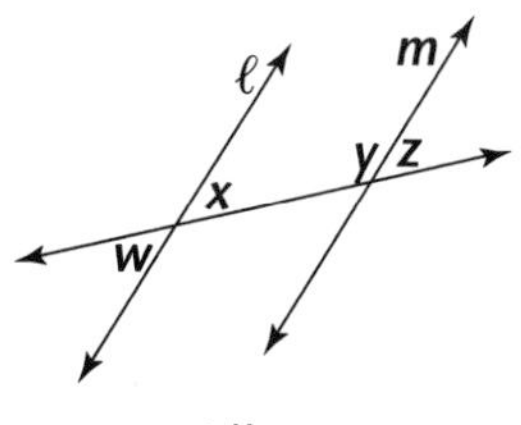

$m\angle w =$ ____

$m\angle y =$ ____

Chapter 3 Supplementary Problems

Use definitions and theorems to complete the statements.

31. $GA \parallel$ _____

32. $\overline{EM} \cong$ _____

33. $\overline{AM} \parallel$ _____

34. $m\angle A + m\angle$ _____ $= 180°$

35. $m\angle M + m\angle$ _____ $= 180°$

36. $m\angle E \cong m\angle$ _____

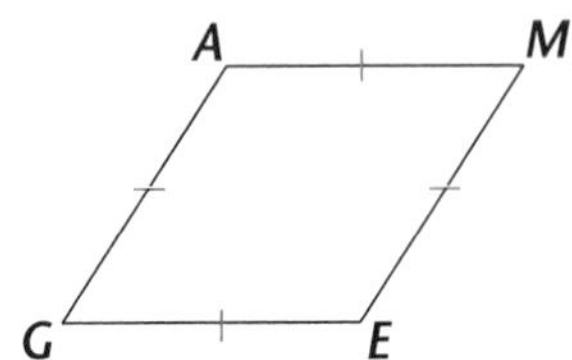

Rhombus *GAME*

Complete the following constructions on a separate sheet of paper. Use only a straightedge and a compass.

37. a square with a $1\frac{1}{2}$-inch base

38. a rectangle with 3-in. and 5-in. sides

39. a trapezoid with a right angle, height of 1 in., and bases of 2 in. and 4 in.

40. a trapezoid with no right angles

Write *parallel* or *not parallel* for each pair of lines crossed by a third line.

41.

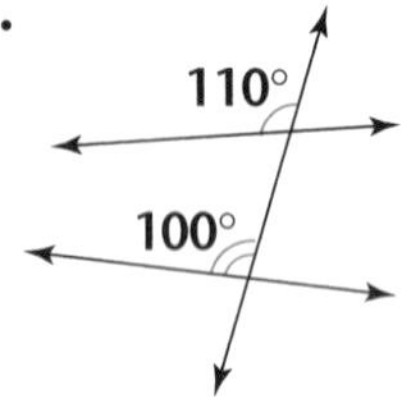

42.

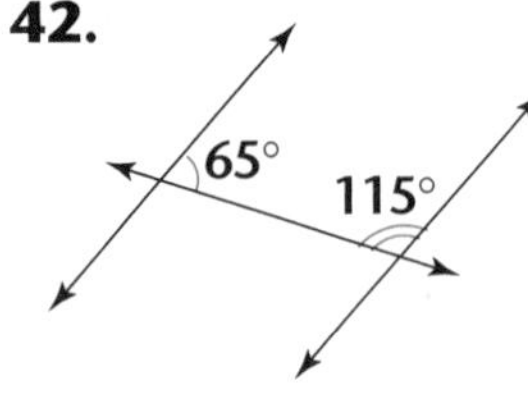

43.

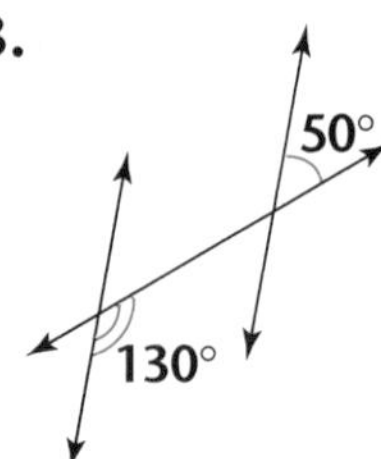

44.

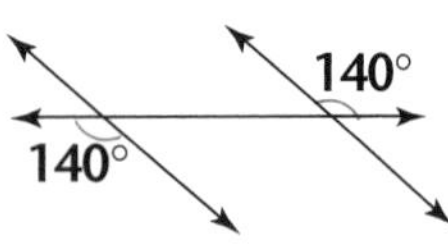

45.

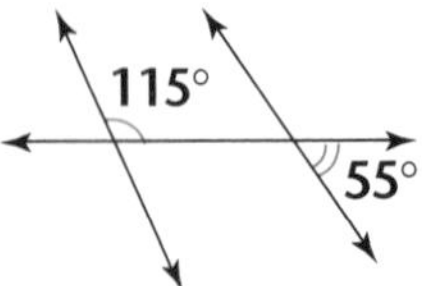

Chapter 4 Supplementary Problems

Name the ordered pair that corresponds to each point.

1. *G*

2. *A*

3. *C*

4. *J*

5. *F*

6. *I*

7. *D*

8. *H*

9. *B*

10. *E*

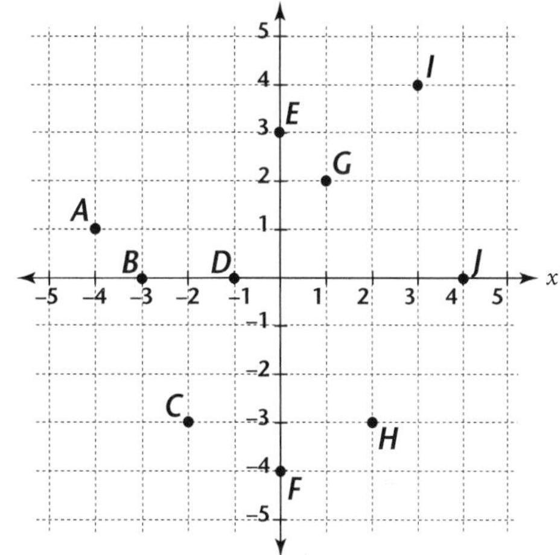

Name the point located at each ordered pair.

11. $(1, 0)$

12. $(4, -3)$

13. $(3, 0)$

14. $(-3, 1)$

15. $(-2, -2)$

16. $(1, 3)$

17. $(4, 4)$

18. $(0, 2)$

19. $(1, -3)$

20. $(0, -2)$

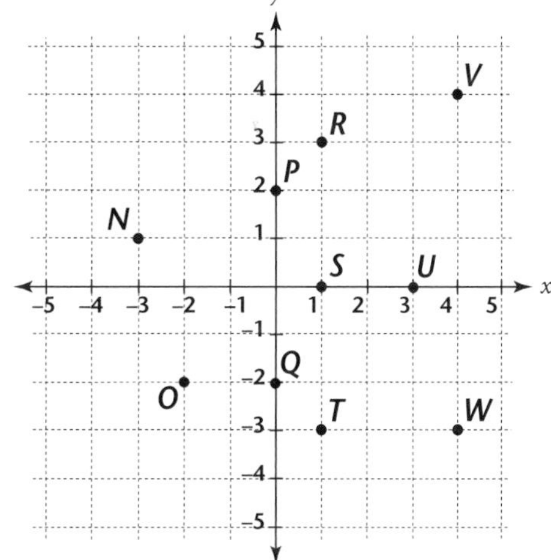

Chapter 4 Supplementary Problems

Find the slope, m, of each line.

21. line ℓ

22. line s

23. line n

24. line p

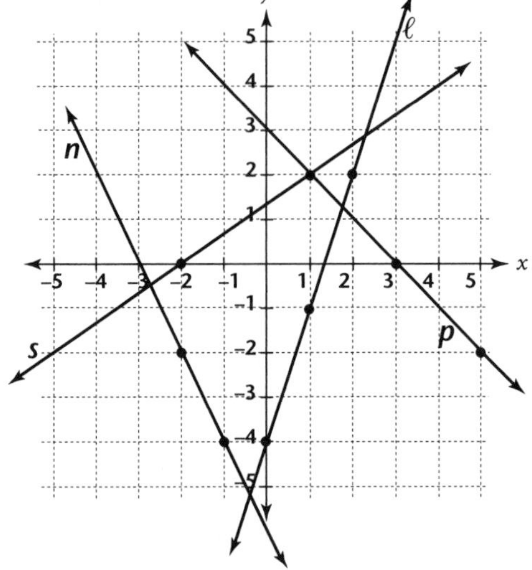

Find the slope, m, of the line that passes through the given points.

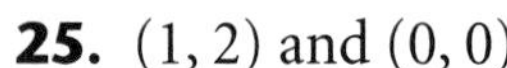

25. $(1, 2)$ and $(0, 0)$

26. $(3, 0)$ and $(2, 0)$

27. $(8, 3)$ and $(4, 1)$

28. $(4, 0)$ and $(2, 2)$

29. $(-3, -3)$ and $(5, 2)$

30. $(10, -6)$ and $(1, -6)$

Write the equation of the line that passes through each pair of points in problems 25–30 above. Use the form $y = mx + b$.

31. problem 25

32. problem 26

33. problem 27

34. problem 28

35. problem 29

36. problem 30

Chapter 4 Supplementary Problems

Find another point on each line using the slope and point given.

37. ℓ; $m = 3$; passes through $(-2, 4)$

38. t; $m = \frac{2}{5}$; passes through $(1, -4)$

39. r; $m = -2$; passes through $(-1, 3)$

40. q; $m = -\frac{3}{4}$; passes through $(0, 0)$

Make a grid and graph each of the lines described in problems 37–40 above. Connect the points with a line.

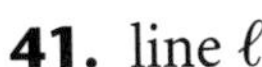

41. line ℓ

42. line t

43. line r

44. line q

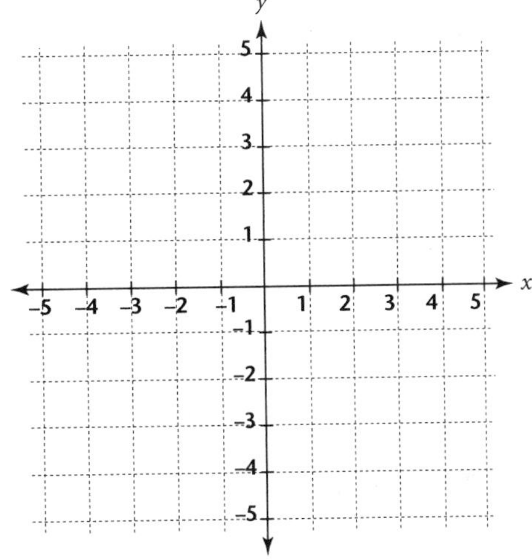

Use the midpoint formula to find the midpoints of line segments having the following endpoints.

45. $(1, 1)$ and $(5, 7)$

46. $(3, 4)$ and $(-1, 2)$

47. $(8, -3)$ and $(-2, 5)$

48. $(12, 8)$ and $(6, -4)$

49. $(0, 6)$ and $(4, 0)$

50. $(1, 5)$ and $(-6, 7)$

Chapter 5 Supplementary Problems

Name the polygon as precisely as you can.

1.

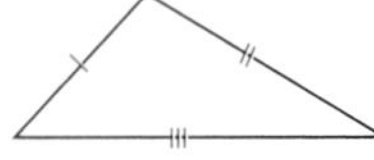

2.

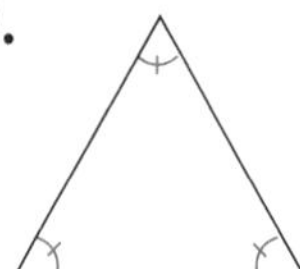

3.

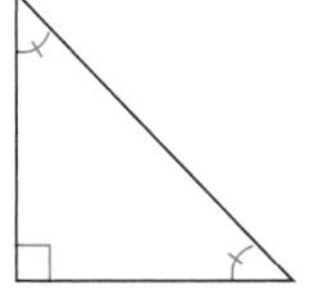

4.

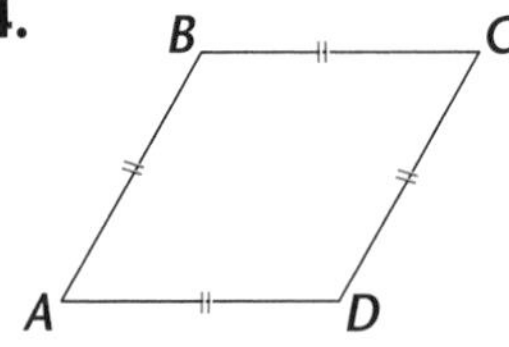

5.

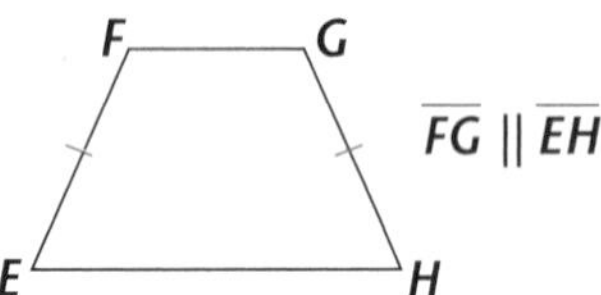

6.

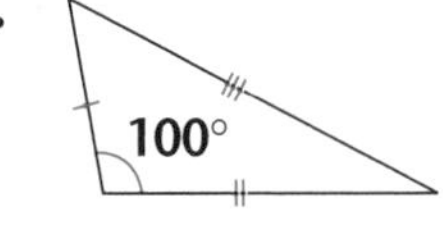

Complete the following constructions on a separate sheet of paper. Use only a straightedge and a compass.

7. Construct an equilateral triangle.

8. Draw any scalene triangle and label the angles X, Y, and Z. Construct the altitude from X to $\overline{YZ}$.

9. Construct a scalene right triangle.

10. Construct a 30°-60° right triangle.

11. Construct ΔLMN with $LM = LN$ and $m\angle L > 90°$.

Chapter 5 Supplementary Problems

Find the measure of $\angle x$.

12.

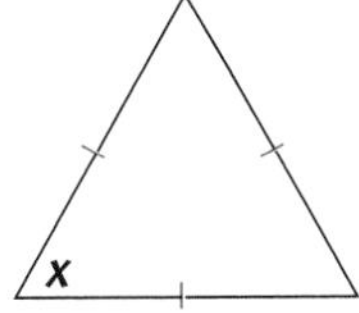

13.

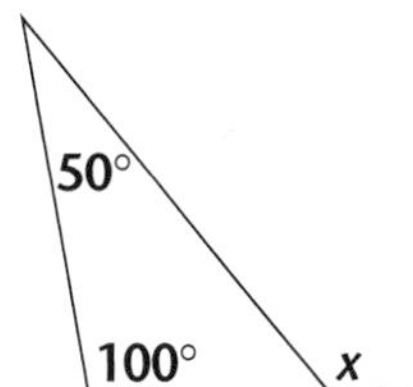

14.

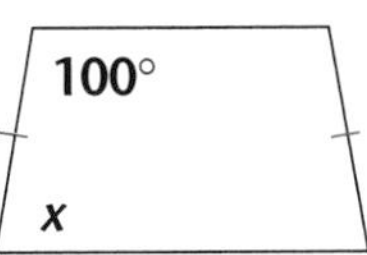

15.

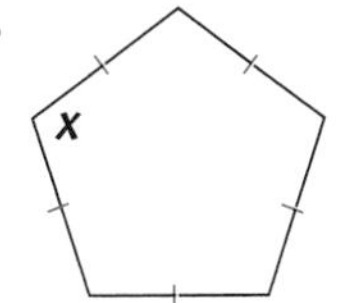

16.

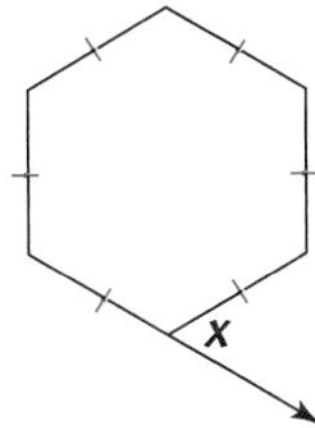

17.

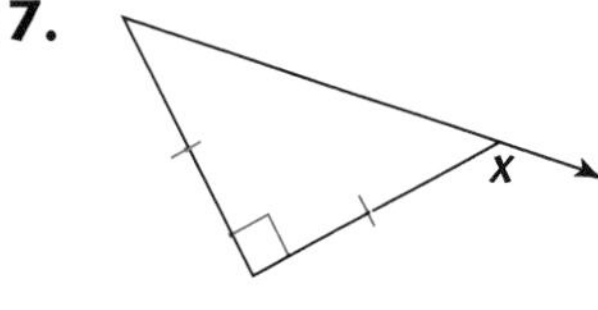

Use the information given to find the angles' measures.

18. m$\angle$2

19. m$\angle$3

20. m$\angle$8

21. m$\angle$5

22. m$\angle$4

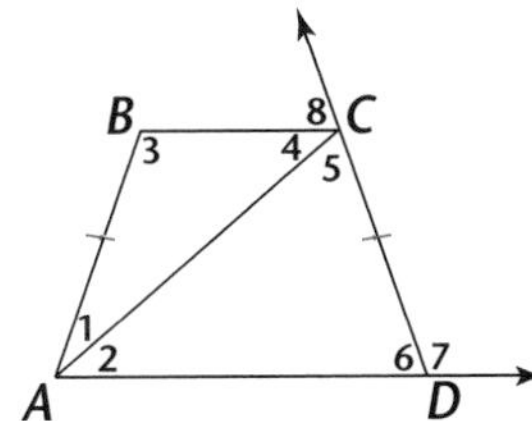

ABCD **is an isosceles trapezoid**
m$\angle$7 = 110°
m$\angle$1 = 30°

Chapter 5 Supplementary Problems

Answer the questions.

23. What is an altitude?

24. What is the sum of the measures of the interior angles of a regular octagon?

25. What is the measure of each angle in an equilateral triangle?

26. What is the measure of each interior angle of a 9-sided regular polygon?

27. How can you find the measure of an exterior angle of a triangle?

28. Is a trapezoid a parallelogram? Why or why not?

29. How can you find the number of triangles formed in a polygon by the diagonals from one vertex?

30. What is a median?

Use the information given to answer the questions.

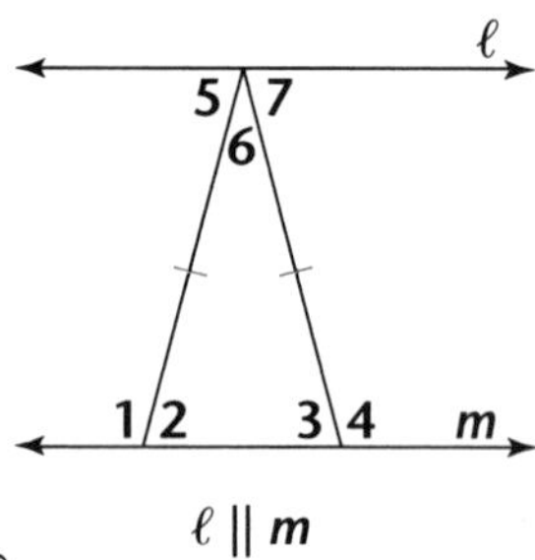

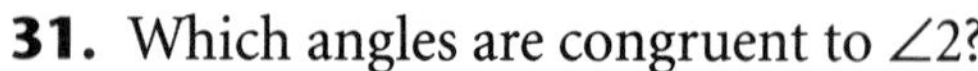

31. Which angles are congruent to $\angle 2$?

32. If $m\angle 6 = 40°$, what is the sum of $m\angle 5$ and $m\angle 7$?

33. If $m\angle 2 = 70°$ and $m\angle 4 = 110°$, what is $m\angle 6$?

34. Which angle measure equals the sum of $m\angle 6$ and $m\angle 2$?

35. Are $\angle 1$ and $\angle 4$ exterior angles? Why or why not?

Chapter 6 Supplementary Problems

Tell whether the triangles in each pair are congruent. Write *yes* or *no*. If your answer is *yes*, name the postulate that supports your answer. If your answer is *no*, explain why.

1.

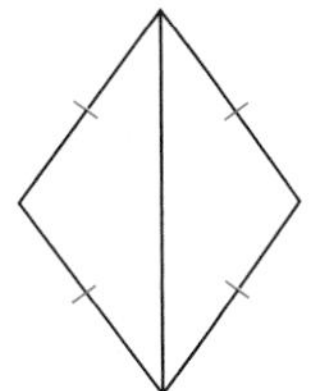

2.

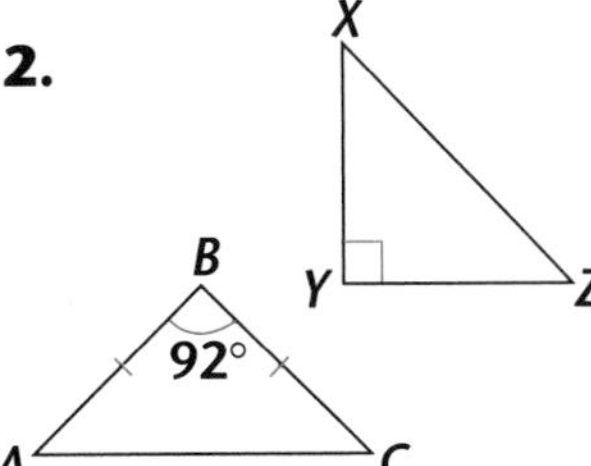

3.

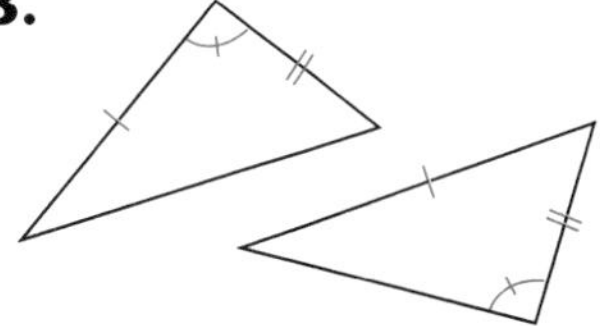

4.

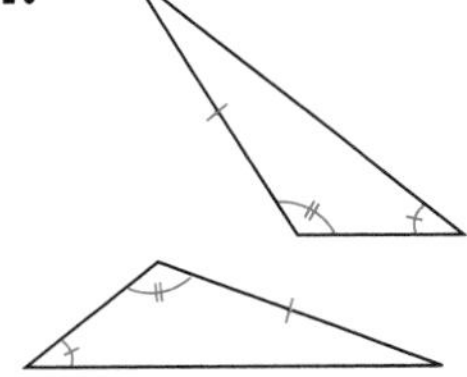

Tell whether you can construct a triangle with the given sides. Write *yes* or *no*.

5. *a*

b *c*

6. $a = 6, b = 3, c = 7$

7. $a = 14, b = 12, c = 5$

8. $a = 5, b = 5, c = 10$

9. *a*

b

c

10. $a = 8, b = 3, c = 4$

11. $a = 5, b = 6, c = 18$

12. $a = 9, b = 9\frac{1}{2}, c = 18$

Chapter 6 Supplementary Problems

Solve the following the problems.

13. $x + 2x + 3x = 180°$

14. $3x + 5x = 120°$

15. If m∠1 is half m∠2, what is m∠1? ∠2?

16. If m∠2 = m∠3, what is m∠2? ∠3?

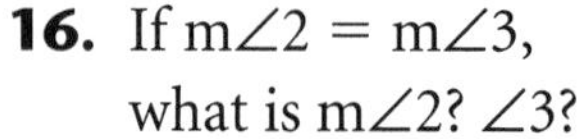

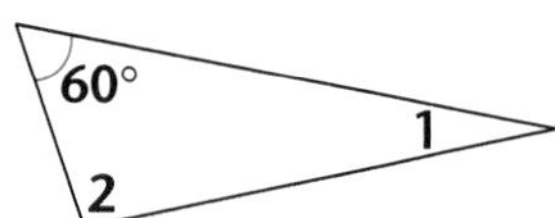

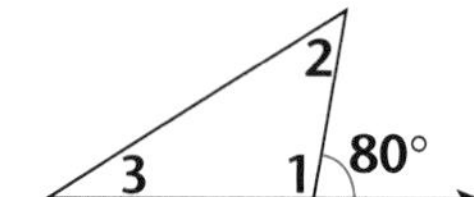

Complete the proof.

Given: ΔABC is an equilateral triangle.
$\overline{BX}$ is a perpendicular bisector.

Prove: $\Delta ABX \cong \Delta CBX$

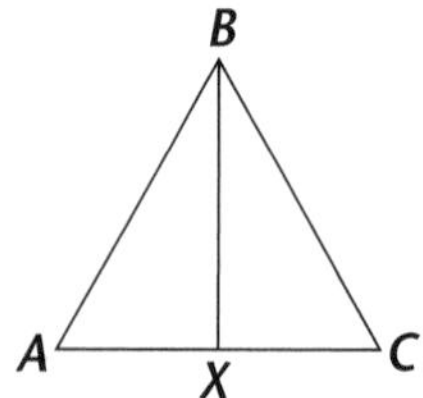

Proof

Statement	Reason
1. $\overline{BX}$ is a perpendicular bisector.	1. **17.**
2. $AB = CB$	2. **18.**
3. $AX = XC$	3. **19.**
4. $BX = BX$	4. **20.**
5. $\Delta ABX = \Delta CBX$	5. **21.**

Chapter 6 Supplementary Problems

Tell how many lines of symmetry each figure has.

22.

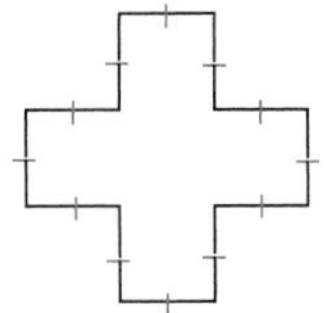

23.

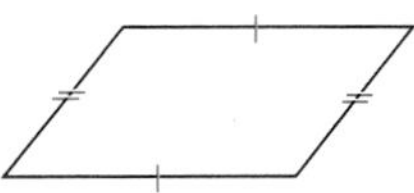

24.

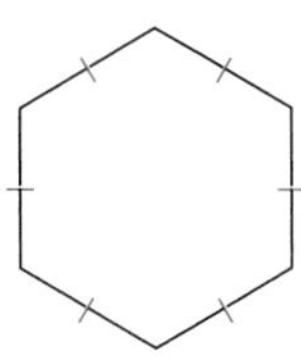

25.

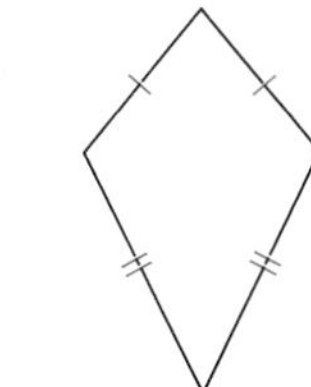

Identify the coordinate of the image of each point under the translation $(x + 3, y - 2)$.

26. $F = (8, 0)$

27. $H = (12, -10)$

28. $T = (9, -7)$

29. $S = (-12, 3)$

30. $R = (3, 2)$

31. $B = (-5, -2)$

32. $P = (-28, -45)$

33. $D = (-3, 4)$

Reflect each image over the indicated axis. Give the coordinates of the image vertices.

34. y-axis

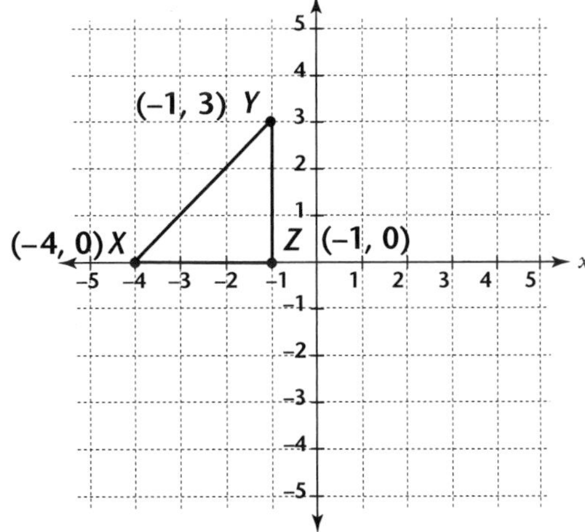

35. x-axis

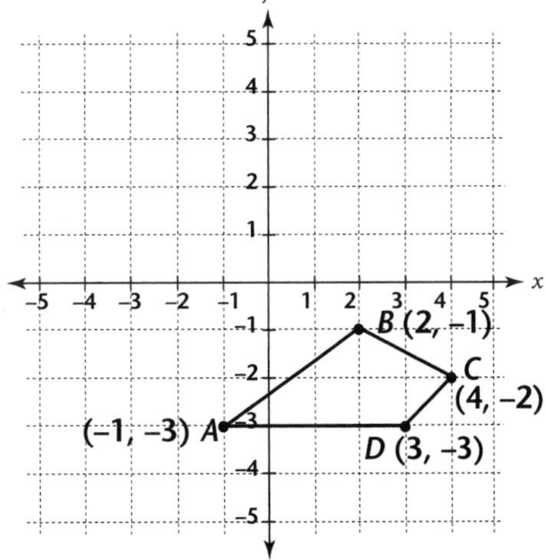

Chapter 7 Supplementary Problems

Are the following ratios equal? Write yes or no.

1. $\frac{6}{7}$ and $\frac{12}{14}$

2. $\frac{1}{3}$ and $\frac{4}{11}$

3. $\frac{2}{5}$ and $\frac{7}{17}$

4. $\frac{6}{7}$ and $\frac{12}{14}$

5. $\frac{9}{12}$ and $\frac{2}{3}$

6. $\frac{5}{8}$ and $\frac{10}{16}$

7. $\frac{11}{10}$ and $\frac{110}{100}$

8. $\frac{8}{3}$ and $\frac{24}{9}$

9. $\frac{7}{16}$ and $\frac{21}{32}$

10. $\frac{3}{25}$ and $\frac{1}{5}$

Find the missing value in each proportion.

11. $\frac{3}{5} = \frac{27}{x}$

12. $\frac{5}{8} = \frac{z}{32}$

13. $\frac{7}{9} = \frac{56}{y}$

14. $\frac{3}{11} = \frac{r}{121}$

15. $\frac{3}{7} = \frac{18}{z}$

16. $\frac{4}{5} = \frac{m}{15}$

Tell whether the triangles in each pair are similar. Answer yes or no. Give reasons for your answer.

17.

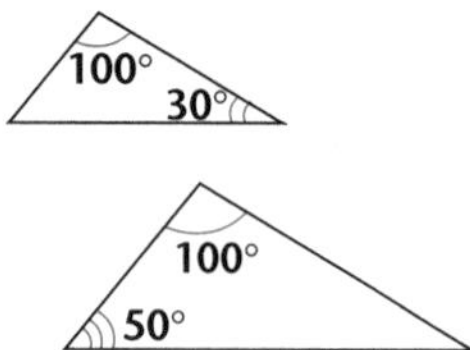

18.

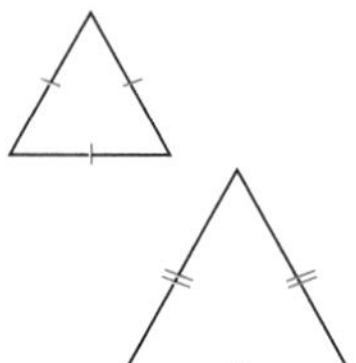

Name the corresponding angles and sides of the similar triangles.

19. m$\angle BDE$ = ■

20. m$\angle C$ = ■

21. $\frac{DB}{AB} = \frac{BE}{■}$

22. $\frac{AC}{■} = \frac{BC}{■}$

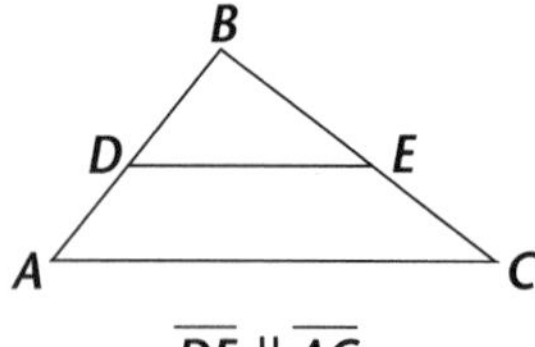

Chapter 7 Supplementary Problems

Find the measure of each interior angle for a regular polygon with the given number of sides.

23. $n = 15$

24. $n = 18$

Complete the following construction on a separate sheet of paper. Use only a straightedge and a compass.

25. Construct a regular hexagon.

Solve for the unknown value in each pair of similar triangles.

26. x

27. y

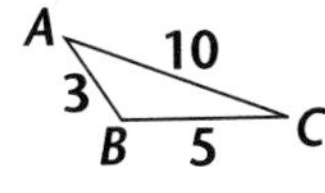

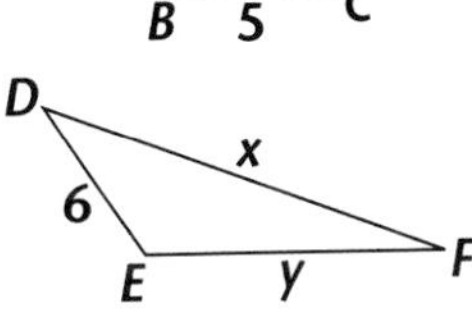

28. x

29. y

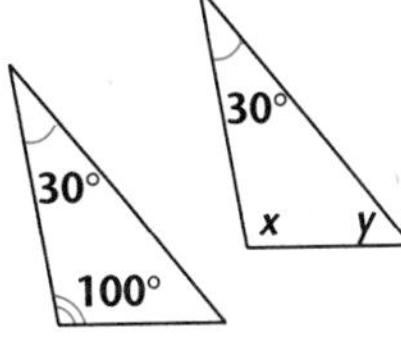

Find the perimeter of each polygon.

30. The ratio of similarity is 3:2

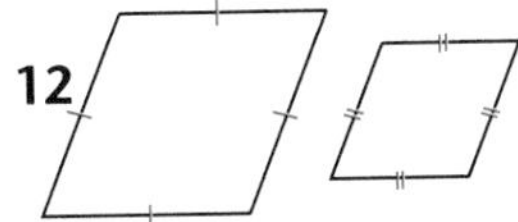

31. The ratio of similarity is 3:1

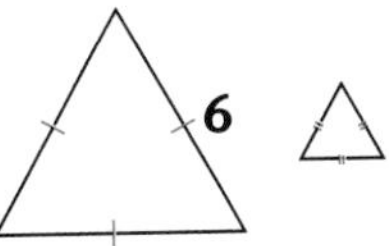

32. The ratio of similarity is 4:5

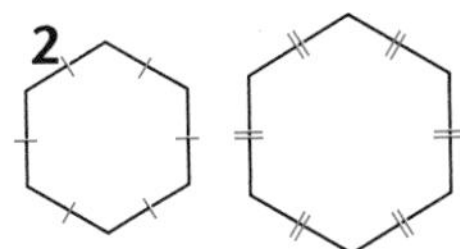

33. The ratio of similarity is 3:4

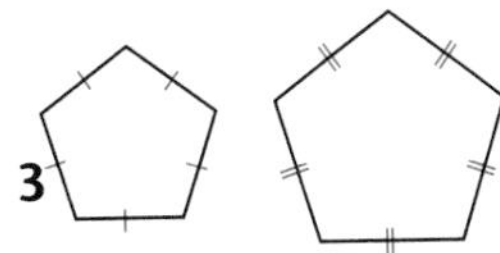

Chapter 7 Supplementary Problems

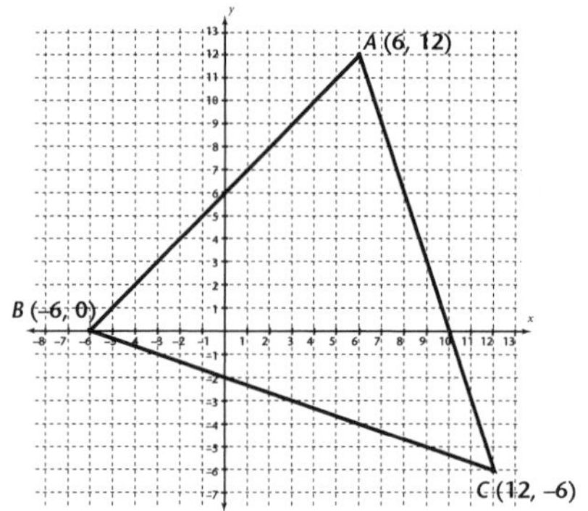

Give the coordinates of the image triangle under the following dilations. Use graph paper to graph the object and its image. (All dilations have (0, 0) as the center of the dilation.)

34. dilation of 3

35. dilation of $\frac{1}{2}$

36. dilation of $\frac{1}{3}$

Solve the following problems.

37. To find the height of a building, an engineer used similar triangles and the height of a smaller building to draw the diagram shown. What is the height of the taller building?

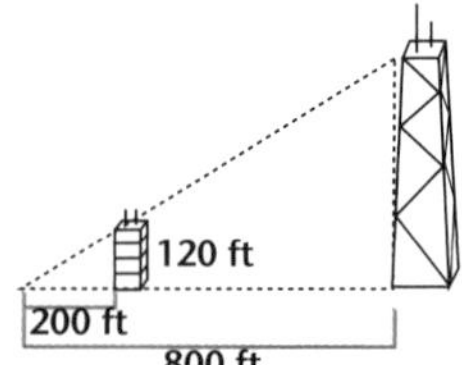

38. Jonas is making a poster by making a 3 × 5-inch photo 4 times larger. He drew the size of the photo on a grid as shown. What will the coordinates of the poster be if Jonas draws its image on the grid?

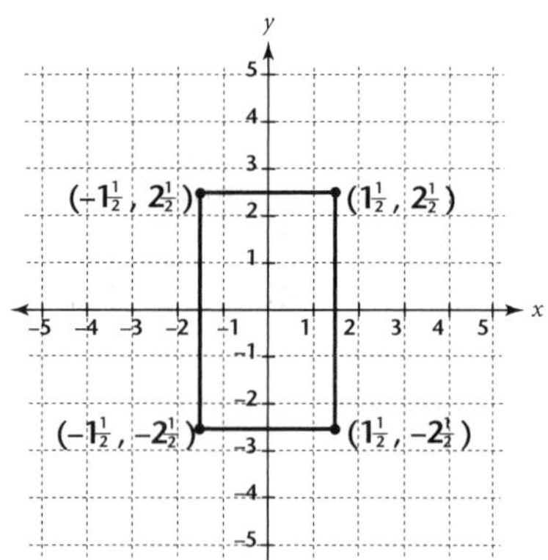

39. A model airplane has a ratio of similarity with the actual airplane of 1:240. If the model measures $4\frac{1}{4}$ inches, what is the measurement of the actual airplane?

40. A model sailboat has a ratio of similarity with an actual sailboat of 1:28. If the actual sailboat measures 42 feet, what is the measurement of the model sailboat?

Chapter 8 Supplementary Problems

Find additional triples using the given triples and multiplier.

1. triple (3, 4, 5) by 2

2. triple (3, 4, 5) by 8

3. triple (3, 4, 5) by 10

4. triple (5, 12, 13) by 2

5. triple (5, 12, 13) by 3

6. triple (5, 12, 13) by 10

Find the length of the unknown side of each right triangle.

7.

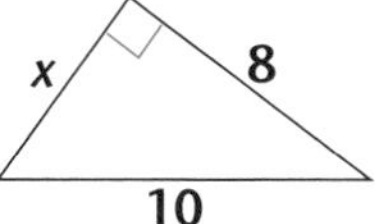

8.

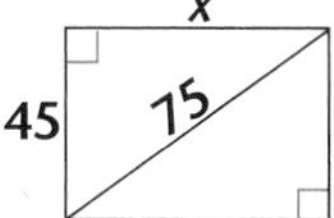

9.

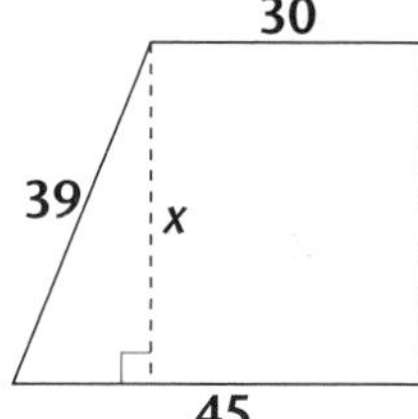

One leg of an isosceles right triangle is given. Solve for the hypotenuse.

10. 5 cm

11. 12 ft

12. 1 in.

13. 2 m

14. 7 mi

15. 25 yd

The hypotenuse of a 30°-60° right triangle is given. Solve for both legs.

16. 18 m

17. 4 yd

18. 12 in.

19. 24 ft

20. 40 cm

21. 2 mi

Chapter 8 Supplementary Problems

Answer the following questions about equilateral ΔABC.

22. What is the length of $\overline{AD}$?

23. What is the length of $\overline{AB}$?

24. What is the length of $\overline{BC}$?

25. What is $m\angle BDC$?

26. What is $m\angle BCD$?

27. What is $m\angle DBC$?

28. What is a name for ΔABD?

29. What is the length of $\overline{BD}$?

Find the area of each trapezoid.

30.

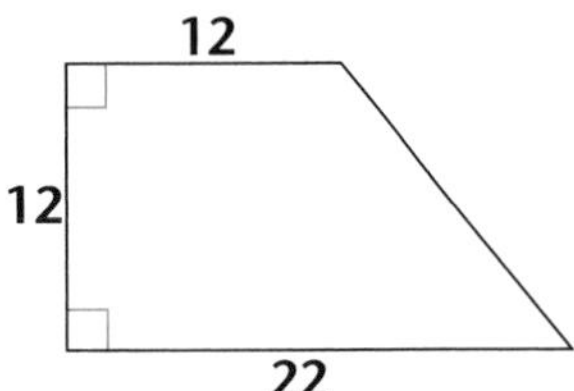

31.

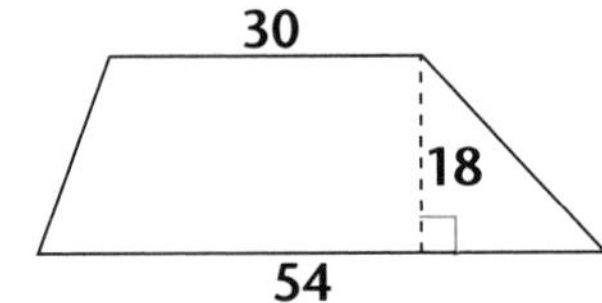

Solve the following problems.

32. A window washer uses a ladder to reach a window 15 feet high. The base of the ladder must be placed at least 4 feet from the wall for safety reasons. Will a 16-foot ladder reach the window?

Chapter 8 Supplementary Problems

33. Charlotte cut a triangular piece of glass to fit in a 90° corner of the frame of a large stained-glass window. After cutting the piece, she measures the lengths of the sides and finds they are $3\frac{1}{2}$ ft, 6 ft, and $7\frac{1}{4}$ ft. Will the piece of glass fit in the corner? Explain your answer.

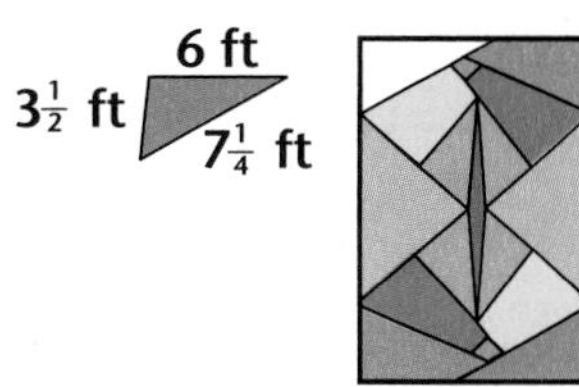

Tell whether or not each triangle is a right triangle. Answer *yes* or *no*. If it is, name the right angle.

34.

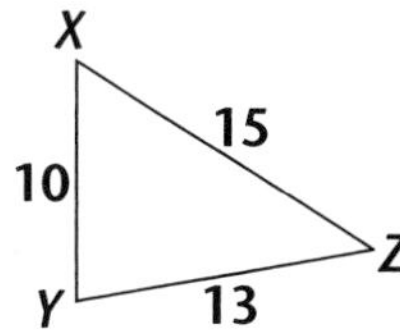

35.

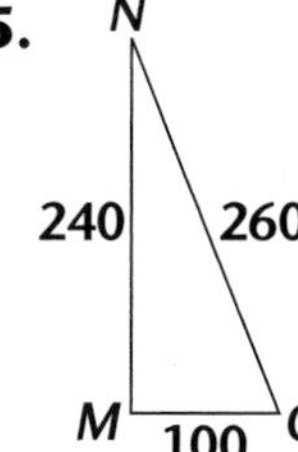

36.

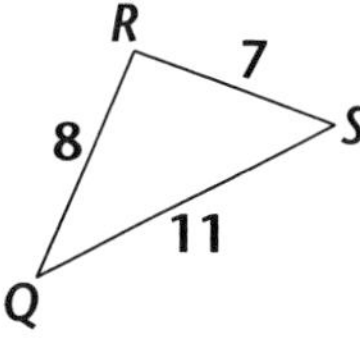

37.

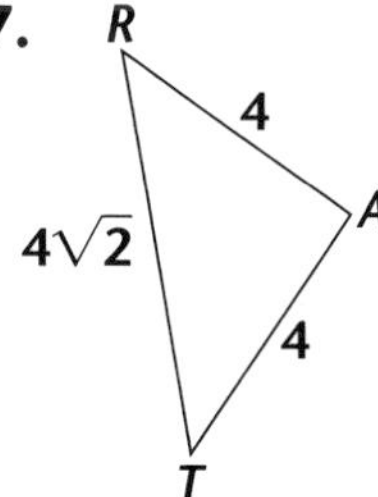

Use the distance formula to find the distances between the given points. Round to the nearest tenth.

38. $(-4, -6)$ and $(8, 10)$

39. $(8, 10)$ and $(20, 32)$

40. $(9, -5)$ and $(20, -10)$

Chapter 9 Supplementary Problems

Find the perimeter of each polygon.

1.

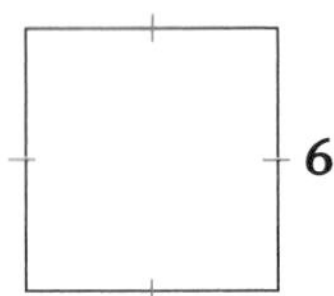

2.

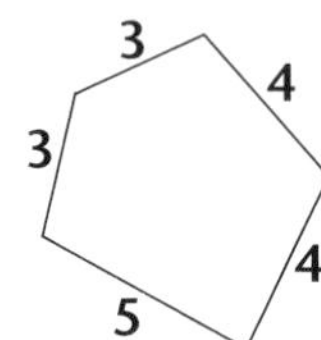

3.

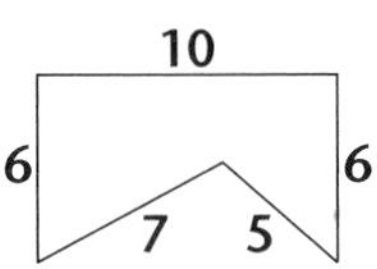

4.

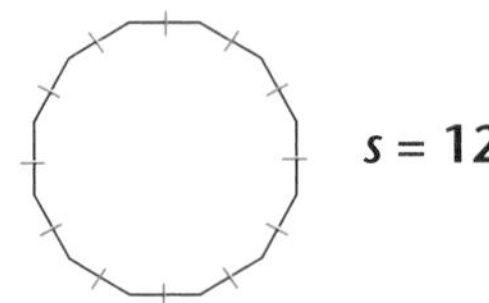

5. rhombus, $s = 125$

6. rectangle, $l = 14$, $w = 10$

Find the perimeter of the following figures. Use the distance formula to find side length, then calculate the perimeter of each figure. (Use a calculator and round to the nearest tenth.)

7. ΔABC

8. $ABCD$

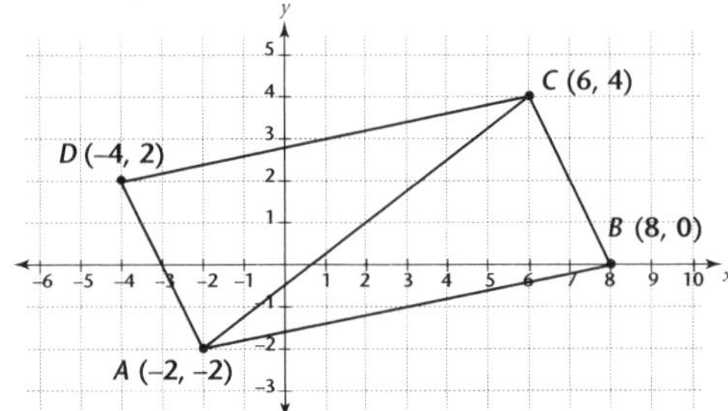

Use the Pythagorean Theorem to find the length of the unknown side. Then find the perimeter.

9.

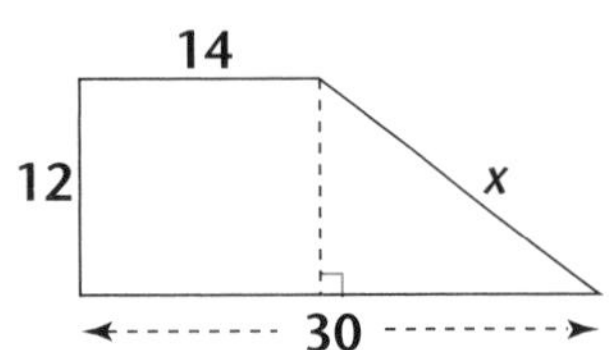

10.

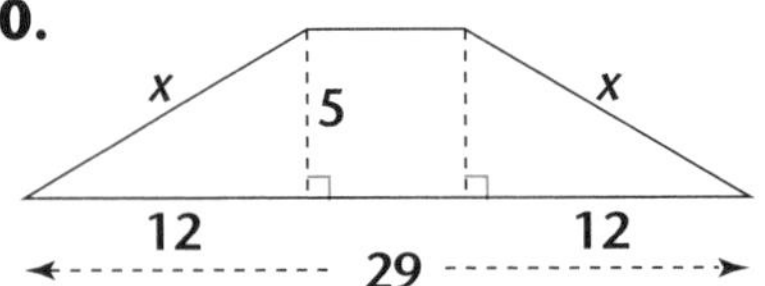

11.

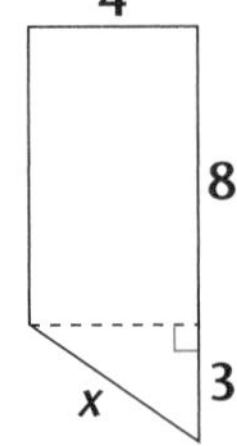

Chapter 9 Supplementary Problems

Solve the following problems.

12. What are the length and width of a rectangle that has a perimeter of 60 and a length 2 times the width?

13. Three times the base of a parallelogram is equal to 4 times the height. The parallelogram has a perimeter of 42. What is its base? Height?

14. What is the length of the diagonal of a square with an area of 64?

15. The length of a rectangle is 4 times the width. The perimeter of the rectangle is 120. What are the length and width of the rectangle?

16. Narinda will put seed on 600 square feet of backyard. Her backyard is 25 feet long. How wide is her backyard?

17. Victor is painting 11 square feet of baseboard around his kitchen. The baseboard is $\frac{1}{4}$ foot wide. The kitchen is 12 feet long. How wide is the kitchen?

Find the length of the unknown side.

18.

$A = 72\text{ ft}^2$ x

9 ft

19.

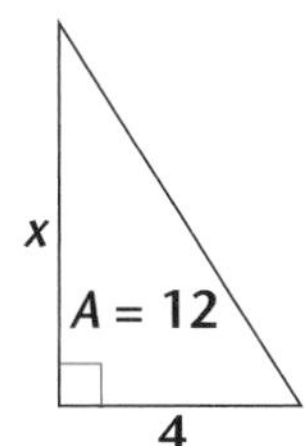

20.

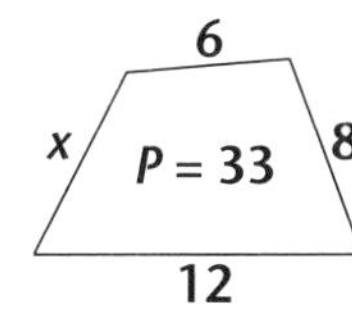

Chapter 9 Supplementary Problems

Find the area of each quadrilateral.

21. 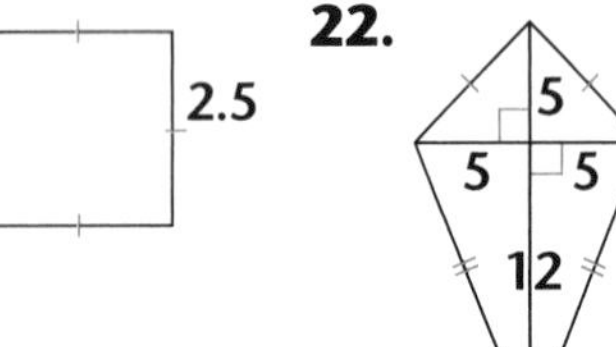

22. 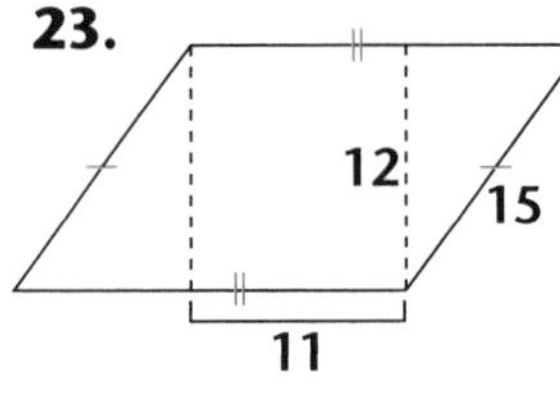

23. 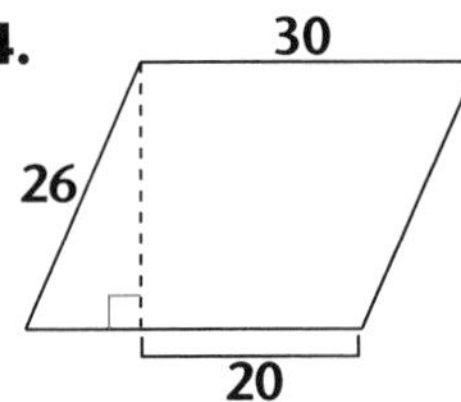

24.

25. 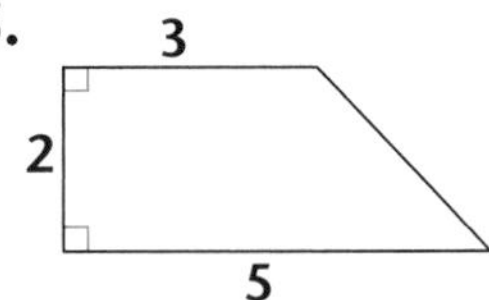

26. 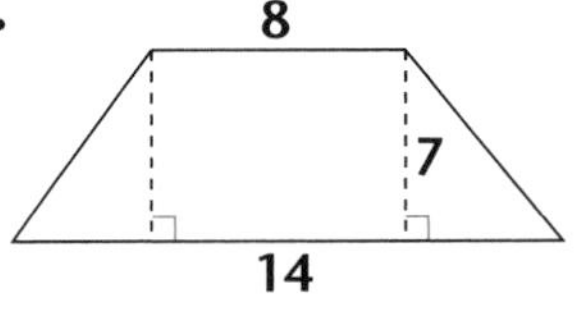

27. 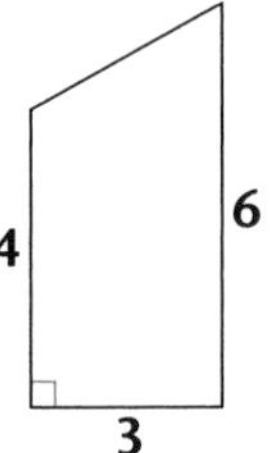

Use Heron's Formula to find the areas of triangles with the given side lengths. Use a calculator and round to the nearest tenth.

28. 9, 10, 13

29. 4, 5, 7

30. 10, 10, 16

31. 12, 12, 12

Find the area of each triangle.

32. 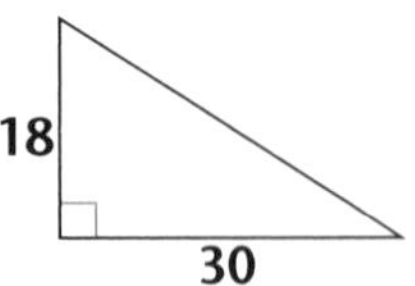

33. 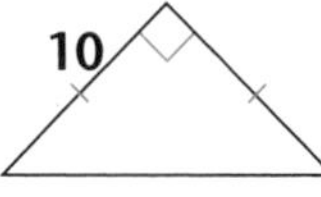

34. 

35. 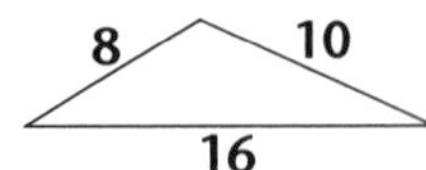

Chapter 10 Supplementary Problems

Estimate the circumference and the area of a circle with the given radius or diameter. Use 3.1 as an approximate value for π.

	Circumference	Area
$r = 1$ in.	**1.** ______	**2.** ______
$d = 1$ cm	**3.** ______	**4.** ______
$r = 20$ ft	**5.** ______	**6.** ______
$d = 30$ m	**7.** ______	**8.** ______
$r = \frac{1}{2}$ in.	**9.** ______	**10.** ______

Find the area of the shaded sector. Give your answer in terms of π.

11.

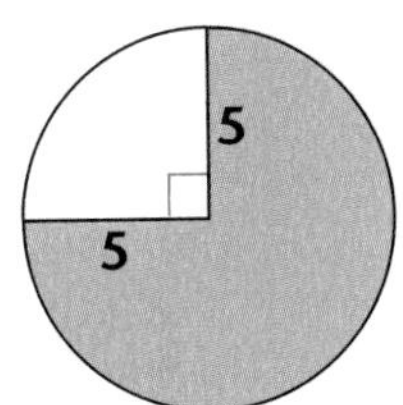

12.

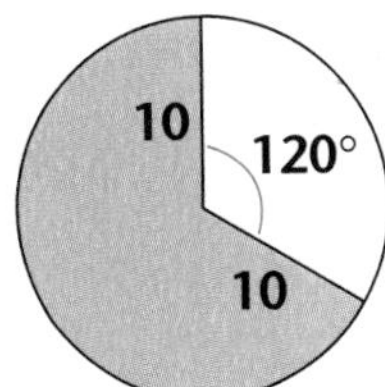

13.

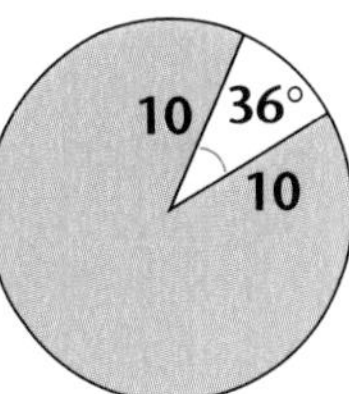

Find the value of the unknown.

14. inscribed angle

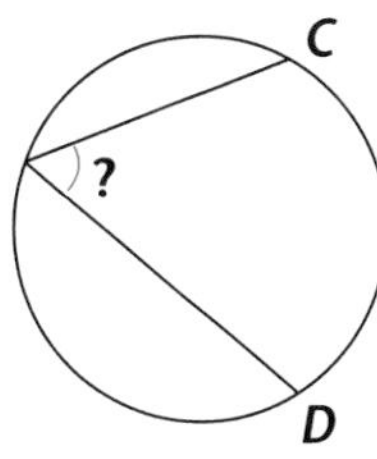

$\overset{\frown}{CD} = 120°$

15. $\overset{\frown}{PR} = ■$

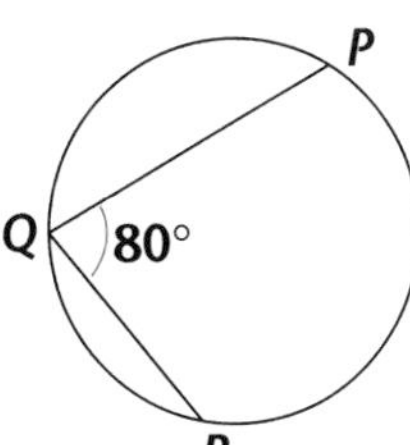

Chapter 10 Supplementary Problems

Find the probabilities.

16. P(shaded area)

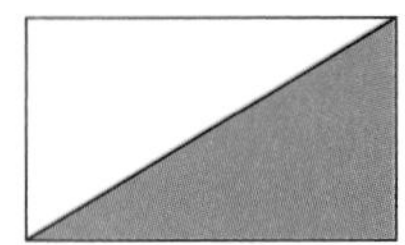

17. P(shaded area)

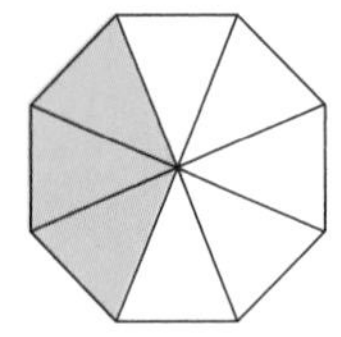

18. P(shaded area)

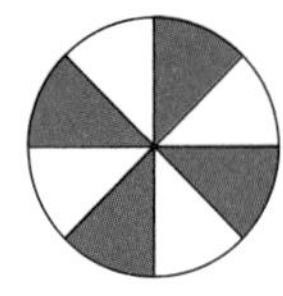

Find the surface area and the volume for each sphere. Give your answer in terms of π.

	Surface Area	Volume
$r = 1$ mi	**19.** ______	**20.** ______
$d = 4$ ft	**21.** ______	**22.** ______
$r = 20$ ft	**23.** ______	**24.** ______
$d = 30$ m	**25.** ______	**26.** ______
$r = \frac{1}{2}$ in.	**27.** ______	**28.** ______

Choose the correct term to complete each sentence.

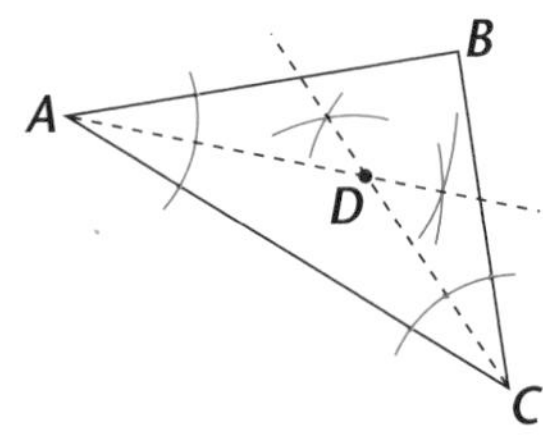

29. In ΔABC, the point D where the angle bisectors meet is the center of the triangle's _____.

A circumcenter **B** incircle **C** circumcircle

30. An incircle of ΔABC touches _____.

A each vertex of the triangle **B** each side of the triangle

C each perpendicular bisector

Chapter 10 Supplementary Problems

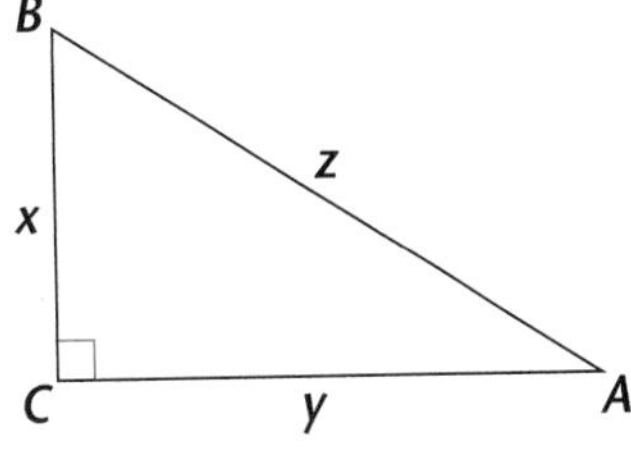

For right ΔABC, find x.
Round your answer to the nearest hundredth.

31. $m\angle A = 30°$, $AB = 15$

32. $m\angle A = 38°$, $AB = 20$

33. $m\angle A = 40°$, $AB = 5$

34. $m\angle A = 60°$, $AB = 14$

35. $m\angle A = 54°$, $AB = 16$

For right ΔABC, find z.
Round your answer to the nearest hundredth.

36. $m\angle B = 60°$, $BC = 10$

37. $m\angle B = 48°$, $BC = 20$

38. $m\angle B = 54°$, $BC = 12$

39. $m\angle A = 45°$, $AC = 3$

40. $m\angle A = 21°$, $AC = 8$

For right ΔABC, find y.
Round your answer to the nearest hundredth.

41. $m\angle A = 40°$, $BC = 21$

42. $m\angle A = 45°$, $BC = 13$

43. $m\angle A = 25°$, $BC = 20$

44. $m\angle A = 30°$, $BC = 6$

45. $m\angle A = 65°$, $BC = 9$

Chapter 11 Supplementary Problems

Find the volumes of these solids.

1.

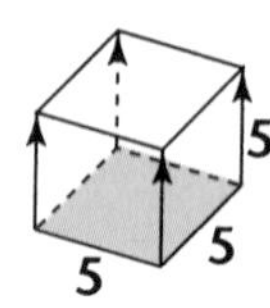

2.

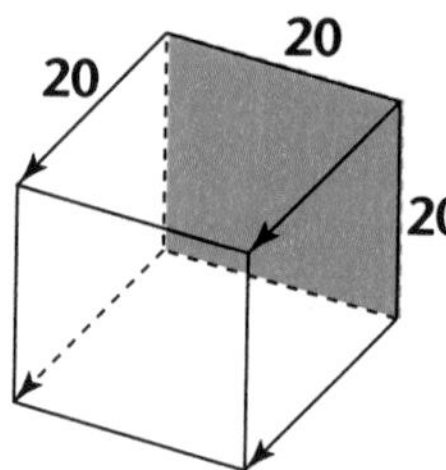

3.

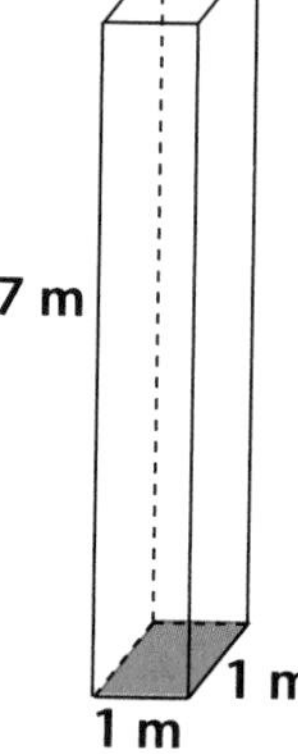

4.

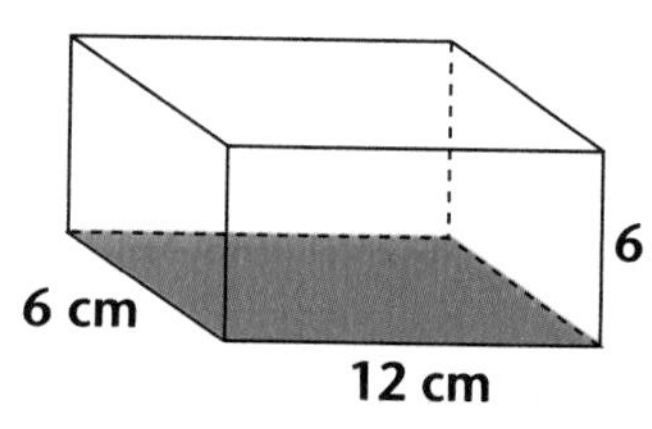

5.

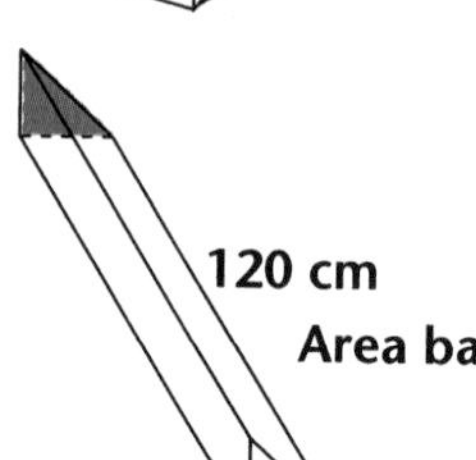

Find the surface area of each figure. Some answers may be in terms of π.

6.

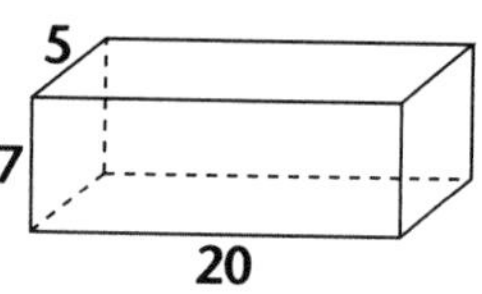

7.

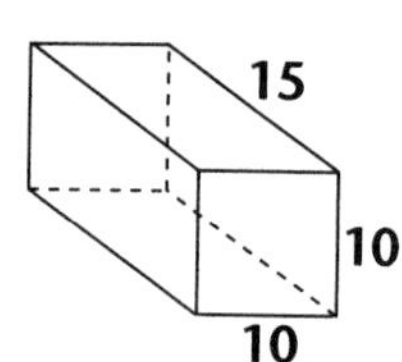

8.

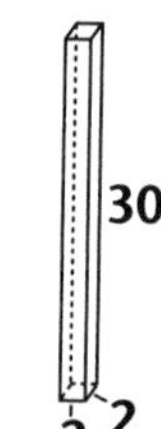

9.

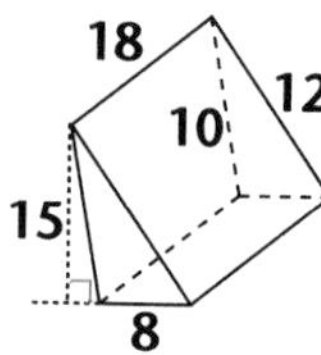

10.

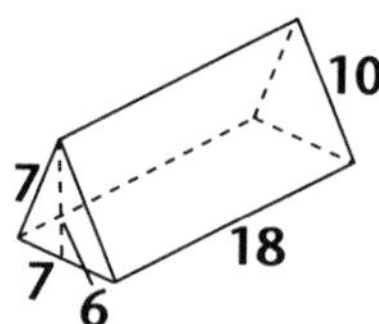

11.

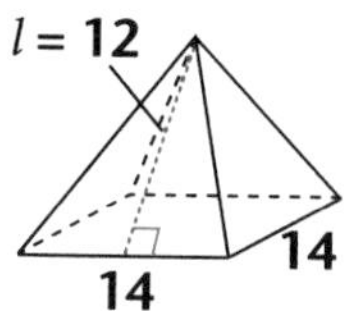

12.

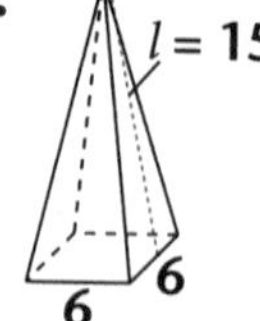

13.

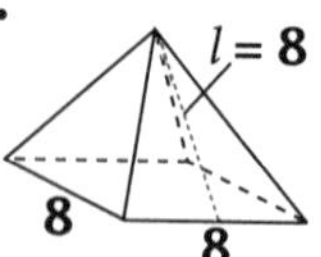

14.

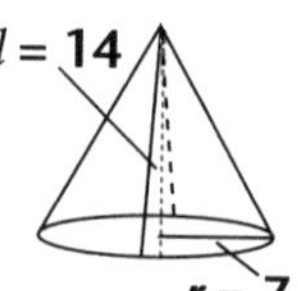

15.

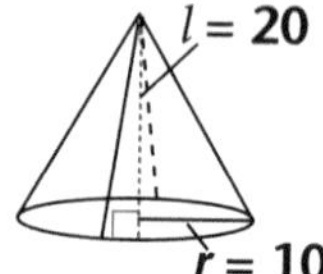

Chapter 11 Supplementary Problems

Find the volume and total surface area for each figure. You may give your answers in terms of π.

16. 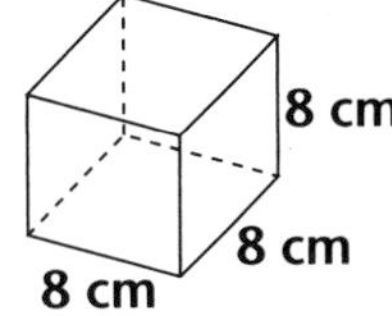

17. 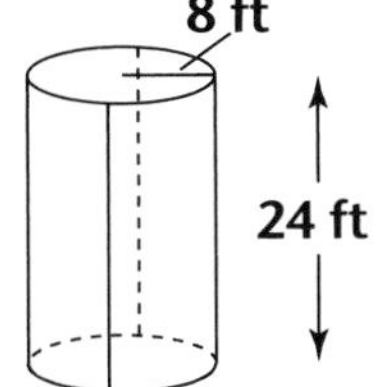

18. 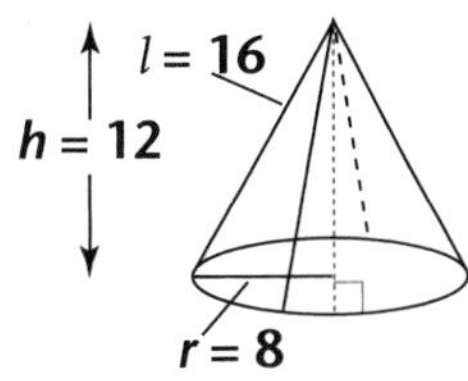

19. 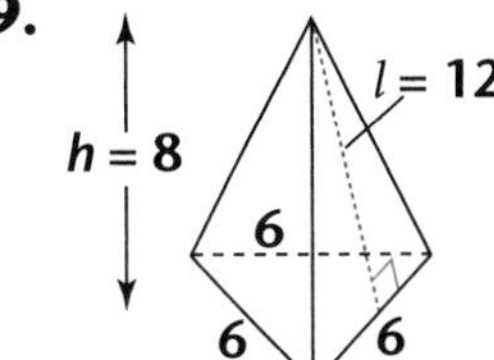

20. 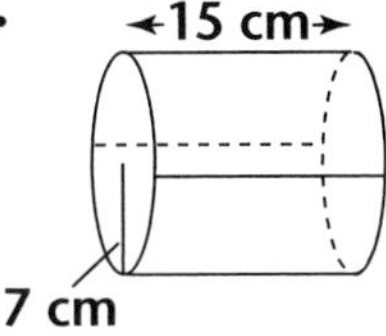

21. 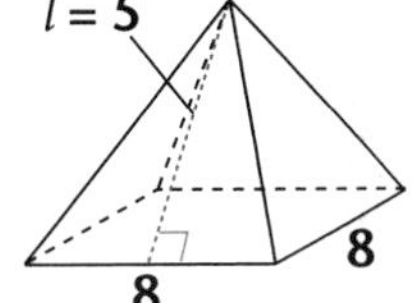

Complete each statement.

22. 6 yd = __________ in.

23. 6 cups = __________ fluid ounces

24. 12 tons = __________ pounds

25. 4 mi = __________ ft

26. 8 pounds = __________ ounces

27. 5 kg = __________ g

28. 8 m = __________ cm

29. 8 cups = __________ gal

30. 12 c = __________ pints

31. 16 ft = __________ in.

32. 3 yd = __________ ft

33. 2 L = __________ ml

Chapter 11 Supplementary Problems

Solve the following problems. You may leave some answers in terms of π.

34. What is the surface area of a triangular door stop whose base measures 6 in. × 6 in. × 6 in. and whose height is 12 in.?

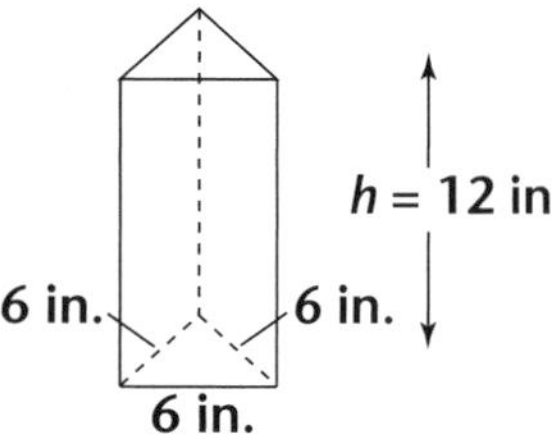

35. Deonne plans to cover the sides and roof of the birdhouse below with copper sheeting. About how much copper will he need? Round to the nearest square centimeter.

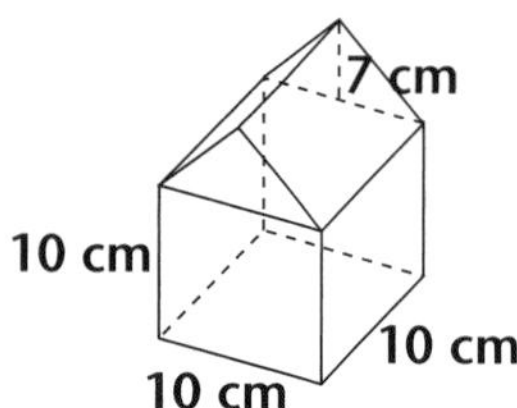

36. Ms. Thomas built a shed that can hold 3,240 cubic feet of storage. It is in the shape of a right prism. It is 18 feet long and 12 feet wide. How high is the shed?

37. What is the surface area of an open aquarium that is 24 in. wide, 14 in. long, and 18 in. deep?

38. Mr. Joungston needs to paint the sides but not the dome of the old corn silo. How many square feet of metal will he be painting?

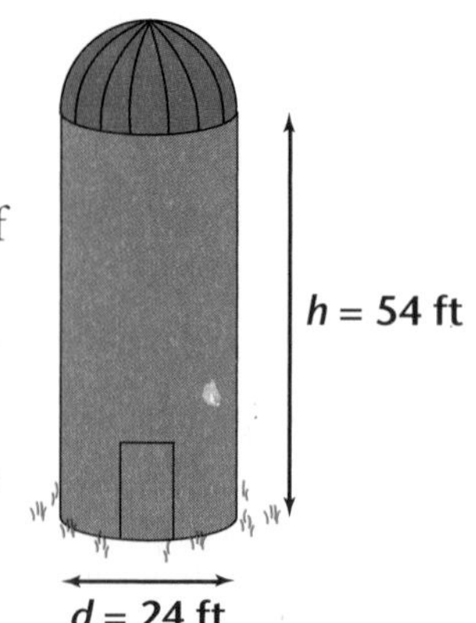

39. How much plastic shrink-wrap is needed to wrap a case of 24 cans of water?

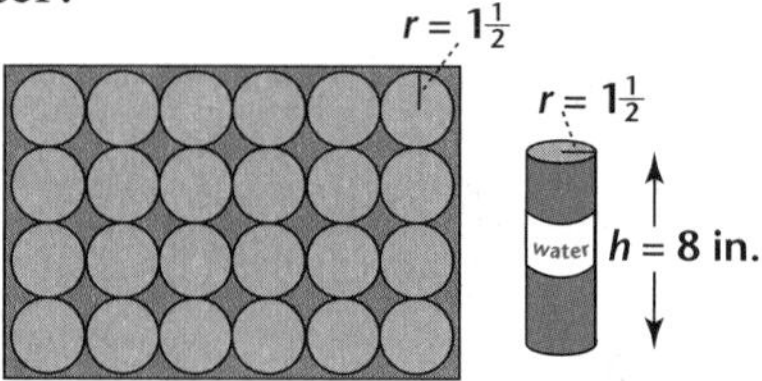

40. Mae Li built a bird feeder shaped like a cylinder. It can hold 150.72 cu in. of birdseed. The area of the base is about 12.56 sq in. What is the height of the bird feeder?

Chapter 12 Supplementary Problems

Sketch and describe the locus of the intersection of the following pairs of figures.

1. A line and a circle have one point in common.
2. A line and a circle have two points in common.
3. A plane and a cone form a circle.
4. A plane and a cone form an oval.
5. Two parallel lines and a circle form 4 points.
6. Two parallel planes and a sphere produce a circle and a great circle.
7. Each of two planes forms a distinct great circle with a sphere.

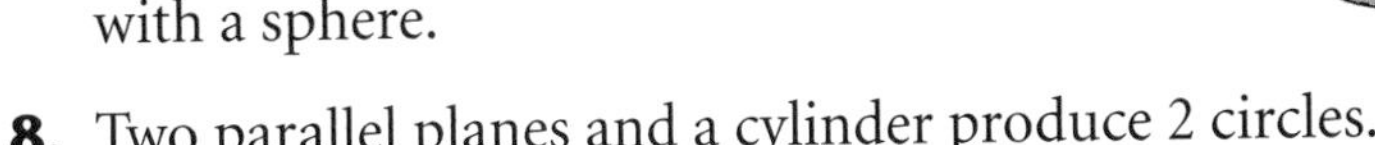

8. Two parallel planes and a cylinder produce 2 circles.
9. Two parallel planes and a cylinder produce 2 ovals.
10. Two parallel planes and a cylinder produce 2 lines.

Draw a sketch and write an equation for each locus.

11. Locus of points 2 units away from $y = \frac{1}{2}$.

12. Locus of points 4 units away from $x = -2$.

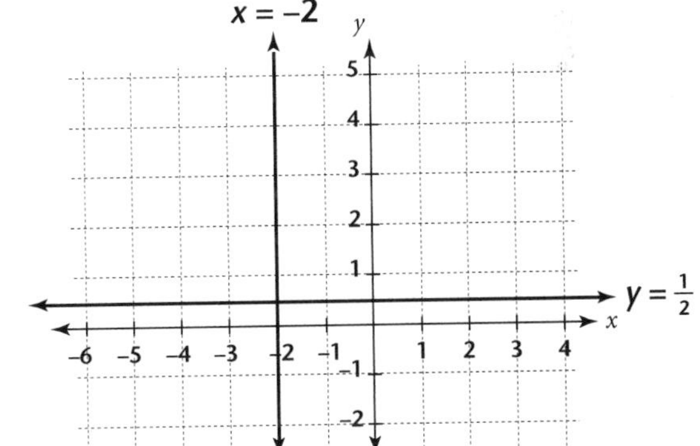

13. Locus of points equidistant from $y = 2$ and $y = 5$.

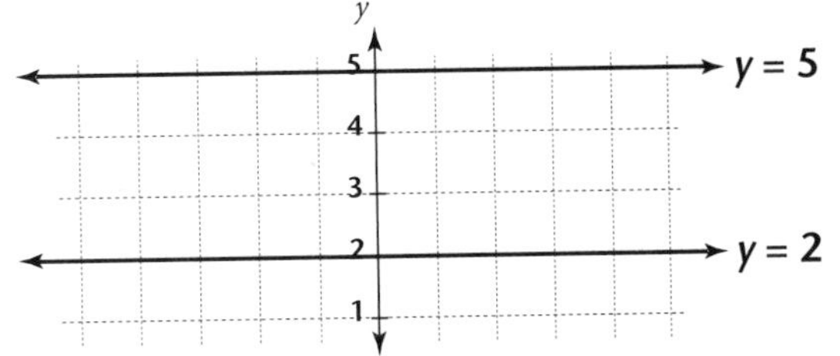

Chapter 12 Supplementary Problems

14. Locus of points equidistant from $y = -x + 2$ and passing through $y = 4$ and $y = 0$.

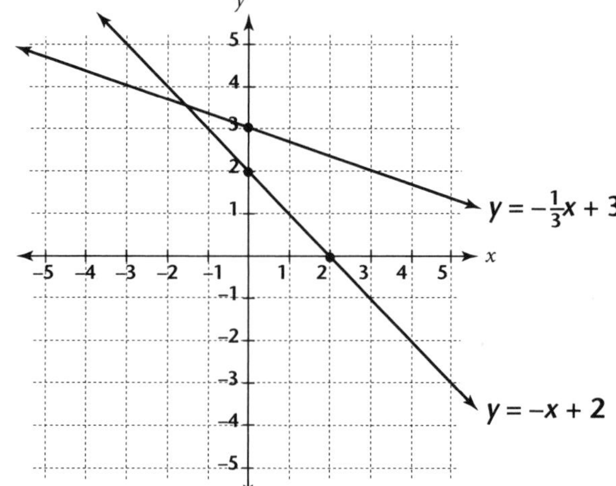

15. Locus of points equidistant from $y = -\frac{1}{3}x + 3$ and passing through $y = 1$ and $y = 5$.

16. Locus of points in a plane 2 units from the origin.

17. Locus of points in a plane $1\frac{1}{2}$ units from the origin.

18. Locus of points in a plane 3.4 units from the origin.

19. Locus of points in a plane equidistant from $(4, 1)$ and $(-2, 1)$.

20. Locus of points in a plane equidistant from $(-3, 2)$ and $(-3, 6)$.

Chapter 12 Supplementary Problems

Sketch and describe these compound loci.

21. The locus of points equidistant from $\overrightarrow{XW}$ and $\overrightarrow{XZ}$ and at a distance of GH from X.

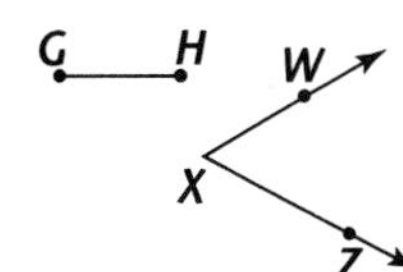

22. The locus of points equidistant from $\overline{XY}$, $\overline{YZ}$, and $\overline{ZX}$.

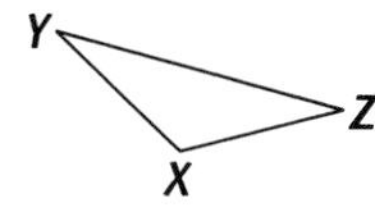

23. The locus of points equidistant from $\angle H$, $\angle I$, and $\angle J$.

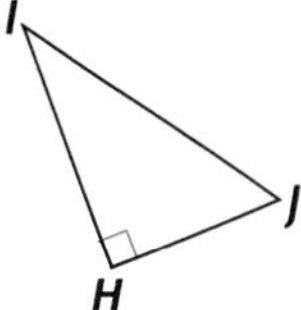

24. The locus of points equidistant from points A and B and equidistant from points C and D.

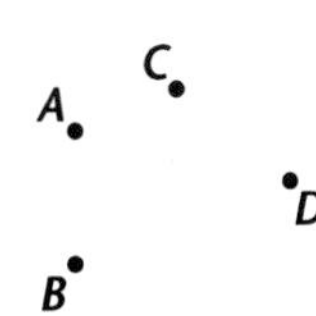

25. The locus of points equidistant from the parallel lines ℓ and m and at a distance of GH from P.

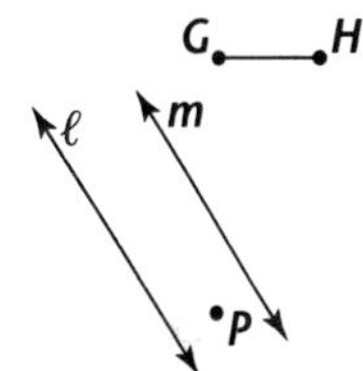

26. The intersection of a plane with a plane.

27. The intersection of two spheres with a line tangent to both spheres.

28. The intersection of a plane and an octagonal pyramid in which the plane is parallel to the base of the pyramid.

29. The intersection of a $5 \times 5 \times 5$ cube with a sphere of diameter 5 inside the cube

30. The intersection of a sphere with a cube that fits snugly inside it.

Selected Answers and Solutions

CHAPTER 1

Lesson 1, pages 4–6

1. *A, F, C;* Use a straightedge to draw a line through any three points that appear to be on the same line. If the line goes through all three, then they are collinear. **3.** *A, B, C; A, D, E; E, F, G;* and *G, H, I* **4.** ray; A ray has one endpoint and one end that extends with no end. **5.** line **7.** ray **9.** line segment **10.** $\overleftrightarrow{GH}$, $\overleftrightarrow{HG}$, and *m;* A line can be named by any two of its labeled points in either order and by a lowercase script letter. **11.** two; A line segment has two endpoints by definition. **13.** one **15.** points **17.** ray **18.** one; Only one line segment can be drawn between two points because a line segment needs two endpoints. **19.** three

Try This

n = number of sides or points; $n \cdot \frac{n-1}{2}$ or count down from $n - 1$ to 1, adding each possibility; square = 4 → 3 + 2 + 1 = 6 segments; 5 points → 4 + 3 + 2 + 1 = 10 segments

Lesson 2, pages 9–10

1. *A* −3, *B* −1, *C* 2, *D* 3.5, *E* 6; The Ruler Postulate states that for every point on the line, there is exactly one real number. **2.** $-3\ A, -\frac{1}{2}\ B, 0\ C, \frac{3}{4}\ D, 2\ E, \pi\ F, 4\ G$ **3.** 3 units; The Ruler Placement Postulate states that given two points, *A* and *B*, on a line, the number line can be chosen so that *A* is at zero and *B* is at a positive number. **5.** 2 inches; Place the ruler so that the left edge of the line segment is at zero and the line segment lines up with the edge of the ruler. Then take a reading of where the right endpoint of the line segment falls on the ruler. **7.** 1 cm; See directions for problem 5. **9.** 3 cm **10.** $AB = 2$, $BC = 4$, $AC = 6$; $AB + BC = 2 + 4 = 6$, so *B* is between *A* and *C*. **11.** $AB = 4$, $BC = 8$, $AC = 12$; $AB + BC = 4 + 8 = 12$, so *B* is between *A* and *C*. **12.** Ruler Postulate; The Ruler Postulate states that the points on a line can be placed in a one-to-one correspondence with the real numbers so that for every point on the line, there is exactly one real number. **13.** Ruler Placement Postulate **15.** no; If the points are not in a straight line, $AB + BC \neq AC$.

Lesson 3, page 14

1. $\angle Q$, $\angle RQP$; An angle can be named by its vertex point or by its vertex point and a labeled point on each ray with the vertex point in the middle. **3.** $\angle QRS$, $\angle SRQ$ **4.** Use the steps on page 12. **5.**

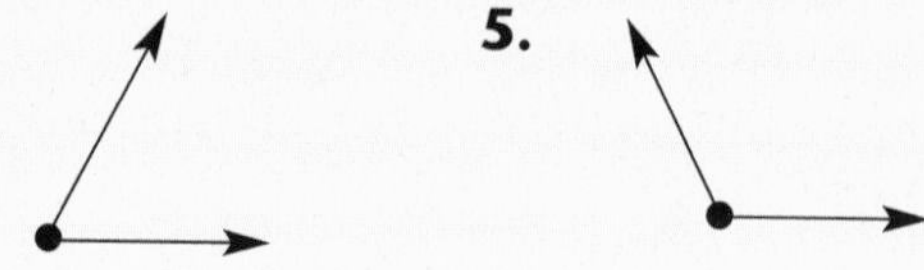

7. Use the steps on page 13. **9.**

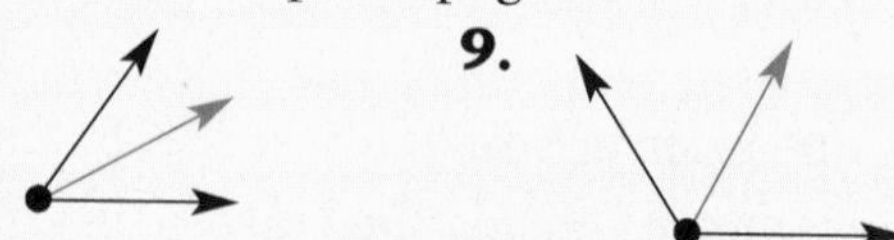

10. Yes, common point *B* could be the vertex of an angle.

Lesson 4, pages 18–19

1. acute; Any angle that measures less than 90° is acute. **3.** straight **5.** acute **7.** obtuse **9.** Angle measurements will vary but should be less than 90°.
11. Angle measurements will vary but should be greater than 90°. **12.** $\ell \perp m$; Lines that form right angles are said to be perpendicular. **13.** $\overline{AB} \perp \overline{BC}$
15. When two perpendicular lines intersect, they form four right angles.

Lesson 5, pages 22–23

1. supplementary; If the sum of two angle measures equals 180°, they are supplementary. **3.** supplementary
5. 80°; Press 180 [–] 100 [ENTER]. The answer is 80. **7.** 118° **9.** 127° **11.** 99° **13.** $\angle m$ and $\angle p$, $\angle o$ and $\angle n$; Vertical angles have a common vertex and their sides are formed by the same lines. **15.** $\angle t$ and $\angle y$, $\angle u$ and $\angle x$, $\angle v$ and $\angle w$, $\angle s$ and $\angle z$
17. 90°; f and c are vertical angles; $m\angle c =$ 90°, so $m\angle f =$ 90° **19.** 45°

Lesson 6, pages 26–27

1. $m\angle a = 100°$, $m\angle b = m\angle c = 80°$; $\angle a$ is a vertical angle to the angle labeled 100°. Therefore, $m\angle a = 100°$. $\angle b$ is supplementary to $\angle a$. $180° - 100° = 80°$. Therefore, $m\angle b = 80°$. $\angle c$ is a vertical angle to $\angle b$. Therefore, $m\angle c = 80°$.
3. $m\angle w = 150°$, $m\angle z = m\angle q = 30°$
4. 48°; $\angle 1$ is complementary to $\angle 2$, which equals 42°. Since the sum of two complementary angles must be equal to 90°, $90° – 42° = 48°$. **5.** 90° **7.** 42°
9. 180°; $\angle 3$, or $\angle EBF$, is supplementary to $\angle CBE$, which is a right angle. Right angles are equal to 90°. $\angle 6$ and $\angle 3$ are vertical angles, so $m\angle 6 = 90°$; $90° + 90° = 180°$. **11.** $\angle 1, \angle 4$; $\angle 2, \angle 5$; and $\angle 3, \angle 6$
13. For any pair of vertical angles, the angles have equal measures. **15.** 36° and 144° **17.** 72° and 108° **19.** 30° and 150°

Lesson 7, page 29

1. a^{10}; $a^7 \cdot a^3 = a^{(7+3)} = a^{10}$ **3.** y^{10} **5.** b^{13}
7. y^{15} **9.** y^1 or y; $y^3 \div y^2 = y^{(3-2)} = y^1 = y$
11. x^6 **13.** z^{10} **15.** y^8 **17.** n^5 **19.** 1
21. $n = 5$; $y^3 \cdot b^2 \cdot y^2 = y^{(3+2)} \cdot b^2 = y^5 \cdot b^2 = b^2 \cdot y^n$; $n = 5$ **23.** $n = 6$ **25.** $n = 12$
27. $n = 7$ **29.** $n = 7$

Application, page 30

1. yes; D to C to B to D to A to B, or start at B and reverse. The network is traversable because you can trace a route along its points without repeating a section. **3.** yes; D to A to C to E to A to B to C to D to E or reverse **5.** yes; B to D to C to B to A to D to F to B to G to F to E to D or reverse

Chapter Review, pages 31–33

1. C **3.** C **5.** C **7.** C **9.** point, X **11.** ray, $\overrightarrow{AT}$ **13.** line, ℓ **15.** 1 inch **17.** 5 cm
19.

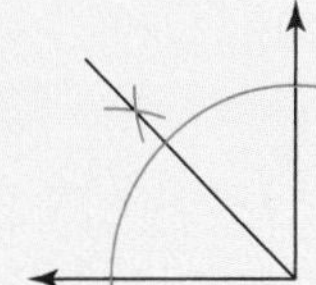

21. obtuse **23.** acute **25.** 60° **27.** 65°
29. 140° **31.** Angle measure should be 180°.

33. 78° **35.** 9°

CHAPTER 2

Lesson 1, pages 39–40

1. *a figure is a triangle,* hypothesis; *it has three sides,* conclusion; The statement that follows the "If" is the hypothesis. The statement that follows the "then" is the conclusion. **3.** *the sum of the measures of two angles is 90°,* hypothesis; *the angles are complementary,* conclusion **5.** *you use SuperBright detergent,* hypothesis; *your clothes will be clean,* conclusion. **6.** True; Right angles always equal 90°. Since the conclusion meets the hypothesis, then the conditional is considered true. **7.** True **9.** False **C11.** If an angle measure is $90° < m < 180°$, the angle is obtuse. The converse of a conditional is the reverse of the hypothesis and conclusion. **C13.** If two angles are complementary, then the sum of their measures is 90°. **C15.** If an animal has four legs, then it is a dog. **D11.** The conditional and its converse are true. An obtuse angle must measure more than 90° and less than 180°. Conversely, any angle that measures more than 90° and less than 180° must be obtuse. **D13.** The conditional and the converse are true. **D15.** The conditional is true and the converse is false.

Try This

Answers will vary.

Lesson 2, pages 44–45

1. Postulate 3, a circle may be described with any center and distance. **3.** Parallel Postulate 5 **5.** Postulate 4, all right angles are equal to one another. **7.** Postulate 1 **9.** Postulate 3 **10.** Lines n and m are parallel; $m\angle d = 90°$ because $\angle a$ and $\angle d$ are supplementary and $m\angle b = 90°$ because $\angle b$ and $\angle c$ are supplementary. Then, since $m\angle c + m\angle d = 180°$, the lines do not meet the requirement for intersection and so they must be parallel.

Lesson 3, pages 47–50

1. Postulate 1, a straight line segment can be drawn from any point to any point. **3.** Postulate 2 **5.** Postulate 2 **7.** Postulates 1 and 3 **9.** Postulates 1 and 3 **11.** Postulate 1; Construction is completed by connecting points K and L with a straightedge. Postulate 1 states that a straight line segment can be drawn from any point to any point.

13. Postulate 4, all four angles are equal.

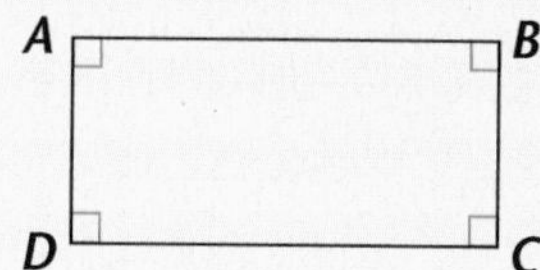

15. Parallel Postulate 5

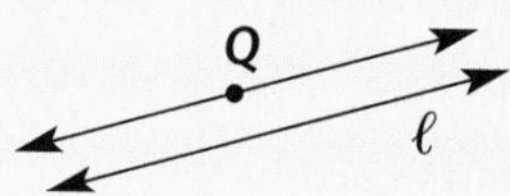

17. Postulate 1

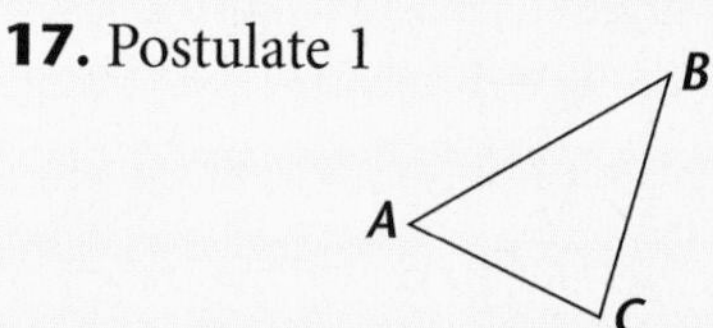

19. Parallel Postulate 5

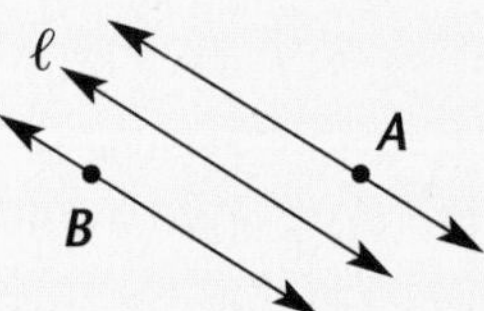

Lesson 4, pages 53–54

1. Axiom 2, which states that if equals are added to equals, the sums are equal. **3.** Axiom 3 **5.** Axiom 2 6. m$\angle BAC <$ 90°; $\angle CAD <$ 90°. Axiom 5, the whole is greater than the sum of the parts. Since $\angle CAD$ and $\angle BAC$ are parts of $\angle BAD$, which measures 90°, then they must each measure less than 90°. **7.** Yes; Axiom 1, substitution for equals. **9.** Angles 1, 2, 3, and 1 + 2, 1 + 3, and 2 + 3 are all less than 180°; Axiom 5, whole is greater than parts 11. 8 pt; Axiom 1, substitution; If 1 quart equals 2 pints, and 1 gallon equals 4 quarts, then 1 gallon = 4 × 2 pints = 8 pints. **13.** 16 oz; Axiom 1, substitution **15.** 3,650 days; Axiom 1, substitution

Lesson 5, pages 56–57

1. Given; The first statement in a proof is given because it is part of the conditional being proven. **3.** $\angle a$ and $\angle b$ are adjacent on m and are supplementary. **5.** Axiom 3, if equals are subtracted from equals, the differences are equal. 6. $x = 60°$, $y = 120°$, $z = 60°$; The Vertical Angle Theorem states that vertical angles are equal. Therefore, m$\angle y$ is equal to its vertical angle, which is equal to 120°. Angles x and z are both supplementary to the angle labeled 120°. Since 180° − 120° = 60°, both x and z are equal to 60°. **7.** $x = 160°$, $y = 20°$, $z = 160°$ **9.** $x = 89°$, $y = 91°$, $z = 89°$ 11. Angles a and b are vertical angles. The theorem states that vertical angles are equal. **13.** m$\angle b$ + m$\angle d$ = 180°, so m$\angle b <$ 180°; Axiom 5, whole is greater than parts 15a. Angles x and w are vertical angles. The theorem states that vertical angles are equal. Angles x and w are right angles. Postulate 4, all right angles are equal to one another. **15b.** Vertical angles are equal. Postulate 4, all right angles are equal to one another. **15c.** Postulate 4, right angles are equal; Axiom 1, substitution.

Lesson 6, page 59

1. 10, 8; $3(10 + 8) = 3 \cdot 10 + 3 \cdot 8$
3. b, x **5.** $5, -y$ 7. $4x + 4y; 4(x + y) = 4 \cdot x + 4 \cdot y = 4x + 4y$ **9.** $ax - ay$
11. $cy - cw$ **13.** $ax + ay - az$
15. $bx - 3b + by$ 16. $a(m + x); am + ax = a \cdot m + a \cdot x = a(m + x)$
17. $3(x - y)$ **19.** $a(x + 3y - w)$

Application, page 60

1. Emmanuel: 16, Javier: 13, Isaac: 8
3. red, blue, green, yellow, orange

Chapter Review, pages 61–63

1. A **3.** B **5.** B **7.** An angle is acute
9. It measures less than 90°. **11.** If an angle measures less than 90°, then the angle is acute. **13.** Postulate 1
15. Postulate 3 **17.** Axiom 5
19. m$\angle a$ + m$\angle c$ = 180°
21. m$\angle a$ + m$\angle c$ = m$\angle a$ + m$\angle b$
23. 60° **25.** 60°

CHAPTER 3

Lesson 1, page 68

1. True; $\overline{AE}$ and $\overline{BD}$ are both perpendicular to $\overline{FC}$ and therefore never meet. Since they never meet and they are both on the same plane, they are parallel lines. **3.** True **5.** False **7.** True **9.** True
11. $\ell \nparallel m$ **13.** $p \parallel q$ **15.** $r \parallel s \parallel t$

Try This

The lines are skew because they are not in the same plane.

Lesson 2, page 71

1. *w, x, s, r;* Exterior angles are outside the parallel lines. Angles *w, x, s,* and *r* are outside the parallel lines ℓ and *m*. **3.** *w* and *p, x* and *q, z* and *s, y* and *r* **5.** *w* and *x, z* and *y, w* and *z, x* and *y, p* and *q, s* and *r, p* and *s, q* and *r* **6.** alternate exterior; *f* and *k* are exterior angles on opposite sides of the transversal. **7.** exterior, supplementary **9.** corresponding **11.** supplementary **13.** corresponding **15.** supplementary, interior **16.** yes; The corresponding angles should appear to be the same exact measure. **17.** no **19.** yes

Lesson 3, pages 74–76

1. 180°; The theorem states that interior angles on the same side of the transversal are supplementary. Since $\angle a$ and $\angle c$ are interior angles on the same side of the transversal, they are supplementary. Therefore, their sum must equal 180°. **3.** $m\angle d$ **5.** $m\angle e$ **7.** $m\angle g$ **9.** $m\angle a$ **11.** $m\angle c$ **13.** 120°; $\angle q$ is supplementary with the angle whose measure is 60°; 180° − 60° = 120°; $m\angle q$ = 120°. **15.** 120°; $\angle q$ and $\angle s$ are vertical angles and therefore equal. **17.** 60°; $\angle x$ and the 60° angle are corresponding angles and therefore equal. **19.** 120°; $\angle z$ and $\angle x$ are supplementary. $m\angle x$ = 60°; 180° − 60° = 120°. **20.** $\angle x$ and $\angle y$ are not supplementary; By indirect proof assumptions, the opposite of the "To prove" statement, which is that $\angle x$ and $\angle y$ are supplementary. **21.** Definition of not supplementary angles **23.** Euclid's Postulate 5 **24.** 90°; corresponding angles are equal **25.** $m\angle x = m\angle y = m\angle i = m\angle j = 45°$ and $m\angle w = m\angle z = m\angle h = m\angle k = 135°$ **26.** 128°; The sum of two supplementary angles is 180°. Press 180° [−] 52° [ENTER]. Display reads 128. **27.** 152° **29.** 117°

Lesson 4, pages 79–80

1. $m\angle z = 135°$, $m\angle y = 45°$, interior angles are supplementary; $\angle z$ and $\angle y$ are interior angles on the same side of the transversal and therefore are supplementary; $m\angle z + m\angle y = 180°$. $m\angle z = 3m\angle y$; $3m\angle y + m\angle y = 180°$. $3m\angle y + m\angle y = 4m\angle y = 180°$. Divide both sides by 4; $m\angle y = 45°$. $m\angle z = 3m\angle y$, or $3 \times 45° = 135°$. Therefore, $m\angle z = 135°$ and $m\angle y = 45°$. **3.** $m\angle a = m\angle z$, corresponding angles are equal; $m\angle z = m\angle a = 162°$; $m\angle w = 18°$ **5.** $m\angle b = m\angle x$, corresponding angles are equal; $m\angle x = m\angle b = 45°$ ($m\angle a = 135°$) **7.** 105°; $\angle o$ is supplementary with the 75° angle. 180° − 75° = 105°. **9.** 105° **11.** 75° **13.** 105° **15.** 75° **17.** 105° **18.**

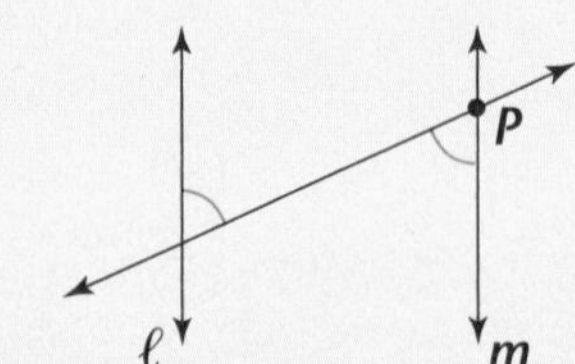

19.

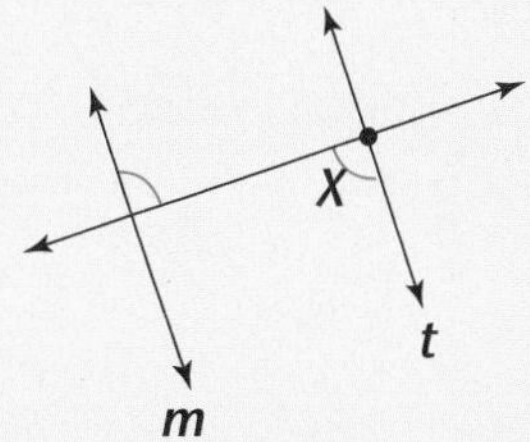

Lesson 5, page 84

1. $\overline{DC}$; A parallelogram is a quadrilateral whose opposite sides are parallel. The opposite side to $\overline{AB}$ is $\overline{DC}$. **3.** $\overline{AD}$, $\overline{BC}$ **5.** 180° **7.** 180° **9.** parallel **10.** Definition of a parallelogram; By definition, the opposite sides of a parallelogram are parallel. **11.** Theorem, interior angles are supplementary **13.** Axiom 2, equals added to equals are equal

14.

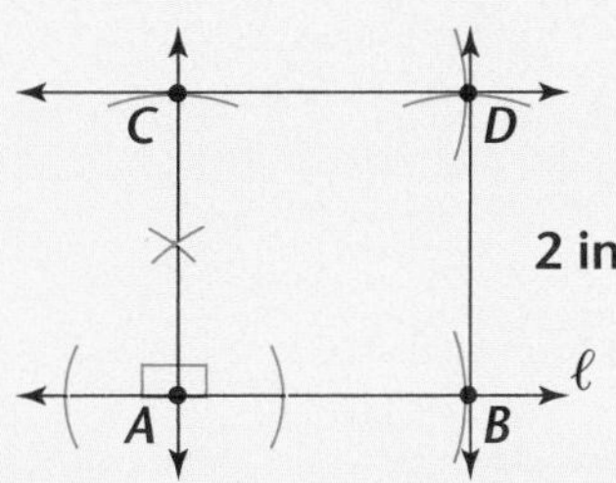

15.

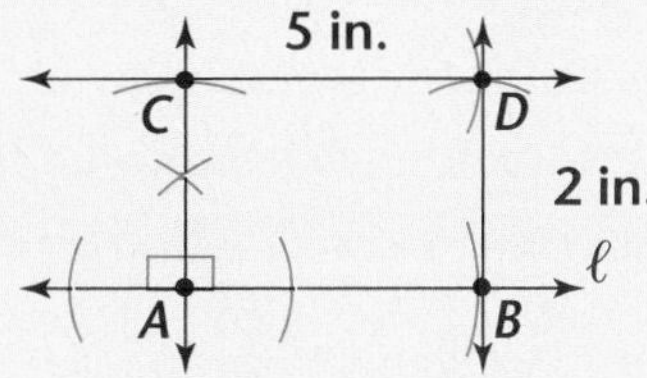

Lesson 6, pages 87–88

1. $\overline{AD}$; A trapezoid is a quadrilateral with exactly one pair of parallel sides. Since $\overline{AB}$ and $\overline{CD}$ are not parallel, $\overline{BC}$ and $\overline{AD}$ must be parallel. **3.** 180° **5.** $\overline{BC}$, $\overline{AD}$, $\overline{CD}$ **6.** $\overline{HG}$; A trapezoid is a quadrilateral with one pair of parallel lines. $\overline{EF}$ and $\overline{HG}$ are parallel sides. **7.** $\overline{EF}$, $\overline{FG}$, $\overline{GH}$ **9.** 180° **11.** 360° **12.** Definition of a trapezoid; A trapezoid is a quadrilateral with exactly one pair of parallel sides. Since $\overline{WZ}$ and $\overline{XY}$, then $\overline{WX}$ and $\overline{YZ}$ must be parallel. **13.** Theorem, interior angles are supplementary **15.** Axiom 2, equals added to equals are equal **16.** True. A rhombus has four equal sides. By theorem, interior angles on the same side of the transversal are supplementary, so the sum of each pair of angles is 180°. If one angle is 90°, then the other angle must be 90°. **18.** True. A rectangle has four right angles; a square also has four right angles.

19.

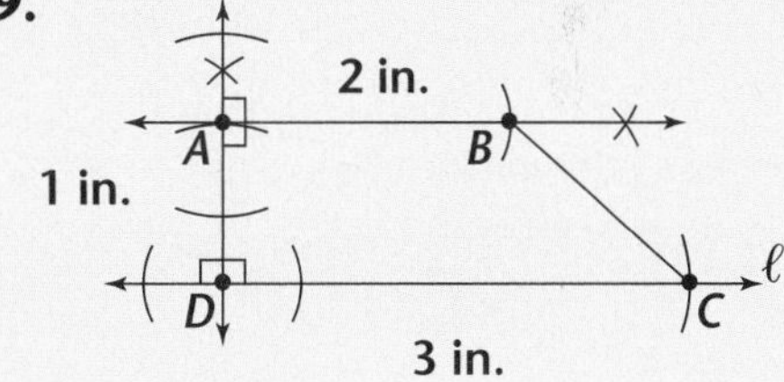

Lesson 7, page 91

1. 110°; alternate interior angles are equal, so m$\angle x$ = 110° **3.** 125° **4.** T; corresponding angles are equal **5.** T **7.** F

9.

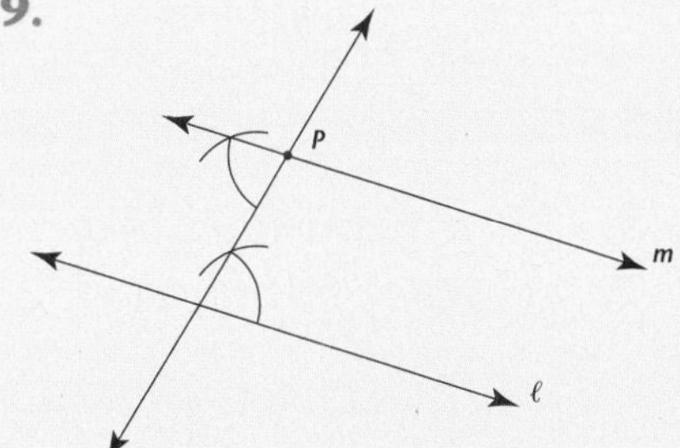

Lesson 8, pages 94–95

1. alternate interior angles equal; $\angle d$ and $\angle e$ are interior angles on opposite sides of the transversal and are therefore alternate interior angles. The Alternate Interior Angles Postulate states that if a transversal intersects two lines so that the alternate interior angles are equal, then the lines are parallel **3.** alternate interior angles equal **5.** corresponding angles equal **7.** interior angles on same side of transversal = 180° **9.** corresponding angles equal **11.** interior angles on same side of transversal = 180°

13.

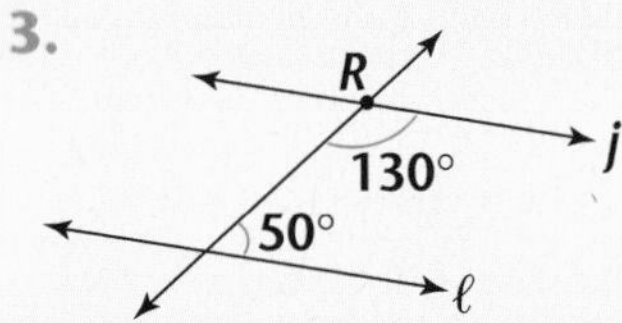

14. The corresponding angles always equal 45° so the lines will always be parallel. **15.** No. The given angles are interior, on the same side of the transversal, and supplementary. Therefore, the paths are parallel.

Lesson 9, page 97

1. $x = 15$; $\frac{2}{3}x = 10$; multiply both sides by $\frac{3}{2}$, $(\frac{3}{2})(\frac{2}{3})x = 10(\frac{3}{2})$; $x = 15$; Check: $(\frac{2}{3})(15) = \frac{30}{3} = 10$ **3.** $x = 18$ **5.** $y = 56$ **7.** $y = -\frac{1}{3}$ **9.** $z = 10$ **11.** $\frac{3}{4}x = 12$, $x = 16$; x = full load; $\frac{3}{4}$ of a full load is 12 cubic yards, so $\frac{3}{4}x = 12$; multiply both sides by $\frac{4}{3}$, $(\frac{4}{3})(\frac{3}{4})x = 12(\frac{4}{3})$; $x = 16$; Check: $(\frac{3}{4})(16) = \frac{48}{4} = 12$ **13.** $x + 3 = 15$, $x = 12$ **15.** $\frac{1}{5}x + 4 = 29$, $x = 125$

Application, page 98

1. not a polygon; A polygon has line segments that intersect at their endpoints. This figure's segments do not meet at their endpoints. **3.** not a polygon; not all segments **5.** polygon **7.** polygon **9.** polygon

Chapter Review, pages 99–101

1. A **3.** D **5.** D **7.** B

9.

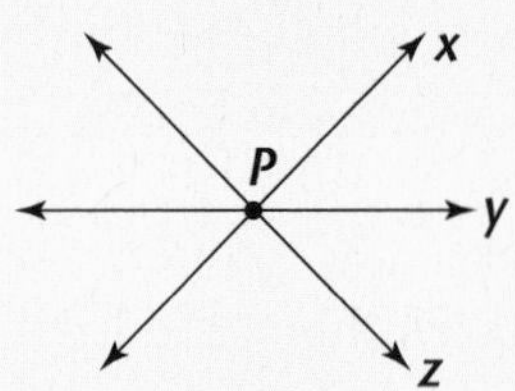

11. ∠*a*, ∠*b*, ∠*g*, and ∠*h* **13.** ∠*a* and ∠*e*, ∠*b* and ∠*f*, ∠*c* and ∠*g*, ∠*d* and ∠*h* **15.** ∠*b*, ∠*c*, ∠*f*, ∠*g* **17.** 45° **19.** 45° **21.** 20° **23.** parallelogram

25. Line *m* should be parallel to ℓ. Point *X* is not on line ℓ.

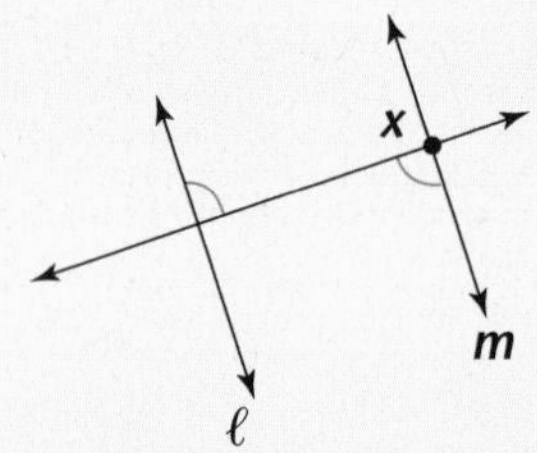

CHAPTER 4

Lesson 1, pages 107–108

1. (1, 1); A point is named by using the *x*- and *y*-values together. The *x*-value is 1 and the *y*-value is 1. **3.** (2, 3) **5.** (−2, 1) **7.** (−1, −3) **9.** (2, −2) **11.** Q; A point is named by using the *x*- and *y*-values together. **13.** *T* **15.** *U* **17.** *R* **19.** *W* **21.** (−2, 0); The *x*-value is −2 and the *y*-value is 0. **23.** (0, 0) 25. (2, 0) **26.** (0, 2); The *x*-value is 0 and the *y*-value is 2. **27.** (0, 1) **29.** (0, −1) **31.** The *x*-values are on the same vertical line, $x = 3$; $-3 \leq y \leq 2$. **33.** $x < 0$, $y = 0$ **35.** Each square can be specified by using a letter-number combination. The coordinate system names intersections or points; the chess system names specific areas.

Lesson 2, pages 110–111

1. $y = 3$, x is any real number; Any point on line ℓ has a y-value of 3; since line ℓ extends in both directions, x is any real number. **3.** $y = 1$, x is any real number **5.** $y = -2$, x is any real number **6.** $(x, 3)$; $x =$ any real number and $y = 3$. **7.** $(x, 2)$ **9.** $(x, -1)$

11.

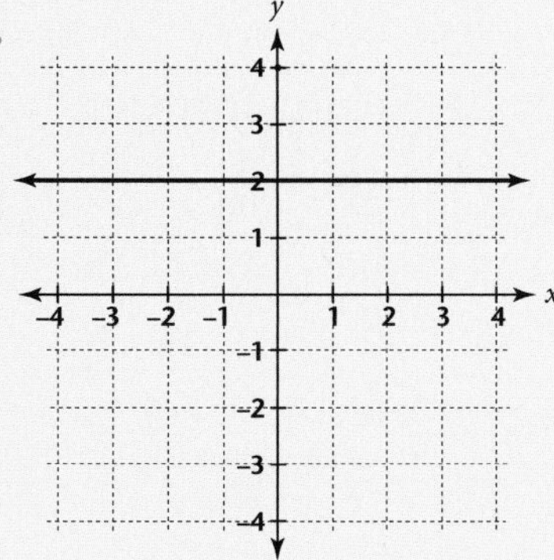

13.

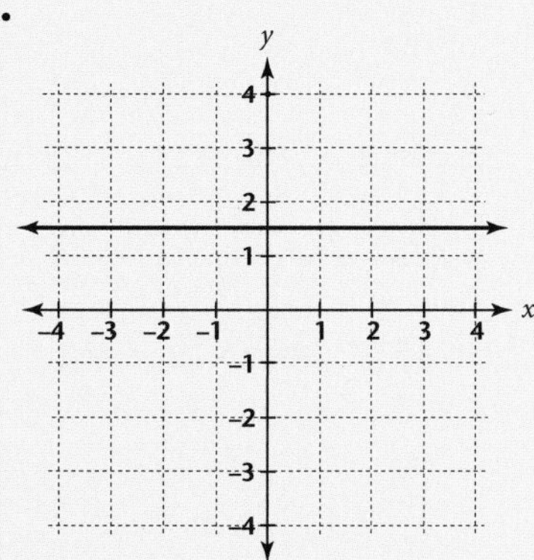

15.

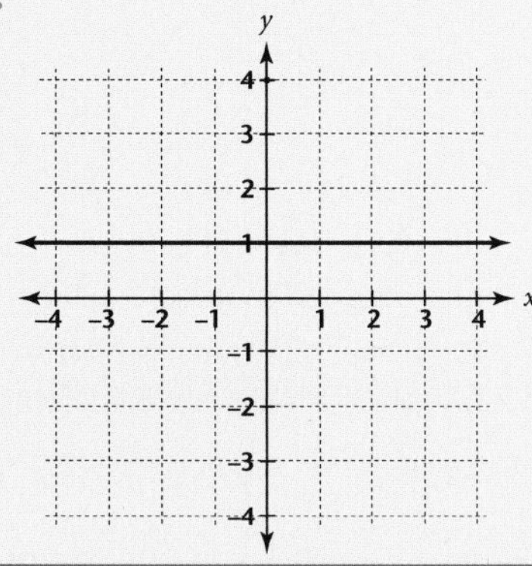

17.

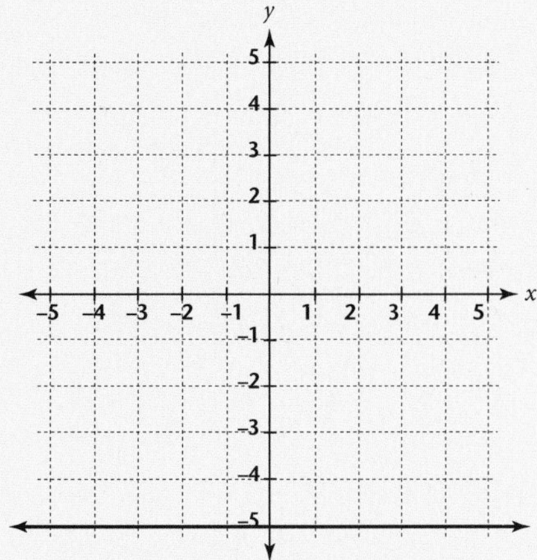

19. $y = 0$, x is any real number; The x-axis is a line perpendicular to the y-axis. It passes through point 0 on the y-axis; its y-value is 0.

Lesson 3, page 114

1. $x = -3$, y is any real number; Any point on line ℓ has an x-value of -3; since line ℓ extends in both directions, y is any real number. **3.** $x = -1$, y is any real number **5.** $x = 2$, y is any real number **6.** $(-3, y)$; $x = -3$ and $y =$ any real number **7.** $(-2, y)$ **9.** $(3, y)$

11.

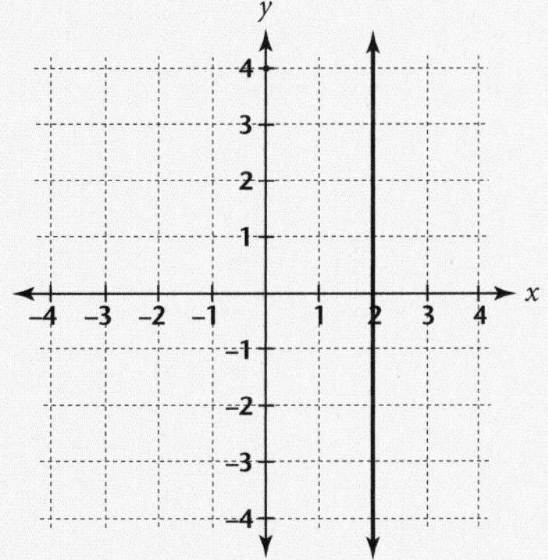

13.

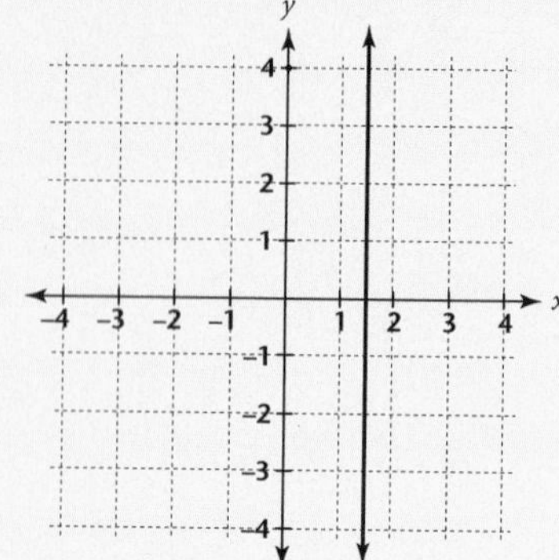

15.

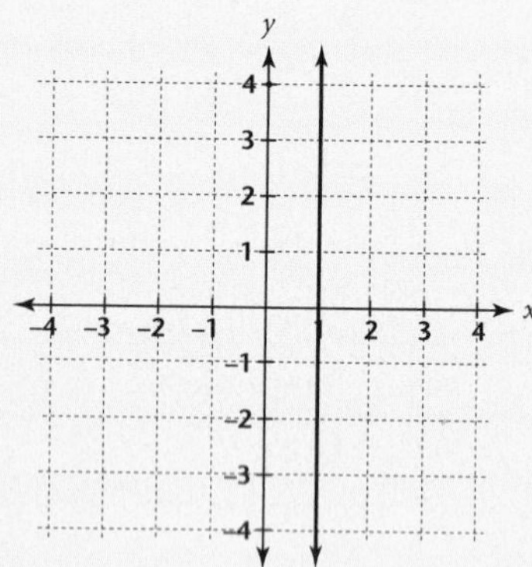

17.

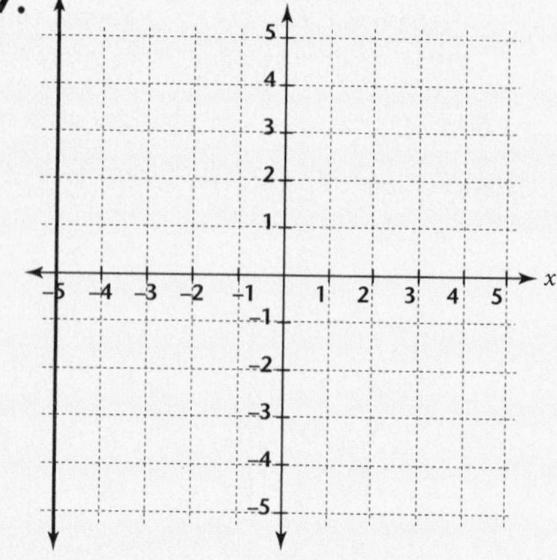

19. $x = 0$, y is any real number; The y-axis is a line perpendicular to the x-axis. It passes through point 0 on the x-axis; its x-value is 0.

Lesson 4, pages 119–120

1. 0.5; Press (6 − 3) ÷ (4 − (−) 2) ENTER. The answer is 0.5. **3.** 0.5 **5.** −0.5 **6.** $m = \frac{1}{3}$; Use the two points listed on the line to formulate the equation to find the slope; $\frac{y_1 - y_2}{x_1 - x_2} = \frac{4 - 3}{5 - 2} = \frac{1}{3}$. **7.** $m = \frac{3}{7}$ **9.** $m = 1$ **10.** $m = 3$; Use the two points to find the slope; $\frac{y_1 - y_2}{x_1 - x_2} = \frac{16 - 4}{7 - 3} = \frac{12}{4} = 3$. **11.** $m = \frac{6}{5}$ **13.** $m = -1$ **14.** Slope of ℓ = slope of m = 1; Use the two points on line ℓ to find the slope; $\frac{y_1 - y_2}{x_1 - x_2} = \frac{6 - (-2)}{2 - (-6)} = \frac{8}{8} = 1$. Use the two points on line m to find the slope; $\frac{y_1 - y_2}{x_1 - x_2} = \frac{0 - (-3)}{3 - 0} = \frac{3}{3} = 1$ **15.** slope of ℓ = slope of $m = -2$

Lesson 5, pages 125–126

1. $x = 2, y = 1$ and $x = 1, y = 2$

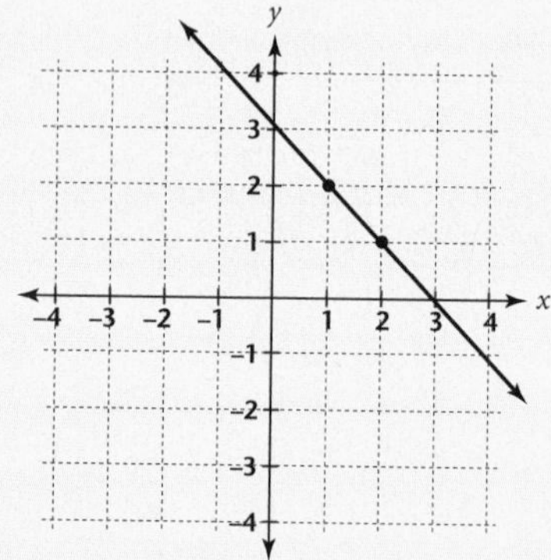

3.

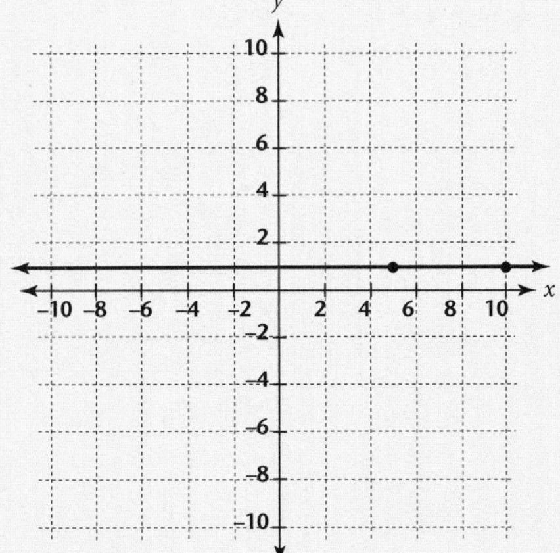

5.

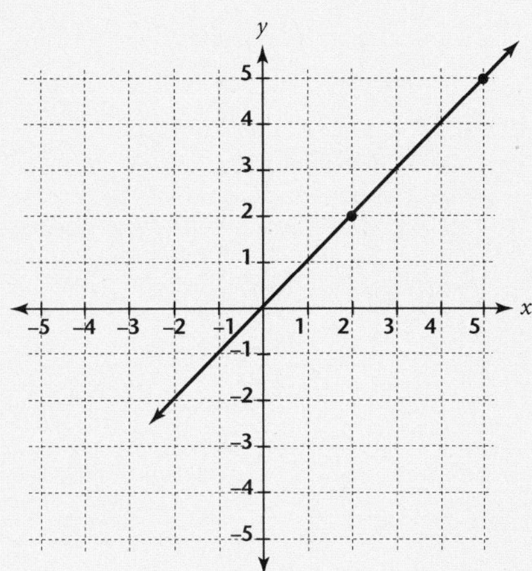

7.

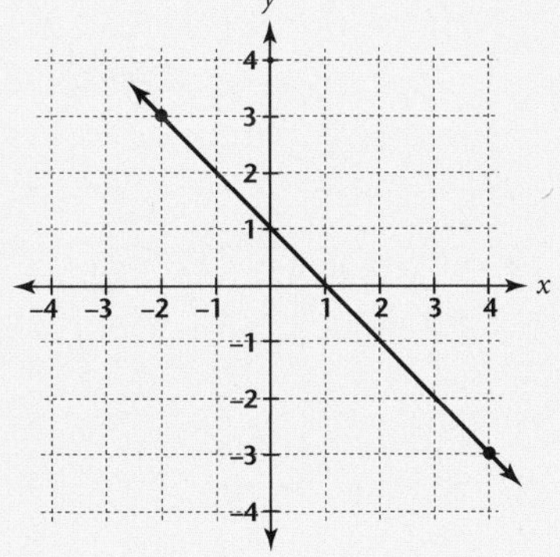

8. Domain: $1 \leq x \leq 2$; Range: $1 \leq y \leq 2$

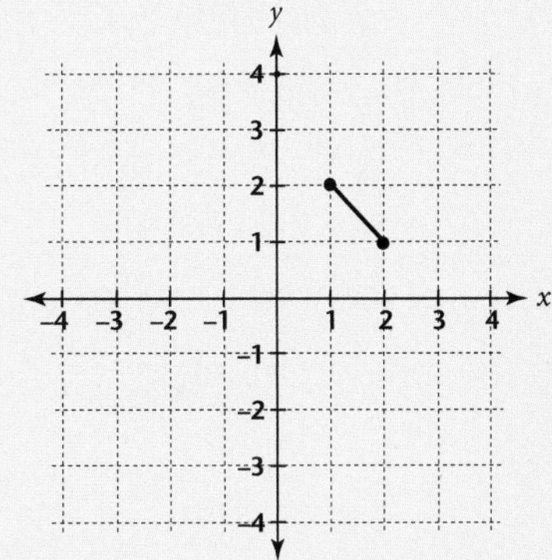

9. Domain: $-2 \leq x \leq 1$; Range: $1 \leq y \leq 6$

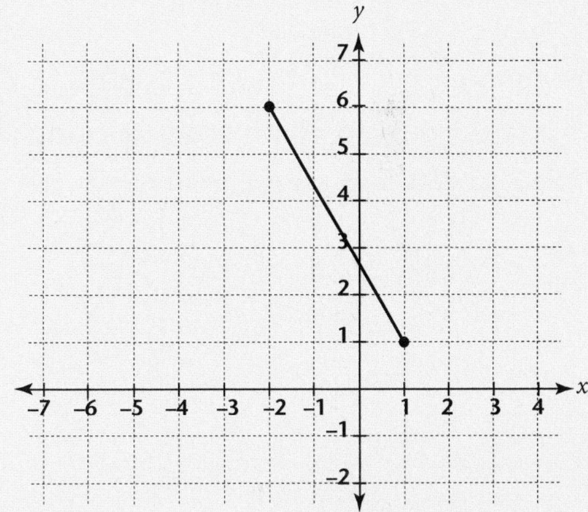

11. Domain: $-1 \leq x \leq 4$; Range: $y = 2$

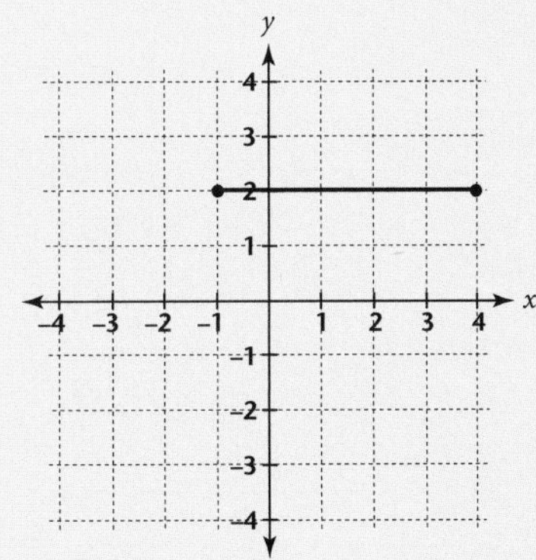

13. $y = -x + 3$; First calculate the slope; slope $= -1$. Then plug in the x- and y-values for one of the points listed along

with the slope to get the value of b. $1 = -1(2) + b$; $1 = -2 + b$; $b = 3$. Then represent the equation using letter values for x and y and real values for b and m.

15. $y = 1$ **17.** $y = x$ **18.** slope $= \frac{7}{10}$ or $-\frac{7}{10}$; Staircase is the y-axis and ground is the x-axis; the measurements result in ordered pairs of (0, 7) and (10, 0); $\frac{y_1 - y_2}{x_1 - x_2} = \frac{7 - 0}{0 - 10} = -\frac{7}{10}$ **19.** slope $= \frac{1}{2}$

Try This

Answers will vary.

Lesson 6, page 130

1. Slope equals 1 or $\frac{1}{1}$; add 1 to both the x- and y-values to graph point B. Connect points A and B to graph the line.

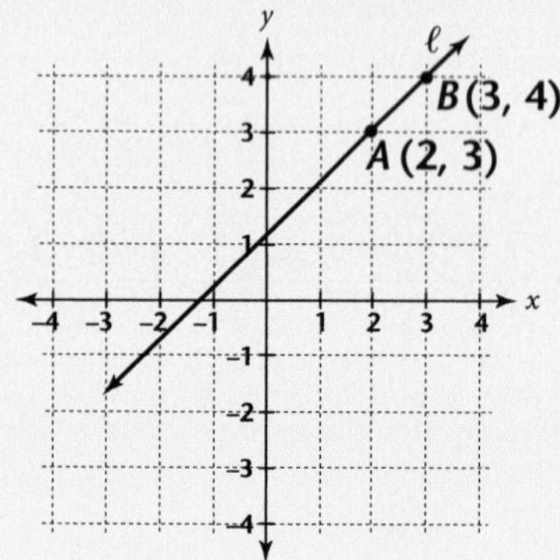

3. $m = -1$

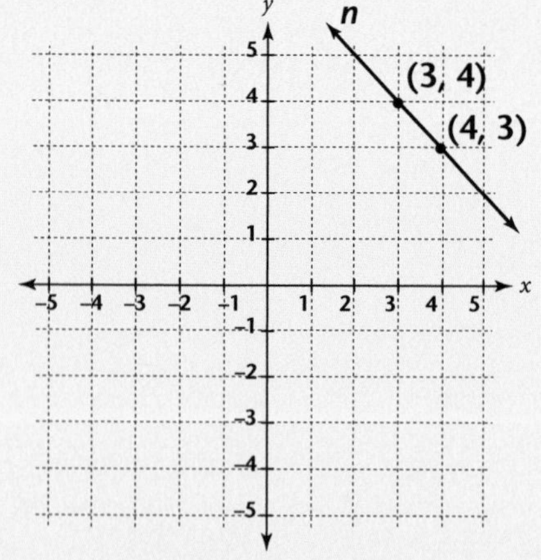

5. $m = 0$

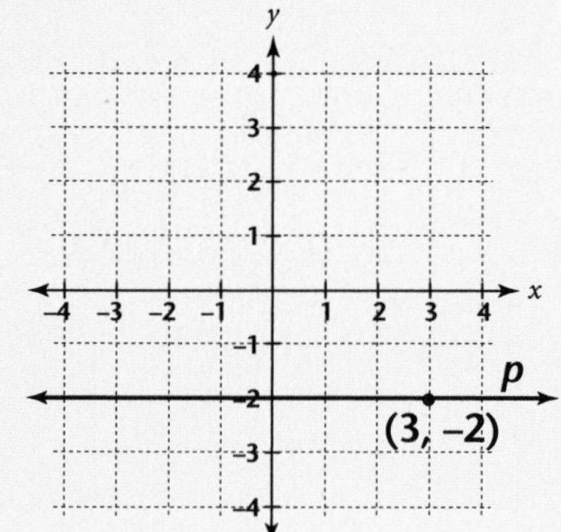

7. $m = 3$

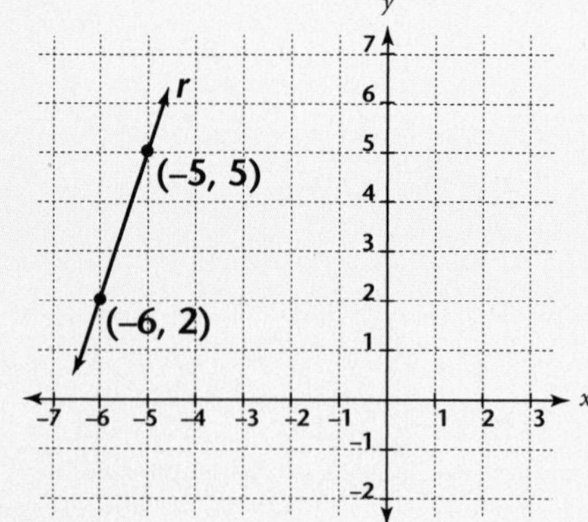

9. $m = -2$

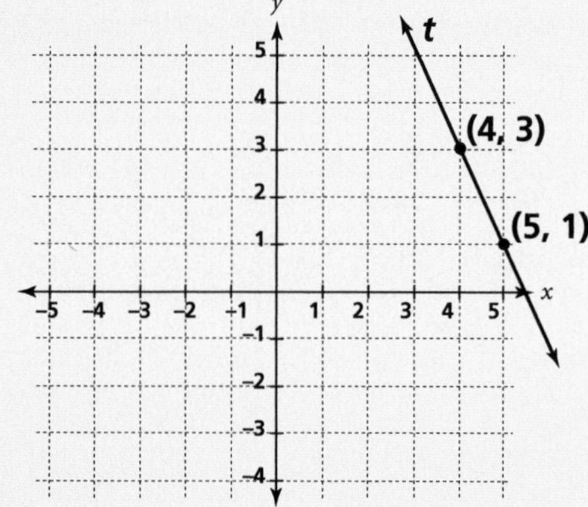

11. $y = x + 1$; Take the slope and a value for x and y; plug these into the slope equation to yield a value of 1 for b. $3 = 1(2) + b$; $3 = 2 + b$; $b = 1$. Then represent the equation with letters for x

and y and the m and b values as numbers. **13.** $y = -x + 7$ **15.** $y = -2, x =$ any real number **17.** $y = 3x + 20$ **19.** $y = -2x + 11$

Lesson 7, pages 134–135

1. $(9, 13\frac{1}{2})$; $(9, 13.5)$; $\frac{x_1 + x_2}{2} = \frac{12 + 6}{2} = 9$ and $\frac{y_1 + y_2}{2} = \frac{18 + 9}{2} = 13.5$ **3.** $(-2, \frac{5}{2})$; $(-2, 2.5)$ **5.** $(-5, 7\frac{1}{2})$; $(-5, 7.5)$

7.

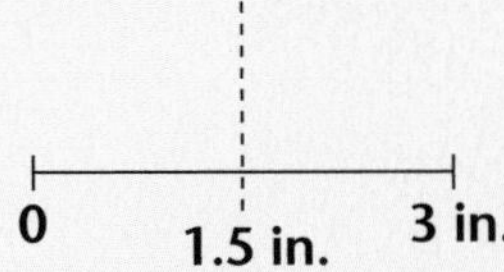

9.

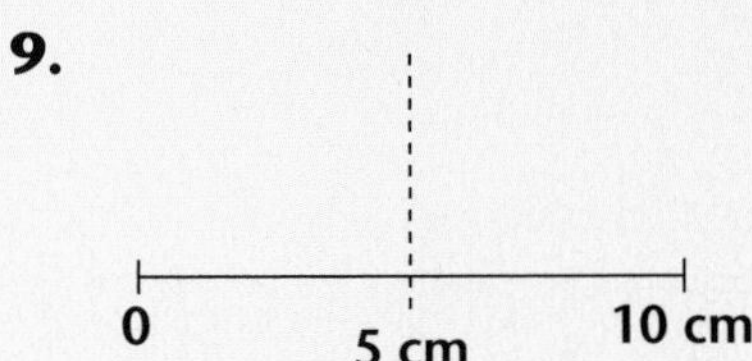

11. Constructions will vary but should include the arcs necessary to find the midpoints. **12.** (4, 3); Use the midpoint formula and plug in the two points given in the problem; $\frac{10 + -2}{2} = 4$ and $\frac{3 + 3}{2} = 3$. This gives the midpoint x- and y-values of 4 and 3. **13.** $(1, -3)$ **15.** $(4, -2)$

Lesson 8, page 137

1. 150 miles; distance (d) = rate (r) • time (t), so $d = 60$ mph • $2\frac{1}{2}$ hours = 150 miles **3.** 39 miles **5.** 60 mph **7.** 50 mph **9.** 4.25 mph

Application, page 138

1. slope = 1.34 **3.** slope = 1.73 **5.** slope = 1.33 **7.** slope = 1 **9.** Beast

Chapter Review, pages 139–141

1. C **3.** A **5.** B **7.** D **9.** 1 **11.** $-\frac{10}{3}$ **13.** $y = 1$ **15.** $y = \frac{1}{2}x$ **17.** $(-4, 8)$

19. $(-3, 7)$

21.

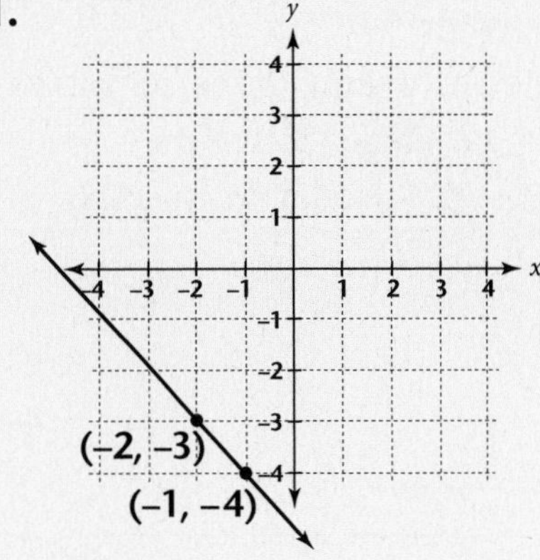

23.

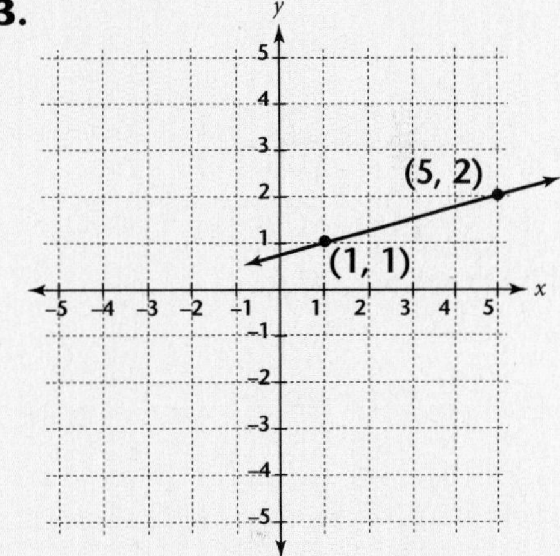

25.

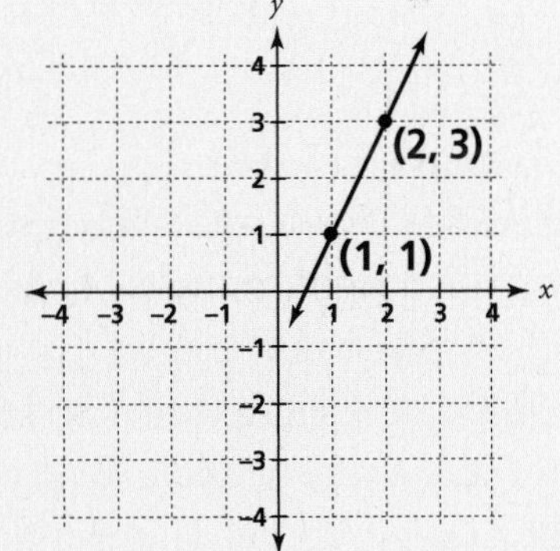

CHAPTER 5

Lesson 1, page 148

1. isosceles; according to the definition of an isosceles triangle. **3.** scalene **5.** isosceles **7.** isosceles **9.** isosceles

11.

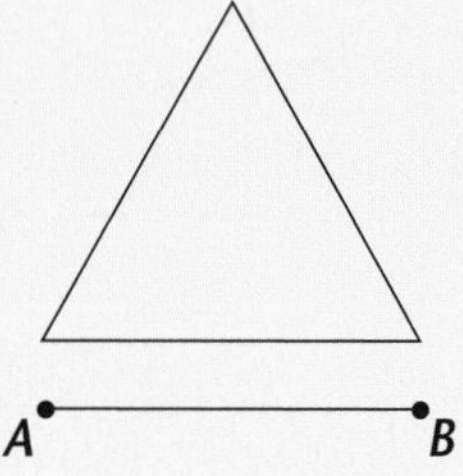

13.

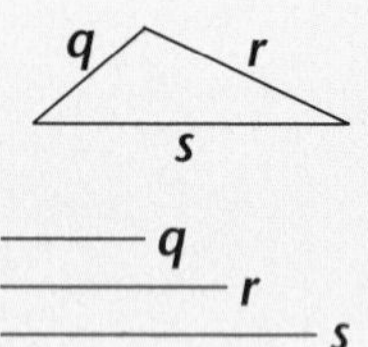

15.

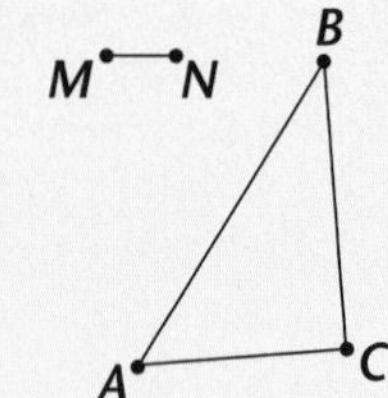

Lesson 2, pages 153–154

1. ΔBAD; ΔBAD has a right angle, so by definition it is a right triangle. **3.** ΔBFD **5.** $\angle ADB$ **7.** They are parallel; corresponding angles are equal, so by theorem ℓ and m are parallel. **9.** $\angle y$ **11.** right triangle; By definition, a triangle with one right angle **13.** acute triangle **15.** equilateral triangle **17.** equilateral triangle **19.** right scalene triangle

21. right isosceles triangle

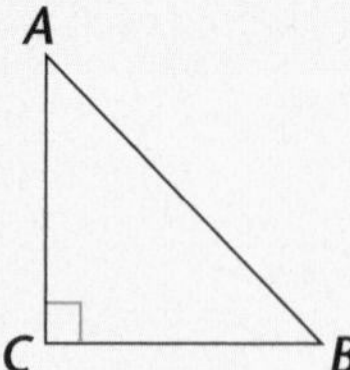

23. obtuse isosceles triangle

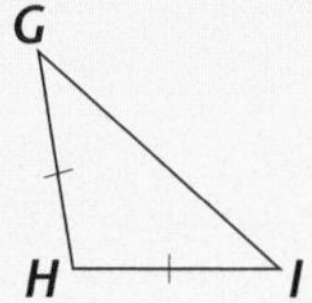

25. right scalene triangle

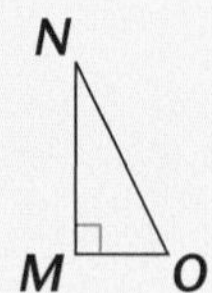

Try This

Constructions will vary. A right triangle cannot be equilateral because it does not have three 60° angles.

Lesson 3, page 157

1. False; A rectangle is also a parallelogram but not a square. **3.** False; isosceles trapezoid **5.** False; not all rhombuses have equal angles **7.** True **8.** Figure with four sides; By definition, a rhombus has four sides **9.** parallel and equal to each other and the other pair of sides as well **11.** rhombus; Four equal sides with angles that are not equal to each other **13.** quadrilateral **15.** rectangle

Lesson 4, page 160

1. definition of parallelogram; It is given that *ABCD* is a parallelogram. By definition, opposite sides are equal and parallel. $\overline{BC}$ and $\overline{AD}$ are opposite sides and therefore parallel. **3.** definition of parallelogram **5.** angle 4; Angle 4 and angle 1 are alternate interior angles on the transversal $\overline{WY}$ crossing parallel lines XY and WZ. By theorem, alternate interior angles are equal. **7.** 25°; Angle 4 and angle 1 are alternate interior angles on the transversal $\overline{EG}$. By theorem, alternate interior angles are equal. **9.** 65° **11.** 65° **12.** 55°; Angle 4 and angle 1 are alternate interior angles on the transversal $\overline{JL}$. By theorem, alternate interior angles are equal. **13.** 55° **15.** 35°

Lesson 5, page 165

1. 180°; The figure shown with one pair of parallel lines at the top and bottom. The left side is a transversal. Angles 1 and 2 are interior angles on the same side of this transversal. By theorem, interior angles on the same side of the transversal are supplementary and equal 180°.
3. 360° **5.** 180° **7.** 40°; The angle x is equal to 180° minus the measures of the other two angles. One of these angles is a right angle that measures 90° and the other is 50°. Therefore, $x = 180° - (90° + 50°)$ or $x = 180° - 140° = 40°$. **9.** 80° **11.** 50° **13.** 30° **15.** 30° **17.** 20° **18.** no; This would give an angle sum greater than 180°; An obtuse angle, by definition, is an angle that measures more than 90°. A right angle measures 90°. Added together, the sum will be more than 180°. By definition, a triangle has three angles whose sum equals 180°. **19.** yes; one angle > 90° and two equal sides

Lesson 6, pages 170–171

1. 5; By definition, a diagonal is a line connecting two nonadjacent vertices, so $n = 5$. **3.** 1,080° **5.** 7 **7.** 7 **9.** 8 **11.** 44 **13.** 1,620° **15.** 54 **17.** regular hexagon; All the angles are equal; only three diagonals are shown. **19.** 720°

Lesson 7, page 174

1.

3.

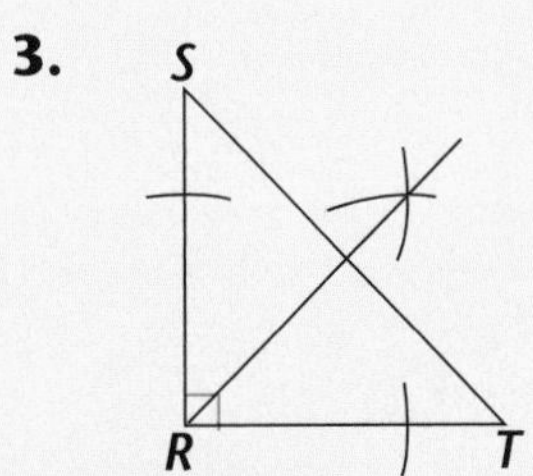

5. yes; $\overline{TP} \parallel \overline{RA}$, alternate angles are equal. Therefore, $\angle RXT = \angle XTP = 90°$, and $\overline{XT}$ is perpendicular to $\overline{RA}$ and $\overline{TP}$.

Try This

Triangles will vary. All perpendicular bisectors divide lines in half and form right angles with them.

Lesson 8, pages 177–178

1.

3. 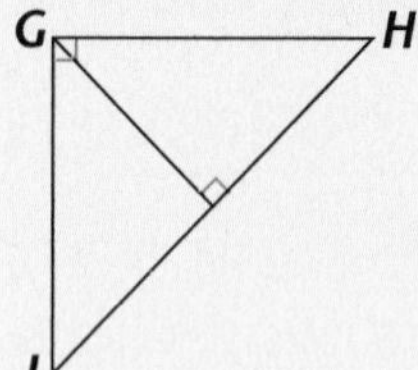

5. 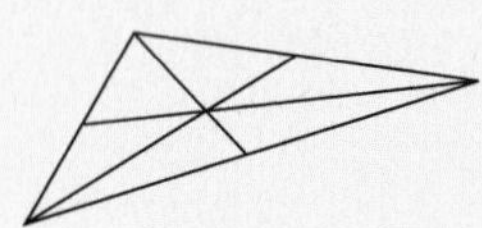

7. 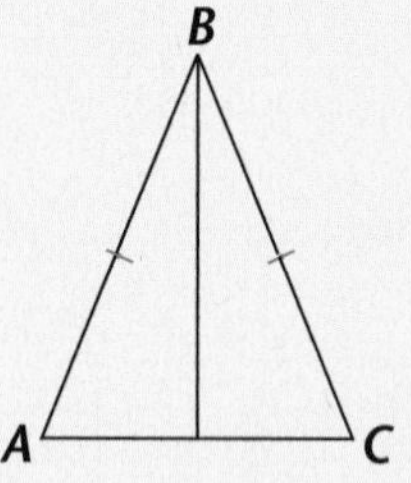

9. 

11. They are the triangle's sides, or legs. The sides that make the right angle are perpendicular to each other. Since the definition of an altitude is that it is perpendicular to one of the triangle's sides, then the sides themselves are the altitudes. **13.** They seem to be the same. **15.** The intersection of the angle bisectors appears to be equidistant from each side of the triangle.

Lesson 9, pages 182–183

1. 30°; Angle 1 is an adjacent angle with the angles labeled 70° and 80° whose exterior sides form a straight line that is equivalent to a straight angle that measures 180°. Therefore, 180° − (70° + 80°) = 180° − 150° = 30°. **3.** 80° **5.** 160° **7.** 180° **9.** 160° **11.** 160° **13.** True; $\angle d$ is an exterior angle and supplementary to $\angle c$; $m\angle d = 180° - m\angle c$. Since the sum of a triangle's angles equal 180°, then the sum of $m\angle a + m\angle b = 180° - m\angle c$. Therefore, $m\angle a + m\angle b = 180° - m\angle c = m\angle d$. **15.** True **17.** False **19.** 60°; If the angles are all equal then they must equal 180° ÷ 3 angles; 180° ÷ 3 = 60°. **21.** 70°; Press 43 [+] 27 [ENTER]. The answer is 70. **23.** 97° **25.** 102°

Lesson 10 page 185

1. $x^2 + 2xy + y^2$; $(x + y)^2 = (x + y)(x + y) = x(x + y) + y(x + y) = x^2 + xy + xy + y^2 = x^2 + 2xy + y^2$
3. $25 + 10x + x^2$ **5.** $81 + 18y + y^2$
7. $a^2 + 4a + 4$ **9.** $x^2 - a^2$; $(x + a)(x - a) = x(x - a) + a(x - a) = x^2 - ax + ax - a^2 = x^2 - a^2$ **11.** $y^2 - z^2$
13. $(c + d)(c - d)$; $c^2 - d^2$ is the difference of two squares; use the model to factor: $a^2 - b^2 = (a + b)(a - b)$, so $c^2 - d^2 = (c + d)(c - d)$
15. $(w + z)(w - z)$ **17.** $c^2 + 3c^2d + 3cd^2 + d^3$; $(c + d)^3 = (c + d)[(c + d)(c + d)] = (c + d)(c^2 + 2cd + d^2) = c(c^2 + 2cd + d^2) + d(c^2 + 2cd + d^2) = c^3 + 2c^2d + cd^2 + c^2d + 2cd^2 + d^3 = c^3 + 3c^2d + 3cd^2 + d^3$ **19.** $x^3 + 15x^2 + 75x + 125$

Try This

$x^3 + 6x^2 + 11x + 6$; $V = l \cdot w \cdot h = (x + 1)(x + 2)(x + 3) = (x + 1)[(x + 2)(x + 3)] = (x + 1)(x^2 + 5x + 6) =$

$x(x^2 + 5x + 6) + 1(x^2 + 5x + 6) = x^3 + 5x^2 + 6x + x^2 + 5x + 6 = x^3 + 6x^2 + 11x + 6$

Application, page 186

1.

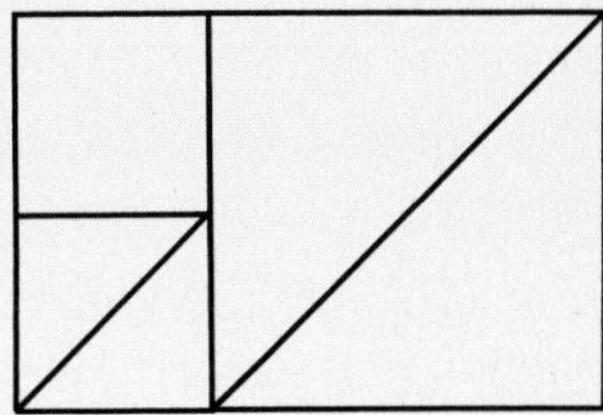

3.

5. Answers will vary.

Chapter Review, pages 187–189

1. A **3.** A **5.** B **7.** 35° **9.** 55° **11.** 55° **13.** 180° **15.** 80° **17.** 120° **19.** 136° **21.** 230°

23.

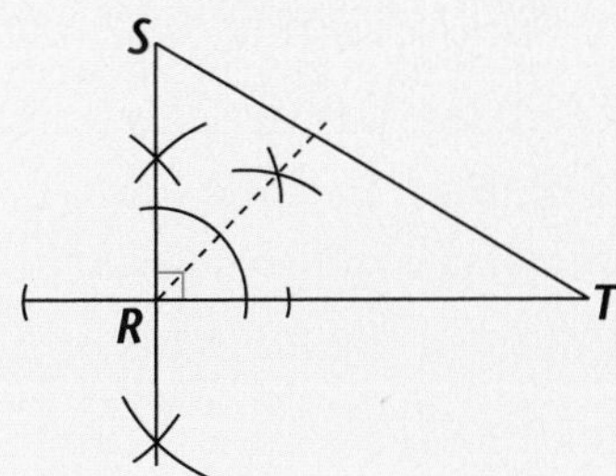

25.

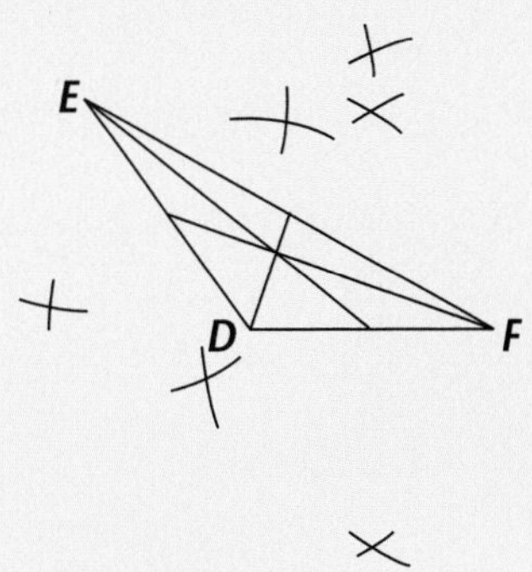

CHAPTER 6

Lesson 1, pages 196–197

1. $\overline{AB} \cong \overline{DE}$, $\angle A \cong \angle D$, $\overline{AC} \cong \overline{DF}$; SAS postulate; A single tick mark on one pair of corresponding sides, double tick marks on the other pair of corresponding sides, and the included angles are marked with arcs **3.** $\overline{HI}$ and $\overline{HK}$, $\overline{HJ}$ and $\overline{HG}$; The included angles between these two pairs of corresponding sides are marked congruent and are equal because they are vertical. For the triangles to be congruent by SAS, the above sides must be congruent. **5.** $\overline{MN}$ and $\overline{ON}$, $\overline{NL}$ and $\overline{NL}$ **7.** Given; This is given as a feature of the figure. **9.** $\angle ACB$ **11.** Given **13.** $\angle EFG \cong \angle HIK$ **15.** 40 paces, SAS congruency; The two triangles are congruent according to the SAS Postulate. If the triangles are congruent, then corresponding sides are congruent. So $\overline{AB}$ and $\overline{A'B'}$ are congruent.

Lesson 2, page 202

1. no, $b + c = a$; Because $b + c$ is not greater than a but only equal to it. **3.** yes, $a + b > c$, $b + c > a$, $a + c > b$ **5.** yes; $14 > 7$, $11 > 10$, $17 > 4$ **7.** yes; $20 > 12$, $23 > 9$, $21 > 11$ **9.** yes; $6 > 5$, $8 > 3$ **11.** $>$; Because $\overline{PQ}$ is not a perpendicular, it cannot be the shortest distance.

13. = **15.** = **17.** >

18.

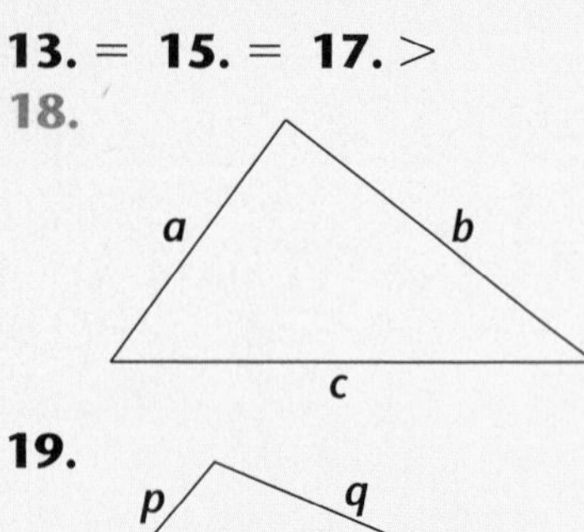

19.

Lesson 3, pages 206–207

1. yes, SSS; The two outer pairs of sides are marked congruent by the single and double tick marks. Both triangles share the third side, which is equal to itself. Therefore, all three sides are equal.
3. Yes, ASA or SAS **5.** Yes, SSS **6.** Given; Given as a feature of the figure **7.** Given
9. $\angle ABE \cong \angle DBC$ **11.** Given
13. Given **15.** $\overline{GI} \cong \overline{GI}$

17.

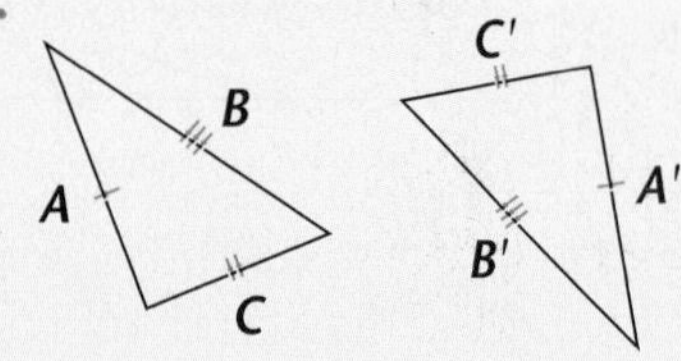

19. no; The problem describes two equilateral triangles. All equilateral triangles have equal angles because all of the angles equal 60°. However, two equilateral triangles can have different length sides.

Lesson 4, pages 212–213

1. SAS; Two pairs of sides and the included angle are shown to be congruent. **3.** AAS **5.** Given; Definition of perpendicular lines. **7.** H-L Theorem **9.** Given; Parallel lines have equal corresponding angles. **11.** $m\angle 1 = m\angle 3$ **13.** $m\angle 1 = 30°$, $m\angle 2 = 60°$; The acute angles in a right triangle are complementary and therefore equal to 90°. $m\angle 2 = 2 \cdot m\angle 1$; $m\angle 2 + m\angle 1 = 90°$; $(2 \cdot m\angle 1) + m\angle 1 = 90°$; $3 \cdot m\angle 1 = 90°$. Divide both sides by 3. $m\angle 1 = 30°$; $90° - 30° = 60°$. $m\angle 2$ is equal to 60°. **15.** $m\angle 3 = 50°$, $m\angle 4 = 40°$ **16.** $x = 20°$; if $5x + x = 120°$, then $6x = 120°$. Divide both sides by 6 to get $x = 20°$. **17.** $x = 20°$ **19.** $x = 24°$

Lesson 5, page 218

1. $A' = (3, -5)$; By definition, a reflection over the x-axis has the same x-value and a negative of the y-value. **3.** $C' = (-3, -5)$ **5.** $E' = (2, 0)$ **7.** $G' = (-4, 2)$; By definition, a reflection over the y-axis has the same y-value and a negative of the x-value. **9.** $I' = (4, 2)$ **11.** $K' = (-3, 0)$ **13.** $A' = (1, 2)$, $B' = (-1, 6)$, $C' = (-2, 2)$, $D' = (-1, -2)$; Since the line of reflection is vertical, the reflected figures' points have the same y-value as the original figure. To find the x-value of each reflected point, subtract 2 from the original x-value. This gives the distance from the line of reflection for the original point. This distance has to be exactly reflected. To find the x-value for the reflected point, subtract this distance from the x-value of the line of reflection, or 2. **15.** $L' = (0, -6)$, $M' = (-2, -2)$, $N' = (-6, -1)$, $O' = (-1, -10)$

Lesson 6, page 220

1. no; The given line does not create coinciding images when the figure is folded along it and is not a line of symmetry. **3.** no **5.** yes **6.** 3; The figure is a triangle. **7.** 4 **9.** It must bisect an interior angle.

Try This

Any diameter seems to be a line of symmetry. There are an infinite number of diameters, so there must be an infinite number of lines of symmetry.

Lesson 7, page 223

1. $A' = (0, 8)$; A slide to the left by any number is made by subtracting the number from the original x-value; $3 - 3 = 0 =$ new x-value. A slide up by any number is made by adding the number to the original y-value; $6 + 2 = 8 =$ new y-value. **3.** $C' = (0, -4)$ **5.** $E' = (-3, 7)$ **7.** $G' = (-3, 2)$ **8.** $A' = (-3, 5)$, $B' = (2, 3)$, $C' = (8, 8)$; To slide the triangle 4 right, add 4 to each x-value for each endpoint. To slide the triangle 2 up, add 2 to each y-value. **9.** $E' = (-5, 1)$, $F' = (0, 5)$, $G' = (0, 0)$ **11.** $(4, 4)$; The point given has an x-value of 3 and a y-value of -1. To find the new values, plug these old values into $x + 1$ and $y + 5$. **13.** $(1, -5)$ **15.** $(7, -1)$ **16.** $(x - 4, y + 4)$; To get new value of x, subtract distance of 4 from old value. To get new value of y, add distance of 4 to old value. **17.** $(x + 3, y + 3)$ **19.** $(x + 2, y - 4)$

Lesson 8, pages 226–227

1.

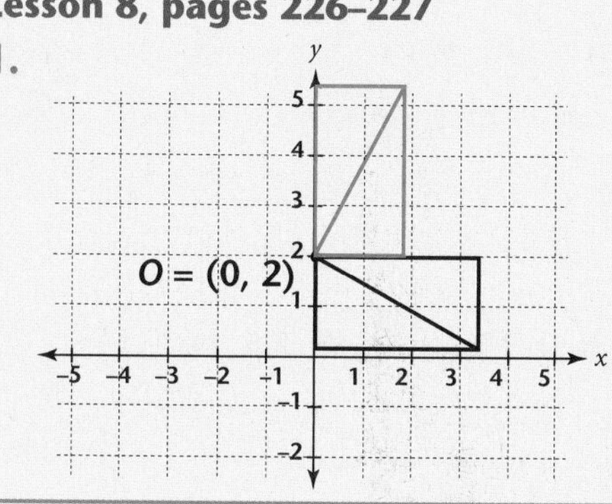

3.

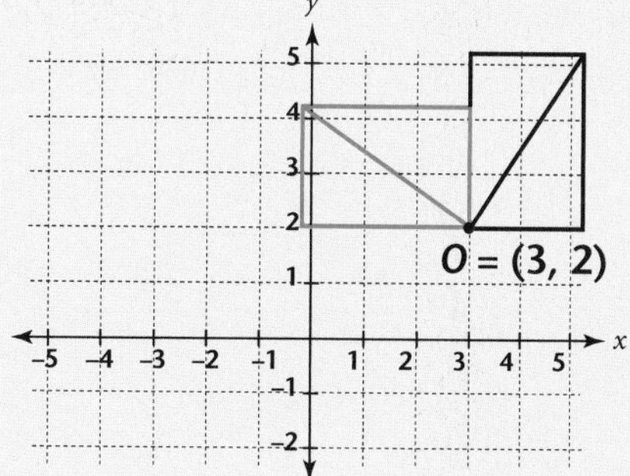

5.

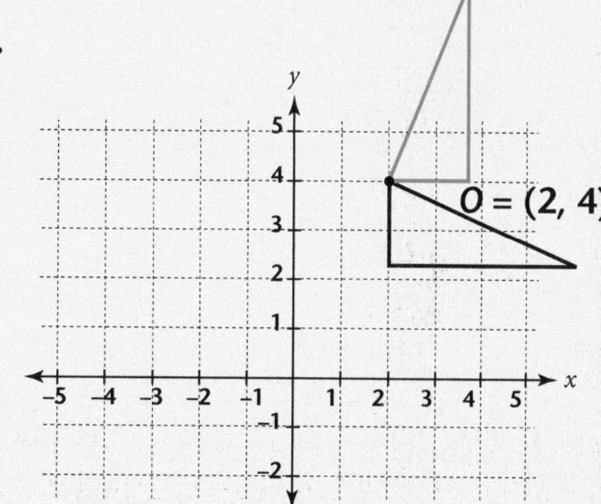

7.

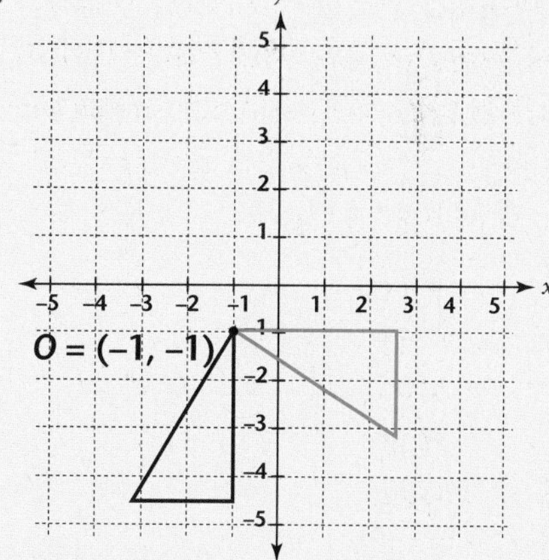

8.

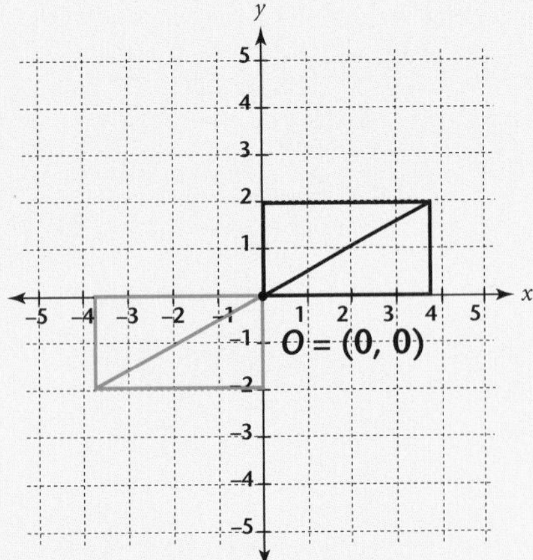

9.

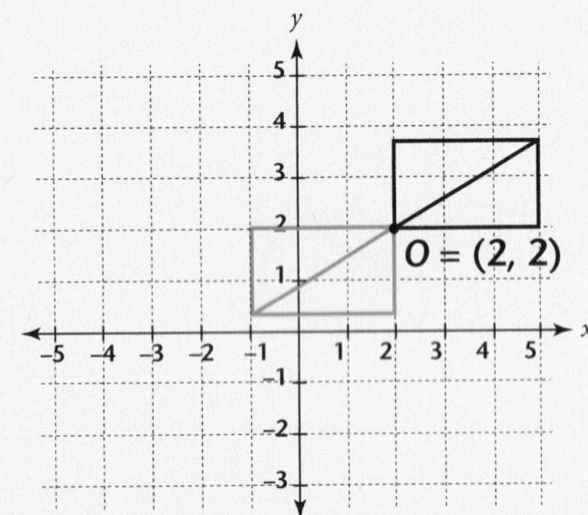

11.

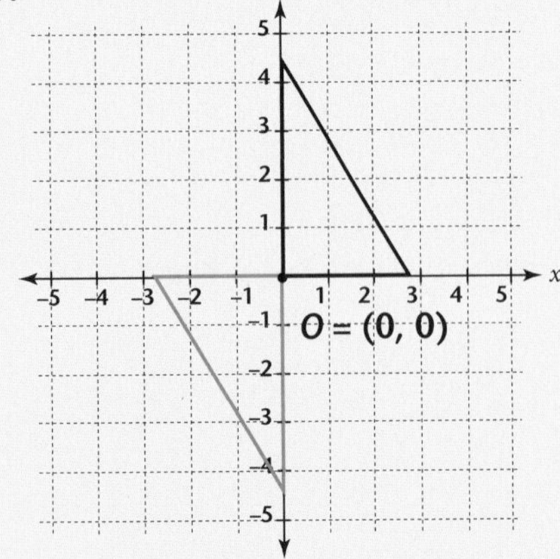

13.

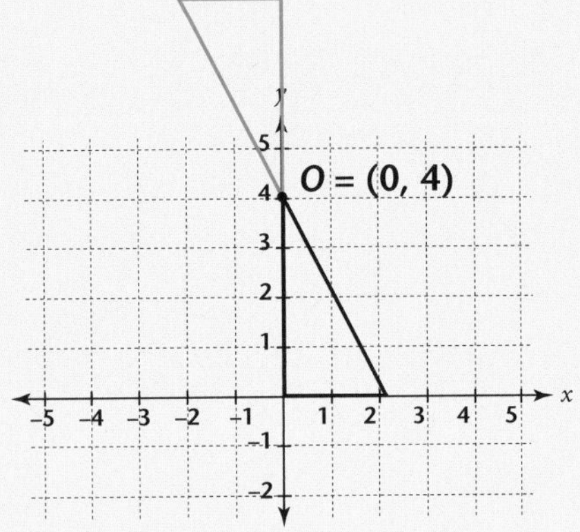

15. $(-4, 5)$; To rotate a point 180°, the distance between the origin and the x- and y-values must be moved in the opposite direction. The distance from the origin to the original point's x-value is $4 - 0 = 4$; the new point's x-value is $0 - 4 = -4$. The distance from the origin to the original point's y-value is $-5 - 0 = -5$; the new point's y-value is $0 - (-5) = 5$. **17.** $(-7, -1)$ **19.** $(-8, 3)$

Lesson 9, page 229

1. $-3, -4$; $x^2 + 7x + 12 = 0$; $(x^2 + 4x) + (3x + 12) = x(x + 4) + 3(x + 4) = (x + 3)(x + 4) = 0$, so $x + 3 = 0$ or $x + 4 = 0$; $x = -3, -4$; Check: $x^2 + 7x + 12 = (-3)^2 + 7(-3) + 12 = 9 - 21 + 12 = 0$; $x^2 + 7x + 12 = (-4)^2 + 7(-4) + 12 = 16 - 28 + 12 = 0$ **3.** $-1, 5$ **5.** $2, -3$ **7.** $8, -3$ **9.** $2, 4$ **11.** $2, -6$; $3x^2 + 12x - 36 = 0$; $(3x^2 + 18x) - (6x + 36) = 3x(x + 6) - 6(x + 6) = (3x - 6)(x + 6) = 0$, so $3x - 6 = 0$, or $x + 6 = 0$; $x = 2, -6$; Check: $3x^2 + 12x - 36 = 3(2)^2 + 12(2) - 36 = 12 + 24 - 36 = 0$; $3x^2 + 12x - 36 = 3(-6)^2 + 12(-6) - 36 = 108 - 72 - 36 = 0$ **13.** $-\frac{3}{2}, -5$ **15.** $\frac{3}{2}, -1$

Try This

$l = (3x + 1)$, $w = (x + 5)$, $P = 8x + 12$; $3x^2 + 16x + 5 = (3x^2 + 15x) + (x + 5) = 3x(x + 5) + 1(x + 5) = (3x + 1)(x + 5)$; $l = (3x + 1)$, $w = (x + 5)$; $P = l + w + l + w = 2l + 2w$; substitute for l and w, $P = 2(3x + 1) + 2(x + 5) = (6x + 2) + (2x + 10) = 8x + 12$

Application, page 230

1. Drawings should reflect the principle that tessellations cover a plane surface without overlapping and without leaving holes. **3.** No **5.** Drawings should reflect the principle that tessellations cover a plane surface without overlapping and without leaving holes.

Chapter Review, pages 231–233

1. C **3.** C **5.** B **7.** B

9.

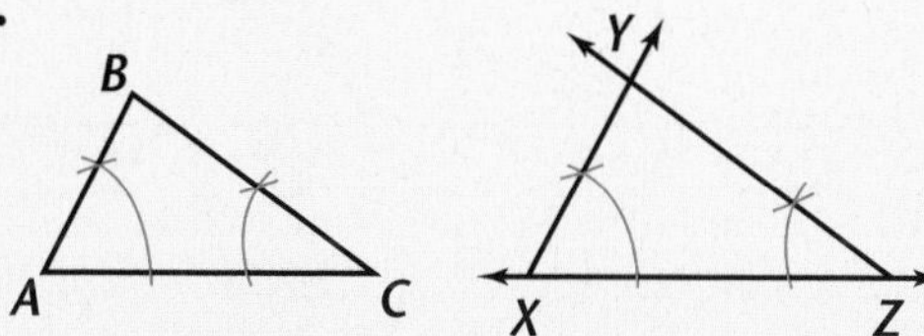

11. $m\angle g = 55°$, $m\angle h = 45°$, $m\angle i = 80°$ **13.** yes **15.** yes **17.** rotation of 90° counterclockwise **19.** slide **21.** $(-4, 2)$ **23.** $(-0, -10)$ **25.** $(3, 7)$

CHAPTER 7

Lesson 1, pages 240–241

1. 6; To solve for x, multiply the extremes together and the means together; $2 \cdot 9 = 3x$; $18 = 3x$; $6 = x$. **3.** 3.5 **5.** 40 **7.** 9 **9.** 14 **11.** 10; Sides $\overline{AC}$ and $\overline{DF}$ are similar sides of the similar triangles that act as one side of the proportion as $\frac{20}{10}$. $\overline{AB}$ and $\overline{DE}$ are also similar. The other side of the proportion is $\frac{DE}{5}$. The whole proportion is $\frac{20}{10} = \frac{DE}{5}$. Multiply extremes and means; $20 \cdot 5 = 10(DE)$; $100 = 10(DE)$; $10 = DE$ **13.** 3 **15.** 6.7 **17.** 19.6 **19.** 11.7 **21.** no, For two ratios to be equal, the extremes multiplied together and the means multiplied together must be equal; $3 \cdot 16 = 48$; $5 \cdot 10 = 50$. The products are not equal, so the ratios are not equal. **23.** yes **25.** no **27.** yes **29.** no

Try This

Give one counterexample (ΔABC with sides 2, 2, 3 and ΔDEF with sides 4, 4, 5).

Lesson 2, pages 245–246

1. yes, 3 equal angles; Each triangle has two angle measures given. To solve for the third angle in each triangle, add together the two given angles and subtract this sum from 180°. The first triangle's given angles' sum is 93°; $180° - 93° = 87°$. The second triangle's given angles' sum is 148°; $180° - 148° = 32°$. Both triangles have angle measures of 61°, 32°, and 87°. **3.** yes, sides are in proportion **5.** yes, using the angle sum and equal base angles **6.** $m\angle D$; $\angle A$ and $\angle D$ are alternate interior angles and are equal. **7.** $m\angle E$ **9.** $\overline{ED}$, $\overline{DC}$ **11.** $m\angle RTS$ **13.** $m\angle TSR$ **15.** $\overline{RS}$, $\overline{TS}$ **16.** 16; Use the ratio formula; $\frac{11}{22} = \frac{8}{x}$; $11x = 176$; $x = 16$. **17.** 12 **19.** 12 **21.** 7.5 **23.** 16 **24.** 343 inches; $\frac{84}{450} = \frac{64}{x}$; $84x = 28{,}800$; $x = 342.85$, which can be rounded up to 343 inches. **25.** 24 feet

Lesson 3, pages 250–252

1. 60°; $180° - \frac{360°}{3} = x$; $180° - 120° = x$; $60° = x$. **3.** 108° **5.** 135° **7.** 150° **9.** 168° **11.** 10; Both triangles are equilateral triangles. One side of the ratio formula is

$\frac{3}{5}$. The other side is the perimeter of the first triangle, 6, over the unknown perimeter of the second triangle, x. The whole equation is $\frac{3}{5} = \frac{6}{x}$; $3x = 30$; $x = 10$. **13.** 75 **15.** 56

16.

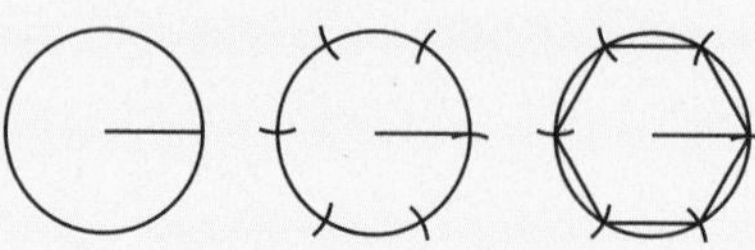

17. Answers may vary. Sample: Equilateral triangle: Connect opposite points on the circle. This will form three diameters, which form 6 equilateral triangles. Dodecagon: Construct three more diameters, each perpendicular to an existing side. Connect each point where the 6 diameters intersect the circle to form 12 equal segments. **19.** Answers may vary. Sample: Construct four more diameters, perpendicular to an existing side. Connect each point where the 8 diameters intersect the circle to form 16 equal segments.

Lesson 4, pages 256–257

1. $A' = (2, 4)$, $B' = (4, 8)$, $C' = (10, 10)$

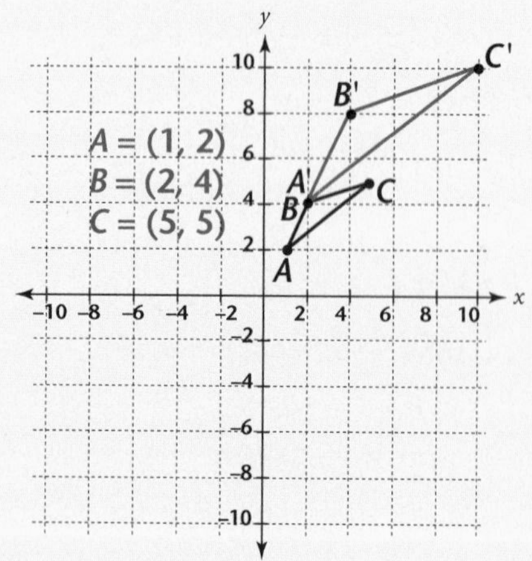

3. $A' = (4, 8)$, $B' = (8, 16)$, $C' = (20, 20)$

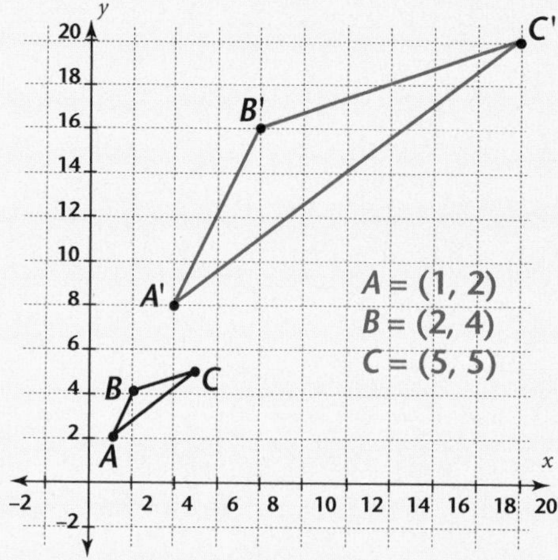

5. $D' = (-6, 6)$, $E' = (9, 3)$, $F' = (6, -6)$

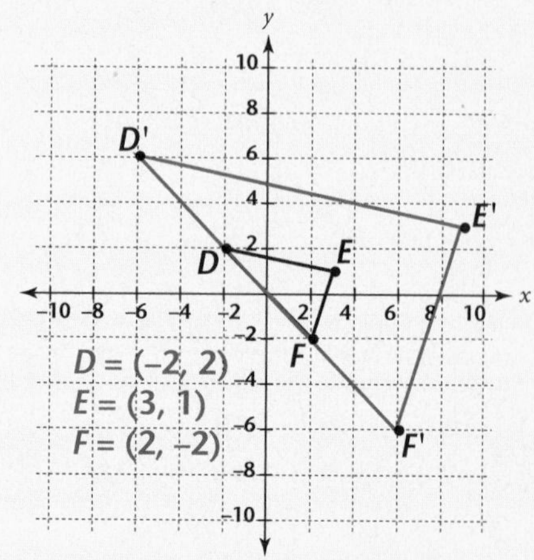

7. $J' = (-9, 3)$, $K' = (-6, 12)$, $L' = (0, 0)$

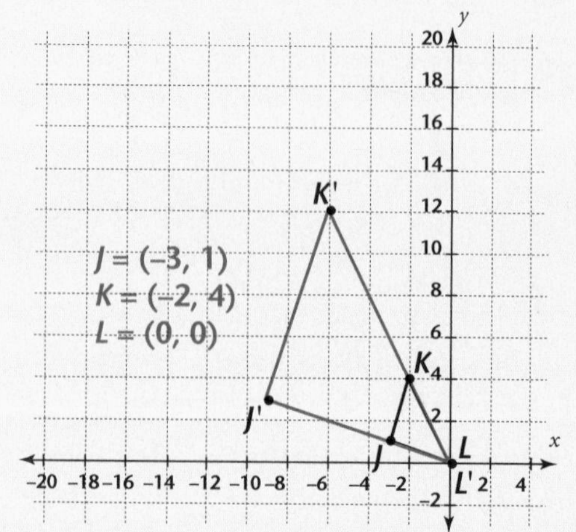

8. $A' = (0, 0)$, $B' = (0, 4)$, $C' = (4, 4)$, $D' = (4, 0)$

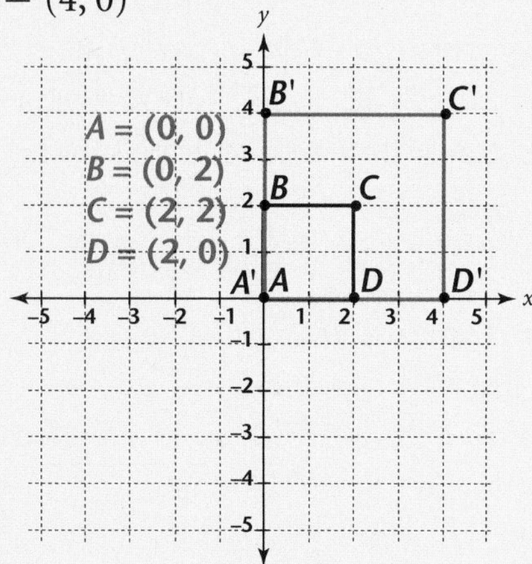

9. $A' = (0, 0)$, $B' = (0, 6)$, $C' = (6, 6)$, $D' = (6, 0)$

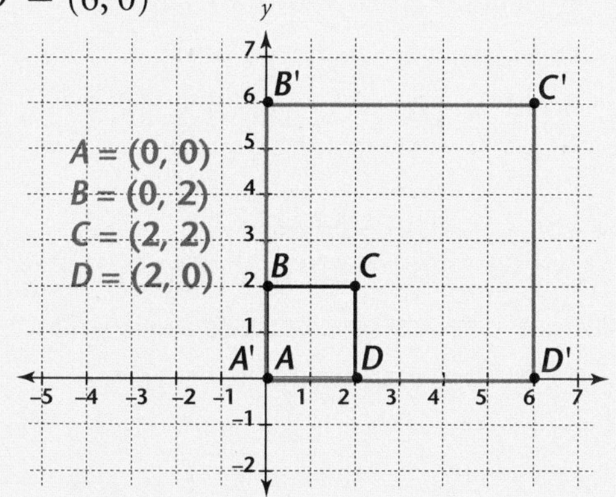

11. $A' = (-4, -4)$, $B' = (-8, 2)$, $C' = (2, 2)$, $D' = (6, -4)$

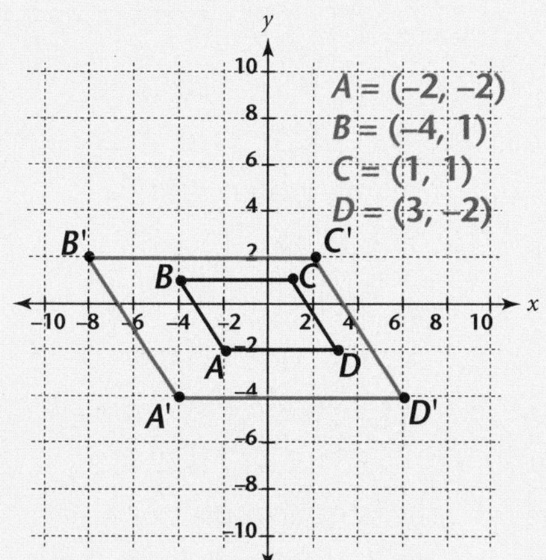

13. 18 inches × 12 inches; For the dimensions of the posters to be 3 times the size of the flyers, multiply each side by the dilation amount; $6 \cdot 3 = 18$ and $4 \cdot 3 = 12$. **15.** The magnitude of the dilation to get 4 × 5s is 2; the magnitude to get 10 × 8s is 4. The vertices have been multiplied by 2 and 4.

Lesson 5, pages 260–261

1. $A' = (-2, -2)$, $B' = (-2, 2)$, $C' = (2, 0)$; Multiply each of the original values by $\frac{1}{2}$ to get the coordinates shown. **3.** $D' = (1, -2)$, $E' = (0, 2)$, $F' = (2, 1)$ **5.** $S' = (0, 0)$, $T' = (0, 1)$, $U' = (1, 1)$, $V' = (1, 0)$; Multiply each of the original values by $\frac{1}{6}$ to get the coordinates shown. **7.** $S' = (0, 0)$, $T' = (0, 4)$, $U' = (4, 4)$, $V' = (4, 0)$ **9.** $S' = (0, 0)$, $T' = (0, 3)$, $U' = (3, 3)$, $V' = (3, 0)$ **11.** 1,120 cm or about 11 m; Put the ratio of 1:80 into the ratio formula as $\frac{1}{80}$. 1 corresponds to the length of the scaled-down car, or 14 cm. To solve for the size of the actual car, or x, write the equation as $\frac{1}{80} = \frac{14}{x}$; $x = 14 \cdot 80$ or $x = 1{,}120$. **13.** 45 inches or $3\frac{3}{4}$ ft
15. 2,750 gallons in 10 minutes, 16,500 in an hour

Lesson 6 page 263

1. 3,628,800; $10! = 10 \cdot 9 \cdot 8 \cdot 7 \cdot 6 \cdot 5 \cdot 4 \cdot 3 \cdot 2 \cdot 1 = 3{,}628{,}800$ **3.** 6; First book: 3 choices; second book: 2 choices; third book: 1 choice; Total possible orders: $3 \cdot 2 \cdot 1 = 6$ **5.** 720

Try This

17,576,000; Each letter can be A–Z, or 26 different options. Each digit can be 0–9, or 10 different options. There are three spots for letters and three spots for numbers. Total number of different license plates possible = (letter combinations) • (number combinations) = (26 • 26 • 26) • (10 • 10 • 10) = 17,576,000

Application, page 264

1. 32,400 inches or 2,700 feet **3.** 59,040 inches or 4,920 feet

Chapter Review, pages 265–267

1. D **3.** B **5.** A **7.** 16 **9.** 30 **11.** 25 **13.** 8 **15.** 24 **17.** $7\frac{1}{3}$ **19.** 56 **21.** $A' = (-1, 0)$, $B' = (-1, 1)$, $C' = (0, 1)$, $D' = (0, 0)$ **23.** $A' = (-2, -4)$, $B' = (-2, 8)$, $C' = (8, 8)$, $D' = (8, -4)$ **25.** $A' = (-3, -6)$, $B' = (-3, 12)$, $C' = (12, 12)$, $D' = (12, -6)$

CHAPTER 8

Lesson 1, page 273

1. 169; The square of 5 is 25. The square of 12 is 144; 25 + 144 = 169. **3.** 400 **5.** 100 **6.** 12, 16, 20; The triple given is 3, 4, 5 and the multiplier is 4; 3 • 4 = 12, 4 • 4 = 16, 5 • 4 = 20 **7.** 15, 20, 25 **9.** 21, 28, 35 **11.** 20, 48, 52 **13.** 30, 72, 78 **15.** 100, 240, 260 **16.** no; Use the formula: $a^2 + b^2 = c^2$. $3^2 + 6^2 = 9^2$; 9 + 36 = 81 is a false statement because 9 + 36 = 45, not 81. **17.** yes **19.** no **21.** 6, 8, 10; Plato's formula is $(2m)^2 + (m^2 - 1)^2 = (m^2 + 1)^2$: Use 3 for *m*; $(2 \cdot 3)^2 + (3^2 - 1)^2 = (3^2 + 1)^2$; $6^2 + (9 - 1)^2 = (9 + 1)^2$; $6^2 + 8^2 = 10^2$, which gives the triple 6, 8, 10. **23.** 20, 99, 101 **25.** 40, 399, 401

Try This

3*m*, 4*m*, 5*m*, where $m > 1$

Lesson 2, page 276

1. 169 sq units; The square measures 13 inches per side. $A = lw$; 13 • 13 = 169 **3.** 7, 49 **5.** yes **6.** 9, 12, 15; Longest side is 15; shortest side is 9; square's side is 3, 3 + 9 = 12 **7.** 54 **9.** 54; Subtract area of small square from area of large square; divide by 4; 225 − 9 = 216; $\frac{216}{4} = 54$; area of each triangle = 54 sq units

Lesson 3, pages 280–281

1. 25; Press 2nd x^2 625 ENTER or 625 2nd x^2. Display reads 25. **3.** 63 **5.** 30; Area of any right triangle is $\frac{1}{2}bh$. The base of each triangle is 5 and the height is 12; $\frac{1}{2}(5 \cdot 12) = \frac{1}{2}(60) = 30$ **7.** 289 **9.** 25 **11.** 60 **13.** the same **14.** 13; For a right triangle, $b^2 + h^2 = \text{hypotenuse}^2$; $5^2 + 12^2 = \text{hypotenuse}^2$; $25 + 144 = 169 = \text{hypotenuse}^2$; $\sqrt{169} = 13$ **15.** 41 **17.** 3.6 **19.** 2

Lesson 4, pages 284–285

1. ΔFGH, ΔFIG, ΔGIH; A perpendicular with the hypotenuse creates two smaller triangles that are similar to the first triangle. **3.** $\angle I = \angle G$, $\angle H = \angle H$, $\angle IGH = \angle F$ **5.** yes, AA Similarity Postulate **6.** 16.64 cm; Clock hands form the base and height of a right triangle; use the formula $b^2 + h^2 = \text{hypotenuse}^2$; $9^2 + 14^2 = \text{hypotenuse}^2$; $81 + 196 = 277$; $\sqrt{277} \approx 16.64$ **7.** 45 feet **9.** 95.39 paces **11.** 14.42 inches **13.** Yes, the opening has a diagonal of 5 feet, which is wide enough. **15.** 721.11 m

Lesson 5, page 289

1. 17 in., 17 in.; The side lengths of an equilateral triangle form the ratio 1:1:1, so if one side = 17 in., (17)1:1:1 = 17:17:17, so the remaining sides also measure 17 in. **3.** 4.5 mi, 4.5 mi **4.** $6\sqrt{2}$

units; The lengths of the sides of an isosceles triangle form a ratio of $1{:}1{:}\sqrt{2}$, so if one leg = 6 units, $(6)1{:}1{:}\sqrt{2} = 6{:}6{:}6\sqrt{2}$, and the hypotenuse = $6\sqrt{2}$ units. **5.** $10\sqrt{2}$ units **7.** $25\sqrt{2}$ in. **9.** $13\sqrt{2}$ ft **10.** $\frac{5}{2}$ units, $\frac{5\sqrt{3}}{2}$units; The lengths of the sides of a 30°-60° right triangle form a ratio of $1{:}\frac{1}{2}{:}\frac{\sqrt{3}}{2}$. If the hypotenuse is 5 units, $(5)1{:}\frac{1}{2}{:}\frac{\sqrt{3}}{2} = 5{:}\frac{5}{2}{:}\frac{5\sqrt{3}}{2}$, and the two legs equal $\frac{5}{2}$ units, and $\frac{5\sqrt{3}}{2}$ units. **11.** $\frac{15}{2}$ units, $\frac{15\sqrt{3}}{2}$ units **13.** 8 m, $8\sqrt{3}$ m **15.** 6 in., $6\sqrt{3}$ in.

Try This

hypotenuse = 12 m, leg = $6\sqrt{3}$m; Side opposite the 30° angle is half the length of the hypotenuse, so the hypotenuse is $6 \cdot 2 = 12$ m. The other leg is $\sqrt{3}$ times the smaller leg, or $6\sqrt{3}$.

Lesson 6, pages 292–293

1. 84; Formula for area of a trapezoid is $\left(\frac{a+b}{2}\right)h$; $\left(\frac{10+18}{2}\right)6 = \left(\frac{28}{2}\right)6 = 14 \cdot 6 = 84$ **3.** 67.5 **5.** 105 **7.** 21 **9.** 19 **10.** 6; Area of any right triangle is $\frac{1}{2}bh$; $\frac{3 \cdot 4}{2} = \frac{12}{2} = 6$ **11.** 6 **13.** 24.5 **15.** 30 **17.** 144.5 **19.** 24 **21.** 98 **23.** 480 **25.** 2,312

Lesson 7, pages 297–298

1. $\sqrt{26}$; $d = \sqrt{(x_2 - x_1)^2 + (y_2 - y_1)^2}$; $d = \sqrt{(-4 - (-5))^2 + (-3 - 2)^2}$; $d = \sqrt{(1)^2 + (-5)^2}$; $d = \sqrt{1 + 25} = \sqrt{26}$ **3.** $\sqrt{52}$ **5.** 11 **7.** $\sqrt{388} = 2\sqrt{97}$ **9.** $\sqrt{325} = 5\sqrt{13}$ **11.** 10; $d = \sqrt{(x_2 - x_1)^2 + (y_2 - y_1)^2}$; $d = \sqrt{(4 - (-2))^2 + (5 - (-3))^2}$; $d = \sqrt{(6)^2 + (8)^2}$; $d = \sqrt{36 + 64} = \sqrt{100} = 10$ **13.** $\sqrt{29}$ **15.** $\sqrt{50} = 5\sqrt{2}$ **16.** $\sqrt{5{,}165}$; $d = \sqrt{(x_2 - x_1)^2 + (y_2 - y_1)^2}$; $d = \sqrt{(30 - (-8))^2 + (-11 - 50)^2}$; $d = \sqrt{(38)^2 + (-61)^2} = \sqrt{1{,}444 + 3{,}721} = \sqrt{5{,}165}$ **17.** $\sqrt{125} = 5\sqrt{5}$ **19.** 5

Lesson 8, page 301

1. yes; For ΔABC, if $(AC)^2 = (AB)^2 + (BC)^2$, then ΔABC is a right triangle. Given sides 3, 4, and 5; $5^2 = 3^2 + 4^2$; $25 = 9 + 16$. Statement is true, so triangle is a right triangle. **3.** no **5.** no **7.** no **9.** no **11.** 12; $a^2 + b^2 = c^2$; $5^2 + (BD)^2 = 13^2$; $25 + (BD)^2 = 169$; subtract 25 from both sides to get $(BD)^2 = 144$; take the square root of each side to get $BD = 12$. **13.** For isosceles triangle, a line from the vertex perpendicular to the base bisects the base. **15.** Both angles are right angles.

Lesson 9, page 303

1. $x = -10$; undefined if denominator $(x + 10) = 0$; $x = 0 - 10 = -10$ **3.** $c = -3$ **5.** $w = 0$; undefined if denominator $(9w^2) = 0$; $w^2 = \frac{0}{9} = 0$; $w = \sqrt{0} = 0$ **7.** $m = \pm 4$ **9.** $b = \pm 10$ **11.** $z = \pm 2$ **13.** $x = \pm 3, -5$; undefined if denominator $(9 - x^2)(x + 5) = 0$; this happens if $(9 - x^2) = 0$ or if $(x + 5) = 0$; $(9 - x^2) = 0$; $-x^2 = 0 - 9 = -9$; $x^2 = 9$; $x = \sqrt{9} = +3$ or -3; $(x + 5) = 0$; $x = 0 - 5 = -5$ **15.** $w = -1, -4$

Application, page 304

1. Answers will vary but should reflect triangles in photos. **3.** Answers will vary but should reflect triangles in photos. **5.** Answers will vary but should include triangles in designs.

Chapter Review, pages 305–307

1. B **3.** C **5.** B **7.** 12 **9.** $x = 13\sqrt{2}$, $y = 13$ **11.** 77 **13.** $\sqrt{41}$ **15.** yes **17.** yes **19.** no

CHAPTER 9

Lesson 1, page 312

1. 35; $10 + 12 + 13 = 35$ **3.** 42 **4.** 10; Let $x =$ the missing side; $8 + 5 + x = 23$; $13 + x = 23$; $x = 10$ **5.** 9 **7.** 9 **8.** $P = 80$ m; $2(15) + 2(25) = P$; $30 + 50 = 80$ **9.** $P = 110$ ft

Lesson 2, pages 315–316

1. $P = 30$; $P = 3s$: $P = 3(10) = 30$ **3.** 56 **5.** 48 **7.** 80 **9.** 14; $P = 2(l + w)$: $P = 2(5 + 2)$; $P = 2(7) = 14$ **11.** 18 **13.** $w = 20$, $l = 60$; $P = 2(l + w)$: l is 3 times w; $P = 2(3w + w)$; $160 = 2(3w + w)$ or $160 = 2(4w)$; $160 = 8w$; $w = 20$. Since l is 3 times w: $3(20) = 60$. **15.** $b = 240$, $s = 160$ **17.** $w = 7.5$, $l = 45$ **18.** 46 in.; $\frac{46}{36}$ rounded to $1\frac{1}{3}$ yards; $P = 2(l + w)$: $P = 2(9 + 14)$; $P = 2(23)$; $P = 46$; (1 yard = 36 inches) **19.** 96 ft

Lesson 3, pages 319–320

1. 11.2, 46.2; Let $x =$ the missing side: $5^2 + 10^2 = x^2$; $25 + 100 = 125$; $x = \sqrt{125} \approx 11.2$; $P \approx 5 + 10 + 20 + 11.2 = 46.2$ **3.** 4.2, 24.2 **5.** 19.3, 44.3 **6.** 12; $P = AB + BC + CA$;
$d = \sqrt{(x_2 - x_1)^2 + (y_2 - y_1)^2}$;
$AB = \sqrt{(2 - 2)^2 + (4 - 1)^2}$;
$AB = \sqrt{(0)^2 + (3)^2} = \sqrt{9} = 3$
$BC = \sqrt{(6 - 2)^2 + (1 - 4)^2}$;
$BC = \sqrt{(4)^2 + (-3)^2}$;
$BC = \sqrt{16 + 9} = \sqrt{25} = 5$
$CA = \sqrt{(2 - 6)^2 + (1 - 1)^2}$;
$CA = \sqrt{(-4)^2 + 0} = \sqrt{16} = 4$;
$P = 3 + 4 + 5 = 12$ **7.** 22.4 **9.** 21.7

Lesson 4, pages 324–325

1. 225 cm^2; $A = s^2$; $15^2 = 225$ **3.** 81 sq in. **5.** 48 cm^2 **7.** 60 km^2 **9.** 9 cm; $\sqrt{A} = s$; $\sqrt{81} = 9$ **11.** 7 in. **13.** $b = 11$ mi; $A = bh$; $110 = 10 \cdot b$; $\frac{110}{10} = b = 11$ **15.** 33 m **16.** 500; $A = bh$; $A = 10 \cdot 50 = 500$ **17.** 1,200 **19.** 33 **21.** 72 **22.** 102 sq ft; Area of $A1 = 8 \cdot 7 = 56$; Area of $A2 = 4 \cdot 4 = 16$; Area of $A3 = 5 \cdot 6 = 30$; $56 + 16 + 30 = 102$ **23.** two; one application area is $75 \cdot 30 = 2{,}250$; $\frac{5{,}000}{2{,}250} \approx 2.2$ **25.** 9 sq ft

Lesson 5, pages 328–329

1. 200; $A = \frac{b_1 + b_2}{2}h$; $\frac{15 + 25}{2}10 = \frac{40}{2}10$; $(20)(10) = 200$ **3.** 210 **5.** 12 **7.** 28 **9.** 168 **11.** 26; $A =$ (average base) $\cdot h$; $156 =$ average base $\cdot 6$; $\frac{156}{6} =$ average base $= 26$ **13.** 7 **15.** 5.5 **16.** 28; $(10 - 4) \div 2 = 3$; $a^2 + b^2 = c^2$; $3^2 + b^2 = c^2$; $9 + b^2 = 25$; $b^2 = 16$; $b = 4$; $A = \frac{b_1 + b_2}{2}h$; $\left(\frac{10 + 4}{2}\right)4 = \left(\frac{14}{2}\right)4 = (7)(4) = 28$ **17.** 56.7 **19.** 349.8

Try This

Yes. Because $b_1 = b_2$ in a rectangle, the average base will be either $\frac{(b_1 + b_1)}{2}$ or $\frac{(b_2 + b_2)}{2} = b_1 = b_2$, giving the results $b \cdot h$ for area, which is equal to $l \cdot w$.

Lesson 6, pages 333–335

1. 7.7; $3 \cdot 4 = 12$; $12 \cdot 5 = 60$; $\sqrt{60} \approx 7.7$ **3.** 35.9 **5.** 21.9 **6.** 12.5; $A = \left(\frac{1}{2}\right)bh$; $(5 \cdot 5) = 25$; $\frac{1}{2}25 = 12.5$. **7.** 24.5 **9.** 72 **11.** 6 **13.** 14 **15.** 225 **17.** 18 **19.** 22.5 **21.** 20.3; $A = \sqrt{s(s-a)(s-b)(s-c)}$ where $s = \frac{1}{2}(a+b+c)$; $s = \frac{1}{2}(6+7+8)$ $= \frac{1}{2}(21) = 10.5$; $A = \sqrt{10.5(10.5-6)(10.5-7)(10.5-8)}$ $= \sqrt{10.5(4.5)(3.5)(2.5)} \approx \sqrt{413.4} \approx$ 20.3 **23.** 71 **25.** 51.9

Try This

$$A = \sqrt{\frac{3x}{2} \cdot \left(\frac{3x}{2} - x\right) \cdot \left(\frac{3x}{2} - x\right) \cdot \left(\frac{3x}{2} - x\right)}$$

$$= \sqrt{\frac{3x^4}{16}} = \frac{x^2\sqrt{3}}{4} \approx (0.4)x^2$$

Lesson 7, page 337

1.

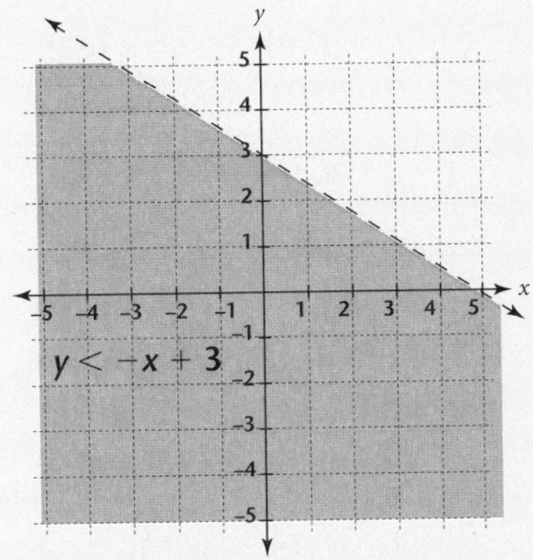

3.

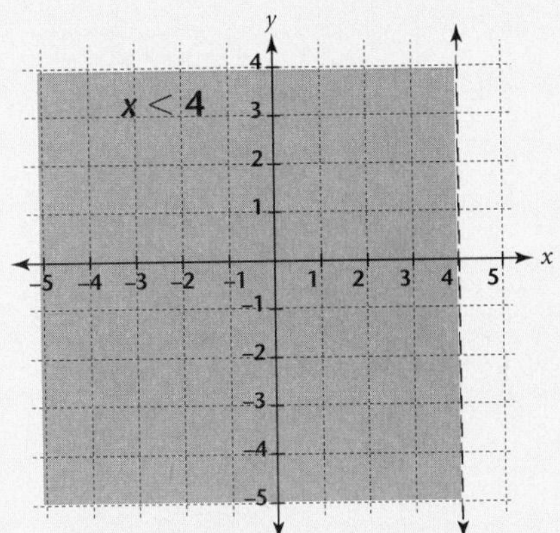

4.

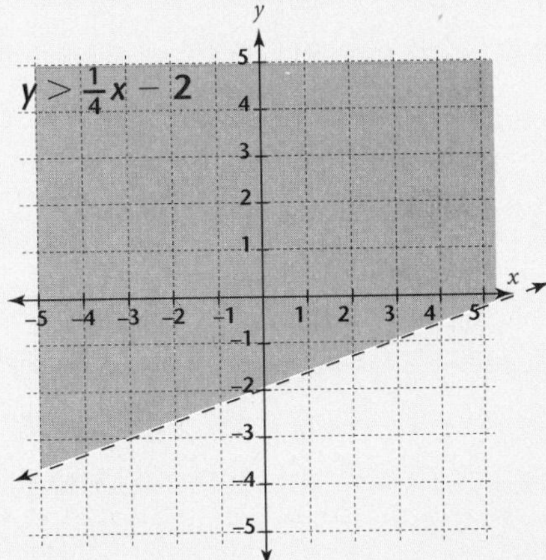

5.

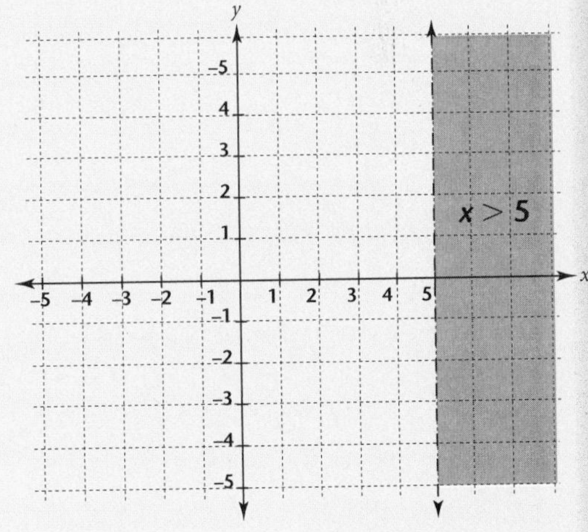

7.

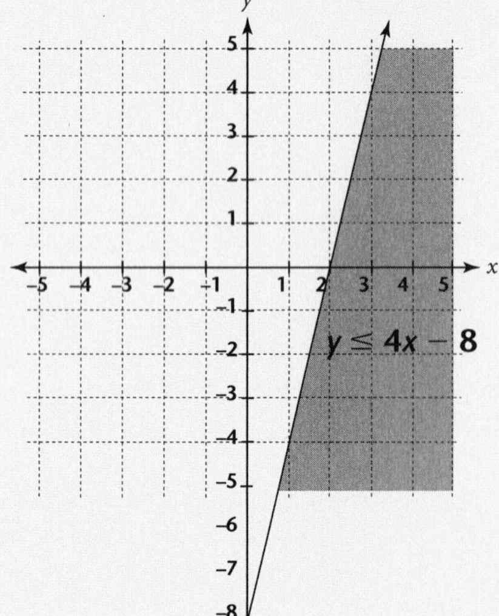

9.

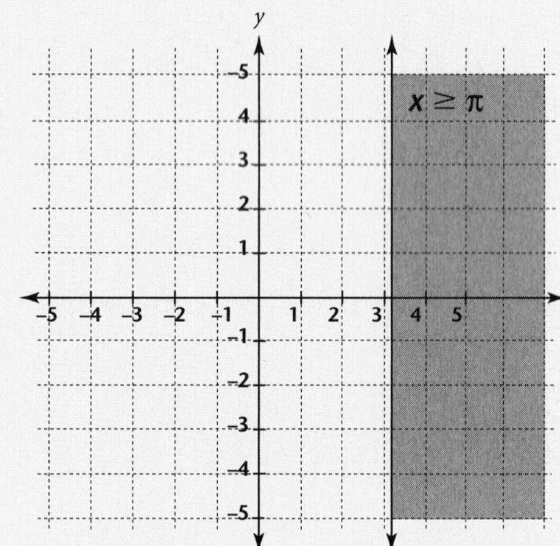

Application, page 338

1. $\frac{9}{16}, \frac{9\sqrt{3}}{64}$ **3.** $\frac{81}{256}, \frac{8\sqrt{3}}{1{,}024}$

Chapter Review, pages 339–341

1. B **3.** A **5.** A **7.** D **9.** 17.6 **11.** $P = 22$, $A = 24$ sq units **13.** $P = 30$, $A = 36$ sq units **15.** $P = 56$, $A = 128$ sq units **17.** $x \approx 5$, $P \approx 45.6$, $A = 50$ sq units **19.** $x = 5$, $P = 36$, $A = 52$ sq units

CHAPTER 10

Lesson 1, page 346

1. center; O is the center of the circle. **3.** diameter **5.** radius **7.** $\overline{BC}$ **9.** C **11.** 12 units; $d = 2r$; $d = 2 \cdot 6 = 12$ **13.** 7 **15.** 12π units, 37.7 units

Lesson 2, page 350

1. 12π units; $C = \pi d$; $C = 12\pi$ **3.** 31π m **5.** 20π in. **7.** 18π ft **9.** $d = 44$ ft, $r = 22$ ft; $C = d\pi = 2r\pi$; $44\pi = d\pi$ and $44\pi = 2r\pi$; $d = 44$ and $2r = 44$; $r = 22$ **11.** $d = 12$ in., $r = 6$ in. **13.** $d = 15$ ft, $r = 7.5$ ft **15.** $d = 22$ cm, $r = 11$ cm **17.** 23 ft; $C = d\pi$; fence $= C$; widest part of garden $= d$; $23\pi = d\pi$; $d = 23$ **19.** 1 to 2 or $\frac{1}{2}$

Lesson 3, page 353

1. large square = 400 sq units, interior square = 200 sq units, estimated area of circle = 300 sq units; A of large square = $4r^2 = 4(10)^2 = 4(100) = 400$; A of interior square = $2r^2 = 2(10)^2 = 2(100) = 200$; A of circle = $\frac{400 + 200}{2} = 300$ **3.** large square = 1,600 sq units; interior square = 800 sq units; estimated area of circle = 1,200 sq units **5.** large square = 2,500 sq units; interior square = 1,250 sq units; estimated area of circle = 1,875 sq units **6.** 48; $A \approx 3r^2$; $A = 3(4^2) = 3(16) = 48$ **7.** 108 **9.** 867 **11.** 432 **13.** 243 **15.** 1,323 **16.** $r = 4$; $A \approx 3r^2$; $48 = 3r^2$; $16 = r^2$; $\sqrt{16} = r = 4$ **17.** $r = 6$ **19.** $r = 10$

Lesson 4, page 355

1. 50%; $\frac{\text{area of desired outcome}}{\text{total area}} = \frac{2}{4} = \frac{1}{2} =$ 50% **3.** 75% **5.** 50%

Try This

A clock face is divided up into 12 hours, so the probability of it being any one particular hour is $\frac{2}{24} = \frac{1}{12}$, or $8\frac{1}{3}\%$.

Lesson 5, pages 358–359

1. 153.94; Press 7 [x^2] [×] [2nd] [^] [ENTER]. Display reads 153.94. **3.** 50.27 **5.** 254.47 **7.** 25 **9.** 1,111 **11.** 9π sq in.; $A = \pi r^2$; $A = \pi(3)^2 = 9\pi$ **13.** 81π m^2 **15.** 225π km^2 **16.** 452.4 sq in.; $A = \pi r^2$; $A = \pi 12^2 = 144\pi$; $144 \cdot \pi \approx 452.4$ **17.** 113.1 ft^2 **19.** 907.9 mm^2 **21.** 452.4 km^2 **23.** 153.9 ft^2 **25.** 6,361.7 mi^2 **26.** $r = 8.2$ cm; $A = \pi r^2$; $210 = \pi r^2$; $66.8 \approx r^2$; $\sqrt{66.8} \approx 8.2$ **27.** $r = 11.3$ in. **29.** $r = 10.0$ km

Lesson 6, page 363

1. 85°; The measure of any central angle is equal to the arc that its endpoints make on the circle; $\angle ACB$ = arc AB.

3. 60° **5.** 125° **6.** $\frac{49}{12}\pi$; The shaded area has a central angle of 30°. A circle has 360°; $\frac{30°}{360°} = \frac{1}{12}$; the shaded area is $\frac{1}{12}$ of the circle. $A = \pi r^2$; $A = \pi 7^2 = 49\pi$; $\frac{1}{12}(49\pi) = \frac{49}{12}\pi$ **7.** 8π **9.** 25°; An inscribed angle is measured by $\frac{1}{2}$ its intercepted arc; $\frac{1}{2}(50) = 25$

Try This

90°

Lesson 7, page 367

1. Given; This statement is part of the given information about the proof.

3. Definition of midpoint. **5.** $m\angle ADX = m\angle BDX$ **7.** Corresponding sides of congruent triangles are equal.

8.

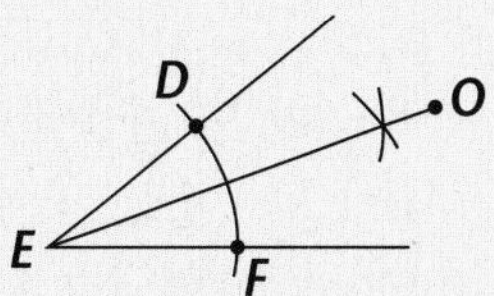

9.

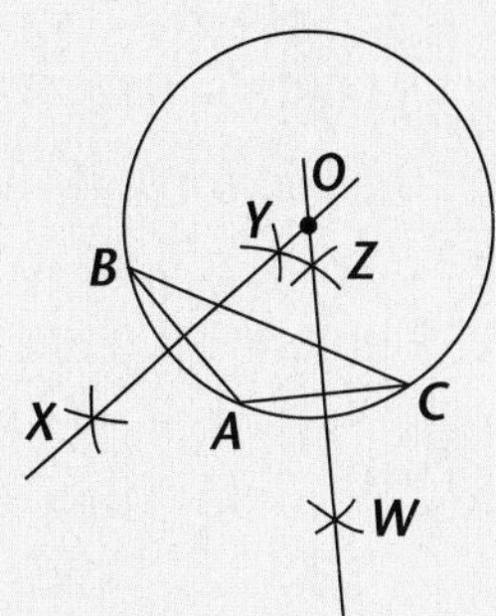

Lesson 8, page 369

1. 0, 1, 0; Press [SIN] 0 [ENTER], display reads 0; Press [COS] 0 [ENTER], display reads 1; Press [TAN] 0 [ENTER], display reads 0. **3.** 0.71, 0.71, 1 **5.** 1, 0, undefined

Lesson 9, page 371

1. 6; $\sin A = \frac{x}{AB}$; $(AB)\sin A = x$; $AB = 12$, $m\angle A = 30°$; $x = (12)\sin 30° = 6$ **3.** 4.90 **5.** 30; $\cos B = \frac{BC}{y}$; $y(\cos B) = BC$; $y = \frac{BC}{(\cos B)}$; $BC = 15$, $m\angle B = 60°$; $y = \frac{15}{(\cos 60°)} = 30$ **7.** 33.23; **8.** 19.08; $\tan A = \frac{BC}{z}$; $z(\tan A) = BC$; $z = \frac{BC}{(\tan A)}$; $BC = 1$; $m\angle A = 3°$; $z = \frac{1}{(\tan 3°)} \approx 19.08$ **9.** 25.03

Try This

$\angle Y = 90°$, $\angle W = 73°$, $WY = 9.3$, $WX = 31.37$

Lesson 10, pages 374–375

1. $S = 36\pi$ sq units, $V = 36\pi$ units^3; Formula for surface area is $S = 4\pi r^2$; $S = 4\pi(3)^2 = 4\pi(9) = 36\pi$. Formula for volume is $V = \frac{4}{3}\pi r^3$; $V = \frac{4}{3}\pi(3)^3 = \frac{4}{3}\pi(27) = 36\pi$ **3.** $S = 64\pi$ sq units,

$V \approx 85.3\pi$ units^3 **5.** $S = 144\pi$ sq units, $V = 288\pi$ units^3 **7.** $S \approx 50.27$ sq units, $V \approx 33.51$ units^3; $S = 4\pi r^2$; $S = 4\pi(2)^2 = 4\pi(4) = 16\pi$; using $\pi = 3.14$: $16 \cdot 3.14 \approx 50.24$. $V = \frac{4}{3}\pi r^3$; $V = \frac{4}{3}\pi(2)^3 = \frac{4}{3}\pi(8) \approx 10.7\pi$; using $\pi = 3.14$: $10.7 \cdot 3.14 \approx 33.51$ units^3. **9.** $S \approx 1{,}520.53$ sq units, $V \approx 5{,}575.28$ units^3 **11.** $S \approx 1{,}256.64$ sq units, $V \approx 4{,}188.79$ units^3 **13.** 36π, 36π; $S = 4\pi r^2$; $S = 4\pi(3)^2 = 36\pi$; $V = \frac{4}{3}\pi r^3$; $V = \frac{4}{3}\pi(3)^3 = \frac{4}{3}\pi(27) = 36\pi$ **15.** 576π, $2{,}304\pi$

Lesson 11, page 377

1. (2, 0); Add the left side of the two equations together, then the right side: $(2x + y) + (3x - y) = 6 + 4$; $5x + 0 = 10$; $5x = 10$; $x = 2$; Insert the answer for x into either equation and solve for y; $2(2) + y = 4$; $4 + y = 4$; $y = 4 - 4 = 0$; $(x, y) = (2, 0)$ **3.** $(-1, 4)$ **5.** $(\frac{1}{2}, \frac{1}{3})$ **7.** $(3, \frac{1}{2})$ **9.** $(-1\frac{1}{2}, \frac{2}{3})$

Application, page 378

1. 27% **3.** 97° **5.** 26% **7.** 26% **9.** 93°

Chapter Review, pages 379–381

1. D **3.** A **5.** C **7.** $C \approx 31.4$ m, $A \approx 78.5$ m^2 **9.** $C \approx 62.8$ km, $A \approx 314.2$ km^2 **11.** 25%

13.

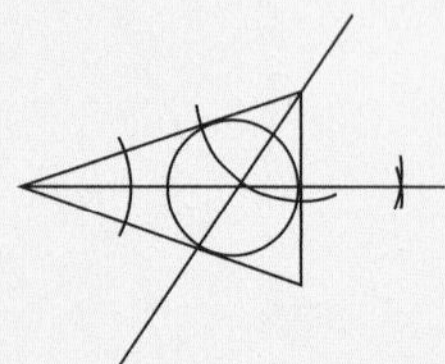

15. 0.72, 0.69, 1.04 **17.** 1.29 **19.** 287.94 **21.** $S = 400\pi$, $V \approx 1{,}333.3\pi$ **23.** $S = 196\pi$, $V \approx 457.3\pi$ **25.** $S = 36\pi$, $V = 36\pi$

CHAPTER 11

Lesson 1, pages 386–387

1. 1,000 m^3; V = area of base • height; area of base = lw; area of base = $10 \cdot 10 = 100$. $V = 100 \cdot$ height; $V = 100 \cdot 10 = 1{,}000$ **3.** 800 cu in. **5.** 144 cu in.; V = area of base • height; $V = 24 \cdot 6 = 144$ **7.** 1,500 cm^3 **8.** $1{,}000\pi$; V = area of base • height; (base is circle with radius of 10) $A = \pi r^2 = \pi(10)^2 = 100\pi$. $V = 100\pi(10) = 1{,}000\pi$ **9.** 3,000 **11.** 3,140 **13.** 375 **15.** 392.5 **16.** $h = 10$; V = area of base • height; $250 = 25 \cdot h$; $h = 10$ **17.** $r = 7$ **19.** $s = 8$

Lesson 2, pages 390–391

1. 333.3π; Formula for volume of cone is $V = \frac{1}{3}\pi r^2 h$; $V = (\frac{1}{3})(\pi 10^2)(10) = \frac{1}{3}(100\pi)(10) = \frac{1}{3}(1{,}000\pi) \approx 333.3\pi$ **3.** 1,033.3 **5.** 144π **7.** 446.4 **9.** 12π **11.** 37.2 **13.** 333.3 cu in.; Formula for volume of pyramid is $V = \frac{1}{3}$(area of base)(height); area $= 10^2 = 100$; $V = \frac{1}{3}(100)(10) = \frac{1}{3}(1{,}000) \approx 333.3$ **15.** 80 cm^3 **17.** 100 m^3 **18.** $w = 4$ cm; Formula for volume of pyramid is $V = \frac{1}{3}$(area of base)(height); area of base = lw; $80 = \frac{1}{3}(6w)(10)$; $80 = 20w$; $w = 4$ **19.** $r = 22.5$ in.

Lesson 3, page 395

1. 96 sq units; Formula for surface area of cube is $S = 6s^2$; $S = 6(4^2) = 6(16) = 96$ **3.** 170π sq units **4.** 112π; Formula for surface area of cylinder is $S = 2\pi r^2 + (2\pi r)h$; (subtract the surface area of one circular base from the equation) $S = \pi r^2 + (2\pi r)h$; $S = \pi 4^2 + 2\pi(4)(12) = 16\pi + 96\pi = 112\pi$ **5.** No, she is planning to paint 516 sq ft.

Lesson 4, pages 398–399

1. 224 sq units; Formula for surface area of pyramid is $S =$ (area of base) + area of each of the triangles. Area of the square base is $A = s^2$; $A = 8^2 = 64$. Formula for area of triangle is $A = \frac{1}{2}(bh)$; $A = \frac{1}{2}(8)(10) = \frac{1}{2}(80) = 40$. $S = 64 + 4(40) = 64 + 160 = 224$ **3.** $120 + 16\sqrt{3}$ sq units **4.** 256, 4; Press 16 [x^2] [ENTER]. The display reads 256. Press 16 [2nd] [x^2] 16 [ENTER]. Display reads 4. **5.** 324, 4.24 **7.** 529, 4.80 **9.** No, he needs a triangle with a base ≥ 50.26 feet; $C = 2\pi r = 2\pi 8 = 16\pi \approx 50.26$

Try This

350 sq units

Lesson 5, page 401

1. 432 in.; A yard is 36 inches long; $12 \times 36 = 432$ **3.** 63,360 **5.** 9 **7.** 15,000 **9.** 1,000,000

Lesson 6, page 403

1. 12; $\sqrt{3x} = 6$; square both sides, $3x = 36$; $x = \frac{36}{3} = 12$ **3.** $\frac{25}{7}$ **5.** 40 **7.** 84 **9.** 76 **11.** 16; $5 - \sqrt{x} = 1$; $\sqrt{x} = 5 - 1 = 4$; square both sides; $x = 16$ **13.** 27 **15.** 6 **17.** 13 **19.** 9

Application, page 404

1. Results will vary based on size of paper. **3.** Results will vary based on size of box. **5.** Results will vary based on size of construction.

Chapter Review, pages 405–407

1. B **3.** C **5.** A **7.** s^3 **9.** $s^2 + 2sl$ **11.** 512π sq ft **13.** 202.5π sq in. **15.** 5.8 cm **17.** 12,000 **19.** 50

CHAPTER 12

Lesson 1, pages 411–412

1. The line is tangent to the cylinder; By definition, a tangent line can share only one point with an object. **3.** The line lies on the surface of the cylinder. **5.** The plane makes a vertical slice through the cylinder. **7.** The plane must "rest against" the side of the cylinder. **9.** A line passed through a circle forming a chord; The circumference of the trunk is comparable to a circle and the board inside the trunk to a line segment.

Lesson 2, pages 415–416

1. $y = 8$ and $y = 2$; For points in a line to be equidistant from a given line, they must form a parallel line. Two lines are parallel to $y = 5$ and they are points 3 units away. They are $y = 8$ and $y = 2$. **3.** $y = -\frac{1}{2}x + 1$ and $y = -\frac{1}{2}x + 3$ **5.** $y = -1$ **7.** $36 = x^2 + y^2$; Points that are equidistant from one point such as the origin create a circle. Each point on the circle has an x- and y-value. A right triangle can be drawn using the radius as the hypotenuse and the axis as the base and height; $\text{hypotenuse}^2 = b^2 + h^2$; $6^2 = x^2 + y^2$ with x equal to the x-value of the point and y equal to the y-value. **9.** $0.25 = x^2 + y^2$ **11.** Two lines, $x = 2$ and $x = 3$. $x = 2\frac{1}{2} + \frac{1}{2} = 3$, $x = 2\frac{1}{2} - \frac{1}{2} = 2$. **13.** One point, the origin, (0, 0). **15.** One point, the origin, (0, 0).

Lesson 3, pages 418–419

1. Two points S and T on the circle and equidistant from ℓ and m

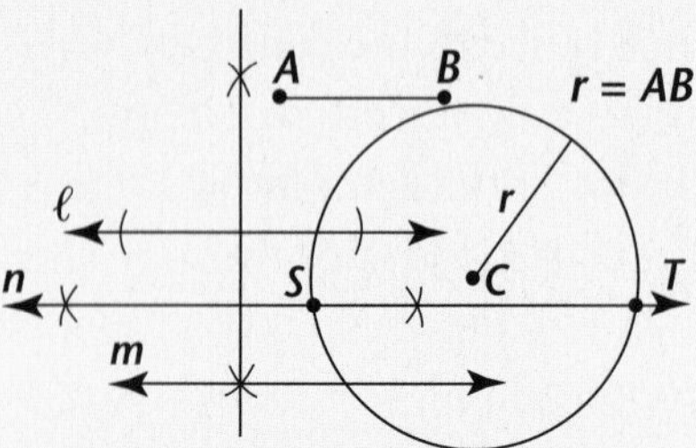

3. The intersection of the perpendicular bisectors of each side of the triangle

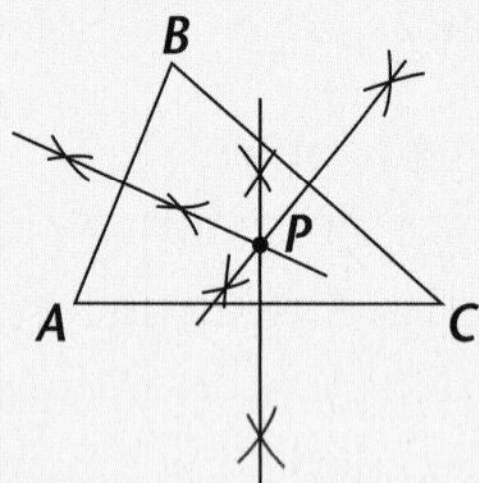

5. a point; A line crossing through a plane will cross at only one point.
7. a square smaller than the base
9. a circle with radius smaller than the radius of the base

Try This

square: intersect perpendicular to length; rectangle: intersect parallel to length; triangle: a line intersecting the length diagonally forms a triangle on the surface of the rectangle

Lesson 4, page 421

1. $x = -\frac{1}{2}$, two complex roots; $ax^2 + bx + c = x^2 + x + 3$; $a = b = 1$, $c = 3$; axis of symmetry has the equation $x = -\frac{b}{2a} = -\frac{(1)}{2(1)} = -\frac{1}{2}$; roots are real if the radicand ≥ 0; $b^2 - 4ac = 1^2 - 4(1)(3) = 1 - 12 = -11$; radicand < 0, so two complex roots **3.** $x = \frac{1}{3}$, two real roots **5.** $x = \frac{3}{2}$, two real roots **6.** $x = 5, 3$; $x^2 - 8x = -15$; $x^2 - 8x + 15 = 0 = ax^2 + bx + c$; $a = 1$, $b = -8$, $c = 15$; $x = \frac{-(-8) \pm \sqrt{(-8)^2 - 4(1)(15)}}{2(1)} = \frac{8 \pm \sqrt{64 - 60}}{2} = \frac{8 \pm \sqrt{4}}{2} = \frac{8 \pm 2}{2} = 4 \pm 1 = 3, 5$
7. $x = 2, -4$ **9.** $x = \pm 5$

Application, page 422

1. The plane is parallel to the base of the cone and cuts either cone at any point other than at the vertex of the cones.
2. The plane is at an angle between being parallel to the base and parallel to the edge of the top cone. **3.** The plane is perpendicular to the bases of the cones, and does not pass through the vertex of the cones. **4.** The plane is parallel to the bases and passes through the point where the two vertices meet. **5.** The plane is parallel to the outer edge of each cone and passes through the point where the vertices meet.

Chapter Review, pages 423–425

1. A **3.** C **5.** D
7. The line passes through the sphere.

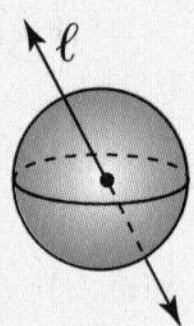

9. The line is on the surface of the cylinder.

11. The plane and the sphere meet at one point only.

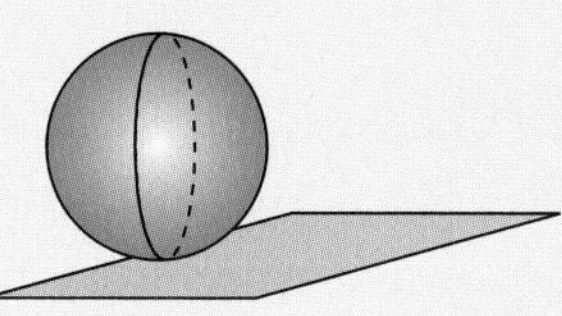

13. $y = -1$

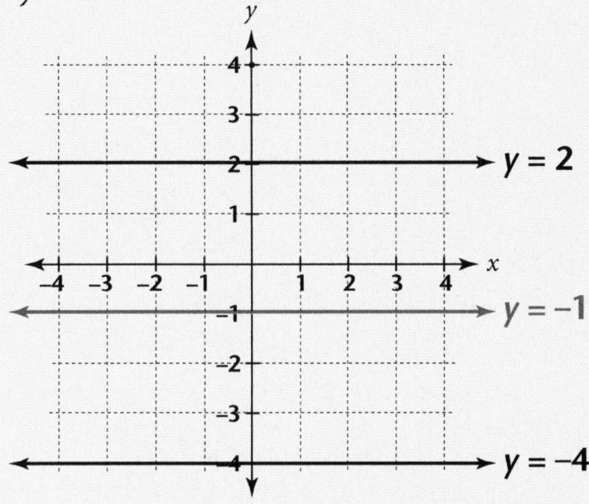

15. $25 = x^2 + y^2$

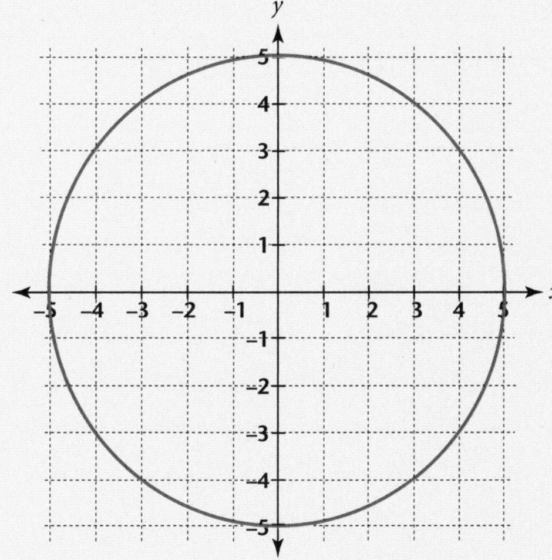

17. $9 = x^2 + y^2$

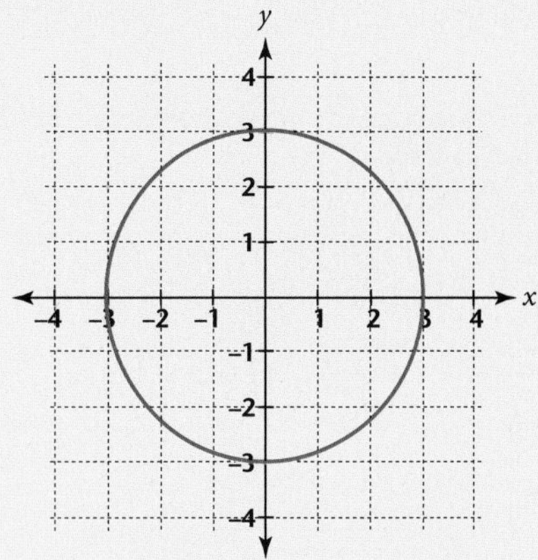

19. two points, each on the circle with center P and radius $\overline{EF}$ and midway between lines m and n

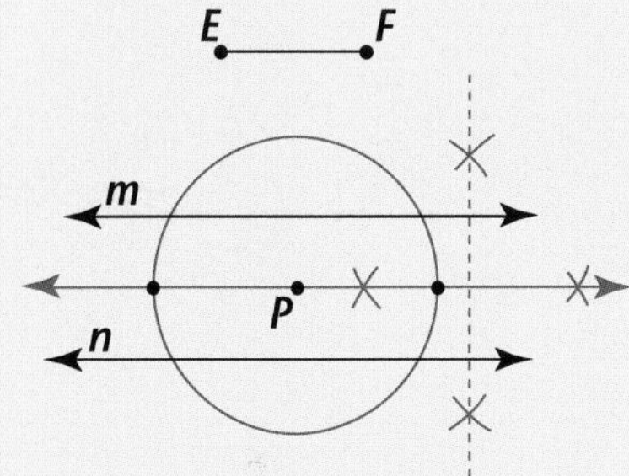

Supplementary Problems

CHAPTER 1

Pages 426–428

1. line, $\overleftrightarrow{XY}$ **2.** ray, $\overrightarrow{PQ}$ **3.** line, *m* **4.** point, *B* **5.** line segment, $\overline{ST}$ **6.** line, *y* **7.** −3 **8.** *B* **9.** 2 **10.** *I* **11.** *C* **12.** 3 **13.** *F* **14.** 0 **15.** $1\frac{1}{2}$ **16.** *D* **17.** 15 **18.** 10 **19.** 5 **20.** 10 **21.** 5 **22.** 10 **23.** 10 **24.** 25 **25.** 15 **26.** 35 **27.** C **28.** C **29.** B **30.** A **31.** $\overleftrightarrow{CA}$ **32.** $\overrightarrow{XY}$ **33.** $\overline{RQ}$ **34.** $\angle DEF$

35.

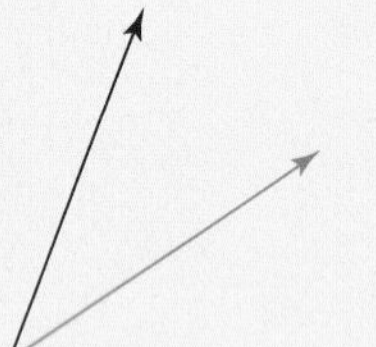

36.

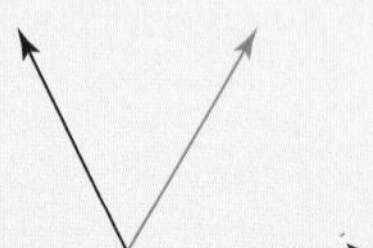

37. right **38.** acute **39.** acute **40.** obtuse **41.** straight **42.** right **43.** 90° **44.** 55° **45.** 35° **46.** 55° **47.** 180° **48.** $m\angle a = 120°$, $m\angle b = 60°$, $m\angle c = 120°$ **49.** $m\angle x = 90°$, $m\angle y = 90°$, $m\angle z = 90°$ **50.** $m\angle q = 50°$

CHAPTER 2

Pages 429–431

1. *an angle is a right angle,* hypothesis; *its measure is 90°,* conclusion **2.** *an angle is a straight angle,* hypothesis; *its measure is 180°,* conclusion **3.** *a figure is a quadrilateral,* hypothesis; *it has 4 sides,* conclusion **4.** *two angles have equal measures,* hypothesis; *they are congruent,* conclusion **5.** *an animal is an insect,* hypothesis; *it has 6 legs,* conclusion **6.** If a figure is a triangle, then it has three sides; true **7.** If the sum of the measures of two angles is 180°, then the angles are supplementary; true **8.** If the sun is not shining, then it is raining; false **9.** If you must pay taxes, then you are a citizen of the United States; false **10.** Postulate 1 **11.** Postulate 3 **12.** Postulate 4 **13.** Parallel Postulate 5 **14.** Postulate 5 **15.** Postulate 3 **16.** yes; Postulate 4 **17.** $m\angle A = 30°$; Axiom 1 **18.** angles *a*, *b*, and *c*; $m\angle a + m\angle b$; $m\angle a + m\angle c$; $m\angle b + m\angle c$; Axiom 5 **19.** yes; Axiom 2 **20.** yes; Axiom 3 **21.** $m\angle R = 90°$, $m\angle S = 45°$, $m\angle Q = 45°$ **22.** $m\angle Q = 30°$, $m\angle R = 150°$, $m\angle S = 150°$ **23.** $m\angle Q = 90°$, $m\angle R = 90°$, $m\angle S = 90°$ **24.** Given **25.** Vertical angles are equal. **26.** Definition of supplementary angles. **27.** Axiom 3 **28.** Axiom 5 **29.** Definition of supplementary angles. **30.** Axiom 5

CHAPTER 3

Pages 432–434

1. lines *x* and *y* **2.** line *q* or *w* **3.** $\angle d$ and $\angle f$, or $\angle l$ and $\angle n$ **4.** $\angle k$ and $\angle m$, or $\angle c$ and $\angle e$ **5.** lines *x* and *q*, or *x* and *w*, or *y* and *q*, or *q* and *w*, or *y* and *w* **6.** $\angle f$ and $\angle l$ **7.** supplementary **8.** alternate interior **9.** alternate exterior **10.** alternate interior **11.** supplementary **12.** alternate exterior **13.** corresponding **14.** supplementary **15.** corresponding **16.** supplementary **17.** 80° **18.** 100°

19. 120° **20.** 120° **21.** 60° **22.** 120° **23.** 80° **24.** 60° **25.** 80° **26.** 80° **27.** 60° **28.** 120° **29.** m∠*b* = 120°; m∠*c* = 60° **30.** m∠*w* = 45°; m∠*y* = 135° **31.** $\overline{EM}$ **32.** $\overline{EG}$, $\overline{GA}$, $\overline{AM}$ **33.** $\overline{GE}$ **34.** *G* or *M* **35.** *E* or *A* **36.** *A*

37.

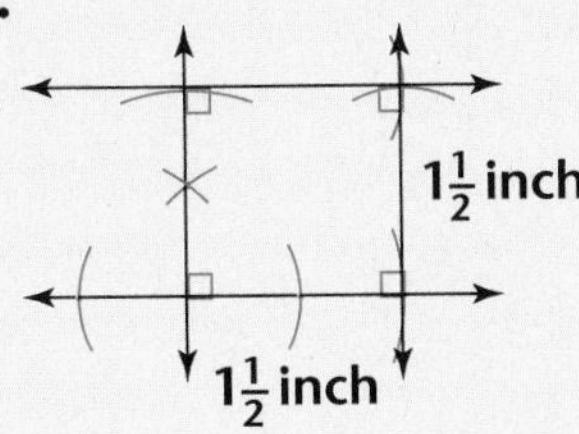

38.

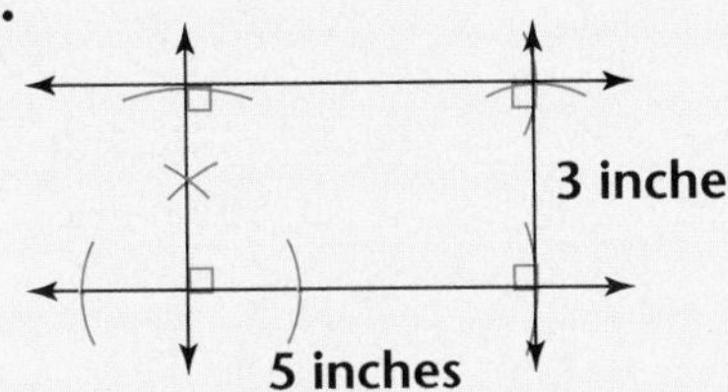

39.

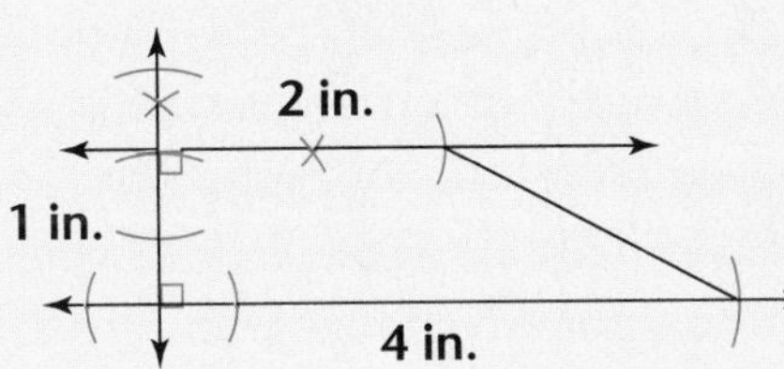

40.

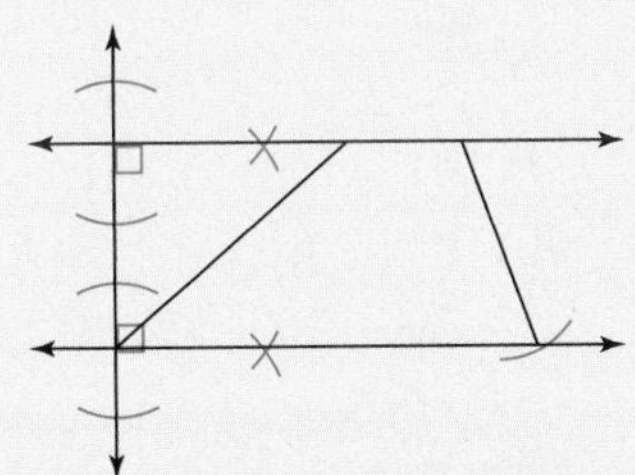

41. not parallel **42.** parallel **43.** parallel **44.** parallel **45.** not parallel

CHAPTER 4

Pages 435–437

1. (1, 2) **2.** (−4, 1) **3.** (−2, −3) **4.** (4, 0) **5.** (0, −4) **6.** (3, 4) *7.* (−1, 0) **8.** (2, −3) **9.** (−3, 0) **10.** (0, 3) **11.** *S* **12.** *W* **13.** *U* **14.** *N* **15.** *O* **16.** *R* **17.** V **18.** *P* **19.** *T* **20.** *Q* **21.** $m = 3$ **22.** $m = \frac{2}{3}$ **23.** $m = -2$ **24.** $m = -1$ **25.** $m = 2$ **26.** $m = 0$ **27.** $m = \frac{1}{2}$ **28.** $m = -1$ **29.** $m = \frac{5}{8}$ **30.** $m = 0$ **31.** $y = 2x$ **32.** $y = 0$ **33.** $y = \frac{1}{2}x - 1$ **34.** $y = -x + 4$ **35.** $y = \frac{5}{8}x - \frac{9}{8}$ **36.** $y = -6$ **37.** (−1, 7) **38.** (6, −2) **39.** (0, 1) **40.** (4, −3) **41.** (−2, 4), (−1, 7)

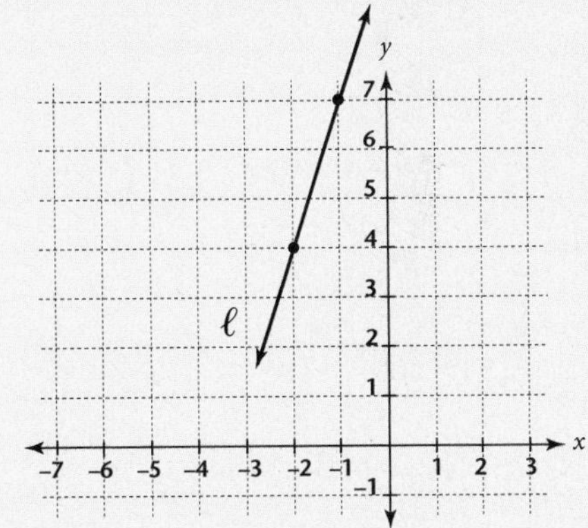

42. (1, −4), (6, −2)

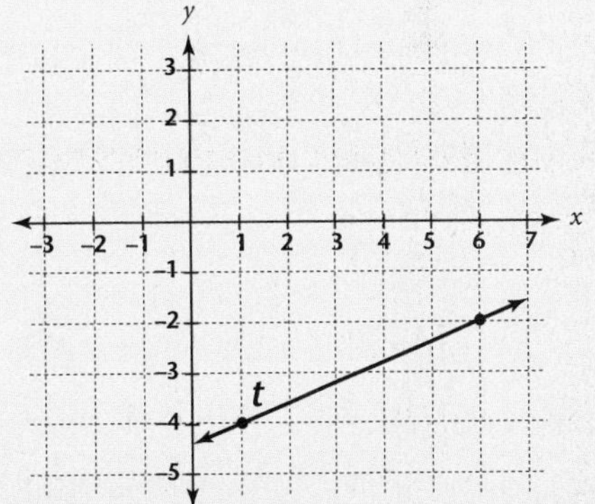

43. $(-1, 3), (0, 1)$

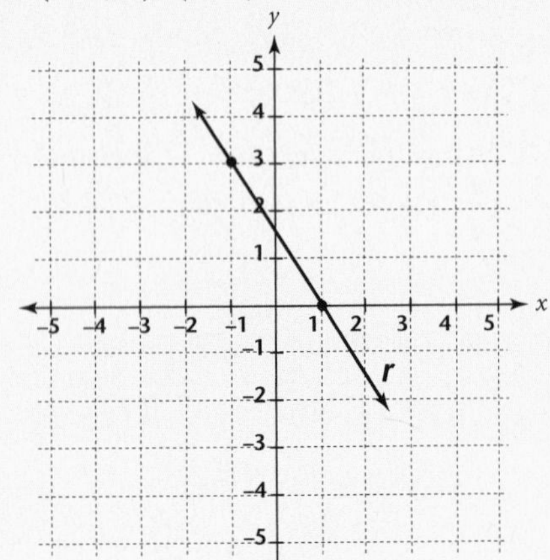

44. $(0, 0), (4, -3)$

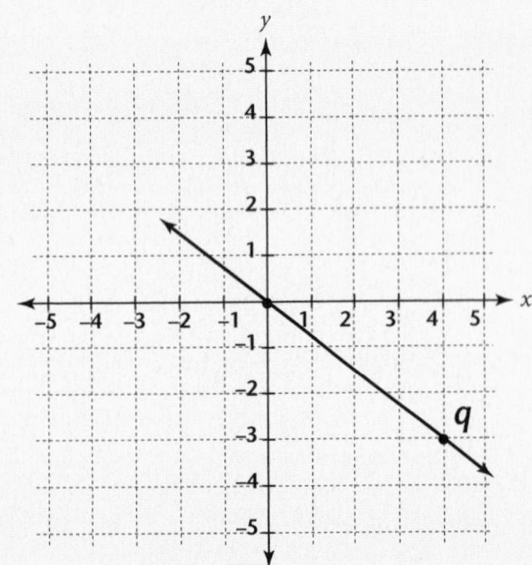

45. $(3, 4)$ **46.** $(1, 3)$ **47.** $(3, 1)$ **48.** $(9, 2)$ **49.** $(2, 3)$ **50.** $(-\frac{5}{2}, 6)$

CHAPTER 5

Pages 438–440

1. scalene triangle **2.** equilateral triangle **3.** isosceles right triangle **4.** rhombus **5.** isosceles trapezoid **6.** obtuse scalene triangle

7.

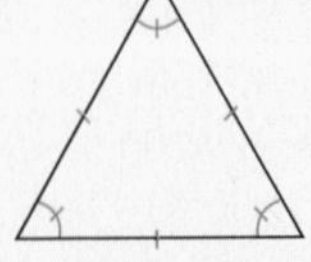

8.

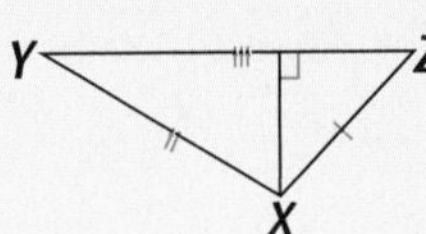

9.

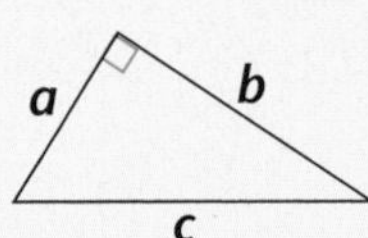

10.

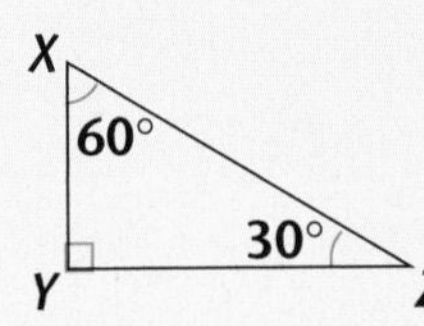

11.

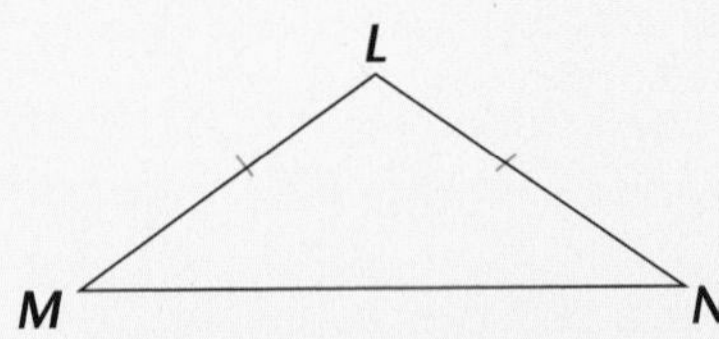

12. 60° **13.** 150° **14.** 80° **15.** 108° **16.** 60° **17.** 135° **18.** 40° **19.** 110° **20.** 70° **21.** 70° **22.** 40° **23.** A line from the vertex of a triangle that is perpendicular to the opposite side **24.** 1,080° **25.** 60° **26.** 140° **27.** Find the sum of the two nonadjacent interior angles. **28.** No, because it has only one pair of parallel sides **29.** Subtract 2 from the number of sides the polygon has. **30.** A line from the vertex of a triangle to the midpoint of the opposite side **31.** $\angle 3, \angle 5, \angle 7$ **32.** 140° **33.** 40° **34.** $m\angle 1$ or $m\angle 4$ **35.** yes; An exterior angle is formed by extending one side of the triangle along any vertex.

CHAPTER 6

Pages 441–443

1. yes; SSS **2.** no; $\angle B$ and $\angle Y$ are not congruent. **3.** no; for SAS, the angle must be the included angle. **4.** yes; AAS **5.** no

6. yes **7.** yes **8.** no **9.** yes **10.** no **11.** no **12.** yes **13.** $x = 30°$ **14.** $x = 15°$ **15.** $m\angle 2 = 80°$; $m\angle 1 = 40°$ **16.** $m\angle 2 = 40°$, $m\angle 3 = 40°$ **17.** Given.
18. Definition of equilateral triangle.
19. Definition of perpendicular bisector.
20. Any item is equal to itself. **21.** SSS
22. 4 **23.** 0 **24.** 6 **25.** 1 **26.** (11, −2)
27. (15, −12) **28.** (12, −9) **29.** (−9, 1)
30. (6, 0) **31.** (−2, −4) **32.** (−25, −47)
33. (0, 2)
34. $X' = (4, 0)$, $Y' = (1, 3)$, $Z' = (1, 0)$

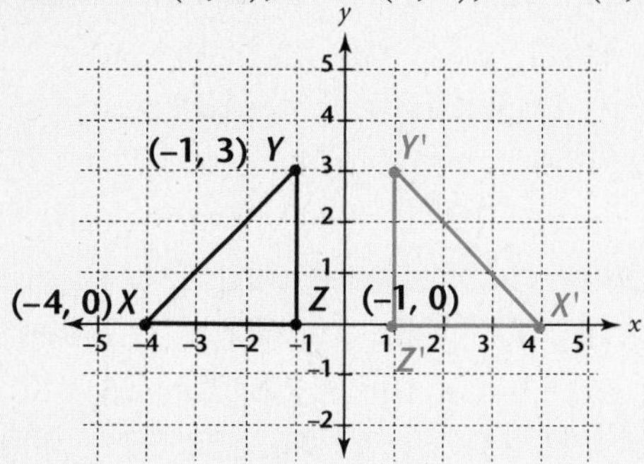

35. $A' = (-1, 3)$, $B' = (2, 1)$, $C' = (4, 2)$, $D' = (3, 3)$

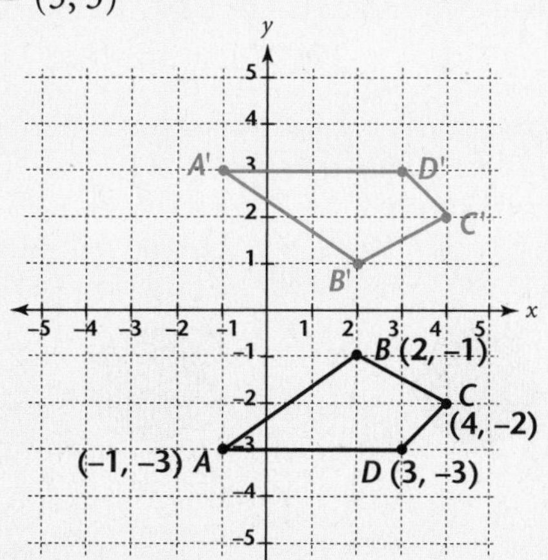

CHAPTER 7

Pages 444–446

1. yes **2.** no **3.** no **4.** yes **5.** no **6.** yes
7. yes **8.** yes **9.** no **10.** no **11.** $x = 45$
12. $z = 20$ **13.** $y = 72$ **14.** $r = 33$
15. $z = 42$ **16.** $m = 12$ **17.** yes; 3 equal angles **18.** yes; all angles are 60°
19. $m\angle A$ **20.** $m\angle BED$ **21.** $\overline{BC}$
22. $\overline{DE}$, $\overline{BE}$ **23.** 156° **24.** 160°
25.

26. 20 **27.** 10 **28.** 100° **29.** 50° **30.** 48, 32
31. 18, 6 **32.** 12, 15 **33.** 15, 20 **34.** $A' = (18, 36)$, $B' = (-18, 0)$, $C' = (36, -18)$
35. $A' = (3, 6)$, $B' = (-3, 0)$, $C' = (6, -3)$
36. $A' = (2, 4)$, $B' = (-2, 0)$, $C' = (4, -2)$
37. 480 feet **38.** (−6, 10) (6, 10) (−6, −10) (6, −10) **39.** 1,020 in. or 85 ft
40. 1.5 ft

CHAPTER 8

Pages 447–449

1. 6, 8, 10 **2.** 24, 32, 40 **3.** 30, 40, 50
4. 10, 24, 26 **5.** 15, 36, 39 **6.** 50, 120, 130
7. $x = 6$ **8.** $x = 60$ **9.** $x = 36$ **10.** $5\sqrt{2}$ cm **11.** $12\sqrt{2}$ ft **12.** $\sqrt{2}$ in. **13.** $2\sqrt{2}$ m
14. $7\sqrt{2}$ mi **15.** $25\sqrt{2}$ yd **16.** 9 m, $9\sqrt{3}$ m **17.** 2 yd, $2\sqrt{3}$ yd **18.** 6 in., $6\sqrt{3}$ in. **19.** 12 ft, $12\sqrt{3}$ ft **20.** 20 cm, $20\sqrt{3}$ cm **21.** 1 mi, $\sqrt{3}$ mi **22.** 3 **23.** 6 **24.** 6
25. 90° **26.** 60° **27.** 30° **28.** 30°-60° right triangle, or 30°-60°-90° triangle **29.** $3\sqrt{3}$
30. $A = 204$ **31.** $A = 756$ **32.** yes

33. no, the cut piece is not a right triangle **34.** no **35.** yes; $\angle M$ **36.** no **37.** yes; $\angle A$ **38.** $d = 20.0$ **39.** $d = 25.1$ **40.** $d = 12.1$

CHAPTER 9

Pages 450–452

1. $P = 24$ **2.** $P = 19$ **3.** $P = 34$ **4.** $P = 144$ **5.** $P = 500$ **6.** $P = 48$ **7.** $P = 24.7$ **8.** $P = 29.3$ **9.** $x = 20, P = 76$ **10.** $x = 13, P = 60$ **11.** $x = 5, P = 28$ **12.** $l = 20, w = 10$ **13.** $b = 12, h = 9$ **14.** $8\sqrt{2}$ **15.** $w = 12, l = 48$ **16.** 24 ft **17.** 10 ft **18.** $x = 8$ ft **19.** $x = 6$ **20.** $x = 7$ **21.** $A = 6.25$ **22.** $A = 85$ **23.** $A = 240$ **24.** $A = 720$ **25.** $A = 8$ **26.** $A = 77$ **27.** $A = 15$ **28.** $A = 44.9$ **29.** $A = 9.8$ **30.** $A = 48.0$ **31.** $A = 62.4$ **32.** $A = 270$ **33.** $A = 50$ **34.** $A = 100$ **35.** $A = 32.7$

CHAPTER 10

Pages 453–455

1. 6.2 in. **2.** 3.1 sq in. **3.** 3.1 cm **4.** 0.78 cm^2 **5.** 124 ft **6.** 1,240 sq ft **7.** 93 m **8.** 697.5 m^2 **9.** 3.1 in. **10.** 0.78 sq in. **11.** $\frac{75}{4}\pi$ **12.** $\frac{200}{3}\pi$ **13.** 90π **14.** 60° **15.** 160° **16.** 50% **17.** 37.5% **18.** 50% **19.** 4π sq mi **20.** $\frac{4}{3}\pi$ cu mi **21.** 16π sq ft **22.** $\frac{32}{3}\pi$ cu ft **23.** $1{,}600\pi$ sq ft **24.** $\frac{32{,}000}{3}\pi$ cu ft **25.** 900π m^2 **26.** $4{,}500\pi$ m^3 **27.** 1π sq in. **28.** $\frac{1}{6}\pi$ cu in. **29.** B **30.** B **31.** $x = 7.5$ **32.** $x = 12.31$ **33.** $x = 3.21$ **34.** $x = 12.12$ **35.** $x = 12.94$ **36.** $z = 20$ **37.** $z = 29.89$ **38.** $z = 20.42$ **39.** $z = 4.24$ **40.** $z = 8.57$ **41.** $y = 25.03$ **42.** $y = 13$ **43.** $y = 42.89$ **44.** $y = 10.39$ **45.** $y = 4.20$

CHAPTER 11

Pages 456–458

1. 125 cu units **2.** 8,000 cu units **3.** 7 m^3 **4.** 432 cm^3 **5.** 6,720 cm^3 **6.** 550 square units **7.** 800 square units **8.** 248 square units **9.** 660 square units **10.** 474 square units **11.** 532 square units **12.** 216 square units **13.** 192 square units **14.** 147π square units **15.** 300π square units **16.** $V = 512$ cm^3, $A = 384$ cm^2 **17.** $V = 1{,}536\pi$ cu ft, $A = 512\pi$ sq ft **18.** $V = 256\pi$ cubic units, $A = 192\pi$ square units **19.** $V = 24\sqrt{3}$ cubic units, $A = 108 + 9\sqrt{3}$ square units **20.** $V = 735\pi$ cm^3, $A = 308\pi$ cm^2 **21.** $V = 64$ cu units, $A = 144$ sq units **22.** 216 **23.** 48 **24.** 24,000 **25.** 21,120 **26.** 128 **27.** 5,000 **28.** 800 **29.** $\frac{1}{2}$ **30.** 6 **31.** 192 **32.** 9 **33.** 2,000 **34.** $216 + 18\sqrt{3}$ sq in. **35.** 672 cm^2 **36.** 642 cm^2 **37.** 1,704 sq in. **38.** $1{,}296\pi$ sq ft **39.** 912 sq in. **40.** 12 in.

CHAPTER 12

Pages 459–461

1.

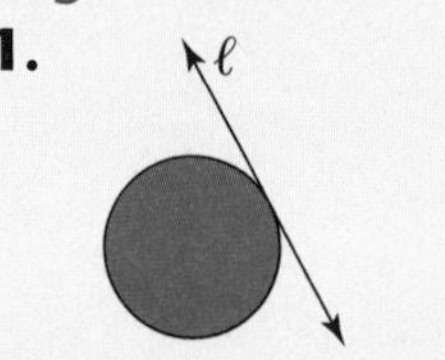

2.

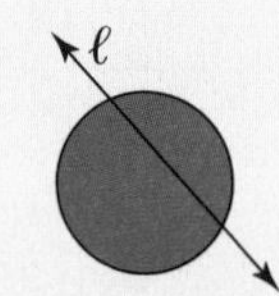

3.

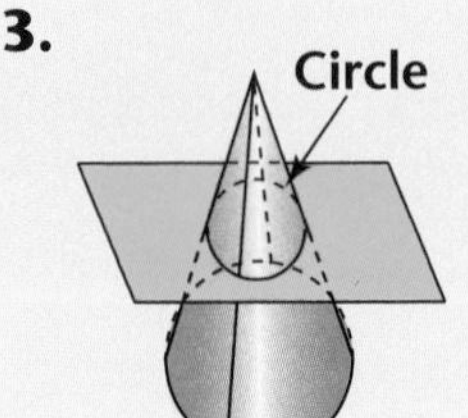

4.

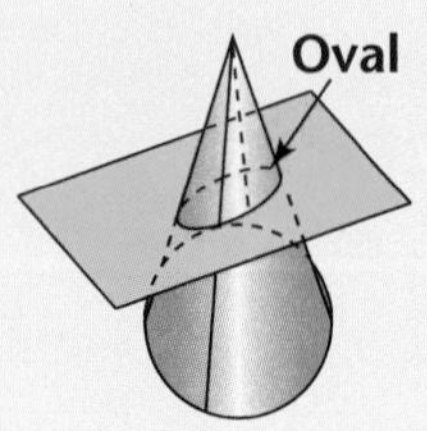

5.

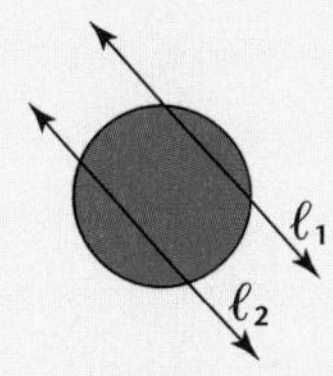

6.

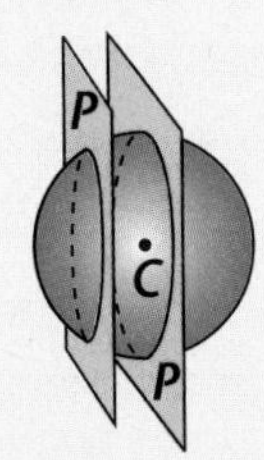

7.

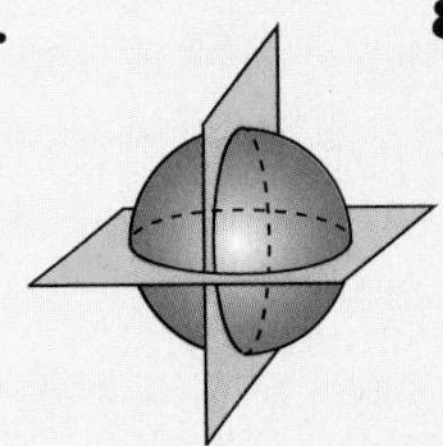

8.

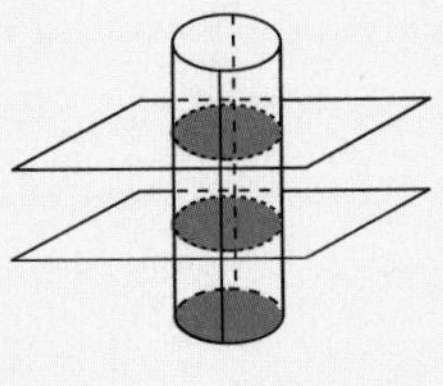

9.

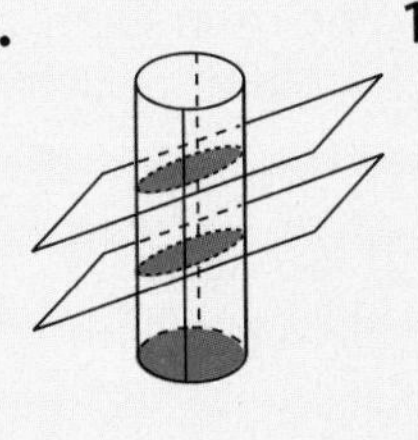

10.

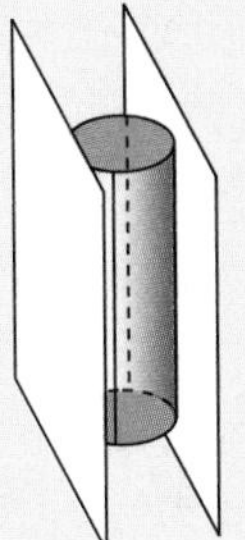

11. $y = 2.5$ and $y = -1.5$

12. $x = -6$ and $x = 2$

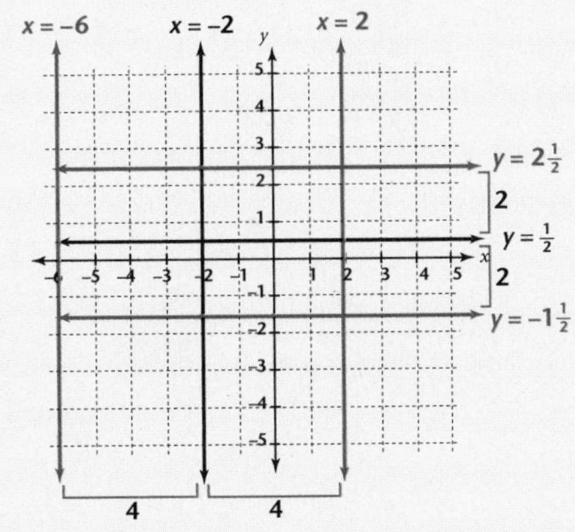

13. $y = 3.5$

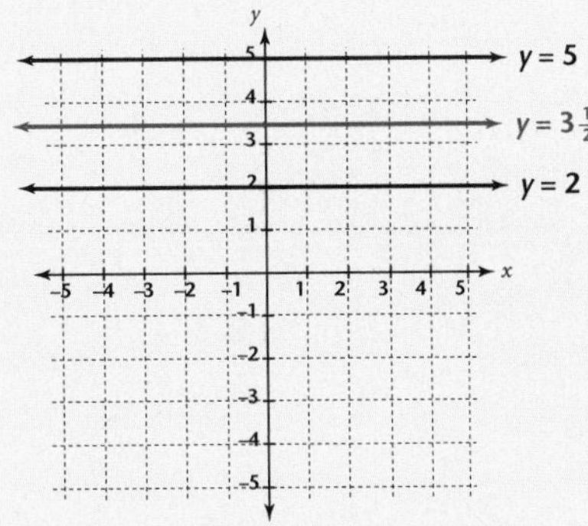

14. $y = -x + 4$ and $y = -x$

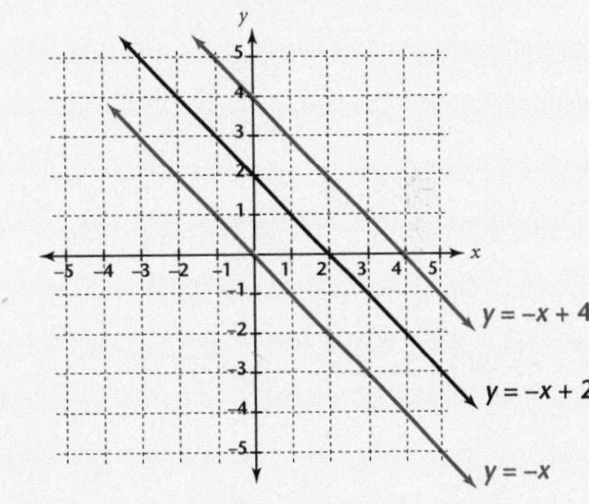

15. $y = -\frac{1}{3}x + 1$ and $y = -\frac{1}{3}x + 5$

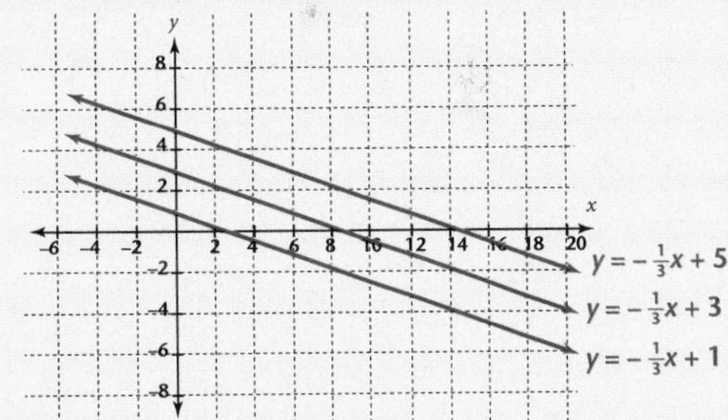

16. $4 = x^2 + y^2$

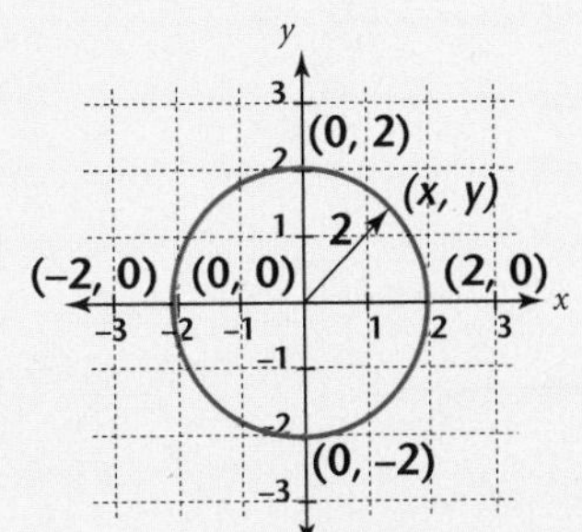

17. $\frac{9}{4} = x^2 + y^2$

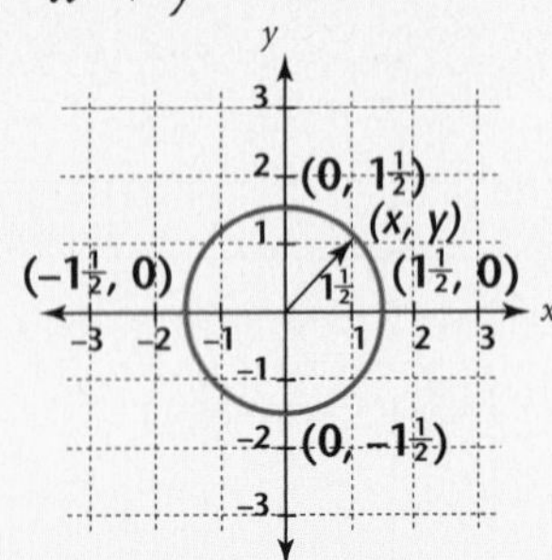

18. $11.56 = x^2 + y^2$

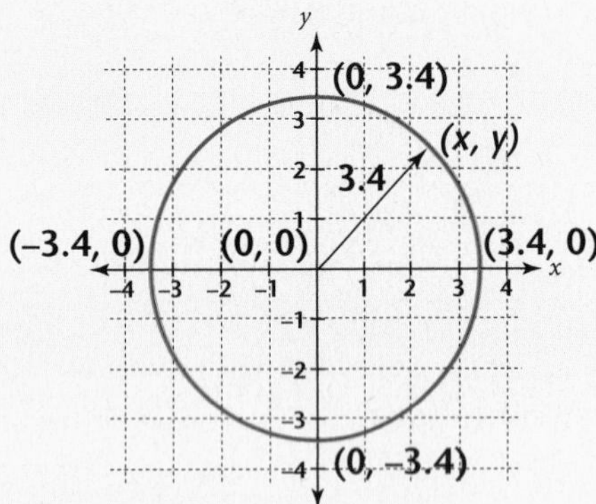

19. $x = 1$

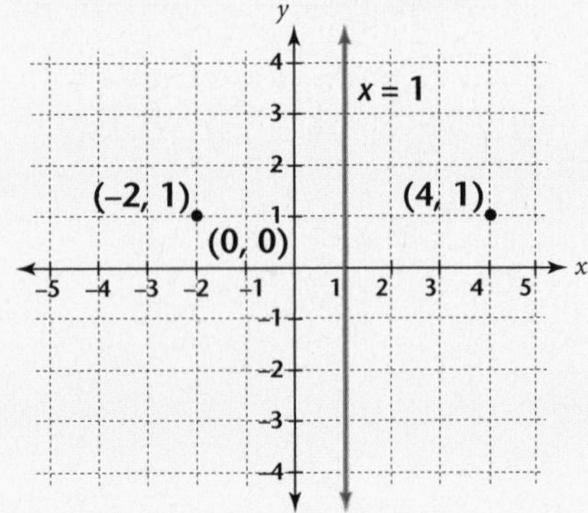

20. $y = 4$

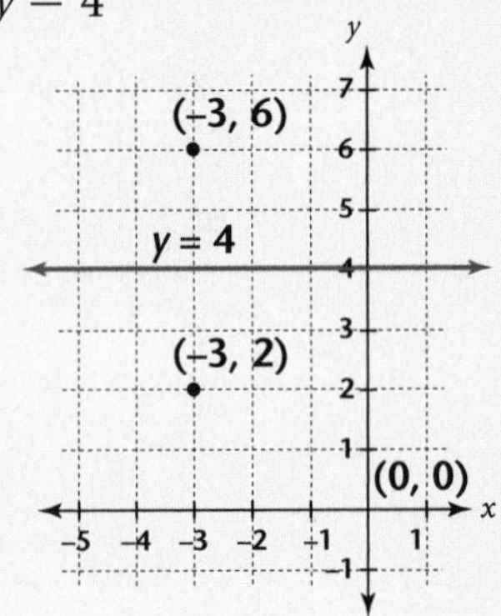

21. one point along the angle bisector and on the circle with radius $\overline{GH}$ **22.** the intersection of the angle bisectors of each angle of the triangle **23.** the intersection of the perpendicular bisectors of each side **24.** the intersection of the perpendicular bisectors of $\overline{AB}$ and $\overline{CD}$ **25.** two points on the circle with radius $\overline{GH}$ and center P and on the perpendicular bisector of a line segment perpendicular to both ℓ and m **26.** A line

27. A point

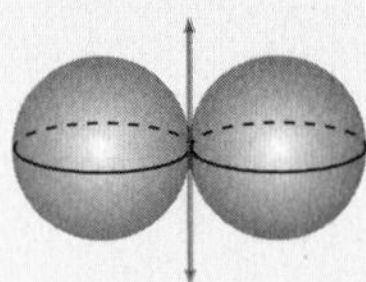

28. An octagon that is smaller than the base

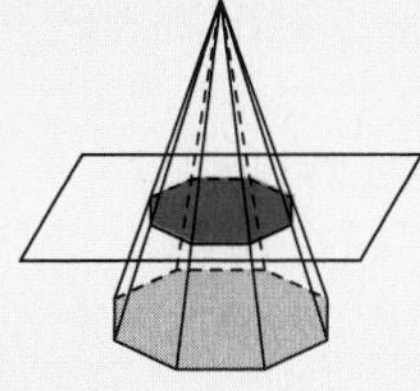

29. 6 points, one in the center of each face of the cube

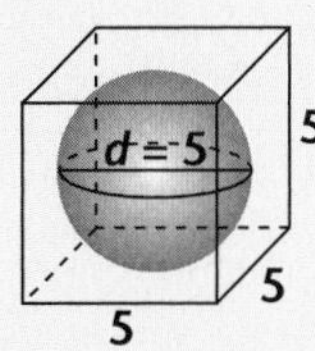

30. 8 points that are the vertices of the cube

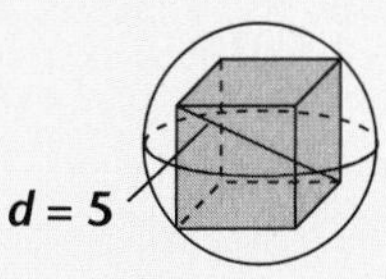

Algebra Review

Page 502

1. 10 **2.** 23 **3.** 20 **4.** 35 **5.** 19 **6.** 4 **7.** 3 **8.** 12 **9.** 5 **10.** 1 **11.** 7 **12.** $1\frac{1}{2}$ **13.** 17 **14.** $6\frac{1}{2}$ **15.** –3 **16.** –4 **17.** $\frac{1}{2}$ **18.** –9 **19.** $3\frac{1}{2}$ **20.** –17

Page 503

1. 2 **2.** 4 **3.** 5 **4.** 15 **5.** 40 **6.** 2 **7.** 4 **8.** 6 **9.** 91 **10.** 20 **11.** –2 **12.** –2 **13.** –6 **14.** –10 **15.** –5 **16.** –4 **17.** –4 **18.** –5 **19.** –20 **20.** –30

Page 505

1. 7 **2.** 3 **3.** 10 **4.** 3 **5.** –2 **6.** $-6\frac{2}{3}$ **7.** $16\frac{1}{2}$ **8.** $1\frac{1}{5}$ **9.** $33\frac{1}{3}$ **10.** $-9\frac{1}{3}$ **11.** 3 **12.** 7 **13.** $6\frac{1}{4}$ **14.** 5 **15.** –16 **16.** 6 **17.** 2 **18.** 7 **19.** 0 **20.** 9 **21.** –7 **22.** 3 **23.** 10 **24.** 6 **25.** 5 **26.** –3 **27.** –8 **28.** 4 **29.** 20 **30.** 8

Page 507

1. 3, 2 **2.** 8, 4 **3.** −5, 1 **4.** −8, 2 **5.** 7, −6 **6.** 7, −4 **7.** −1 **8.** −4, −10 **9.** 8, −1 **10.** −11, 3 **11.** −2, −8 **12.** 3, 9 **13.** −1, −4 **14.** 17, 3 **15.** −9, 8 **16.** 20, −5 **17.** −2, −7 **18.** 9, −3 **19.** 10 **20.** −10, 9 **21.** −1, −3 **22.** 3, 4 **23.** 12, −5 **24.** $-\frac{1}{3}$, 1 **25.** $-\frac{5}{2}$, $-\frac{3}{2}$ **26.** −2, 1 **27.** 7, −5 **28.** $\frac{4}{3}$, 2 **29.** −2, $\frac{3}{2}$ **30.** $-\frac{6}{5}$, 2

Algebra Review 1

Solution of Equations Using Addition/Subtraction

EXAMPLE 1 Solve for x when $x - 5 = 7$

$x - 5 = 7$	given
$+ 5 = + 5$	add 5 to both sides
$x = 12$	answer

Check: Substitute 12 for x in $x - 5 = 7$

$12 - 5 = 7$ is True, $x = 12$ is correct

EXAMPLE 2 Solve for x when $x + 5 = 7$

$x + 5 = 7$	given
$- 5 = - 5$	subtract 5 from both sides (or add -5)
$x = 2$	answer

Check: Substitute 2 for x in $x + 5 = 7$

$2 + 5 = 7$ is True, $x = 2$ is correct

Exercise Solve for x and check.

1. $x - 3 = 7$

2. $x - 10 = 13$

3. $x - 4 = 16$

4. $x - 15 = 20$

5. $x - 9 = 10$

6. $x + 3 = 7$

7. $x + 10 = 13$

8. $x + 4 = 16$

9. $x + 15 = 20$

10. $x + 9 = 10$

11. $x - 2 = 5$

12. $x - \frac{1}{2} = 1$

13. $x - 13 = 4$

14. $x - 1\frac{1}{2} = 5$

15. $x - 7 = -10$

16. $x + 7 = 3$

17. $x + \frac{1}{2} = 1$

18. $x + 13 = 4$

19. $x + 1\frac{1}{2} = 5$

20. $x + 7 = -10$

Algebra Review 2

Solution of Equations Using Multiplication/Division

Example 1 Solve for x when $3x = 12$

$3x = 12$ given

$3x \div 3 = 12 \div 3$ divide both sides by 3 (or multiply by $\frac{1}{3}$)

$x = 4$ answer

Check: Substitute 4 for x in $3x = 12$

$3 \bullet 4 = 12$ is True, $x = 4$ is correct

Example 2 Solve for x when $5x = -30$

$5x = -30$ given

$\frac{1}{5}(5x) = \frac{1}{5}(-30)$ multiply both sides by $\frac{1}{5}$ (or divide by 5)

$x = -\frac{30}{5} = -6$ answer

Check: Substitute -6 for x in $5x = -30$

$5(-6) = -30$ is True, $x = -6$ is correct

Exercise Solve for x and check.

1. $3x = 6$
2. $4x = 16$
3. $7x = 35$
4. $10x = 150$
5. $15x = 600$
6. $5x = 10$
7. $15x = 60$
8. $8x = 48$
9. $10x = 910$
10. $40x = 800$
11. $3x = -6$
12. $5x = -10$
13. $6x = -36$
14. $10x = -100$
15. $15x = -75$
16. $7x = -28$
17. $6x = -24$
18. $9x = -45$
19. $16x = -320$
20. $40x = -1,200$

Algebra Review 3

Solving Equations

EXAMPLE 1 Solve for x when $3x + 5 = 17$

Remember, the strategy is to get x = some number.

$3x + 5 = 17$	given
$3x = 12$	subtract 5 from both sides
$x = 4$	divide both sides by 3
$x = 4$	answer

Check: Substitute 4 for x in $3x + 5 = 17$

$(3 \bullet 4) + 5 = 17$ is True, $x = 4$ is correct

EXAMPLE 2 Solve for x when $\frac{3}{2}x + 2 = -9$

$\frac{3}{2}x + 2 = -9$	given
$\frac{3}{2}x = -11$	subtract 2 from both sides
$\frac{2}{3}(\frac{3}{2}x) = \frac{2}{3}(-11)$	multiply both sides by $\frac{2}{3}$ to make $1x$
$x = -\frac{22}{3}$	answer

Check: Substitute $-\frac{22}{3}$ for x in $\frac{3}{2}x + 2 = -9$

$\frac{3}{2}(-\frac{22}{3}) + 2 = -9$

$-11 + 2 = -9$ is True, $x = -\frac{22}{3}$ is correct

Algebra Review 3

Solving Equations *(continued)*

Exercise Solve for x and check.

1. $2x + 5 = 19$

2. $6x + 3 = 21$

3. $4x + 9 = 49$

4. $3x - 2 = 7$

5. $7x + 2 = -12$

6. $\frac{3}{2}x + 1 = -9$

7. $\frac{2}{3}x - 1 = 10$

8. $\frac{5}{6}x + 1 = 2$

9. $\frac{3}{10}x - 7 = 3$

10. $\frac{3}{4}x - 3 = -10$

11. $3x + 4 = 13$

12. $5x + 6 = 41$

13. $\frac{4}{5}x + (-5) = 0$

14. $2x - 3 = 7$

15. $\frac{3}{4}x + 12 = 0$

16. $2x - 6 = 6$

17. $4x - 1 = 7$

18. $2x + 3 = 17$

19. $-9x - 4 = -4$

20. $3x - 4 = 23$

21. $-\frac{2}{7}x - 6 = -4$

22. $9x - 25 = 2$

23. $3x - 25 = 5$

24. $-6x + 20 = -16$

25. $4x + 5 = 25$

26. $-4x + 2 = 14$

27. $-\frac{1}{2}x + 2 = 6$

28. $2x - (-10) = 18$

29. $3x + 40 = 100$

30. $2x - 8 = 8$

Algebra Review 4

Solving Quadratic Equations

Some quadratic equations can be solved by factoring. Others are difficult or impossible to solve by factoring. For these, you can use the quadratic formula.

EXAMPLE 1 Solve $x^2 - 6x + 8 = 0$ for x by factoring. Then check.

Step 1 Factor

$x^2 - 6x + 8 = 0$

$(x - \quad)(x - \quad) = 0$ Look at the equation. Ask yourself: What two numbers multiply to 8 and add to 6?

$(x - 4)(x - 2) = 0$

Step 2 Set each factor equal to 0.

$x - 4 = 0$

$x - 4 + 4 = 0 + 4$ Add 4 to both sides to solve.

$x = 4$

$x - 2 = 0$

$x - 2 + 2 = 0 + 2$ Add 2 to both sides to solve.

$x = 2$

Check: When $x = 4$, $x^2 - 6x + 8 = 4^2 - 6(4) + 8 = 16 - 24 + 8 = 0$.
When $x = 2$, $x^2 - 6x + 8 = 2^2 - 6(2) + 8 = 4 - 12 + 8 = 0$.

EXAMPLE 2 Use the quadratic formula to solve $3x^2 - x - 10 = 0$ for x. Then check.

$x = \frac{-b \pm \sqrt{b^2 - 4ac}}{2a}$ Write the quadratic formula.

$a = 3, b = -1, c = -10$ Identify a, b and c from the equation ($ax^2 + bx + c = 0$).

$x = \frac{-(-1) \pm \sqrt{(-1)^2 - 4(3)(-10)}}{2(3)}$ Substitute for a, b and c in the quadratic formula.

$x = \frac{1 \pm \sqrt{1^2 - (-120)}}{6}$ Solve for x.

$= \frac{1 \pm \sqrt{121}}{6}$

$= \frac{1 \pm 11}{6}$

$= \frac{12}{6}$ or $\frac{-10}{6}$

$= 2$ or $-\frac{5}{3}$

Check: When $x = 2$, $3x^2 - x - 10 = 3(2)^2 - 2 - 10 = 12 - 2 - 10 = 0$.
When $x = -\frac{5}{3}$, $3x^2 - x - 10 = 3\left(-\frac{5}{3}\right)^2 - \left(-\frac{5}{3}\right) - 10 = \frac{25}{3} + \frac{5}{3} - \frac{30}{3} = 0$.

Algebra Review 4

Solving Quadratic Equations *(continued)*

Exercise A Solve for x by factoring.

1. $x^2 - 5x + 6 = 0$
2. $x^2 - 12x + 32 = 0$
3. $x^2 + 4x - 5 = 0$
4. $x^2 + 6x - 16 = 0$
5. $x^2 - x - 42 = 0$
6. $x^2 - 3x - 28 = 0$
7. $x^2 + 2x + 1 = 0$
8. $x^2 + 14x + 40 = 0$
9. $x^2 - 7x - 8 = 0$
10. $x^2 + 8x - 33 = 0$
11. $x^2 + 10x + 16 = 0$
12. $x^2 - 12x + 27 = 0$
13. $x^2 + 5x + 4 = 0$
14. $x^2 - 20x + 51 = 0$
15. $x^2 + x - 72 = 0$
16. $x^2 - 15x - 100 = 0$

Exercise B Use the quadratic formula to solve for x.

17. $x^2 + 9x + 14 = 0$
18. $x^2 - 6x - 27 = 0$
19. $x^2 - 20x + 100 = 0$
20. $x^2 + x - 90 = 0$
21. $x^2 + 4x + 3 = 0$
22. $x^2 - 7x + 12 = 0$
23. $x^2 - 7x - 60 = 0$
24. $3x^2 - 2x - 1 = 0$
25. $4x^2 + 16x + 15 = 0$
26. $x^2 + x = 2$
27. $x^2 = 2x + 35$
28. $3x^2 - 10x + 8 = 0$
29. $2x^2 + x - 6 = 0$
30. $5x^2 - 4x - 12 = 0$

Axioms, Postulates, and Theorems

Axioms

Axiom 1 Things that are equal to the same thing are equal to each other. (p. 51)

Axiom 2 If equals are added to equals, the sums are equal. (p. 51)

Axiom 3 If equals are subtracted from equals, the differences are equal. (p. 51)

Axiom 4 Things that are alike or coincide with one another are equal to one another. (p. 51)

Axiom 5 The whole, or sum, is greater than the parts. (p. 51)

Postulates

Ruler Postulate The points on a line can be placed in a one-to-one correspondence with the real numbers so that

1. for every point on the line, there is exactly one real number.
2. for every real number, there is exactly one point on the line.
3. the distance between any two points is the absolute value of the difference of the corresponding real numbers. (p. 7)

Ruler Placement Postulate Given two points, A and B on a line, the number line can be chosen so that A is at zero and B is at a positive number. (p. 8)

Segment Addition Postulate If B is between A and C, then $AB + BC = AC$. (p. 8)

Euclid's Postulate 1 A straight line can be drawn from any point to any point. (p. 41)

Euclid's Postulate 2 A finite straight line can be extended continuously in a straight line. (p. 42)

Euclid's Postulate 3 A circle may be described with any center and distance. (p. 42)

Axioms, Postulates, and Theorems

Euclid's Postulate 4 All right angles are equal to one another. (p. 42)

Euclid's Postulate 5 If two lines ℓ and m are cut by a third line t, and the two inside angles, a and b, together measure less than two right angles, then the two lines ℓ and m, if extended, will meet on the same side of t as the two angles a and b. (p. 43)

Parallel Postulate 5 If there is a line ℓ and a point P not on ℓ, then there is only one line that passes through P and is parallel to ℓ. (p. 43)

Alternate Interior Angles Postulate If a transversal intersects two lines so that the alternate interior angles are equal, then the lines are parallel. (pp. 77, 90)

SAS (Side-Angle-Side) Postulate If two sides and the included angle of one triangle are congruent to the corresponding two sides and included angle of a second triangle, the triangles are congruent. (p. 193)

SSS (Side-Side-Side) Postulate If three sides of a triangle are congruent to three sides of a second triangle, then the triangles are congruent. (p. 203)

ASA (Angle-Side-Angle) Postulate If two angles and the included side of a triangle are congruent to the corresponding angles and included side of a second triangle, then the triangles are congruent. (p. 204)

AA Similarity Postulate If two angles of a triangle have the same measures as two angles of a second triangle, then the two triangles are similar. (p. 244)

Theorems

Vertical Angle Theorem (2.5.1) If angles are vertical angles, then their measures are equal.
(p. 55)

Theorem 3.3.1 If two lines are parallel, then the interior angles on the same side of the transversal are supplementary. (p. 72)

Axioms, Postulates, and Theorems

Theorem 3.3.2 If two lines cut by a transversal are parallel, then the corresponding angles are equal. (p. 73)

Theorem 3.3.3 If two lines cut by a transversal are parallel, then the alternate interior angles are equal. (p. 74)

Theorem 3.5.1 If a figure is a parallelogram, then its angle sum is 360°. (p. 84)

Theorem 3.6.1 If a figure is a trapezoid, then its angle sum is 360°. (p. 88)

Theorem 3.7.1 If corresponding angles are equal, then the lines are parallel. (p. 90)

Theorem 3.8.1 If two lines are cut by a transversal so that the angles on the same side of the transversal are supplementary, then the lines are parallel. (p. 92)

Theorem 5.4.1 In rectangle *ABCD* with diagonal $\overline{AC}$, $m\angle 1 = m\angle 4$ and $m\angle 2 = m\angle 3$. (p. 158)

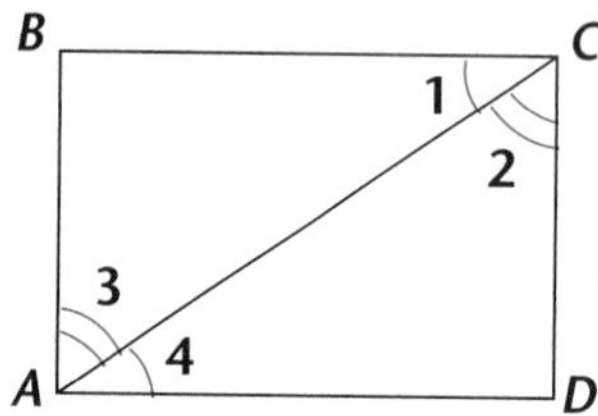

Angle Sum Theorem (5.9.1) The sum of the angle measures in any triangle is 180°. (p. 180)

Corollary to the Angle Sum Theorem (5.9.2) If ΔABC is any triangle, then an exterior angle of *ABC* has the same measure as the sum of the measures of the two nonadjacent interior angles. (p. 180)

Shortest Distance Theorem (6.2.1) The perpendicular segment from a point to a line is the shortest segment from that point to the line. The length of the perpendicular segment is called the *distance* from the point to the line. (p. 200)

Triangle Inequality Theorem (6.2.2) The sum of the lengths of any two sides of a triangle must be greater than the length of the third side. (p. 200)

Axioms, Postulates, and Theorems

AAS (Angle-Angle-Side) Theorem (6.4.1) If two angles and one side not included between those angles are congruent to two angles and the corresponding side of a second triangle, then the two triangles are congruent. (p. 208)

Theorem 6.4.2 The acute angles in any right triangle are complementary. (p. 209)

Hypotenuse-Leg (H-L) Theorem (6.4.3) Two right triangles are congruent if the hypotenuse and leg of one triangle are congruent to the hypotenuse and corresponding leg of the second triangle. (p. 210)

Theorem 7.1.1 In any proportion, the product of the extremes equals the product of the means. (p. 238)

Theorem 7.2.1 If one acute angle of a right triangle has the same measure as one acute angle of a second right triangle, then the two right triangles are similar. (p. 244)

Pythagorean Theorem (8.2.1) If a triangle is a right triangle with legs a and b and hypotenuse c, then $a^2 + b^2 = c^2$. (p. 275)

(8.4.1) In any right triangle ABC, with hypotenuse $\overline{AC}$, $(AC)^2 = (AB)^2 + (BC)^2$. (p. 282)

Theorem 8.5.1 The angles opposite equal sides in a triangle are equal. (p. 286)

Theorem 8.5.2 In a 30°-60° right triangle, the side opposite the 30° angle is one-half the length of the hypotenuse. (p. 288)

Converse of the Pythagorean Theorem (8.8.1) If for ΔABC, $(AC)^2 = (AB)^2 + (BC)^2$, then ΔABC is a right triangle. (p. 299)

Theorem 10.6.1 The measure of an inscribed angle is half the measure of its intercepted arc. (p. 362)

Geometric Symbols and Formulas

Symbols

$\angle A$	angle A	$\perp$	is perpendicular to
$m\angle A$	measure of angle A in degrees	$\not\perp$	is not perpendicular to
$\overleftrightarrow{AB}$	line through points A and B	$\parallel$	is parallel to
$\overline{AB}$	segment AB with endpoints A and B	$\nparallel$	is not parallel to
ΔABC	triangle ABC	$n°$	n degrees
$\overrightarrow{AB}$	ray AB, with endpoint A and passing through B	$\therefore$	therefore
$\cong$	is congruent to	$a \Rightarrow b$	If a then b
$\not\cong$	is not congruent to	π	$\frac{\text{circumference}}{\text{diameter of a circle}}$
		$\odot$	circle

Formulas

$C = \pi d$ $C =$ circumference
$d =$ diameter

$d = 2r$ $r =$ radius

$\pi = \frac{c}{d}$ π as a ratio

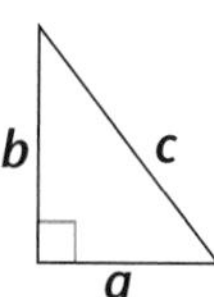

$a^2 + b^2 = c^2$ Pythagorean Formula

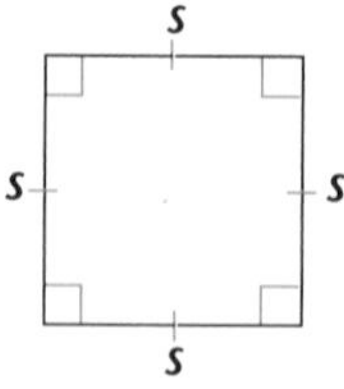

Perimeter of a square $= 4s$

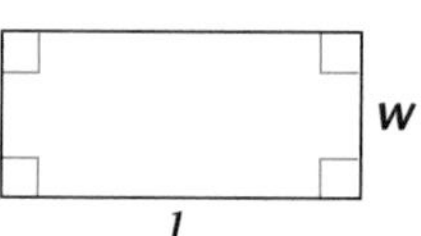

Perimeter of a rectangle $= 2l + 2w$

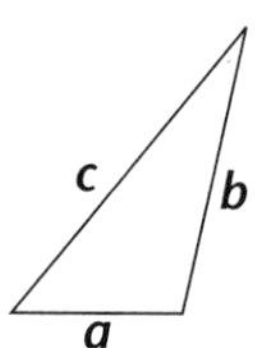

Perimeter of a scalene $\Delta = a + b + c$

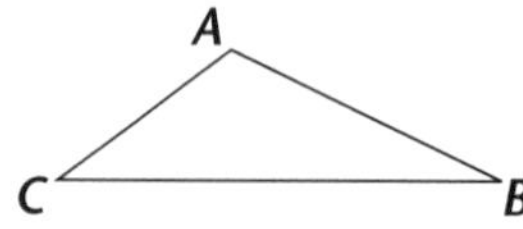

$m\angle A + m\angle B + m\angle C = 180°$

Geometric Symbols and Formulas

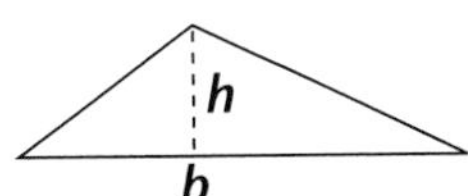

Area of a $\Delta = \frac{1}{2}bh$

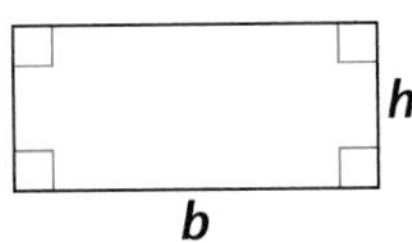

Area of a rectangle $= bh$

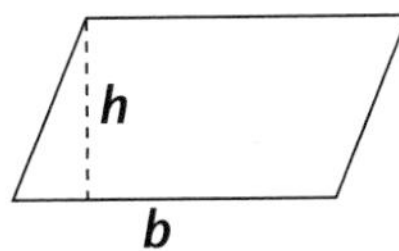

Area of a parallelogram $= bh$

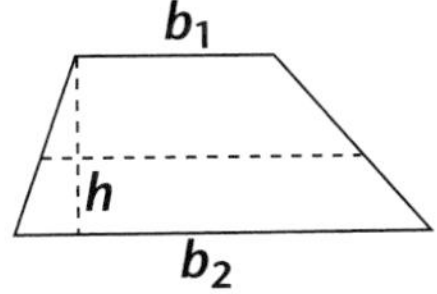

Area of a trapezoid $= h\left(\frac{b_1 + b_2}{2}\right)$

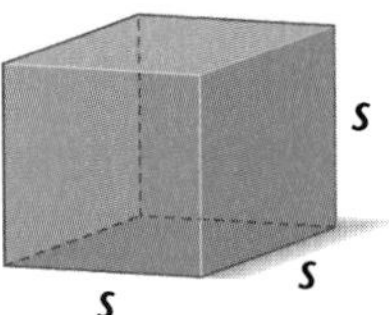

Volume of a cube $= s^3$

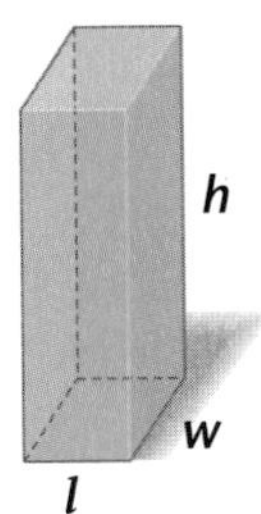

Volume of a rectangular box $= lwh$

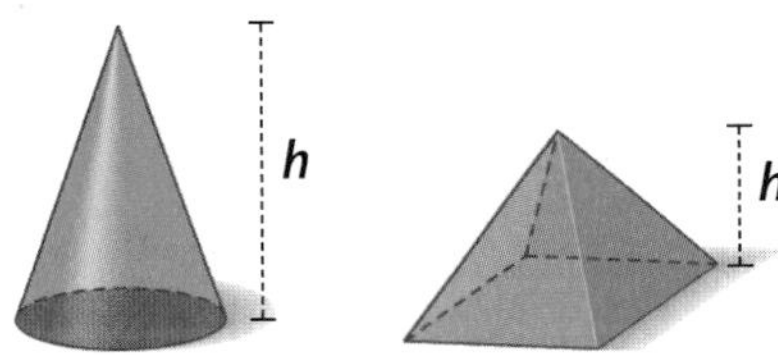

Volume of a cone or a pyramid
$= \frac{1}{3}h$(area of base)

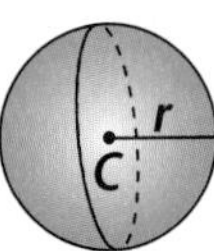

Volume of a sphere $= \frac{4}{3}\pi r^3$

Measurement Conversion Factors

Metric Measures

Length

1,000 meters (m) = 1 kilometer (km)
100 centimeters (cm) = 1 m
10 decimeters (dm) = 1 m
1,000 millimeters (mm) = 1 m
10 cm = 1 decimeter (dm)
10 mm = 1 cm

Area

100 square millimeters (mm^2) = 1 square centimeter (cm^2)
10,000 cm^2 = 1 square meter (m^2)
10,000 m^2 = 1 hectare (ha)

Volume

1,000 cubic meters (m^3) = 1 cubic centimeter (cm^3)
100 cm^3 = 1 cubic decimeter (dm^3)
1,000,000 cm^3 = 1 cubic meter (m^3)

Capacity

1,000 milliliters (mL) = 1 liter (L)
1,000 L = 1 kiloliter (kL)

Mass

1,000 kilograms (kg) = 1 metric ton (t)
1,000 grams (g) = 1 kg
1,000 milligrams (mg) = 1 g

Temperature Degrees Celsius (°C)

0°C = freezing point of water
37°C = normal body temperature
100°C = boiling point of water

Time

60 seconds (sec) = 1 minute (min)
60 min = 1 hour (hr)
24 hr = 1 day

Customary Measures

Length

12 inches (in.) = 1 foot (ft)
3 ft = 1 yard (yd)
36 in. = 1 yd
5,280 ft = 1 mile (mi)
1,760 yd = 1 mi
6,076 feet = 1 nautical mile

Area

144 square inches (sq in.) = 1 square foot (sq ft)
9 sq ft = 1 square yard (sq yd)
43,560 sq ft = 1 acre (A)

Volume

1,728 cubic inches (cu in.) = 1 cubic foot (cu ft)
27 cu ft = 1 cubic yard (cu yard)

Capacity

8 fluid ounces (fl oz) = 1 cup (c)
2 c = 1 pint (pt)
2 pt = 1 quart (qt)
4 qt = 1 gallon (gal)

Weight

16 ounces (oz) = 1 pound (lb)
2,000 lb = 1 ton (T)

Temperature Degrees Fahrenheit (°F)

32°F = freezing point of water
98.6°F = normal body temperature
212°F = boiling point of water

Measurement Conversion Factors

To change	To	Multiply by
centimeters	inches	0.3937
centimeters	feet	0.03281
cubic feet	cubic meters	0.0283
cubic meters	cubic feet	35.3145
cubic meters	cubic yards	1.3079
cubic yards	cubic meters	0.7646
feet	meters	0.3048
feet	miles (nautical)	0.0001645
feet	miles (statute)	0.0001894
feet/second	miles/hour	0.6818
gallons (U.S.)	liters	3.7853
grams	ounces avdp	0.0353
grams	pounds	0.002205
hours	days	0.04167
inches	millimeters	25.4000
inches	centimeters	2.5400
kilograms	pounds avdp	2.2046
kilometers	miles	0.6214
liters	gallons (U.S.)	0.2642
liters	pecks	0.1135
liters	pints (dry)	1.8162
liters	pints (liquid)	2.1134
liters	quarts (dry)	0.9081
liters	quarts (liquid)	1.0567

To change	To	Multiply by
meters	feet	3.2808
meters	miles	0.0006214
meters	yards	1.0936
metric tons	tons (long)	0.9842
metric tons	tons (short)	1.1023
miles	kilometers	1.6093
miles	feet	5,280
miles (statute)	miles (nautical)	0.8684
miles/hour	feet/minute	88
millimeters	inches	0.0394
ounces avdp	grams	28.3495
ounces	pounds	0.0625
pecks	liters	8.8096
pints (dry)	liters	0.5506
pints (liquid)	liters	0.4732
pounds avdp	kilograms	0.4536
pounds	ounces	16
quarts (dry)	liters	1.1012
quarts (liquid)	liters	0.9463
square feet	square meters	0.0929
square meters	square feet	10.7639
square meters	square yards	1.1960
square yards	square meters	0.8361
yards	meters	0.9144

Glossary

A

Acute angle (ə kyüt´ ang´gəl) an angle whose measure is greater than 0° and less than 90° (p. 16)

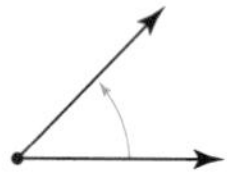

Acute triangle (ə kyüt´ trī´ ang gəl) a triangle whose angles are all less than 90° (p. 149)

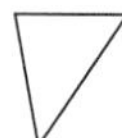  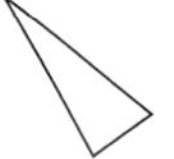 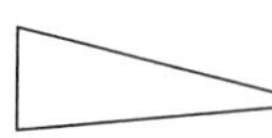

Adjacent (ə jā´ snt) sharing a common side (p. 158)

Adjacent angles (ə jā´ snt ang´ gəlz) angles with a common vertex and one common side (p. 20)

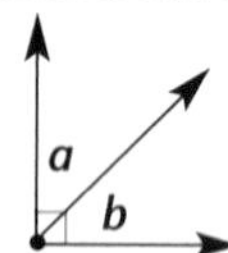

Adjacent vertices (ə jā´ snt vėr´ tə sēz) vertices that share a common side (p. 158)

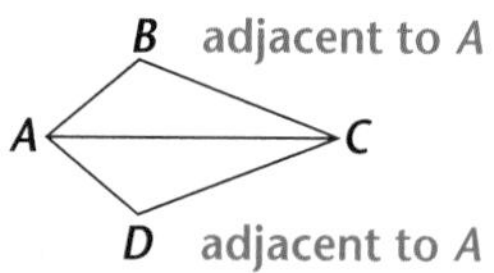

Alternate exterior angles (ȯl´ tər nit ek stir´ ē ər ang´ gəlz) pairs of exterior angles on opposite sides of the transversal (p. 70)

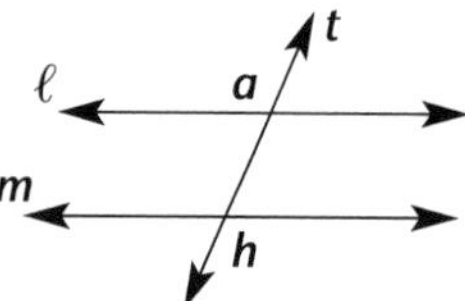

Alternate interior angles (ȯl´ tər nit in tir´ ē ər ang´ gəlz) pairs of interior angles on opposite sides of the transversal (p. 70)

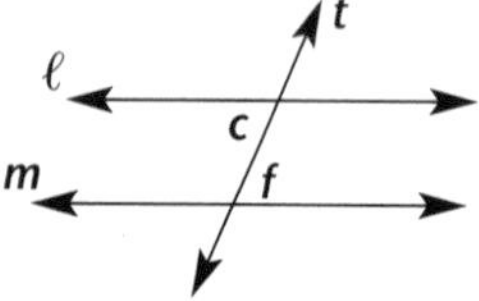

Altitude (al´ tə tüd) line segment from the vertex of a triangle that is perpendicular to the opposite side (p. 175)

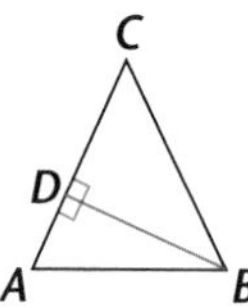

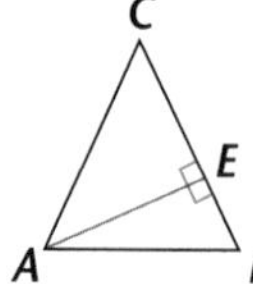

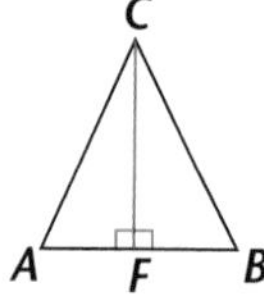

Angle (ang´ gəl) a figure made up of two sides, or rays, with a common endpoint (p. 11)

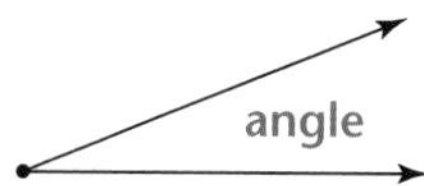

Angle bisector (ang´ gəl bī sek´ tər) ray that divides an angle into two equal parts (p. 13); locus of points equidistant from the sides of the angle (p. 366)

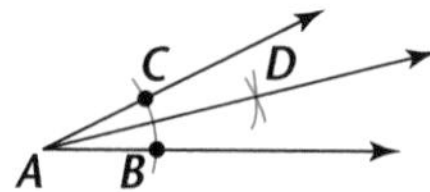

Angle sum (ang´ gəl sum) the sum of the measures of all the interior angles in an enclosed figure (p. 85)

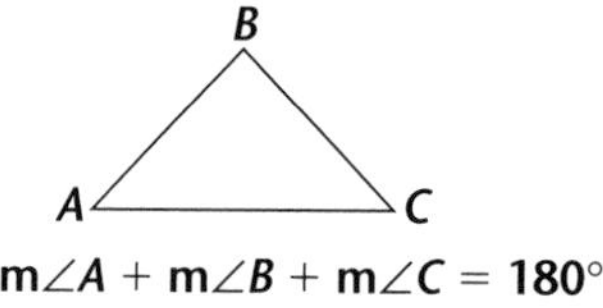

Arc (ärk) part of a circle (p. 12); a portion of a circle bounded by two distinct points on the circle (p. 360)

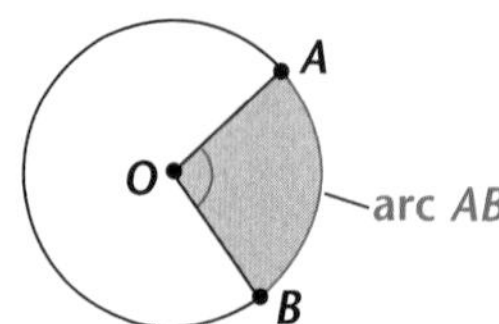

Area (âr´ ē ə) the number of square units inside a closed region (p. 274)

5 • 5 = 25 sq units

5

5

Argument (är´ gyə mənt) course of reasoning (p. 72)

Assumption (ə sump´ shən) something taken to be true without proof (p. 72)

Average (av´ ər ij) a number found by dividing the sum of all the quantities by the number of quantities (p. 290)

$$\frac{(a+b)}{2} = \text{average of } a \text{ and } b$$

Average base (av´ ər ij bās) the line that connects the midpoints of the nonparallel sides of a trapezoid (p. 326)

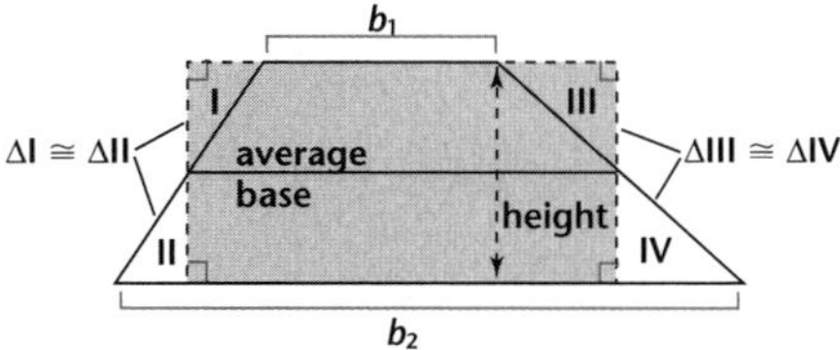

Axiom (ak´ sē əm) a statement assumed to be true without proof (p. 51)

B

Base (bās) the number being multiplied by itself (p. 28)

Binomial (bī nō´ mē əl) the sum or difference of two numbers or variables (p. 184)

Bisect (bī´ sekt) to divide into two equal parts (pp. 13, 132)

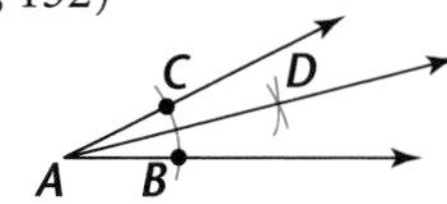

C

Capacity (kə pas´ ə tē) the amount a container will hold when full (p. 400)

Center of the dilation (sen´ tər uv ꟸHə dī lā´ shen) the origin of the rays passing through the vertices of the dilated images (p. 254)

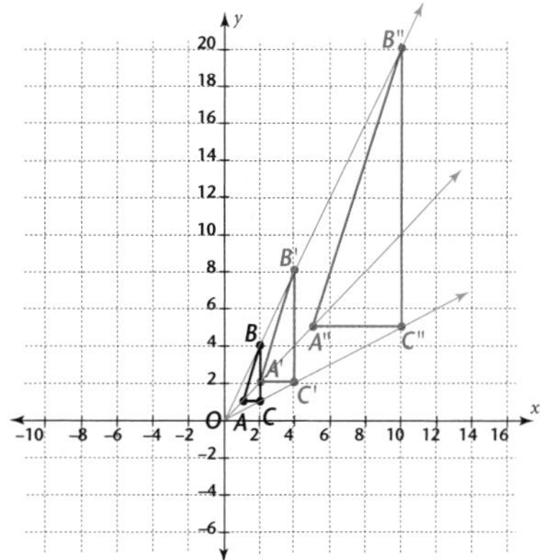

O (0,0) is the center of the dilation

Central angle (sen´ trəl ang´ gəl) an angle with its vertex at the center of a circle and the circle's radii as its sides (p. 360)

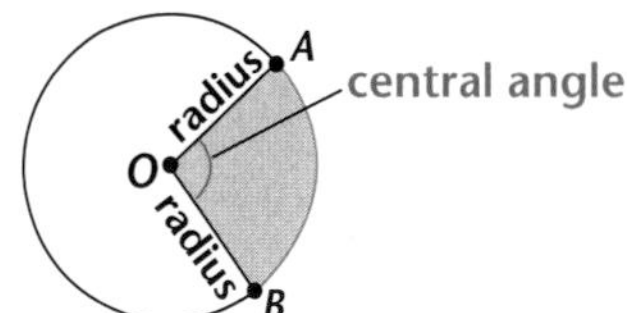

Centroid (sen´ troid) point where the three medians of a triangle intersect (p. 176)

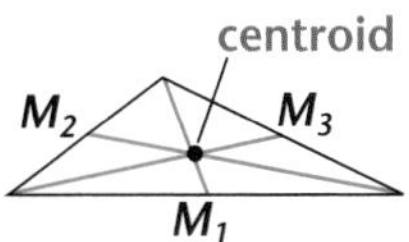

Characteristics (kâr ik tə ris´ tik) special features or qualities (p. 290)

Chord (kôrd) line segment joining two points on a circle (p. 344)

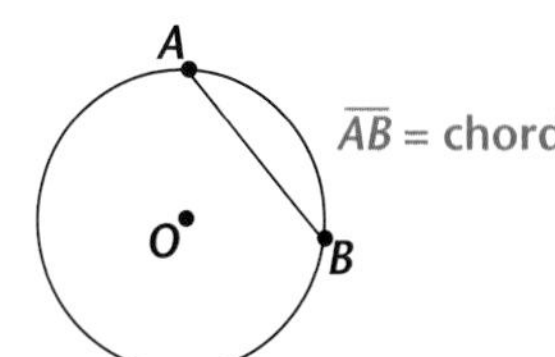

a	hat	e	let	ī	ice	ô	order	u̇	put	sh	she	ə { a	in about
ā	age	ē	equal	o	hot	oi	oil	ü	rule	th	thin	e	in taken
ä	far	ėr	term	ō	open	ou	out	ch	child	ꟸH	then	i	in pencil
â	care	i	it	ȯ	saw	u	cup	ng	long	zh	measure	o	in lemon
												u	in circus

Circle (sėr´ kəl) set of points at the same distance from a given point (p. 344)

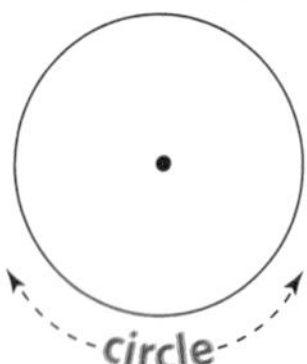

Circumcenter (sėr kəm sen´ tər) center of a circumcircle and located at the intersection of the perpendicular bisectors of any two sides of a triangle (p. 366)

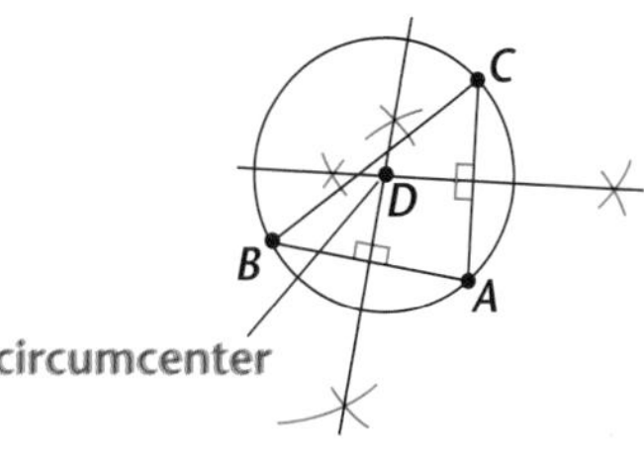

Circumcircle (sėr kəm sėr´ kəl) circle that passes through the three vertices of a triangle (p. 366)

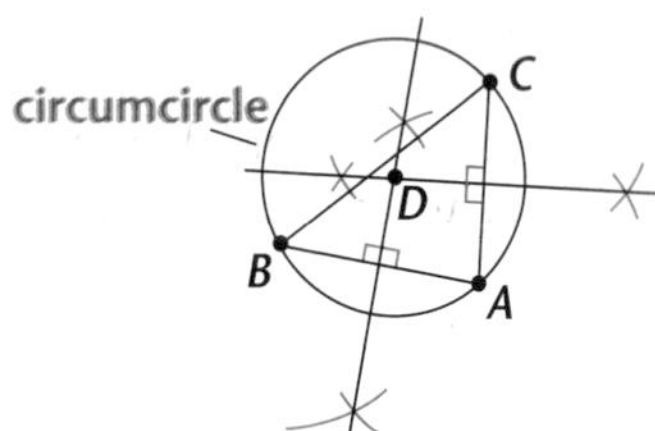

Circumference (sər kum´ fər əns) the complete length of a circle (p. 344)

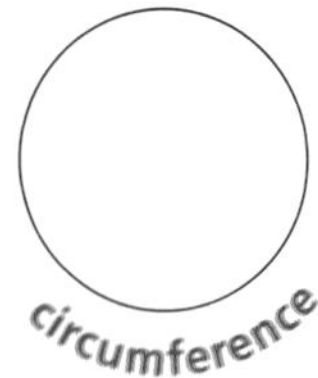

Coincide (kō in sīd´) to be alike or occupy the same position at the same time (pp. 51, 161)

Collinear (kō lin´ ē ər) points on the same line (p. 3)

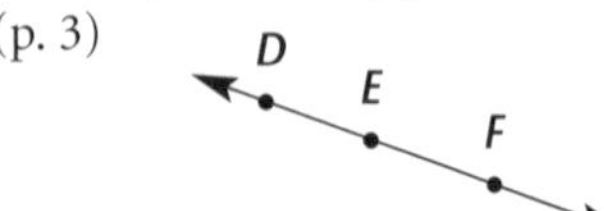

Common factor (kom´ ən fak´ tər) a multiplier shared by the terms in an expression (p. 58)

Compass (kum´ pəs) a tool used to draw circles and parts of circles called arcs (p. 12)

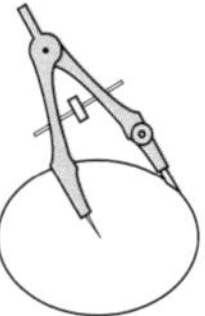

Complementary angles (kom plə men´ tər ē ang´ gəlz) two angles whose measures add up to 90° (p. 20)

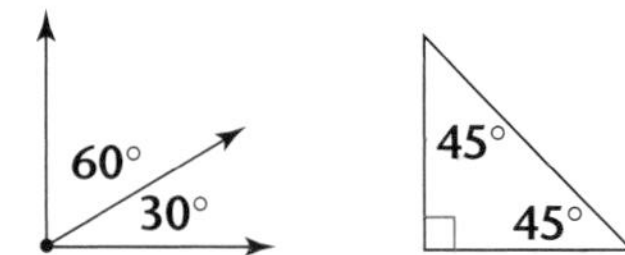

Compound locus (kom´ pound lō´ kəs) a set of points satisfying more than one condition at a time (p. 417)

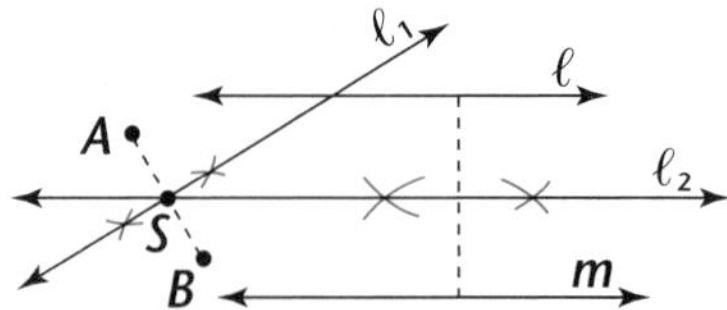

S is the compound locus of points equidistant from ℓ and m, and points A and B.

Concave polygon (kon kāv´ pol´ e gon) a polygon for which a segment joining any two points in the interior does not lie entirely within the figure (p. 166)

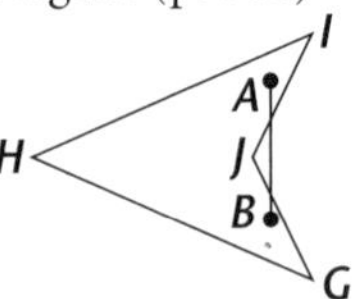

Conclusion (kən klü´ zhən) the "*then*..." part of a conditional (p. 36)

Condition (kən dish´ ən) something on which something else depends; a requirement (p. 36)

Conditional (kən dish´ ə nəl) a statement in the form "*If*...*then*..." (p. 36)

Cone (kōn) a three-dimensional figure whose base is a circle and all segments that join the circle to a vertex, *V*, not in the plane of the circle (p. 388)

Congruent (kən grü′ ənt) having the exact same size and shape (p. 192)

Congruent angles (kən grü′ ənt ang′ gəlz) angles that have equal measures (p. 192)

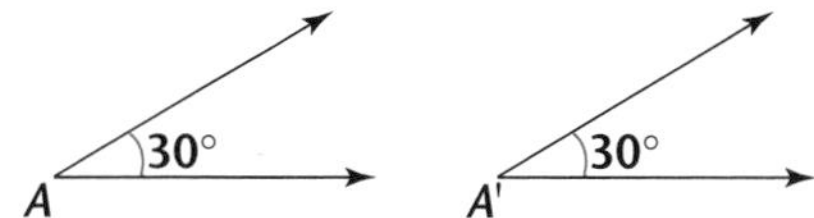

Congruent segments (kən grü′ ənt seg′ mənt) segments that have the same length (p. 192)

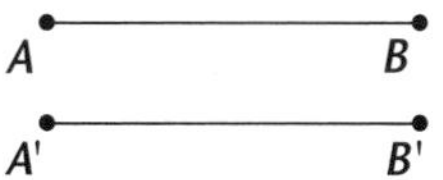

Congruent triangles (kən grü′ ənt trī′ ang gəlz) triangles whose corresponding angles and sides are congruent (p. 192)

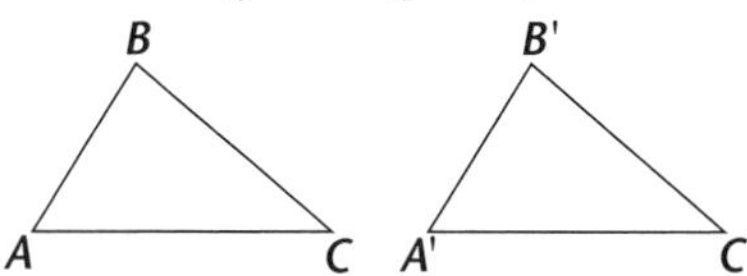

Construction (kən struk′ shən) process of making a line, angle, or figure according to specific requirements (p. 12)

Contradiction (kon trə dik′ shən) a statement that can be shown to be true and false (p. 72)

Converse (kən vėrs′) a new conditional formed from a given conditional in which the hypothesis and conclusion are switched (p. 38)

Convex polygon (kon′ veks pol′ ē gon) a polygon for which the line segment joining any two points in the interior lies entirely within the figure (p. 166)

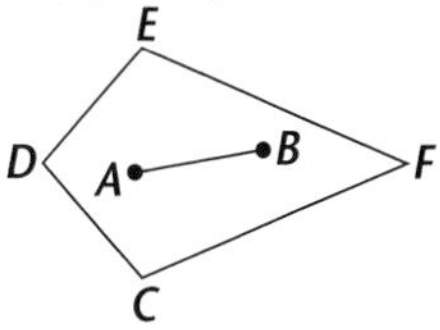

Coordinate plane (kō ôrd′ n it plān) plane formed by placing two real number lines at right angles (p. 104)

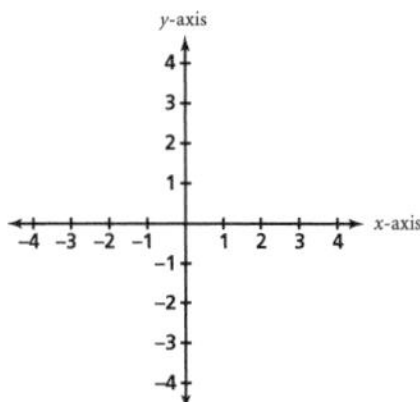

Coplanar (kō plā′ nər) lines or points in the same plane (p. 66)

Corollary (kôr′ ə ler ē) a conclusion that follows easily from a given theorem (p. 180)

Corresponding angles (kôr ə spon′ ding ang′ gəlz) pairs of angles in similar positions (pp. 70, 192)

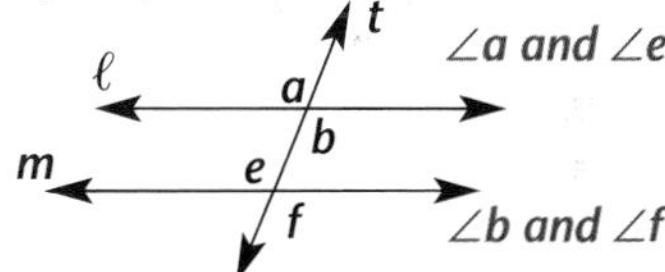

Cosine (cos) (kō′ sīn) for an angle of a right triangle (not the right angle), the ratio of the length of its adjacent leg to the length of the hypotenuse (p. 368)

Counterexample (koun′ tər eg zam′ pəl) a single example that proves a statement false (p. 156)

Customary (kus′ tə mer ē) usual or common, ordinary; a system of measurements used mostly in the United States; inches and cups are basic units (p. 400)

a	hat	e	let	ī	ice	ô	order	ů	put	sh	she	ə	a	in about
ā	age	ē	equal	o	hot	oi	oil	ü	rule	th	thin		e	in taken
ä	far	ėr	term	ō	open	ou	out	ch	child	ᴛʜ	then		i	in pencil
â	care	i	it	ȯ	saw	u	cup	ng	long	zh	measure		o	in lemon
													u	in circus

D

Deductive (Deductive Thinking) (di duk´ tiv) logical reasoning in which a conclusion necessarily follows from the propositions stated (see pp. 55–56 for first example of proof)

Degree (di grē´) a unit of angle measurement (p. 15)

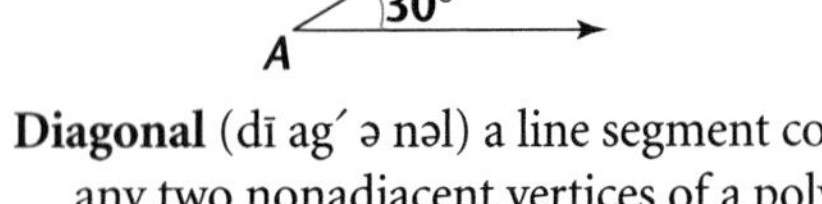

Diagonal (dī ag´ ə nəl) a line segment connecting any two nonadjacent vertices of a polygon (p. 158)

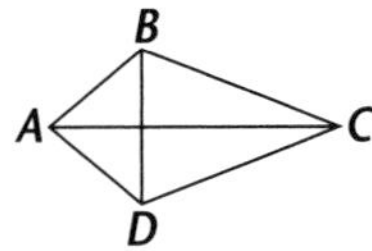

Diameter (dī am´ ə tər) distance across a circle through the center (p. 236); a chord that passes through the center of a circle (p. 344)

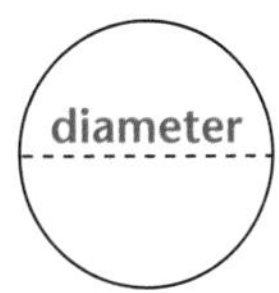

Dilation (dī lā´ shən) process by which a geometric figure is enlarged or shrunk (p. 253)

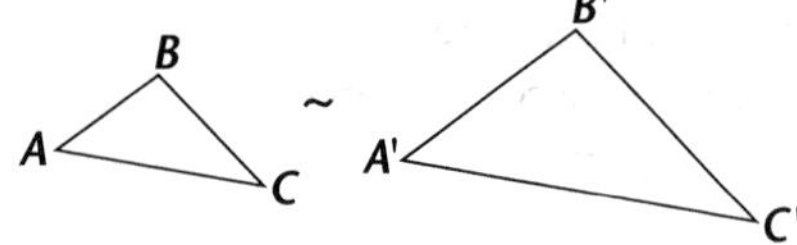

Distributive property (dis trib´ yə tiv prop´ ər tē) $a(b + c) = ab + ac$ (p. 58)

Domain (dō mān´) the *x*-values of a function (p. 122)

E

Endpoints (end´ points) *A* and *B* are the endpoints of $\overline{AB}$ where $\overline{AB}$ is the set of points *A*, *B*, and all the points between *A* and *B* (p. 3)

Equation (i kwā´ zhən) a mathematical sentence stating that two quantities are equal (p. 96)

Equiangular triangle (ē kwē ang´ gyə lər trī´ ang gəl) a triangle with three equal angles (p. 286)

Equidistant (ē kwə dis´ tant) at an equal distance (p. 365)

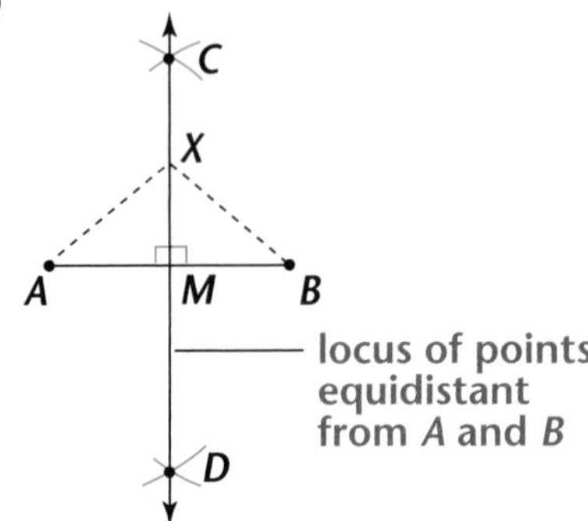

Equilateral triangle (ē kwə lat´ ər əl trī´ ang gəl) a triangle with three equal sides (p. 144)

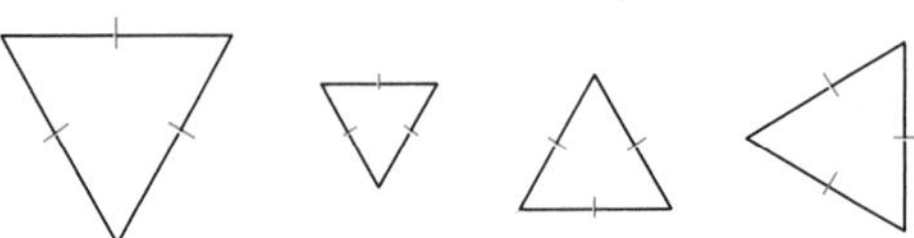

Exponent (ek spō´ nənt) the number of times a base is multiplied by itself (p. 28)

Exterior angle (ek stir´ ē ər ang´ gəl) angle outside the parallel lines (p. 69); angle formed by extending one side of a triangle through any vertex (p. 180)

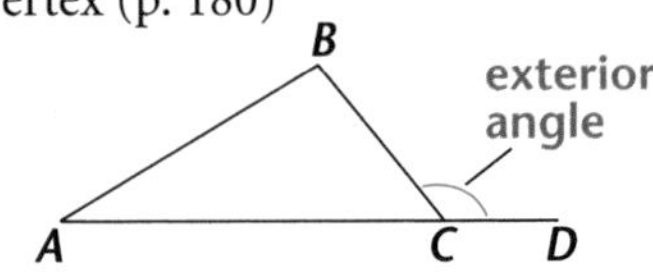

F

Factor (fak´ tər) to write an expression as the product of its multipliers (p. 58)

Factorial (fak´ tôr´ ē əl) the product of all positive integers from 1 to *n* (p. 263)

$n! = n \bullet (n - 1) \bullet (n - 2) \bullet \ldots . \bullet 3 \bullet 2 \bullet 1$

Function (fungk´ shən) a rule that pairs every *x*-value with one and only one *y*-value (p. 122)

Fundamental counting principle (fun də men´ tl koun´ ting prin´ sə pəl) a rule that states if one task can be done *p* different ways and another can be done *q* different ways, then both can be done *pq* different ways (p. 262)

G

Geometry (jē om´ ə trē) the study of points, lines, angles, surfaces, and solids (p. 2)

Given (giv′ ən) specified (p. 55)

Graph (graf) a diagram showing how one quantity depends on another (p. 104)

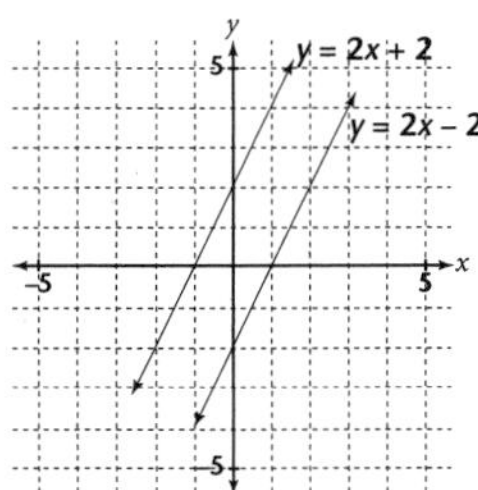

Great circle (grāt sėr′ kəl) circle on a sphere whose center is the center of the sphere and whose radius equals the radius of the sphere (p. 372)

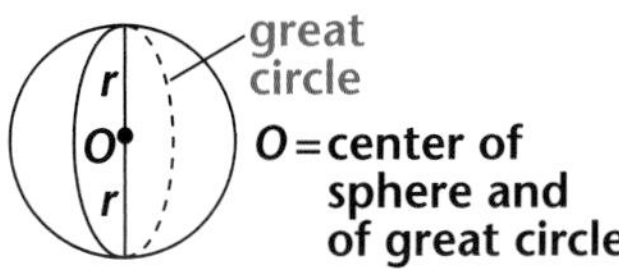

H

Hemisphere (hem′ ə sfir) half of a sphere (p. 373)

Hexagon (hek′ sə gon) a six-sided polygon (p. 248)

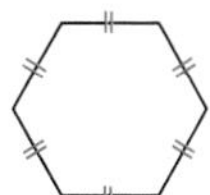

Horizontal (hôr ə zon′ tl) parallel to the horizon (p. 104)

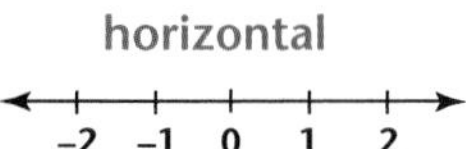

Hypotenuse (hī pot′ n üs) the side opposite the right angle in a right triangle (pp. 149, 200)

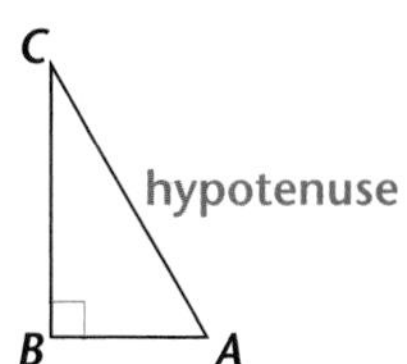

Hypothesis (hī poth′ ə sis) the given or "*If*..." part of a conditional (p. 36)

I

Image (im′ ij) reflection of an object (p. 214)

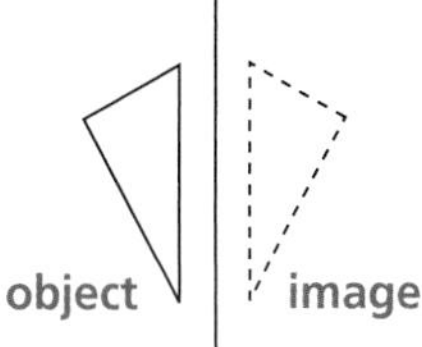

In-center (in sen′ tər) the point where the angle bisectors of the angles of a triangle intersect (p. 176)

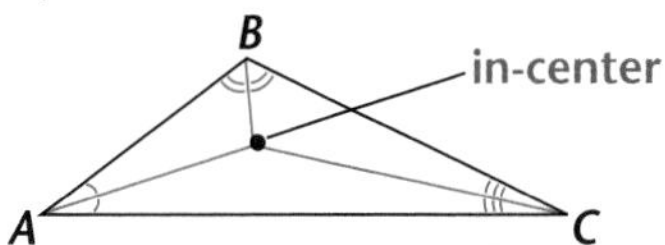

Incircle (in sėr′ kəl) circle inside a triangle and tangent to each of the triangle's sides (p. 366)

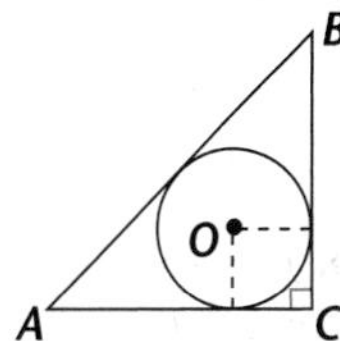

Indirect proof (in də rekt′ prüf) a proof that shows that the conclusion cannot be false because accepted facts would be contradicted (p. 72)

Inductive (in duk′ tiv) using the similarities of particular cases to make a general statement (pp. 85, 161)

Inequality (in i kwol′ ə tē) the state of being unequal; shown by the less than, greater than, and unequal to signs (p. 336)

$5 > 2 \quad 5 < 7 \quad 5 \neq 4$

Integer (in′ tə jər) one of the set of positive and negative whole numbers including zero (p. 270)

. . . –3, –2, –1, 0, 1, 2, 3, . . .

a	hat	e	let	ī	ice	ô	order	u̇	put	sh	she	ə { a	in about
ā	age	ē	equal	o	hot	oi	oil	ü	rule	th	thin	e	in taken
ä	far	ėr	term	ō	open	ou	out	ch	child	ᴛʜ	then	i	in pencil
â	care	i	it	ȯ	saw	u	cup	ng	long	zh	measure	o	in lemon
												u	in circus

Interior (in tir´ ē ər) inside (p. 166); segment *AB* is in the interior of the polygon

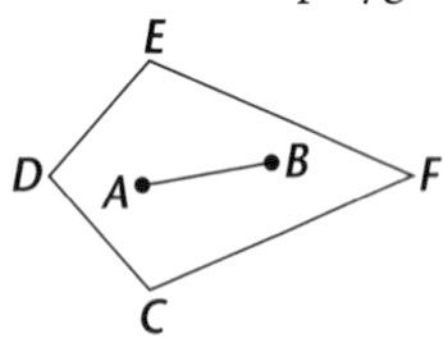

Interior angle (in tir´ ē ər ang´ gəl) angle inside the parallel lines (p. 69)

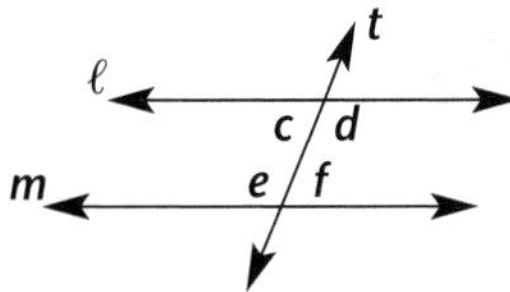

Intersect (in tər sekt´) to meet at a point; to cross or overlap each other (p. 21)

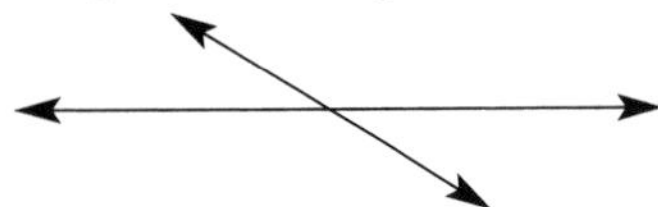

Isosceles (i sos´ ə lēz) a geometric figure with two sides of equal length (p. 85)

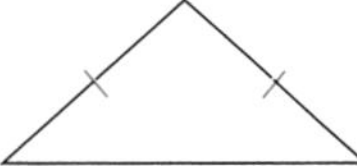

Isosceles triangle (i sos´ ə lēz trī´ ang gəl) a triangle with two equal sides (p. 144)

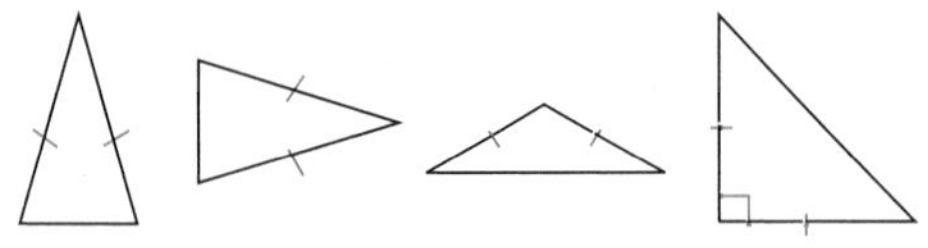

L

Legal (lē´ gəl) allowed by mathematical laws (p. 89)

Line (līn) a set of many points that extend in opposite directions without ending (p. 2)

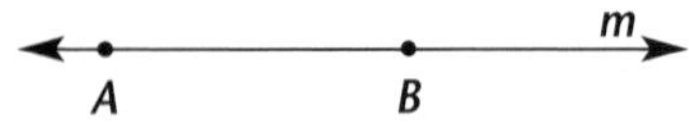

Line of reflection (līn ov re flek´ shən) the line halfway between an object and its reflected image (p. 214)

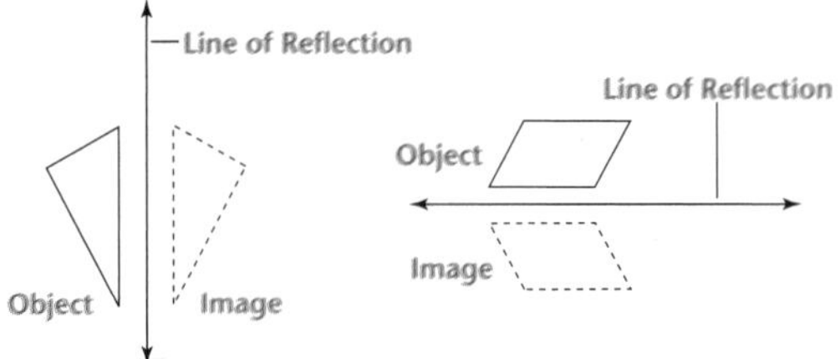

Line of symmetry (līn ov sim´ ə trē) reflection line of an object for which the object coincides with the image (p. 219)

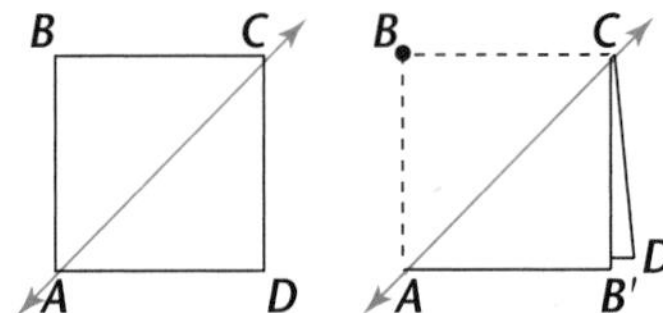

Line segment (līn seg´ mənt) segment *AB* is the set of points *A*, *B*, and all of the points between *A* and *B* (p. 3)

Linear equation (lin´ ē ər i kwā´ zhən) equation whose graph is a straight line (p. 336)

Locus of points (lō´ kəs ov points) location of points (plural *loci*) (p. 344); a set of points that satisfy a certain condition

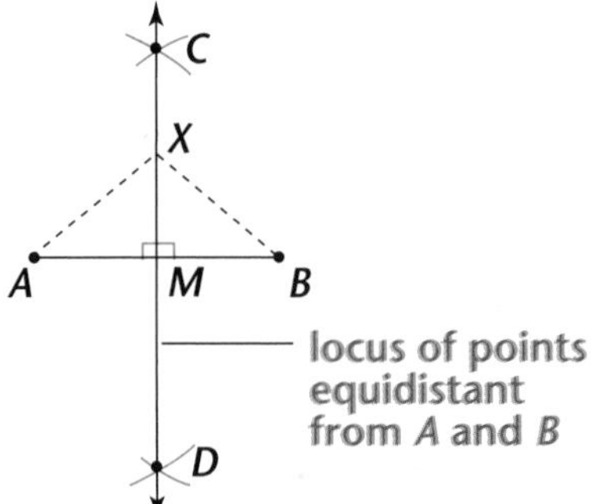

M

Median (mē´ dē ən) line from a vertex of a triangle to the midpoint of the opposite side (p. 176)

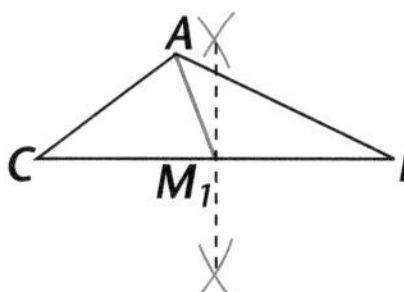

Metric (met´ rik) system of measurement based on powers of ten; gram and meter are basic units (p. 400)

Midpoint (mid´ point) point that divides a line segment into two equal parts (p. 131)

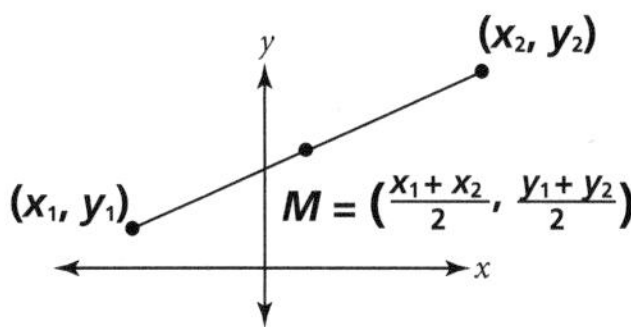

N

Net (net) the two-dimensional representation of the surface of a three-dimensional figure (p. 392)

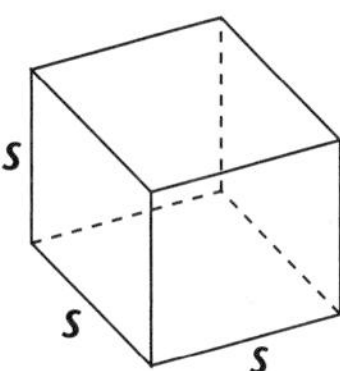

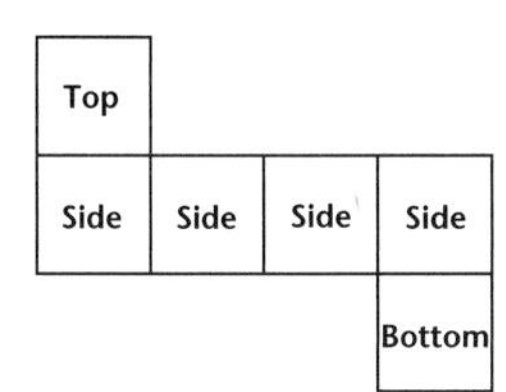

Nonadjacent (non ə jā´ snt) not having a common side (p. 158)

Nonadjacent vertices (non ə jā´ snt vėr´ tə sēz) vertices that do not share a common side (p. 158)

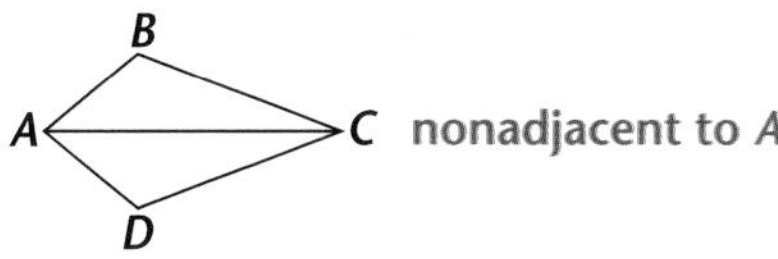

Notion (nō´ shən) idea (p. 51)

O

Obtuse angle (əb tüs´ ang´ gəl) an angle whose measure is greater than 90° but less than 180° (p. 17)

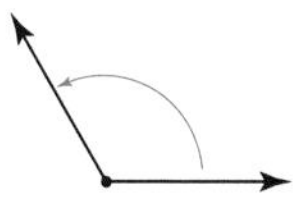

Obtuse triangle (əb tüs´ trī´ ang gəl) a triangle having one angle greater than 90° (p. 149)

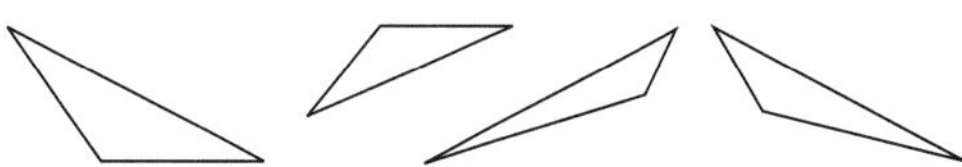

Octagon (ok´ tə gon) an eight-sided polygon (p. 251)

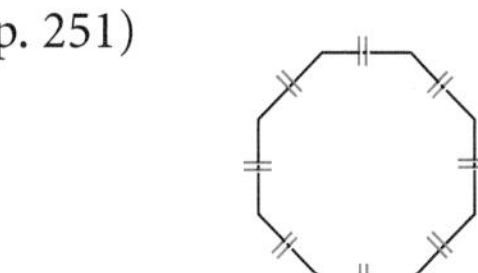

Ordered pair (ôr dəred pâr) a set of two real numbers that locate a point on a plane (p. 105)

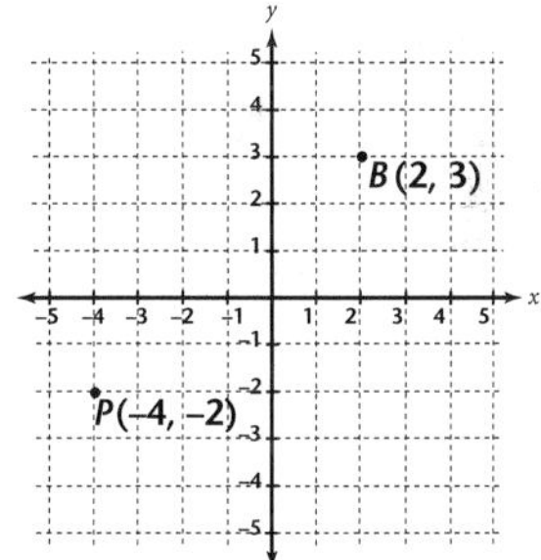

a	hat	e	let	ī	ice	ô	order	u̇	put	sh	she	ə { a	in about
ā	age	ē	equal	o	hot	oi	oil	ü	rule	th	thin	e	in taken
ä	far	ėr	term	ō	open	ou	out	ch	child	ᴛʜ	then	i	in pencil
â	care	i	it	ȯ	saw	u	cup	ng	long	zh	measure	o	in lemon
												u	in circus

Origin (ôr´ ə jin) the point at which the y-axis and the x-axis in the coordinate system intersect (p. 105)

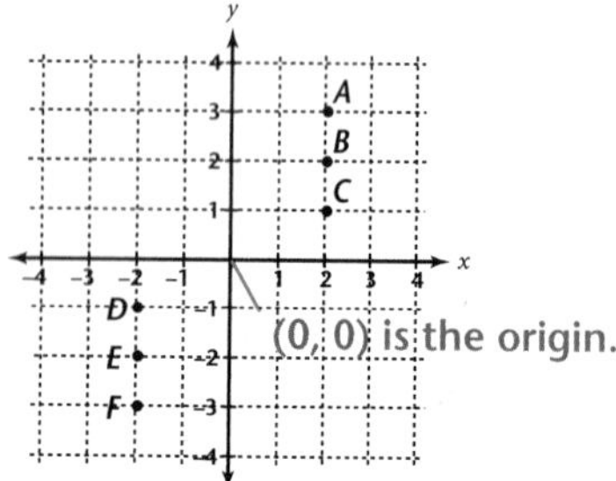

Orthocenter (ôr thə sen´ tər) the point where the altitudes of a triangle meet (p. 175)

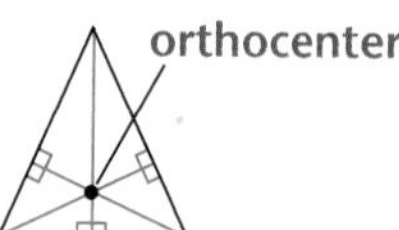

P

Parallel lines (par´ ə lel līnz) lines in the same plane that never meet (p. 66)

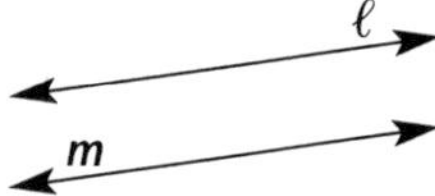

Parallelogram (par ə lel´ ə gram) a quadrilateral whose opposite sides are parallel (pp. 81, 155)

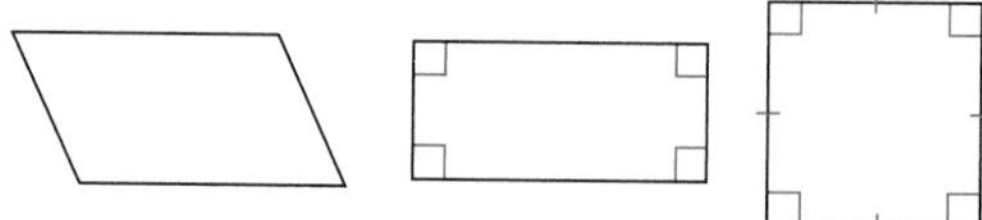

Pentagon (pen´ tə gon) a five-sided figure (p. 247)

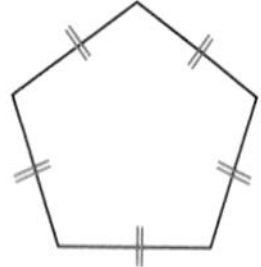

Perimeter (pə rim´ ə tər) the distance around the outside of a shape (p. 249)

$P = a + b + c + d + e$

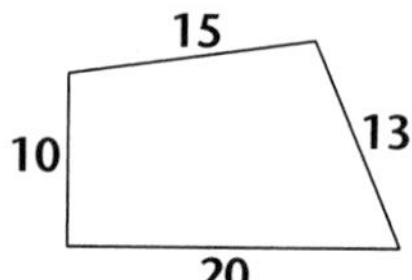

Perimeter of a polygon (pə rim´ ə tər ov ə pol´ e gon) sum of the lengths of all the sides of the polygon (p. 310)

Perimeter = 10 + 15 + 13 + 20

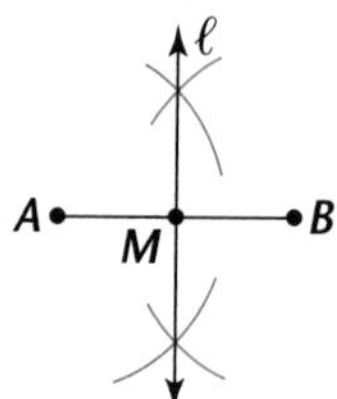

Perpendicular bisector (pėr pən dik´ yə lər bī sek´ tər) line that bisects a given line segment and forms a right angle with it (p. 172); set of points equidistant from two given points (p. 365)

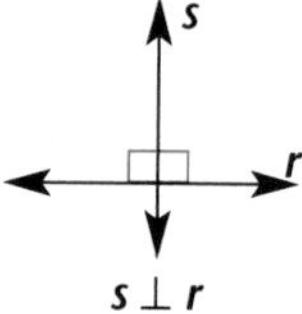

Perpendicular lines (pėr pən dik´ yə lər līnz) lines that form right angles (p. 17)

$s \perp r$

Pi (pī) ratio of the circumference of a circle to its diameter (p. 347)

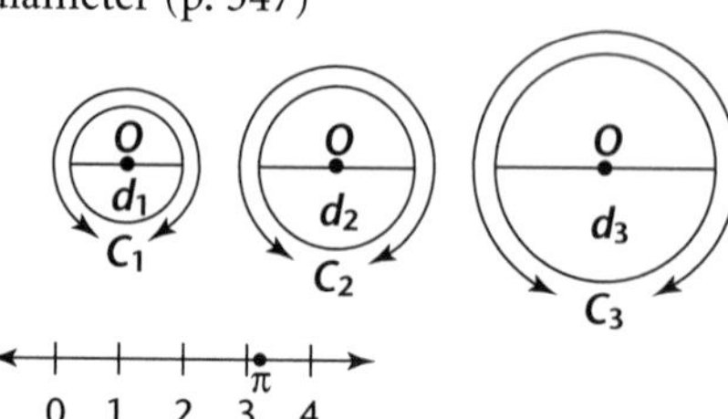

Plane (plān) two-dimensional flat surface (p. 2)

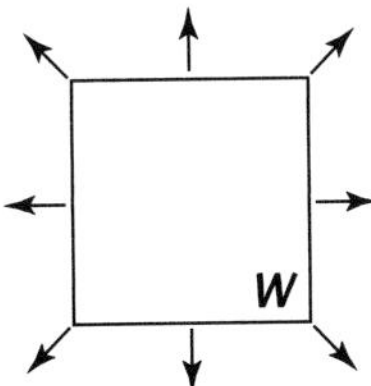

Point (point) a location in space represented by a dot (p. 2)

Point of tangency (point ov tan′ jen sē) the point where the tangent touches the circle (p. 364)

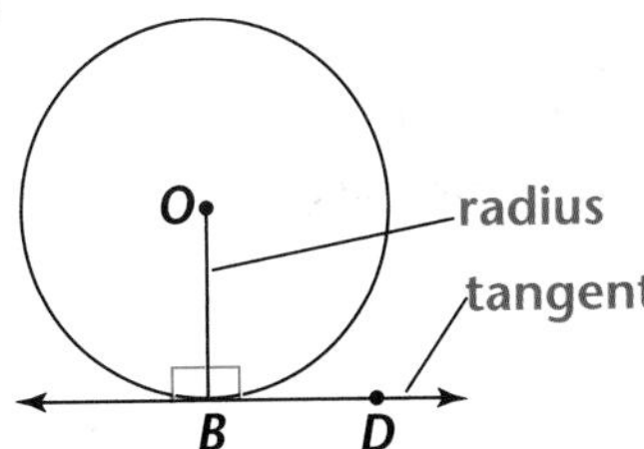

B is the point of tangency

Poles (pōlz) endpoints of the diameter of a sphere (p. 373)

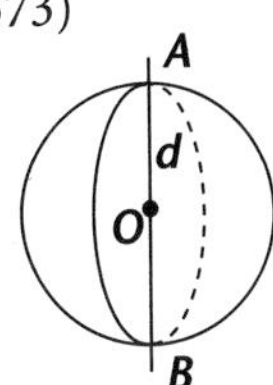

Polygon (pol′ ē gon) a closed, many-sided geometric figure (p. 166)

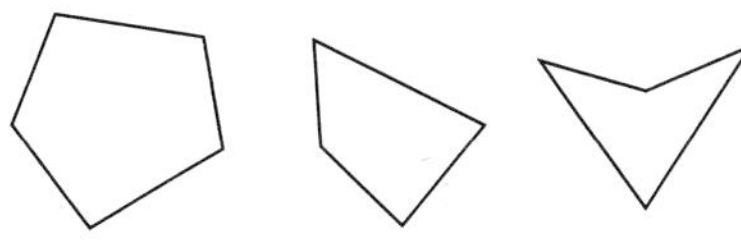

Postulate (pos′ chə lit) a statement about geometric figures accepted as true without proof (p. 7)

Prism (priz′ əm) a three-dimensional figure that has congruent polygons as bases in parallel planes and whose sides are parallelograms (p. 384)

Probability (prob ə bil′ ə tē) the chance or likelihood of an event occurring (p. 354)

Proof (prüf) a series of true statements leading to a desired conclusion (p. 55)

Proportion (prə pôr′ shən) the equality of two ratios (p. 238)

$$\frac{a}{b} = \frac{c}{d}$$

Protractor (prō trak′ tər) a tool used to draw or measure angles (p. 15)

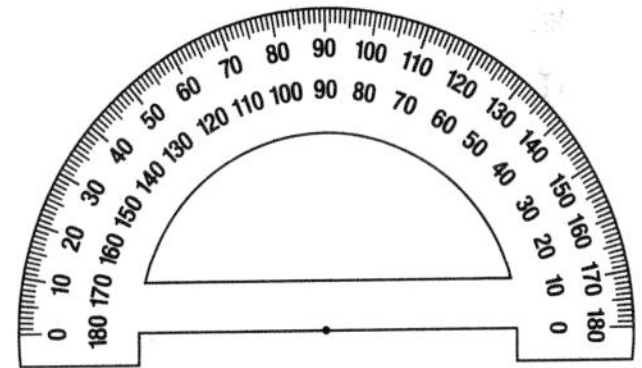

Prove (prüv) to show that a conclusion is true (p.55)

Pyramid (pir′ ə mid) a three-dimensional figure with a single base and sides that are triangles (p. 388)

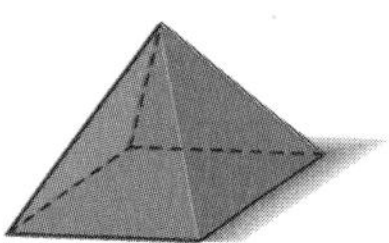

Pythagorean Triple (pə thag ə rē′ ən trip′ əl) integers *a*, *b*, and *c* such that $a^2 + b^2 = c^2$ (p. 271)

a	hat	e	let	ī	ice	ô	order	u̇	put	sh	she	ə { a	in about
ā	age	ē	equal	o	hot	oi	oil	ü	rule	th	thin	e	in taken
ä	far	ėr	term	ō	open	ou	out	ch	child	ᴛʜ	then	i	in pencil
â	care	i	it	ȯ	saw	u	cup	ng	long	zh	measure	o	in lemon
												u	in circus

Q

Quadrant (kwäd′ rənt) one-fourth of the coordinate plane (p. 106); one-fourth of a circle (p. 345)

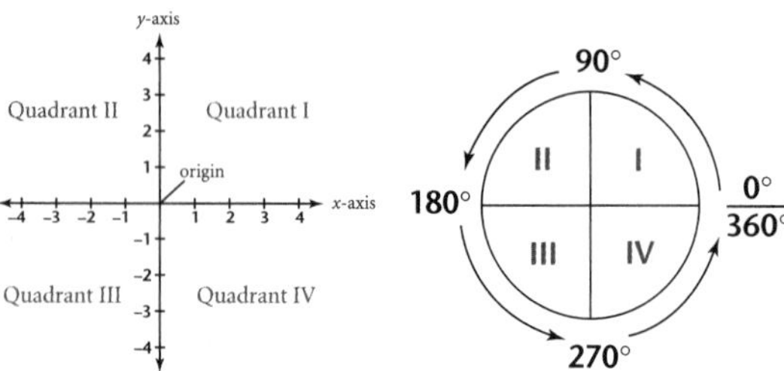

Quadratic equation (kwä drat′ ik i kwā′ zhən) an equation in which the highest power of the variable is the second power (p. 228)

Quadratic formula (kwä drat′ fôr′ myə lə) formula that can provide roots of any quadratic equation (p. 420)

Quadrilateral (kwäd rə lat′ ər əl) a geometric figure with four sides (p. 81)

R

Radical (rad′ ə kəl) an expression written with a radical sign, such as $\sqrt{2}$ (p. 402)

Radicand (rad ə kand′) expression inside a radical sign Example: in $\sqrt{a + b}$, $a + b$ is the radicand (p. 402)

Radius (rā′ dē əs) distance from the center of the circle to the circle (p. 247); distance between the center of a circle and any point on the circle (pp. 247, 344)

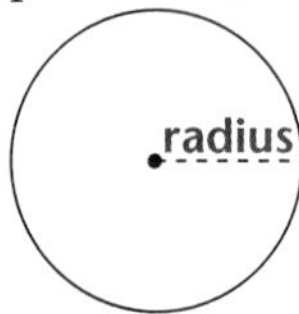

Range (rānj) the *y*-values of a function (p. 122)

Rate (rāt) quantity measured in proportion to something else (p. 136)

Ratio (rā′ shē ō) comparison of two like quantities *a* and *b* (p. 236)

$$\frac{a}{b} \quad \text{or} \quad a : b \quad \text{or} \quad a \text{ to } b$$

Ratio of similarity (rā′ shē ō ov sim ə lar′ ə tē) a ratio comparing the relative sizes of similar figures (p. 236)

Rational number (rash′ ə nəl num′ bər) an integer divided by another integer *b* where $b \neq 0$ (p. 302)

Ray (rā) a set of points that is part of a line; a ray has one endpoint and extends in one direction with no end (p. 4)

Rectangle (rek′ tang gəl) a parallelogram with four right angles (pp. 81, 155)

Regular polygon (reg′ yə lər pol′ ē gon) a polygon with sides of equal length and angles of equal measure (p. 166)

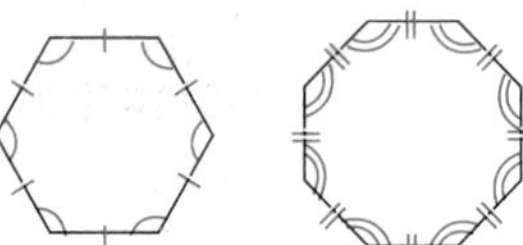

Rhombus (rom′ bəs) a parallelogram with four equal sides (pp. 81, 155)

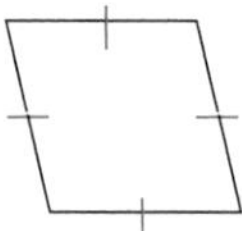

Right angle (rīt ang′ gəl) an angle whose measure is 90° (p. 16)

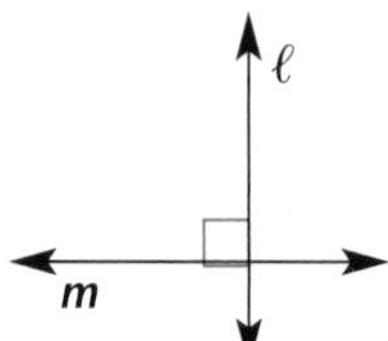

Right prism (rīt priz´ əm) prism in which the base and the sides are at right angles (p. 393)

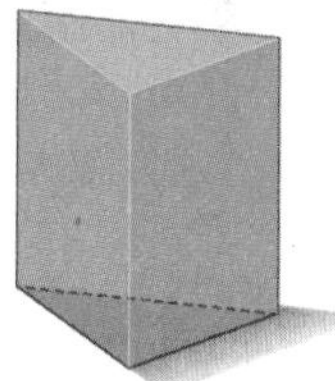

Right triangle (rīt trī´ ang gəl) a triangle having one right angle (p. 149)

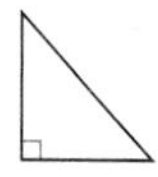

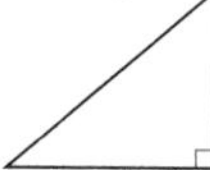

Root (rüt) a value of x that satisfies the equation $ax^2 + bx + c = 0$ (p. 420)

Rotation (rō tā´ shən) transformation in which a geometric figure turns around a center without affecting its size or shape (p. 224)

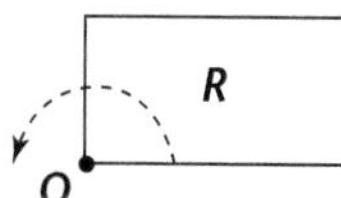

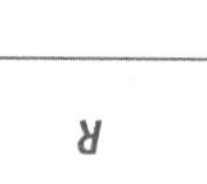

S

Scalene (skā´ lēn) a geometric figure with sides of unequal length (p. 85)

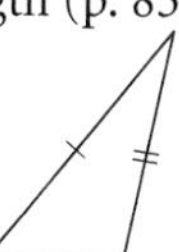

Scalene triangle (skā´ lēn trī´ ang gəl) a triangle with no equal sides (p. 145)

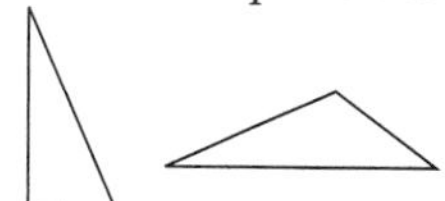

Sector (sek´ tər) the area enclosed within a central angle of a circle (p. 360)

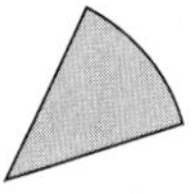

Set (set) a collection of particular things, like the set of points on a line segment (p. 2)

Similar (sim´ ə lər) having the same shape (p. 236)

Similar triangles (sim´ ə lər trī´ ang gəlz) triangles whose corresponding angles are equal and whose corresponding sides are in proportion (p. 242)

Sine (sin) (sīn) for an angle of a right triangle (not the right angle), the ratio of the length of the opposite leg to the length of the hypotenuse (p. 368)

Skew lines (skyü līnz) lines in space that are not coplanar and never meet (p. 66)

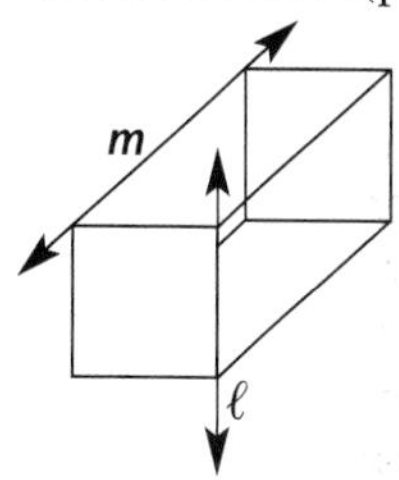

Slant height (slant hīt) distance from the base of a cone to the vertex or from the midpoint of a base side to the vertex of a pyramid (p. 396)

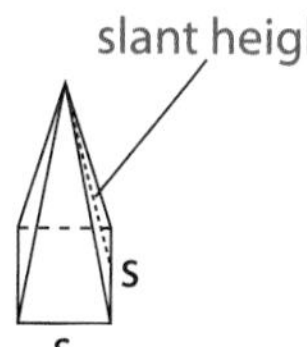

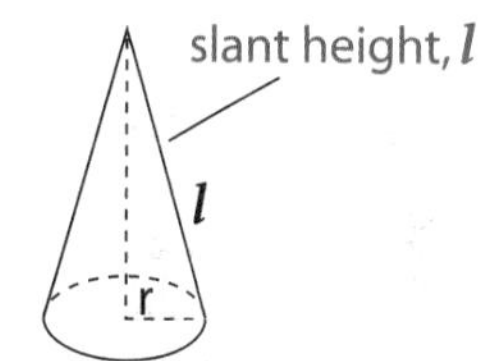

Slope of a line (slōp ov ə līn) ratio of the difference in y-values to the difference in x-values of any two points on a line (p. 115)

$$\text{slope} = \frac{\text{rise}}{\text{run}}$$

a	hat	e	let	ī	ice	ô	order	ů	put	sh	she	ə { a	in about
ā	age	ē	equal	o	hot	oi	oil	ü	rule	th	thin	e	in taken
ä	far	ėr	term	ō	open	ou	out	ch	child	ᴛʜ	then	i	in pencil
â	care	i	it	ȯ	saw	u	cup	ng	long	zh	measure	o	in lemon
												u	in circus

Sphere (sfir) locus of points in space equidistant from a fixed point (p. 372)

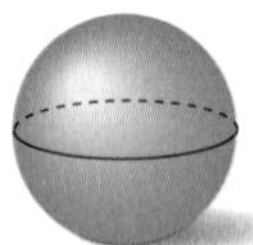

Square (skwâr) a rectangle with sides of equal length (p. 81)

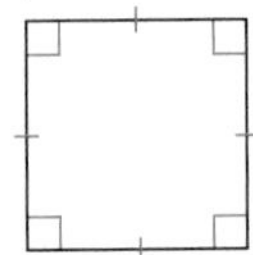

Straight angle (strāt ang´ gəl) an angle whose measure is 180° (p. 17)

Strict (strikt) exact and precise (p. 36)
Supplementary angles (sup lə men´ tər ē ang´ gəlz) two angles whose measures add to 180° (p. 21)

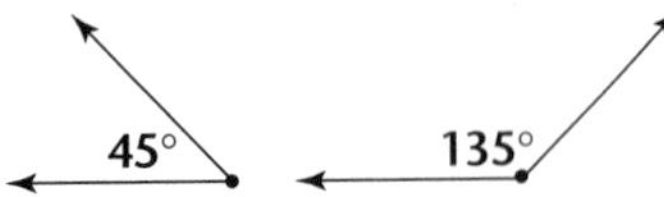

System of linear equations (sis´ təm ov lin´ ē ər i kwā´ zhənz) a system of equations for two or more straight lines (p. 376)

Tangent (tan) (tan´ jənt) for an angle of a right triangle (not the right angle), the ratio of the length of the opposite leg to the length of the adjacent leg (p. 368)
Tangent (tan´ jənt) line that touches but does not intersect a circle (p. 364)

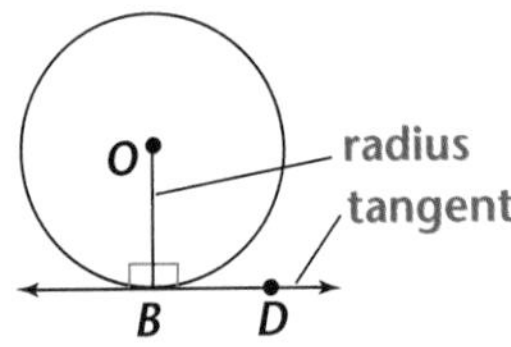

Tessellation (tas´ əl ā shən) an arrangement of shapes that cover a plane surface without overlapping and without leaving holes (p. 230)
Theorem (thē´ ər əm) a statement that can be proven true (p. 55)

Transform (tran sfôrm´) to change the size or shape of a figure (p. 254)
Transformation (tran sfər mā´ shən) movement of a geometric figure from one location to another (p. 221)
Translation (tran slā´ shən) transformation in which a geometric figure slides from one location to another without affecting its size or shape (p. 221)

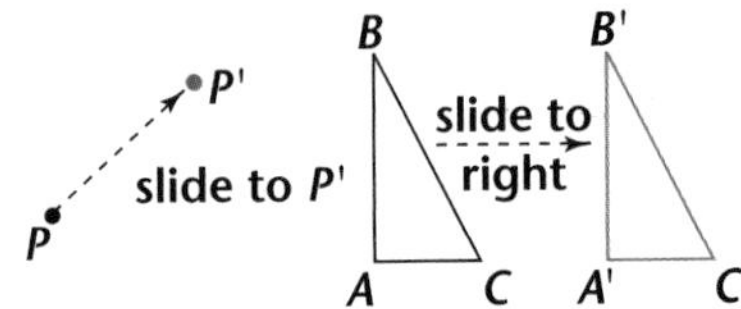

Transversal (trans vėr´ səl) a line that crosses parallel lines (p. 69)

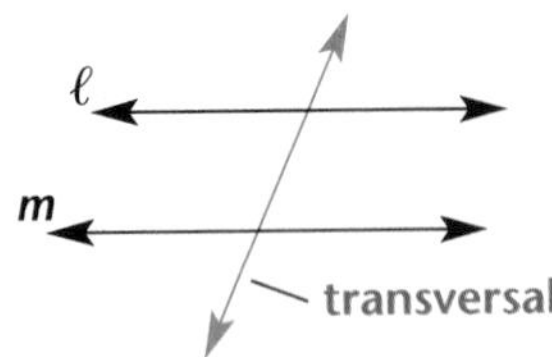

Trapezoid (trap´ ə zoid) a quadrilateral with exactly one pair of parallel sides (pp. 85, 156)

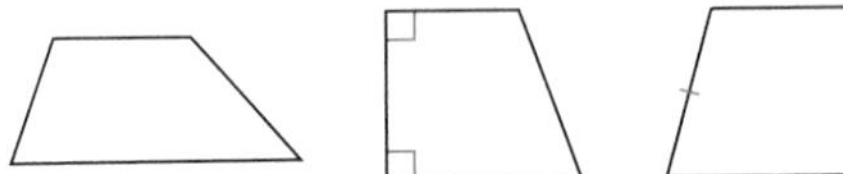

Trigonometry (trig ə nom´ ə trē) branch of mathematics dealing with relations between the sides and angles of triangles (p. 369)

Undefined (un di fīnd´) cannot be expressed numerically (p. 117)
Unit circle (yü´ nit sėr´ kəl) Circle whose radius is one (p. 368)

Valid (val´ id) based on evidence or fact (p. 72)
Variable (vâr´ ē bəl) the unknown quantity in an equation (p. 96)
Vertex (vėr´ teks) the point common to both sides of an angle (p. 11)

Vertical (vėr′ tə kəl) straight up and down (p. 104)

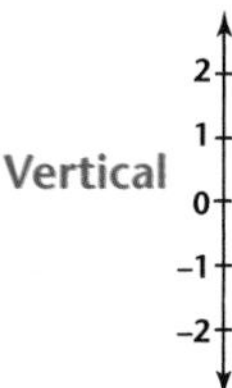

Vertical angles (vėr′ tə kəl ang′ gəlz) angles that have a common vertex and whose sides are formed by the same lines (p. 21)

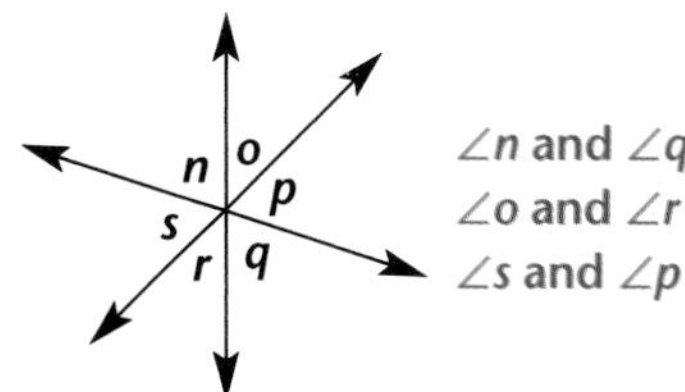

Vertices (vėr′ tə sēz) plural of *vertex* (p. 158)

Volume (vol′ yəm) the measure of the number of unit cubes in a solid figure (p. 384)

Y

***Y*-intercept** (y in tər sept′) the *y*-value of the point where a line crosses the *y*-axis (when $x = 0$) (p. 122)

a	hat	e	let	ī	ice	ô	order	ů	put	sh	she	ə	a	in about
ā	age	ē	equal	o	hot	oi	oil	ü	rule	th	thin		e	in taken
ä	far	ėr	term	ō	open	ou	out	ch	child	ᴛʜ	then		i	in pencil
â	care	i	it	ȯ	saw	u	cup	ng	long	zh	measure		o	in lemon
													u	in circus

Index

D

E

L

M

N

O

P

Q

R

S

T

U

V

W

X

Y

Z

Photo Credits

Cover, © Ltd, Fullerton Technology Co/Index Stock Imagery; p. xviii, © James H. Pickerell/Folio, Inc.; p. 10, © STScI/NASA/Science Source/Photo Researchers, Inc.; p. 19, © Gary Conner/PhotoEdit; p. 30, © Tony Freeman/PhotoEdit; p. 34, © Robert Llewellyn/Folio, Inc.; p. 41, © The Granger Collection, New York; p. 46, © Michael Brennan/Corbis; p. 47, © Howard Grey/Stone/Getty Images; p. 60, © Eyebyte/Alamy; p. 64, © Kathleen Kliskey-Geraghty/Index Stock Imagery; p. 66, © Michael Wong/Corbis; p. 67, © Court Mast/Taxi/Getty Images; p. 68, © Dan McCoy/Rainbow; p. 76, © Lowell Georgia/Corbis; p. 89, © Joe Sohm/Photo Researchers, Inc.; p. 95, © Richard T. Nowitz/Corbis; p. 98, © John Warden/SuperStock; p. 102, © AFP/Corbis; p. 108, © Mark Cooper/Corbis; p. 110, © Gregory Sams/Science Photo Library/Photo Researchers, Inc.; p. 111, © John Fullbright/Rainbow; p. 126, © Brad Wrobleski/Masterfile; p. 138, © AFP/Corbis; p. 142, © Allan Davey/Masterfile; p. 144, © Philip James Corwin/Corbis; p. 163, © Mark Schneider/Visuals Unlimited; p. 171, © Gerber Oppermans/Stone/Getty Images; p. 171, © Superstock; p. 183, © Art Montes de Oca/Taxi/Getty Images; p. 190, © Dick Thomas/Visuals Unlimited; p. 195, © Lucidio Studio, Inc/SuperStock; p. 214, © Cameron Attree/Alamy; p. 222, © Richard Cummins/Folio, Inc.; p. 230, © Jonathan Nourok/PhotoEdit; p. 234, © David Young-Wolff/PhotoEdit; p. 236, © Michael Newman/PhotoEdit; p. 253, © Tim Brown/Stone/Getty Images; p. 261, © Pictor Images/ImageState; p. 264, © Melissa Farlow/National Geographic Image Collection; p. 268, © (ZF) J. Raga/Masterfile; p. 270, © Hulton Archive/Getty Images; p. 301, © Calvin Larsen/Photo Researchers, Inc.; p. 304, © Joseph Sohm; ChromoSohm Inc./Corbis; p. 304, © Andre Jenny/Alamy; p. 308, © Sean Ellis/Stone/Getty Images; p. 311, © John & Dallas Heaton/Corbis; p. 335, © Ralph A. Clevenger/Corbis; p. 342, © Howard Sokol/Index Stock Imagery; p. 355, © Sadik Demiroz/SuperStock; p. 361, © John de Visser/Masterfile; p. 373, © David Jeffrey/Image Bank/Getty Images; p. 378, © Yellow Dog Productions/Image Bank/Getty Images; p. 382, © Koji Kitagawa/SuperStock; p. 399, © Keren Su/China Span; p. 404, © Photodisc; p. 408, © Doug Wilson/Corbis; p. 416, © BSIP Agency/Index Stock Imagery; p. 419, © (ZF) Hackenberg/Masterfile; p. 422, © Douglas Pulsipher/Alamy